SQL Functions Programmer's Reference

SQL Functions Programmer's Reference

Arie Jones
Ryan K. Stephens
Ronald R. Plew
Robert F. Garrett
Alex Kriegel

Wiley Publishing, Inc.

SQL Functions Programmer's Reference

Published by
Wiley Publishing, Inc.
10475 Crosspoint Boulevard
Indianapolis, IN 46256
www.wiley.com

Copyright © 2005 by Wiley Publishing, Inc., Indianapolis, Indiana

Published simultaneously in Canada

ISBN 13   978-0-7645-6901-2

ISBN 10   0-7645-6901-5

Manufactured in the United States of America

10 9 8 7 6 5 4 3 2 1

1B/RU/QU/QV/IN

For general information on our other products and services or to obtain technical support, please contact our Customer Care Department within the U.S. at (800) 762-2974, outside the U.S. at (317) 572-3993 or fax (317) 572-4002.

For technical support, please visit www.wiley.com/techsupport.

Wiley also publishes its books in a variety of electronic formats. Some content that appears in print may not be available in electronic books.

Library of Congress Cataloging-in-Publication Data:

SQL functions programmer's reference / Arie Jones ... [et al.].

    p. cm.

  Includes bibliographical references and index.

  ISBN 0-7645-6901-5 (paper/website : alk. paper)

 1. SQL (Computer program language) I. Jones, Arie.

  QA76.73.S67S674 2005

  005.13'3--dc22

               2005002765

About the Authors

Arie Jones

Arie Jones is a senior database administrator for Perpetual Technologies, Inc. (www.perptech.com). He holds a master's degree in physics from Indiana State University and also works as the chief Web architect/DBA for the USPFO for Indiana. Arie's main specialty is in developing .NET-based database solutions for the government. He and his wife and family live outside of Indianapolis, Indiana.

Ryan K. Stephens

Ryan Stephens is the president and CEO of Perpetual Technologies, Inc. (www.perptech.com), an Indianapolis-based IT firm specializing in database technologies. Ryan has been working with SQL and databases for 15 years and has held the positions of project manager, database administrator, and programmer/analyst. Ryan has been teaching database courses for local universities since 1997 and has authored several internationally published books on topics such as database design, SQL, database architecture, database administration, and Oracle. Ryan enjoys discovering new ways to optimize the use of technology to streamline business operations, as well as empowering others to do the same. Ryan and his wife live in Indianapolis with their three children.

Ronald R. Plew

Ronald R. Plew is vice president and CIO for Perpetual Technologies, Inc. (www.perptech.com) in Indianapolis, Indiana. Ron is a Certified Oracle Professional. He has coauthored several internationally published books on SQL and database technology. Ron is also an adjunct professor for Vincennes University in Indiana, where he teaches SQL and various database courses. Ron holds a bachelor of science degree in business administration/management from Indiana Institute of Technology out of Fort Wayne, Indiana. Ron recently retired from the Indiana Army National Guard, where he served as a programmer/analyst. His hobbies include automobile racing, chess, golf, and collecting Indy 500 memorabilia. Ron resides in Indianapolis with his wife Linda.

Robert F. Garrett

Bob Garrett is the software development manager at Perpetual Technologies, Inc. (www.perptech.com). Bob's languages of preference are Java, C++, and English. He has extensive experience integrating applications with relational databases. Bob has a degree in computer science and mathematics from Purdue University, and lives with his wife and daughter near Indianapolis.

Alex Kriegel

Alex Kriegel is a professional database systems analyst with a major manufacturing firm in Oregon. He has more than 10 years of database experience working with Microsoft SQL Server, Oracle, DB2, Sybase, and PostgreSQL both as developer and DBA. Alex has a bachelor of science degree in solid-state physics from State Polytechnic Institute of Minsk, Belarus, and has earned the Microsoft Certified Solution Developer (MCSD) accreditation. He is the author of *SQL Bible*. Alex wrote the first draft of approximately two-thirds of this book.

Contributing Authors

Joshua Stephens

Joshua Stephens is a systems administrator/DBA for Perpetual Technologies, Inc. (www.perptech.com). He has eight years of experience in various IT areas. As a former technical writer and trainer, he continues to enjoy helping others through writing. He holds a bachelor of arts degree in pure mathematics and physics from Franklin College. He lives in Franklin, Indiana, with his wife and daughter.

Richard Bulley

Richard is a Ferris State University graduate and received a master of arts degree from Ball State University. He has had 20 years of data processing experience with the United States Air Force and is a United States Air Force Reserves Retiree and currently has over six years of experience as a Sybase and MS SQL Server system DBA.

Credits

Acquisitions Editor
Jim Minatel

Development Editor
Kevin Shafer

Production Editor
Gabrielle Nabi

Technical Editor
Wiley-Dreamtech India Pvt Ltd

Copy Editor
Publication Services, Inc.

Editorial Manager
Mary Beth Wakefield

Vice President & Executive Group Publisher
Richard Swadley

Vice President and Publisher
Joseph B. Wikert

Project Coordinator
Ryan Steffen

Graphics and Production Specialists
April Farling, Carrie Foster, Denny Hager,
Julie Trippetti

Quality Control Technicians
Joe Niesen
John Greenough

Proofreading and Indexing
TECHBOOKS Production Services

I would like to dedicate this book to my wife, Jacqueline, for being understanding and supportive during the long hours that it took to complete this book.

— *Arie Jones*

For Tina, Daniel, Autumn, and Alivia. You are my inspiration.

— *Ryan Stephens*

For Linda

— *Ron Plew*

For Becky and Libby

— *Bob Garrett*

Acknowledgments

Shortly after we accepted this project, it became clear how much of a team effort would be needed to make this book a must-have for anyone's SQL library. Fortunately, I have an incredible technical team that knows how to come together and get the job done. Most of my thanks go to Arie Jones. Arie stepped up when I needed the most help, unafraid of commitment, confidently accepting another aggressive assignment. Our author team included Arie Jones, Ron Plew, Bob Garrett, Alex Kriegel, and myself. Contributing authors were Joshua Stephens and Richard Bulley. I cannot say enough about their professionalism and technical proficiency. Thank you for being part of another successful project!

Probably as no surprise to the Wiley audience, the author team thanks the editorial staff at Wiley, which is one of the best with whom we have had the pleasure of working. Specifically, we appreciate Jim Minatel's efforts and confidence in our team, Kevin Shafer's strict attention to detail, and the technical editorial team's thoroughness. Their dedication, patience, and thoroughness, we believe, reflect directly on the quality and timely delivery of this book, which would not have been possible without each of them, as well as the unmentioned Wiley staff behind the scenes.

— *Ryan Stephens and the author team*

Contents

Contents

Contents

Contents

Contents

Contents

Contents

Contents

Contents

Contents

Contents

Contents

Contents

Contents

Contents

Contents

Introduction

This book is a complete SQL functions reference for all of the major RDBMS vendors in today's market. Structured Query Language (SQL) is the standard language used to communicate with relational databases. SQL is a simple, English-like (yet powerful) language that allows the database user to effectively store, manipulate, and retrieve data from a database. Among the most robust features of SQL is its ability to mine data from a database and flexibly display that data in a format that suits the user's exact needs. SQL functions comprise a huge part of the SQL language and play a critical role in determining what data is retrieved, how it is retrieved, and how it is to be displayed. Once you learn to query a database with SQL, learning how to intelligently use functions will allow you to quickly master the art of retrieving data from any relational database. This book will contribute to your mastery of effective data retrieval using SQL, regardless of the vendor implementation you are using.

The SQL implementations covered in this book include ANSI SQL, Oracle, Microsoft SQL Server, Sybase, IBM Universal Database (UDB) DB2, MySQL, and PostgreSQL. As a SQL programmer, you will find that there is a growing need to effectively use SQL functions, yet there are few resources to serve as an aid. You will also encounter the need to cross-reference different SQL implementations, at times having to integrate data between, say, Oracle and SQL Server. Migrations of data from one implementation to another is also very common in data warehousing environments, and as organizations make the commitment to go with another vendor's relational database management system (RDBMS) to better support evolving business needs. This book is the necessary tool to facilitate expedient function referencing, cross-referencing between implementations, creating userdefined functions (UDFs), and providing tips and examples for applying the use of functions to real-world data-retrieval situations.

If you have purchased this book, thank you. We know that you will find this book to be an invaluable reference for SQL functions for all the major players in the RDBMS market. If you are considering this book, please take a minute to flip through this reference, making note of the reference material, the trailing chapters describing real-world practical applications of SQL functions, and particularly Appendix A, which cross-references all the functions contained in this book by vendor. You should find this book to be thorough and inclusive of all functions currently available in each of the major RDBMS vendor implementations.

Who This Book Is For

This book is for the SQL programmer, and any software developer who has a need to effectively retrieve data from a relational database, or to integrate applications with RDBMS implementations. Database administrators and other database users will also discover great value. This book is for readers of all levels, and has been organized in an easy-to-understand format that allows quick search and reference. This book is packed with realistic examples, allowing the reader to immediately apply SQL functions concepts to the job at hand.

Although the intent of this book is not to teach you SQL, the introductory chapters we have provided serve as an introduction to the world of SQL, explaining basic SQL concepts and describing how to use SQL to query a database, either with or without the use of functions. The trailing chapters of this book show numerous applications of SQL functions in the modern database world.

How This Book Is Organized

This book has been organized into four major sections for your convenience and ease of use. We have also included several appendixes for supplemental reference related to SQL functions. Following are brief descriptions.

Introduction to Functions

The introductory chapters in this book (Chapters 1–4) provide an overview of SQL, SQL built-in functions, UDFs, and major vendor implementations of RDBMS and SQL functions. These chapters are meant to serve as an introduction to SQL function architecture and concepts for those readers who need to increase their knowledge and sharpen their skills. Following is a breakdown of those introductory chapters:

- ❑ *Chapter 1*—Exploring popular SQL implementations
- ❑ *Chapter 2*—Concepts and architecture of functions
- ❑ *Chapter 3*—Comparison of SQL built-in functions by vendor
- ❑ *Chapter 4*—SQL procedural extensions and user-defined functions

Functions Reference by Vendor

Chapters 5–11 contain the primary reference material for built-in SQL functions for all of the major RDBMS vendors. Each chapter includes an introduction with SQL query syntax and a summary in addition to the core reference material. Detailed examples are included with each and every function, along with function syntax and detailed explanations. Reference chapters include thorough coverage of the following vendor implementations.

- ❑ *Chapter 5*—ANSI SQL
- ❑ *Chapter 6*—Oracle
- ❑ *Chapter 7*—IBM DB2 UDB
- ❑ *Chapter 8*—SQL Server
- ❑ *Chapter 9*—Sybase
- ❑ *Chapter 10*—MySQL
- ❑ *Chapter 11*—PostgreSQL

Creating User-Defined Functions by Vendor

Chapters 12–18 contain the secondary reference material for SQL functions for all of the major RDBMS vendors, discussing the concepts of creating UDFs. Each chapter is written in an easy-to-understand format, explaining exactly how UDFs are created through the use of numerous examples. Detailed examples are included throughout each chapter, including syntax and detailed explanations. The reference chapters in this section include thorough coverage of the following vendor implementations.

- *Chapter 12—ANSI SQL*
- *Chapter 13—Oracle*
- *Chapter 14—IBM DB2 UDB*
- *Chapter 15—SQL Server*
- *Chapter 16—Sybase*
- *Chapter 17—MySQL*
- *Chapter 18—PostgreSQL*

Functions in Action

Chapters 19–27 contain valuable material showing functions "in action." In other words, we have identified several common instances in which SQL functions are used every day by most organizations. This content is more instructional versus a reference lookup, and reveals SQL function uses that are widely unknown to many database users. Topics in this section include the following:

- *Chapter 19—Reporting and ad hoc queries*
- *Chapter 20—Using functions for migrating data*
- *Chapter 21—Using functions to feed a data warehouse*
- *Chapter 22—Using embedded functions and other advanced uses*
- *Chapter 23—Generating SQL with SQL and functions*
- *Chapter 24—Embedding SQL functions in an application*
- *Chapter 25—Empowering the query with functions and views*
- *Chapter 26—Understanding the impact of SQL functions on query and database performance*
- *Chapter 27—Utilizing useful queries from the system catalog (by vendor implementation)*

Appendixes

Several appendixes have been included to offer quick access to SQL function-relevant material. Following is a breakdown of the appendixes:

- *Appendix A*—This includes a built-in function cross reference table and index, listing all functions covered in the book. You will quickly see the value of this resource because it allows you to quickly and easily locate functions supported by each vendor, compare coverage in other SQL implementations, and find similar functions in different implementations. This appendix is particularly useful for the programmer who deals with more than one RDBMS implementation.
- *Appendix B*—This provides a quick reference to ANSI SQL and vendor-specific SQL keywords.
- *Appendix C*—This provides a quick reference to ANSI SQL and vendor-specific data types.
- *Appendix D*—This provides a quick reference to various types of database permissions by vendor.

❏ *Appendix E*—This provides an Open Database Connectivity (ODBC) quick reference, showing how to establish an ODBC database connection via an application. ODBC is one of the most common methods for integrating an application and a database.

❏ *Appendix F*—This is a Java Database Connectivity (JDBC) quick reference, showing how to establish a JDBC database connection via an application. JDBC is another common method for integrating an application and a database.

❏ *Glossary*—This provides a listing of common database and SQL terminology.

How to Use This Book

This book was primarily created as a comprehensive SQL function reference book for the programmer, although we have included supplemental material to increase its value to you as the reader and database user. Following are our recommendations on how to use this book.

As a Reference

To use this book as a complete reference, you may find the following useful:

❏ *Table of contents*—This is best used to navigate to a high-level topic, particularly reference chapters for vendor-dependent SQL functions. The table of contents is also a good way to quickly navigate to a desired appendix, and to find introductory or trailing chapters with special-interest content.

❏ *Index*—This is best used to find a specific function based on function name or concept.

❏ *Appendix A*—This is best used to cross-reference all functions covered in this book. This appendix is particularly useful if you are dealing with multiple RDBMS versions.

❏ *Flip method*—The reference material in this book is organized both logically and alphabetically for the reader who likes to manually flip through the book.

For Understanding SQL Concepts

To aid in the understanding of SQL concepts, you may find the following useful:

❏ *Introductory material*—Read Chapters 1–4 sequentially to better understand SQL and the architecture and concepts behind SQL functions.

❏ *Function references*—Each reference chapter (Chapters 5–18) can be read individually to grasp a better understanding of a specific SQL implementation. Each chapter includes an introduction, explanation of SQL query syntax, and summary. Additionally, the reference material is organized logically and written in a manner to facilitate reader comprehension.

❏ *Trailing chapters*—Chapters 19–27 are designed to be read individually to better understand how SQL functions can best be applied on the job. Each chapter is standalone and can be referenced directly, based on the reader's specific interest.

Conventions

To help you get the most from the text and keep track of what's happening, we've used a number of conventions throughout the book.

> **Boxes like this one hold important, not-to-be-forgotten information that is directly relevant to the surrounding text.**

Tips, hints, tricks, and asides to the current discussion are offset and placed in italics like this.

As for styles in the text:

- ❏ We highlight new terms and important words *in italics* when we introduce them.
- ❏ We show keyboard strokes like this: Ctrl+A.
- ❏ We show file names, URLs, and code within the text like so: `persistence.properties`.
- ❏ We present code in two different ways:

```
In code examples we highlight new and important code with a gray background.
```

```
The gray highlighting is not used for code that's less important in the present
context, or has been shown before.
```

Errata

We make every effort to ensure that there are no errors in the text or in the code. However, no one is perfect, and mistakes do occur. If you find an error in one of our books, like a spelling mistake or faulty piece of code, we would be very grateful for your feedback. By sending in errata you may save another reader hours of frustration and at the same time you will be helping us provide even higher quality information.

To find the errata page for this book, go to `http://www.wrox.com` and locate the title using the Search box or one of the title lists. Then, on the book details page, click the Book Errata link. On this page you can view all errata that have been submitted for this book and posted by Wrox editors. A complete book list including links to each book's errata is also available at `www.wrox.com/miscpages/booklist.shtml`.

If you don't spot "your" error on the Book Errata page, go to `www.wrox.com/contact/techsupport.shtml` and complete the form there to send us the error you have found. We'll check the information and, if appropriate, post a message to the book's errata page and fix the problem in subsequent editions of the book.

p2p.wrox.com

For author and peer discussion, join the P2P forums at `p2p.wrox.com`. The forums are a Web-based system for you to post messages relating to Wrox books and related technologies and interact with other readers and technology users. The forums offer a subscription feature to e-mail you topics of interest of your choosing when new posts are made to the forums. Wrox authors, editors, other industry experts, and your fellow readers are present on these forums.

Introduction

At `p2p.wrox.com` you will find a number of different forums that will help you not only as you read this book, but also as you develop your own applications. To join the forums, just follow these steps:

1. Go to `p2p.wrox.com` and click the Register link.
2. Read the terms of use and click Agree.
3. Complete the required information to join, as well as any optional information you wish to provide and click Submit.
4. You will receive an e-mail with information describing how to verify your account and complete the joining process.

   You can read messages in the forums without joining P2P, but in order to post your own messages, you must join.

Once you join, you can post new messages and respond to messages other users post. You can read messages at any time on the Web. If you would like to have new messages from a particular forum e-mailed to you, click the Subscribe to this Forum icon by the forum name in the forum listing.

For more information about how to use the Wrox P2P forums, be sure to read the P2P FAQs for answers to questions about how the forum software works as well as many common questions specific to P2P and Wrox books. To read the FAQs, click the FAQ link on any P2P page.

For More Information

For more information about this book, supplemental material, Wiley Publishing, and other useful books and resources, visit Wiley's Web site at `www.wiley.com`.

For more information about the authors of this book, Perpetual Technologies, and additional database and SQL resources, visit the Perpetual Technologies Web site at `www.perptech.com`.

Thanks again, and good luck empowering your database environment with SQL functions!

Exploring Popular SQL Implementations

Any tour into the realm of writing SQL functions should begin with a solid foundation of the basic principles of SQL. In this chapter, we will be discussing the ins and outs of creating, querying, and modifying databases using basic SQL syntax. This chapter is the basis upon which we will build in the following chapters. This will help you unravel the mystery of using the power of built-in functions available across the various relational database management systems (RDBMS) platforms and to introduce new functionality into your applications by developing your own user-defined functions (UDFs).

Introduction to SQL

Structured Query Language (otherwise known as SQL and pronounced "SEE-kwul") was first developed by IBM in the mid- to late 1970s for their DB2 platform RDBMS. At the time, its purpose was to provide a way in which the RDBMS could retrieve data in a declarative way. Declarative "programming" was a way in which the RDBMS developer could specify what data would be selected, inserted, updated, or deleted without having to necessarily know where the data was or how it was stored. That was the job of the RDBMS. The main goal of SQL was to provide the following functionality to the RDBMS:

❑ Query the database to retrieve the data stored therein.

❑ Update existing data within the database.

❑ Insert new data into the database.

❑ Remove unwanted data from the database.

❑ Add permissions to RDBMS objects (databases, tables, and so on).

❑ Modify a database's structure.

❑ Change security settings.

Oracle released the first commercial RDBMS that used SQL in 1978. Soon after that, in the mid-1980s, Sybase released its own RDBMS, SQL Server. In 1988, this was ported to OS/2 by Sybase and Microsoft, and eventually to Windows NT. In 1993, the partnership parted ways and Sybase eventually renamed their product *Adaptive Server Enterprise (ASE)* to differentiate it from the Microsoft version. However, since that time, Open Source RDBMS solutions such as MySQL and PostgreSQL have taken hold in the marketplace and are among the fastest growing. Even though all of these systems follow or attempt to follow the same base SQL implementation, each has its own unique characteristics and extensions that make it stand out from the rest.

Understanding the SQL Standard

The "standard" of SQL is laid out by both the American National Standards Institute (ANSI) and the International Standards Organization (ISO). It is fundamentally a set of base standards that, in theory, is the agreed-upon example of what the SQL syntax and logic in an RDBMS should be. The original ANSI standard was put forth in 1986 and then later developed into ANSI SQL:1989 or, simply, SQL 89. The former version laid out a basic pattern of the following three separate ways in which SQL could be implemented:

❑ **Embedded** — This refers to embedding SQL statements within a program separate from the RDBMS instance. Patterns for this implementation were written to reflect the programming languages of the day (COBAL, FORTRAN, Pascal, and PL/1).

❑ **Direct** — The implementer could provide specific direct implementation of SQL to the developer.

❑ **Module** — Modules enable calls from procedures within programs and return a value to the calling program.

This baseline was further expanded with the release of ANSI 1992 or SQL 92, which included such things as connections to databases, dynamic SQL, and outer joins. This was in addition to establishing levels of compliance (entry, intermediate, and full) that the RDBMS system could tout to their user base. SQL:1999 again extended the standard by including more data types in the mix, such as arrays, user-defined types (UDTs), Boolean, BLOB, and CLOB. SQL:2003 expands upon the data types available, along with some new built-in functions.

However, it should be noted that the standards for core compliance have not been changed from the SQL:1999 version. This effectively means that anything that is SQL 99-compliant will automatically be SQL:2003-compliant as well. Therefore, it is important to understand that even though a specific RDBMS implementation may by SQL:2003-compliant, it does not mean that it has implemented all of the changes proposed within the new standard. In actuality, it has just prescribed to a set of core compliance standards, and you will have to check the specific instance of your RDBMS documentation to see which parts have truly been implemented.

Overview of Vendor Implementations of SQL

Another important aspect of understanding the basics of ANSI SQL is to know the different implementations of available RDBMS packages. This book is based upon what we see as the top six RDBMS implementations that use the ANSI SQL standard. It is important to realize that even though the ANSI SQL standard is something that every database should strive to emulate, each vendor implementation of that standard is unique and has nuances that the other implementations will not have. This section provides an overview of each of the six different RDBMS implementations discussed in this book to give you a good understanding of their backgrounds before going into the technical details of each implementation.

Oracle

Oracle is the market leader in the commercial RDBMS market. As mentioned in the previous section, Oracle released the first commercially available RDBMS in 1978. With the release of its commercial version 10g, Oracle claims SQL:2003 compliance, as well as a full set of features and tool sets for the developer. In addition, Oracle provides several different editions that fit a wide variety of operating environments (UNIX, Linux, and Windows) and levels of use.

IBM DB2 UDB

IBM created SQL for their DB2 database platform in the mid- to late 1970s. IBM is the world's leading hardware vendor, and their DB2 database platform has evolved into their Universal Database line. As of this writing, the current version is 8.2, and they offer several different editions to fit a number of operating platforms and uses.

Microsoft SQL Server and Sybase

As mentioned earlier, Sybase produced the original SQL Server and Microsoft later entered into a code-velopment agreement with them. Later in 1988, Microsoft ported the database from OS/2 over to their Windows platform. In 1993, the two companies discontinued their agreement and parted ways.

Since the split in 1993, Sybase has renamed their products *Sybase Adaptive Server Enterprise* and *Sybase IQ*. Originally developed for the OS/2 environment, Sybase's RDMS is now available for a wide variety of platforms, such as Windows, Linux, Solaris x86/64-bit, and Mac.

Microsoft is now the world's largest software developer. SQL Server 2000 is now their flagship database version, and they will soon release SQL Server 2005 (its beta version is currently available). Microsoft touts the ease of use of their database system, rather than total ANSI compliance. They provide a feature-rich set of administration tools, but are limited to the Microsoft Windows platform. SQL Server's most obvious difference from other SQL implementations is its use of Microsoft's extension language T-SQL. In Microsoft's version, there is no apparent difference to distinguish T-SQL from the standard version of SQL: they are treated as one and the same.

MySQL

Possibly the world's most-used Open Source RDBMS, MySQL is the product of its parent company MySQL AB, which was founded in Sweden in the 1980s. Although its solution is marketed as Open Source, it does have a commercial license if developers want to produce closed-source solutions with it. MySQL was initially developed with speed in mind and, as such, has suffered somewhat from its lack of a full feature set compared with some of its competitors. However, in recent releases (such as MySQL 4.0 and 5.0 Alpha), MySQL is starting to tout both its speed and compliance with the new SQL:2003 standard.

PostgreSQL

PostgreSQL (pronounced "Post-gres-Q-L") was developed in 1986 at the University of California at Berkeley. Today, it is considered to be the most powerful of the available Open Source RDBMS packages. Initially, PostgreSQL was written to perform on a number of versions of the UNIX operating system. As of this writing, PostgreSQL is in version 8.0 Beta 4, and is available since the initial release of version 8.0 on Windows NT-based systems. Whereas MySQL was written to be fast, PostgreSQL was developed to be "full featured." However, the trend has shifted with each subsequent release to make it faster.

Connecting to SQL Databases

To connect to an RDBMS, you must have two things: an SQL client and a CONNECTION statement. The SQL client acts as (or at least is perceived to be) a part of the specific SQL implementation. In addition, it also helps keep track of the state of all three parts of the connection instance: itself, the SQL agent, and the SQL server. Different vendors will have their own versions (even though the functionality is similar) of the SQL client. Oracle has SQL-PLUS and SQLPlus Worksheet, Microsoft had their own version in Query Analyzer, MySQL has MySQLGUI, and the list goes on. Once you have your particular client that matches your RDBMS of choice, connecting to a database is a rather simple matter. This is done by issuing the following SQL command:

```
CONNECT TO <database_name>
```

If your SQL client is set up with a default database to connect to, then you can simply issue the default connection command, which is the following:

```
CONNECT TO DEFAULT
```

Please note that if there is no default database established for the SQL client, then an exception error will be thrown by the client because it will not be able to establish a connection. However, depending on which RDBMS system you have and how your security context is set up, after issuing the command, you will more often than not be challenged for a username/password combination to access the database itself.

Once you are connected to your particular database instance, you can change to another database by issuing another CONNECT statement, naming the connection, and then issuing the SET statement to move between your different named connections, as shown here:

```
CONNECT TO DATABASE1 AS FIRSTDB USER sa;
CONNECT TO DATABASE2 AS SECONDDB USER sa;
SET CONNECTION FIRSTDB;
// Now we are working with the first database... //
SET CONNECTION SECONDDB;
// Now we are working with the second database.... //
```

Once you are finished working within your database(s), it is also necessary to disconnect from your session using the DISCONNECT statement, as shown here:

```
DISCONNECT <connection_name>;
// Or if you have multiple connections that you want to close... //
DISCONNECT ALL;
```

ANSI SQL Data Types

The ANSI SQL standard also specifies different data types in which to hold your data. In general, each RDBMS implementation will vary from these as each uses its own unique set to provide some uniqueness to the environment. The basic set of SQL data types can be broken down into the categories shown in the following table.

Type	ANSI SQL Data Types
Boolean	BOOLEAN
String	CHAR
	VARCHAR
Numeric	NUMERIC
	DECIMAL
	DOUBLE PRECISION
	FLOAT
	INTEGER
	REAL
	SMALLINT
	BIGINT
Date Time	DATE
	TIME
	TIMESTAMP

Since each RDBMS implementation differs, it is always best to refer to the documentation of your specific vendor to determine which data types it supports. The preceding table should merely serve as a guideline for some of the basic data types that are supported by the ANSI standard. Your particular vendor could have more or less, depending on the implementation. It is equally important to read the vendor descriptions of data types carefully, because, even though two vendors may provide data types with the same name, their precision and range may differ.

Creating SQL Databases

To create a new SQL database, you must issue the following command:

```
CREATE DATABASE <database_name>
```

This is the basic syntax for the CREATE DATABASE statement. There are plenty of optional clauses that can be used with the statement, but they differ from implementation to implementation. Clauses include those that specify everything for location of data files, database collation, and database state. It is best to check with your RDBMS systems documentation for the particular variance that they support.

Once the foundation of the database has been created, it is time to focus on creating the tables that will hold the various data you need within the database. The basic syntax for the CREATE TABLE statement is as follows:

```
CREATE TABLE <table_name>
(
<column_name1> data_type,
<column_name2> data_type,
.......
)
```

The columns can be identified using any of the ANSI-supported data types detailed earlier in this chapter.

At least one column name of a specific data type must be designated at the time of creation. If all columns are not named when the table is created, then the table may be altered using the ALTER TABLE syntax detailed here:

```
ALTER TABLE <table_name>
         [ADD COLUMN <column name> data type]
         [ALTER COLUMN <column name> new data type]
         [DROP COLUMN <column name>]
```

As you can see from this syntax, the ALTER TABLE syntax can be used not only to add columns to your table, but also to either modify them or drop them altogether.

Additionally, at most one column of the table can be designated as an identity column. An identity column is automatically assigned values based on an internal sequence generator every time a new row is inserted into the table. These identity columns are important in database table design because they ensure that each row is unique in at least one column. You can implement an identity column in your table by using syntax similar to the following:

```
CREATE TABLE employees
(
EMP_ID INTEGER
                GENERATED ALWAYS AS IDENTITY
                START WITH 1
                        INCREMENT 1
                        MINVALUE 1
                        NO MAXVALUE
                        NO CYCLE,
EMP_NAME        VARCHAR (30),
EMP_ADDRESS     VARCHAR (50),
EMP_CITY        VARCHAR (20),
EMP_STATE       CHAR (2),
EMP_SALARY      DECIMAL (10, 2)
)
```

A table may also be created with an *index*, which is the equivalent of a table of contents for your table. Indices are created separately from the actual data within the table, and are used to speed up queries on the table. There are several different implementations of placing indices on tables, as shown in the following syntax:

```
CREATE [UNIQUE] INDEX <index name>
     ON <table_name> (column_name1,column_name2,.......)
```

You may optionally use the UNIQUE keyword on your index to specify that any two index values must be unique across your index on the table. Additionally, you may specify more than one column on which to place the index, in which case it is commonly referred to as a *covering index*. It should also be specified that in order to speed up your queries, the index must be placed on a column(s) that your queries are using. In our previous example of creating the employees table, if we place an index on EMP_ID and perform a query on EMP_NAME our index would not be used.

Carefully planning your database creation will keep you from having to spend excess time and resources reconfiguring different aspects of your database structure.

Querying SQL Databases

Querying information from the database involves using the SELECT statement, whose basic syntax is as follows:

```
SELECT select_list
FROM table_source
```

The breakdown of the SELECT statement is similar to any SQL query in that it is composed of keywords and clauses. *Keywords* are the individual SQL statements. In this case, SELECT and FROM would be the keywords. *Clauses* are everything else within the statement and are objects that shape what data the keywords operate upon. In a simple example, we could pull the First_Name and Last_Name from a table named "Authors" in our database, as follows:

```
SELECT FIRST_NAME, LAST_NAME
FROM AUTHORS;
FIRST NAME          LAST NAME
Tennessee           Williams
Steven              King
Danielle            Steeley
Margo               Hennesay
Jordan              Michaels
```

By looking closely at the example, you can see several characteristics of the SELECT statement that are true for all SQL statements in general. The first thing that you should see is that the objects in the select list (FIRST_NAME, LAST_NAME) are pulled from the database in the order that they were named. Our SQL query is written in uppercase, but it should be noted that SQL is a case-insensitive language. This means that it does not matter in what case we specify our SQL statements. We could have used the following statement and received the same results:

```
Select first_name, last_name
From authors;

FIRST NAME          LAST NAME
Tennessee           Williams
Steven              King
Danielle            Steeley
Margo               Hennesay
Jordan              Michaels
```

It is important to remember, however, that the data within your database is case-sensitive. So, if we were to add a WHERE clause to our previous query in order to pull any authors with the last name of "King" from our database, it would be important to know in which case King was stored within the database. "King," "KING," "king," and "KinG" are all considered different from our WHERE clause.

```
// Incorrect case for King //
SELECT FIRST_NAME, LAST_NAME
FROM AUTHORS
WHERE LAST_NAME='king';


FIRST NAME          LAST NAME
No rows selected




// Correct case for King //
SELECT FIRST_NAME, LAST_NAME
FROM AUTHORS
WHERE LAST_NAME='King';


FIRST NAME          LAST NAME
Steven              King
```

There are other clauses that can also be added to our SELECT statement to further shape and restrict the data that is returned to us from our query. DISTINCT is used to restrict the query to return only distinct values and to drop all duplicates from the query.

```
SELECT DISTINCT <select_list> FROM <table_name>
```

TOP N is used to return the first N number of rows from the query results returned by the rest of the statement.

```
SELECT TOP <number or rows> <select_list> FROM <table_name>
```

ORDER BY is used to order the data from the query based upon the designated columns.

```
SELECT <select_list> FROM <table_name>
ORDER_BY <column_name1,column_name2,.......>
```

Using our previous example of the Authors table, we can combine several of these clauses to our SELECT statement to alter our result set.

```
SELECT TOP 2 FIRST_NAME, LAST_NAME
FROM AUTHORS
ORDER BY LAST_NAME;


FIRST NAME          LAST NAME
Margo               Hennesay
Steven              King
```

The last thing to note before we change our focus to the manipulation of data in SQL databases is that the query statements in this example use the semicolon as the terminating value. It should be noted that some implementations use this syntax and will not process a query statement without it (such as Oracle). However, others (such as SQL Server) make the syntax optional, so you can use it or not at your leisure. As always, it is best to check your specific version of RDBMS documentation to find out the proper syntax you should be using.

Manipulating Data in SQL Databases

Manipulating data within the database is centered on the use of the following three SQL statements:

- ❏   INSERT
- ❏   UPDATE
- ❏   DELETE

The INSERT statement handles the insertion of new data rows into the tables of your database. It can be called using either specific values or the SELECT statement to populate the new rows in your table. When you want to populate a single row in a table within your database, it is best to use the following version of the statement:

```
INSERT INTO <table_name> (<column_name1,column_name2,.....>)
VALUES (<value1,value2,........)
```

The most important things to remember about the INSERT statement are that the arguments in the column list and the value list must be equal in number, and that they must appear in the same order. So, using an example with our Authors table, we could use the following:

```
// Values are in incorrect order with respect to the Columns //
INSERT INTO Authors( First_Name, Last_Name)
VALUES ('King','Steven')

// Values are in the correct order with respect to the Columns //
INSERT INTO Authors( First_Name, Last_Name)
VALUES ('Steven','King')
```

This is a good example because it shows how the column names must align themselves with the values in both number and order. Another interesting fact is that both of these statements will execute because neither of them violates the structure of the table itself. The Last_Name and First_Name fields are obviously both character fields, and, as far as the database is concerned, they would both be valid values. This illustrates how careful the developer must be to make sure that the data being entered into the database is always entered in the correct fields to prevent complications down the road.

The other instance in which you would be entering data into a table would be one in which you wanted to insert multiple rows with a single SQL statement. In this case, you would use a SELECT statement in place of the VALUES statement.

```
INSERT INTO <table_name> (<column_name1, column_name2,.....>)
SELECT <select_list>
FROM <table_name>
```

In essence, you are inserting the results of your SELECT statement into the specified table within your database. In this instance, it is important to remember that the column list specified on the first line above must match the select list of the SELECT statement in both number and order. Failing to pay close attention to this will result in the possibility of incorrect values being loaded into your tables without an exception being raised, as detailed in our previous example.

Once your data is loaded into the tables of your database, it may become necessary to change some of the values. In order to accomplish this, you use the UPDATE statement.

```
UPDATE <table_name>
SET column_name1 = value1, column_name2 = value2, .......
WHERE
<search condition>
```

The UPDATE statement is called detailing which column values are to be changed, what they are to be changed to, and a search condition to limit the number of rows affected. Please remember that if you do not specify a search condition when issuing this command, then *all* of the rows within your table will be modified to the new value(s), possibly an unintended result. The following provides an example of the possible implementation of an UPDATE query on our theoretical Authors table:

```
// A query to check our original values //
SELECT FIRST_NAME, LAST_NAME FROM AUTHORS
WHERE LAST_NAME = 'King';
FIRST NAME          LAST NAME
Steven              King
// Now we update the First_Name of the row to Mike //
UPDATE Authors
SET First_Name = 'Mike'
WHERE
Last_Name = 'King';


// Now we query the table again to confirm the row has been changed //
SELECT FIRST_NAME, LAST_NAME FROM AUTHORS
WHERE LAST_NAME = 'King';
FIRST NAME          LAST NAME
Mike                King
```

At some point in time, it may become necessary to completely remove rows of old data from the tables within the database. To accomplish this, you would use the DELETE statement.

```
DELETE FROM <table_name>
WHERE <search condition>
```

The syntax of the DELETE statement is simple, but like the UPDATE statement, if you do not include the search condition, then *all* rows are affected. Following our previous example, the DELETE statement can be implemented like this:

```
// Verify that the row we are going to delete exists //
SELECT FIRST_NAME, LAST_NAME FROM AUTHORS
WHERE LAST_NAME = 'King';
FIRST NAME          LAST NAME
Mike                King
// Now we say goodbye to Mr. King //
DELETE
FROM Authors
WHERE
Last_Name = 'King';


// Let's verify that the row is gone //
SELECT FIRST_NAME, LAST_NAME FROM AUTHORS
WHERE LAST_NAME = 'King';
FIRST NAME          LAST NAME
No rows selected
```

Summary

You should now have a general understanding of the basics of SQL history and structure. SQL has been around since the late 1970s and has been set forth as the standard for the RDBMS industry. The standard is maintained by ANSI, but they no longer test for compliance with the standard. Considering that, you should always rely on your RDBMS documentation to determine if the specific implementation provides the level of compliance you desire.

In addition, you should also have a reasonable understanding of the major RDBMS implementations that will be used throughout this book. The differences between these systems will become more apparent as you traverse the chapters of this book. These differences are an important point to remember before taking the leap of deciding on a specific RDBMS implementation. These slight differences can lead to major problems if existing code must be ported to another vendor's implementation.

We have also detailed the basic functions (SELECT, INSERT, UPDATE, DELETE) used to maintain the data within the tables of your database. We will use this basic knowledge as a building block in later chapters in order to show the power and functionality of using functions within your database's schema. In the next chapter, we will discuss the basic concepts of built-in and user-defined SQL functions, which comprise the majority of this book.

Functions: Concept and Architecture

Functions supply the cornerstone of any RDBMS development project. To clearly understand the power and flexibility that functions can bring to your environment, you must first understand the basics. This chapter demystifies some of the basic conceptual and architectural features of functions. It begins with a discussion of what is actually classified as a function, and progresses on to how functions are created, compiled, executed, and classified. Along the way, we will provide several examples to illustrate the usefulness of functions in the SQL programming environment.

What Is a Function?

A *function* is a fragment of program code to which the program execution may jump (or *branch*) from another location. It ends by returning the program execution to the location immediately following the branch point. Generally, a function accepts one or more arguments and returns a value. How does it do this?

Every time a program executes, a data structure called the *program stack* is associated with it. A stack is just a block of memory accessed at a single point, the "top," where things may be "pushed" onto the stack (placed in that memory) or "popped" off it (removed from that memory). This sort of structure is classified as Last In, First Out (LIFO), and it is useful for processes that recursively backtrack their steps (such as spanning a tree structure).

When a function is called (that is, when the program execution branches off to a function), the address of the instruction (following the branch point) is pushed onto the stack. This is how the function knows where to return after its execution. When it is finished, the last thing that happens is the current top of the stack (which is the address of the next instruction in the main program) is popped into the instruction pointer (a CPU register, containing the address of the next instruction to be processed).

How can we be sure that the top of the stack after the function finishes is the address of the next instruction? Contemporary high-level languages normally ensure the proper manipulation of the stack, which guarantees this. One of the great bogies of assembly language programming used to be "stack imbalance," which happened if the programmer did not carefully balance each push with the corresponding pop in the right order. In those cases, a function was liable to "return to Neverland" instead of returning where it was expected.

Before a function is called, the calling program pushes the function's arguments onto the stack. In principle, it does not matter in what order this is done, so long as the corresponding popping is accomplished in the reverse order (LIFO, remember). But because there are several ways of doing this (if there is more than one argument), each compiler does it differently. Fortunately, there are only two conventions: push the last argument first, or push the first argument first. For some unfathomable reason, no one has invented pushing the middle argument first, or the last-but-one argument last. The two conventions are usually referred to as the C-style and the Pascal-style of argument passing (C pushes the last argument first).

This is critical because you must know which convention the SQL compiler uses and which language the compiler uses to ensure compatibility. In the end, both compilers must use the same argument-pushing order.

If a database management system (DBMS) offers a compiler to write functions, you can safely assume that the compiler uses the correct argument-pushing order. However, if the DBMS offers a way to add in a *compiled* function, you must dig around to avoid this potential problem. Usually, compilers provide switches or some other means of overriding the default argument-pushing order.

Of course, functions on different platforms can be structured in different ways. To highlight the difference between a function in an operating system versus those created within an RDBMS implementation, we will discuss a few brief examples.

Simple UNIX Shell Function Example

An excellent example of a UNIX shell function is one that provides the uppercase version of a string. In the following example, ToUpper() takes a single string value as a parameter and returns that value in uppercase.

```
ToUpper()
{
    echo $1 | tr 'abcdefghijklmnopqrstuvwxyz' \
              'ABCDEFGHIJKLMNOPQRSTUVWXYZ'
}
```

UNIX uses $x, with x equal to a numeral from 0 to 9, as its syntax for positional parameters passed into a function. In our example, one can readily see that $1 is using the first parameter to pass into the UNIX translate command (tr) to perform the simple uppercase translation. Executing the function in UNIX would give the following result:

```
$ ToUpper david
  DAVID
```

Simple SQL Function Example

The idea of a function in SQL is similar in reasoning to a UNIX shell function even though the syntax varies dramatically. In the following example, we create a simple Oracle function called `Get_Tax`. The purpose of `Get_Tax` is to pass it a dollar amount and have it return the sales tax the customer owes based on a 5 percent rate.

```
Create or replace function Get_Tax (aAmount IN NUMBER(10,2))
    Return NUMBER
    Is
    Tax_owed NUMBER(10,2);
Begin
    Select aAmount * 0.05 into Tax_owed;
    Return(Tax_owed);
End;
```

This example uses the `CREATE OR REPLACE FUNCTION` syntax to declare the function within the Oracle system. A developer familiar with Oracle would recognize that our function takes a number parameter of length 10 and decimal accuracy of 2 identified by `aAmount`. Furthermore, the Oracle developer would note that it returns a number identified by the variable `Tax_owed`. The value in `aAmount` is multiplied by our tax rate of 5 percent and stuffed into the variable `Tax_owed`, and `Tax_owed` is returned to the user or calling routine.

ANSI SQL Functions

The Committee on Data Systems and Languages (CODASYL) chartered the American National Standards Institute (ANSI) International Committee for Information Technical Standards (INCITS) H2 committee to create a standard for what then was seen as *the* model for data operations: the Network Data Model. By 1980, the Data Definition Language (DDL) part of the emerging standard was complete, followed by Data Manipulation Language (DML) in 1982. The DML included some provisions for what eventually became known as SQL functions.

The Relational Data Model abstracts the logical implementation of the data from the physical implementation and provides a declarative interface. By late 1982, it was obvious that the Relational Data Model offered certain advantages over the Network Data Model, and efforts were redirected toward incorporate this new fad. The "fad" has survived for more than two decades, and shows no signs of abating.

Throughout the 1980s, the only game in town for enterprise systems was IBM DB2, which was little surprise, given the cost of entry into the mainframe software business. Every vendor entering the field crafted database systems to be at least somewhat compatible with IBM DB2. It was IBM's Phil Shaw who submitted the Relational Database Language (RDL) specification for approval. It was accepted, and after several iterations became an ANSI SQL standard in 1986. The resulting SQL86 (also known as SQL1) standard had two levels of compliance: Entry (Level 1) and Full (Level 2). It was relatively simple at only 105 pages, and was immediately implemented by a number of software vendors who sensed their chance to challenge IBM's iron grip on the field.

Some things were missing though, most notably referential integrity. This called for a revision, and a new SQL 89 standard was born. Mercifully, the specification still contained only 120 pages. The list of SQL functions mandated by the new standard included fewer than 10.

A variety of RDBMS packages featuring SQL as the built-in language appeared. Oracle emerged as RDBMS vendor of choice for small and mid-range computers, leapfrogging Ingres (which was using QUEL as a query language), Informix, and IBM System R (replaced by the DB2 intergalactic standard in 1982).

The rise of personal computers opened the floodgates for hundreds of new vendors, most of which have since faded away (RIM, RBASE 5000, Dbase III/IV, and WatcomSQL, to name a few). And they (almost) all spoke the same SQL language! Whether it was because the standard was not enforced, or because vendors used originality to attract and retain customers, SQL became fragmented by the various new dialects. Nowhere was this more noticeable than in the built-in SQL functions implemented by the vendors. Each "real-world" RDBMS sported dozens of these SQL functions in their products, even though the standard called for a much smaller count.

As the capabilities of computers grew, so did the appetites of users for RDBMS features. Vendors were gaining expertise, and new players were entering the RDBMS market. It was time for another SQL standard. The new standard was released in 1992, and the full length of the document describing it was a whopping 575 pages. At the same time, the list of the "standard" functions grew to more than 20.

When the gold rush in the early RDBMS markets was over, customers began to realize that they must ensure their business RDBMS continuity. Facing a flood of "one-night stand" vendors, they felt it would be better to stick to some kind of standard. The ANSI SQL compliance came into vogue.

To claim SQL 92 compliance, an RDBMS must comply with Entry Level SQL 92. For the next standard (SQL 99, otherwise known as SQL3), the minimum compliance is called Core SQL 99. The current standard, aptly called SQL:2003, requires Core SQL:2003 compliance.

Oracle claims Core SQL 99 compliance for its Oracle 9i and 10g flagship database product. IBM DB2 UDB in its version 8.1 also claims Core SQL 99 compliance, while Sybase, Microsoft, and MySQL adhere to the Entry Level SQL 92. The PostgreSQL (quite possibly the most standards-compliant RDBMS in existence) claims the Core SQL 99 compliance.

As we've pointed out before, there weren't many SQL functions mandated by the original SQL standards committee. Therefore, every RDBMS could claim full (well, almost full) compliance with SQL 92 standards in this regard. The SQL 99 and Core SQL:2003 standards are a different matter, because more advanced functions were introduced in these standard specifications. Nevertheless, most RDBMS packages discussed in this book did comply with these, if not in letter, then in spirit.

Built-in Functions

A built-in function library is one of the most powerful resources available to the SQL programmer. Built-in functions provide the programmer with precoded logic that can be used multiple times, and embedded within SQL queries, third-generation programming languages (3GLs), or fourth-generation programming languages (4GLs), which are discussed later in this chapter in the section "Creating, Compiling, and Executing a SQL Function." In this section, we will illustrate the execution and common uses of built-in SQL functions.

Executing Built-in Functions

Executing a built-in function is a relatively simple matter that only requires that you call the function and pass it the required variables it needs to execute. This lends itself to a wide variety of uses, and this flexibility is what makes functions such powerful tools for the developer. In this first example, we will create a variable and then set its value equal to the built-in function GETDATE() return value.

```
DECLARE @THISDATE DATETIME
SELECT @THISDATE=GETDATE()
```

Likewise, we could also use this built-in function in conjunction with the ADD_MONTHS function within a SELECT statement that pulls invoice numbers from the database that are over six months old.

```
SELECT INVOICE_NUM
FROM ORDERS
WHERE
    INVOICE_DATE < ADD_MONTHS(GETDATE(),-6)
```

Practical Uses of Functions

The two most compelling uses of functions revolve around the reusability of your code and the simplification of complex queries. One of the biggest advantages of using functions is that you can use them in place of code that would normally have to be written over and over again; entire chunks of code are compressed into a compact, reusable format. Consider the simplest of instances: you want to get the maximum value of the Amount column in a Sales table to find the largest sale of the day using SQL Server. Without the use of built-in functions, this would require the impractical use of things such as cursors and variables, making the developer write lines and lines of code if used throughout the project. Luckily for us, there is already a built-in function, MAX(), that will return the maximum value within the column and can be utilized like this:

```
CREATE TABLE SALES(
                    AMOUNT    NUMERIC(5,2)
                    );

INSERT INTO SALES(AMOUNT) VALUES(100.00);
INSERT INTO SALES(AMOUNT) VALUES(1435.50);
INSERT INTO SALES(AMOUNT) VALUES(456.87);
INSERT INTO SALES(AMOUNT) VALUES(4500.00);
INSERT INTO SALES(AMOUNT) VALUES(564.55);
INSERT INTO SALES(AMOUNT) VALUES(3456.34);

SELECT MAX(AMOUNT) AS BIG_SALE FROM SALES;

BIG_SALE
4500.00
```

The other biggest practical use of functions is the ability to encapsulate complex code that both simplifies your code and increases its readability. Suppose that a government agency needs a series of reports showing expenditures based on its fiscal year. While this would be a simple matter if the government adhered to the calendar, sadly, the government's fiscal year starts on October 1, which adds an element of complexity to the problem. One option is to just write out the queries without a function using the straight SQL Server syntax.

```
SELECT
      INVOICE_NUM, AMOUNT
FROM EXPENDITURES
WHERE
      FISCAL_YEAR =
            CASE
                  WHEN MONTH(GETDATE())>= 10
                  THEN YEAR(GETDATE()) + 1
                  ELSE YEAR(GETDATE())
            END
ORDER BY INVOICE_NUM
```

Although this is a perfectly legitimate way in which to write this query, we can simplify the code by using a function that calculates the fiscal year for us. Following that logic, we would use the following bit of code to create our function:

```
CREATE FUNCTION DBO.CURRENT_FISCAL_YEAR(@ADATE DATETIME)
RETURNS INT AS
BEGIN
DECLARE @RTNDATE INT
SELECT @RTNDATE =
                  CASE
                        WHEN MONTH(@ADATE)>= 10
                        THEN YEAR(@ADATE) + 1
                        ELSE YEAR(@ADATE)
                  END
RETURN @RTNDATE
END
```

Now, we can not only reuse this code as was explained in the previous example, but we will have reduced the amount of complexity in our query. This not only lessens the amount of coding that we have to do, but also makes our code more readable, which, in turn, makes our code easier to maintain. We can see this by the implementation of our expenditures query using the new function:

```
SELECT
      INVOICE_NUM, AMOUNT
FROM EXPENDITURES
WHERE
      FISCAL_YEAR = DBO.CURRENT_FISCAL_YEAR(GETDATE())
ORDER BY INVOICE_NUM
```

Creating, Compiling, and Executing a SQL Function

A function is, ideally, an isolated, "black-box" piece of code that solves a single, well-defined problem and returns a single result. An isolated piece of code that does not have a defined return value is customarily called a *procedure*. Because of the overwhelming popularity of C (which consists of nothing but functions), the term *function* frequently describes procedures as well. In the context of SQL, the distinction between functions and procedures is an important one. A well-designed SQL program is composed of procedures and functions — unless it is composed of objects, which interact with other parts of the program with methods (which are nothing more, nor less, than procedures or functions).

Some of the more sophisticated software development systems (for example Visual Basic) provide *built-in* functions, which we don't have to write for ourselves. For example, to take apart a string, we may use built-in functions `Left`, `Right`, and `Mid`. We don't have to figure out how to read the system clock, thanks to the built-in function `Now`.

Visual Basic is designed to make it easier for a programmer to write a program. It has a compiler that reads the programmer-written code and translates it into computer-readable, executable instructions. It also has function libraries (collections of functions) that are written, translated, and made available for incorporation into other programs. That is all a built-in function is: a stand-alone function, written as part of a programming system (rather than as part of a particular program), for use and reuse.

A DBMS also is a collection of programs, albeit with a somewhat different purpose (namely, storage and retrieval of data). Data storage and retrieval is a particularly involved matter, with many different parameters and combinations of parameters. SQL is an entire language created to explain DBMS requirements. SQL is to a DBMS what a programming language is to a computer system. Just as a computer system must translate (compile) a program, so must a DBMS compile a SQL statement. And, just as a computer system helps programs along by providing built-in functions, so does a DBMS have built-in functions that a SQL statement (that is, a little program written in SQL) may call.

Languages such as C, Pascal, Ada, and Basic are third-generation languages (3GLs). These languages are used to teach a computer system *how* to perform a task.

SQL, on the other hand, is an example of a fourth-generation language (4GL). A 4GL tells the computer *what* needs to be done. An important assumption is implicit here: a 4GL expects the system to know how to do things ahead of time.

So, in a 3GL, we might write the following:

```
read a record
while record id does not match the specified key do
    if not the end of file then
            read a record
    else
            stop reading
    end if
end while
if not the end of file then
 record.field = value
end if
```

In 4GL, we just write the following:

```
UPDATE table SET field=value
```

This is much simpler, of course, but how does this magic happen?

A 4GL includes stored algorithms and serves as the middle manager. We tell it what needs to be done; it turns around and tells the system how to do it. Essentially, a 4GL compiler replaces the name of each task with the corresponding algorithm.

But what if we ask it to perform a task it does not know how to do? We then have to teach it.

Recalling and rewriting every compiler whenever a new command must be added would be tiresome, not to mention time-consuming. It's more efficient to define, ahead of time, the means of *extending* the 4GL's store of knowledge. Even more helpful would be the means to add new functionality without altering existing compilers. This, then, is a function library.

If we were to look under the hood of a SQL compiler, we would discover that it converts commands such as UPDATE and SELECT into calls to procedures and functions from its accompanying libraries. So, all we do to extend the language capabilities is add some more functions to its libraries, or some more libraries for the compiler to dip into.

Why not also give the users a means to add new functions, written in some suitable 3GL? Some vendors provide a proprietary 3GL (such as Oracle PL/SQL). Others provide a compiler for a standard 3GL (such as C or Java). Some allow you to incorporate your own algorithms into the system by linking in precompiled functions and libraries.

Why do we talk about SQL *functions* but not SQL *procedures*? Because SQL is a highly specialized language designed for dealing with databases. We can only do so many things to a database, and the designers of the language have provided adequate SQL commands to perform each such action. Consequently, there's no room for extending the language. A function, remember, is there, not so much to perform a job, but to map one or more values (or even zero values, to make mathematicians suffer) onto a single value (which, of course, may be a bit of a job in itself, but that's of secondary importance). Not even the cleverest bunch of language designers can foresee and provide for every possible contingency where a value must be procured or computed. More importantly, it can be argued that *logically* a language such as SQL must not concern itself with facilities for procurement of values. Its job is to do things to a database. If the things to be done require some values to be computed, that's the job of a *language extension* (that is, a logically separate entity). That is why SQL may be extended with functions, but not procedures.

There are very useful procedures that organize database operations (expressed in SQL) and other needful things such as the order that things are done (expressed in 3GLs) into sequences of actions, as will be seen in the next section. These procedures extend our ability to *use* SQL, but they don't extend the capabilities *of* SQL.

Let us consider, briefly, a 3GL procedure with some SQL statements incorporated in it. Such a procedure may be written, for example, in an Oracle language: Procedural Language/SQL (PL/SQL) or Pro*C. PL/SQL is a language designed and developed specifically to write procedures with SQL statements embedded in them. Pro*C is itself an extension, this time of the C language, whose purpose is to enable the programmer to embed SQL statements in a procedure (a C function, in this case).

What happens when this procedure is compiled? Two separate processes take place: the 3GL code is processed by the 3GL compiler and the SQL statements are processed by the SQL processor. At some point, the results of the two compilations are merged into the one executable.

This can be very clearly seen when using Oracle's Pro*C. Pro*C is a precompiler, so its output is, in fact, the proper C code. By studying it, you can see what the SQL processor has done to the SQL statements. It converts them to a C code sequence, loading the parameters into some data structures and calling some functions (remember, in C, every subroutine is a function) with these data structures as arguments. In this case, the "merging" happens quite early on. In fact, the C compiler only sees the proper C code, all SQL stuff having been translated already.

Here are some excerpts from a small program written in Pro*C. This is the source code. Note that the uppercase code is not C, but SQL code. A regular C compiler would be confused by it. This code is processed by the Pro*C precompiler *before* the regular C compilation happens.

```
/* Declare section for host variables */
EXEC SQL BEGIN DECLARE SECTION;

VARCHAR userid[20];
VARCHAR passwd[20];
VARCHAR prod_name[15];

EXEC SQL END DECLARE SECTION;
<some code goes here . . .>
/* Catch errors automatically and go to error handling routine */
    EXEC SQL WHENEVER SQLERROR GOTO error;
<some code goes here . . .>
    EXEC SQL CONNECT :userid IDENTIFIED BY :passwd;
<some code goes here . . .>
```

Following is the precompiled code. Now we see that all the SQL code has been mapped onto C code. The original SQL statements have been retained as comments.

```
/* Declare section for host variables */
/* EXEC SQL BEGIN DECLARE SECTION; */

/*note how variable declarations are translated into data structures */
/* VARCHAR userid[20]; */
struct { unsigned short len; unsigned char arr[20]; } userid;

/* VARCHAR passwd[20]; */
struct { unsigned short len; unsigned char arr[20]; } passwd;
/* VARCHAR prod_name[15]; */
struct { unsigned short len; unsigned char arr[15]; } prod_name;
/* EXEC SQL END DECLARE SECTION; */
<some code goes here . . . >
/* Catch errors automatically and go to error handling routine*/
/* EXEC SQL WHENEVER SQLERROR GOTO error; */

    /* Connect to Oracle */

    /* EXEC SQL CONNECT :userid IDENTIFIED BY :passwd; */
```

Note the expansion of the CONNECT statement. A large data structure was declared and loaded with various necessary data and, in the last lines, a C function was called to perform the connection and error checking. The result is as follows:

```
{
  struct sqlexd sqlstm;
  sqlstm.sqlvsn = 10;
  sqlstm.arrsiz = 4;
  sqlstm.sqladtp = &sqladt;
  sqlstm.sqltdsp = &sqltds;
  sqlstm.iters = (unsigned int  )10;
  ... (lots and lots more lines like these here!) ...
  sqlstm.sqphss = sqlstm.sqhsts;
  sqlstm.sqpind = sqlstm.sqindv;
  sqlstm.sqpins = sqlstm.sqinds;
  sqlstm.sqparm = sqlstm.sqharm;
  sqlstm.sqparc = sqlstm.sqharc;
  sqlstm.sqpadto = sqlstm.sqadto;
  sqlstm.sqptdso = sqlstm.sqtdso;
finally, here's the function call:
  sqlcxt((void **)0, &sqlctx, &sqlstm, &sqlfpn);
  if (sqlca.sqlcode < 0) goto error;
}
```

This example shows how the 4GL "magic" happens: each brief 4GL statement is translated into some 3GL code that manipulates data and calls functions in the usual 3GL fashion.

Passing Parameters by Value or by Reference

A *parameter* is any variable used by a function that must be assigned a value before the function's calculations can be performed. As you know, parameters may be passed either *by value* or *by reference*. "By value" means that *a copy* of the passed value is provided to the function. "By reference" means that the actual variable, containing the passed value, is made available to the function. In C, where this difference is not explicitly defined, passing by reference is accomplished by passing, not the variable itself, but a pointer to (or the address of) the variable.

For a SQL function, the most obvious use of passing a parameter by reference is passing a buffer (that is, a container variable), which the function is to fill with some data retrieved from the database. (The key, by which the data is to be found, would normally be passed by value.)

Let us take a closer look at the mechanism of passing arguments by value and by reference. Let's begin with a quick overview of the famously arcane topics of memory, memory addressing, and pointers.

Program variables are stored in memory. From the program's point of view, *memory* is a contiguous block of slots, rather like mailboxes in a large apartment complex, or a bank of pigeonholes upon an efficient secretary's desk. Each memory slot is numbered sequentially.

Actually, a better image for these slots would be land plots along a town street. They, too, are numbered. However, a developer may decide to combine two adjacent land plots and build a larger-than-usual house. The address of the house will be that of the first land plot. To the casual observer, the house would appear to occupy one land plot, just like any other. Just like that casual observer, we will say that each memory slot is capable of containing a value, never mind its size.

Each such slot that contains (or is capable of containing) a useful value to the program is called a *program variable*. The program knows of its variables by their addresses (the slot numbers). As programmers, we usually assign to program variables some more or less useful or cryptic names, depending on our upbringing and mental constitution. The program couldn't care less. It doesn't even try. When it is compiled, all our clever names are replaced by memory addresses, and that's all. (Or, rather, they are replaced with offsets from a certain base memory address, so that the program may be loaded into different memory spaces at different times, but let's just say memory addresses, for simplicity. Also for the sake of simplicity, let us pretend that these memory addresses look like four-digit numbers, though these days, they are somewhat more complex. It does not alter our present story.)

When a program needs a value from a variable, it just says to the CPU, "Get me what's at address [1800]." Conversely, it may ask the CPU to place a value in memory at address [1800], as shown here:

```
int x = 5; /* place value at address 1800 */
...|___|_5_|___|...
 1799 1800 1801
x = x * 3; /* get value from the address at 1800, multiply it by 3 and put it into
the same spot */
...|___|15_|___|...
 1799 1800 1801
```

Note in the previous code that a *value* is quite independent of the *variable* that stores it. We may get the value 5 out of [1800], triple it, extract the cubic root and do other strange things to it. As long as we *do not put it back* to [1800], the variable at [1800] will continue to contain the value of 5. (In the previous code, we did put it back to [1800], in which case, of course, the content of [1800] did change.)

Now, just for fun, let us imagine a set of instructions a program wants to perform on a series of similar values.

Instead of repeatedly coding the instructions for each variable, we might set up a loop where the program, each time it enters it, says, "Now go to memory [2156] and get its value." *This is the address of the variable to use* this time around. Here we have a *pointer* variable, or a variable containing the memory address of another variable. (Something inside the loop will have to change the contents of memory slot 2156, of course.)

```
...|___|_5_|_3_|_7_|12_|...
 1799 1800 1801 1802 1803
int *xp = &x;
...|___|1800|___|...
 2155  2156 2157
```

When passing by value, the program says, "Get a value from [1800]; push it on the stack." When passing by reference, it says, "Push '1800' on the stack." In the first case, the stack might contain the value "5;" in the second case, it will contain "1800." Also, the function knows whether the variable it got has been passed by value or by reference.

With arguments passed by value, the function does as it pleases, and nobody is the wiser. It may have received the value of 5, turned it into 15 or 357; the original value of 5, which was taken from memory at [1800] is still there and is still 5, not 15, nor yet 357! This is because when arguments are passed by value, it essentially creates a local "cloned" version of the variable that exists only within the scope of the function.

Not so in the other case, because the function, recognizing a variable passed by reference, does not pass the value along to the stack (in this case 5), but instead passes a reference to the location within memory where the value is stored. So, it might still turn 5 into 15, but it will do that by saying, "Get the value that was passed, use its *address, and get the value from memory at that address*, triple it, get the value that was passed, use its *address again and put the new tripled value into memory at that address.*"

And now, the function may have been long finished and gone, but the new value of 15 is there for all of the program to see. In the other case, of course, whatever the function was doing to the value perished along with the function (see the section "Scope of a Function" later in this chapter), unless it was communicated to the rest of the program in some other way *and became an entirely different variable* in the process.

> *While it is possible to pass by-reference parameters to a function and return more than one value in this way, this is not considered a good practice. Most of the time, if a function must return more than one value, it is a good indication that the function attempts to do more than one job, which is not good design. Returning values in output parameters should be avoided also because a function that does that could not possibly be used in a SQL statement.*

In an RDBMS, the only place where you could specify "by value" or "by reference" is user-defined functions (UDFs) and stored procedures. This applies to the functions and procedures created with custom procedural extensions languages (PL/SQL, Transact-SQL, and so on). The SQL built-in functions are designed to accept parameters by reference. This topic is covered in greater depth in Chapter 3.

Scope of a Function

A code block is a logically distinct piece of code. It may be big or small. It may be a function or a group of functions. It may be the body of a loop or it may be a conditional clause (IF *condition* THEN *block* ELSE *block* ENDIF). The important bit for us right now is that we may define things inside a block so that these things exist, and are known, only inside the block. A variable declared inside the block is accessible only within that block. (Moreover, unless we make a special effort to the contrary, it actually *does not exist* outside the block. It is created when the block is entered and destroyed before exit.) This is called *encapsulation*, and it is important for several reasons. We will consider two:

❏ **Logical thinking** — If we have defined, let us say, a function inside a block, and then eventually find ourselves wanting to call this function from the outside, we are alerted to the inconsistency, and we may stop to ponder what has gone wrong. Are we trying to do *outside* what ought to be done *inside*? Or, is our function really of a more general nature than just one block? This helps to keep our thinking crisp.

❏ **Debugging and limiting damage** — If a variable is defined inside a block, it is easier to determine which code may possibly alter or destroy its contents, because, obviously, no code *outside* the block can reach that variable. The code from which a variable (or a function, or any other program object) is *visible* (that is, accessible) is called the *scope* of that object. Code blocks are hierarchical (meaning that a block may contain other blocks). The scoping rules usually dictate that an object's scope is the block where the object is defined and all the blocks defined inside that block, directly or otherwise.

Better Security

Scoping also helps with security, in that if a whole scope is protected by some access control, then, obviously, so is everything within the scope. For example, if your function is inside a package, a user must be granted proper privileges to the package in order to execute the function, even though programmatically the function might be within the scope accessible for the user. Most RDBMS packages provide for fine-grained level of control by assigning different access privileges to the database object (a function in our case). Only users to whom the EXECUTE privilege was granted are allowed to invoke the function.

Various SQL extensions define large scoping blocks to contain a number of related database objects (such as functions, procedures, tables, and so on). Oracle defines packages and schemas. MS SQL Server and Sybase define a whole database as one scoping block, and so on.

In Oracle, one database may contain several packages, so a function in one package may access a function from another package, even though, by scoping rights, it shouldn't be able to. The way to do it is to access the package itself, first, like this: <package_name>.<function_name>. The same is true when a function declared in one schema makes use of a function contained in another schema. The syntax in this case would also include the schema name: <schema_name>.<package_name>.<function_name>. Of course, proper privileges must be in place for such a call to succeed.

Overloading

Overloading is a concept borrowed from object-oriented programming (OOP). The gist of it is that *the same job* may need to be done in *different ways* depending on the circumstances.

If you have twins and one of them phones you and asks you to bring home her favorite treat, you only have to perform the BuyTreatForKid task. Depending on which twin made the request, you will implement the job differently.

Of course, we could talk about two different tasks, BuyTreatForKatie and BuyTreatForJanie, but, really, it would mean unduly concentrating on *implementation details* at the time when we ought to be interested in the concept. What's to be done? BuyTreatForKid. Which kid? Well, that depends on the circumstances (on the *input argument*).

In SQL, "overloaded" means that two or more functions have the same name, but different argument lists or return data types. The argument lists must differ either in the number of arguments, or in the data types (or both).

Consider the following example (written in Oracle PL/SQL):

```
create or replace function AddSomething
(
   arg1 IN number,
   arg2 IN number
) return number
is
begin
return arg1 + arg2;
end AddSomething;
```

```
create or replace Function AddSomething
(
   arg1 IN varchar,
   arg2 IN varchar
) return varchar
is
begin
return arg1 || arg2;
end AddSomething;
```

These functions have exactly the same name, but differ in their arguments' data types and return data types. The first function accepts two numbers, adds them together, and returns a sum (also a number). The second function accepts two strings, and returns a string (a result of concatenation of the passed-in parameters). When the AddSomething function is called, Oracle decides which one to use based on the data type of the arguments the calling routine sends in, and the expected data type of the result.

> *The overloaded functions in Oracle could only be created as a part of a package. You cannot create an overloaded stand-alone function.*

It must be emphasized, that overloading functions is an extremely useful *design tool*. As with any tool, it may be misused. The most likely damage from misusing it is a confused and muddled picture of the original design idea.

It is difficult to provide an isolated example of bad overloading (precisely because it is a design question, whether the thing is good or bad, and so it would need some context). However, when deciding whether to overload a function or to define a new function, the rule of thumb is this: *conceptually*, do these functions perform *the same* task? Would you, explaining yourself to a subordinate, say, "Look, here is *a job* I want to you do, now go and decide how you do it!" If the answer is "Yes," then overload. If you would say to the subordinate, "Here are *a couple of jobs* I want you to do; they are pretty similar, so if you figure one of them out, you won't have any trouble with the other," then do not overload. Write separate functions.

Overloading is a part of the SQL 99 standard. It is defined in the package called "SQL/MM support" as "feature T322." This is a rather advanced feature, so not every RDBMS vendor has chosen to implement it.

❏ Oracle supports overloading for functions defined as part of a package.

❏ IBM DB2 supports overloading for functions defined in different schemas.

❏ Microsoft SQL Server and Sybase explicitly disallow overloading. Any attempt to create a function (or any other database object) using the name of the existing one would result in compile error. This should come as no surprise, considering the fact that every created object has an entry in the SYSOBJECTS table for the given database, which has a UNIQUE constraint declared for it. Consequently, every object must have a unique name.

❏ PostgreSQL fully supports overloading of its functions, be they built-in or user-defined. In fact, you could easily create your own version of any built-in function.

❏ MySQL does not support overloading.

Classifying SQL Functions: Deterministic and Non-Deterministic Functions

The need to organize and classify things is part of human nature. It brings a sense of order and stability, and often makes life easier.

Classifying means grouping together things that share some common attributes, characteristics, or because we simply know them to "belong together." If you think this is far from being scientific, you are right. Yet, that is exactly how the categories of SQL functions are organized.

The number of SQL function classifications is practically limitless, and you could easily come up with one of your own. The SQL standards do not mandate any specific classification, so each vendor structures its documentation according to its own preferences.

Knowing the basic function classification of each RDBMS vendor is definitely of value to anyone who is dealing with more than one RDBMS product, but what is most important is to understand how SQL function classifications (and non-SQL function classifications, for that matter) fall into two broad categories: deterministic and non-deterministic functions.

The first level of classification hierarchy is *deterministic* and *non-deterministic* functions. It is mentioned by the SQL 99 ANSI standard (in the package "SQL/Persistent Storage Module"), and more or less every RDBMS subscribes to this. There are no ironclad rules for recognizing a SQL routine as either deterministic or non-deterministic. The SQL 99 standard introduces a keyword DETERMINISTIC that declares a SQL routine as such. Even that is no more than declaration of the intent.

The definition is quite simple. A function of the first type always returns exactly the same result any time it is called with the exactly the same set of arguments. A function of the second type does not. An example of a deterministic function is the function LENGTH. When passed an argument of a string data type, it returns the length of the argument passed. Calling it with the same argument over and over again will yield exactly the same result.

A function that takes no arguments is called *niladic*. Merriam Webster's dictionary may not contain this word, but it is quite plausible to assume that the word was fashioned after the mathematical term "dyadic," which refers to a mathematical operator in which two vectors are written side by side without a dot or cross between them (that is, A B). The root is the Greek word "dyo," meaning "two." Consequently, there are derivatives such as *monadic* (single), *dyadic* (twofold) or *triladic* (treefold), the latter being extensively used by the SQL Standards Committee. "Niladic," then, would mean "none" ("nil-adic").

Here is an example of this function executed through Oracle's SQL*Plus interface:

```
SELECT  LENGTH('word') word_length FROM DUAL;
word_length
----------------
              4
```

For a non-deterministic function example, we may use a SQL function, GETDATE(), implemented by Microsoft SQL Server. When called without any arguments, it returns system time of the server:

```
SELECT GETDATE() whatstime_now
WAITFOR DELAY '00:00:01'
SELECT GETDATE() whatstime_again

whatstime_now
------------------------------------------------------
2003-10-30 22:50:08.110
 (1 row(s) affected)

whatstime_again
------------------------------------------------------
2003-10-30 22:50:09.108
 (1 row(s) affected)
```

As you can see, a one-second delay introduced between the two queries executed in SQL Server Query Analyzer (plus some incalculable distractions, depending on the server processes running at the same time), produced completely different results from identical queries.

Here is yet another example of a non-deterministic function, GENERATE_UNIQUE from IBM DB2 Universal Database (UDB). It was specifically designed to return a unique value (that is, unique among all other results returned by the function, but it could be used as a unique ID generator).

```
db2 => select generate_unique() as unique_id from sysibm.sysdummy1

UNIQUE_ID
---------------------------
x'20031106225757157066000000'
1 record(s) selected.
```

The same query run a second time brings a completely different value:

```
db2 => select generate_unique() as unique_id from sysibm.sysdummy1
UNIQUE_ID
---------------------------
x'20031106230106388183000000'

1 record(s) selected.
```

Some RDBMS packages (such as Microsoft SQL Server and IBM DB2) find the distinction quite significant (as discussed later in this chapter), but others barely mention it at all. To add to the confusion, the same function might be considered either deterministic or non-deterministic, depending on the context. For example, Oracle's built-in analytic function FIRST_VALUE is supposed to return the first value from an ordered set. Since the set could be ordered in at least two ways (for example, ascending or descending), the function's determinism depends on the ORDER BY clause. If a SQL function is invoked within a transaction, the transaction isolation level may have a significant impact of the determinism of the function, especially levels other than SERIALIZABLE.

Of those vendors who allow for creating UDFs (that is, every RDBMS discussed in this book, in some way or other), some (such as Oracle and IBM) provide special clauses in SQL syntax designating the function as either deterministic or non-deterministic, and some (such as MS SQL Server) designate the UDF based on the type of objects the function invokes. UDFs are discussed in Chapter 4.

Almost every vendor has some restrictions concerning the usage of non-deterministic functions within their respective RDBMS, be it built-in or user-defined ones. This distinction is significant in every SQL-compliant RDBMS, even those that do not even mention it in their documentation.

Oracle

Oracle does not emphasize the deterministic/non-deterministic character of its SQL functions in documentation. Nevertheless, the concept does apply, notably in *analytic* functions. The following list presents some of the restrictions concerning usage of non-deterministic functions in Oracle:

❑   Non-deterministic functions cannot be used in CHECK constraints. In addition, the constraint cannot contain calls to user-defined functions.

❑   Non-deterministic functions are disallowed in function-based indexes. Any user-defined function used for this purpose must be created with the DETERMINISTIC clause.

❑   Some optimization techniques (such as ENABLE QUERY REWRITE) rely on functions used in creating an object (view, materialized view) to be deterministic.

IBM DB2 UDB

With IBM DB2 UDB, non-deterministic functions (sometimes also called *variant* functions in this vendor's documentation) have numerous restrictions on their usage. Here are some of the common restrictions on usage of the non-deterministic functions in IBM DB2 UDB environment:

❑   Non-deterministic functions cannot be used in a FULL OUTER join condition of a SELECT statement.

❑   Non-deterministic functions cannot be used in CASE expressions.

❑   Non-deterministic functions cannot be used in a CHECK constraint.

❑   Non-deterministic functions cannot be used in a function-defined index, or in a CREATE INDEX EXTENSION statement.

❑   Non-deterministic functions cannot be used in a REFRESH IMMEDIATE SUMMARY TABLE object.

❑   Non-deterministic functions cannot be used to create typed views and sub-views, or views created by the WITH CHECK option.

❑   Non-deterministic UDFs cannot be created as a PREDICATE.

❑   Non-deterministic UDFs cannot use the ALLOW PARALLEL clause in their syntax (one that determines whether function invocation/execution could be parallelized — that is, run on multiple processors).

❑   Non-deterministic functions cannot be used with On-Line Analytical Processing (OLAP) functions with ORDER BY and PARTITION BY clauses.

Whenever these (and some other) restrictions are violated, IBM DB2 UDB produces an error: SQLSTATE 42845.

When you think about it, it does make perfect sense. How could you create a FULL OUTER JOIN based on matching criteria defined by a non-deterministic function? Each criterion in a WHERE clause that employs a non-deterministic function could evaluate to "match" or "no match" for the same set of values! Or, consider the ORDER BY clause used with a non-deterministic function. If it returns different values for the ordering expression, how could we be sure of an order, even for identical sets of data? Yet, some other restrictions are less obvious, and have much to do with particulars of the implementation. Although some might argue that this is a useful case scenario, and has its place in business logic programming, we insist that the user creating such a query must understand the ramifications of employing non-deterministic functions.

Microsoft SQL Server

There are two main restrictions on the use of non-deterministic functions in Microsoft SQL Server:

❑ An index cannot be created on a computed column if the expression that makes up that column contains non-deterministic functions.

❑ A clustered index cannot be created on a view that contains non-deterministic functions.

Unlike IBM DB2 UDB and Oracle, Microsoft SQL Server does not make as much fuss about non-deterministic functions being used with a CHECK constraint, though most of the other restrictions do apply.

Here is an example. The table CHECK_TEST contains only one column, called FIELD1, declared with default value of the current system date. At the same time, the CHECK constraint makes sure that the inserted value is never the current system date (yes, completely useless, since the default value contradicts the constraint, but it proves the point).

```
CREATE TABLE check_test
(
    field1 DATETIME NOT NULL DEFAULT GETDATE()
    CHECK (field1 < GETDATE())
)

The command(s) completed successfully.
```

Once the table is created, we could execute the following INSERT statement, which fails because of constraint violation:

```
INSERT INTO check_test VALUES (default)

Server: Msg 547, Level 16, State 1, Line 1
INSERT statement conflicted with COLUMN CHECK constraint
'CK__check_tes__field__40EF84EB'. The conflict occurred in database 'master', table
'check_test', column 'field1'.
The statement has been terminated.
```

At the same time, this statement goes through smoothly:

```
insert check_test VALUES(GETDATE()-1)

(1 row(s) affected)
```

As you can see, you cannot assume that a restriction, even of such a general nature, would hold true for different RDBMS packages.

An attempt to do the same in Oracle would generate an exception: "ORA-02436: date or system variable wrongly specified in CHECK constraint." IBM DB2 UDB also will reject an attempt to create a table with a CHECK constraint referencing CURRENT DATE register. Sybase, because of its shared ancestry with Microsoft SQL Server, will behave identically to it (that is, it will allow for the table to be created, and generates an error message for the insert of a default value). The PostgreSQL take on this is similar to that of Oracle. As of this writing, the CHECK constraint is not yet implemented in MySQL.

Whereas some vendors (Oracle, IBM) introduce a special clause that defines the behavior of the UDF as either deterministic or non-deterministic, Microsoft favors a circumstantial approach. In SQL Server, a UDF is considered to be deterministic if:

❑ The function is schema bound (that is, a function created with SCHEMABINDING option, meaning that the objects this function references cannot be altered or destroyed).

❑ Every function (built-in or user defined) used within that function's body is deterministic.

❑ The body of the function does not reference any database objects (for example, tables, views, other functions) outside its scope.

❑ The function does not call extended stored procedures (which might alter the database state).

Every UDF that does not comply with these requirements is non-deterministic by default.

Sybase

There aren't any specific rules in regard to non-deterministic functions in Sybase, simply because Sybase disallows many of the scenarios accommodated by other vendors. For example, there are no indexes on computed columns or views. Even though your RDBMS might not complain about a particular syntax, it would not be a good idea to use non-deterministic functions in a FULL OUTER JOIN query, simply because results will be unpredictable. The same goes for the use of the non-deterministic functions in GROUP BY and ORDER BY clauses.

> Sybase does not provide any mechanism for creating UDFs, except with the Java programming language. The syntax in SQLJ (the dialect used to create Java functions and procedures) does provide deterministic and non-deterministic keywords "for syntactic compatibility with the ANSI standard," but its documentation states that these keywords are not yet implemented.

MySQL and PostgreSQL

The two leading Open Source RDBMS packages do not have any specific guidelines concerning the use of non-deterministic functions. This is partly because they lack many features provided by their "closed-source" RDBMS rivals, and partly because, in general, they are trying to keep things simple.

Most of the restrictions imposed by the enterprise-level RDBMS packages (Oracle, IBM, and Microsoft) are non-issues with either MySQL or PostgreSQL. Either they are not allowed, or they are considered to be a "feature." It would be only prudent to follow the general rules of the SQL. Do not use non-deterministic functions in FULL OUTER JOIN query GROUP BY or ORDER BY clauses unless you understand all the ramifications.

Summary

You should now have a general understanding of the mechanics of employing functions in SQL, as well as the basis for their classification. Additionally, you should clearly understand how the various RDBMS implementations all adhere to a common thread by attempting to adhere, at least in part, to the ANSI standard.

SQL standards go back to the 1978 mandate of the CODASYL subcommittee. Since then, the number of SQL functions specified by the standard has grown steady with each release, playing the catch-up game with the hundreds of SQL built-in functions implemented by RDBMS vendors. SQL:2003, adopted officially in 2004, includes new data types (such as BIGINT, MULTISET, and XML) and new aggregate functions (such as COLLECT, FUSION, and INTERSECTION).

SQL functions are part of the core of the ISO/ANSI standards, and are, therefore, required in the implementation to claim compatibility. Most of the RDBMS vendors claim at least SQL 92 (SQL2) compliance in the current versions of their software, with some (Oracle, IBM DB2 UDB, and PostgreSQL) aspiring to SQL:2003 compliance. It is important to keep in mind that the compliance is tied to a specific version of the product (that is, Oracle8i is SQL 92 compliant, while Oracle 9i/10g claims SQL:2003 compliance). This is important because, as functionality and breadth are added to the SQL standard, you may not receive all the functionality of a new standard when using an older version.

Classification is an arbitrary process of grouping objects based on some similar features. Applied to SQL functions, it yields a surprising variety of groupings. All SQL functions could be split into two major categories: deterministic and non-deterministic. The difference between the two is that the functions of the first category always return the same result when called with an identical set of arguments, and the functions in the latter category do not.

Chapter 3 compares the different built-in SQL functions based on the vendors who distribute them.

3

Comparison of Built-in SQL Functions by Vendor

The SQL standard lists only a handful of built-in SQL functions, all of which are covered in this chapter. SQL 99 was updated with mostly statistical, Business Intelligence (BI) functions. All RDBMS vendors stuff their toolboxes with hundreds of built-in functions, in addition to the ability to create custom functions. The standard is really a template to create these built-in functions, but even if a vendor includes the function in its implementation, it is not obliged to call it the same name, or even provide full functionality. We will go into details of usage of the standard-compliant functions in Chapter 13.

This chapter begins with a brief overview of the main types of functions used within the SQL environment, followed by a discussion of the classification and different built-in functions available by vendor. Examples of the functions are found in the relevant implementations chapters (Chapters 5–11), as there is no SQL function without an RDBMS.

Types of Functions

The SQL 99 standard has two basic types of functions: *aggregate* and *scalar*. The aggregate functions are those that operate against a collection of values to return a single value. The number of values that are processed by the function is wholly dependent on the number of queried rows. The basic example of this is the SUM statement, which computes the sum of the values of a particular column and is only constrained by how many rows are generated by the SELECT statement. The SQL:2003 standard specifies a particular subclassing of the aggregate functions given in the following table.

Category	Usage
Group	These functions deal with the grouping operation or the group aggregate function.
Window	These functions compute their aggregate values the same as a group function, except that they aggregate over the window frame of a row and not over a group of a grouped table.
Unary Group	These functions take an arbitrary `<value expression>` as an argument.
Binary Group	These functions take a pair of arguments, a dependent one and an independent one, both of which are numeric expressions. They remove `NULL` values from the group, and if there are no remaining rows, they evaluate to 0.
Inverse Distribution	There are only two inverse functions: `PERCENTILE_CONT` and `PERCENTILE_DISC`. Both functions take an argument between 0 and 1.
Hypothetical Set	These functions are related to the window functions `RANK`, `DENSE_RANK`, `PERCENT_RANK`, and `CUME_DIST`.

Scalar functions, on the other hand, require no arguments, or at most one argument, to be passed to them; they return a single value that is based on the input value. Furthermore, scalar functions can be broken down into the subcategories shown in the following table, based upon their intended use:

Category	Usage
Built-in	These functions perform operations on values and settings that are built into the database (such as specifics dealing with the user session).
Date and Time	These functions perform operations on datetime fields.
Numeric	These functions perform operations on numeric values.
String	These functions perform operations on character values such as `CHAR`, `VARCHAR`, `NCHAR`, `NVARCHAR`, and `CLOB`, and they can return either numeric or string values.

Classifying Built-in SQL Functions

The next level of hierarchy defines categories of the functions. As we have mentioned before, these classifications are rather arbitrary, and they usually reflect the vendor-specific approach. They should be regarded as such (no more, no less).

SQL:1999 (also known as SQL 99 and SQL3) defines a number of categories for the functions that every aspiring RDBMS implementation should support at different compliance levels. The Paragraph 6 (Scalar

Expressions) and Paragraph 10 (Additional Common Elements of the SQL/Foundation) documents list the following categories (listed alongside their respective paragraph numbers):

❑ `<window function>` — In ANSI/ISO lingo, this category is defined by a "window," which is "a transient data structure associated with a `<table expression>`." Loosely translated into English, it means a data set returned by the query. In other words, a window function would return a result for any given row based on the entire data set. It could return a rank, or distribution, or row number, or even an aggregate value for the set such as COUNT, SUM, and so on. (6.10)

❑ `<numeric value function>` — This is any scalar function returning a numeric result. (6.27)

❑ `<string value function>` — This specifies a function yielding a value of type character string or binary string. (6.29)

❑ `<datetime value function>` — This specifies a function yielding a value of type datetime. (6.31)

❑ `<interval value function>` — This specifies a function yielding a value of type interval. (6.33)

❑ `<multiset value function>` — This specifies a function yielding a value of a multiset type (see Oracle's analytic functions later in this chapter). (6.38)

❑ `<aggregate function>` — This is defined as a function whose result is based on aggregation of rows; that is, it returns a value computed from a collection of rows. (10.9)

These categories were designed to be as generic as possible, to provide guidance for those who would implement it in code. Each category might be divided into subcategories and additional groups. To claim SQL 99 (or any previous standard) compliance at a certain level, a specified number of the features (including functions) must be implemented. Most vendors are specified at SQL 92 level (with selected advance SQL 99 features), with PostgreSQL being closest to the full SQL 99 compliance.

Oracle

Oracle groups SQL functions first by the data set to which the function is applied (that is, row-based versus column-based data), and then by the data types of the arguments the functions accept. The first brings in the distinction between *scalar functions* (that is, row-based, dealing with discrete values) and *column functions*; the second brings in the functional categorization (that is, system functions, security functions, and so on).

Oracle employs overloading (also found in IBM DB2 UDB and PostgreSQL), which occurs when one name can invoke different functions, depending on data type and/or number of arguments passed. For example, the AVG aggregate function (calculating averages of the data set and returning a single value) is listed as belonging both to aggregate functions and analytic functions groups, where a data set of rows is returned.

❑ *Single-Row (Scalar) Functions* — The functions of this type are applied to each and every row returned by the query. Oracle differentiates the single-row functions further, based on input arguments' data type(s).

    ❑ *Character* functions are further divided into character functions returning character values and character functions returning numeric values. An example of the first kind could be the function LOWER, which turns all characters of a string argument into lowercase characters. An example of the latter kind would be the LENGTH function, which returns the length of the string argument, in characters.

❑ *Conversion* functions perform explicit conversion between different compatible data types. Unlike many other RDBMS packages, Oracle sports a large number of type-specific conversion functions in addition to generic CAST and CONVERT. For example, you could use Oracle's specific TO_NUMBER function, or the more generic CONVERT one, to convert a compatible string into a numeric value. The results would be identical. Although using data type–specific functions makes code more readable, it makes the code less portable at the same time.

❑ *Date and Time* functions perform operations on date and time values (Oracle's data type DATE). For example, the LAST_DAY function returns the last day of the month for the date passed in as the argument.

❑ *Numeric* functions accept numeric-type arguments and return a numeric result. They include such elementary math functions as SQRT (square root function) and LN (natural logarithm function).

❑ *Miscellaneous Single-Row* functions include every single-row function that cannot be reliably classified into any of the preceding categories. The functions in this group include new XML-related functions, the DECODE function (Oracle's version of CASE expression mandated by the ANSI SQL standard), and many others.

❑ *Aggregate Functions* — An *aggregate function* returns a single result for a group of rows. An example of an aggregate function is the function SUM, which sums up all the values in the column for the row set returned by the query. When used with a GROUP BY clause, it is applied to a row set in each group. Otherwise, the whole row set is affected.

❑ *Analytic Functions* — The main difference between aggregate and analytic functions is that the latter return a set of values, as opposed to the single value result produced by aggregate functions. The multiple rows returned for each group are called "windows," which is defined by the analytic clause in the query. These functions are the last to be executed in a SQL query, so they cannot be used anywhere but the SELECT clause and the ORDER BY clause.

❑ *Object Reference Functions* — These functions were introduced to manipulate object data types, which is a relatively new addition to the RDBMS world. Oracle introduced object tables and views starting with Oracle 8i.

IBM DB2 UDB

IBM employs the most succinct classification. It orders all the built-in functions by the type of the object they are applied to. There are only three groups in IBM DB2 UDB: *scalar* functions, *column* functions, and *table* functions.

❑ *Scalar Functions* — When a SQL query containing a scalar function returns a set of rows, the function is applied to one row at a time. This category includes everything that many other vendors elaborate into more granular categories. Here, IBM DB2 UDB puts character functions, date and time functions, numeric functions — you name it. You can create your own functions of this type either in DB2 SQL Procedural Language (internal) or in C (external) using interfaces provided by IBM DB2 UDB.

❑ *Column Functions* — As the name implies, column functions work on the "vertical" set of values. This category includes what other RDBMS packages call *aggregate functions*. Examples of the functions in this category are AVG, SUM, and COUNT. Creating column UDFs requires rather advanced skills, but it is not impossible.

❑ *Table Functions* — This is the only category of functions that can be used in the FROM clause of a SQL query. An example of such a function is the MQRECEIVEALL function, which retrieves messages from IBM MQSeries message queuing server and presents them as a table to the SQL query. IBM DB2 UDB also allows for creating custom UDFs that return data of the TABLE type.

Microsoft SQL Server and Sybase ASE

Microsoft and Sybase are very similar in their approach to the classification of the built-in functions, which should come as no surprise, considering their common roots. Even though the categories themselves might sound identical, do not assume that the function distribution will follow the pattern. Two RDBMS products have diverged considerably since the last common version (4.2). And, beginning with version 7.0, Microsoft has made a clean break with the Sybase legacy code, while Sybase has carried it onto versions 11, 12, and 12.5. One important distinction concerns creation and use of the UDFs. SQL Server allows for creation of these using C/C++ (external functions), Transact-SQL (internal), and .NET languages. Sybase (in its latest incarnation ASE 12.5) allows for the use of Java to create custom functions, but nothing more.

Both vendors use a mixed approach to the classification of SQL functions. Some of the functions are classified on the basis of the data type (data type domain, rather) that the functions accept, return, or manipulate (string functions, date and time functions, mathematical functions, text and image functions, cursor functions, rowset functions), and some are based on the functionality (metadata, configuration functions, security and system functions, system statistical functions).

> *Though not recognized as a separate category, Microsoft SQL Server sports quite a few undocumented functions (that is, functions distributed with SQL Server installation but not documented in the Books-on-Line or anywhere else in official manuals). These functions are being used by SQL Server, and are not devised for users. This means that, in addition to being undocumented, any of these functions could be renamed, redesigned, or dropped altogether. You should never use these functions in your applications.*

❑ *String Functions (Microsoft and Sybase)* — These perform operations on string data-type arguments (CHAR or VARCHAR). The return types may be either string or numeric. Some examples of the string functions are LEN (which returns the length of the string passed into it) and LOWER (which converts the argument string to lowercase).

❑ *Mathematical Functions (Microsoft and Sybase)* — These perform mathematical calculations upon input parameters and return a numeric result. An example of this class of functions is SQUARE (which returns the square of the value passed as the argument).

❑ *Aggregate Functions (Microsoft and Sybase)* — This class of functions is recognized and implemented by virtually every database vendor with a SQL-compliant product. The idea behind the aggregate functions is to accept a set of data and return a single value. The function AVG performs operations on the set of values and returns the average for the entire set.

❑   *Configuration Functions (Microsoft and Sybase)* — These return information about the current configuration of the RDBMS server and on the state of the processes. In the older versions of SQL Server (and in Sybase, including the latest version), these functions used to be called *global variables*. They always start with double character @@. For example, the unary function @@LANGUAGE returns the default language set up for the RDBMS installation.

❑   *Conversion Functions (Sybase)* — Sybase ASE 12.5 defines a category of conversion functions. Microsoft SQL Server bundles these functions (somewhat unjustifiably) into the *system functions* category. These functions assist in explicit conversion between different data types.

❑   *Cursor Functions (Microsoft and Sybase)* — The cursor construct is introduced in many RDBMS packages to facilitate row-by-row processing of the data. As such, it is outside the pure SQL and is part of the procedural extension (Transact-SQL) language. A cursor cannot be used in a SQL query, but it can be used in custom UDFs. The purpose of the cursor functions is to return information about the CURSOR object state.

❑   *Metadata Functions (Microsoft)* — Metadata functions supply information about various database objects: tables, columns, database files, and so on. For example, the metadata function DB_NAME returns the name of the database defined in the current installation of SQL Server.

❑   *Rowset Functions (Microsoft)* — These functions are found in Microsoft SQL Server and have no analogue in Sybase Advanced Server. They return an object (a virtual table) that can be used in a SQL query's FROM clause (compare to IBM DB2 UDB table functions). Microsoft SQL Server also allows for creation of the custom functions returning table-valued results.

❑   *Security Functions (Microsoft and Sybase)* — Each RDBMS implements security features that govern access to the database objects. The security functions return information about the security arrangement within the system (roles, users, privileges, and so on). For example, a SQL Server function USER returns the system-supplied username for the current session.

❑   *System Functions (Microsoft and Sybase)* — This is a broad category of functions. It deals with information about values, objects, and system settings within the RDBMS server.

❑   *System Statistical Functions (Microsoft)* — These return statistical information about the system (CPU access time, read/write activity, and so on). Usually, these functions are part of the system-monitoring and -tuning procedures in the DBA toolbox.

❑   *Text and Image Functions (Microsoft and Sybase)* — Life was easy when a database contained only numeric and character data. Today we can store virtually anything in RDBMS packages: images, audio data, video data, the text of an entire book. The SQL Server text and image functions perform operations on text/image data–type input parameters. Return results usually contain information about these. The PATINDEX function is as close as you can get to a regular expressions search in pure SQL.

Undocumented functions are used by the RDBMS server for its internal purposes. It is not recommended to use them as there is no guarantee they would be present (or behave identically) in any subsequent release. For the Open Source databases, where it is possible to create one's own built-in functions, this category might include the user's modifications. The rule of thumb in any case would be to avoid any undocumented function, because it might render your SQL code nonportable not only between different RDBMs, but also between different versions and flavors of the same RDBMS package.

MySQL

As with every Open Source project, the MySQL RDBMS is always "in progress," and nothing is ever cast in stone. The classification of the SQL functions built into the latest release of MySQL is taken directly from the Open Source community documents, and is by no means final.

As of this writing, there is no MySQL-specific procedural SQL extension language, and the only way to add UDFs to it is by using C/C++ interface. MySQL also allows for creating built-in custom functions through modifying and recompiling the source code (which is open). This flexibility is a double-edged sword. You can have any function you could conceive and implement built right into your very own MySQL server; at the same time, it renders business logic based on this function nonportable.

❑ *Aggregate Functions* — These return a single numeric value calculated for the entire range of the input values from the table column. MySQL provides a standard set of the aggregate built-in functions.

❑ *Date and Time Functions* — These functions were designed to work with dates. Examples of such a function are CURRENT_DATE (which returns the current date of the system) and DAYNAME (which returns day of the week from the date argument). The functions in this category accept input arguments and return results in a variety of formats and data types.

❑ *Numeric Functions* — These perform mathematical calculations and other operations with numbers. The input and output data types are numeric.

❑ *String Functions* — These perform operations with character-based data. This category includes the usual string functions found in other RDBMS (such as LOWER and LENGTH) and also has some of its own (for example, ORD, FIND_IN_SET).

❑ *System Functions* — These return information about the database system. An example of such functions could be DATABASE, which returns the name of the current database for the session.

❑ *Security Functions* — This category includes all data security functions (that is, DES_ENCRYPT or SHA1), as well as system security functions (for example, PASSWORD).

❑ *Miscellaneous Functions* — This is the one handy category under which you could list any function. We use it as the last resort for a function that does not fit into any of the preceding categories.

PostgreSQL

PostgreSQL is probably the most advanced among the Open Source RDBMS packages. By saying this, we do not imply that it is the fastest or easiest to administer, or the most robust. This RDBMS is the most compliant with SQL standards, and it possesses some advanced features lacking in MySQL, or even in the heavyweights of the database world. Where functions are concerned, not only does it supply virtually hundreds of built-in functions, but it also allows for creating your own functions in a language of your choice — in addition to providing several SQL Procedural extensions (such as pgSQL/PL).

The classification presented here is based on the PostgreSQL documentation posted on the dedicated site (www.postgresql.org). As with MySQL, it is possible to make any UDF a built-in "native" function. The price to pay is limited portability of the applications utilizing this feature.

❑ *Aggregate Functions* — These return a single numeric value calculated for the entire range of the input values from the table column.

❑ *Conversion Functions* — Although functions for data-type conversions are found in each and every RDBMS package discussed here, only Oracle, Sybase, and PostgreSQL list them in a separate category. These functions convert (cast) between different data types, and they format output (optionally).

❑ *Geometric Functions* — This set of built-in functions is unique to PostgreSQL, and probably reflects its academic roots. These functions assist in performing operations on spatially-related data sets.

❑ *Network Functions* — This is further evidence of PostgreSQL's scientific heritage. The functions perform calculations and transformations of network-related data.

❑ *Numeric Functions* — These perform mathematical calculations. They are not different (at least in spirit) from those found in all other RDBMS packages covered in this book.

❑ *Sequence Manipulation Functions* — Sequence objects are found in many RDBMS packages (Oracle and IBM DB2 UDB being the most notable examples). Essentially, a *sequence* is a construct that returns the number, sequential and unique for this particular object. The Sequence Manipulation Functions are used, not surprisingly, to manipulate sequences, including the return of information about the past, current, and future values generated by the sequence.

❑ *String Functions* — These functions correspond directly to Oracle character functions and to Microsoft SQL Server and MySQL string functions. DB2 UDB lists these under scalar functions. Their purpose is to transform and modify string-based data.

❑ *Date and Time Functions* — Again, this is a category found in every other RDBMS package discussed in this book (with the exception of IBM DB2 UDB, which dumps them into the Scalar Functions category). These functions perform operations/calculations on date and time–related data.

❑ *Miscellaneous Functions* — All functions that are not included in any of the previous categories are in this one. PostgreSQL puts all system, security, and configuration functions into this category.

Overview of Built-in Functions by Vendor

The latest standard proposes to make a part of SQL a handful of new analytic functions that hitherto have been in the Business Intelligence domain (for example, STDDEVPOP_, which deals with statistical distribution of the data values). Some vendors (such as Oracle and IBM) have already added these functions (and more of their ilk) to their SQL implementations. Others (such as Microsoft) have made it part of Multidimensional Expressions (MDX) language for SQL Server Analysis Services, and yet others are relying on programmers to add the necessary logic.

The following table lists the functions the ISO/ANSI SQL Standards Committee deemed necessary to be included in the SQL specifications. As discussed before, classifying functions is an arbitrary process at best, and the SQL 99 standard does not provide any classifications for the functions it does specify. With the addition of the SQL:2003 standard, there are several newer functions, but they are not required for core compliance. You should always check your vendor-specific documentation to see if a function is supported or not.

First Introduced	SQL Standard Identifier	SQL Function	Description
SQL 92	E021-04	CHARACTER_LENGTH (<string>)	Returns the length of the expression, usually a string, in characters.
SQL 92	E021-05	OCTET_LENGTH (<string>)	Returns the length of the expression in *bytes* (each byte containing 8 bits).
SQL 92		BIT_LENGTH (<string>)	Returns the length of the expression, usually a string, in bits.
SQL 92	E021-06	SUBSTRING (<string> FROM <position> FOR <length>)	Returns a string part of a *string*, from the *start* position up to specified *length*.
SQL 92	E021-08	UPPER(<string>)	Converts character string from lowercase (or mixed case) into uppercase letters.
SQL 92	E021-08	LOWER(<string>)	Converts character string from uppercase (or mixed case) into lowercase letters.
SQL 92	E021-09	TRIM (BOTH <char> FROM <string>)	Returns string from a string expression where *both* char characters are removed.
SQL 92	E021-09	TRIM (LEADING <char> FROM <string>)	Returns string from a string expression where *leading* char characters are removed.
SQL 92	E021-09	TRIM (TRAILING <char> FROM <string>)	Returns string from a string expression where *trailing* char characters are removed.
SQL 92	E021-11	POSITION (<chat> IN <string>)	Returns the position of the char in the source string.
SQL 92		TRANSLATE (<string> USING <mask>)	Returns string translated into another string according to specified rules.
SQL 99	E091-01	AVG(expression)	Returns the average value of an expression; usually used with GROUP BY.
SQL 99	E091-02	COUNT	Returns the number of selected rows or input values.

Table continued on following page

First Introduced	SQL Standard Identifier	SQL Function	Description
SQL 99	E091-03	MAX	Returns the highest of the input values.
SQL 99	E091-04	MIN	Returns the lowest of the input values.
SQL 99	E091-05	SUM	Returns the sum of the input values.
SQL 92	F051-06	CURRENT_DATE	Returns the current date in the session's time zone.
SQL 92	F051-06	CURRENT_TIME	Returns the current time in the session's time zone.
SQL 92	F051-06	CURRENT_TIMESTAMP	Current date and time in the session's time zone are returned as TIMESTAMP data type.
SQL 99	F051-07	LOCALTIME	Result is the current time (meaning: "now") in the RDBMS server's time zone returned as a TIME data type.
SQL 99	F051-08	LOCALTIMESTAMP	Current date and time in the RDBMS server's time zone are returned as TIMESTAMP data type.
SQL 92	F201	CAST (expression AS type)	Converts supplied value from one data type into another *compatible* data type.
SQL 99	T441	ABS(<n>)	Returns the absolute value of n.
SQL 99	T441	MOD(<m>,<n>)	Returns the remainder of m divided by n. Returns m if n is 0.
SQL:2003	T621	CEILING(<n>)	Returns the smallest integer greater than or equal to n.
SQL:2003	T621	FLOOR(<n>)	Returns the largest integer equal to or less than n.
SQL:2003	T621	LN (<n>)	Returns the natural logarithm of n, where n is greater than 0.
SQL:2003	T621	EXP(<n>)	Returns e raised to the nth power, where $e = 2.71828183$.
SQL:2003	T621	POWER(<m>, <n>)	Returns m raised to the nth power.
SQL:2003	T621	SQRT(<n>)	Returns the square root of n.

First Introduced	SQL Standard Identifier	SQL Function	Description
SQL:2003	T621	STDDEV_POP	Computes the population standard deviation and returns the square root of the population variance.
SQL:2003	T621	STDDEV_SAMP	Computes the cumulative sample standard deviation and returns the square root of the sample variance.
SQL:2003	T621	VAR_POP	Returns the population variance of a set of numbers after discarding the NULLs in this set.
*SQL:2003	T621	VAR_SAMP	Returns the sample variance of a set of numbers after discarding the NULLs in this set.
*SQL:2003	T621	REGR_COUNT	Returns the number of rows remaining in the group.
*SQL:2003	T621	COVAR_POP	Returns the population covariance. This is defined as the sum of the products of the difference of the independent variable expression from its mean times the difference of the dependent variable expression from its mean, divided by the number of rows remaining. This can be defined by the expression (SUM(X * Y) - SUM(Y) * SUM(X) / n) / n, where *n* is the number of pairs (X,Y) in which neither value is Null.
*SQL:2003	T621	COVAR_SAMP	This is based on the population covariance explained previously, but it is divided by the number of rows remaining minus 1.
*SQL:2003	T621	CORR	Returns the ratio of the population covariance divided by the product of the population standard deviation of the independent variable and the population standard deviation of the dependent variable. This can be summed up by the equation COVAR_POP (x, y) / STDDEV_POP (x) * STDDEV_POP (y).

Table continued on following page

First Introduced	SQL Standard Identifier	SQL Function	Description
*SQL:2003	T621	REGR_R2	Returns the square of the correlation coefficient.
*SQL:2003	T621	REGR_SLOPE	Returns the slope of the least-squares-fit linear equation determined by the independent, dependent pairs.
*SQL:2003	T621	REGR_INTERCEPT	Returns the y-intercept of the least-squares-fit linear equation determined by the independent, dependent pairs.
*SQL:2003	T621	REGR_SXX	Returns the sum of the squares of the independent variable.
*SQL:2003	T621	REGR_SYY	Returns the sum of the squares of the dependent variable.
*SQL:2003	T621	REGR_SXY	Returns the sum of the products of the independent variable times the dependent variable.
*SQL:2003	T621	REGR_AVGX	Returns the average of the independent variable expression.
*SQL:2003	T621	REGR_AVGY	Returns the average of the dependent variable expression.
*SQL:2003	T621	PERCENTILE_CONT	Returns the interpolation of the value received by considering the pair of consecutive rows that are indicated by the argument (a value between 0 and 1), treated as a fraction of the total number of rows in the group. This function primarily deals with three values: the Row Number (RN), the Floor(RN) denoted by FRN, and the Ceiling(RN) denoted by CRN. If RN = CRN = FRN, then this is evaluated as the expression from the row at RN. Otherwise, this is evaluated as `(CRN-RN)*(value of expression at row at FRN) + (RN-FRN)*(value of expression at row CRN)`.

First Introduced	SQL Standard Identifier	SQL Function	Description
*SQL:2003	T621	PERCENTILE_DISC	Given a value P, the PERCENTILE_DISC function first sorts the values by the ORDER BY clause, then selects the one with the smallest cumulative distribution, based on the ordering.
*SQL:2003	T621	RANK	Returns the rank of row R, defined as 1 plus the number of rows that precede R and are not peers of R.
*SQL:2003	T621	DENSE_RANK	Returns the rank of row R, defined as the number of rows preceding and including R that are distinct with respect to the window ordering.
*SQL:2003	T621	PERCENT_RANK	Returns the relative rank of row R, defined as (RK-1)/(NR-1), where RK is defined to be the Rank of R and NR is defined to be the number of rows in the window partition of R.
*SQL:2003	T621	CUME_DIST	Returns the relative rank of row R defined as NP/NR, where NP is defined to be the number of rows preceding (or peer to) row R in the window ordering of the window partition (or R), and NR is defined to be the number of rows in the window partition R.

*These functions are all advanced numeric functions defined within the SQL:2003 standard. They do not provide any bearing on the compliance with the SQL:2003 standard since RDBMSs are compliant with SQL:2003 if they were compliant with SQL:1999. Therefore, we will not be discussing these functions further within this book. We can't guarantee that this is a complete list of functions, but it should be reasonably comprehensive.

The SQL standard names the functions and specifies the functionality they are supposed to provide. Details of implementations are handled by the vendors — and handle them they do. Only a handful of functions from the preceding table were implemented the way the committee had specified across all the RDBMSs discussed in this book.

Most of the time, the difference is just a matter of syntax, though often the required functionality was achieved using a different approach. Take, for example, the SQL function CHARACTER_LENGTH. It is called LENGTH in IBM DB2 UDB and Oracle, but it appears as LEN in Sybase and MS SQL Server. MySQL dutifully implemented CHARACTER_LENGTH, while PostgreSQL decided upon the shortened version of CHAR_LENGTH. These discrepancies, while frustrating by themselves, have valid historical reasons, and were the major drive behind this book.

The following table lists the standard SQL functions and marks the level of compliance within each RDBMS. *Full* stands for total compliance in both syntax and name, *partial* indicates that the function is present albeit in modified form, and *X* means that the feature was not implemented.

SQL Function	Oracle	IBM	Microsoft	Sybase	MySQL	Post-greSQL
CHARACTER_LENGTH	Partial	Partial	Partial	Partial	Full	Full
OCTET_LENGTH	Partial	Partial	Partial	Partial	Full	Full
BIT_LENGTH	Partial	X	X	X	Full	Full
SUBSTRING	Partial	Partial	Full	Full	Full	Full
UPPER	Full	Full	Full	Full	Full	Full
LOWER	Full	Full	Full	Full	Full	Full
POSITION	Partial	Partial	Partial	Partial	Full	Full
TRANSLATE	Full	Full	X	X	X	Full
AVG	Full	Full	Full	Full	Full	Full
COUNT	Full	Full	Full	Full	Full	Full
MAX	Full	Full	Full	Full	Full	Full
MIN	Full	Full	Full	Full	Full	Full
SUM	Full	Full	Full	Full	Full	Full
CURRENT_DATE	Partial	Full	Full	Full	Full	Full
CURRENT_TIME	Partial	Full	Full	Full	Full	Full
CURRENT_TIMESTAMP	Partial	Full	Full	Full	Full	Full
LOCALTIME	Partial	Partial	Partial	Partial	Full	Full
LOCALTIMESTAMP	Full	Partial	Partial	Partial	Partial	Full
CAST	Full	Full	Full	Full	Full	Full
ABS	Full	Full	Full	Full	Full	Full
MOD	Full	Full	Partial	Partial	Full	Full

SQL Function	Oracle	IBM	Microsoft	Sybase	MySQL	Post-greSQL
CEILING	Full	Full	Full	Full	Partial	Partial
FLOOR	Full	Full	Full	Full	Full	Full
LN	Full	Full	Partial	Full	Full	Full
EXP	Full	Full	Full	Full	Full	Full
POWER	Full	Full	Full	Full	Full	Partial
SQRT	Full	Full	Full	Full	Full	Full
STDDEV_POP	Full	Full	X	X	X	X
STDDEV_SAMP	Full	Full	X	X	X	X
VAR_POP	Full	Full	X	X	X	X
VAR_SAMP	Full	Full	X	X	X	X

The fact that a certain feature was not implemented does not mean that you cannot achieve the same functionality either using a combination of built-in functions or coding yourself a user-defined one. For example, the function TRIM(BOTH...FROM) is not implemented in Microsoft SQL Server, but you could use RTRIM(LTRIM(<expression>)) instead.

There are two competing strategies in developing SQL applications: one is to adhere to the notion of portability, and another is to squeeze the last drop of performance out of the vendor's software using its proprietary extensions. The first option implies avoidance of the vendor's extensions at any cost. The second calls for tight coupling of the coded logic with the RDBMS (and, possibly, operating system the RDBMS runs on). The call is yours; there is no "one size fits all" solution, though we personally favor the former approach.

Remember the heyday of Sybase? It had less than 3 percent of the RDBMS market in 2003. Remember almighty Oracle? It's in steady decline since its bitter rivals (IBM DB2 and Microsoft) are gaining their respective market shares. Ever hear of MySQL in the middle of the 1990s? It is the fastest-growing share of RDBMS market right now. Although it is true that the future cannot be avoided, it can be prepared for. Implementing your SQL logic using the most generic approach may not result in the fastest or most concise piece of code, but it certainly would have the best chance to be the longest lasting.

The SQL standard is not cast in stone. It is driven by ever-accelerating advances in hardware and software engineering, and (most importantly) by the business community needs. Today it consumes data that comes not only as text, but also in a variety of formats, most of which were unheard of just a decade ago. SQL has shown a remarkable resiliency in adapting to these demands by introducing new data types, new storage formats, and new built-in functions. Some of these innovations will eventually become a part of a new standard; some will remain "vendor-specific extensions." It always will be up to the user to differentiate between the two. In the case of SQL, it is the vendors who are pushing for new things, leaving ISO/ANSI to play the catch-up game and to reign in the rogues.

Summary

You should now have a better understanding of the types, classifications, and availability of built-in functions within your specific RDBMS implementation. Studying these functions will be the cornerstone in developing unique functions to deploy within your own environment.

In addition to the universal types of functions discussed in the first section, each vendor's documentation contains its own proprietary classification of the built-in SQL functions. The two most common approaches are to group functions based on the nature of the data set these functions are applied to (column, table, row — IBM DB2 UDB), or group them based on the data type these functions accept and/or return. Learning about a vendor's specific classifications helps you find your way through that vendor's documentation and facilitates understanding of the mindset behind the RDBMS product.

The different implementations (Oracle, SQL Server, MySQL, and so on) sponsor hundreds of built-in SQL functions that don't necessarily enter the ANSI standard domain. Therefore, it would be prudent to stay with the standardized functions whenever possible, as it would alleviate many problems should you ever decide to change your RDBMS vendor. This is further discussed in Chapter 4, where we will look at ANSI SQL guidance for procedural extensions.

SQL Procedural Extensions and User-Defined Functions

One of the biggest advantages of SQL is its ability to manipulate data within an RDBMS package from a single line of code. However, this is also one of its drawbacks. Since the syntax of the base version of SQL was concerned only with the manipulation of data in a declarative fashion, it lacked the fundamental means in which to control those statements in a step-by-step fashion. In the early days of SQL, this meant that a developer had to embed SQL code within a 3GL or 4GL to control the processing of the SQL statements. Soon vendors produced their own "extensions" to the SQL language that provided for such necessary things as looping, branching, and flow of control. In doing so, they not only provided the developer with the means to ensure that their code would execute in a stepwise fashion, but also gave them the means to develop their own form of built-in functions called *user-defined functions* (UDFs).

Procedural versus Declarative Languages

SQL is a typical example of a declarative language. Although it is different from some general-purpose languages (being a set-based language), it is nevertheless a 4GL language. A *declarative language* is a language that specifies *what* needs to be done without going into the details of *how* it should be done. This is different from *procedural languages*, which put more emphasis on *how*.

Consider the following analogy. You are ordering a dessert at a Japanese restaurant and you choose Kuri Fukume-ni. You can determine *what* are you ordering from the menu (this would be the sweet chestnuts, by the way), but you don't care *how* the dish is prepared, as long it's brought to your table in a reasonable amount of time. This is a *declarative* approach.

If you were a *procedural* type of person, you would explicitly instruct the cook to "take 15 chestnuts and 4 tablespoons of sugar; cut a deep groove in the flat, soft side of each chestnut. Put the chestnuts into a 2-quart saucepan, cover them with cold water, and bring it to boil. After cooking them for about 3 minutes, remove the chestnuts from the pan and peel off their shells. Bring 23 cups of water to a boil and simmer the peeled chestnuts in it for 20 minutes, then drain and set aside. Prepare light sugar syrup, combining 1 cup of cold water and 3 tablespoons of sugar in a

1.5-quart saucepan, and cook for another 20 minutes; stir in 1 more tablespoon of sugar, cook for some additional 5-7 minutes, and cool to room temperature in the same liquid. Drain the chestnuts and bring them to me."

Let's emphasize the major differences between these approaches:

❏ A declarative language (both in restaurant and in RDBMS environment) is useful only when you have a knowledgeable cook (a database engine) who understands the order, knows what to do with it, and has all the ingredients at hand. It is always a one-line command, no matter how long the line is. You are utterly dependent on the cook (database engine) to understand what is required and find the optimal way to produce results.

❏ A procedural language requires an interpreter or compiler to communicate instructions. It goes into great detail explaining the steps to be taken to achieve the final result. It involves numerous lines (statements) to get anything done. You are, however, in *almost* total control over the preparation and execution of your final results.

The declarative nature of SQL is the source of its power. It is also the reason for its inherent weakness. There is nothing more beautiful than a tight SQL code extracting information from an unlikely bunch of relational tables.

On the other hand, your SQL statement is only as good as the algorithms implemented by the RDBMS vendor, and you have very little say in the way your final results are returned. To counter these potential drawbacks, you may choose to:

❏ Handle the final transformation in the client application (that is, use the programming logic of the client application to modify and process the data returned by RDBMS)

❏ Employ vendor-supplied SQL functions inside your statements (if such functionality was anticipated by the vendor)

❏ Create your own function using a general programming language and register the function with the RDBMS (if the vendor has provided this capability)

❏ Create your own UDF using the SQL procedural extension language supplied by the vendor

❏ Wait for the next version of your favorite RDBMS, or switch vendors altogether

Creating your own routines to use within the RDBMS calls for persistent modules (that is, blocks of programming logic capable of being called and executed by the RDBMS). SQL persistent modules first became a standard in 1996 [ISO/IEC 9075-4:1996(E) Database Language SQL — Part 4: Persistent Stored Modules (SQL/PSM)]. This standard was later enhanced to accommodate emerging software paradigms. In the meantime, RDBMS vendors left to their own devices designed and implemented their own versions of procedural SQL.

Oracle, Microsoft, IBM, Sybase, and PostgreSQL all provide some built-in procedural languages to use when you are programming for their respective RDBMS, while MySQL uses C to achieve the same results (with a promise to implement the functionality of its more mature rivals in the next version, MySQL 5.0, currently in alpha stage).

Procedural extensions combine standard SQL features (a 4GL, set-based language) with 3GL features such as control structures (IF-THEN-ELSE), strongly typed variables, cursors, use of custom data types, and so on. A SQL statement operates on a set of data, while its procedural extension allows row-by-row manipulation, as well as calls to additional resources (such as procedures and functions).

Many vendors allow users to create custom functions (UDFs) within their RDBMS packages that are nearly identical to the built-in functions. The UDFs may be created with either the vendor's proprietary *procedural extension* language or one of the general programming languages (most notably C and Java).

ANSI SQL Guidance for Procedural Extensions to SQL

Although SQL:2003 does provide guidance on procedural extensions to SQL, its guidance is limited at best. This narrow scope leads to a lack of portability with respect to moving code from one database to another. Some would argue that this lack of portability is intentional by the RDBMS community as a way in which to produce "vendor lock-in." However, this compatibility issue is arguably from the following list of reasons:

❑ The SQL standard suffers from ambiguity because, even though it does precisely specify syntax, it does not specify the semantics of the constructs.

❑ Most vendors are unwilling to adopt certain standards that would break their backward compatibility with previous versions of their products.

❑ The sheer complexity of the SQL:1999 standard alone means that not all databases can implement the entire standard. Therefore, some database systems may have variants of their own for certain SQL data types.

❑ Although the standard is complex, it does not address certain important behaviors (such as indexes).

Because of the variations that these problems introduce in the various RDBMS systems, it is rare that code can be ported to another system without major modifications. However, SQL:2003 does provide a "syntax" guidance for procedural extensions to SQL, as shown in the following table.

Statement Type	Implementation
Variable declaration	`DECLARE variable VARCHAR(20)`
Assignment	`SET variable='XXX'`

Compound statements	`BEGIN`
	`<SQL statement list>`
	`END`

If statements	`IF <conditional statement> THEN`
	`.....`
	`ELSE .....`

Table continued on following page

51

Statement Type	Implementation

For statements	`FOR <result set>  AS .....`
	`DO....`
	`END FOR`

Case statements	`CASE  variable`
	`WHEN <conditional statement> THEN...`
	`WHEN ....`
	`END`

Loop statements	`LOOP`
	`<SQL statement list>`
	`END LOOP`

While statements	`WHILE <conditional statement>`
	`DO ......`
	`END WHILE`

Return statement	`RETURN 'XXX'`

Repeat statement	`REPEAT ......`
	`UNTIL <conditional statement>`
	`END REPEAT`

Leave statements	`LEAVE`
Signal/ Resignal statements	`SIGNAL   division_by_zero`
Call statements	`CALL procedure_name(X,Y,Z)`

SQL Procedural Extensions by Vendor

This section provides an overview of SQL procedural extensions by each major SQL database vendor. Chapters 12 through 18 provide specialized coverage of the creation of UDFs in each vendor's implementation.

Oracle PL/SQL

Procedural Language/SQL (PL/SQL) was designed to augment deficiencies of set-based SQL in Oracle's flagship database. Later it was incorporated into other Oracle products (that is, Oracle Developer).

PL/SQL is a very powerful language. Admittedly, it lacks the conciseness of SQL (which is a 4GL). In fact, some find it quite verbose. On the other hand, it has all the procedural constructs of a 3GL language: strongly typed variables, loops, control structures (IF-THEN-ELSE), ability to call other procedures and functions (SQL can only call functions, including these built in PL/SQL), and the power to use object-oriented types and methods (version 8 and higher).

Starting with version 2.0, PL/SQL allows you to organize its compiled modules (stored procedures and functions) within packages. None of the other major database vendors allow you to do so. The idea behind a package is to group together related functions and procedures. They are subsequently invoked with the name of the procedure, preceded by the name of the package. In addition to being a sound concept of structured programming, it allows for fine-grained security, whereby privileges to execute the package can be granted to or revoked from a database user.

Unlike many of its 3GL/4GL cousins, PL/SQL cannot be used to create stand-alone applications (nor can any of the other SQL procedural extension languages, for that matter). It exists only within the Oracle RDBMS environment and Oracle Developer forms as an interpreted language (though it is possible to compile PL/SQL procedures into a native machine code using the C compiler; more about this is covered in Chapter 13). PL/SQL modules (both functions and stored procedures) can be invoked through the SQL*Plus interface (supplied with the Oracle RDBMS) or from client applications once a connection with the RDBMS is established.

PL/SQL v1.0 was first released with Oracle version 6 in 1991 and quickly progressed to PL/SQL v2.0 in Oracle RDBMS version 7. After three incremental releases (versions 2.1, 2.4, and 2.3), PL/SQL was upgraded to version 8 with the release of the Oracle8 database. From there it went through version 8.1 (Oracle8i RDBMS), version 9.0 (Oracle9i RDBMS Release 1), version 9.2 (Oracle9i Release 2), up to the latest version of PL/SQL 10, (incorporated into Oracle10g RDBMS). The following table provides brief descriptions of the features introduced with each release.

Oracle RDBMS Version	PL/SQL Version	Brief Description
Oracle6	1.0	The very first version of PL/SQL, it could not even create named reusable modules, let alone UDFs.
Oracle6	1.1	This release supported client-side subprograms to execute stored code transparently.
Oracle7	2.0	This major upgrade from version 1.0 introduced support for stored procedures, UDFs, packages, and many other features (such as PL/SQL tables and user-defined records).
Oracle7.1	2.1	This version enables use of the UDFs within SQL statements (previously they could only be used within other functions and stored procedures) and introduces custom subtypes and the ability to execute dynamic SQL with the DBMS_SQL package.
Oracle7.2	2.2	This version introduced cursor variables and further enhancement for PL/SQL tables.
Oracle7.3	2.3	This version completed implementation of cursor variables and improved I/O capabilities with the UTL_FILE package.
Oracle8	8.0	This version reflects Oracle's effort to synchronize version numbers across the range of its products. It adds support for object-oriented features, collections, arrays (VARRAY, nested table), and queuing (with the Oracle Advanced Queuing Facility).

Table continued on following page

Oracle RDBMS Version	PL/SQL Version	Brief Description
Oracle8i	8.1	This version adds a new version of Dynamic SQL, Java support, autonomous transactions, and performance enhancements.
Oracle9i Release 1	9.0	This version adds support for inheritance in object types, table functions, and cursor expressions, as well as CASE expressions (in addition to the ancient DECODE function).
Oracle9i Release 2	9.2	This release, prompted by increasing XML popularity, introduced additional support for XML. It also added the ability to use associative arrays (indexed by VARCHAR) and record-based INSERT statements.
Oracle10g	10	The PL/SQL compiler was completely rewritten, resulting in increased speed and performance. Some restrictions of Oracle9i regarding compilation of PL/SQL modules into native code were removed. XML support was enhanced. Tracing information was expanded to help manage performance (through identifying potentially poorly performing units at compile time).

Each version constitutes an improvement upon the previous one, adding new features and rendering the old ones obsolete. Because PL/SQL is tightly coupled with the Oracle RDBMS, you can never assume full backward compatibility, or expect to use new features with older versions.

> SQLJ is an ANSI/ISO standard designed for embedding SQL into Java. Initially called JSQL, it changed names after some legal issues. It requires Java Virtual Machine (JVM) and Java Database Connectivity (JDBC) (which is one of the standard Java API interfaces supporting dynamic SQL). SQLJ was created when Java was all the rage and considered a silver bullet for every programming problem. Initial enthusiasm has subsided, but the concept of using an embedded general programming language was carried on—virtually every vendor has added support for some general programming language within its environment, be it Java, C, VB, or C#. Creating procedures in Java incurs significant overhead, and they tend to perform more poorly than native PL/SQL procedures. Nevertheless, this might not be an issue when clarity and flexibility are more important then raw speed.

Microsoft or Sybase Transact-SQL

Sybase (one of the RDBMS pioneers) created a procedural database language of its own: Transact-SQL. Later, because of partnering with Microsoft for producing an RDBMS on the Windows platform, the language was also adopted for Microsoft SQL Server. Unlike Sybase, Microsoft makes very little distinction between SQL proper and its procedural extension Transact-SQL. Since it is used only within RDBMS, there has been no versioning of Transact-SQL. It simply exists in every Microsoft or Sybase SQL Server.

New features appear and old features are made obsolete with every new release of its host environment (RDBMS software). The only way to track the changes would be to follow versions of the RDBMS.

Since version 7.0 of its RDBMS product, Microsoft no longer shares its code base with Sybase. In the future, you can expect even more divergence between the two. At present, the difference is mostly in the variety of built-in functions available for use within Transact-SQL code, chained transactions support found only in Sybase, minor differences in cursor scope, and usage syntax.

> **Sybase does not allow use of its version of Transact-SQL to be used for the creation of UDFs. Everything we say about this particular procedural extension in this book refers to Microsoft SQL Server.**

Similar to Oracle PL/SQL, Transact-SQL represents a cross between 4GL and 3GL. It employs SQL (4GL) in addition to the strongly typed variables, control structures, and constructs of a typical 3GL environment.

The compiled modules (stored procedures and functions), stored in the RDBMS itself, allow for faster execution compared to a stand-alone SQL statement; in addition, there is a reduction of overhead when transferring information through the network. The compiled module is stored as a byte-code (this seems to be the same across all major RDBMSs), and its source Transact-SQL code is stored in system tables.

Microsoft SQL Server allows for creation of *extended stored procedures*. Extended stored procedures are dynamic-link libraries (DLLs) that SQL Server can dynamically load and execute. These are usually written in C, and they reside outside the RDBMS server. The procedure must implement a specific callable interface defined by the Microsoft SQL Server Open Data Services and be registered with it through a system-stored procedure `sp_addextendedproc`.

Some of the features of Transact-SQL have equivalents in PL/SQL, but most do not. Even similarly named objects (that is, cursor variables) exhibit different behavior. Although source code of both PL/SQL and Transact-SQL is simple ASCII text, it could not possibly be compiled in an environment it was not created for, at least not without a translation.

Sybase, while supporting its own dialect of Transact-SQL, disallows the use of it for the purpose of creating UDFs, opting for Java instead. The UDFs were introduced with Sybase ASE 12.0, and were considerably improved with version 12.5.

The Sybase UDF is executed through a dedicated JVM inside the Adaptive Server Enterprise (ASE) server. This requires you to license a separate ASE_JAVA option (that is, you cannot use just any JVM that happens to be installed on your machine).

IBM Procedural SQL

IBM is firmly established in the world of mainframe databases, but it is a newcomer to the PC world of RDBMS. As of this writing, its latest "PC" database is IBM DB2 UDB version 8.1.

Originally, the stored procedures for IBM RDBMSs were developed in C (actually, any programming language supported by IBM DB2 UDB Pre-compilers; the list of languages also includes REXX, FORTRAN, Java, and COBOL). When procedural logic was compiled into UNIX, shared libraries (or Windows

DLLs) were stored outside the RDBMS. The SQL queries were separated and statically compiled into sections of a package (refer to IBM documentation for more information on packages) and stored inside the RDBMS. During the execution of such a procedure, there was a context switch between the library (DLL) and IBM database engine whenever a SQL statement had to be executed (the SQL queries in such a scenario were compiled only once whenever the stored procedure was compiled).

This was a huge drag on performance. In version 8, the SQL procedures ran in *unfenced mode*, which meant that they ran within the same memory space as the database engine. In this scenario, *switch of context* refers to a switch between layers of the same application (as opposed to a switch between two different processes within an operating system).

> *If you are looking to squeeze the last drop of performance from your IBM DB2 UDB database, you might consider programming your most resource-intensive procedures in C (unfenced mode).*

SQL functions are compiled *in-line* (that is, into the query that uses the SQL function). As a result, the whole compilation process is repeated every time the query that uses the function is compiled. Unlike a stored procedure, the code of an in-line function is executed in the same layer as the database process, avoiding costly context switching altogether. Although certain exceptions do exist (see Chapter 14 for more information), procedural logic will execute much faster if implemented as a function rather than as a stored procedure.

IBM introduced its first procedural SQL constructs in DB2 UDB version 7, initially for stored procedures only. It was not until version 7.2 that the user was able to create functions and triggers using this language. Version 8 brought in the name SQL PL as the official name for its new built-in language.

> *Although the existence of the SQL procedural extension language in IBM DB2 UDB was widely adver-tised, its name was a well-kept secret. You had to search hard for the SQL PL term in IBM documenta-tion prior to 2003. Various names were used in the books on IBM DB2: TSQL, IBM SQL, and DB2 SQL. Fortunately, IBM Press released a book titled DB2 SQL Procedural Language for Linux, UNIX and Windows, by Paul Yip et al. (Upper Saddle River, N.J.: Prentice Hall, 2002) that put to rest all the guesswork.*

SQL PL has all the usual constructs found in Oracle's PL/SQL or Transact-SQL, although it includes a number of additional restrictions regarding usage of SQL PL for creating UDFs. Following are the most important:

- ❑ SQL queries cannot modify any data.
- ❑ PREPARE, EXECUTE, and EXECUTE IMMEDIATELY are not allowed.
- ❑ There is no support for exception handlers.
- ❑ There is no support for stored procedure calls from a UDF.
- ❑ There is no support for the INSERT INTO statement in a UDF.

IBM DB2 UDB also supports SQLJ and Java for stored procedures/UDF development using JDBC drivers (types 1 through 4).

MySQL

Until its very recent release (version 5.0, still in alpha stage as of this writing), there were no such things as stored procedures or UDFs in MySQL. The same goes for the cursors, views, and constraints, which are supposed to debut in the upcoming version 5.1 (available in a snapshot release).

The closest thing you can use right now is a script (for example, Perl) stored in the database, pulled out and parsed on demand, and executed by some external run-time environment. More advanced users may also add a required procedure or SQL function directly to the database run time by modifying the source code.

The syntax of the new procedural SQL extension will be similar to Oracle PL/SQL, but according to MySQL AB "not identical." A promise was made to hook in external languages (compare to PostgreSQL features). The effort will be based on the SQL 99 standard. MySQL's current progress can be followed on their corporate Web site, at www.mysql.com.

PostgreSQL

PostgreSQL allows users to add new programming languages for creating functions and procedures. Unlike the procedural languages of Oracle, Microsoft SQL Server, Sybase, and IBM DB2 UDB, these are defined outside the PostgreSQL server, and they rely on an appropriate compiler/interpreter. Whenever a procedure or function is invoked, the processing task is passed to a special handler that knows the details of a particular language. It can parse, compile, and execute the procedure itself, or pass it on to an existing implementation of the language. The handler itself is a special module compiled (in C language) into a shared object (DLL, in Microsoft Windows), and it is loaded on demand.

A PostgreSQL installation must be made aware of a particular procedural language by adding ("installing") it to each database in which the language will be available.

> *Procedural languages installed in the database TEMPLATE1 are available to all subsequently created databases.*

The PostgreSQL comes with a standard PL/pgSQL language. It can be installed using the program createlang right away, but all other languages must be added to the template manually. Although virtually any language can be installed for that purpose as long as it satisfies certain criteria, the following languages are most commonly used:

❑   PL/pgSQL

❑   PL/Tcl

❑   PL/Perl

❑   PL/PythonU

These can be installed with the standard PostgreSQL installation if support is configured on the server.

Summary

This chapter offers a brief overview of the SQL procedural languages implemented by the RDBMS vendors discussed in the book. While every RDBMS has built-in functions that can be used in a regular SQL query, the need for procedural processing led to the creation of SQL procedural extensions. Procedural extensions were introduced to alleviate restrictions imposed by SQL's declarative nature: inability to work with data *during* execution of the code and limited support (through SQL functions) for data transformation. Gradually, the procedural extension languages were given the capability to create custom functions to be used in a SQL query.

Not every vendor provides such a language with its product (MySQL has just added its own implementation loosely based on Oracle's PL/SQL), and even those that do provide it may restrict its usage from creation of UDFs (for example, Sybase).

The details of implementation and execution vary from RDBMS to RDBMS, rendering such procedural code nonportable (essentially, it must be rewritten for each and every vendor). SQL proper is, by and large, a vendor-neutral language (if it follows ANSI SQL Standard).

For some vendors, the performance of a procedural extension–coded routine differs very little from a "native" function's performance. For some, the difference is significant. However, learning the nuances of your chosen RDBMS system will allow you to extend the functionality of your code significantly. In the following chapters, we will begin to delve into the specifics of each of the different RDBMS systems' query syntax and functions in order to help you reach that end.

In Chapter 5, we begin to cover the built-in functions of each SQL implementation, beginning with the ANSI SQL Standard. Keep in mind in Chapter 5 that the ANSI SQL Standard is just a standard and not an implementation itself; it lays the groundwork for each vendor's implementation of the standard.

5

Common ANSI SQL Functions

Even though the SQL standard is a nonbinding recommendation, many RDBMS vendors share some SQL functions. Whether this happened by accident or because of the commitment to the common standards, we cannot say. This chapter is the first of several that examine some of the most commonly used functions, found in the majority (if not all) of RDBMS implementations discussed in this book.

Some of the material found in this chapter also appears in an RDBMS-specific chapter later in this book. The redundancy is intentional. Throughout the chapter, you may see cross-references to vendor-specific chapters. The following table provides a handy guide to help you locate those chapters.

Vendor	Function Reference by Vendor	User-Defined Function by Vendor
ANSI SQL	Chapter 5	Chapter 12
Oracle	Chapter 6	Chapter 13
IBM DB2	Chapter 7	Chapter 14
SQL Server	Chapter 8	Chapter 15
Sybase	Chapter 9	Chapter 16
MySQL	Chapter 10	Chapter 17
PostgreSQL	Chapter 11	Chapter 18

This chapter begins by examining the basics of ANSI query syntax. The discussion then shifts to specific types of functions, including aggregate functions, string functions, mathematical functions, and miscellaneous functions.

ANSI Query Syntax

The ANSI SQL query syntax is based upon the SELECT statement. The ANSI standard is a quite complicated document that may make it difficult to decipher all the nuances of the SELECT statement. Following is an example of the basic SELECT statement:

```
SELECT [ <set_quantifier> ] <select_list> <table_expression>
```

One possible interpretation of this syntax is that a SELECT statement can contain an optional `<set_quantifier>` followed by at least a `<select_list>` and a `<table_expression>`. A `<set_quantifier>` is either a DISTINCT or an ALL modifier. To find out what a `<select_list>` is, we must dig deeper.

The following syntax tells us that a `<select_list>` is either an `<asterisk>` (*) (which means select all objects from the `<table expression>`) or a comma-delimited list of the `<select_sublist>`.

```
<select_list> ::= <asterisk>
    | <select_sublist> [ { <comma> <select_sublist> }... ]
```

A `<select_sublist>` is basically a value expression that equates to a column, function, variable, or other item that is value-based. The last item to look at is the `<table_expression>`, which is detailed here:

```
<table_expression> ::=
    <from_clause>
    [ <where_clause> ]
    [ <group_by_clause> ]
    [ <having_clause> ]
```

The `<table_expression>` is merely the back end of our query statement that tells the SELECT statement where to get the information we desire. In Chapter 1, this would be equivalent to everything in the SELECT statement starting at the FROM clause and moving to the right. It can also contain WHERE, GROUP BY, and HAVING clauses to restrict and shape the data that is pulled from the table(s).

It should be noted that the preceding breakdown of the `<table expression>` is by no means a complete list, and there are many more options that the developer can choose from. To get a full listing of options, you must look at the actual ANSI SQL standard. However, this should give you a good reference from which to start.

Aggregate Functions

An *aggregate SQL function* summarizes the results of an expression for the group of rows (selected from a table, view, or table-valuated function) and returns a single value for that group. Following is generic syntax of an aggregate function:

```
<aggregate_function_name> ([DISTINCT | ALL] <expression>)
```

The modifiers DISCTINCT and ALL affect the behavior of the function. The DISTINCT modifier instructs the function to consider only distinct values for the argument, ignoring the duplicates. The ALL modifier tells the function to include all values. When no modifier is supplied, ALL is assumed, by default. Therefore, the ALL modifier is rarely (if ever) used.

The full list of aggregate functions supported by each of the RDBMS implementations discussed in this book is given in Appendix A. A select group of common functions discussed in this chapter is shown in the following table.

SQL Function	Oracle	IBM	Microsoft	Sybase ASE	MySQL	PgSQL	Notes
AVG	Yes	Yes	Yes	Yes	Yes	Yes	Calculates the average of the set of numbers; NULL values are ignored.
COUNT	Yes	Yes	Yes	Yes	Yes	Yes	Returns the number of records.
MAX	Yes	Yes	Yes	Yes	Yes	Yes	Returns a single maximum value in a given set.
MIN	Yes	Yes	Yes	Yes	Yes	Yes	Returns a single minimum value in a given set.
SUM	Yes	Yes	Yes	Yes	Yes	Yes	Returns the sum of the values in a set.

The aggregate functions usually use the GROUP BY clause. If this clause is omitted, the function will be applied to all rows in the view/table/table-valued function. All examples in this section will be based on the table CARS, which contains make, model, and price information for cars, created with the following generic SQL syntax. It will execute without modification in every one of the RDBMS implementations discussed in this book.

```
CREATE TABLE cars
(
  MAKER  VARCHAR (25),
  MODEL  VARCHAR (25),
  PRICE  NUMERIC
)

INSERT INTO CARS VALUES('CHRYSLER','CROSSFIRE',33620);
INSERT INTO CARS VALUES('CHRYSLER','300M',29185);
INSERT INTO CARS VALUES('HONDA','CIVIC',15610);
INSERT INTO CARS VALUES('HONDA','ACCORD',19300);
```

```
INSERT INTO CARS VALUES('FORD','MUSTANG',15610);
INSERT INTO CARS VALUES('FORD','LATESTnGREATEST',NULL);
INSERT INTO CARS VALUES('FORD','FOCUS',13005);
```

AVG()

Syntax:

```
AVG ([DISTINCT]|[ALL] <numeric expression>)
```

The function `AVG()` calculates the arithmetic average of the series of numbers of its argument. For example, the following queries could be used to gather some statistical information about the cars in the CARS table:

```
SELECT
      AVG(price) average_price
FROM cars;

average_price
--------------------
21055
```

This summed all the prices (in column PRICE) and divided them by the number of entries. Now, to find the average of the uniquely priced cars, we use the DISTINCT modifier:

```
SELECT
    AVG(DISTINCT price) average_price
FROM cars;

average_price
--------------------
22144
```

To find out the average price for each manufacturer, we would use the GROUP BY clause:

```
SELECT
    maker,
    AVG(price) average_price
FROM cars
GROUP BY maker;

Maker                   average_price
----------------        -------------
CHRYSLER                31402.5
FORD                    14307.5
HONDA                   17455
```

While usefulness of the obtained information is questionable, now we know that the average (?) car costs about $21,000, and Ford produces the least-expensive cars on average.

This function is supported across all the RDBMS implementations covered in this book, though some differences do exist. For example, the use of the DISTINCT clause is supported by Microsoft SQL Server,

Sybase ASE, IBM DB2 UDB, and PostgreSQL. However, the DISTINCT clause cannot be used with MySQL's version of the AVG() function (though it is allowed in its COUNT() function).

COUNT()

Syntax:

```
COUNT([DISTINCT]|[ALL] <expression>)
```

This function would answer the question, "How many cars do we have on the lot?" Consider the following example:

```
SELECT
    COUNT(*) cars_count
FROM cars

CARS_COUNT
---------------------
7
```

Using GROUP BY would tell us how many cars from each vendor we have on the lot:

```
SELECT
    Maker,
    COUNT(price)cars_count
FROM cars
GROUP BY maker;

MAKER             CARS_COUNT
----------------  -------------
CHRYSLER          2
FORD              2
HONDA             2
```

The COUNT(*) function reports that the CARS_COUNT value equals 7, while COUNT(price) insists that we have only six cars, which makes sense — price-wise we know about only six cars, though on the lot we see seven. Looking back at the original CARS table, we see that one Ford model had a price of NULL.

```
SELECT
    Maker,
    COUNT(*)        total_count,
    COUNT(price)    car_prices
FROM cars
GROUP BY maker;

MAKER             TOTAL_COUNT     CAR_PRICES
----------------  -------------   -----------
CHRYSLER          2               2
FORD              3               2
HONDA             2               2
```

This behavior pertains to the COUNT() and GROUPING() functions. The rest of the aggregate functions ignore NULLs.

You should also be aware of GROUP BY clause behavior when it encounters NULL — all NULLs will be grouped into a group of their own and placed at the bottom of the returned result set. The order is determined by the fact that ORDER BY (ascending) is implicitly performed whenever GROUP BY is executed and a NULL value will always be at the end of the ascending sort order.

The functionality and syntax of COUNT() is identical across all RDBMS implementations in their current versions, although this might not be true for previous versions. This is one of the functions where MySQL allows the DISTINCT modifier.

MAX() and MIN()

Syntax:

```
MAX ([DISTINCT]|[ALL] <expression>)
      MIN([DISTINCT]|[ALL] <expression>)
```

The names of these functions are self-describing. They allow you to display maximum and minimum values in a set. To find the highest and lowest prices of cars on the lot, the following query could be used:

```
SELECT
    MAX(price) max_price,
    MIN(price) min_price
FROM cars;

max_price           min_price
----------------    -------------
33620               13005
```

To find the price range for the cars on the lot in relation to the manufacturer, the GROUP BY clause must be used:

```
SELECT
    Maker,
    MAX(price) max_price,
    MIN(price) min_price
FROM cars
GROUP BY maker;
Maker           max_price       min_price
------------    -----------     ------------
CHRYSLER        33620           29185
FORD            15610           13005
HONDA           19300           15610
```

The MIN() and MAX() functions behave identically to the AVG() function in the handling of NULL values.

The functionality and syntax is identical across all RDBMS implementations. This is one of the functions where MySQL allows DISTINCT modifier.

SUM()

Syntax:

```
SUM([DISTINCT]|[ALL] <numeric_expression>)
```

The SUM() function does just what the name implies—sum the values. For example, to find the total price for all the cars on the lot, we would issue the following query:

```
SELECT
    SUM(price) total
FROM cars;

TOTAL
---------------
126330
```

The GROUP BY function would produce yet another angle on the data: inventory totals distributed across different vendors:

```
SELECT
    Maker,
    SUM(price) total
FROM cars
GROUP BY maker;

Maker                total
----------------     -------------
CHRYSLER             62805
FORD                 28615
HONDA                34910
```

The functionality and syntax is identical across all RDBMS implementations. This is one of the functions where MySQL allows the DISTINCT modifier.

String Functions

Although numbers comprise the bulk of the data contained in RDBMS implementations, and new data formats (such as binary pictures, movies, and sounds) spread rapidly, character data is a staple in every database. Reflecting this, all RDBMS implementations have vast collections of built-in functions to manipulate strings. The following table lists some of the built-in SQL functions found in all six RDBMS implementations discussed in this book.

Function	Oracle	IBM	Microsoft	Sybase ASE	MySQL	PgSQL	Brief description
ASCII	Yes	Yes	Yes	Yes	Yes	Yes	Returns ASCII code of the first character of a string.
CHR or CHAR	Yes	Yes	CHAR	CHAR	CHAR	CHR	Returns the character corresponding to the ASCII code that is passed to it.
CONCAT	Yes	Yes	Yes	Yes	Yes	Yes	Returns the result of concatenation of two (or more) strings.
LEN or LENGTH	Yes	Yes	LEN	LEN	CHAR_ LENGTH	CHAR_ LENGTH	Returns number of characters in a string.
LOWER	Yes	Yes, and LCASE	Yes	Yes	Yes, and LCASE	Yes	Converts all characters in a string to lowercase.
REPLACE	Yes	Yes	Yes	STR_ REPLACE	Yes	Yes	Replaces all occurrences of string1 within string2 with string3.
UPPER	Yes	Yes, and UCASE	Yes	Yes	Yes, and UCASE	Yes	Converts all characters in a string to uppercase.

ASCII()

Syntax:

```
ASCII(<expression>)
```

This function returns the numeric value of the leftmost character of the string. It returns 0 if the string is the empty string. It returns NULL if the string is NULL. ASCII() works for characters with numeric values from 0 to 255. Any character out of this range would either be ignored or return an error. For example, this code will run in every one of the six RDBMS implementations discussed in this book. Note that this function only applies to the leftmost character and ignores the rest of the string.

```
SELECT
   ASCII('A')    uppercase_a,
   ASCII('abc') lowercase_a

uppercase_a     lowercase_a
-----------     -----------
65              97
```

As the name implies, the function only deals with ASCII characters. For national UNICODE/UTF/EBCDIC equivalents, see respective vendor's chapters.

CHR() or CHAR()

Syntax:

```
CH[A]R(<numeric_expression>)
```

The CHR() function is the opposite of the ASCII function. It returns a character when given its ASCII code. For inputs outside this range, the behavior is dependent on the particular RDBMS implementation. See the specific vendor chapters for more information. For example, consider the following:

```
SELECT
   CHR(65)      uppercase_a,
   CHR(97)      lowercase_a

uppercase_a     lowercase_a
-----------     -----------
A               a
```

Except for a small syntactic difference (Microsoft SQL Server, Sybase, and MySQL use CHAR(), while the rest of the discussed RDBMS implementations discussed in this book use CHR()), the usage for the ASCII-range characters is identical.

CONCAT()

Syntax:

```
CONCAT(<expression>,<expression>)
```

The CONCAT() function simply concatenates two (or more) strings. MySQL allows concatenation of more than two strings, while IBM DB2 UDB and Oracle insist on exactly two. Consider the following example:

```
SELECT
   CONCAT('Hello ', ' ,world') result

RESULT
--------------
Hello, world
```

In addition to the CONCAT() function, Oracle employs the operator "||" for concatenation, as does IBM DB2 UDB. Microsoft SQL Server and Sybase both overload the plus ("+") operator (and Sybase ASE has the "||" operator as well). MySQL relies on the CONCAT() function only, while PostgreSQL only uses the "||" operator.

LOWER() and UPPER()

Syntax:

```
LOWER(<numeric expression>)
    UPPER(<numeric expression>)
```

The LOWER() and UPPER() functions complement each other. The former converts all the characters in a string into lowercase and the latter converts them into uppercase. Consider the following example:

```
SELECT
    LOWER('STRING') lowercase,
    UPPER('STRING') uppercase

LOWERCASE         UPPERCASE
------------      -------------
string            STRING
```

The functions are found in every RDBMS discussed in this book. IBM DB2 UDB and MySQL also have synonyms for the UPPER() and LOWER() functions—UCASE() and LCASE(). The syntax and usage are identical across the implementations.

LENGTH() or LEN()

Syntax:

```
LEN[GTH](<expression>)
```

The LENGTH() function returns the number of character in a given string. The SQL 99 standard includes BIT_LENGTH(), CHAR_LENGTH(), and OCTET_LENGTH() functions. All of these are implemented in the RDBMS implementations discussed in this book, though each vendor did it differently. The LENGTH() function is found in every RDBMS implementation (in the form of CHAR_LENGTH() of the SQL Standard, MySQL, and PostgreSQL).

The following example returns the number of characters in a literal:

```
SELECT
    LENGTH('test') TEST

TEST
--------
    4
```

In general, there is a correspondence between the number of characters and the number of bytes in a word. This is true where ASCII characters are concerned. This is complicated once some national character sets come into play. For example, the MySQL's CHAR_LENGTH() (length in characters) and LENGTH() (length in bytes) will both return the same result for an ASCII word, but they might be different for any national character set. To avoid confusion, ensure that you are using the proper function.

The LENGTH() function returns the length in characters for IBM DB2 UDB, Oracle, Microsoft SQL Server, and Sybase (the name is LEN() for the last two). PostgreSQL and MySQL both employ the CHAR_LENGTH() function for this purpose.

REPLACE()

Syntax:

```
REPLACE (<string_expression>,<search_string> [,<replacement_string>])
```

The REPLACE() function replaces every occurrence of the string specified as the search_string with the replacement_string. If the replacement_string is an empty string, the found matches for the search_string are removed from the resulting character string (Oracle allows you to omit the third argument for the same purpose).

The following example replaces each uppercase "A" in a string with an asterisk ("*") in the first field. The second field, where the third argument is omitted, returns a string with all occurrences of "A" removed.

```
SELECT
    REPLACE ('ABCDA', 'A','*')   replace_A,
    REPLACE ('ABCDA', 'A','')    remove_A

REPLACE_A   REMOVE_A
---------   --------
*BCD*       BCD
```

All arguments of the REPLACE() function can be any of the character data types, and some of the RDBMS implementation perform an implicit conversion for compatible data types. The returned string is of VARCHAR data type, and is in the same character set as replacement_string.

This function exists in Oracle, IBM DB2 UDB, Microsoft SQL Server, MySQL, and PostgreSQL. Sybase ASE 12.5 has the STR_REPLACE() function, which abides by the same rules as REPLACE() in other RDBMS implementations. Some RDBMS implementations have additional uses for the function, as well as syntax peculiarities. Please see vendor specific chapters for more information.

Mathematical Functions

Implementation of mathematical functions is fairly standard across all RDBMS implementations discussed in this book. Nevertheless, some confusion does exist in names, execution details, and so on. The following table lists most of the mathematical functions as they are implemented by the RDBMS vendors.

Function	Oracle	IBM	Microsoft	Sybase	MySQL	PgSQL	Brief description
ABS	Yes	Yes, and ABSVAL	Yes	Yes	Yes	Yes	Returns the absolute value of n.
ACOS	Yes	Yes	Yes	Yes	Yes	Yes	Returns the arccosine of n.
ASIN	Yes	Yes	Yes	Yes	Yes	Yes	Returns the arcsine of n.
ATAN	Yes	Yes	Yes	Yes	Yes	Yes	Returns the arctangent of n.
ATAN2	Yes	Yes	ATN2	ATN2	Yes	Yes	Returns the arctangent of n and m.
CEIL	Yes	Yes, and CEIL-ING	CEILING	CEILING	Yes, and CEIL-ING	Yes	Returns the smallest integer greater than or equal to n.
COS	Yes	Yes	Yes	Yes	Yes	Yes	Returns the cosine of n.
COSH	Yes	Yes	No	No	No	No	Returns the hyperbolic cosine of n.
COT	No	Yes	Yes	Yes	Yes	Yes	Returns the cotangent of the specified angle (in radians) in the given float expression.
DEGREES	No	Yes	Yes	Yes	Yes	Yes	Given an angle in radians, returns the corresponding angle in degrees.
EXP	Yes	Yes	Yes	Yes	Yes	Yes	Returns e raised to the nth power, where e = 2.71828183....
FLOOR	Yes	Yes	Yes	Yes	Yes	Yes	Returns the largest integer equal to or less than n.

Function	Oracle	IBM	Microsoft	Sybase	MySQL	PgSQL	Brief description
LN	Yes	LOG	LOG	LOG	Yes, and LOG	Yes	Returns the natural logarithm of n, where n is greater than 0.
LOG2	No	No	No	No	Yes	No	Returns the base-2 logarithm of x.
LOG10	No	Yes	Yes	Yes	Yes	No	Returns the base-10 logarithm of x.
LOG	Yes	No	No	No	Yes	Yes	Returns the base-m logarithm of n.
MOD	Yes	Yes	"%" operator	"%" operator	Yes	Yes	Returns the remainder of m divided by n; returns m if n is 0.
PI	No	No	Yes	Yes	Yes	Yes	Returns pi (approx. 3.1415926...).
POWER	Yes	Yes	Yes	Yes	Yes, and POW	POW	Returns m raised to the nth power.
RADIANS	No	Yes	Yes	Yes	Yes	Yes	Returns radians when a numeric expression, in degrees, is entered.
RAND	No	Yes	Yes	Yes	Yes	No	Returns a random float value from 0 to 1.
ROUND	Yes	Yes	Yes	Yes	Yes	Yes	Returns a numeric expression rounded to the specified length or precision.
SIGN	Yes	Yes	Yes	Yes	Yes	Yes	Returns −1 if $n < 0$, 0 if $n = 0$, and 1 if $n > 0$.

Table continued on following page

Function	Oracle	IBM	Microsoft	Sybase	MySQL	PgSQL	Brief description
SINH	Yes	Yes	No	No	No	No	Returns the hyperbolic sine of *n*.
SQUARE	No	No	Yes	Yes	No	No	Returns the expression raised to the power of 2; equivalent to POWER (number,2).
SQRT	Yes	Yes	Yes	Yes	Yes	Yes	Returns the square root of *n*.
TAN	Yes	Yes	Yes	Yes	Yes	Yes	Returns the tangent of *n*.
TANH	Yes	Yes	No	No	No	No	Returns the hyperbolic tangent of *n*.
TRUNC or TRUNCATE	TRUNC	Yes, both	No	No	TRUN-CATE	TRUNC	Returns the number *x*, truncated to *D* decimals. If *D* is 0, the result will have no decimal point or fractional part. If *D* is negative, the integer part of the number is zeroed out.

ABS()

Syntax:

```
ABS(<numeric expression>)
```

The ABS() function returns the absolute value of a numeric input argument. As the following examples show, the number returned will always be positive:

```
SELECT
    ABS(-100) negative,
    ABS(100)  positive;

NEGATIVE    POSITIVE
---------   ---------
100         100
```

Some RDBMS implementations impose restrictions on the size of the number passed in. Microsoft will not process numbers exceeding the maximum precision of 38, and Sybase ASE and IBM DB2 UDB will stop at the maximum for the internal machine representation (33 bytes for 32-bit computers, 255 characters long). Oracle, PostgreSQL, and MySQL will handle virtually any number.

Also, you must take into consideration the rounding/truncation errors. Sybase ASE would truncate the result for a maximum precision of 38, while Oracle and MySQL would round them. PostgreSQL and Microsoft SQL Server will keep the original number up to the system limits (and the former has no self-imposed limitations — it will process virtually any number you want to supply).

The previous syntax would work in Microsoft SQL Server, Sybase ASE, MySQL, and PostgreSQL; Oracle requires a FROM dual clause, and IBM DB2 UDB needs FROM sysibm.sysdummy1. (Alternatively, IBM DB2 UDB uses VALUES <function> syntax.)

ACOS()

Syntax:

```
ACOS(<numeric expression>)
```

The ACOS() function is used to return the arccosine of the <numeric expression> passed to it. The <numeric expression> must be a float value in the range –1 to 1 and the value returned will be in radians. The following code gives an example of the use of the ACOS() function:

```
SELECT
    ROUND(DEGREES(ACOS(.5)),0) as FIRST_ANGLE,
    ROUND(DEGREES(ACOS(.75)),0) as SECOND_ANGLE,
    ROUND(DEGREES(ACOS(1.0)),0) as THIRD_ANGLE
```

FIRST_ANGLE	SECOND_ANGLE	THIRD_ANGLE
60.0	41.0	0.0

This function is supported across all of the RDBMS implementations discussed in this book.

ASIN()

Syntax:

```
ASIN(<numeric expression>)
```

The ASIN() function returns the arcsine of the <numeric expression> passed to it. The <numeric expression> must generally be in the range –1 to 1 and the value returned will be in radians. The following code gives an example of the use of the ASIN() function:

```
SELECT
    ROUND(DEGREES(ASIN(.5)),0) as FIRST_ANGLE,
    ROUND(DEGREES(ASIN(.75)),0) as SECOND_ANGLE,
    ROUND(DEGREES(ASIN(1.0)),0) as THIRD_ANGLE
```

FIRST_ANGLE	SECOND_ANGLE	THIRD_ANGLE
30.0	49.0	90.0

This function is supported across all of the RDBMS implementations discussed in this book.

ATAN() and ATAN2()

Syntax:

```
ATAN(<numeric expression>)
ATAN2(<numeric expression1>,<numeric expression2>)
```

The `ATAN()` and `ATAN2()` functions are used to return some form of the arctangent of the arguments passed to them. In the case of `ATAN()`, the function returns the arctangent of the `<numeric expression>` argument passed to it. The `ATAN2()` function returns the arctangent of the angle whose tangent is defined by the *x* and *y* coordinates defined by `<numeric expression1>` and `<numeric expression2>`, respectively. The following code is an example of the use of both of these functions:

```
SELECT
    ATAN(.5) AS FIRST_RESULT,
    ATAN2(.5,1.0) AS SECOND_RESULT
FROM DUAL;
```

FIRST_RESULT	SECOND_RESULT
.463647609	.463647609

The `ATAN()` and `ATAN2()` functions are supported in all of the implementations, except that `ATAN2()` is not supported in Microsoft SQL Server and Sybase. In these two databases, there is an equivalent function `ATN2()` that serves the same purpose.

CEIL() or CEILING() and FLOOR()

Syntax:

```
CEIL[ING](<numeric expression>)
FLOOR(<numeric expression>)
```

Both of these functions round the numbers, albeit differently. `CEIL()` rounds up to the nearest integer value; `FLOOR()` rounds down (or truncates) to get to the next-least-integer value. Consider the following example:

```
SELECT
    CEIL(109.19)  ceil_val,
    FLOOR(109.19) floor_val
```

CEIL_VAL	FLOOR_VAL
110	109

The functions act in a way similar to the TRUNC() and ROUND() functions, and could be interchanged in certain circumstances.

IBM DB2 UDB and MySQL accept both the CEIL() and CEILING() syntaxes of the function. Microsoft SQL Server and Sybase only recognize CEILING(), and Oracle and PostgreSQL standardized on CEIL().

COS()

Syntax:

```
COS(<numeric expression>)
```

The COS() function returns the cosine of the <numeric expression> argument that is passed to it. The <numeric expression> argument is a float value that represents the angle in radians from which to obtain the cosine. The following example demonstrates the use of the COS() function:

```
SELECT
    COS(RADIANS(0)) AS FIRST_ANGLE,
    COS(RADIANS(45)) AS SECOND_ANGLE,
    COS(RADIANS(90)) AS THIRD_ANGLE

FIRST_ANGLE             SECOND_ANGLE            THIRD_ANGLE
-------------           ---------------         -------------
1.0                     1.0                     0.54030230586813977
```

The COS() function is available in all of the RDBMS implementations discussed in this book.

COSH()

Syntax:

```
COSH(<numeric expression>)
```

The COSH() function returns the hyperbolic cosine of <numeric expression>. The <numeric expression> argument is the angle expressed in radians from which the hyperbolic cosine is to be calculated. The following code gives an example of the use of the COSH() function on the Oracle platform:

```
SELECT COSH(.5) AS RESULT FROM DUAL;

    RESULT
----------
1.12762597
```

The COSH() function is available only on the Oracle and IBM DB2 implementations.

COT()

Syntax:

```
COT(<numeric expression>)
```

The COT() function is used to return the cotangent of <numeric expression>. The <numeric expression> argument is the angle expressed in radians whose cotangent is to be calculated. The following code provides an example of the use of the COT() function:

```
SELECT
    COT(RADIANS(90)) AS ANGLE

ANGLE
----------------------
0.64209261593433076
```

The COT() function is available in all the RDBMS implementations discussed in this book except for Oracle.

DEGREES() and RADIANS()

Syntax:

```
DEGREES(<numeric expression>)
    RADIANS(<numeric expression>)
```

The DEGREES() and RADIANS() functions complement each other. The former takes in radians and returns degrees, while the latter performs the reverse operation. Consider the following example:

```
SELECT
    RADIANS(45)   radian,
    CEIL(DEGREES (0.7853981633))  degree

RADIAN              DEGREE
------------        ----------
0                   45
```

The CEIL() function in this example rounds up the resulting degrees, which, because of the double-precision data type, would return as 44.999999994416.

The functions are supported by every RDBMS implementation, with the notable exception of Oracle.

EXP()

Syntax:

```
EXP(<numeric expression>)
```

The EXP() function returns e raised to the nth power (n is the <numeric_expression> value), where e is the base of the natural logarithm and is equal to approximately 2.71828183. The syntax and usage are identical across all RDBMS implementations discussed in this book. Consider the following example:

```
SELECT
    EXP(10) exponent
EXPONENT
--------------------
22026.465794806718
```

There are no restrictions on the use of zero, fractional, or negative values as input arguments for the EXP() function. The only difference between the RDBMS implementations would be in the calculated precision of the returned results.

LOG(), LN(), LOG2(), and LOG10()

Syntax:

```
LOG(<base>, <numeric expression>)
    LN(<numeric expression>)
    LOG2(<numeric expression>)
    LOG10(<numeric_expression>)
```

Logarithmic functions are common tools in mathematical calculations. Their implementation among different RDBMS implementations is somewhat confusing. The natural logarithm function is spelled as LN in Oracle, IBM DB2 UDB, and PostgreSQL. The same function is spelled as LOG() in Sybase, Microsoft SQL Server, and MySQL. To add to the confusion, the identically named LOG() function returns the regular (base must be specified) logarithm in the former group. Let's take it step by step.

Natural logarithm is LN() in mathematical notation. Its base is a number equal to approximately 2.71828183. Essentially, LN() returns a standard logarithm with base 2.71828183. The natural logarithm is especially useful in calculus because of its simple derivative (as opposed to the derivative of logarithms with any other base).

Keep the following in mind:

❑ The LOG() function in IBM DB2 UDB, Sybase, and Microsoft SQL Server returns a natural logarithm of the expression. MySQL overloads the LOG function. When called with only one argument it returns the natural algorithm.

❑ The LOG() function in Oracle, PostgreSQL, and MySQL accepts two arguments, and returns a standard logarithm for the base specified as the second argument.

❑ The LN() function is present in every RDBMS implementation with the exception of Sybase ASE and Microsoft SQL server. It returns the natural logarithm of the expression.

❑ The LOG10() function is decimal logarithm (a logarithm with base 10). It is equivalent to LOG(10, N). This function is present in every database discussed in this book except for Oracle and PostgreSQL.

❑ The LOG2() function is found in MySQL only. It is equivalent to LOG(2, N).

MOD()

Syntax:

```
MOD(<numeric_expression1>,<numeric_expression2>)
```

The MOD() function returns the remainder of <numeric_expression1> divided by <numeric_expression2>, as shown in the following example:

```
SELECT
    MOD(10,5) remainder1,
    MOD(10,3) remainder2

REMAINDER1     REMAINDER2
-----------    -----------
0              1
```

Of course, specifying the second parameter as zero would result in the "division by zero" error. This is true for every RDBMS implementation, with the exception of Oracle, which returns the first parameter in this case. For example, the MOD(10, 0) expression in Oracle yields 10.

The second argument can acquire fractional values in PostgreSQL and Oracle. See the vendor-specific chapters for examples. Fractional values are disallowed in IBM DB2, Microsoft SQL Server, Sybase, and MySQL, which require integer values to perform the operation.

When supplied with negative arguments, the MOD() function differs from the standard formula. This affects only Oracle and MySQL discussed in this book. The rest of the RDBMS implementations follow and calculate the result identically in both cases.

The standard formula is defined as follows

```
NUM1 - NUM2*(FLOOR(NUM1/NUM2))
```

The following table illustrates the difference in processing between the RDBMS implementations discussed in this book. (Note that there is no discrepancy between the MOD() function result and execution of the classical formula expressions in IBM, Sybase, Microsoft, and PostgreSQL implementations.)

NUM1	NUM2	MOD Function	Classic Formula in Oracle & MySQL	Classic Formula in Sybase ASE, IBM DB2 UDB, SQL Server, PostgreSQL
11	4	3	3	3
11	-4	3	-1	3
-11	4	-3	1	-3
-11	-4	-3	-3	-3

The MOD() function is implemented as a modulo operator "%" in Sybase ASE and Microsoft SQL Server. This operator is also valid for MySQL and PostgreSQL (in addition to the MOD() function syntax). Starting from version 4.1, MySQL also allows <numeric_expression1> MOD <numeric_expression2> syntax.

PI()

Syntax:

```
PI()
```

The `PI()` function returns the constant value of pi. The following code demonstrates the result of the `PI()` function:

```
SELECT
    PI() AS RESULT_OF_PI

RESULT_OF_PI
------------------------
3.1415926535897931
```

The `PI()` function is available in the SQL Server, Sybase, MySQL, and PostgreSQL platforms. Oracle and IBM DB2 do not support its use.

POWER()

Syntax:

```
POWER(<numeric_expression>,<power>)
```

The `POWER()` function returns the <numeric_expression> raised to the power of <power>. Here is an example raising 10 to the power of 2:

```
SELECT
    POWER(10,2) power_2

POWER_2
-----------
100
```

The syntax and the usage are very straightforward for all RDBMS implementations. PostgreSQL has a different name for the function — `POW()`. MySQL accepts `POW()` as a synonym for `POWER()`.

Most RDBMS implementations of this function follow all the standard mathematical rules. A number to the power of 1 equals the number itself. A number raised to the power of 0 becomes 1 (the number itself cannot be 0). Fractional power values yield the root of the corresponding values (1/2 is a square root, 1/3 is a cubic root, and so on), and a number raised to a negative power equals its reciprocal raised to the opposite positive power. Consider the following example:

```
SELECT
POWER(100, 1)  power_1,
POWER(100,0.5) square_root,
POWER(100,-2)  one_ten_thousandth

POWER_1     SQUARE_ROOT ONE_TEN_THOUSANDTH
----------  ----------- ------------------
100         10              .0001
```

This behavior is not uniform across the RDBMS implementations discussed in this book. IBM DB2 UDB, Sybase ASE, and Microsoft SQL Server would return zero for a number raised into a negative power. Oracle, MySQL, and PostgreSQL would interpret it as shown in the previous example.

RAND()

Syntax:

```
RAND(<numeric_expression>)
```

The RAND() function is used to generate some random numbers at run time. The syntax and usage are almost identical for IBM DB2 UDB, MS SQL Server, Sybase ASE, and MySQL. Neither Oracle nor PostgreSQL provide such a function with their RDBMS implementations. Consider the following example:

```
SELECT
    RAND() random_num

RANDOM_NUM
-------------------------
0.65631908425718
```

The RAND() function accepts an optional seed argument (integer) and will produce a pseudo-random float number in the range between 1 and 0 (inclusive). There are some nuances to RAND() function usage that should be noted. Called several times within a session with the same seed value, it will produce exactly the same output. To get different pseudo-random numbers, you must specify different seed values, or use different sessions.

To produce a pseudo-random number within a range outside of the 0-to-1 limit, you could multiply the output of the function by the range factor, and then TRUNCATE() or ROUND() the result. Here is an example of producing a set of pseudo-random generated values in the range of 0 to 10,000 in MS SQL Server 2000 syntax:

```
SELECT
    ROUND((RAND()* 10000),0) from_zero_to_10000

from_zero_to_10000
-------------------------
8134.0
```

ROUND()

Syntax:

```
ROUND(<numeric expression>,<precision>)
```

This function rounds a number to a specific length or precision, and works almost identically in all RDBMS implementations. The numeric expression can be any number in an allowable range, and the precision can only take integer values (both positive and negative). In the following example, a number is rounded to one decimal place:

```
SELECT
    ROUND(109.09 ,1) rounded

ROUNDED
------------
109.10
```

Since our query requested precision of 1, the number was rounded up to the nearest decimal. Note that some RDBMS implementations (Microsoft SQL Server, Sybase ASE, and IBM DB2 UDB) preserve the original number of digits even though some are zeroes. The others (Oracle, PostgreSQL, and MySQL) would drop the zero in the previous example (100.1). Some of this behavior can be changed with the database parameters settings. Refer to the respective vendor's documentation for more information.

Specifying negative precision will round numbers on the left side of the decimal point, as shown here:

```
SELECT
    ROUND(109.09 ,-1) rounded

ROUNDED
------------
110.00
```

Here, the last digit of the number on the left of the decimal point was rounded up. The digits on the right side subsequently went to zero. Again, only IBM DB2 UDB, Microsoft SQL Server, and Sybase ASE would display the zeroes to the right of the decimal point.

Microsoft SQL Server's version of the ROUND() function behaves somewhat differently than its equivalents in the other RDBMS implementations because it has a third optional argument (default 0). When this argument is omitted or explicitly set to 0, the result is rounding—exactly as seen in the previous examples. When the value is other than 0, the result will be truncated.

Oracle, PostgreSQL, and MySQL also overload the ROUND() function. They have a version of the function that accepts only a single argument. When only a single argument is supplied, the number is rounded up to the nearest integer.

SIGN()

Syntax:

```
SIGN(<numeric expression>)
```

The SIGN() function returns –1 when the input argument is negative, 1 when the argument is positive, and 0 when the argument is zero, as shown here:

```
SELECT
    SIGN(-50) minus,
    SIGN(50)  plus,
    SIGN(0)   zero,
    SIGN(NULL) null_value
```

```
MINUS        PLUS        ZERO     NULL_VALUE
---------    --------    -------  -----------
-1           1           0        NULL
```

The function returns NULL for any NULL argument passed, and this behavior is consistent across all six databases discussed in this book.

SINH()

Syntax:

```
SINH(<numeric expression>)
```

The SINH() function returns the hyperbolic sine of <numeric expression>. The <numeric expression> argument is a float value that represents the angle in radians. The following code demonstrates the use of the SINH() function on the Oracle platform:

```
SELECT SINH(.5) AS RESULT FROM DUAL;

    RESULT
----------
.521095305
```

The SINH() function is only available on the Oracle and IBM DB2 implementations.

SQUARE()

Syntax:

```
SQUARE(<numeric expression>)
```

The SQUARE() function is used to return the <numeric expression> raised to the power of 2 (in other words, <numeric expression> * <numeric expression>). The following code demonstrates the use of the SQUARE() function:

```
SELECT
    SQUARE(2) AS SQUARE_OF_2,
    SQUARE(3) AS SQUARE_OF_3,
    SQUARE(4) AS SQUARE_OF_4

SQUARE_OF_2             SQUARE_OF_3             SQUARE_OF_4
------------            -----------             -----------
4.0                     9.0                     16.0
```

The SQUARE() function is only available on the Microsoft SQL Server and Sybase implementations. Similar functionality can be achieved in the other database platforms by using either the POWER() (for Oracle, IBM DB2, and MySQL) or the POW() (for PostgreSQL) function.

SQRT()

Syntax:

```
SQRT(<numeric expression>)
```

The SQRT() function extracts the square root from the input argument. It accepts only positive arguments, and returns an error when a negative argument is passed in. Consider this example:

```
SELECT
    SQRT(100) root

ROOT
-------
10.0
```

The only difference between the RDBMS implementations will be in the precision of the returned arguments.

Raising an expression to the power of ½ would produce the same results. See the section POWER earlier in this chapter.

TAN()

Syntax:

```
TAN(<numeric expression>)
```

The TAN() function returns the tangent of the <numeric expression> argument passed to it. The <numeric expression> argument represents the angle in radians for which the tangent is to be calculated. The following code gives an example of the use of the TAN() function:

```
SELECT
    TAN(36) AS RESULT

RESULT
--------------------
7.7504709056991477
```

The TAN() function is available in all of the RDBMS implementations discussed in this book.

TANH()

Syntax:

```
TANH(<numeric expression>)
```

The TANH() function returns the hyperbolic tangent of <numeric expression>. The <numeric expression> argument is the angle expressed in radians from which the hyperbolic tangent is to be calculated. The following code gives an example of the use of the TANH() function on the Oracle platform:

```
SELECT TANH(.5) AS RESULT FROM DUAL;

    RESULT
----------
.462117157
```

The TANH() function is only available in the Oracle and IBM DB2 implementations.

TRUNC() or TRUNCATE()

Syntax:

```
TRUNC(<numeric expression>, <decimal_places>)
     TRUNCATE(<numeric_expression>,<decimal_places>))
```

The function TRUNC() returns its argument truncated to the number of decimal places specified with the second argument. The keyword TRUNC() is for Oracle and PostgreSQL. MySQL insists on TRUNCATE(), and IBM DB2 UDB accepts both TRUNC() and TRUNCATE(). Consider the following example:

```
SELECT
    TRUNC(109.29, 1) truncated

TRUNCATED
------------
109.20
```

The value 109.29 was truncated to the single digit on the left side of the decimal point. Similar to the ROUND() function, the TRUNC() function also accepts negative values for the <decimal_places> argument. The result is truncation on the left of the decimal point, as shown here:

```
SELECT
    TRUNC(109.29, -1) truncated

TRUNCATED
------------
100
```

Oracle overloads the TRUNC() function with the DATE data type argument. See Chapter 6 for the Oracle-specific information on this function.

Also, PostgreSQL and Oracle overload the function with a single input argument. When the <decimal_places> argument is not specified, the number is truncated to the nearest integer.

MS SQL Server does not have this function because it uses the ROUND() function to truncate. See the Microsoft-specific chapter (Chapter 8) and the Sybase-specific chapter (Chapter 9) for more information.

Sybase ASE simply does not have the TRUNCATE() function in its repertoire, though its functionality could be replicated with either a UDF or combination of built-in functions.

Miscellaneous Functions

Miscellaneous functions are generally the most vendor-specific. As such, there are not many of these that are common across the different RDBMS implementations. The following table lists some of the functions from this category that are found in all six databases discussed in this book.

Function	Oracle	IBM	Microsoft	Sybase	MySQL	PgSQL	Brief Description
COALESCE	Yes	VALUE	Yes	Yes	Yes	Yes	Returns first non-NULL expression in the list.
NULLIF	Yes	Yes	Yes	Yes	Yes	Yes	Compares two expressions; if they are equal, returns NULL; otherwise returns the first expression.

COALESCE()

Syntax:

```
COALESCE (<exp1>,<exp2> . . . <expN>)
```

The COALESCE() function returns the first non-null expression in the expression list. At least one expression must not be the literal NULL. If all expressions evaluate to NULL, then the function returns NULL. Consider the following example:

```
SELECT
    COALESCE (NULL, NULL, 'NOT NULL', NULL) test

TEST
------------
NOT NULL
```

The syntax in this example is valid for Oracle, Microsoft SQL Server, PostgreSQL, and MySQL. It will not work with IBM DB2 UDB, which has somewhat different ideas about how this function should be used. Please refer to the Chapter 7 for more details on IBM's implementation of the COALESCE() function.

The COALESCE() function is the most generic version of the NVL() function, and could be used instead of it. The syntax and usage are identical across all RDBMS implementations discussed in this book.

NULLIF()

Syntax:

```
NULLIF( <expression1>,<expression2>)
```

The function `NULLIF()` compares two expressions. If they are equal, it returns `NULL`. Otherwise, it returns the first expression. Here is an example:

```
SELECT
    NULLIF('ABC','ABC')  equal,
    NULLIF ('ABC','DEF') diff

EQUAL    DIFF
------   -----
NULL     ABC
```

The `NULLIF()` function is found in IBM DB2 UDB, Microsoft SQL Server, Sybase ASE, PostgreSQL, and MySQL. The syntax and usage are identical.

Summary

The chapter describes some functions for which functionality and syntax are very similar, if not identical, across all six RDBMS implementations discussed in this book. It should not be assumed, however, that using supported functions guarantees portability of an application among the different vendors. These are merely a subset of the vast number of functions available across the six RDBMS platforms discussed in this book that are based upon the ANSI standard, and the details of their implementation still vary from vendor to vendor. When porting your applications to a different platform, you must be diligent in checking the documentation of your new RDBMS implementation to ensure that the integrity of your code will remain intact.

In the next chapter, we will deal with the specific built-in functions available on the Oracle RDBMS implementation. Now you will get the chance to see the correlation between the ANSI standard and the functionality implemented by the Oracle system.

Oracle SQL Functions

In its latest incarnation (version 10g), Oracle supports more than 200 built-in functions. Some of them have been around since the beginning of time; some were added to spice up the newest release. A detailed discussion of every one of the SQL functions supplied in the Oracle RDBMS would take a book of its own. The selections discussed here represent some of the most useful functions, including several whose usage is less than obvious.

This chapter begins with a discussion of the Oracle query syntax. The discussion then focuses on aggregate functions, analytic functions, character functions, regular expressions, conversion functions, date and time functions, numeric functions, object reference functions, and miscellaneous single-row functions. Additionally, we have formatted the output columns to display the full column name in an attempt to increase the readability of the code. However, you should understand that some of your results might have truncated column headings.

Oracle Query Syntax

The base Oracle version of the SELECT statement is similar to the ANSI SQL version introduced in Chapter 5. It can be broken down into specific parts to get a better understanding of its use and meaning. The following code provides a breakdown of the basic SELECT statement on the Oracle platform:

```
SELECT  [hint]
[ DISTINCT | ALL ]
<select_list>
FROM <table_reference>
[WHERE <condition>]
[START WITH <condition> CONNECT BY <condition>]
[GROUP BY <elements> ]
[HAVING <condition> ]
[ORDER BY <elements> ]
```

Following this syntax, the first optional element that you can add to your statement is a [hint]. *Hints* are objects that tell the cost-based optimizer how to process the query. The query hint syntax is as follows:

```
/*+  <query_hint_type>(hint_object)  */
```

Oracle has three hint types that are useful when dealing with various queries: FULL, ROWID, and INDEX. The first two are related to table operations, and the latter is used when you want to specify a particular index for a query. The FULL hint is used in conjunction with a table name to tell the optimizer to perform a full table scan on the table to retrieve the information. This is useful when your table is small. It is more effective than using an index. The ROWID hint uses the row IDs to access and return rows quickly whenever the tables are large. To use this option, you must actually know which row IDs are needed, or use an index. The INDEX hint directs the optimizer to use a specific index instance when accessing the object for data. This will force the optimizer to use an index in cases, such as a small table, where it would normally choose not to. When using a specific index, you must pass both the table name and index values, as shown in the following:

```
Select  /*  index( users       users$userid)  */  Roles
From USERS
 WHERE USERNAME='BigDave';
```

The next optional section is to tell the query whether to select all the rows (using the ALL syntax) or to give you only those rows with unique values (using the DISTINCT syntax). By default, ALL is always selected, so there is no need to actually specify the value.

The next two sections deal with the select_list and the FROM clause. The select_list includes the columns that you want included in the result set of your query. These can actually be any form of a column: the column name, a variable, an equation, or a function. The column element can also be given a column alias by using the keyword AS followed by the alias. The FROM clause is used to specify where the select_list should be drawn from. It can contain any number of tables, views, or subqueries, which can also be given aliases. However, unlike the column aliases, they can be used anywhere throughout the SELECT statement and, once aliased, the alias *must* be used.

The next three sections will be dealt with together because they have the same ability — to restrict the amount of data that is drawn from the initial part of the SELECT statement. Their purpose is to act as a valve on the stream of data coming from the SELECT statement. The first one is the WHERE clause. Its basic syntax is set up by having a set of conditions connected with either AND or OR objects. These conditions can be equality conditions that would cause natural joins to be formed, or they can be restrictions on the type of data that is returned. Following is an example of the two basic types:

```
// Illustrates a basic equality condition that would create a natural join

Employees.EmpID = Managers.MngrID

// Illustrates a condition that just restricts the amount of data returned

Employees.Country =  'England'
```

CONNECT BY and START WITH are most often used in the syntax that follows, as shown here:

```
CONNECT BY [PRIOR] expression = [PRIOR] condition
START WITH expression = expression
```

The main purpose of this syntax is in developing a "family tree" or "linked list" of items from the query using a parent-child relationship. The location of the PRIOR command determines which elements in the CONNECT BY statement are treated as the root, and which ones are treated as the branches. The START WITH expression is used to determine where within the list to begin that traversal of the tree. A good example of this would be if you had an Employees table in which there were EmpID (Employee IDs) and MngrID (Manager IDs). Each employee would have one and only one manager, while every manager would also need to be an employee. So, how would you find *all* of the employees who reported to, say, "Bob," the European Operations Manager? If you knew that Bob's EmpID = 5, then you could perform the following query:

```
SELECT Employee_Name
FROM EMPLOYEES
WHERE MngrID = 5
ORDER BY Employee_Name;
```

While this query is perfectly logical and returns all the employees who have Bob as their direct manager, it is incorrect. It does not take into account those people who directly report to Bob who may also be managers, with employees underneath them. Of course, you could do a subquery for that level, but that would defeat the purpose because you may have another level beyond that. A much simpler approach would be to treat the structure as a linked list and use the CONNECT BY ...START WITH syntax as follows:

```
SELECT Employee_Name
FROM EMPLOYEES
CONNECT BY PRIOR MgrID = EmpID
START WITH EmpID = 5
ORDER BY Employee_Name;
```

This code is much more reliable because it will work anywhere within the "tree" and for any number of levels.

The GROUP BY, HAVING, and ORDER BY clauses are the last ones in the SELECT statement to analyze. The GROUP BY clause is used to return summary row information on one or more columns within the SELECT statement. To use a column from your select_list in the GROUP BY clause, it must be at least one of the following:

❑   A group function (AVG, COUNT, MAX, MIN, or SUM)

❑   The same as an expression contained in the GROUP BY clause

❑   A constant or a function that does not take parameters

These are restrictions for using columns only from within the select_list. Any column can be used in the GROUP BY clause as long as it is contained in the tables of your query. The HAVING clause is much like the WHERE clause in that it is used to restrict the data from the query. While the WHERE clause would restrict the amount of data placed in the groups of the GROUP BY clause, the HAVING clause restricts which groups are to be used. The ORDER BY clause is used to determine the order in which the data is returned. This can be determined by a column name, alias, expression, or even a column number. The order can be selected as Ascending (ASC) or Descending (DESC) and can be more than one column because the ordering is done in a hierarchal fashion starting with the first element in the ORDER BY clause. If ORDER BY is not used in the SELECT statement, then the order is arbitrary and may change from execution to execution.

You should now have a good understanding of the basics of the Oracle platform. This will give you a basis on which to get a better understanding of the use of the different functions, enabling you to decipher the examples given throughout this chapter.

Aggregate Functions

An aggregate SQL function summarizes the results of an expression for the group of rows (selected from a table, view, or table-valuated function) and returns a single value for that group. The generic syntax of every aggregate function in Oracle is as follows:

```
<aggregate_function_name> ([DISTINCT | ALL] <expression>)
```

The modifiers DISTINCT and ALL affect the behavior of the function. The DISTINCT instructs the function to consider only distinct values for the argument, ignoring the duplicates. The ALL modifier tells the function to include all values. When no modifier is supplied, the ALL is assumed.

The full list of the aggregate functions supported by Oracle is given in Appendix A. The select group discussed in this chapter is shown in following table.

SQL Function	Input Arguments	Return Arguments	Notes
AVG	Numeric Expression	Single numeric value	Calculates the average of the set of numbers; NULL values are ignored.
CORR	Numeric Set Expression 1, Numeric Set Expression 2	Single numeric value	Oracle applies the function to the set of (expr1, expr2) after eliminating the pairs for which either expr1 or expr2 is NULL. The function would return NULL if applied to an empty set.
COUNT	Numeric Expression	Single numeric value	Returns the number of records.
GROUPING	Aggregate Set	Single numeric value	This function allows for identifying the aggregate rows from the aggregated sets (so-called superaggregates, or group of groups), which have value of NULL.
MAX	Numeric Expression	Single numeric value	This function returns a single maximum value in a given set.

SQL Function	Input Arguments	Return Arguments	Notes
MIN	Numeric Expression	Single numeric value	Returns a single minimum value in a given set.
STDDEV		Single numeric value	The statistical STDDEV function returns standard deviation value for the set of numerical values.
SUM	Numeric expression	Single numeric value	Returns the sum of the values in a set.

The aggregate functions usually use the GROUP BY clause. If this clause is omitted, the function will be applied to all rows in the view/table/table-valuated function. All examples in this section will be based on the table CARS, which contains make, model, and price information for cars, as shown here (and originally presented in Chapter 5):

```
CREATE TABLE cars
(
  MAKER   VARCHAR2 (25),
  MODEL   VARCHAR2 (25),
  PRICE   NUMBER
)

INSERT INTO CARS VALUES('CHRYSLER','CROSSFIRE',33620);
INSERT INTO CARS VALUES('CHRYSLER','300M',29185);
INSERT INTO CARS VALUES('HONDA','CIVIC',15610);
INSERT INTO CARS VALUES('HONDA','ACCORD',19300);
INSERT INTO CARS VALUES('FORD','MUSTANG',15610);
INSERT INTO CARS VALUES('FORD','LATESTnGREATEST',NULL);
INSERT INTO CARS VALUES('FORD','FOCUS',13005);
```

AVG()

Syntax:

```
AVG([DISTINCT]|[ALL] <numeric expression>)
```

The function AVG() calculates the arithmetic average of the series of numbers of its argument. For example, the following queries could be used to gather some statistical information about the cars in the CARS table:

```
SELECT
   AVG(price) average_price
FROM cars;

average_price
--------------------
21055
```

This summed all the prices and divided them by the number of entries. Now, to find the average of the uniquely priced cars, we use the DISTINCT modifier:

```
SELECT
    AVG(DISTINCT price) average_price
FROM cars;

average_price
--------------------
22144
```

To find out the average price for each manufacturer, we would use the GROUP BY clause:

```
SELECT
    maker,
    AVG(price) average_price
FROM cars
GROUP BY maker;

Maker                   average_price
----------------        -------------
CHRYSLER                31402.5
FORD                    14307.5
HONDA                   17455
```

While usefulness of the obtained information is questionable, we know that the average (?) car costs about $21,000, and Ford produces the least-expensive cars on average.

The AVG() function could also be used as an analytic function (see the section "Analytic Functions" later in this chapter).

This function is supported across all the RDBMS implementations covered in this book, though some differences do exist. For example, the use of the DISTINCT clause is supported by Microsoft SQL Server, Sybase ASE, IBM DB2 UDB, and PostgreSQL, but it cannot be used with MySQL.

CORR()

Syntax:

```
CORR(<numeric expression1>,<numeric_expression2>)
```

The CORR() function returns the coefficient of correlation for a pair of numbers. Both arguments must be group-set. The function belongs to the realm of statistical analysis functions. First, the function is applied to the set of the two argument expressions (pairs where if either argument is NULL, it is eliminated), and the results are manipulated through the following formula:

```
COVAR_POP(expr_1, expr_2) / (STDDEV_POP(expr_1) * STDDEV_POP(expr_2))
```

The function could be used, for example, to find whether there is any correlation in entry-level car prices manufactured by Honda and Ford, or how closely correlated the list price and actual selling price are for the different models of the cars. To run these examples, you would need a much more elaborate setup than allowed by this book.

Coefficient of correlation is a statistical representation of how closely the two numbers correlate with each other. The range is from –1 (negative correlation), through 0 (no correlation), to +1 (perfect positive correlation).

The CORR() function also could be used as an analytical function (see the section "Analytic Functions" later in this chapter).

With the exception of IBM DB2 UDB, there is no correspondence for this function in any of the other databases covered in the book (though its functionality sometimes can be emulated through using combination of other functions. The algorithm calculating it is fairly straightforward, though, and it could be implemented in virtually any procedural language.

MySQL provides VARIANCE() and STDEV() functions (since version 4.1). PostgreSQL has support for STDDEV() in version 7.1 or later, and Microsoft added STDEV()/STDEVP() and VAR()/VARP() statistical functions in version 7.0, but Sybase leaves you on your own, though it has added some of these functions to Adaptive Server Anywhere (ASA).

COUNT()

Syntax:

```
COUNT([DISTINCT]|[ALL] <expression>)
```

This function would answer the question, "How many cars do we have on the lot?" Consider the following example:

```
SELECT
    COUNT(*) cars_count
FROM cars

CARS_COUNT
---------------------
7
```

Using GROUP BY would tell us how many cars of each vendor we have on the lot:

```
SELECT
    Maker,
    COUNT(price)cars_count
FROM cars
GROUP BY maker;

MAKER               CARS_COUNT
----------------    -------------
CHRYSLER            2
FORD                2
HONDA               2
```

The COUNT(*) function reports that the CARS_COUNT value equals 7, while COUNT(price) insists that we have only 6 cars, which makes sense — price-wise, we know about only six cars, though on the lot we see seven. Looking back at the original CARS table, we see that one Ford model had a price of NULL.

```
SELECT
    Maker,
    COUNT(*)        total_count,
    COUNT(price)  car_prices
FROM cars
GROUP BY maker;

MAKER                   TOTAL_COUNT       CAR_PRICES
----------------        -------------     ------------
CHRYSLER                2                 2
FORD                    3                 2
HONDA                   2                 2
```

This behavior pertains to the COUNT() and GROUPING() functions; the rest of the aggregate functions ignore NULLs.

Oracle's COUNT() function can also be used as an analytical function (see the "Analytic Functions" section later in this chapter).

You should also be aware of GROUP BY clause behavior when it encounters NULL. All NULLs will be grouped into a group of their own and placed at the bottom of the returned result set. The order is determined by the fact that ORDER BY (ascending) is implicitly performed whenever GROUP BY is executed and a NULL value will always be at the end of the ascending sort order. This behavior is fairly consistent across all databases covered in this book, and is mandated by the SQL standard.

The function COUNT() is part of every RDBMS implementation in its current version, though this might not be true for the previous versions.

GROUPING()

Syntax:

```
GROUPING(<expression>)
```

This function allows for identifying the aggregate rows from the aggregated sets (so-called *superaggregates*, or groups of groups), which have the value of NULL. It is used with the GROUP BY extensions, such as ROLLUP() or CUBE(). A value of 1 would indicate a super aggregate row, while a value of 0 would indicate a "regular" aggregate row, not added by the ROLLUP() and CUBE(). The function and the keywords it supports are part of the On-line Analytical Programming (OLAP) group of functions, and as such are beyond the scope of the book.

This function is found in Oracle, Microsoft SQL server, and IBM DB2 UDB. Sybase ASE does not have this function (though it is present in Sybase ASA). Neither MySQL nor PostgreSQL provide an equivalent of the function in their current versions (5.0 and 7.4, respectively).

MAX() and MIN()

Syntax:

```
MAX([DISTINCT]|[ALL] <expression>)
MIN([DISTINCT]|[ALL] <expression>)
```

The names of these functions are self-describing. They allow you to display maximum and minimum values in a set. To find the highest and lowest prices of cars on the lot, the following query could be used:

```
SELECT
    MAX(price) max_price,
    MIN(price) min_price
FROM cars;

max_price           min_price
----------------    -------------
33620               13005
```

To find the price range for the cars on the lot in relation to the manufacturer, the GROUP BY clause must be used:

```
SELECT
    Maker,
    MAX(price) max_price,
    MIN(price) min_price
FROM cars
GROUP BY maker;

Maker         max_price      min_price
------------  -----------    -----------
CHRYSLER      33620          29185
FORD          15610          13005
HONDA         19300          15610
```

The MIN() and MAX() functions behave identically to the AVG() function in the handling of NULL values.

STDDEV()

Syntax:

```
STDEV(<numeric_expression>)
```

The statistical STDDEV() function returns a standard deviation value for the set. A *standard deviation* is a statistical value that tells you just how tightly the values follow the *mean value* calculated from the set (defined as sum of all the values divided by the number of the values). For example, the STDDEV() statistics applied to the car prices on the lot would be as follows:

```
SELECT
    maker,
    STDDEV(price)  deviation,
    AVG(price)     mean
FROM cars
GROUP BY maker;

Maker          deviation    mean
------------   ----------   ------------
CHRYSLER       3136.01857   31402.5
FORD           1842.01316   14307.5
HOND           2609.22402   17455
```

This function is found in every RDBMS implementations discussed in this book, with the notable exception of Sybase ASE. (It is provided with Sybase ASA.)

SUM()

Syntax:

```
SUM([DISTINCT]|[ALL] <numeric_expression>)
```

The SUM() function does just what the name implies — sum the values. For example, to find the total price for all the cars on the lot, we would issue the following query:

```
SELECT
    SUM(price) total
FROM cars;

TOTAL
---------------
126330
```

The GROUP BY function would produce yet another angle on the data: inventory totals distributed across different vendors:

```
SELECT
    Maker,
    SUM(price) total
FROM cars
GROUP BY maker;

Maker              total
----------------   ------------
CHRYSLER           62805
FORD               28615
HONDA              34910
```

This function is found in all RDBMS implementations discussed in this book.

Analytic Functions

Analytic functions are unique to Oracle and differ from their aggregate counterparts in returning multiple rows for each group (aggregate functions always return one row). They are a precursor to and a part of the larger domain of OLAP. Oracle lists 30 analytic functions altogether, though some of them are over-loaded versions of aggregate functions (AVG, CORR, COUNT, MAX, MIN, and SUM, to name a few). A discussion of these functions is beyond the scope of this book (in fact, they deserve a book, or a chapter at the very least, of their own), because the analytic clause for these functions could easily become unwieldy.

The idea behind analytic functions is to define a special window — a group of rows from which calculations for any given current row are conducted. Window sizes can be based on either a physical number of rows, or a logical interval such as time. The analytic functions find their usage in a data warehousing practice in conjunction with OLAP operations. One example could be calculating the *moving averages* (that is, averages of the values over certain period of time).

They are the last set of operations performed in a query except for the final ORDER BY clause. All joins and all WHERE, GROUP BY, and HAVING clauses are completed before the analytic functions are processed. Therefore, analytic functions can appear only in the select_list or ORDER BY clause.

These functions are usually a part of the OLAP extensions in mature RDBMS implementations such as IBM DB2 UDB or Microsoft SQL Server. They are not found in MySQL or PostgreSQL.

Character Functions

As the name implies, the character functions help with character data manipulations. Oracle's character data types include (N) VARCHAR, (N) CHAR, and CLOB.

SQL Function	Input Arguments	Return Arguments	Notes
CHR	Numeric expression for a given character set (for example, ASCII code).	VARCHAR2	Returns the character corresponding to the ASCII code number passed in as the argument. The CHR function with the USING NCHAR_CS is equivalent to the NCHAR function.
INITCAP	Character data types; CLOB data type will be implicitly converted to VARCHAR2, if possible.	VARCHAR2	Returns the character string passed into it with the first letter of each word capitalized.

Table continued on following page

SQL Function	Input Arguments	Return Arguments	Notes
LPAD	Character data types; other data types will be implicitly converted into VARCHAR2, if possible.	VARCHAR2	Returns input argument padded with blank spaces or characters from the left.
LTRIM	Character data types; other data types will be implicitly converted into VARCHAR2, if possible.	VARCHAR2	Returns the input argument with trimmed off characters and blank spaces from the left side.
RTRIM	Character data types; other data types will be implicitly converted into VARCHAR2, if possible.	VARCHAR2	Returns the input argument with trimmed off characters and blank spaces from the right side.
RPAD	Character data types; other data types will be implicitly converted into VARCHAR2, if possible.	VARCHAR2	Returns input argument padded with blank spaces or characters from the left.
REPLACE	Character data types; other data types will be implicitly converted into VARCHAR2, if possible.	VARCHAR2	Replaces every occurrence of the string specified as the search_string in the input string with the replacement_string; if the replacement_string is omitted, the found matches for the search_string are removed from the resulting character string.
SOUNDEX	Character data types; other data types will be implicitly converted into VARCHAR2, if possible.	VARCHAR2	Returns a character string containing the phonetic representation of character.

SQL Function	Input Arguments	Return Arguments	Notes
SUBSTR	Character data types; other data types will be implicitly converted into VARCHAR2, if possible.	VARCHAR2	Returns a portion of string, beginning at numeric_position up to a specified substring_length characters long; if the last argument (substring_ length is omitted, then the length will be until the end of the string_ expression). If numeric position is positive (> 0) then the characters are searched and counted from the beginning. If it is negative (< 0), the search starts from the end and continues toward the end of the string; 0 is treated as positive 1.
TRIM	Character data types; other data types will be implicitly converted into VARCHAR2, if possible.	VARCHAR2	Returns the input argument with trimmed off leading, trailing, or both characters and blank spaces.
TRANSLATE	Character data types; other data types will be implicitly converted into VARCHAR2, if possible.	VARCHAR2	Returns input argument string where all occurrences of the from_ template are replaced with corresponding characters in the to_template.

CHR() and NCHR()

Syntax:

```
CHR(<numeric_code> [USING NCHAR_CS])
NCHR(<numeric_code>)
```

The CHR() function returns a character corresponding to the number passed in as the argument. The returned character (a VARCHAR2 data type) could be either in the database character set, or national character set. The function has an optional clause USING NCHAR_CS. Specifying this clause would result in the multibyte (data type NVARCHAR2) national character set being returned by the function.

The code 65 corresponds to an uppercase "A" in the standard ASCII code set. The following example returns both characters, because the database character set and the national character set are identical on the test machine. Results could differ if national character sets are installed.

```
SELECT
   CHR(65)    "DB_CS",
   CHR(65 USING NCHAR_CS)    "N_CS"
FROM dual;


DB_CS      N_CS
------     ------
A          A
```

For single-byte character sets (such as ASCII), when the argument exceeds 256 (the maximum value for the ASCII character set), the binary equivalent of (<argument> MOD 256) is returned. For multibyte character sets, the argument must correspond to the single valid code defined for the national character.

The NCHR() function is essentially equivalent to the function CHR() with the USING NCHAR_CS clause.

These functions correspond to the other RDBMS functions CHAR() (Microsoft, Sybase, and MySQL) and CHR() (IBM and PostgreSQL).

INITCAP()

Syntax:

```
INITCAP(<character_string>)
```

This function returns the character string passed into it with the first letter of each word capitalized, as shown here:

```
SELECT
    INITCAP('hello world') "HELLO"
FROM dual;

HELLO
------------
Hello World
```

The word identifiers (separators) are blank spaces and nonprintable characters. The argument could be of CHAR, VARCHAR2, NCHAR, and NVARCHAR2 data types. The CLOB data type is implicitly converted when passed as an argument to the function; as such, it is subject to the data-type restrictions (that is, VARCHAR2 could only accommodate 4,000 bytes).

There are no equivalents of this function in any other RDBMS implementation discussed in this book, with the exception of PostgreSQL.

LPAD() and RPAD()

Syntax:

```
LPAD(<character string>, <length_of_resulting_string> [,<padding_string>])
RPAD(<character string>, <length_of_resulting_string>  [,<padding_string>])
```

These functions are used to pad the input parameter of character data types with blanks (or another character) from the left or right, respectively. They both accept three input parameters, the first of which is the one to be padded, the second the total length of the resulting string, and the last one the optional string of characters to pad with. (If omitted, the first input parameter will be padded with blank spaces.) Here is an example:

```
SELECT
    LPAD('ABC',6,'***') result
FROM dual;

RESULT
-------
***ABC
```

If the character to be padded is longer than the requested total length, it will be trimmed to the exact total. Similarly, the padding characters will be trimmed if the resulting string would be longer than the specified length, as shown here:

```
SELECT
    LPAD('ABC',6,'***') result1,
    LPAD('ABC',4,'***') result2,
    LPAD('ABC',2,'***') result3
FROM dual;

RESULT1  RESULT2 RESULT3
-------  ------- -------
***ABC   **ABC   AB
```

The RPAD() function's behavior is identical to that of LPAD(), the only difference being the padding side. The previous example for the RPAD() function would be as follows:

```
SELECT
    RPAD('ABC',6,'***') result1,
    RPAD('ABC',4,'***') result2,
    RPAD('ABC',2,'***') result3
FROM dual;

RESULT1    RESULT2    RESULT3
-------    -------    -------
ABC***     ABC*       AB
```

The returned string is in the same character set as the input argument. The length of the returned string usually corresponds to the number of characters in the string. However, for some multibyte character sets, this might not be true.

Identical functions are found in MySQL and PostgreSQL. There are no direct equivalents of these functions in the other RDBMS, though the functionality could be simulated through employing analogue functions such as SPACE (IBM and Microsoft, Sybase), REPEAT (IBM), REPLICATE (Microsoft and Sybase), and STUFF (Microsoft and Sybase).

TRIM(), LTRIM(), and RTRIM()

Syntax:

```
TRIM([trim_char]|[[LEADING | TRAILING|BOTH trim_char]] [FROM] <trim_string>)
LTRIM(<trim character string> [,<trim char>])
RTRIM(<trim character string> [,<trim char>])
```

These functions do the exact opposite of the LPAD() and RPAD() functions. They trim off characters and blank spaces. Both LTRIM() and RTRIM() are the specialized versions of the TRIM() function. Consider the following example:

```
TRIM([trim_char]|[[LEADING | TRAILING|BOTH trim_char]] [FROM] <trim_string>)
```

The function allows you to trim leading or trailing characters or both from the character <trim_string>. Specifying the LEADING, TRAILING, or BOTH modifiers instructs Oracle to remove all matching characters in the respective directions. Omitting these modifiers defaults to BOTH. The function would look for all occurrences of the specified trim characters. If none were specified, the default will be blank spaces.

The following example demonstrates the different scenarios for the function:

```
SELECT
    TRIM('A' FROM 'ABCA')        both,
    TRIM(LEADING  'A' FROM 'ABCA')     lead,
    TRIM(TRAILING 'A' FROM 'ABCA')     trail,
    TRIM(' ABC ')        blank
FROM dual;

BOTH     LEAD     TRAIL   BLANK
-------  -------  ------  -----
BC       BCA      ABC     ABC
```

The LTRIM() and RTRIM() functions' respective functionality is identical to that of the TRIM() function with corresponding modifiers; they involve less code because there is no need to specify LEADING (for LTRIM()), or TRAILING (for RTRIM()) modifiers.

Specifying NULL as either trim or trimmed character string would result in NULL output from the TRIM() function.

Both trim character string and trimmed character string can be any of the data types: CHAR, VARCHAR2, NCHAR, NVARCHAR2, CLOB, or NCLOB. The string returned is of VARCHAR2 data type and is in the same character set as trimmed character string.

REPLACE()

Syntax:

```
REPLACE(<string_expression>, <search_string> [, <replacement_string>])
```

The REPLACE() function replaces every occurrence of the string specified as the search_string with the replacement_string. If the replacement_string is omitted, the found matches for the search_string are removed from the resulting character string.

The following example replaces each uppercase "A" in a string with an asterisk ("*") in the first field. The second field, where the third argument is omitted, returns a string with all occurrences of "A" removed. The third field demonstrates a situation where the search string is NULL; the intact string expression is returned.

```
SELECT
    REPLACE ('ABCDA', 'A','*')  replace_A,
    REPLACE ('ABCDA', 'A')      remove_A,
    REPLACE ('ABCDA',NULL)      null_search
FROM dual;

REPLACE_A   REMOVE_A    NULL_SEARCH
---------   --------    -----------
*BCD*       BCD         ABCDA
```

All arguments of the REPLACE() function can be any of the following data types: CHAR, VARCHAR2, NCHAR, NVARCHAR2, CLOB, or NCLOB. The returned string is of VARCHAR2 data type, and is in the same character set as replacement_string.

It is possible to achieve the same functionality using the TRANSLATE function, though it is limited to replacing only single characters. See the section "TRANSLATE()" later in this chapter.

This function exists in IBM DB2 UDB, Microsoft SQL Server 2000 (also see its STUFF() function), MySQL, and PostgreSQL. Sybase ASE 12.5 has a built-in function, STUFF(), which could be used to emulate this functionality to a certain extent, as well as STR_REPLACE(), which is equivalent.

SOUNDEX()

Syntax:

```
SOUNDEX(<character_string>)
```

This is a rather advanced SQL standard function, implemented in every RDBMS with the exception of PostgreSQL. It returns a character string containing the phonetic representation of a character and lets you compare words that are spelled differently, but sound alike in English, based on the four-character code.

For example, the SOUNDEX codes for the two following expressions are identical because they sound similar in English:

```
SELECT
    SOUNDEX('OLD TIME')  ENGLISH,
    SOUNDEX('OLDE TYME') OLD_ENGLISH
FROM dual;

ENGLISH    OLD_ENGLISH
-------    -----------
O433       O433
```

Identical values mean that a search for "OLD TIME" would be equivalent to one for "OLDE TYME," if SOUNDEX is employed as the search criterion in a SQL query. The argument could be CHAR, VARCHAR2 (and national equivalents); CLOB data type is supported through implicit conversion into VARCHAR2.

> *The rules for assigning the SOUNDEX codes are defined in* The Art of Computer Programming, Volume 3: Sorting and Searching, *by Donald E. Knuth (Boston: Addison-Wesley, 1998).*

While existing implementations deal only with English sound-alikes, there are versions of the custom implementations for other languages.

SUBSTR()

Syntax:

```
SUBSTR(<string_expression>, <numeric_position> [,<substring_length>])
```

The SUBSTR() function returns a portion of string, beginning at numeric_position up to a specified substring_length characters long. If the last argument, substring_length, is omitted, then the length will be until the end of the *string_expression*. If a numeric position is positive (> 0), then the characters are searched and counted from the beginning. If it is negative (< 0), the search starts from the end and continues toward the end of the string (0 is treated as positive 1).

SUBSTR() calculates lengths using characters as defined by the input character set. The following example extracts first and second words from the expression "HELLO, WORLD":

```
SELECT
    SUBSTR('HELLO, WORLD', 1,5) first_word,
    SUBSTR('HELLO, WORLD', 8)   last_word,
    SUBSTR('HELLO, WORLD',-5)   back
FROM dual;
FIRST_WORD    LAST_WORD   BACK
----------    ---------   -----
HELLO         WORLD       WORLD
```

The blank spaces inside the expression will be considered as characters and counted toward the total length.

The SUBSTR() function comes in four additional flavors: SUBSTRB(), SUBSTRC(), SUBSTR2(), and SUBSTR4(). Their functionality is equivalent to that of the SUBSTR(), with some distinctions. SUBSTRB() is similar in functionality to the SUBSTR() function, with the exception of using bytes instead of characters for the string's length; SUBSTRC() uses Unicode complete characters for this purpose; and SUNSTR2() and SUBSTR4() use UCS2 and UCS4 Unicode representation, respectively.

Oracle's SUBSTR() function has its direct equivalents in IBM DB2, Microsoft SQL Server 2000, Sybase ASE 12.5, MySQL, and PostgreSQL, though actual implementation might differ.

TRANSLATE()

Syntax:

```
TRANSLATE(<string_expression>, <from_template>, <to_template>)
```

The TRANSLATE() function returns a string where all occurrences of the from_template are replaced with corresponding characters in the to_template. For example, to translate the output of a Visa credit card number, the following query could be used:

```
SELECT
     TRANSLATE ('4428-2174-5093-1501'
               ,'0123456789-'
               ,'XXXXXXXXXX*') hide_num
FROM dual;

HIDE_NUM
-------------------
XXXX*XXXX*XXXX*XXXX
```

Every single number in this example was replaced with "X," and the dash character ("-") was replaced with an asterisk. If the string_expression character is not in the from_template, it will not be replaced.

The from_template argument can contain more characters than to_template. The characters at the end of the from_template that have no corresponding values in the to_template will be removed from the return string. The following example shortens the to_template by one character:

```
SELECT
     TRANSLATE('4428-2174-5093-1501'
              ,'0123456789-'
              ,'XXXXXXXXXX*')  hide_num
FROM dual;

HIDE_NUM
-------------------
XXXX*XXXX*XXXX*XXXX
```

As you can see, all dashes ("-") were dropped from the translated string, and the digit "9" was translated into an asterisk. This could be useful in getting rid of the characters in a string. Consider the following example:

```
SELECT
     TRANSLATE('4428-2174-5093-1501'
              ,'0123456789-'
              ,'0123456789') numbers_only
FROM dual;

NUMBERS_ONLY
----------------
4428217450931501
```

The blank spaces can be removed using the TRANSLATE() function just as any other character (a dash "-", in the preceding example). At the same time, the empty string cannot be used to remove characters listed in the from_template from the <string_expression>. Oracle treats an empty string as NULL, and if any of the arguments of the TRANSLATE function are NULL, the return result will always be NULL.

This function is also found in IBM DB2 UDB and PostgreSQL. There are no direct equivalents in Microsoft SQL Server, Sybase, and MySQL.

Regular Expressions

Regular expressions, a longtime staple of the general programming languages, were introduced into Oracle's SQL in version 10g. The main uses of the regular expressions are search, data validation, and string parsing.

Regular expressions are the most recent addition to Oracle, and have been a long-standing feature of MySQL and PostgreSQL databases. Neither Microsoft SQL Server 2000, Sybase ASE, nor IBM DB2 UDB have built-in functions (though UDF versions could be created quite easily).

Conversion Functions

Most conversion functions could be traced to SQL's standard CAST() function, introduced in the SQL2 specification. In many cases the CAST() function was introduced retroactively, leaving questions as to why there are CONVERT(), TO_CHAR(), TO_DATE() functions, which are virtually identical to the standard CAST() in functionality.

The following table shows Oracle conversion functions:

SQL Function	Input Arguments	Return Arguments	Notes
CAST	Data type	Data type	Converts between compatible data types.
COMPOSE	Character data	VARCHAR2	Returns a Unicode representation of the input argument.
CONVERT	Character data	VARCHAR2	Converts between two different character sets.
DECOMPOSE	Character data	VARCHAR2	Composed characters will be disassembled into separate units.
TO_CHAR	Character data types Date/time data types Numeric data types	VARCHAR2	Converts the expression into character data.

SQL Function	Input Arguments	Return Arguments	Notes
TRANSLATE ... USING	Character set data	Character set data	Used to translate a text between different character sets.
UNISTR	Character expression	National character set	Accepts string argument and returns its representation in a national character set.

CAST()

Syntax:

```
CAST(<expression> | [(subquery)] | [MULTISET (subquery)] AS type_name)
```

This is the SQL Standard function, introduced in Oracle version 9i. It allows you to convert one built-in data type (cast) into another; it also could be used for casting compatible collection types from one into one another. The compatibility of the built-in types for the CAST() function is shown in the following table.

	VARCHAR2 CHAR	NCHAR/ NVCHAR2	NUMBER	DATETIME/ INTERVAL	RAW	ROWID/ UROWID
VARCHAR2 CHAR	Yes	No	Yes	Yes	Yes	Yes
NUMBER	Yes	No	Yes	No	No	No
DATE / TIMESTAMP INTERVAL	Yes	No	No	Yes	No	No
RAW	Yes	No	No	No	Yes	No
ROWID / UROWID	Yes	No	No	No	No	Yes
NCHAR / NVARCHAR2	No	Yes	Yes	Yes	Yes	Yes

In many cases, Oracle performs implicit conversions. For example, if a query includes concatenation of a character and a number, the whole result will be implicitly converted into VARCHAR2. The need for explicit casting arises whenever Oracle cannot manage unambiguous explicit conversion. For example, if a date is represented as a VARCHAR2 string, you cannot use it to increment the date by, say, three days. The result will produce an error: ORA-01722: invalid number. To accomplish the task, the VARCHAR2 date string must be converted into a date first:

```
SELECT
    CAST('05-JUN-2004' AS DATE) + 3  threedaysahead
FROM dual;

THREEDAYSAHEAD
---------------
08-JUN-2004
```

When converting numeric data types, a loss of precision might occur. For example, converting the number 1.0123 into an INTEGER would result in 1, and there would be no warning. Beginning from version 8i, Oracle recommends using its generic NUMBER data type, which accommodates all compatible numeric types. Nevertheless, it will not prevent the lost of precision when specific numeric types are used for a column definition or variable declaration.

You can cast an unnamed operand (such as a date or the result set of a subquery) or a named collection (such as a VARRAY or a nested table) into a type-compatible data type or named collection.

The CAST() function is found in IBM DB2 UDB, Microsoft SQL Server, PostgreSQL, and MySQL. Sybase has only the CONVERT() function.

COMPOSE()

Syntax:

```
COMPOSE(<character_expression>)
```

The COMPOSE() function returns a Unicode representation of the input argument, no matter what compatible data type the input argument was. The allowable data types are CHAR, VARCHAR2, NCHAR, NVARCHAR2, CLOB, or NCLOB. For example, \00C4' UNICODE stands for the character "Ä" (uppercase "A umlaut" in German). The same character could be obtained by composing the umlaut character ("\0308") and a regular ASCII character "A" (in both cases, you would use UNISTR() function to correctly translate hexadecimal code into a Unicode character):

```
SELECT
    UNISTR ('\00C4')   a_umlaut,
    COMPOSE('A' || UNISTR('\0308')   composed,
    'A' || UNISTR('0308'))    concatenated
FROM dual;

A_UMLAUT  COMPOSED    CONCATENATED
--------  ----------  -----------------
Ä         Ä           A0308
```

There is no direct correspondence to this function among other RDBMS implementations discussed in this book.

CONVERT()

Syntax:

```
CONVERT(<character_expression>, <target_charset> [,<source_charset>])
```

Oracle's CONVERT() function converts between two different character sets. The returned value's data type is VARCHAR2. The input character could be of any of the following data types: CHAR, VARCHAR2, NCHAR, NVARCHAR2, CLOB, or NCLOB. If the source character set is not specified, the default database character set is assumed. For example, to convert a German character "A-umlaut" into an English "A," the following statement could be used:

```
SELECT
    CONVERT ('Ä', 'US7ASCII') ascii_a
FROM dual;

ASCII_A
--------
A
```

Both the destination and source character set arguments must be one of the predefined character sets, with either supplied as literals from a lookup of table columns. Some of the most commonly used formats are listed in the following table:

Character Set	Description
US7ASCII	U.S. 7-bit ASCII character set
WE8DEC	West European 8-bit character set
WE8HP	Hewlett-Packard West European LaserJet 8-bit character set
F7DEC	DEC French 7-bit character set
WE8EBCDIC500	IBM West European EBCDIC Code Page 500
WE8PC850	IBM PC Code Page 850
WE8ISO8859P1	ISO 8859-1 West European 8-bit character set

If some of the characters to be translated are not present in the target character set, they will be substituted with replacement characters. The replacement characters could be defined as a part of the character set definition: The default is a question mark ("?"). For example, the character "Ø" is found in many Scandinavian languages, but has no correspondence in the English alphabet:

```
SELECT
    CONVERT ('Ä'||'Ø', 'US7ASCII') ASCII_A
FROM dual;

ASCII_A
--------
A?
```

The CONVERT() function has its equivalents in every RDBMS. Microsoft SQL Server uses its CAST/CONVER functions, Sybase ASE uses CONVERT() function, IBM DB2 UDB deploys a variety of modifiers with its data conversion functions, PostgreSQL specifically provides over 100 specialized character set conversion functions, and MySQL supports both the CONVERT...USING function and a CHARACTER SET option in its CAST() function.

DECOMPOSE()

Syntax:

```
DECOMPOSE(<character_expression> [,[CANONICAL]|[COMPATIBILITY]] )
```

The DECOMPOSE() function is used for Unicode characters only. It is an exact opposite of the COMPOSE() function because the composed characters will be disassembled into separate units.

The two optional parameters are CANONICAL and COMPATIBILTY. The first is a default parameter. It ensures that the decomposed result could be composed again into the same character using the COMPOSE() function. The second, COMPATIBILITY mode, is useful, for example, when decomposing half-width and full-width katakana characters, where recomposition might not be desirable without external formatting or style information. To decompose the previous examples, the following query could be used:

```
SELECT
    COMPOSE('A' || UNISTR('\0308')    composed,
    DECOMPOSE('Ä')    decomposed
FROM dual;

COMPOSED    DECOMPOSED
--------    -----------
   Ä           Ä
```

Just as with its COMPOSE() counterpart, there are no direct equivalents of the DECOMPOSE () function in the RDBMS implementations discussed in this book.

TO_CHAR()

Syntax:

```
TO_CHAR(<expression> [,[FORMAT] [,NLS_PARAM]] )
```

The TO_CHAR() function converts the expression into character data.

The function is overloaded; it accepts NCHAR, NVARCHAR2, CLOB, or NCLOB and converts them into the database character set. It converts DATE, TIMESTAMP, TIMESTAMP WITH TIMEZONE, or TIMESTAMP WITH LOCAL TIME ZONE data types into VARCHAR2 according to the format specified in the FORMAT parameter, and it converts NUMBER data type into a VARCHAR2 using the optional FORMAR parameter.

The optional NLS_PARAM argument pertains to the latter two versions of the TO_CHAR() function. In the case of the DATE-accepting version, the NLS_PARAM specifies the language in which month and day names and abbreviations are returned. In the case of NUMBER version, the NLS_PARAM designates characters that are returned by number format (decimal character, group separator, local currency symbol, and international currency symbol).

There is nothing that could be demonstrated using literals as input arguments for the TO_CHAR() function because the results would appear identical for CHAR and NCHAR varieties. Internal representation does change, though. Consider the following example, where the function LENGTHB() returns the number of bytes in the character Ø (Unicode codepoint 216):

```
SELECT
   LENGTHB(NCHR(216))  national,
   LENGTHB(TO_CHAR(NCHR(216))) converted
FROM dual;
NATIONAL  CONVERTED
--------  ---------
2         1
```

As you can see, the "raw" character Ø consists of 2 bytes, while its converted TO_CHAR() version has only 1.

The following table details the format parameter options available on the Oracle platform and examples of their implementations:

Format Element	Description	Example
AD	AD indicator	TO_CHAR (SYSDATE,'YYYY AD')
AM	Meridian indicator (am/pm)	TO_CHAR (SYSDATE,'HH:MI:SS AM')
BC	BC indicator (Before Common era/Before Christ)	TO_CHAR (SYSDATE,'YYYY BC')
D	Day of the week (from 1 to 7)	TO_CHAR (SYSDATE,'D')
DAY	Name of the day, padded with blank spaces to the total length of nine characters	TO_CHAR (SYSDATE,'DAY')
DD	Day of the month (from 1 to 31)	TO_CHAR (SYSDATE,'DD')
DDD	Day of the year (from 1 to 366)	TO_CHAR (SYSDATE,'DDD')
DY	Abbreviated name of the day	TO_CHAR (SYSDATE,'DY')
HH	Hour of the day (from 1 to 12)	TO_CHAR (SYSDATE,'HH')
HH12	Hour of the day (from 1 to 12)	TO_CHAR (SYSDATE,'HH12')
HH24	Hour of the day (from 0 to 23)	TO_CHAR (SYSDATE,'HH24')
MI	Minute (from 0 to 59)	TO_CHAR (SYSDATE,'MI')
MM	Month (from 01 to 12)	TO_CHAR (SYSDATE,'MM')
MON	Abbreviated name of the month	TO_CHAR (SYSDATE,'MON')
MONTH	Name of the month, padded with blankspaces to the total length of nine characters	TO_CHAR (SYSDATE,'MONTH')
PM	Meridian indicator (am/pm)	TO_CHAR (SYSDATE,'PM')
RM	Roman numeral month (from I to XII)	TO_CHAR (SYSDATE,'RM')
RR	Calculates full year given two digits	TO_CHAR (SYSDATE,'RR')
SS	Second (from 0 to 59)	TO_CHAR (SYSDATE,'SS')

The following example is for the TO_CHAR(datetime) version of the function. It returns the current date (obtained through SYSDATE() function, which is discussed in the section, "Date and Time Functions," later in this chapter) in a long format specified by the format mask:

```
select
    TO_CHAR(SYSDATE,'DD-DAY-MONTH-YEAR') LONG_DATE
FROM dual;

LONG_DATE
------------------------------------
06-SUNDAY-JUNE-TWO THOUSAND FOUR
```

For a NUMBER version of the TO_CHAR() function, the following example converts a negative number into one with a trailing "minus sign," using a format mask from the preceding table that details the format elements available in the Oracle implementation:

```
SELECT
    TO_CHAR(-1234,'9999MI') result
FROM dual;

RESULT
-----------
1234-
```

The following table details the various numerical format elements that can be used in format masks on the Oracle platform.

Format Element	Description	Example
$	Returns value with appended dollar sign at the beginning.	TO_CHAR(1234,'$9999')
0	Returns leading and/or trailing zeroes.	TO_CHAR(1234,'09999')
9	Returns value of the specified number of digits, adding leading blank space for positive numbers or leading minus sign for negatives.	TO_CHAR(1234,'9999')
B	Returns blanks for the integer of a fixed point number, where integer part of the number is zero.)	TO_CHAR(1234,'B9999'
C	Returns ISO currency symbol (as defined by Oracle's NLS_ISO_CURRENCY parameter) in the requested position.	TO_CHAR(1234,'C9999')
D	Returns ISO decimal character (as defined by Oracle's NLS_NUMERIC_CHARACTER parameter) in the requested position.	TO_CHAR(1234.5,'99D99')
EEEE	Returns value in scientific notation.	TO_CHAR(1234,'9.9EEEE')

Format Element	Description	Example
FM	Returns value with no leading or trailing blank spaces.	`TO_CHAR(1234,'FM9999')`
MI	Returns negative value with the trailing minus sign; positive values are returned with a trailing blank space.	`TO_CHAR(-1234,'9999MI')`
PR	Returns a negative value in the angle brackets, and returns a positive value with leading and trailing blank spaces.	`TO_CHAR(-1234,'9999PR')`
RN / rn	Returns value as a Roman numeral in uppercase/or lowercase.	`TO_CHAR(1234,'RN')`
S	Appends minus or plus signs ether in the beginning or at the end of the number.	`TO_CHAR(1234,'S9999')`
X	Returns hexadecimal value of the specified number of digits; noninteger values get rounded.	`TO_CHAR(1234,'XXXX')`

The `TO_CHAR()` conversion function has its equivalent in the IBM DB2 UDB `CHAR` function. It could be emulated using Microsoft SQL Server's `CAST()` and `CONVERT()` functions and Sybase ASE's `CONVERT()` function. MySQL sports both `CAST()` and `CONVERT()`, as does PostgreSQL.

TRANSLATE...USING

Syntax:

```
TRANSLATE(<text> USING [CHAR_CS|NCHAR_CS])
```

The `TRANSLATE...USING` function is used to translate a text between different character sets — namely, a database character set and one of the national character sets. Oracle indicates that this function is supported only for ANSI/ISO compatibility, and recommends using `TO_CHAR()` and `TO_NCHAR()` functions instead because they accept wider range of data types.

Specifying `CHAR_CS` in the second part of the function would result in data returned as `VARCHAR2` data type, while `NCHAR_CS` would return `NVARCHAR2` data type result.

The functionality is identical to that of the `CONVERT()` function, with a notable exception. The `TRANSLATE....USING` function must be used when dealing with `NCHAR` and `NVARCHAR2` data types.

UNISTR()

Syntax:

```
UNISTR(<string_expression>)
```

The UNISTR() function accepts a string argument and returns its representation in a national character set. The national character set of the database can be either AL16UTF16 or UTF8. The function supports Unicode literals by allowing you to specify hexadecimal codes (in UCS-2 format) instead of characters. A code must be preceded by backslash (for example, "\00C4" "stands for the character Ä, or an uppercase "A umlaut" in German).

```
SELECT
    UNISTR('OE ' || '\00C4\00E9') diff
FROM dual;

DIFF
-----------
OE Äé
```

It is recommended to use ASCII characters and Unicode hexadecimal values to increase portability of your data and to avoid ambiguity.

To include the backlash itself into the string, precede it with an escape character (the backslash itself, as in \\ ).

The UNISTR() function is analogous to the Microsoft SQL Server 2000 function NCHAR(), encoding conversion functions in PostgreSQL, and the Sybase ASE function TO_UNICHAR(). There are no built-in equivalent functions in IBM DB2 UDB and MySQL.

Date and Time Functions

The Date and Time functions are some of the most numerous in Oracle's arsenal. They provide a means for manipulating dates, as well as providing date/time information about the environment, as shown in the following table

SQL Function	Input Arguments	Return Arguments	Notes
ADD_MONTHS	DATE	DATE	Returns the input argument date with the specified number of months added.
DBTIMEZONE SESSIONTIMEZONE	n/a	VARCHAR2	These two niladic functions (that is, called without arguments) return the database time zone and the client session time zone, respectively.
EXTRACT	DATETIME, Date-Part String	VARCHAR2	Returns the value of a specified datetime field from a datetime or interval value expression.

SQL Function	Input Arguments	Return Arguments	Notes
MONTH_BETWEEN	DATE, DATE	NUMBER	The function calculates the number of months between two dates. If the date_one is earlier than date_two, the returned number is negative; otherwise, a positive number is returned.
NEW_TIME	DATE, time-zone string, time-zone string	DATETIME	Returns the <zone_two> equivalent of the <zone_one> date.
ROUND	DATE, Format String	DATE	Returns the date rounded to the unit specified by the format string. If the latter is omitted, then the date is rounded to a nearest day.
SYSDATE	n/a	DATE	Returns the Oracle server's current date and time.
TRUNC	DATE, Format String	DATE	Returns a date with the time portion of the day truncated to the unit specified by the format string. If format is omitted, then date will be truncated to the nearest day.

ADD_MONTHS()

Syntax:

```
ADD_MONTHS(<date>, <months_to_add>)
```

The ADD_MONTHS() function returns the date plus the number of months specified as a second argument. The <months_to_add> argument can be any integer value. The following example demonstrates its usage by adding exactly one month to today's date (the niladic SYSDATE() function is used to return the today's date on the Oracle system):

```
SELECT
    add_months(SYSDATE, 1) month_from_now,
SYSDATE                    today
FROM dual;
MONTH_FROM_NOW    TODAY
--------------    ----------
05-JUL-04         05-JUN-04
```

If the date specified is the last day of the month, or if the resulting month has fewer days than the day component of the date argument, the last day of the resulting month will be returned. For example, the same query run on June 30, 2004, would return July 31, 2004.

The equivalent functions in the RDBMS implementations covered in this book would be DATEADD() for Microsoft SQL Server and Sybase ASE and DATE_ADD() and ADDDATE() for MySQL. There are no equivalent built-in functions for IBM DB2 UDB and PostgreSQL, where you could use operators to achieve the same results.

DBTIMEZONE and SESSIONTIMEZONE

Syntax:

```
DBTIMEZONE
SESSIONTIMEZONE
```

These two niladic functions (that is, called without arguments) return the database time zone and the client session time zone, respectively.

The return type is a time zone offset (a character type in the format [+|-]TZH:TZM) or a time zone region name, depending on the database settings. For example, the following query returns the time zone offset for both the database server and the client session:

```
SELECT
    DBTIMEZONE      db_time,
    SESSIONTIMEZONE   session_time
FROM dual;

DB_TIME         SESSION_TIME
---------       -------------
+00:00          +00:00
```

Since both client and server are set for the same time zone, the results are predictably the same. Of course, this example is assuming that the user's RDBMS implementation is running in the 00:00 GMT time zone. If your implementation's time zone differs, then your results for the preceding code will differ as well.

If we alter the session with the ALTER SESSION statement and set the session's time zone forward by, say, nine hours, we'll get somewhat different results:

```
ALTER SESSION SET TIME_ZONE = '+9:00';
Session altered.


SELECT
    DBTIMEZONE      db_time,
    SESSIONTIMEZONE   session_time
FROM dual;

DB_TIME         SESSION_TIME
--------        -------------
+00:00          +09:00
```

There are many more functions that return date and time information, including ones that deal with UTC time (Coordinated Universal Time) and conversion between different zones. Refer to Appendix A for full list of such functions.

The IBM DB2 UDB implements similar functionality using special registers. Microsoft SQL Server and Sybase ASE have the GETUTCDATE() and GETDATE() functions. PostgreSQL has the LOCALTIME(), NOW(), and CURENT_TIME() functions, while MySQL has a variety of functions, such as NOW(), CURRENT_TIME(), CURRENT_DATE(), UTC_DATE(), and the modifier AT TIME ZONE. Refer to Appendix A for more information on the time zone functions.

EXTRACT()

Syntax:

```
EXTRACT([[YEAR]|[MONTH]|[DAY]|[HOUR]|[MINUTE]|[SECOND]]|
[[TIMEZONE_HOUR]|[TIMEZONE_MINUTE]|[TIMEZONE_REGION]|[TIMEZONE_ABBR])
```

The EXTRACT() function returns the value of a specified datetime field from a datetime or interval value expression. For example, to find out a year from a date, the following query could be used:

```
SELECT
    EXTRACT(YEAR FROM SYSDATE) current_year
FROM dual;

CURRENT_YEAR
------------
2004
```

The FROM clause within the function signature must also be of an appropriate data type. The YEAR, MONTH, and DAY could be extracted only from a DATE value, and TIMEZONE_HOUR and TIMEZONE_MINUTE could be extracted only from the TIMESTAMP WITH TIME ZONE data type. In the following example, the TIMEZONE_ABBR argument is used with the SYSTIMESTAMP() function that does contain all the necessary information:

```
SELECT
    EXTRACT(TIMEZONE_ABBR from SYSTIMESTAMP)     timezone,
    SYSTIMESTAMP     sys_stamp
FROM dual;

TIMEZONE        SYS_STAMP
-----------     -----------------------------------
UNK             05-JUN-04 09.22.07.020000 PM -07:00
```

The returned value UNK stands for "unknown." Whenever Oracle cannot resolve an ambiguity for certain arguments passed into the function, the return value is "unknown." In the previous example, the timezone is specified through offset and could potentially correspond to more than one region.

For the TIMEZONE_REGION and TIMEZONE_ABBR (abbreviation) arguments, the function returns a string with the appropriate time zone name or abbreviation. For all other parameters, the value returned is in the Gregorian calendar; an extract from a datetime with a time zone value results in a UTC value being returned.

For a full list of `timezone` names and their corresponding abbreviations, you can query the `V$TIMEZONE_NAMES` dynamic performance view. It contains more than 1,300 records.

This function is overloaded. In addition to the `datetime` data types, it could accept XML.

Equivalents of this function are found in many other RDBMS implementations. Microsoft SQL Server and Sybase ASE provide the `DATEPART()` function, and IBM DB2 UDB has a variety of specialized functions, such as `YEAR()`, `DAY()`, `HOUR()`, and so on. PostgreSQL has the `DATE_PART()` function, and MySQL sports its own version of `EXTRACT()`.

MONTH_BETWEEN()

Syntax:

```
MONTH_BETWEEN(<date_one>,<date_two>)
```

This function calculates the number of months between two dates. If `date_one` is earlier than `date_two`, the returned number is negative; otherwise, a positive number is returned.

If `date1` and `date2` are either the same days of the month or are both the last days of months, then the result is always an integer; otherwise the fractional portion of the result based on a 31-day month is calculated, and the difference in time components is also taken into consideration. The following example returns the number of months between today and the same day a year from now. It also calculates the number of months between today and tomorrow, both of which fall within the same months.

```
SELECT
    months_between(SYSDATE, SYSDATE+365) one_year,
    months_between(SYSDATE, SYSDATE+1) one_day
FROM dual;

ONE_YEAR      ONE_DAY
----------    ----------
-12           -.03225806
```

The `ONE_DAY` field reports that the one-day difference is 1/32 of a month, while 365 days in the future correctly results in 12 months difference.

Microsoft SQL Server and Sybase ASE provide the `DATEDIFF()` function to serve this purpose, while IBM DB2 UDB relies on date arithmetic used together with the `MONTH()` function. PostgreSQL uses date and time arithmetic and MySQL has the `DATE_DIFF()` function, as well as `PERIOD_DIFF()` and `TIME_DIFF()`. MySQL also allows date arithmetic following the IBM style.

NEW_TIME()

Syntax:

```
NEW_TIME(<date>, <zone_one>,<zone_two>)
```

The `NEW_TIME()` function returns the `<zone_two>` equivalent of the `<zone_one>` date. For example, to find out what would be the Atlantic Standard Time equivalent for the current date and time on the Pacific Coast, you could use the following:

```
SELECT
    NEW_TIME(SYSDATE, 'PST','AST')    ast_time,
    SYSDATE    pst_time
FROM dual;

AST_TIME              PST_TIME
-------------------- --------------------
05-JUN-2004 21:05:31 05-JUN-2004 17:05:31
```

The PST stands for Pacific Standard Time, and AST stands for Atlantic Standard Time. A full list of the acceptable values is listed in the following table:

Time Zone	Description
AST (ADT)	Atlantic Standard (or Daylight Time)
BST (BDT)	Bering Standard (or Daylight Time)
CST (CDT)	Central Standard (or Daylight Time)
EST (EDT)	Eastern Standard (or Daylight Time)
GMT	Greenwich Mean Time
HST (HDT)	Alaska-Hawaii Standard Time or Daylight Time
MST (MDT)	Mountain Standard or Daylight Time
NST	Newfoundland Standard Time
PST (PDT)	Pacific Standard or Daylight Time
YST (YDT)	Yukon Standard or Daylight Time

Prior to using the function, set the NLS_DATE_FORMAT to display 24-hour time

Oracle also provides the FROM_TZ() function, which is much more flexible and allows for wider spectrum of the time zone values.

There are no direct equivalents of this function in any of the other RDBMS implementations discussed in this book, though equivalent functionality could be easily achieved using date and time operators in conjunction with date and time functions and UTC offset values. IBM provides special registers such as CURRENT TIMEZONE to assist with this task.

ROUND()

Syntax:

```
ROUND(<date>, [<format>])
```

The overloaded version of the ROUND() function accepts two arguments—the date and an optional format string. The returned result represents the date rounded to the unit specified by the format string. If the latter is omitted, then the date is rounded to the nearest day. The full list of acceptable formats could be found in the table shown in the "NEW_TIME" section, earlier in this chapter. For example, to round today's date as returned by the SYSDATE() function to the nearest month, the following query could be used:

```
SELECT
    ROUND(SYSDATE, 'MONTH')  near_month,
    SYSDATE    today
FROM DUAL;
NEAR_MONTH  TODAY
----------_ ---------
 01-JUN-04   06-JUN-04
```

The ROUND() function has several similarities with the TRUNC() function, but they are not equal. If, for example, you were to truncate and round a date that falls into the second part of a year, the results would be different:

```
SELECT
    SYSDATE + 100                 fall_date,
    TRUNC(SYSDATE + 100, 'YEAR') truncated,
    ROUND(SYSDATE + 100, 'YEAR') rounded
FROM DUAL;

FALL_DATE  TRUNCATED  ROUNDED
---------  ---------  ---------
 14-SEP-04  01-JAN-04  01-JAN-05
```

While virtually every RDBMS has its equivalent of the ROUND() function, none of the databases discussed in this book applies it to the DATE data type, except for Oracle.

SYSDATE

Syntax:

```
SYSDATE
```

SYSDATE returns the current date and time of the local Oracle server. The data type of the returned value is DATE. The function requires no arguments, and we have used it to provide the date and time values in the numerous examples earlier in this section. Here is a simple example:

```
SELECT
    sysdate
FROM dual;

SYSDATE
---------
05-JUN-2004 22:14:39
```

Note that the CURRENT_DATE() function returns the date and time of the session, not the server itself, and its value affected by ALTER SESSION statements.

Oracle disallows the use of this function as the CHECK constraint for a table, which is one of the few restrictions on the use of nondeterministic functions.

The equivalent of this function is found in every single RDBMS database discussed in this book. Microsoft SQL Server and Sybase ASE have the GETDATE() function, while IBM DB2 UDB has the CURRENT DATE special register. PostgreSQL has the CURRENT_DATE() and NOW() functions, while MySQL has the CURENT_DATE(), NOW(), and SYSDATE functions.

TRUNC()

Syntax:

```
TRUNC(<date>, [FMT])
```

The TRUNC() function applied to a DATE data type returns a date with the time portion of the day truncated to the unit specified by the format model FMT. If the format is omitted, then the date will be truncated to the nearest day. For example, to truncate a value returned by the SYSDATE() function to the nearest YEAR, nearest MONTH, and nearest DAY, the following query could be used:

```
SELECT
    TRUNC(SYSDATE, 'YEAR')   year_start,
    TRUNC(SYSDATE, 'MONTH')  month_start,
    TRUNC(SYSDATE, 'DAY')    day_start
FROM DUAL;

YEAR_START MONTH_START    DAY_START
---------  -----------    ---------
01-JAN-04  01-JUN-04      06-JUN-04
```

Applying the formats could get tricky. For the complete list of formats used with the TRUNC() function for the DATE data type, refer to the following table. (These formats are fully applicable to ROUND() date function, as well.)

Format Element	Description	Example
CC	One greater than the first two digits of a four-digit year.	ROUND(SYSDATE,'CC')
SCC	One greater than the first two digits of a four-digit year.	ROUND(SYSDATE,'SCC')
Year		
SYYYY	Year; rounds up on July 1.	ROUND(SYSDATE,'SYYYY')
YYYY	Year; rounds up on July 1.	ROUND(SYSDATE,'YYYY')
YEAR	Year; rounds up on July 1.	ROUND(SYSDATE,'YEAR')
YYY	Year; rounds up on July 1.	ROUND(SYSDATE,'YYY')
YY	Year; rounds up on July 1.	ROUND(SYSDATE,'YY')
Y	Year; rounds up on July 1.	ROUND(SYSDATE,'Y')
IYYY	ISO year.	ROUND(SYSDATE,'IYYY')

Table continued on following page

Format Element	Description	Example
IY	ISO year.	ROUND(SYSDATE,'IY')
I	ISO year.	ROUND(SYSDATE,'I')
Q	Quarter; rounds up on sixteenth day of the second month of the quarter.	ROUND(SYSDATE,'Q')
Month		
MONTH	Month; rounds up on sixteenth day.	TRUNC(SYSDATE,'MONTH')
MON	Month; rounds up on sixteenth day.	TRUNC(SYSDATE,'MON')
MM	Month; rounds up on sixteenth day.	TRUNC(SYSDATE,'MM')
RM	Month; rounds up on sixteenth day.	TRUNC(SYSDATE,'RM')
Week		
WW	Same day of the week as the first day of the year.	TRUNC(SYSDATE,'WW')
IW	Same day of the week as the first day of the ISO year.	TRUNC(SYSDATE,'IW')
W	Same day of the week as the first day of the month.	TRUNC(SYSDATE,'W')
Day		
DD	Day of the month (from 1 to 31).	ROUND(SYSDATE,'DD')
DDD	Day of the year (from 1 to 366).	ROUND(SYSDATE,'DDD')
J	Day.	ROUND(SYSDATE,'J')
D	Starting Day of the week.	
DY	Starting Day of the week.	TRUNC(SYSDATE,'DY')
DAY	Starting Day of the week.	TRUNC (SYSDATE,'DAY')
HH	Hour of the day (from 1 to 12).	TRUNC (SYSDATE,'HH')
HH12	Hour of the day (from 1 to 12).	TRUNC (SYSDATE,'HH12')
HH24	Hour of the day (from 0 to 23).	TRUNC (SYSDATE,'HH24')
MI	Minute (from 0 to 59).	TRUNC (SYSDATE,'MI')

While virtually every RDBMS has its equivalent of the TRUNC() function, none of the databases discussed in this book apply it to the DATE data type, except for Oracle and PostgreSQL, which provide the DATE_TRUNC() function.

Numeric Functions

Oracle provides a small number of numeric functions whose main purpose is to provide processing of basic numeric operations. The following table details the functions available:

SQL Function	Input Arguments	Return Arguments	Notes
ABS	NUMBER	NUMBER	Returns the absolute value of a numeric expression.
BITAND	NUMBER, NUMBER	NUMBER	Computes the result of the binary and between two arguments.
CEIL	NUMBER	NUMBER	Returns a rounded-up integer value based on the input argument.
FLOOR	NUMBER	NUMBER	Returns a rounded-down integer value based on the input argument.
MOD	NUMBER, NUMBER	NUMBER	Returns the remainder of the first argument divided by the second.
SIGN	NUMBER	NUMBER	Returns –1 if the argument is negative, 0 if the argument is zero, and 1 if the argument is positive.
ROUND	NUMBER	NUMBER	Returns the integer closest in value to the argument.
TRUNC	NUMBER, [format mask]	NUMBER	Returns its input argument truncated to a certain number of decimal places specified by the second argument.

ABS()

Syntax:

```
ABS(<numeric expression>)
```

The ABS() function returns the absolute value of a numeric input argument. Consider the following example:

```
SELECT
    ABS(-100) negative,
    ABS(100)  positive
FROM DUAL;

NEGATIVE   POSITIVE
---------  ---------
100        100
```

The number returned will be positive. Some RDBMS implementations impose restrictions on the size of the number passed in, but Oracle will handle virtually any number.

The ABS() function is available in all of the RDBMS implementations discussed in this book.

BITAND()

Syntax:

```
BITAND(<argument1>, <argument2>)
```

This function computes the result of the binary and, given two arguments. The arguments passed in must resolve to non-negative integers. The function allows you to tell whether a particular bit is turned ON or OFF. This is useful for applying the bit masks and reading the status of bit flags. The following example shows the status of the first, second, and third bit for the binary number 11110101 (decimal 245):

```
SELECT
    BITAND(245,1)+0   first_bit,
    BITAND(245,2)+0   second_bit,
    BITAND(245,4)+0   third_bit
FROM DUAL;

Firstbit     secondbit    thirdbit
---------    ---------    --------
1            0            4
```

Values greater than 0 indicate ON (binary 1 detected); zeroes (binary 0 detected) indicate OFF status.

The only RDBMS implementation that has implemented a similar function is Microsoft SQL Server 2000.

CEIL() and FLOOR()

Syntax:

```
CEIL(<numeric_expression>)
FLOOR(<numeric_expression>)
```

The CEIL() function returns a rounded-up integer value based on the input argument, as shown here:

```
SELECT
    CEIL(10.2)   close_to_10,
    CEIL(10.9)   close_to_11
FROM dual;
close_to_10      close_to_11
-----------      -----------
11               11
```

The decimal number was rounded up to the nearest integer (11 in this example).

The FLOOR() function acts in a manner similar to the CEIL() function, rounding down to the lowest possible integer value. Consider the following example:

```
SELECT
    FLOOR(10.2)  close_to_10,
    FLOOR(10.9)  close_to_11
FROM dual;

close_to_10      close_to_11
-----------      -----------
10               10
```

The decimal number is rounded *down* to the nearest integer (10 in this example).

Compare the FLOOR() and CEIL() functions with the TRUNC() and ROUND() functions discussed later.

The FLOOR() and CEIL() functions are available in all of the RDBMS implementations discussed in this book.

MOD()

Syntax:

```
MOD(<numeric_expression1>,<numeric_expression2>)
```

This is the mathematical *modulus* function. It returns the remainder of the first argument divided by the second. The following simple query demonstrates the usage:

```
SELECT
    MOD(100,50)    noremainder,
    MOD(100,99)    remainder
FROM dual;

Noremainder      remainder
-----------      -----------
0                1
```

This function is useful for checking completeness of a cycle, or for implementing computational algorithms.

The MOD() function is implemented in all of the RDBMS implementations discussed in this book except for Microsoft SQL Server and Sybase. Both SQL Server and Sybase use the "%" operator instead of the MOD() function.

SIGN()

Syntax:

```
SIGN(<numeric_expression>)
```

While the ABS() built-in function returns the absolute value of a number, it might be important to know whether the number was positive or negative to begin with. This could be easily achieved by comparing the number with zero in the WHERE clause, but the SIGN() function (or its custom UDF equivalent) is the only way to do it in the SELECT clause of a query. The function returns a –1 if the argument is negative, 0 if the argument is zero, and 1 if it is positive, as shown here:

```
SELECT
    SIGN(-100)    negative,
    SIGN(0)       zero,
    SIGN(100)     positive
FROM dual;

Negative    zero    positive
---------   -------  --------
-1           0       1
```

If the argument is NULL, a NULL will be returned.

The SIGN() function is found in all of the RDBMS implementations discussed in this book.

ROUND()

Syntax:

```
ROUND(<numeric_expression>, [decimal_places])
```

The ROUND() function is fairly intuitive. It rounds the numeric value according to a specific set of rules, which are given in the second argument. The function returns its input argument rounded up to a certain number of decimal places specified by the second optional argument. If the second argument is omitted, the number will be rounded to zero decimal places, as shown here:

```
SELECT
    ROUND(10.12345)      omitted,
    ROUND(10.12345, 1)   onedigit,
    ROUND(10.12345, 2)   twodigits,
    ROUND(109, -1)       round_left
FROM dual;

OMITTED    ONEDIGIT    TWODIGITS    ROUND_LEFT
---------  ----------  ---------    ----------
10         10.1        10.12        110
```

If the argument is negative, it rounds the numbers on the left side of the decimal point (so ROUND(199,-1) evaluates to 200—the first digit on the left—while ROUND(199,-3) evaluates to 0—the third digit on the left—and DROUND(599,-3) would return 1000).

The function has an overloaded version that accepts DATE as the input data type.

The ROUND() function is found in every RDBMS implementation discussed in this book, though some input parameters might differ.

TRUNC()

Syntax:

```
TRUNC(<numeric_expression>, [decimal_places])
```

The TRUNC() function is fairly intuitive. It truncates a numeric value, given a certain input mask. The function returns its input argument truncated to a certain number of decimal places specified by the second argument, as shown here:

```
SELECT
    TRUNC(10.12345, 1)   onedigit,
    TRUNC(10.12345, 2)   twodigits,
    TRUNC(109, -1)       left
FROM dual;

Onedigit    twodigits   left
---------   ----------  --------
10.1        10.12       100
```

If the second argument is omitted, the number is truncated to zero decimal places. If the argument is negative, it truncates the numbers on the left side of the decimal point (so TRUNC(199,-1) evaluates to 190, while TRUNC(199,-2) evaluates to 100).

The function has an overloaded version that accepts DATE as the input data type.

The TRUNC() function is also found in IBM DB2 UDB, PostgreSQL, and MySQL, while Sybase and Microsoft SQL Server both use the ROUND() function for this purpose.

Object Reference Functions

The object reference functions represent the ability to get as close as you could possibly get to obtaining pointer reference on an object within a database. The reference could be established to a row in an object view or in an object table. Using these functions allows for utilization of the object-oriented features in Oracle and is beyond the scope of this book. For a complete list of Oracle's object-reference functions, refer to Appendix A, and refer to the vendor's documentation for examples of their usage.

Miscellaneous Single-Row Functions

As the saying goes, virtually anything could be classified under the miscellaneous category. Most of the functions we have bundled into this section were introduced to compensate for the nonprocedural nature of the SQL. Some, like the DECODE() function, are on their way to becoming obsolete, or are being replaced by the SQL-standard CASE expression; some are very Oracle-specific. We would like to remind you that every classification is arbitrary.

The following table shows the miscellaneous single-row functions discussed in this chapter:

SQL Function	Input Arguments	Return Arguments	Notes
COALESCE	List of expressions	Expression	Returns first expression from the list that is not NULL.
DECODE	Two expressions	Expression	Compares two expressions; if they are null, returns NULL; otherwise the first expression is returned.
DUMP	Character Value, Optional: Numeric mask, Start Position, Length	VARCHAR2	Returns a VARCHAR2 value containing the data type code, length in bytes, and internal representation of expression.
GREATEST	List of expressions	Expression	Returns the greatest of the list of expressions.
NULLIF	Two expressions	Expression	Compares two expressions. If they are equal, it returns NULL; otherwise, it returns the first expression.
NVL	Expression	Expression	Checks whether expression is null; if it is, returns the specified value.
NVL2	Expression	Expression	If the expression is NULL, returns the first value; otherwise, returns the second one.
NULLIF	Two expressions	Expression	Compares two expressions. If they are null, returns NULL; otherwise, the first expression is returned.
UID	n/a	INTEGER	Returns an integer that uniquely identifies the session user.
VSIZE	Expression	Number	Returns the number of bytes in the internal representation of expression.

COALESCE()

Syntax:

```
COALESCE(<exp1>,<exp2> . . . <expN>)
```

The COALESCE() function returns the first non-null expression in the expression list. At least one expression must not be the literal NULL. If all expressions evaluate to null, then the function returns NULL. Consider the following example:

```
SELECT
    COALESCE (NULL, NULL, 'ALEX', NULL) test
FROM dual;

TEST
------------
ALEX
```

The COALESCE() function is the most generic version of the NVL() function and could be used in its place.

This function is found in every RDBMS discussed in this book.

DECODE()

Syntax:

```
DECODE
```

The DECODE() function is Oracle's invention. Every other RDBMS of this level provides the CASE statement, which is also a part of the SQL standard.

The function compares <expression> to each <search_value > one-by-one. If the expression is equal to the search, the corresponding result is returned. If no match is found, then Oracle returns the default, or if the default is omitted, it returns NULL. The character data is compared using the nonpadded semantics, and the result can be of any of the following data types: CHAR, VARCHAR2, NCHAR, and NVARCHAR2; the return value is always VARCHAR2 if the first result is either NULL or CHAR. For example, the following query could be used to produce the list of cars segregated by the domestic and foreign manufacturers (using the table set up for the aggregate functions in the beginning of the chapter):

```
SELECT
    model,
    DECODE(maker, 'CHRYSLER','DOMESTIC'
           ,'FORD','DOMESTIC'
           ,'FOREIGN')
FROM cars;

MODEL                        DECODE
------------------------     -------
CROSSFIRE                    DOMESTIC
300M                         DOMESTIC
CIVIC                        FOREIGN
ACCORD                       FOREIGN
MUSTANG                      DOMESTIC
LATESTnGREATEST              DOMESTIC
FOCUS                        DOMESTIC
```

This statement could be easily rewritten using the CASE statement

```
SELECT
        model,
        CASE maker
        WHEN 'CHRYSLER'      THEN 'DOMESTIC'
        WHEN 'FORD'          THEN 'DOMESTIC'
        ELSE                 'FOREIGN'
        END
  FROM cars;

MODEL                        CASEMAKE
------------------------     --------
CROSSFIRE                    DOMESTIC
300M                         DOMESTIC
CIVIC                        FOREIGN
ACCORD                       FOREIGN
MUSTANG                      DOMESTIC
LATESTnGREATEST              DOMESTIC
FOCUS                        DOMESTIC
```

Oracle implicitly converts every expression and each search value to the data type of the first search value before proceeding with comparison.

In a DECODE() function, Oracle considers two nulls to be equivalent; this is not the case in a regular SELECT statement comparison.

The maximum number of components in the DECODE() function, including expressions, searches, results, and default, is 255.

There is no direct equivalent for the DECODE() function in the other RDBMS implementations discussed in this book because they implement the CASE statement, which provides the same functionality. Beginning with version 8i, Oracle also supports this statement.

DUMP()

Syntax:

```
DUMP(<expression> [,RETURN_FORMAT [START_POSITION] [LENGTH]])
```

The DUMP() function returns a VARCHAR2 value containing the data type code, length in bytes, and internal representation of the expression.

The RETURN_FORMAT can have any of the following values:

❑   8 returns result in octal notation.

❑   10 returns result in decimal notation.

❑   16 returns result in hexadecimal notation.

❑   17 returns result as single characters.

The return value contains no character set information by default. To include it, you must specify the RETURN_FORMAT value plus 1,000, as shown here:

```
SELECT
   DUMP('ABC',1010)  type_info
FROM dual;

TYPE_INFO
------------------------------------------------
Typ=96 Len=3 CharacterSet=WE8MSWIN1252: 65,66,67
```

To decipher the obtained information, refer to Appendix C for a list of the built-in data-type codes and their descriptions. It the previous example, code 96 corresponds to CHAR data type, the length is three characters, the character set is WE8MSWIN1252, and the codes for the displayed characters "ABC" are 65, 66, and 67, respectively.

The START_POSITION specifies which character in the supplied string to start with, and the optional length specifies how many characters to consider. For example, to return the value for the first character in the previous string, the following query could be used:

```
SELECT
   DUMP('ABC',1010,1)  type_info
FROM dual;

TYPE_INFO
------------------------------------------------
Typ=96 Len=3 CharacterSet=WE8MSWIN1252: 65,66,67
```

The function supports all character data (CLOB is supported through implicit conversion to VARCHAR2, which imposes certain restrictions regarding the length of the data).

There is no single function in any of the RDBMS implementations discussed in this book that has similar functionality, though the information could be obtained through a combination of some other built-in functions, and a UDF solution could be created easily.

GREATEST()

Syntax:

```
GREATEST(<expression1>,<expression2>. . . <expression>)
```

The GREATEST() function returns the greatest of the list of expressions. Before comparison, all expressions on the list are converted to the data type of the first expression. The expressions are compared according to the data comparison rules: character comparison is based on the value of the character in the database character set, while numerical values are compared in a manner similar to the MAX() function. The value returned is of the same data type as the first expression; if it is character data, then its data type is always VARCHAR2. The following example selects the greatest value from a list of integers, and a list of names:

```
SELECT
   GREATEST('ALEX','WALTER','PHILLIP')   names,
   GREATEST(10,20,135)       numbers
FROM dual;
```

```
NAMES    NUMBERS
------   --------
WALTER   135
```

Oracle compares the values based on nonpadded comparison semantics. The following table lists some of Oracle's comparison rules for different types of expressions:

Data Type	Rule
Numeric Values	A larger value is considered greater than a smaller one. All negative numbers are less than zero, and all positive numbers.
Date Values	A later date is considered greater than an earlier one. This applies not only to the date part, but also to the hours, minutes, and seconds, as supplied.
Character String Values	**Blank-Padded Comparison Semantics:** Whenever the two values have different lengths, Oracle first adds blanks to the end of the shorter one so their lengths are equal. Oracle then compares the values character-by-character up to the first character that differs. The value with the greater character in the first differing position is considered greater. If two values have no differing characters, then they are considered equal. This rule means that two values are equal if they differ only in the number of trailing blanks. Oracle uses blank-padded comparison semantics only when both values in the comparison are expressions of data types CHAR and NCHAR, text literals, or values returned by the USER function. **Nonpadded Comparison Semantics**: Two values are compared character-by-character up to the first character that differs. The value with the greater character in that position is considered greater. If two values of different length are identical up to the end of the shorter one, then the longer value is considered greater. If two values of equal length have no differing characters, then the values are considered equal. Oracle uses nonpadded comparison semantics whenever one or both values in the comparison have the data type VARCHAR2 or NVARCHAR2.
Single Characters	Oracle compares single characters according to their numeric values in the database character set. One character is greater than another if it has a greater numeric value than the other character set. Oracle considers blanks to be less than any character, which is true in most character sets.

The function has its equivalent in MySQL, but there is no direct correspondence in Microsoft SQL Server, Sybase ASE, IBM DB2 UDB, or PostgreSQL.

NULLIF()

Syntax:

```
NULLIF( <expression1>,<expression2>)
```

The NULLIF() function compares two expressions. If they are equal, it returns NULL; otherwise, it returns the first expression. Here is an example:

```
SELECT
    NULLIF('ABC','ABC') equal,
    NULLIF ('ABC','DEF') diff
FROM dual;
EQUAL    DIFF
------   -----
NULL     ABC
```

The NULLIF() function is found in IBM DB2 UDB, Microsoft SQL Server, Sybase ASE, PostgreSQL, and MySQL. The syntax and usage are identical in all cases.

NVL()

Syntax:

```
NVL(<expression1>,<expression2>)
```

The NVL() function evaluates the result of the <expression1>. If it is NULL, it returns <expression2>; otherwise, <expression1> is returned. It also lets you replace a null (blank) with a string in the results of a query. Both <expression1> and <expression2> could be of any data type. If the data types of the expressions are different, the <expression2> is always converted into the <expression1> data type. For example, if you need to add two numbers, none of the addends can be NULL:

```
SELECT
    NVL(NULL, 0) + 10  "sum"
FROM dual;

SUM
---------
10
```

The data type of the return value is always the same as the data type of <expression1>. If the <expression1> is of character data type, a VARCHAR2 is returned.

This function has its equivalents in the IBM DB2 UDB COALESCE() function, as well as the Microsoft SQL Server and Sybase ASE ISNULL() function. MySQL has the IFNULL() function, and PostgreSQL provides the NULLIF() function. For all of these, the use of the COALESCE() function is also an option.

NVL2()

Syntax:

```
NVL2(<expression1>,<expression2>,<expression3>)
```

The NVL2() function evaluates the <expression1> and returns <expression2> if the result is not NULL; <expression3> is returned otherwise. The <expression1> could be of any data type, while <expression2> and <expression3> cannot be LONG. In addition, Oracle implicitly converts <expression3> to be of the same data type as <expression2>. The following query demonstrates the functionality:

```
SELECT
    NVL2(NULL, 'not NULL','is NULL') test
FROM dual;

TEST
--------
is NULL
```

The data type of the return value is always the same as the data type of <expression2>. If <expression2> is of character data type, a VARCHAR2 is returned.

There are no direct equivalents to this function, though a combination of the built-in functions could be used to provide similar functionality.

UID

Syntax:

```
UID
```

The niladic UID() function returns an integer that uniquely identifies the session user. Here is an example of usage:

```
SELECT
 UID
FROM dual;

UID
---------
5
```

This function has its equivalents in every RDBMS implementation discussed in this book. Microsoft SQL Server and Sybase ASE have the SUSER_ID() function. IBM DB2 UDB utilizes special registers, and PostgreSQL and MySQL both provide the USER function (returns a unique character ID).

VSIZE()

Syntax:

```
VSIZE(<expression>)
```

The VSIZE() function returns the number of bytes in the internal representation of an expression. If the expression is NULL, then NULL is returned. The functionality of VSIZE() is very similar to the LENGTH family of functions (especially the LENGTHB() function).

For example, assuming the single byte internal representation, the following query would return 5 (the number of bytes, which also happens to be the number of characters):

```
SELECT
    VSIZE('hello') bytes
FROM dual;

BYTES
------
5
```

The function supports all character data types, though the CLOB data type is implicitly converted into VARCHAR2.

The analogs of this function are DATALENGTH() in Microsoft SQL Server and Sybase ASE. MySQL provides the LENGTH() and BIT_LENGTH() functions. IBM DB2 UDB provides the LENGTH() function, which is capable of returning the number of bytes in the expression. PostgreSQL has the OCTET_LENGTH() function, which is also a SQL 99 standard function.

Summary

In this chapter, we discussed the various built-in functions available to the Oracle RBDMS implementations. The built-in functions were discussed in relation to their relevant grouping (aggregate, character, regular expressions, conversion, date/time, numeric, object reference, and miscellaneous). This should have made the material more readily available to the reader.

In the next chapter, we will turn our attention to the IBM DB2 UDB platform and the built-in functions available to that implementation.

7

IBM DB2 Universal Database (UDB) SQL Functions

IBM DB2 has been around since the 1970s. It went through all the stages of hierarchical and networking paradigms, and eventually became the relational type as we now know it. Its DB2 flagship database comes in several different flavors and runs on a variety of platforms, the latest addition being IBM DB2 Universal Database (UDB) for Linux, UNIX, and Windows — IBM DB2 UDB LUW, for short. The current version, 8.1, and the upcoming Stinger support a surprisingly large number of SQL functions, and have the ability to create these in C/C++, Java, and (with the release of Stinger) the .NET family of languages. This chapter takes a look at some of the most useful built-in SQL functions in the IBM DB2 UDB LUW arsenal.

IBM classifies its SQL functions as either scalar, column, or table functions. This chapter is going to group the functions into areas of specialization — string functions, date and time functions, and so on. In our opinion, this format makes it more useful as a look-up reference. The full list of functions in IBM's preferred classification format is provided in Appendix A.

All built-in SQL functions in IBM DB2 reside in either the SYSIBM or SYSFUN schemas; these functions can be called without the schema qualifier. The main difference is that the functions contained in SYSIBM are "true" built-in functions developed and compiled in C, while functions contained in SYSFUN are developed as user-defined functions (UDFs) in either C or SQL/PL.

A user cannot add or drop functions in the SYSIBM or SYSFUN schemas (or any schema beginning with SYS, for that matter).

IBM DB2 UDB allows for overloading, and some of the built-in functions are overloaded. The overloaded built-in functions are usually split between the SYSIBM and SYSFUN schemas. You must be aware of the function name resolution upon invocation: the search for the specified function goes according to the order specified in the SQL path parameter. When the SYSIBM schema is omitted from the SQL path, it will be assumed that it is the very first schema on the list. If a user schema is specified first (preceding SYSIBM) and contains a function with the required number, order, and type of arguments, it will be called first. Therefore, it is advisable to qualify the name of each SQL function with the schema name to avoid ambiguity.

Overloading capability also leads to strict handling of the parameters passed into functions as arguments—the data types must match exactly; there is no implicit conversion. This means that trying to pass a REAL data type instead of a required INTEGER would result in an error message such as the following:

```
SQL0440N  No authorized routine named <function_name> of type "FUNCTION" having
compatible arguments was found.
```

DB2 UDB Query Syntax

The IBM DB2 UDB SELECT statement is based upon the ANSI SQL standard discussed in Chapter 5. To gain a better understanding of the syntax, the SELECT statement will be broken into segments so you can examine each in succession. The basic syntax of the DB2 UDB SELECT statement is outlined in the following code:

```
SELECT [DISTINCT | ALL]
select_list
FROM clause
[WHERE expression [AND|OR] ....]
[GROUP BY expression]
[HAVING expression]
[ORDER BY expression]
[FETCH FIRST expression]
[OPTIMIZE FOR expression]
```

The first optional elements in the SELECT statement are the DISTINCT and ALL objects. DISTINCT constricts a query to return only those rows that have unique values. The ALL option returns all the rows of the query, but it is the SELECT default, so it is rarely used.

The select_list is the list of columns that the user wants to have returned in the result set. These can be any of the following: column name, literal, expression, special register, or a subquery that returns a single row. These items may also be aliased by using the AS clause and may be given a correlation name.

The FROM clause details from which sources the select_list information will be drawn in the SELECT statement. These objects can be either a table, a view, an alias to another table, or a subquery. The elements in the FROM clause may be given a correlation name either by using the AS syntax, or by following the element name with a space and then the correlation name (for example, Employee_table A).

The WHERE clause constricts the output of the SELECT statement by using a series of conditional statements. These conditional statements can either be relating an object to another object (thus creating a natural join), or relating objects to an expression or literal value. There may be multiple conditional statements that are linked by AND/OR statements. The AND statement links two conditional statements together so that both must be satisfied for the resultant row to be added into the result set. An OR statement links two conditional statements so that if either of the statements is satisfied, then the resultant row is added to the result set.

The GROUP BY and HAVING clauses return summary rows of information about the columns in the select_list. This is done by combining rows into distinct sets based on one or more columns. Developers can use the GROUPING SETS clause to define multiple independent GROUP BY clauses in one query. This is the longhand version of the CUBE and ROLLUP clauses, which can be used to get similar results. The following code gives an example of using the GROUPING SETS and its equivalent ANSI SQL syntax, using the following consideration: given an Employees table in which you have the Country, Division, and Salary columns to group by:

```
GROUPING SETS ( (Country,Division,Salary),(Country,Division),(Salary) )

// Equivalent SQL syntax...........
GROUP BY Country,Division,Salary
UNION ALL
GROUP BY Country,Division
UNION ALL
GROUP BY Salary
```

The CUBE and ROLLUP statements are equivalent to specific instances of the use of the GROUPING SETS clause. CUBE returns all possible groupings of the items in the grouping list, while ROLLUP returns a hierarchal grouping of the grouping list. Using the previous example, you can show what the ANSI SQL equivalent is for a similar CUBE and ROLLUP statement:

```
GROUP BY CUBE (Country,Division,Salary)

//Equivalent SQL syntax..........
GROUP BY Country,Division,Salary
UNION ALL
GROUP BY Country,Division
UNION ALL
GROUP BY Country,Salary
UNION ALL
GROUP BY Division,Salary
UNION ALL
GROUP BY Country
UNION ALL
GROUP BY Division
UNION ALL
GROUP BY Salary
UNION ALL
(grand-total)

// ROLLUP statement
GROUP BY ROLLUP(Country,Division,Salary)

// Equivalent SQL Statement
GROUP BY Country,Division,Salary
UNION ALL
GROUP BY Country,Division
UNION ALL
GROUP BY Country
UNION ALL
(grand total)
```

The HAVING clause will restrict the grouping sets that are produced by the SELECT statement. This is different than the WHERE clause, which restricts the rows that are put into the grouping sets.

The ORDER BY clause orders the result set by the columns defined in the clause. This ordering is hierarchal based on the order of the columns in the list, so it will order by the first column, then the second column, and so on. The ordering can be either ascending (ASC) or descending (DESC), and can be identified differently per column.

The FETCH FIRST clause will limit the number of rows returned by the SELECT statement. It can be used as in the following syntax:

```
FETCH FIRST 10 ROWS ONLY
```

The FETCH FIRST clause can also be used with the OPTIMIZE FOR clause to improve the query performance on large tables. The following example demonstrates the syntax:

```
FETCH FIRST 10 ROWS ONLY
OPTIMIZE FOR 10 ROWS
```

Now you should have a good understanding of the basics of the IBM DB2 UDB platform. This will be a basis on which to get a better understanding of the use of the different functions, as well as being able to decipher the examples given throughout this chapter.

String Functions

The SQL string functions reside in the SYSIBM schema. They are used to manipulate character data. The following table shows the string functions discussed in this chapter.

SQL Function	Input	Output	Description
CONCAT	<char_expression1>, <char_expression2>	<char_expression1>	Returns result of the concatenation of two strings.
INSERT	<char_expression1>, <start_integer>, <remove_chars>, <char_expression2>	<char_expression>	Returns a string where <remove_chars> have been deleted from expression1 beginning at <start_integer>, and where <char_expression2> has been inserted into expression1 beginning at <start_integer>.
LEFT	<char_expression>, INTEGER	<char_expression>	Returns n number of characters starting from the left.
LENGTH	<expression>	INTEGER	Returns the number of characters in a string.

SQL Function	Input	Output	Description
LOCATE	`<char_expression1>, <char_expression2> [,<start_integer>]`	`INTEGER`	Returns the position of an occurrence of a substring within the string.
LTRIM	`<char_expression>`	`<char_expression>`	Trims leading spaces off the string. (SYSIBM and SYSFUN schemas).
POSSTR	`<char_expression1>, <char_expression2>`	`INTEGER`	Returns the position of an occurrence of a substring within the string. The POSSTR test is case sensitive.
REPEAT	`<char_expression>, <times_integer>`	`<char_expression>`	Returns the string expression repeated *n* times.
REPLACE			Replaces all occurrences of expression2 in expression1 with expression3.
RIGHT	`<char_expression>, INTEGER`	`<char_expression>`	Returns a string consisting of the rightmost expression2 bytes in expression1.
RTRIM	`<char_expression>`	`<char_expression>`	Returns the characters of the argument with trailing blanks removed.
SOUNDEX	`<char_expression>`	`CHAR(4)`	Returns a four-character code representing the sound of the words in the argument.
SPACE	`INTEGER`	`<char_expression>`	Returns a string of *n* blanks.
SUBSTR	`<char_expression>, <start_integer> [,<length_integer>]`	`<char_expression>`	Returns a part of a string starting from the *n*th character for the length of *m* characters.
TRUNC or TRUNCATE	`<numeric_value>, <decimal_places>`	`<numeric_expression>`	Returns *n* truncated to *m* decimal places.

CONCAT()

Syntax:

```
CONCAT(<char_expression1>,<char_expression2>)
```

The CONCAT() function returns the result of the concatenation of two strings. The function has two notations: prefix and postfix.

Consider the following example:

```
SELECT
    CONCAT('ABC', 'DEF') AS prefix_concat,
    ('ABC' CONCAT 'DEF') AS postfix_concat,
    'ABC' || 'DEF'   AS operator_concat
FROM SYSIBM.SYSDUMMY1

PREFIX_CONCAT POSTFIX_CONCAT OPERATOR_CONCAT
------------- -------------- ---------------
ABCDEF        ABCDEF         ABCDEF
```

As mentioned previously, unlike many other databases, IBM DB2 UDB is very strict and will not allow implicit conversion for disparate data types, or any data types save for character. This is because of overloading; the RDBMS would consider the call to the CONCAT() function with, say, INTEGER input parameters as an attempt to invoke an overloaded version of the function.

The CONCAT() function is found only in MySQL, which allows more than one string to be concatenated. Oracle and PostgreSQL utilize only the concatenation operator (||). Microsoft SQL Server and Sybase ASE use the overloaded operator (+).

INSERT()

Syntax:

```
INSERT(<char_expression1>, <start_integer>,<remove_chars>,<char_expression2>)
```

The INSERT() function removes the specified number of characters <remove_chars> from the <char_expession1> beginning at the start position <start_integer>, replacing them with characters specified in the <char_expression2>. The function accepts the VARCHAR data type as argument, as well as BLOB and CLOB. Consider the following example:

```
SELECT
    INSERT('ABCDEFG',4,2,'**')   AS  two_asterisks,
    INSERT('ABCDEFG',4,2,'***')  AS  three_asterisks,
    INSERT('ABCDEFG',4,2,'')     AS empty_string
FROM SYSIBM.SYSDUMMY1;

two_asterisks            three_asterisks       empty_string
--------------------     ----------------      ----------------
ABC**FG                  ABC***FG               ABCFG
```

The specified number of characters to remove will always be removed, even though <char_expression2> might be shorter or longer. The resulting string will be shifted or stretched to ensure the best fit. Specifying an empty string in place of the <char_expression2> will result in the deletion of the <remove_chars>.

The total length of the returned string will always be VARCHAR(4000).

The Microsoft SQL Server and Sybase ASE equivalent of the INSERT() function is the STUFF() function.

LEFT() and RIGHT()

Syntax:

```
LEFT(<char_expression>, <chars_number>)
RIGHT(char_expression>, <chars_number>)
```

Both of these functions return a string consisting of the leftmost or rightmost <chars_number> bytes in <char_expression>. The first parameter can be of any character data type (that is, CHAR, VARCHAR, CLOB, or BLOB). Consider the following example:

```
SELECT
    LEFT('ABCDEFG',4)   AS  four_left,
    RIGHT('ABCDEFG',4)  AS  four_right
FROM SYSIBM.SYSDUMMY1;

four_left               four_right
-------------------     ----------------
ABCD                    DEFG
```

Blanks are considered characters and will be taken into consideration by the functions. The returned value is invariably a VARCHAR(4000).

Both the LEFT() and RIGHT() functions have their direct equivalents in Microsoft SQL Server, Sybase ASE, Oracle, and MySQL. PostgreSQL does not implement the functions, relying on the more generic SUBSTRING() function instead.

LENGTH()

Syntax:

```
LENGTH(<expression>)
```

This function returns the internal length of the data type, except for of character data types CHAR, VARCHAR, and CLOB, where the returned value reflects the length of the data in characters. Consider the following example:

```
SELECT
    LENGTH(1)   AS integer_length,
    LENGTH('ABCDEFG') AS string_length
FROM SYSIBM.SYSDUMMY1;
```

```
integer_length    string_length
---------------   -------------
4                       7
```

This function corresponds to the DATALENGTH() function in Microsoft SQL Server and Sybase ASE.

LOCATE() and POSSTR()

Syntax:

```
LOCATE(<char_expression1>, <char_expression2>[,<start_integer>])
LOCATE(<char_expression2>, <char_expression1>)
```

The LOCATE() function returns the position of the first occurrence of a substring (<char_expression1>) within a string (<char_expression2>). When no match is found, a zero will be returned. The return value is of the INTEGER data type. Consider the following example:

```
SELECT
    LOCATE('B', 'ABCDABCD'),
    LOCATE('B','ABCDABCD',3),
    LOCATE('B','ABCDABCD', 8)
FROM SYSIBM.SYSDUMMY1

1             2             3
-----------   -----------   -----------
2             6             0
```

When no starting position is specified, the very beginning of <char_expession2> is assumed. Only the position of the first occurrence of <char_expression1> is returned. When no match found, the function returns zero. The position is always calculated as absolute position (that is, from the start of the string).

IBM DB2 UDB also has the somewhat similar POSSTR() function. The order of arguments for this function is reversed in comparison to LOCATE(), and there is no way to specify the beginning point, as shown here:

```
SELECT
    POSSTR('ABCDABCD','B')
FROM SYSIBM.SYSDUMMY1

1
-----------
2
```

The equivalents of this function are Microsoft SQL Server and Sybase ASE's CHARINDEX() function.

LTRIM() and RTRIM()

Syntax:

```
LTRIM(<char_expression>)
RTRIM(<char_expression>)
```

Both functions return the characters of the argument with respectively leading or trailing blanks removed. The following example uses a string with both trailing and leading blanks added to it. To make things visible, asterisks are concatenated with the result from both sides.

```
SELECT
'*' || '   ABCD   ' || '*',
'*' || LTRIM('   ABCD   ') || '*',
'*' || RTRIM('   ABCD   ') || '*'
FROM SYSIBM.SYSDUMMY1


1                2                3
-----------      -----------      -----------
*   ABCD   *     *ABCD   *        *   ABCD*
```

These functions have their equivalent in Sybase ASE, Microsoft SQL Server, and PostgreSQL. Oracle uses the TRIM() function, which incorporates the functionality of both LTRIM() and RTRIM().

REPEAT()

Syntax:

```
REPEAT(<char_expression>,<times_integer>)
```

This function returns the string expression repeated <times_integer> number of times. Consider the following example:

```
SELECT
REPEAT('ABC', 3)  AS three_times
FROM SYSIBM.SYSDUMMY1


THREE_TIMES
-----------
ABCABCABC
```

There are direct equivalents of this function in Oracle, PostgreSQL, and MySQL. Microsoft SQL Server and Sybase ASE have the REPLICATE() function to perform essentially the same operation.

REPLACE()

Syntax:

```
REPLACE(<char_expresssion1>, <char_expression2>,<char_expression3>)
```

This function replaces all occurrences of <char_expression2> within <char_expression1> with <char_expression3>. Consider the following example:

```
SELECT
    REPLACE('ABCD','BC','*')
FROM SYSIBM.SYSDUMMY1


1
-----------
A*D
```

The REPLACE() function is case sensitive, and its return value is of the VARCHAR(4000) data type.

The function has direct equivalents in Microsoft SQL Server, Sybase ASE, PostgreSQL, and MySQL. Oracle 10g provides a new regular expression syntax that uses the REGEXP_REPLACE() function, which is equivalent.

SOUNDEX()

Syntax:

```
SOUNDEX(<char expression>)
```

This function returns a four-character code to evaluate the similarity between the sounds of two character expressions. SOUNDEX() evaluates an alpha string and returns a four-character code to find similar-sounding words or names. The first character of the code is the first character of <char_expression> and the second through fourth characters of the code are numbers. Vowels in <char_expression> are ignored unless they are the first letter of the string. The function could be used to specify search criteria for similar-sounding words, and is, of course, case insensitive. For example, the following query finds all three words to be similar sounding:

```
SELECT
    SOUNDEX('GOOD') AS upper_case,
    SOUNDEX('good') AS lower_case,
    SOUNDEX('GUT')  AS something_else
FROM SYSIBM.SYSDUMMY1

upper_case lower_case something_else
---------- ---------- --------------
G300       G300       G300
```

The SOUNDEX() function is implemented across all of the RDBMS implementations discussed in this book.

SPACE()

Syntax:

```
SPACE(<times_integer>)
```

The SPACE() function returns a string consisting of <times_integer> blanks. The returned result is of the VARCHAR(4000) data type. The following example produces a string of four blanks. The function LENGTH() is used to verify the length of the return result.

```
SELECT
    LENGTH(SPACE(4) ) AS four_blanks
FROM SYSIBM.SYSDUMMY1

FOUR_BLANKS
-----------
4
```

Only integer values are allowed as the input arguments.

The SPACE() function is also found in Microsoft SQL Server, Sybase ASE, and MySQL. Both Oracle and PostGreSQL provide similar functionality using the LPAD() and RPAD() functions.

SUBSTR()

Syntax:

```
SUBSTR(<char_expression>, <start_integer> [,<length_integer>])
```

The SUBSTR() function returns a part of the string <char_expression> starting from position <start_integer> for the length of <length_integer> characters. Consider the following example:

```
SELECT
    SUBSTR('ABCDEFG', 4) AS  four_chars,
    SUBSTR('ABCDEFG', 4, 4) AS  padded_four_chars
FROM SYSIBM.SYSDUMMY1
FOUR_CHARS          PADDED_FOUR_CHARS
----------          -----------------
DEFG                DEFG
```

The <length_integer> is an optional argument. If provided, and the requested length is less than the rest of the string, the result will be truncated to the exact number of characters. If the specified <length_integer> is greater than the remaining characters, an exception will be thrown (SQL0138N The second or third argument of the SUBSTR function is out of range.). The return value is of the VARCHAR data type; if the optional third argument is used, the returned result is a fixed-length CHAR.

The function is represented by SUBSTRING() function in Microsoft SQL Server, Sybase ASE, and PostgreSQL (the latter also accepting the shortened SUBSTR() syntax).

TRUNC() or TRUNCATE()

Syntax:

```
TRUNCATE(<numeric_value>,<decimal_places>)
TRUNC(<numeric_value>,<decimal_places>)
```

The TRUNCATE() function returns <numeric_value> truncated to <decimal_places> decimal places. The first argument can be any numeric value, and the second is an integer that can be positive, negative, or zero. When the <decimal_places> argument is positive, the function returns the <numeric_value> truncated on the right of the decimal point; with a negative <decimal_places> argument, the values truncated are on the left of the decimal point; and zero truncates to the INTEGER value. Consider the following example:

```
SELECT
    TRUNCATE(1234.56, 1)    AS  one_decimal,
    TRUNCATE(1234.56,0)     AS  no_decimals,
    TRUNCATE(1234.56,-1)    AS  left_side
FROM SYSIBM.SYSDUMMY1;

ONE__DECIMAL      NO_DECIMALS      LEFT_SIDE
----------------  ------------     ----------
1234.50           1234.00          1230.00
```

The last field needs some more explanation. The truncation specified with a negative `<decimal_places>` would truncate to the nearest 10, 100, 1,000, and so on, moving left for each digit added. Consider the following example:

```
SELECT
    TRUNCATE(1234.56, -1)    AS  tens
    TRUNCATE(1234.56,-2)     AS  hundreds,
    TRUNCATE(1234.56,-3)     AS  thousands,
FROM SYSIBM.SYSDUMMY1;
TENS           HUNDREDS      THOUSANDS
-----------    ------------  ----------
1230.00        1200.00       1000.00
```

Note that the number preserves the original precision.

The TRUNCATE() function is found in Oracle 9 (which also overloads it for the DATE data type). PostgreSQL uses the TRUNC() function, and MySQL implemented TRUNCATE(). Both Sybase ASE and Microsoft SQL Server use the ROUND() function (with appropriate arguments) to do the truncation.

Date and Time Functions

IBM DB2 UDB has a wealth of date- and time-related functions, probably more than any other of the RDBMS discussed in the book. The following table shows the date and time functions discussed in this section:

SQL Function	Input	Output	Description
DATE	`<expression>`	DATE	Returns a date from a value.
DAY	`<expression>`	INTEGER	Returns the day part of a value.
DAYNAME	`<expression>`	VARCHAR	Returns a mixed-case character string containing the name of the day for the day portion of the argument, based on the locale where the database was started.
DAYOFWEEK	`<expression>`	INTEGER	Returns the day of the week in the argument as an integer value in the range of 1–7, where 1 represents Sunday.
DAYOFWEEK_ISO	`<expression>`	INTEGER	Returns the day of the week in the argument as an integer value in the range of 1–7, where 1 represents Monday.
DAYOFYEAR	`<expression>`	INTEGER	Returns the day of the year in the argument as an integer value in the range of 1–366.

SQL Function	Input	Output	Description
DAYS	`<expression>`	INTEGER	Returns an integer representation of a date.
HOUR	`<expression>`	INTEGER	Returns the hour part of a value.
JULIAN_DAY	`<expression>`	INTEGER	Returns an integer value representing the number of days from January 1, 4713 B.C. (the start of the Julian date calendar) to the date value specified in the argument.
MICROSECOND	`<expression>`	INTEGER	Returns the microsecond part of a value.
MIDNIGHT_ SECONDS	`<expression>`	INTEGER	Returns an integer value that represents the number of seconds between midnight and the time value specified in the argument.
MINUTE	`<expression>`	INTEGER	Returns the minute part of a value.
MONTH	`<expression>`	INTEGER	Returns the month part of a value.
MONTHNAME	`<expression>`	VARCHAR	Returns a mixed-case character string containing the name of month for the month portion of the argument, based on the locale where the database was started.
SECOND	`<expression>`	INTEGER	Returns the seconds part of a time-value expression.
TIME	`<expression>`	TIME	Returns a time part from a value.
TIMESTAMP	`<datetime_expression>` `[,<time_expression>]`	TIMESTAMP	Returns a timestamp from a value or a pair of values.
TIMESTAMPDIFF	`<interval_identifier>,` `<timestam1> -` `<timestamp2>`	INTEGER	Returns an estimated number of intervals of the type defined by the first argument, based on the difference between two timestamps.

Table continued on following page

SQL Function	Input	Output	Description
TIMESTAMP_ FORMAT	`<timestamp_expression>, <format_string>`	TIMESTAMP	Returns a TIMESTAMP value from a compatible character input based on specific timestamp format.
TIMESTAMP_ISO	`<datetime_expression>`	TIMESTAMP	Returns an ISO timestamp value based on date, time, or timestamp argument.
WEEK	`<expression>`	INTEGER	Returns the week of the year of the argument as an integer value in the range of 1–54. The week starts with Sunday.
WEEK_ISO	`<expression>`	INTEGER	Returns the week of the year of the argument as an integer value in the range 1–53.
YEAR	`<expression>`	INTEGER	Returns the year part of a value.

DATE()

Syntax:

```
DATE(<expression>)
```

The DATE() function returns a date from a value. The expression could be a numeric or character one, and the rules of conversion are as follows:

❑ The numeric input is assumed to represent the number of days since the date 01-01-0001 (that is, January 1, 1); the fractional part of a numeric value is ignored.

❑ CHAR or VARCHAR input is assumed to be in format of *YYYYnnn* where *YYYY* is a year, and *nnn* represent number of days since the start of the year (that is, 001 through 366).

The actual conversion also takes the length of the supplied data into consideration. Here is an example that illustrates the points:

```
SELECT
    DATE('2004185')      AS  half_year,
    DATE(005)            AS long_time_ago,
    DATE('10-07-2004')   AS today,
    DATE(CURRENT DATE)   AS today2
FROM SYSIBM.SYSDUMMY1

HALF_YEAR       LONG_TIME_AGO     TODAY         TODAY2
----------      -------------     ----------    ----------
07/03/2004      01/05/0001        10/07/2004    12/08/2004
```

Note that the CHAR or VARCHAR values must be enclosed in quotes; otherwise, they will be interpreted as numeric input. For invalid input, an exception will be thrown. Input arguments are considered invalid if the value is out of range (for example, "2004-55-55"), or if the string representation cannot be translated into DATE.

The equivalent of the function in Oracle would be TO_DATE().

DAY()

Syntax:

```
DAY(<expression>)
```

The DAY() function returns a day of the month from a date value (or its equivalent, which could be converted into a date). Consider the following example:

```
SELECT
    DAY('2004-10-07')    AS  from_char,
    DAY(CURRENT DATE)    AS  from_date,
    CURRENT DATE         AS  today
 FROM SYSIBM.SYSDUMMY1;

 from_char       from_date       today
 ----------      ----------      --------
 7               11              07/11/2004
```

SQL Server and Sybase provide a similar function, MySQL has the DAYOFMONTH() function, and PostgreSQL provides the DATE_PART() function. The equivalent for Oracle is the EXTRACT() function.

DAYNAME()

Syntax:

```
DAYNAME(<expression>)
```

This function returns a mixed-case character string containing the name of the day for the day portion of the argument based on the locale where the database was started. Consider the following example:

```
SELECT
    DAYNAME('2004-10-07')    AS  from_char,
    DAYNAME(CURRENT DATE)    AS  from_date,
    CURRENT DATE             AS  today
FROM SYSIBM.SYSDUMMY1;

 from_char       from_date       today
 ----------      ----------      --------
 Thursday        Sunday          07/11/2004
```

MySQL provides a similar function called DAYNAME(). Similar functionality could be achieved in the other RDBMS implementations by using several different functions. An example of similar functionality in Oracle would be the following:

```
SELECT TO_CHAR( SYSDATE, 'DAY' ) as Today_Is
FROM dual;
Today_Is
------------
Tuesday
```

DAYOFWEEK()

Syntax:

```
DAYOFWEEK(<expression>)
```

The function returns the day of the week in the argument as an integer value in the range of 1–7, where 1 represents Sunday, as shown here:

```
SELECT
    DAYOFWEEK('2004-10-07')   AS  from_char,
    DAYOFWEEK(CURRENT DATE)   AS  from_date,
    CURRENT DATE              AS  today
FROM SYSIBM.SYSDUMMY1;

from_char       from_date       today
-----------     -----------     --------
5               1               07/11/2004
```

The value returned corresponds to the U.S. standard, where Sunday is considered the first day of week. In comparison, the DAYOFWEEK_ISO() function considers Monday to be the first day of the week.

Similar functionality can be achieved using the DATE_PART() function in SQL Server and Sysbase. MySQL has the DAYOFWEEK() function, while Oracle could use another version of the TO_CHAR() function.

DAYOFWEEK_ISO()

Syntax:

```
DAYOFWEEK_ISO(<expression>)
```

Returns the day of the week in the argument as an integer value in the range of 1–7, where 1 represents Monday. Consider the following example:

```
SELECT
    DAYOFWEEK_ISO('2004-10-07')   AS  from_char,
    DAYOFWEEK_ISO(CURRENT DATE)   AS  from_date,
    CURRENT DATE                  AS  today
FROM SYSIBM.SYSDUMMY1;

from_char       from_date       today
-----------     -----------     --------
4               7               07/11/2004
```

Similar functionality can be achieved using SQL Server and Sysbase's DATE_PART() function. MySQL has the DAYOFWEEK() function, while Oracle could use another version of the TO_CHAR() function.

DAYOFYEAR()

Syntax:

```
DAYOFYEAR(<expression>)
```

This function returns the day of the year in the argument as an integer value in the range of 1–366.

```
SELECT
    DAYOFYEAR('2004-10-07')    AS  from_char,
    DAYOFYEAR(CURRENT DATE)    AS  from_date,
    CURRENT DATE               AS  today
  FROM SYSIBM.SYSDUMMY1;

 from_char       from_date          today
 -----------     -----------        --------
 281             194                07/12/2004
```

Similar functionality to extract this can be found in all of the other RDBMS implementations discussed in this book.

DAYS()

Syntax:

```
DAYS(<expression>)
```

Returns an integer representation of a date — the number of days passed since 01-01-0001, inclusive. For example, you could find the number of days passed since January 1, 1 till today as follows:

```
SELECT
    DAYS(CURRENT DATE)        AS  days_since,
    CURRENT DATE          AS  today
FROM SYSIBM.SYSDUMMY1;

DAYS_SINCE       TODAY
-----------      ---------
731774           07/12/2004
```

Similar functionality can be achieved in the other RDBMS implementations discussed in this book by using a combination of functions.

HOUR()

Syntax:

```
HOUR(<expression>)
```

The HOUR() function returns the hour part of a time expression. The data must be compatible with the time format. Consider the following example:

```
SELECT
   HOUR('22:12:55')      AS  char_val,
   CURRENT TIME          AS  now,
   HOUR(CURRENT TIME)    AS  hour_val
FROM SYSIBM.SYSDUMMY1;

CHAR_VAL      NOW        HOUR_VAL
-----------   ---------  ----------
22            19:31:34   19
```

MySQL provides an HOUR() function that is similar. The closest equivalent in the other RDBMS implementations would be the EXTRACT() function found in Microsoft SQL Server, Oracle, and Sybase ASE.

The following table illustrates some of the basic date formats available on the IBM DB2 UDB platform:

Format	Template	Example
International Standard Organization (ISO); Japanese Industrial Standard Christian Era (JIS)	YYYY-MM-DD	2002-09-12
IBM USA Standard	MM/DD/YYYY	09/12/2002
IBM European Standard	DD.MM.YYYY	12.09.2002
Database Custom-Defined	Depends on the database country code	N/A

The following table displays the available time formats on the IBM DB2 UDB platform:

Format	Template	Example
International Standard Organization (ISO); Japanese Industrial Standard Christian Era (JIS)	HH.MM.SS	22.45.02
IBM USA Standard	HH:MM AM/PM	10.45 PM
IBM European Standard	HH.MM.SS	22.45.02
Database Custom-Defined	Depends on the database country code	N/A

JULIAN_DAY()

Syntax:

```
JULIAN_DAY(<expression>)
```

Returns an integer value representing the number of days from January 1, 4712 B.C. (the start of the Julian date calendar) to the date value specified in the argument. Consider the following example:

```
SELECT
    JULIAN_DAY('0001-01-01-00.00.00')  AS till_BC
FROM SYSIBM.SYSDUMMY1

till_BC
----------------
1721426
```

The Julian Day number system was invented by Dutch astronomer Joseph Justus Scaliger in 1583. In 1752, the English-speaking countries converted to the Gregorian calendar we are using now.

The closest functionality is provided by Oracle by using a version of the TO_CHAR() function. The Julian date can be calculated on most other RDBMS implementations by using simple date arithmetic.

MICROSECOND()

Syntax:

```
MICROSECOND(<expression>)
```

The MICROSECOND() function returns an integer value, which represents the number of microseconds in the time value specified in the argument. The input arguments could be of TIMESTAMP, TIME, or character data in date-time format. Consider the following example:

```
SELECT
    MICROSECOND(CURRENT TIMESTAMP) AS Micro_Seconds,
    CURRENT TIMESTAMP  AS now
FROM SYSIBM.SYSDUMMY1

Micro_Seconds          NOW
-------------          --------------------------
557001                 2004-07-12-21.54.24.557001
```

Similar functionality can be achieved by using the DATE_FORMAT() function in MYSQL or the EXTRACT() function in Oracle, SQL Server, and Sybase.

MIDNIGHT_SECONDS()

Syntax:

```
MIDNIGHT_SECONDS(<expression>)
```

The MIDNIGHT_SECONDS() function returns an integer value, which represents the number of seconds between midnight and the time value specified in the argument. The input arguments could be of TIMESTAMP, TIME, or character data in date-time format. Consider the following example:

```
SELECT
    MIDNIGHT_SECONDS(CURRENT TIMESTAMP) AS md_sec,
    CURRENT TIMESTAMP  AS now
FROM SYSIBM.SYSDUMMY1
```

```
MD_SEC       NOW
-----------  --------------------------
78864        2004-07-12-21.54.24.557001
```

The TIMESTAMP data type has its own peculiarities. Refer to Appendix C for more information on data types.

Similar functionality can be achieved in other RDBMS implementations through the use of date-time arithmetic operations.

MINUTE()

Syntax:

```
SELECT MINUTE(<expression>)
```

The MINUTE() function returns the minute part of a time value (or its equivalent, which could be converted into a time-compatible data type). Consider the following example:

```
SELECT
   MINUTE('22:56:19')    AS  from_char,
   MINUTE(CURRENT TIME)  AS  from_time,
   CURRENT TIME          AS  now
 FROM SYSIBM.SYSDUMMY1;


FROM_CHAR      FROM_TIME      NOW
-----------    -----------    --------
56             36             18:36:34
```

MySQL provides the same function. The equivalent could be the EXTRACT() function in Oracle, SQL Server, and Sybase.

MONTH()

Syntax:

```
SELECT MONTH(<expression>)
```

The MONTH() function returns the MONTH part of a date value (or its equivalent, which could be converted into a date-compatible data type). Consider the following example:

```
SELECT
   MONTH('2004-07-08')   AS  from_char,
   MONTH(CURRENT DATE)   AS  from_date,
   CURRENT DATE          AS  today
FROM SYSIBM.SYSDUMMY1;

FROM_CHAR      FROM_DATE      TODAY
-----------    -----------    -----------
7              7              07/12/2004
```

The equivalent could be the EXTRACT() function in MS SQL Server, Sybase, and Oracle. MySQL provides an equivalent Month() function.

MONTHNAME()

Syntax:

```
SELECT MONTHNAME(<expression>)
```

This function returns a mixed-case character string containing the name of month for the month portion of the argument, based on the locale where the database was started. The output format is VARCHAR(100).

```
SELECT
    MONTHNAME('2004-10-07')   AS   from_char,
    MONTHNAME(CURRENT DATE)   AS   from_date,
    CURRENT DATE              AS   today
 FROM SYSIBM.SYSDUMMY1;

from_char        from_date        today
-----------      -----------      --------
October          July             07/11/2004
```

This function also exists on the MySQL platform.

SECOND()

Syntax:

```
SECOND(<expression>)
```

The SECOND() function returns the seconds part of a time value (or its equivalent, which could be converted into a time-compatible data type). Consider the following example:

```
SELECT
    SECOND('22:56:19')      AS   from_char,
    SECOND(CURRENT TIME)    AS   from_time,
    CURRENT TIME            AS   now
FROM SYSIBM.SYSDUMMY1;

FROM_CHAR        FROM_TIME        NOW
-----------      -----------      --------
19               27               18:45:27
```

The equivalent could be the EXTRACT() function in MS SQL Server, Sybase, and Oracle. MySQL provides the same function on its platform.

TIME()

Syntax:

```
TIME(<expression>)
```

The `TIME()` function returns a time part from a value. The input argument is of the `TIME` data type, or character expressions of a compatible format; the return parameter is `TIME`. Consider the following example:

```
SELECT
    TIME('22:56:19')         AS  from_char,
    TIME(CURRENT TIMESTAMP)  AS  from_timestamp,
    CURRENT TIMESTAMP        AS  now
 FROM SYSIBM.SYSDUMMY1


 FROM_CHAR      FROM_TIME      NOW
 -----------    -----------    ---------------------------
 22:56:19       20:32:01       2004-07-12-20.32.01.968001
```

Similar functionality can be achieved using the `DATE_FORMAT()` function with the `Time` specifier in MySQL or the `EXTRACT()` function in Oracle, SQL Server, and Sybase.

TIMESTAMP()

Syntax:

```
TIMESTAMP(<datetime_expression> [,<time_expression>])
```

The `TIMESTAMP()` function returns a timestamp from a value or a pair of values. The `<datetime_expression>` could be any of the following: a timestamp value (or a character string of compatible format), or a 14-byte character expression in *YYYYMMDDHHMMSS* format. Consider the following example:

```
SELECT
    TIMESTAMP('2004-07-12-20.33.12')    AS from_char,
    TIMESTAMP('20040712203312')         AS from_format
FROM SYSIBM.SYSDUMMY1

FROM_CHAR                   FROM_FORMAT
--------------------------  --------------------------
2004-07-12-20.33.12.000000  2004-07-12-20.33.12.000000
```

When two arguments are supplied, the `<datetime_expression>` should be a date (or a character string of a compatible format), while the `<time_expression>` should be time (or a character string of compatible format). Consider the following example:

```
SELECT
    TIMESTAMP(CURRENT DATE,CURRENT TIME)  AS FROM_CURRENT,
    TIMESTAMP('2004-07-12','20.33.12')    AS FROM_TWO_CHAR
FROM SYSIBM.SYSDUMMY1

FROM_CURRENT                FROM_TWO_CHAR
--------------------------  --------------------------
2004-07-12-20.37.04.000000  2004-07-12-20.33.12.000000
```

Similar functionality can be achieved using the `DATE_FORMAT()` function with the Time specifier in MySQL or the `EXTRACT()` function in Oracle, SQL Server, and Sybase.

TIMESTAMPDIFF()

Syntax:

```
TIMESTAMPDIFF(<interval_identifier>, <timestam1> - <timestamp2>)
```

This function returns an estimated number of intervals of the type defined by the first argument, based on the difference between two timestamps converted into CHAR. The following table shows the different interval identifiers that can be used with this function:

Value	Description
1	Return difference in microseconds.
2	Return difference in seconds.
4	Return difference in minutes.
8	Return difference in hours.
16	Return difference in days.
32	Return difference in weeks.
64	Return difference in months.
128	Return difference in quarters.
256	Return difference in years.

The following example returns the number of hours between the CURRENT TIMESTAMP value and one converted from a character expression:

```
SELECT
    CHAR(CURRENT TIMESTAMP - TIMESTAMP('2004-07-10-19.43.10')),
    TIMESTAMPDIFF(8,CHAR(CURRENT TIMESTAMP - TIMESTAMP('2004-07-12-20.33.12')))
FROM SYSIBM.SYSDUMMY1


1                          2
----------------------     -----------
00000002154206.328001      63
```

You should use this function with caution because the values calculated might not be exact, but rather an estimate.

The notion of a timestamp in Microsoft SQL Server and Sybase is radically different than in IBM DB2 UDB, where it represents date and time data. In Microsoft SQL Server it is a version-controlling value for table rows, which is binary 8 bytes and bears no direct relation to date and/or time.

Similar functionality may be achieved in the SQL Server and Sybase implementations by using the DATEDIFF() function.

TIMESTAMP_FORMAT()

Syntax:

```
TIMESTAMP_FORMAT(<timestamp_expression>,<format_string>)
```

The `TIMESTAMP_FORMAT()` returns a `TIMESTAMP` value from a compatible character input based on specific timestamp format. The input parameter is in the *YYYY-MM-DD HH:MI:SS* format, as shown here:

```
SELECT
    TIMESTAMP_FORMAT('2004-07-12-20.33.12','YYYY-MM-DD HH:MI:SS')
FROM SYSIBM.SYSDUMMY1

1
---------------------------
2004-07-12-20.33.12.000000
```

Similar functionality can be achieved using the `DATE_FORMAT()` function in SQL Server and Sybase. Oracle can use the `TO_CHAR()` function, while MySQL has a special `TIME_FORMAT()` function. PostgreSQL does not provide similar functionality within its scope of built-in functions.

TIMESTAMP_ISO()

Syntax:

```
TIMESTAMP_ISO(<datetime_expression>)
```

Returns an ISO timestamp value based on date, time, or timestamp argument in ISO format (*YYYY-MM-DD HH:MI:SS:NNNNNN*) converted from the IBM internal format. Consider the following example:

```
SELECT
    TIMESTAMP_ISO(CURRENT DATE),
    TIMESTAMP_ISO(CURRENT TIME)
FROM SYSIBM.SYSDUMMY1

1                             2
---------------------------   ---------------------------------
2004-07-12-00.00.00.000000    2004-07-12-21.19.10.000000
```

If the input argument is supplied as `TIME`, the current date is also inserted as part of the return value.

Similar functionality can be gained through the use of the various date-time functions in the other RDBMS implementations, although none of them specifically are used to convert from the IBM internal format.

WEEK()

Syntax:

```
WEEK(<expression>)
```

The WEEK() function returns the week part of a date value (or its equivalent, which could be converted into a date-compatible data type). Both the first and the last week might not contain a full seven days. The week starts with Sunday, or the first day of the year. Consider the following example:

```
SELECT
    WEEK('2000-01-01')  AS  from_char,
    WEEK(CURRENT DATE)  AS  from_date,
    CURRENT DATE            AS  today
FROM SYSIBM.SYSDUMMY1;

FROM_CHAR        FROM_DATE          TODAY
-----------      -----------        -----------
1                29                 07/12/2004
```

Similar functionality can be gained in SQL Server and Sybase by using the DATEPART() function. Oracle users can benefit from the use of the TRUNC() function. MySQL and PostgreSQL do not have a directly correlated function.

WEEK_ISO()

Syntax:

```
WEEK_ISO(<expression>)
```

This function returns the week of the year of the argument as an integer value in the range 1–53. An ISO week begins on Monday, and does not have an exact ending or start at the exact end of the year. By definition, the first week is the very first week after January 1 that contains a Thursday. Consider the following example:

```
SELECT
    WEEK_ISO('2000-01-01')  AS  from_char,
    WEEK_ISO(CURRENT DATE)  AS  from_date,
    CURRENT DATE            AS  today
 FROM SYSIBM.SYSDUMMY1;

FROM_CHAR        FROM_DATE          TODAY
-----------      -----------        -----------
52               29                 07/12/2004
```

Similar functionality can be gained in SQL Server and Sybase by using the DATEPART() function in conjunction with the @@DATEFIRST variable. Oracle users can benefit from the use of the TRUNC() function. MySQL and PostgreSQL do not have a directly correlated function.

YEAR()

Syntax:

```
YEAR(<expression>)
```

Returns the year part of a value in the range of 0001 to 9999. The input types are DATE or TIMESTASMP (or its equivalent, which could be converted into a date-compatible data type). Consider the following example:

```
SELECT
   YEAR('2000-01-01')     AS  from_char,
   YEAR(CURRENT DATE)     AS  from_date,
   CURRENT DATE           AS  today
 FROM SYSIBM.SYSDUMMY1;

FROM_CHAR        FROM_DATE           TODAY
-----------      -----------         -----------
2000             2004                07/12/2004
```

The equivalent could be the EXTRACT() function in Microsoft SQL Server, Oracle, and Sybase. MySQL provides an equivalent version.

Conversion Functions

The conversion functions of the IBM DB2 implementation are used in instances where explicit conversion of data types is needed. The following table details the conversion functions available on the IBM DB2 UDB platform:

SQL Function	Input	Output	Description
DEC[IMAL]	<expression> [,<precision> [,<scale> [,<decimal_char>]]])	DECIMAL	Returns a decimal representation of a number, a character string representation of a decimal number, or a character string representation of an integer number.
HEX	<expression>	HEX	Returns a hexadecimal representation of a value as a character string.
DOUBLE[_PRECISION]	<expression>	FLOAT	Returns a floating-point number corresponding to a number (if the argument is a numeric expression character string) or a representation of a number (if the argument is a string expression).
INT[EGER]	<expression>	INTEGER	Returns an integer representation of a number or character string in the form of an integer constant.

SQL Function	Input	Output	Description
SMALLINT	<expression>	SMALLINT	Returns a small integer representation of a number or character string in the form of a small integer constant.
TRANSLATE	<expression> [,<to_string>, <from_string> [,<pad_char>]]	<expression>	Replaces all occurrences of string1 within string2 with string3.
VARCHAR	<expression> [,<output_length>]	VARCHAR	Returns a varying-length character string representation of a character string, datetime value, or graphic string.

DEC or DECIMAL

Syntax:

```
DEC[IMAL](<numeric_expression> [,<precision> [,scale]])
    DEC[IMAL](<char_expression> [,<precision> [,<scale>[,<decimal_char>]]])
```

This function returns a decimal representation of a number, a character string representation of a decimal number, or a character string representation of an integer number. The <numeric_expression> could be of any numeric data type; the <precision> value is an INTEGER in the range of 1 to 31 (The exact uppermost value depends on the numeric data type being converted into DECIMAL. For floating-point numbers and decimals, the maximum value is 15, for BIGINT it is 19, for INTEGER it is 11, and SMALLINT goes up to 5.) The value for <scale> matches that for <precision>, with the default being zero. Consider the following example:

```
SELECT
    DEC(1234),
    DEC(1234,6,2),
    DEC('1234#99', 6, 2, '#')
FROM SYSIBM.SYSDUMMY1;

1               2               3
-----------     -----------     -----------
1234            1234.00         1234.99
```

Conversion of the character value into DECIMAL requires a few more restrictions:

❑   An expression for the <char_expression> cannot exceed 4,000 characters (that is, no CLOB or LONG VARCHAR data types are accepted).

❑   All leading and trailing blanks will be trimmed from the expression.

❏ An expression will be converted into a code page to match the code page of the specified decimal character.

❏ As with <numeric_expression>, the <precision> value could range from 1 to 31, with a default of 15; the <scale> value matches the <precision> value, with a default of 0.

❏ The specified decimal character must be a single-byte character and cannot appear more than once within the <char_expression>; it cannot be blank, minus ("-"), or plus ("+").

An error will occur if the number of significant decimal digits required to represent the whole part of the number is greater than <precision> – <scale>.

Similar functionality can be found using the CAST() function in Oracle, SQL Server, and Sybase.

HEX()

Syntax:

```
HEX(<expression>)
```

This function returns a hexadecimal representation of a value as a character string. You can feed virtually any data type into the function and get the HEX out of it. Consider the following example:

```
SELECT
    HEX('string')    AS from_char,
    HEX(1234)        AS from_number,
    HEX(CURRENT DATE)   AS from_date
FROM SYSIBM.SYSDUMMY1

FROM_CHAR        FROM_NUMBER      FROM_DATE
-------------    -----------      -----------
737472696E67     D2040000         20040713
```

The Microsoft SQL Server's ENCRYPT() function very closely resembles the functionality of the HEX function.

DOUBLE or DOUBLE_PRECISION

Syntax:

```
DOUBLE[_PRECISION](<expression>)
```

The function returns a floating-point number corresponding to a number (if the argument is a numeric expression), character string, or a representation of a number (if the argument is a string expression). Consider the following example:

```
SELECT
    DOUBLE(1234),
    DOUBLE('    1234    ')
FROM SYSIBM.SYSDUMMY1;
```

```
    1                              2
--------------------         --------------------
+1.23400000000000E+003        +1.23400000000000E+003
```

In the SYSIBM schema, FLOAT and DOUBLE_PRECISION could be used as synonyms for the function, though an overloaded version that accepts character data belongs to the SYSFUN schema.

Similar functionality can be found using the CAST() function in Oracle, SQL Server, and Sybase.

INT() or INTEGER() and SMALLINT()

Syntax:

```
INT[EGER](<expression>)
```

This function returns an integer representation of a number or character string in the form of an integer constant. For numeric equivalents containing a decimal point, the result is an integer part of the number; for character input, the presence of a decimal point result in the following exception: SQL0420N Invalid character found in a character string argument of the function 'INTEGER'. SQLSTATE= 22018. Consider the following example:

```
SELECT
    INT(4.99)          AS from_char,
    INT('+123')        AS from_number,
    INT(CURRENT DATE)  AS from_date
FROM SYSIBM.SYSDUMMY1


FROM_CHAR          FROM_NUMBER      FROM_DATE
-------------      -----------      -----------
4                  123              20040713
```

The SMALLINT() function follows the same rules, but the range of convertible values is restricted by the data type.

Similar functionality can be found using the CAST() function in Oracle, SQL Server, and Sybase.

TRANSLATE()

Syntax:

```
TRANSLATE(<expression> [,<to_string>,<from_string>[,<pad_char>]])
```

This function replaces all occurrences of <to_string> within <expression> translated into <from_string> and can include a padding character for nonconverted characters. This is a smart version of the REPLACE() function. It uses pattern matching to find and replace characters within a string. The acceptable <char_expression> data types are CHAR, VARCHAR, GRAPHIC, and VARGRAPHIC.

The following example query replaces all numbers (from 0 through 9) with 0, and all letters (except "K") with an asterisk ("*"). The letter "K" is replaced with "X":

```
SELECT
    TRANSLATE('2KRW229'
              ,'0000000000**********X***************'
              ,'0123456789ABCDEFGHIJKLMNOPQRSTUVWXYZ'
              ) translate_example
FROM SYSIBM.SYSDUMMY1;

translate_example
--------------------
0X**000
```

The returned result is of the same data type and code page as `<char_expression>`; if no translation for the specified character exists, the character will be replaced with the `<pad_char>` specified in the function's argument. (If it is omitted, a double-byte blank will be used instead.)

When only one input parameter (`<char_expression>`) is specified, the returned result will be in uppercase for single-byte characters; multibyte characters will remain unchanged.

The `TRANSLATE()` function is found in Oracle (watch for order of arguments). PostGreSQL has a similar function, but neither Microsoft SQL Server nor Sybase have it.

VARCHAR()

Syntax:

```
VARCHAR(<expression> [,<output_length>])
```

The function `VARCHAR()` returns a varying-length character string representation of a character string, datetime value, or graphic string. The optional `<output_length>` specifies the resulting length of the converted expression. If it is omitted, the returned parameter length will be that of the expression, up to a maximum of 4,000. Both leading and trailing blanks are taken into consideration as a part of the expression. Consider the following example:

```
SELECT
    VARCHAR('simple string')    AS from_char,
    VARCHAR('simple string',5)  AS five_varchar,
    VARCHAR(CURRENT DATE)       AS from_date
FROM SYSIBM.SYSDUMMY1

FROM_CHAR        FIVE_VARCHAR    FROM_DATE
-------------    ------------    -----------
simple string    simple          07/14/2004
```

In the case where the requested length of the returned `VARCHAR` data is less than `<expression>`, the data will be truncated, and the following warning will be issued: '`SQL0445W Value "<expression>"` `has been truncated. SQLSTATE=01004`'

Similar functionality can be found using the `CAST()` function in Oracle, SQL Server, and Sybase.

Security Functions

The IBM DB2 UDB platform also contains a limited number of security functions. These functions mainly deal with aspects associated with data encryption and decryption. Most of these functions are in limited use because most have been replaced with custom encryption methods. The following table details the various security functions available on the IBM DB2 platform:

SQL Function	Input	Output	Description
DECRYPT_BIN	<encrypted_data> [,<password>]	CLOB, BLOB	Returns a value that is the result of decrypting encrypted data.
DECRYPT_CHAR	<encrypted_data> [,<password>]	CHAR, VARCHAR	Returns a value that is the result of decrypting encrypted data.
ENCRYPT	<data_to_encrypt> [,<password> [,<hint>]]	Binary VARCHAR	Returns a value that is the result of encrypting a data-string expression.
GETHINT	<encrypted_data>	CHAR, VARCHAR	Returns the password hint if one is found in the encrypted data.

DECRYPT_BIN()

Syntax:

```
DECRYPT_BIN(<encrypted_data> [,<password>])
```

This function returns a value that is the result of decrypting encrypted data (that is, results of the ENCRYPT() function, which is discussed later in this chapter). The data type for the input and output arguments can be the binary data types BLOB or CLOB. If the password is omitted, a special register must be set to supply it.

```
create table binary_emp (MyPassword varchar(124) for bit data);
set encryption password = 'password';

insert into binary_emp (MyPassword) values(encrypt(x'4269672042697264'));
insert into binary_emp (MyPassword) values(encrypt(x'536D616C6C20446F67'));
insert into binary_emp (MyPassword) values(encrypt(x'477265656E2046726F67'));
select decrypt_bin(MyPassword) from binary_emp;

1
------------------
x'4269672042697264'x'536D616C6C20446F67'
x'477265656E2046726F67'
```

See the ENCRYPT() function later in this chapter for details.

The only equivalent to a decryption-type function in the RDBMS implementations discussed in this book is PostgreSQL's DECODE() function.

DECRYPT_CHAR()

Syntax:

```
DECRYPT_CHAR(<encrypted_data> [,<password>]))
```

This returns a value that is the result of decrypting encrypted data (that is, results of the ENCRYPT() function, which is discussed later in this chapter). The data type for the input arguments can be of any character type. If the password is omitted, a special register must be set to supply it. Consider the following example, which demonstrates the use of the DECRYPT_CHAR() function:

```
create table emp (MyPassword varchar(124) for bit data);
set encryption password = 'password';

insert into emp (MyPassword) values(encrypt('Big Bird'));
insert into emp (MyPassword) values(encrypt('Small Dog'));
insert into emp (MyPassword) values(encrypt('Green Frog'));
select decrypt_char(MyPassword) from emp;


1
------------Big BirdSmall DogGreen Frog
```

The only equivalent to a decryption-type function in the RDBMS implementations discussed in this book is PostgreSQL's DECODE() function.

ENCRYPT()

Syntax:

```
ENCRYPT(<data_to_encrypt>[,<password> [,<hint>]])
```

The ENCRYPT() function returns a value that is the result of encrypting a data-string expression. The input parameters are of the CHAR or VARCHAR data types, and the return result is binary VARCHAR. Consider the following example:

```
SELECT
    ENCRYPT('some data','password') as no_hint
FROM SYSIBM.SYSDUMMY1

NO_HINT
-------------------------------------------------------------------
x'00728E09E404A2D573616D6520776F72647246740D2B6C9DD4EE1699A172AEC1EC'
```

Both password and hint values are optional. Nevertheless, to function properly without a password, the password value must be set using the SET ENCRYPTION PASSWORD statement. Valid encryption passwords must be within a range of no less than 6 bytes and no greater than 127 bytes; the valid hint value must not exceed 32 bytes. The maximum value that could be encrypted using the function is 32,633 bytes.

PostgreSQL has an ENCODE() function available. SQL Server has an ENCRYPT() function, but interestingly enough there is not an equivalent DECRYPT() function.

GETHINT()

Syntax:

```
GETHINT(<encrypted_data>)
```

The GETHINT() function returns the password hint if one is found in the encrypted data. Using the previous example, you feed the output of the ENCRYPT() function into the GETHINT() function as follows:

```
SELECT
    GETHINT(ENCRYPT('some data','password','same')) as hint
FROM SYSIBM.SYSDUMMY1

HINT
---------
Same
```

This function is unique to IBM DB2 UDB. None of the other RDBMS implementations discussed in this book have an equivalent function.

IBM DB2 UDB Special Registers

The *special registers* in IBM DB2 UDB are defined as storage areas allocated for an application process by the database manager. These areas are used to store information. The equivalent of IBM DB2 UDB's special registers are unary (niladic) functions, which are found in all other databases. The main difference is that special registers are represented by one, two, or more separate words, while unary functions are a single word (sometimes requiring parentheses to signify a function as opposed to a keyword; found in Microsoft SQL Server and Sybase ASE). The following table provides a listing of the special registers on the IBM DB2 UDB platform, followed by brief explanations of what we deem to be the most important ones in the context of this book:

Special registers are in the database code page.

SQL Function	Description
CURRENT DATE	Returns the date of the server at the time the SQL statement that contains it is executed.
CURRENT DEFAULT TRANSFORM GROUP	Returns a VARCHAR(18) value that identifies the name of the transform group used by dynamic SQL statements for exchanging user-defined structured type values with host programs.
CURRENT DEGREE	Returns the degree of intra-partition parallelism for the execution of dynamic SQL statements.
CURRENT EXPLAIN MODE	Returns a VARCHAR(254) value that controls the behavior of the Explain facility with respect to eligible dynamic SQL statements.
CURRENT EXPLAIN SNAPSHOT	Returns a CHAR(8) value that controls the behavior of the Explain snapshot facility.

Table continued on following page

SQL Function	Description
CURRENT NODE	Returns an INTEGER value that identifies the coordinator node number (the partition to which an application connects). For a database not configured for partitioning, it returns zero.
CURRENT PATH	Returns a VARCHAR(254) value that identifies the *SQL path* to be used to resolve function references and data type references that are used in dynamically prepared SQL statements. SET CURRENT PATH is used to set the value.
CURRENT QUERY OPTIMIZATION	Returns an INTEGER value that controls the class of query optimization performed by the database manager when binding dynamic SQL statements. The corresponding statement SET CURRENT QUERY OPTIMIZATION is used to set the value.
CURRENT REFRESH AGE	Returns a timestamp duration value of a data type of DECIMAL(20,6). It specifies maximum duration, since a REFRESH TABLE statement has been processed on a REFRESH DEFERRED summary table such that the summary table can be used to optimize the processing of a query. SET CURRENT REFRESH AGE is used to set the value.
CURRENT SCHEMA	Returns a VARCHAR(128) value that identifies the schema name used to qualify unqualified database object references in a SQL statement. Initial value is the authorization ID of the current session user. SET CURRENT SCHEMA is used to set or change the value.
CURRENT SERVER	Returns a VARCHAR(18) value that is the name of the RDBMS server where database is running. It is *not* the name of the computer.
CURRENT TIME	Returns the time of the server at the time the SQL statement that contains it is executed.
CURRENT TIMESTAMP	Returns the current timestamp of the server read at the moment the query was executed.
CURRENT TIMEZONE	Returns the difference between UTC (Coordinated Universal Time) and the local time at the application server. The difference is represented by a decimal number in which the first two digits are the number of hours, the next two digits are the number of minutes, and the last two digits are the number of seconds.
USER	Returns the run-time authorization ID passed to the database manager when an application starts on a database. The data type of the register is VARCHAR(128).

CURRENT DATE

Syntax:

```
CURRENT DATE
```

The CURRENT DATE special register returns the date of the server at the time the SQL statement that contains it is executed. Consider the following example:

```
SELECT
   CURRENT DATE  as CUR_DATE
FROM SYSIBM.SYSDUMMY1

CUR_DATE
----------------------
06/24/2004
```

The date is that of the server, not the client who submits the query. For a single-batch query, the reading also occurs once, meaning that all returned values from the query will be identical. While it does not seem significant for a date, it has clear implications when the register read is CURRENT TIME or CURRENT TIMESTAMP.

In federated systems, CURRENT DATE can be used in a query intended for data sources. When the query is completed, the date returned will be that of the federated server, not from the data sources.

CURRENT DEFAULT TRANSFORM GROUP

Syntax:

```
CURRENT DEFAULT TRANSFORM GROUP
```

The CURRENT DEFAULT TRANSFORM GROUP register returns the name of the transform group used by dynamic SQL statements for exchanging user-defined structured type values with host programs. Consider the following example:

```
SELECT CURRENT DEFAULT TRANSFORM GROUP  as GROUP FROM SYSIBM.SYSDUMMY1
GROUP                  ------------------
```

CURRENT DEGREE

Syntax:

```
CURRENT DEGREE
```

The CURRENT DEGREE register returns the degree of intra-partition parallelism for the execution of dynamic SQL statements. Consider the following example:

```
SELECT CURRENT DEGREE  as DEGREE FROM SYSIBM.SYSDUMMY1
DEGREE
-------
1
```

CURRENT EXPLAIN MODE

Syntax:

```
CURRENT EXPLAIN MODE
```

The CURRENT EXPLAIN MODE special register is a VARCHAR(254) that sets the behavior for the Explain facility, at least with respect to any dynamic SQL statements. The Explain facility is what inserts and updates information into the Explain tables. There are a few possible values for the register, including YES, EXPLAIN, NO, REOPT, RECOMMEND 7 INDEXES, and EVALUATE INDEXES. The following example demonstrates using the register to find out the current mode of the database:

```
SELECT CURRENT EXPLAIN MODE FROM SYSIBM.SYSDUMMY1

-------------
NO
```

This register returns information about the current state of the Explain facility in the IBM DB2 UDB database. The Explain facility generates the query execution plan information, and inserts it into system tables. The initial (default) is NO. The allowable values for the register are shown in the following table:

Value	Description
YES	Enables the Explain facility and causes Explain information for a dynamic SQL statement to be captured when the statement is compiled.
NO	Disables the Explain facility (default).
EXPLAIN	Enables the Explain facility, like YES. However, the dynamic statements are not executed.
RECOMMEND INDEXES	For each dynamic query, a set of indexes is recommended. The ADVISE_INDEX table is populated with the set of indexes.
EVALUATE INDEXES	Dynamic queries are explained as if the recommended indexes existed. The indexes are picked up from the ADVISE_INDEX table.

Its value can be changed by the SET CURRENT EXPLAIN MODE statement.

CURRENT EXPLAIN SNAPSHOT

Syntax:

```
CURRENT EXPLAIN SNAPSHOT
```

The CURRENT EXPLAIN SNAPSHOT register is used to return the value that controls the behavior of the Explain snapshot facility. Consider the following example:

```
SELECT CURRENT EXPLAIN SNAPSHOT  as SNAPSHOT FROM SYSIBM.SYSDUMMY1
SNAPSHOT--------NO
```

CURRENT ISOLATION

Syntax:

```
CURRENT ISOLATION
```

The CURRENT ISOLATION special register is a CHAR(2) variable that holds the current isolation level of any dynamic SQL statements currently running in the session. There are five separate values that the register can be set to:

- ❑ **(blanks)** — Not set
- ❑ **UR** — Uncommitted Read
- ❑ **CS** — Cursor Stability
- ❑ **RR** — Repeatable Read
- ❑ **RS** — Read Stability

The following example demonstrates checking the current isolation level on the user's database:

```
SELECT CURRENT ISOLATION FROM SYSIBM.SYSDUMMY1
1
--------
```

CURRENT NODE

Syntax:

```
CURRENT NODE
```

The CURRENT NODE register returns an integer that represents the partition to which the application connects. If the database in question is not configured for partitioning, then the register will return 0. Consider the following example:

```
SELECT CURRENT NODE  as Node FROM SYSIBM.SYSDUMMY1
NODE
-----------0
```

CURRENT PATH

Syntax:

```
CURRENT PATH
```

The CURRENT PATH register identifies the SQL path that is to be used for resolving function and datatype references for dynamic SQL statements. The register contains a comma-delimited list of schema names enclosed by double quotation marks that represent the path to be taken and the order in which to take it. The following example displays the default CURRENT PATH value:

```
SELECT CURRENT PATH FROM SYSIBM.SYSDUMMY1

1
------------------------------------------------------------------
"SYSIBM","SYSFUN","SYSPROC","DB2ADMIN"
```

The SYSIBM schema does not need to be specified. If it is not included in the SQL path, it is implicitly assumed as the first schema.

CURRENT QUERY OPTIMIZATION

Syntax:

```
CURRENT QUERY OPTIMIZATION
```

The CURRENT QUERY OPTIMIZATION register returns an integer value that reflects the class of query optimization performed by the database manager when binding dynamic SQL statements. Consider the following example:

```
SELECT
    CURRENT QUERY OPTIMIZATION as OPTIMIZATION
FROM SYSIBM.SYSDUMMY1
OPTIMIZATION
-----------
5
```

SET CURRENT QUERY OPTIMIZATION is used to set the value.

CURRENT REFRESH AGE

Syntax:

```
CURRENT REFRESH AGE
```

The CURRENT REFRESH AGE register is used to return the maximum duration since a REFRESH_TABLE statement has been processed on a REFRESH_DEFERRED summary table so that the summary table can be used to optimize the processing of a query. Consider the following example:

```
SELECT
    CURRENT REFRESH AGE as AGE
FROM SYSIBM.SYSDUMMY1
AGE
----------------------0.000000
```

SET CURRENT REFRESH AGE is used to set the value.

CURRENT SCHEMA

Syntax:

```
CURRENT SCHEMA
```

The CURRENT SCHEMA register contains the value that identifies the schema name used to qualify any dynamic SQL queries. Initially, this value is the authorization ID of the current session user. The following query demonstrates the usage of the register:

```
SELECT CURRENT SCHEMA FROM SYSIBM.SYSDUMMY1

1
----------
DB2ADMIN
```

CURRENT SERVER

Syntax:

```
CURRENT SERVER
```

The CURRENT SERVER register is used to return the name of the current RDBMS server on which the database is running. This should not be confused with the name of the computer. Consider the following example:

```
SELECT
    CURRENT SERVER as SERVER
FROM SYSIBM.SYSDUMMY1
SERVER
------------------
SAMPLE
```

CURRENT TIME

Syntax:

```
CURRENT TIME
```

The CURRENT TIME register contains the current time of the server read at the moment the query was executed. Consider the following example:

```
SELECT
    CURRENT TIME  as CUR_TIME
FROM SYSIBM.SYSDUMMY1

CUR_TIME
----------------------
19:47:49
```

Again, using more than one CURRENT TIME statement would yield identical values for each, because the register is read only once during the query execution.

The time is that of the server, not the client who submits the query. In federated systems, CURRENT TIME can be used in a query intended for data sources. When the query is completed, the time returned will be that of the federated server, not the data sources.

CURRENT TIMESTAMP

Syntax:

```
CURRENT TIMESTAMP
```

This register contains the current timestamp of the server read at the moment the query was executed. Having more than one CURRENT TIMESTAMP statement would yield identical values for them, because the register is read only once during the query execution (and this is the place where you could actually see it). Consider the following example:

```
SELECT
    CURRENT TIMESTAMP  as ONE,
    CURRENT TIMESTAMP  as TWO
FROM SYSIBM.SYSDUMMY1

ONE                        TWO
-------------------------  -------------------------
2004-06-24-19.54.11.953000 2004-06-24-19.54.11.953000
```

CURRENT TIMEZONE

Syntax:

```
CURRENT TIMEZONE
```

The CURRENT TIMEZONE register specifies the difference between UTC (Coordinated Universal Time) and local time at the application server. The difference is represented by a decimal number in which the first two digits are the number of hours, the next two digits are the number of minutes, and the last two digits are the number of seconds. The hour range is between 24 and –24, exclusive. Subtracting CURRENT TIMEZONE from a local time converts that local time to UTC. The time is calculated from the operating system time at the moment the SQL statement is executed. Consider the following example:

```
SELECT
    CURRENT TIMEZONE  as tz,
    CURRENT TIMESTAMP as LOCAL,
    CURRENT TIMESTAMP - CURRENT TIMEZONE  as UTC
FROM SYSIBM.SYSDUMMY1

TZ       LOCAL                      UTC
-------- -------------------------  -------------------------
-70000   2004-06-26-16.07.58.953000 2004-06-26-23.07.58.953000
```

The CURRENT TIMEZONE special register can be used in arithmetic date operations where any expression returning the DECIMAL(6,0) data type is used.

The CURRENT TIMEZONE value is determined from C run-time functions, and is subject to the particular library implementations for the specific platform.

SESSION_USER

Syntax:

```
SESSION_USER
```

The SESSION_USER register is a synonym for the USER register. Thus, it holds the authorization ID of the current session user, which was used to connect to the database. The following example demonstrates the use of the register:

```
SELECT SESSION_USER FROM SYSIBM.SYSDUMMY1

1
```

```
--------------
DB2ADMIN
```

USER

Syntax:

```
USER
```

The USER register is used to return the run-time authorization ID passed to the database manager when an application starts on a database. The following example demonstrates the use of the register:

```
SELECT
    USER  as USER
FROM SYSIBM.SYSDUMMY1
USER
--------------
DB2ADMIN
```

Miscellaneous Functions

Miscellaneous functions are those built-in functions that do not necessarily fall neatly into one of the other groups. Most are used to compensate for the nonprocedural nature of the ANSI SQL standard. The following table details the various miscellaneous functions available on the IBM DB2 platform.

SQL Function	Input	Output	Description
COALESCE	<list_of_ expressions>	<expression>	Returns the first argument that is not NULL in the list.
DIGITS	<numeric_ expression>	VARCHAR	Returns a character-string representation of a number.
GENERATE_ UNIQUE	None	CHAR(13)	Returns a bit-data character string 13 bytes long (CHAR(13) FOR BIT DATA) that is unique when compared to any other execution of the same function.
NULLIF	<expression1>, <expression2>	<expression>	Returns a NULL value if the arguments are equal; otherwise, it returns the value of the first argument.
RAND	[seed_integer]	FLOAT	Returns a random floating-point value between 0 and 1 using the argument as the optional seed value.
TABLE_NAME	<char_alias>, <alias_schema>	<char_ expression>	Returns the unqualified name of the object found after any alias chains have been resolved.

Table continued on following page

SQL Function	Input	Output	Description
TYPE_ID	`<reference_ expression>`	`INTEGER`	Returns the internal type identifier of the dynamic data type of the expression.
TYPE_NAME	`<reference_ expression>`	`VARCHAR(18)`	Returns the unqualified name of the dynamic data type of the expression.
VALUE	`<list_of_ xpressions>`	`<expression>`	Returns the first argument that is not NULL.

COALESCE() and VALUE()

Syntax:

```
COALESCE(<list_of_expressions>)
     VALUE(<list_of_expressions>)
```

Both of these functions return the first argument that is not NULL on the list. The COALESCE() function is a SQL standard implemented by virtually every RDBMS in existence, while the VALUE() function is a synonym for the former and is a legacy from the IBM mainframe days. The functions will not accept literal values, so a table must be constructed and populated to illustrate them, as shown here:

```
CREATE TABLE tblTEST
(
   field1 VARCHAR(10),
   field2 INT
)

INSERT INTO tblTEST (field1) VALUES ('test')
INSERT INTO tblTEST( field2) VALUES (1)

SELECT
   field1,
   field2,
   COALESCE(field1,'NULL'),
   COALESCE(field2,0)
FROM tblTEST

FIELD1     FIELD2     3          4
---------- ---------- ---------- ---------
test       -          test       0
```

As you can see, the NULL values were tested for the first record, and FIELD1 was found to contain a string, "test"; field FIELD2 has NULL, so the next non-NULL value on the list was returned — zero. For the second record, the situation was reversed. FIELD1 had a NULL value. Therefore, the second argument on the list (a string "NULL") was returned for FIELD1; FIELD2 has a non-NULL value of 1.

The function has its direct equivalents in Oracle, Sybase ASE, Microsoft SQL Server, MySQL, and PostgreSQL.

DIGITS()

Syntax:

```
SELECT DIGITS(<numeric_expression>)
```

This function returns a character-string representation of a number, translating the INTEGER or DECIMAL numbers into a leading zeroes–padded integer value. Consider the following example:

```
SELECT
    DIGITS(1)        AS one,
    DIGITS(100)      AS hundred,
    DIGITS(-2)       AS minus2,
    DIGITS(12.34)    AS decimal_val
FROM tblTEST

ONE           HUNDRED        MINUS2         DECIMAL_VAL
----------    -----------    -----------    ------------
0000000001    0000000100     0000000002     1234
```

The actual number of the digits is determined by the IBM DB2 UDB configuration. Note that the +/- signature of the number is lost with the translation, and converted decimal values are not padded.

Similar functionality can be found in Oracle, SQL Server, and Sybase by using the CAST() function, while the PostgreSQL implementation provides the CONVERT() function.

GENERATE_UNIQUE()

Syntax:

```
SELECT GENERATE_UNIQUE()
```

Returns a bit-data character string 13 bytes long (CHAR(13) FOR BIT DATA) that is unique when compared to any other execution of the same function (that is, reasonably unique). Since it uses a computer's clock as one of the ingredients, resetting the clock could eventually produce duplicate values. Consider the following example:

```
SELECT
    GENERATE_UNIQUE(),
    GENERATE_UNIQUE()
FROM SYSIBM.SYSDUMMY1

1                                 2
------------------------------    -----------------------------
x'20040713233425061587000000'    x'20040713233425061577000000'
```

A closer look at the returned values shows a striking resemblance to TIMESTAMP, which, indeed, composes the largest part of the value.

Microsoft SQL Server has the NEWID() function, which could serve as equivalent to GENERATE_UNIQUE().

NULLIF()

Syntax:

```
NULLIF(<expression1>,<expression2>)
```

Returns a NULL value if the arguments are equal; otherwise it returns the value of the first argument. Consider the following example:

```
SELECT
    NULLIF(1,1)  AS equal,
    NULLIF(1,2)       AS non_equal,
    NULLIF('equal','equal') AS equal_string
FROM SYSIBM.SYSDUMMY1

Equal          non_equal      equal_string
----------     -----------    ------------
-              1              -
```

The first field was evaluated to NULL (a dash is the way IBM DB2 UDP displays a NULL). Because the values were equal, the second expression returned the first value of 1. The same goes for the third field, which demonstrates that the function accepts a variety of data types. The data types of both arguments must match precisely.

The NULLIF() function is represented across all the RDBMS implementations discussed in this book.

RAND()

Syntax:

```
RAND([seed_integer])
```

This function returns a random floating-point value between 0.0 and 1.0, using the argument as the optional seed value. It accepts an optional parameter as a seed value, and returns a double-precision floating-point number. Consider the following example:

```
SELECT
    RAND() AS first,
    RAND() AS second
FROM SYSIBM.SYSDUMMY1

FIRST                      SECOND
-----------------------    -----------------------
+8.96633808404798E-002    +8.25708792382580E-001
```

When the function is invoked without a seed value, it uses a seed generated randomly at server startup. If it is initialized to a specific seed, the function will return exactly the same number, unless the seed is changed. Consider the following example:

```
SELECT
   RAND(1) AS first,
   RAND(1) AS second
FROM SYSIBM.SYSDUMMY1
FIRST                     SECOND
-----------------------   -----------------------
+1.25125888851588E-003    +1.25125888851588E-003
```

To receive random numbers in a range other than 0 and 1, you may use a combination of the built-in functions and operators. For example, to produce a pseudo-random number in a range between 0 and 100, the following statement could be used:

```
SELECT
   TRUNC(RAND()*100,0) AS first,
   ROUND(RAND()*100,0) AS second
FROM SYSIBM.SYSDUMMY1

first                    second
---------------------    --------------------
+3.50000000000000E+001   +4.70000000000000E+001
```

Encapsulating this functionality in the UDF would be a logical solution to the problem.

The RAND() function is present in every RDBMS implementations discussed in this book, except PostgreSQL, which implements the function RANDOM().

TABLE_NAME()

Syntax:

```
TABLE_NAME(<char_alias>,<alias_schema>)
```

This returns the unqualified name of the object found after any alias chains have been resolved. The function accepts two parameters, with the second one, <alias_schema>, being optional. If another is not provided, a default schema is assumed. The returned result is of the VARCHAR(18) data type. The following example demonstrates creating an alias for the Sales table, which is available in the SAMPLE database, and finding the base table name using the TABLE_NAME function:

```
CREATE ALIAS S1
FOR SALES;

SELECT
  TABLE_NAME('S1') AS BASE_TABLE
FROM SYSIBM.SYSDUMMY1;

BASE_TABLE
SALES
```

There is no equivalent function in the RDBMS implementations discussed in this book. However, similar functionality can still be obtained through the use of system views.

TYPE_ID()

Syntax:

```
TYPE_ID(<reference_expression>)
```

This function returns the internal type identifier of the user-defined structured data type. The return result is of the INTEGER data type. The following example demonstrates creating a simple user defined type and then using the TYPE_ID expression:

```
CREATE TYPE  DEPT AS
    (DEPT_NAME      VARCHAR(30),
     NO_OF_EMPLOYEES INT)
REF USING INT
MODE  DB2SQL;
```

The TYPE_ID function is unique to the IBM DB2 implementation.

TYPE_NAME()

Syntax:

```
TYPE_NAME(<reference_expression>)
```

This function returns the unqualified name of the user-defined structured data type. The returned result is of the VARCHAR(18) data type.

The TYPE_NAME function is unique to the IBM DB2 implementation.

Summary

In this chapter, we discussed the built-in functions specifically available to the IBM DB2 platform. The IBM DB2 platform contains a robust and wide array of functions available to the developer. To that end, relevant functions were grouped into pertinent sections in an effort to make the information readily available to the reader.

In the next chapter, we will turn our attention to the Microsoft SQL Server platform. The reader should try to notice some of the distinct differences between the SQL Server platform and the other RDBMS implementations discussed in the book.

Microsoft SQL Server Functions

The SQL functions described in this chapter are not part of Microsoft SQL Server. Rather, they are part of the Transact-SQL language that Microsoft shares (to a certain extent) with Sybase. The two dialects diverge more with every new release of the respective RDBMS packages. This process affects the SQL functions as each vendor introduces new features, old functions get overhauled, and new functions are added.

We will be specifically discussing several different families of functions within the Transact-SQL framework: string, date and time, metadata, configuration, security, system, system statistical, and undocumented functions. As with the previous chapters, each section will provide you with a table of the various functions within the section for quick reference, and a detailed explanation of the implementation involved with each. By the end of this chapter, you should have a thorough understanding of the different types and implementations of the various functions available to you on the MS SQL Server platform.

SQL Server Query Syntax

The basis of the Microsoft SQL Server SELECT statement is the same as the ANSI standard discussed in Chapter 5, and shown here:

```
SELECT select_list
[ INTO new_table ]
FROM table_source
[ WHERE search_condition ]
[ GROUP BY group_by_expression ]
[ HAVING search_condition ]
[ ORDER BY order_expression [ ASC | DESC ] ]
```

However, once we look at the specifics of the SELECT statement, we will notice that some things are done differently. First, let's break down the SELECT statement into a more complex version showing most of the attributes. Then we may take each part in turn to provide a short description. Consider the following example:

```
SELECT statement ::=
    < query_expression >
    [ ORDER BY { order_by_expression | column_position [ ASC | DESC ] }
        [ ,...n ]    ]
    [ COMPUTE
        { { AVG | COUNT | MAX | MIN | SUM } ( expression ) } [ ,...n ]
        [ BY expression [ ,...n ] ]
    ]
    [ FOR { BROWSE | XML { RAW | AUTO | EXPLICIT }
            [ , XMLDATA ]
            [ , ELEMENTS ]
            [ , BINARY base64 ]
        }
    ]
    [ OPTION ( < query_hint > [ ,...n ]) ]
```

The <query expression> is the basis of the SELECT statement and we will go into more detail regarding it shortly. The next statement is the optional ORDER BY clause. The purpose of this clause is to determine which columns of data are sorted and how the sorting is accomplished. The columns can be specified as column names, aliases, or non-negative numbers specifying column locations in the result set. The way in which the columns are sorted is specified by either the ASC (ascending) or DESC (descending) operator. Otherwise, the columns are sorted as ASC by default. Ordering of the columns is important because it determines the hierarchy of what gets ordered first. In addition, ordering of columns need not appear in the select list unless a UNION operator or SELECT DISTINCT statement is used.

The next area is the optional COMPUTE clause. Its purpose is to provide *additional* summary columns at the end of the result set. These can be grouped into sets if the BY clause is used (similar to the GROUP BY clause); this optional clause adds breaks and subtotals in the result set. You may use any of the following aggregate functions to provide the summary information: AVG, COUNT, MAX, MIN, or SUM. If you use the COMPUTE BY clause, then you must also use ORDER BY in your statement. In fact, your ORDER BY statement *must* include all of the objects in the COMPUTE clause, or at least a subset of those.

The FOR clause is used to relate the use of either the BROWSE or the XML options. The BROWSE option allows updates to be made to a table while it is being browsed with a browse mode cursor. In order for this to be available, the table in question must have a timestamp column and a unique index, and the SELECT statement cannot use the UNION operator. The XML option states that the result set is to be returned as XML in the three following modes:

❑   *RAW*—This mode transforms each row of the result set into an XML element with a generic row identifier.

❑   *AUTO*—This will return the results in a nested set of XML elements. Each of the tables specified in the FROM clause that have columns in the result will be represented by elements in the resulting XML.

❑   *EXPLICIT*—This mode determines that the XML returned should be in a specific format. To use this mode, you must specially structure your SELECT statement so that the result set returned can be transformed into a well-defined XML document. However, this is beyond the scope of this book.

The OPTION clause is for specifying that a *query hint* is to be used in evaluating the SELECT statement. A query hint is a call to the query optimizer to force it to use a particular type of operation when working with objects such as joins, unions, and groupings. This clause is for the experienced database administrator

(DBA) because it requires some analysis to determine whether the query hint will help or hinder the operations being performed. In most cases, Microsoft's query analyzer will determine an optimal path, and this statement can be ignored.

Lastly, we will look at the <query expression>, which can be made up of one or more <query specifications> joined by the UNION operator. The syntax is as follows:

```
SELECT [ ALL | DISTINCT ]
    [ { TOP integer | TOP integer PERCENT } [ WITH TIES ] ]
    < select_list >
[ INTO new_table ]
[ FROM { < table_source > } [ ,...n ] ]
[ WHERE < search_condition > ]
[ GROUP BY [ ALL ] group_by_expression [ ,...n ]
    [ WITH { CUBE | ROLLUP } ]
]
[ HAVING < search_condition > ]
```

You will notice right away that this is almost identical to the basic SELECT statement discussed in Chapter 5. There are notable differences, such as the TOP option. This option specifies that either the TOP n (number) or TOP n PERCENT of rows from the result set are returned. If the ORDER BY clause is used, then the results are determined from the ordered set. Otherwise, the results returned are arbitrary. The WITH TIES option specifies that any additional rows returned in the result set that have the same value in the ORDER BY columns be pushed to the end of the TOP n rows. Of course, since this option is dependent upon the ORDER BY clause, it can only be used when ORDER BY is specified. Lastly, you may notice the CUBE and ROLLUP options, which are subsets of the GROUP BY clause. These two statements are used to return additional rows in the result set that contain summary information. In the case of CUBE, it returns summary rows for every possible combination of objects in the GROUP BY clause. ROLLUP, however, applies hierarchical ordering based on the GROUP BY clause and, therefore, the ordering of the GROUP BY elements may affect the number of summary rows returned.

Now you should have a good understanding of the basics of the Microsoft SQL Server platform. This will be a basis on which to build a better understanding of the use of the different functions, and will enable you to decipher the examples given throughout this chapter.

String Functions

This family of functions performs various operations on string and binary inputs, and returns values in either a string or numeric format. Most of these functions can only be used on CHAR, NCHAR, VARCHAR, and NVARCHAR data types, but a few can be used with BINARY and VARBINARY types as well. The following table details the different string functions that we will be discussing in this section.

Function Name	Input	Output	Description
CHARINDEX	<char_expression1>, <char_expression2>	INTEGER	Returns the first position of the first occurrence of one expression within another expression.

Table continued on following page

Function Name	Input	Output	Description
DIFFERENCE	`<char_expression1>,` `<char_expression2>`	INTEGER	Returns the integer difference between two SOUNDEX expressions. The range is 0 through 4.
LEFT	`<char_expression>,` `<length_integer>)`	`<char_expression>`	Returns part of the expression starting from a specific character to the left.
LEN	`<char_expression>`	INTEGER	Returns the number of characters in the expression, excluding trailing blank spaces.
LTRIM	`<char_expression>`	`<char_expression>`	Returns an expression without left trailing blanks.
NCHAR	`<integer_code>`	NCHAR	Returns a Unicode character from the code number.
REPLACE	`<char_expression1>` `<char_expression2>` `<char_expression3>`	`<char_expression>`	Returns a string in which all occurrences of the second expression within the first expression are replaced with the third expression.
QUOTENAME	`<char_expression>` `[,<quote_identifier>]`	`<char_expression>`	Returns a Unicode expression with delimiters added for validation.
REPLICATE	`<expression>` `<times_integer>`	`<expression>`	Returns an expression consisting of the first argument repeated n times.
REVERSE	`<expression>`	`<expression>`	Returns a reversed character expression (first character last, last character first).
RIGHT	`<char_expression>,` `<lengh_integer>`	`<char_expression>`	Returns part of the expression starting from a specific character to the right.
RTRIM	`<char_expression>`	`<char_expression>`	Returns the expression with trailing blanks removed.
SOUNDEX	`<char_expression>`	`<char_expression>`	Returns a four-character code to evaluate similarity between the sounds of two expressions.
SPACE	INTEGER	`<char_expression>`	Returns a string composed of n blank spaces.

Function Name	Input	Output	Description
STR	`<number_float` `[,<length_integer>` `[,<decimal_integer]]`	`<char_ expression>`	Returns character data of numeric data type.
STUFF	`<char_expression1>` `<start_integer>` `<length_integer>` `<char_expression2>`	`<char_ expression>`	Deletes a specified number of characters, and inserts another set of characters at the specified point.
SUBSTRING	`<expression>` `<start_integer>` `<length_integer>`	`<char_ expression>`	Returns part of a string, starting from a specified point and spanning a specified number of characters.
UNICODE	`<nchar_expression>`	INTEGER	Returns a Unicode integer code for the first character in the expression.

ASCII()

Syntax:

```
ASCII(<expression>)
```

This function returns the numeric value of the leftmost character of the string. It returns 0 if the string is an empty string. It returns NULL if the string is NULL. ASCII() works for characters with numeric values from 0 to 255. Any character out of this range will either be ignored, or an error will be returned.

```
SELECT
    ASCII('A')   uppercase_a,
    ASCII('abc') lowercase_a

uppercase_a       lowercase_a
-----------       -----------
65                97
```

This function is available in all of the RDBMS implementations discussed in this book.

CHAR()

Syntax:

```
CHAR(<numeric_expression>)
```

The CHAR() function is the opposite of ASCII(). It returns a character given an ASCII code. For the characters outside this range, the behavior is dependent on the particular RDBMS implementation. For example, consider the following:

```
SELECT
    CHAR(65)        uppercase_a,
    CHAR(97)        lowercase_a


uppercase_a     lowercase_a
-----------     -----------
A               a
```

Sybase and MySQL both use the CHAR() function; the other RDBMS implementations use the CHR() syntax.

CHARINDEX()

Syntax:

```
CHARINDEX(<char_expression1>, <char_expression2>)
```

The CHARINDEX() function searches <expression2> for the first occurrence of the <expression1> and returns an integer specifying the beginning position of the occurrence. Both expressions can be any of the character data types. Consider the following example:

```
SELECT
    CHARINDEX('E', 'ABCDEFG') AS position
position
---------
5
```

This function does not allow use of wildcards commonly used in regular expressions or LIKE statements. CHARINDEX() treats all wildcards as literals. If <char_expression1> is not found within <char_expression2>, the function will return zero.

> *If either <char_expression1> or <char_expression2> is NULL, CHARINDEX returns NULL when the database compatibility level is 70 or later. When the database compatibility level is 65 or earlier, the function returns NULL only when both <char_expression1> and <char_expression2> are NULL.*

This function is also available on the Sybase platform.

DIFFERENCE()

Syntax:

```
DIFFERENCE(<char_expression1>, <char_expression2>)
```

The DIFFERENCE() function returns the difference between two SOUNDEX values—<char_expression1> and <char_expression2>. (The SOUNDEX() function is discussed later in this chapter.) These values represent four-character codes corresponding to phonetic equivalence of the string. For example, to find out how close the pronunciation of "time" and "tyme" would be, the following query could be used:

```
SELECT
    SOUNDEX('time')     as time,
    SOUNDEX('tyme')     as tyme,
```

```
    DIFFERENCE('time', 'tyme')    as diff

time  tyme  diff
----  ----  ----------
T500  T500  4
```

As you can see, the SOUNDEX values are a perfect match and the DIFFERENCE is 4—the best match possible (0 being the lowest).

The DIFFERENCE() function is found in IBM DB2 UDB, Sybase ASE, and MySQL (version 3.2 and later). Oracle provides the SOUNDEX() function but not DIFFERENCE(), and, as of version 7.4.2, PostgreSQL does not have either SOUNDEX() or DIFFERENCE() functions implemented.

LEFT() and RIGHT()

Syntax:

```
LEFT(<char_expression>,<length_integer>)
RIGHT(<char_expression>,<length_integer>)
```

The LEFT() function returns the leftmost part of the expression to the specified length, and the RIGHT() function returns the rightmost part of the expression to the specified length. For example, the following queries return the three rightmost characters of the string "ABCDEF" and the three leftmost characters of the same string:

```
SELECT
    RIGHT('ABCDEF', 3) AS three_last,
    LEFT('ABCDEF', 3) AS three_first

three_last    three_first
----------    -----------
DEF           ABC
```

These functions are special cases of the more generic SUBSTRING() function. Both LEFT() and RIGHT() functions are also found in Sybase ASE.

LEN()

Syntax:

```
LEN(<char_expression>)
```

The LEN() expression returns the length of the expression, which can be of any character data type. Leading blanks are included in the calculation, while trailing blanks are not. For example, the following query returns 5, taking into consideration the one leading blank, but ignoring the four trailing blanks:

```
SELECT LEN(' ABCD    ') AS total_length

total_length
------------
5
```

The number returned is the number of characters in the string, not the number of bytes. So Unicode and ASCII expressions will return exactly the same value, even though the latter might occupy two times less space. For non-character data types of the input argument, Microsoft will attempt to implicitly convert all compatible data types into characters prior to evaluating it.

Sybase has CHAR_LENGTH() for this purpose (but also employs synonym LEN()). Oracle provides a family of equivalent LENGTH() functions. IBM DB2 UDB also supports the LENGTH() function. MySQL has CHAR_LENGTH() and CHARACTER_LENGTH() functions, while PostgreSQL supports both LENGTH() and CHAR_LENGTH() functions.

LOWER()

Syntax:

```
LOWER(<numeric expression>)
```

The LOWER() function converts all the characters in a string into lowercase. Consider the following example:

```
SELECT
    LOWER('STRING') lowercase

LOWERCASE
-----------
string
```

This function is found in every database implementation discussed in this book. IBM DB2 UDB and MySQL also have a synonym for the LOWER() function: LCASE(). The syntax and usage is identical across the implementations.

LTRIM() and RTRIM()

Syntax:

```
LTRIM(<char_expression>)
RTRIM(<char_expression>)
```

LTRIM() and RTRIM() functions return the specified <char_expression> with trimmed leading or trailing blanks, respectively. Only characters that correspond to the blank space character in the current character set will be removed. The input parameter can be of any character data type or their Unicode equivalents. The returned result will be of the same data type. For Unicode expressions, the function returns the lowercase Unicode equivalent of the specified expression. Characters in the expression that have no lowercase equivalent will be left unchanged. Here is an example where the string to be trimmed is padded by three blanks on each side:

```
SELECT
    ( '*' + LTRIM ('   ABC   ') + '*') AS left_trimmed,
    ( '*' + RTRIM ('   ABC   ') + '*') AS right_trimmed

left_trimmed right_trimmed
------------ -------------
*ABC   *        *   ABC*
```

Asterisk markers were added to both sides of each result to make the trim results visible.

Versions prior to 7.0 will evaluate the functions differently. Setting compatibility levels within later versions of SQL Server will have identical effect.

These functions have their equivalents in every RDBMS discussed in this book.

NCHAR()

Syntax:

```
NCHAR(<integer_code>)
```

The NCHAR() function returns a Unicode character from the code number, defined by the Unicode standard. The <integer_code> is a positive whole number from 0 through 65,535. For values outside this range, NULL will be returned. For example, the code 1041 defines a letter "B" in the Russian alphabet, as shown here:

```
SELECT
    NCHAR(1041)   AS russian_B,
    NCHAR(1040)   AS russian_A,
    NCHAR(65)    AS ASCII_A

russian_B russian_A ASCII_A
--------- --------- -------
_         _         A
```

Although the two uppercase "As" appear indistinguishable, they have different Unicode values. The byte length of the character will be two, even for the ASCII character, because it was padded with an additional byte being returned from a Unicode function.

PATINDEX()

Syntax:

```
PATINDEX(<pattern_expression>,<string_expression>)
```

The PATINDEX() function returns the starting position of the first instance of <pattern expression> in the <string expression>. If the pattern is not found, then zeroes are returned. Consider the following example:

```
SELECT
    PATINDEX('%CAT%','CATASTROPHE') AS A_MATCH,
    PATINDEX('%MISSY%','MISSISSIPPI') AS NO_MATCH

A_MATCH      NO_MATCH
----------- -----------
1            0
```

This function is also available in Sybase.

REPLACE()

Syntax:

```
REPLACE(<string_expression1> , <string_expression2> , <string_expression3>)
```

Returns a string in which all occurrences of the second expression within the first expression are replaced with the third expression. The expressions can be either character or binary data. Consider the following example:

```
SELECT
    REPLACE('ABCDEFG','CDE','*') AS no_CDE

no_CDE
-------------
AB*FG
```

Compatible data types of the expressions will be implicitly converted into a common equivalent prior to evaluation.

The REPLACE() function is available in all of the databases discussed in this book.

QUOTENAME()

Syntax:

```
QUOTENAME(<char_expression> [,<quote_identifier>])
```

This function returns a Unicode expression with delimiters added for validation of the string. The <quote_identifier> can be a single quotation mark ('), a left or right bracket ([or]), or a double quotation mark ("). Whenever <quote_ identifier> is omitted, brackets will be used. If an invalid identifier is used (none of the three listed), the function returns NULL. Consider the following example:

```
SELECT
    QUOTENAME('abdef',CHAR(39)) AS single_quote,
    QUOTENAME('abdef','"') AS double_quote,
    QUOTENAME('ab[]def') AS brackets

single_quote      double_quote      brackets
---------------   ----------------  -----------
'abdef'                "abdef"       [ab[]]def]
```

Notice that the right bracket in the third field of the result set is doubled to specify an escape character for the bracket itself.

This function is unique to Microsoft SQL Server.

REPLICATE()

Syntax:

```
REPLICATE(<expression>,<times_integer>)
```

The REPLICATE() function returns a string consisting of the specified expression repeated the given number of times. The character expression can be of any of the character data types. The <times_integer> parameter can be of INTEGER data type or any of its subtypes. The return data type will be implicitly converted into VARCHAR. Consider the following example:

```
SELECT
    REPLICATE('A',5)    AS five_a,
    REPLICATE('',5)     AS five_blanks,
    REPLICATE(5,2)      AS two_times_five

five_a five_blanks two_times_five
------ ----------- --------------
AAAAA              55
```

The results of this query may need some explanation: they are uppercase "A" repeated five times, the blank space character repeated five times (here, an empty string '' and a space character ' ' are treated the same—as a blank character), and the number "5" repeated two times.

Microsoft SQL Server versions prior to 7.0 would evaluate the functions differently; setting compatibility levels within later versions of SQL Server will have an identical effect.

The function is also found in Sybase ASE, though it behaves slightly differently from the Microsoft version.

REVERSE()

Syntax:

```
REVERSE(<expression>)
```

The REVERSE() function returns the string passed into it with the characters in reverse order. The expression can be any of the character data types. Any other data type will be implicitly converted, if possible. Consider the following example:

```
SELECT
    REVERSE('ABCD')    AS backwards_char,
    REVERSE(12345)     AS backwards_numeric

backwards_char backwards_numeric
-------------- -----------------
DCBA           54321
```

As you can see, the function recognizes the data type passed to it and reverses it appropriately. A character expression must be placed in quotes—double or single. If the <expression> is NULL, a NULL will be returned.

This function is also found in Sybase ASE, though it behaves slightly differently from the Microsoft version.

SOUNDEX()

Syntax:

```
SOUNDEX(<char_expression>)
```

193

This function returns a four-character code to evaluate similarity between the sounds of two character expressions. SOUNDEX() evaluates an alphabetic string and returns a four-character code to find similar-sounding words or names. The first character of the code is the first character of <char_expression> and the second through fourth characters of the code are numbers. Vowels in <char_expression> are ignored unless they are the first letter of the string. The function can be used to specify search criteria for similar-sounding words, and is, of course, case-insensitive. For example, the following query finds all three words to be similar-sounding:

```
SELECT
    SOUNDEX('GOOD') AS upper_case,
    SOUNDEX('good') AS lower_case,
    SOUNDEX('GUT')  AS something_else

upper_case lower_case something_else
---------- ---------- --------------
G300       G300       G300
```

The function SOUNDEX() is found in every RDBMS implementation discussed in this book.

SPACE()

Syntax:

```
SPACE(<expression>)
```

The SPACE() function returns a string consisting of blanks, repeated to a specified number of single-byte space characters. The accepted input parameters can be of any integer type (INTEGER and its sub-types). The following example uses the DATALENGTH() function to count the number of spaces produced (because the LEN() function truncates trailing spaces):

```
SELECT
    DATALENGTH(SPACE(5)) AS five_spaces

five_spaces
-----------
5
```

This function is also present in Sybase ASE.

STR()

Syntax:

```
STR(<number_float [,<length_integer> [,<decimal_integer]]])
```

The STR() function returns the character equivalent of the specified number. It accepts three arguments, specifying the numeric value to be converted into a string, the number of the resulting characters to be returned, and the number of decimal places (default is zero). The last two parameters are optional, and can never be negative. If all of the optional parameters are omitted, the result will be rounded up or truncated to the integer portion of the number. Consider the following example:

```
SELECT
    STR(1234.5678, 4)      AS four_chars
    STR(1234.5678, 7,2)    AS seven_chars
    STR(1234.5678, 3,1)    AS not_enough_space

four_chars  seven_chars  not_enough_space
----------  -----------  ----------------
1235           1234.57    ***
```

Since no decimals were specified for the <four_chars> field, none were returned. In addition, the result was rounded up to fit within the specified length. In the case of the <seven_chars> field, the returned string contains seven characters (decimal point is included in the count, as is a minus sign), and exactly two decimals (which are rounded up because the remainder of the decimal values is closer to the ceiling than to the floor; otherwise the number will be truncated). The last field displays three asterisks because the specified length (3) cannot accommodate the five digits of the integer portion of the number. The length must at the very least be equal to the integer portion of the number.

This function is also present in Sybase ASE.

STUFF()

Syntax:

```
STUFF(<char_expression1> ,<start_integer> , <length_integer> , <char_expression2>)
```

The STUFF() function returns the string created by deleting a specified number of characters from <string_expression1> and inserting another set of characters (<string_expression2>) at the specified point. If the <start_integer> is negative, or the <length_integer> value exceeds <string_expression1>, a NULL will be returned. Consider the following example:

```
SELECT
    STUFF('ABCDABCD',5,4,'EFG') as alphabet

alphabet
---------
ABCDEFG
```

In the previous example, the function was supplied arguments to replace four characters in the first argument string with the fourth argument string, starting with the fifth character. The function can also be used to delete characters inside a string, or to replace them with blank spaces. Consider the following example:

```
SELECT
    STUFF('ABCDABCD',5,3,NULL)    AS remove3,
    STUFF('ABCDABCD',5,3,' ')     AS blank,
    STUFF('ABCDABCD',5,3,'')      AS empty_string

remove3 blank   empty_string
------- ------  ------------
ABCDD   ABCD D  ABCDD
```

Notice that the first and the last fields yield identical results.

This function is also present in Sybase ASE.

SUBSTRING()

Syntax:

```
SUBSTRING(<expression>,<start_integer>,<length_integer>)
```

The SUBSTRING() function returns part of a string, starting from a specified point and spanning a specified number of characters. The acceptable data types for the expression can be any of the character and BINARY (VARBINARY) data types. For example, to extract the first three characters of an expression, the following query could be used:

```
SELECT
    SUBSTRING('ABCDEFG',1,3) AS first_three,
    SUBSTRING(0x001101,1,2)  AS first_binary

first_three first_binary
----------- ------------
ABC         0x0011
```

The function returned three characters for the first field and 2 bytes for the second.

This function is present in Sybase ASE, PostgreSQL, and MySQL. Both Oracle and IBM DB2 UDB have implemented the SUBSTR() function with identical behavior.

UNICODE()

Syntax:

```
UNICODE(<nchar_expression>)
```

The UNICODE() function returns a Unicode integer code for the first character in the expression. For example, 1041 is the code for the uppercase Russian letter "_." The following example uses the function NCHAR() to pass an actual letter into the UNICODE() function:

```
SELECT
    UNICODE(NCHAR(1041))   AS unicode_B,
    NCHAR(1041)    AS russian_B

unicode_B    russian_B
-----------  ---------
1041         _
```

The USCALAR() function in the Sybase platform provides similar functionality.

UPPER()

Syntax:

```
UPPER(<numeric expression>)
```

The UPPER() function converts all the characters in a string into uppercase. Consider the following example.

```
SELECT
    UPPER('STRING') uppercase

UPPERCASE
-------------
STRING
```

This function is found in every RDBMS implementation discussed in this book. IBM DB2 UDB and MySQL also have synonyms for the UPPER function—UCASE(). The syntax and usage is identical across the implementations.

Date and Time Functions

Microsoft classifies the date and time functions as those that perform operations on date/time input and return a variety of data types (DATETIME, VARCHAR, and so on). Most of the functions derive from the Sybase legacy, but some were added only recently. The following table documents the date and time functions that we will examine in this section.

Function Name	Input	Output	Description
DATEADD	<datepart>, <how_many_integer>, <add_to_date>	DATETIME or SMALLDATETIME	Returns a new DATETIME value based on the passed value plus the specified interval.
DATEDIFF	<datepart>, <date_expression1>, <date_expression2>	INTEGER	Returns the number of time units (seconds, days, years, etc.) passed between two dates.
@@DATEFIRST	N/A	INTEGER	Returns an integer indicating the setting for SET DATEFIRST, which determines the starting day of the week.
DATENAME	<date_expression>	<char_ expression>	Returns a character string representing the specified part of the date.
DATEPART	<date_part>, <date_expression>	INTEGER	Returns an integer representing the specified part of the date.
DAY	<date_expression>	INTEGER	Returns an integer representing the day part of a date.
GETDATE	N/A	DATETIME or SMALLDATETIME	Returns the current system's date and time.
GETUTCDATE	N/A	DATETIME or SMALLDATETIME	Returns date/time value for the current UTC time.

Table continued on following page

Function Name	Input	Output	Description
MONTH	<date_expression>	INTEGER	Returns an integer representing the month part of a date.
YEAR	<date_expression>	INTEGER	Returns an integer representing the year part of a date.

DATEADD()

Syntax:

```
DATEADD(<datepart>,<how_many_integer>,<add_to_date>)
```

The DATEADD() function returns a new DATETIME value based on the passed value plus a specified interval. For example, the following query adds four months to today's date:

```
SELECT
    DATEADD(month,4, GETDATE()) as four_months_ahead

four_months_ahead
-----------------------------------------------------
2004-11-07 17:00:29.237
```

This example uses the GETDATE() function to supply the current date and time as the third argument. A character representation of a date is also acceptable because it will be implicitly converted into a DATETIME data type. For example, the query could be rewritten as follows:

```
SELECT
    DATEADD(month, 4, '2004-11-07') as four_months_ahead

four_months_ahead
-----------------------------------------------------
2005-03-07 00:00:00.000
```

The time format must be one of SQL Server's recognized formats to be accepted, and it must be enclosed in single quotes. The following TIME formats are recognized:

❑ HH:MI

❑ HH:MI:SS

❑ HH:MI:SS.X

❑ H[AM/PM]

❑ [0]H[:MI:SS:MS] AM

The DATE format follows standard *MM/DD/YY[YY]* formats. The default date format depends upon your system settings. For a detailed table outlining the different default date formats see the CONVERT() function in the section "System Functions" later in this chapter.

This function has a direct equivalent in Sybase ASE.

DATEDIFF()

Syntax:

```
DATEDIFF(<datepart>,<date_expression1>,<date_expression2>)
```

The `DATEDIFF()` function returns the number of time units (seconds, days, years, and so on) passed between two dates. The calculation always involves a `DATETIME` data type. Even if `SMALLDATETIME` arguments are supplied, SQL Server would convert them implicitly into `DATETIME`, with seconds and milliseconds set to 0.

For example, to find out how many days are between today and, say, January 1, 1900, the following query could be used:

```
SELECT
      DATEDIFF (day, '1900-01-01', GETDATE()) AS days
days
-----------
38274
```

If `<date_expression2>` happens to be earlier than `<date_expression1>` the result will be negative (that is, if the second and third arguments in this example had been switched).

The return parameter is of `INTEGER` data type; therefore it cannot exceed a value of 2,147,483,647, be it days, months, minutes, or seconds. This means that the function cannot be used to calculate seconds passed since (as of this writing), June 17, 1936 (maximum of 68 years worth of seconds).

Since a character expression representing a date will always be converted into `DATETIME` (or `SMALLDATETIME`), the function cannot accept parameters specifying a date earlier than January 1, 1753. This restriction is because of design decisions made by Sybase and MS SQL Server architects.

This function has a direct equivalent in Sybase ASE.

@@DATEFIRST()

Syntax:

```
SELECT @@DATEFIRST
```

The `@@DATEFIRST` function returns the current value of the `SET DATEFIRST` parameter, which indicates the specified first day of each week: 1 for Monday, 2 for Tuesday, and so on through 7 for Sunday. Consider the following example:

```
SELECT
   @@DATEFIRST AS first_day
first_day
---------
7
```

This function is also available on the Sybase platform.

DATENAME()

Syntax:

```
DATENAME(<date_expression>)
```

The DATENAME() function returns the full name of the date part specified extracted from the date. For example, to find the name of the current month, the following query could be used:

```
SELECT
   GETDATE()   AS full_date,
   DATENAME( month, GETDATE())   AS month_name

full_date                 month_name
----------------------    -------------------
2004-07-07 16:50:11.700   July
```

The first field supplies the current date using the GETDATE() function, while the second extracts the name of the month from the returned date.

This function has a direct equivalent in Sybase ASE.

DATEPART()

Syntax:

```
DATEPART(<date_part>,<date_expression>)
```

The DATEPART() function extracts parts of a date/time expression, where <date_part> is one of the predefined identities shown in the following table, and <date_expression> can be of DATETIME, SMALLDATETIME, or character data types in date/time format.

Date Part	Abbreviations
YEAR	YY, YYYY
QUARTER	QQ, Q
MONTH	MM, M
Day of Year	DY, Y
Week	WK, WW
Hour	HH
Minute	MI, N
Seconds	SS, S
Milliseconds	MS

For example, the following query returns year part extracted from the current date:

```
SELECT
    DATEPART(year, GETDATE()) as current_year

current_year
------------
2004
```

It is recommended to use DATETIME and SMALLDATETIME for dates on or later than January 1, 1753, and use character strings in date/time format for earlier dates.

The results of the function are affected by the DATEFIRST setting. The syntax is SET DATEFIRST <integer_value>. The integer value indicating the first day of the week can be any of those listed in the following table.

Day of Week	Description
1	Monday
2	Tuesday
3	Wednesday
4	Thursday
5	Friday
6	Saturday
7	Sunday (default for U.S. English)

The function @@DATEFIRST is used to check the value of this setting.

If the year is specified as two digits rather than four digits, Microsoft SQL Server employs logic based on the *two-digit year cutoff* configuration option (configured using the sp_configure system stored procedure). The default setting for the option is 2049. This means that a year specified as 50 will be interpreted as 1950, while a year specified as 49 will be considered to be 2049. When the <date_expression> is represented by a number, the number is converted into DATETIME (or SMALLDATETIME) prior to execution; all the rules of the data type conversion apply. Consider the following example:

```
SELECT
    CAST(1460 AS DATETIME) AS cast_value,
    DATEPART(YY, 1460) as year_extract

cast_value                      year_extract
------------------------------- ------------
1904-01-01 00:00:00.000         1904
```

This function has a direct equivalent in Sybase ASE, though some rules might differ.

DAY()

Syntax:

```
DAY(<date_expression>)
```

The DAY() function returns an integer representing the day part of a date. Consider the following example:

```
SELECT
    DAY(GETDATE())    AS current_day,
    GETDATE()   AS 'current_date'

current_day    current_date
-----------    ------------------------
7              2004-07-07 19:45:24.023
```

For all practical purposes the DAY() function is equivalent to the DATEPART(day, <date_expression>) function, and is subject to the same rules and limitations.

Sybase provides a similar function, MySQL has the DAYOFMONTH() function, and PostgreSQL provides the DATE_PART() function. The equivalent for Oracle is the EXTRACT() function.

GETDATE() and GETUTCDATE()

Syntax:

```
GETDATE()
GETUTCDATE()
```

The GETDATE() function returns the current system's date and time, while GETUTCDATE() returns current UTC time (Universal Time Coordinate or Greenwich Mean Time). Consider the following example:

```
SELECT
    GETUTCDATE()    AS utc_time,
    GETDATE()   AS local_time

utc_time                       local_time
------------------------       ------------------------
2004-03-07 23:33:23.940        2004-03-07 16:33:23.940
```

The equivalent of the Microsoft SQL Server GETDATE() function in Sybase is GETDATE(), while the IBM DB2 UDB equivalent is the special register CURRENT DATE. Oracle implemented the SYSDATE pseudo-column (which can be considered a function for all practical purposes).

MONTH()

Syntax:

```
MONTH(<date_expression>)
```

The MONTH() function returns an integer representing the month part of a date. Consider the following example:

```
SELECT
    MONTH(GETDATE())    AS current_month,
    GETDATE()   AS 'current_date'
```

```
current_month    current_date
------------      ------------------------
7                2004-07-07 19:45:24.023
```

For all practical purposes, the function MONTH() is equivalent to the function DATEPART(month, <date_expression>), and is subject to the same rules and limitations.

The EXTRACT() function in SQL Server, Sybase, and Oracle offers similar functionality. MySQL provides an equivalent MONTH() function.

YEAR()

Syntax:

```
YEAR(<date_expression>)
```

The YEAR() function returns an integer representing the year part of a date. Consider the following example:

```
SELECT
    YEAR(GETDATE())   AS current_year,
    GETDATE()    AS 'current_date'

current_year    current_date
------------     ------------------------
2004             2004-07-07 19:45:24.023
```

For all practical purposes, the YEAR() function is equivalent to the DATEPART(year, <date_expression>) function, and is subject to the same rules and limitations.

The EXTRACT() function in Oracle and Sybase offers similar functionality. MySQL and IBM DB2 provide an equivalent version.

Metadata Functions

These types of scalar functions return information about the database and also about structures within the database. The following table details the functions that we will discuss in this section.

Function Name	Input	Output	Description
COL_LENGTH	<object_name>, <column_name>	INTEGER	Returns the defined length of a column.
DB_ID	[<database_ name>]	INTEGER	Returns the database identification number.

Table continued on following page

203

Function Name	Input	Output	Description
DB_NAME	[<databaseid>]	<char_ expression>	Returns the current database name.
FILE_ID	<logical_file_ name>	INTEGER	Returns the file identification number for a given logical file.
FILE_NAME	<file_id>	<char_ expression>	Returns the filename from a given identification number.

COL_LENGTH()

Syntax:

```
COL_LENGTH(<object_name>, <column_name>)
```

The COL_LENGTH() function returns the length defined for a given column in a given table, view, default, rule, trigger, or procedure's arguments. The names must be enclosed in quotes, and fully qualified names are accepted (that is, the name can be in the format <server>.<database>.<database_owner> .<object>). For the columns defined as non-variable data types (INTEGER, BINARY, etc.), the length returned will be that of the data type. For example, the following table is created to contain columns of several built-in data types:

```
CREATE TABLE  tblTEST
(
    field1    CHAR(10),
    field2    VARCHAR(25),
    field3    INTEGER,
    field4    MONEY,
    field5    BIT
)
```

The following COL_LENGTH() query against this table would yield the following results:

```
SELECT
    COL_LENGTH('tblTEST', 'field1') AS char10,
    COL_LENGTH('tblTEST', 'field2') AS varchar25,
    COL_LENGTH('tblTEST', 'field3') AS integer4,
    COL_LENGTH('tblTEST', 'field4') AS money8,
    COL_LENGTH('tblTEST', 'field5') AS bit1,
    COL_LENGTH('tblTEST', 'field6') AS invalid

char10    varchar25   integer4    money8      bit1        invalid
--------- ----------- ----------- ----------- ----------- -----------
10        25          4           8           1           NULL
```

Each column reported its defined length, and the last column ("field6"), which was never defined in the table tblTEST, returned NULL. For the columns of TEXT or IMAGE data types, the length will always be that of BINARY(16), which is the length of a pointer to an actual storage location. For Unicode character data types, the length will be defined by the number of characters specified for the type, not the number of bytes.

The COL_LENGTH() function returns the length of the column, not the length of the data it stores. To find the actual data length, use the DATALENGTH() function.

This function is also found in Sybase ASE.

DB_ID()

Syntax:

```
DB_ID([<database_name>])
```

The DB_ID() function returns the ID number for the specified database name. If no name is specified, the ID of the current database is returned, and if the name argument is invalid, the function returns NULL. Consider the following example:

```
USE tempdb
SELECT
    DB_ID('master')    AS master_id,
    DB_ID()    AS current_db,
    DB_ID('nosuchthing')    AS invalid_db

master_id    current_db  invalid_db
-----------  ----------- -----------
1            2                NULL
```

This batch switches context to TEMPDB, and then executes the query. The ID of the master database is always 1, while the current database has ID of 2. For the nonexistent database name the function returns NULL.

This function is also found in Sybase ASE.

DB_NAME()

Syntax:

```
DB_NAME([<database_id>])
```

The DB_NAME() function returns a database name when it is passed a valid database ID. Consider the following example:

```
SELECT DB_NAME (1) AS db

db
------
master
```

The numeric ID for the master database is 1, and the function returned master when passed the ID 1. To find valid ID(s) for a database, you can query the SYSDATABASES system table, as shown here:

```
SELECT
    Name AS database_name,
    dbid  AS database_id
```

```
FROM master.dbo.sysdatabases

database_name               database_id
--------------------        -----------
master                      1
tempdb                      2
model                       3
msdb                        4
pubs                        5
Northwind                   6
acme                        7
```

If no database ID is supplied, the function returns the ID of the current database.

This function is also found in Sybase ASE.

FILE_ID()

Syntax:

```
FILE_ID(<logical_file_name>)
```

This function returns the file identification number for a given logical file that corresponds to the column in the SYSFILES system table. Consider the following example:

```
USE tempdb
SELECT
    FILE_ID('tempdev')    AS tempdb_fileID

tempdb_fileID
-------------
1
```

Each database has at least two files—a database file and a log file. Here is an example of a query executed against the SYSFILES table in the TEMPDB database:

```
USE tempdb
SELECT
    fileid,
    name
FROM SYSFILES

fileid name
------ ------------
1      tempdev
2      templog
```

The argument passed represents a logical, not physical, name of the file, which in this example would be under the FILENAME column of the SYSFILES table.

There is no direct equivalent available in the other RDBMS implementations discussed in this book.

FILE_NAME()

Syntax:

```
FILE_NAME(<fileID_integer>)
```

This function returns the logical filename for the given file identification (ID) number. The idea behind the function is an action opposite to the FILE_ID() function. Consider the following example:

```
USE tempdb
SELECT
    FILE_NAME(1)   AS tempdb_file

tempdb_file
-------------
tempdev
```

There are no direct equivalent functions in the other RDBMS implementations discussed in this book.

Configuration Functions

This set of scalar functions returns various information regarding the current configuration option settings. This can be particularly helpful in diagnosing performance issues on the RDBMS. An example would be to check the configuration settings on client connections to determine whether client settings are affecting database performance. The following table lists the various functions that we will discuss in this section.

Function Name	Description
@@CONNECTION	Returns the number of opened or attempted connections.
@@LANGUAGE	Returns the name of the language for the current session/database.
@@LANGID	Returns ID of the language for the current session/database.
@@LOCK_TIMEOUT	Returns lock timeout in milliseconds.
@@MAX_CONNECTIONS	Returns the maximum number of simultaneous user connections.
@@NESTLEVEL	Returns the nesting level of the current stored procedure.
@@OPTIONS	Returns bitmask information about current SET options.
@@SPID	Returns the Server Process ID (SPID) of the current process/session.
@@VERSION	Returns the date, version, and processor type for the current version of SQL Server.

@@CONNECTION

Syntax:

```
SELECT @@CONNECTION
```

The @@CONNECTION function returns the number of opened or attempted connections, including the number of user logins attempted for the RDBMS server. The number includes all connections, not just active ones. This is important to remember if you are using this function as a performance counter measurement because the total connections can include those that are considered to be "sleeping" and not active. Consider the following example:

```
SELECT
    @@CONNECTION as total_connections

total_connections
-----------------
2
```

This function is also found in Sybase ASE.

@@LANGID

Syntax:

```
SELECT @@LANGID
```

The @@LANGID function returns the current local language ID number of the language that is in use on the system. The following code gives an example of the use of the @@LANGID function.

```
SELECT @@LANGID AS DB_LANGUAGE

DB_LANGUAGE
-----------------
0
```

This result would indicate that the us_english language was the local language currently in use on the system. The sp_helplanguage procedure returns a listing of the various language settings, including a breakdown of the language IDs.

The @@LANGID function can also be found in the Sybase ASE implementation.

@@LANGUAGE

Syntax:

```
SELECT @@LANGUAGE
```

This function returns the language description assigned to a particular language ID (for example, us_english) from the table syslanguages. This is an important function to consider if you would like your code to work in a multiple region environment. Consider the following example, which displays the current language setting for the database:

```
SELECT
    @@LANGUAGE AS server_language
```

```
server_language
---------------
us_english
```

The following table shows the various languages that are installed with MS SQL Server.

Language	SQL Server Message Group ID
ARABIC	1025
BRAZILIAN	1046
BULGARIAN	1026
CHINESE (SIMPLIFIED)	2052
CHINESE (TRADITIONAL)	1028
CROATIAN	1050
CZECH	1029
DANISH	1030
DUTCH	1043
ENGLISH (USA)	1033
ENGLISH (British)	1033 (NT LCID 2057)
ESTONIAN	1061
FINNISH	1035
FRENCH	1036
GERMAN	1031
GREEK	1032
HUNGARIAN	1038
ITALIAN	1040
JAPANESE	1041
KOREAN	1042
LATVIAN	1062
LITHUANIAN	1063
NORWEGIAN	2068
POLISH	1045
PORTUGUESE	2070
ROMANIAN	1048
RUSSIAN	1049

Table continued on following page

Language	SQL Server Message Group ID
SLOVAK	1051
SLOVENE	1060
SPANISH	3082
SWEDISH	1053
TURKISH	1055
THAI	1054

This function is also found in Sybase ASE.

@@LOCK_TIMEOUT

Syntax:

```
SELECT @@LOCK_TIMEOUT
```

This returns the lock timeout in milliseconds. It allows an application to set the maximum time that a statement waits on a blocked resource. When a statement has waited longer than the LOCK_TIMEOUT setting, the blocked statement is automatically canceled, and an error message is returned to the application.

This function is also available on the Sybase platform.

@@MAX_CONNECTIONS

Syntax:

```
SELECT @@MAX_CONNECTIONS
```

The @@MAX_CONNECTIONS function returns the number of simultaneous connections for which the given environment is configured. The number is dependent upon the type of licenses purchased. Consider the following example:

```
SELECT
    @@MAX_CONNECTIONS AS max_out

max_out
-----------
32767
```

You can use the sp_reconfigure system stored procedure to change the setting. Understanding the maximum number of connections that MS SQL Server will allow is crucial for understanding performance issues related to such things as connection pooling.

This function is also found in Sybase ASE.

@@NESTLEVEL

Syntax:

```
SELECT @@NESTLEVEL
```

The @@NESTLEVEL function returns the current nesting level for the procedure. The maximum allowable value is 32; once that level is exceeded the transaction is terminated. The function is rarely useful in a SQL statement, except when you want to ensure that a stored procedure or trigger is not fired past a specific nesting level.

This function is also found in Sybase ASE.

@@OPTIONS

Syntax:

```
SELECT @@OPTIONS
```

This function returns the bitmask information from the current SET options. To find out whether the bitmask contains a specific flag, use the bitwise "&" operator. For example, the following shows a current setup that does not have option XACT_ABORT set on (value 16384):

```
SELECT
    @@OPTIONS & 16384 AS bit_value
GO

bit_value
-----------
0
```

The options can be configured using the sp_configure system stored procedure. For example, setting the option ON will produce different results:

```
SET XACT_ABORT ON
SELECT
    @@OPTIONS & 16384 AS bit_value
GO

bit_value
-----------
16384
```

Refer to the vendor's documentation for more information on the SET options. This function is also found in Sybase ASE.

@@SPID

Syntax:

```
SELECT @@SPID
```

This function returns the number (ID) of the current process/session. Consider the following example:

```
SELECT
    @@SPID AS process_id

process_id
-----------
51
```

This example returns the current server process ID number that the user is using to execute the statement. This information is important to know when troubleshooting locking/blocking issues for the database.

For more detailed information about processes, use the system-stored procedure sp_who.

The same function can be found in the Sybase implementation.

@@VERSION

Syntax:

```
SELECT @@VERSION
```

The @@VERSION function returns the date, version, and processor type for the current version of SQL Server. The function accepts no arguments, and the return data is of NVARCHAR data type. For example, our installation returns the following:

```
SELECT @@VERSION

--------------------------------------------------------------------
Microsoft SQL Server  2000 - 8.00.760(Intel X86)
Dec 17 2002 14:22:05
Copyright (c) 1988-2003 Microsoft Corporation
Developer Edition on Windows NT 5.0 (Build 2195: Service Pack 3)
```

Use the extended stored procedure xp_msver to get more detailed information in tabular form.

This function is available on the Sybase platform and returns the same type of information for the Sybase Adaptive Server instance.

Security Functions

These scalar functions return information pertaining to users and roles in the current security context. The following table details the various functions that we will discuss in this section.

Function Name	Input	Output	Description
HAS_DBACCESS	<database_name>	INTEGER	Indicates whether the current user has access to the specified database.
SUSER_SID	[login]	VARBINARY(85)	Returns user's security identification number (SID) from login name.
SUSER_SNAME	[<userID_binary>]	char_expression	Returns user's login name from security identification number (SID).
USER_ID	[<user_name>]	INTEGER	Returns user's database identification number from username.
USER_NAME	[<user_id>]	char_expression	Returns database user's name from identification number.
USER	N/A	char_expression	Returns the current user's database name.

HAS_DBACCESS()

Syntax:

```
SELECT HAS_DBACCESS(<database_name>)
```

This function indicates whether the current user has access to the specified database. The return integer 0 is interpreted as lack of access, while 1 is returned for a database to which the user has access (this follows C world definitions). The user is implicitly assumed to be the current one. Consider the following example:

```
SELECT
    HAS_DBACCESS ('master') AS sys_admin

sys_admin
-----------
1
```

There is no equivalent function available in the other RDBMS implementations discussed in this book.

SUSER_SID()

Syntax:

```
SELECT SUSER_SID([login])
```

This function returns the user's security identification number (SID) given a login name. If `login` is omitted, an ID for the current user is returned. Consider the following example:

```
SELECT
    SUSER_SID() AS windows_user,
    SUSER_SID('sa') AS sa_user

windows_user                                                sa_user
---------------------------------------------------------   ----------
0x010500000000000515000000A1F40462DDE8E41C16C0EA32E8030000   0x01
```

The first, scary-looking ID is generated for the Windows-authenticated user connected to the SQL Server. Specifying the username from a Windows user profile (for example, "ALEX-TEST\sql_test") would yield identical results.

An equivalent function, `SUSER_ID()`, is available on the Sybase RDBMS platform.

SUSER_SNAME()

Syntax:

```
SUSER_SNAME([<userID_binary>])
```

This function returns a user's login name given a security identification number (SID) as a `VARBINARY` data type. Its action is opposite that of the `SUSER_SID` function—it returns a username from the user ID. An invalid user ID would result in `NULL`. Consider the following example:

```
SELECT
    SUSER_SNAME(0x01)    AS sa_login
    SUSER_SNAME(0x023)   AS invalid_ID

sa_login       invalid_id
----------     --------------
sa             NULL
```

If the `<userID_binary>` value is omitted, the function returns the default current user.

An equivalent function, `SUSER_NAME()`, is available on the Sybase RDBMS platform.

USER

Syntax:

```
SELECT USER
```

This function is used to return the current database user's username. Essentially this function is the same as the system function USER_NAME. Consider the following example:

```
SELECT USER

----------------
dbo
```

The USER function is available in all of the RDBMS implementations discussed in this book.

USER_ID()

Syntax:

```
SELECT USER_ID([user_name])
```

This function returns a user's database identification number from the username. If the name is omitted, the current user's ID number is returned. Consider the following example:

```
SELECT
    USER_ID() AS current_user_id

current_user_id
----------------------
1
```

When <user_name> is supplied as CHAR data type, it will be implicitly converted into NCHAR.

The USER_ID function is also available on the Sybase ASE platform. Oracle provides a similar function called UID that uniquely identifies the current session user.

USER_NAME()

Syntax:

```
SELECT USER_NAME([user_id])
```

This function returns a database user's name given the identification number. If the number is omitted, the current username is returned. Consider the following example:

```
SELECT
    USER_NAME(2) AS user_2,
    USER_NAME() AS default_user

user_2       default_user
--------     --------------
guest        dbo
```

When `user_id` is not specified, the function defaults to the `USER()` function. The information about users is stored in the system table `SYSUSERS`. The following query gives an example of what this table contains:

```
SELECT
    Uid,
    name
FROM master..sysusers
ORDER BY uid

Uid    name
------ ----------------------
0      public
1      dbo
2      guest
3      INFORMATION_SCHEMA
4      system_function_schema
16384  db_owner
16385  db_accessadmin
16386  db_securityadmin
16387  db_ddladmin
16389  db_backupoperator
16390  db_datareader
16391  db_datawriter
16392  db_denydatareader
16393  db_denydatawriter
```

The `USER_NAME()` function is also available in the Sybase ASE implementation. Of course, without the parameter setting, the function behaves as the `USER()` function and, thus, has an equivalent that is available in all of the RDBMS implementations discussed in this book.

System Functions

These functions return information on and perform operations on various objects, values, and settings in the database. The following table details the various functions involved.

Function Name	Input	Output	Description
APP_NAME	None	<expression>	Returns the application name of the current session if set by an application.
CASE	<input expression>	<expression>	Evaluates a list of conditional statements and returns a result expression based upon those conditions.

Function Name	Input	Output	Description
CAST	<expression> AS <data_type>	<expression>	Explicitly converts one data type into another data type.
COALESCE	<expession1>, <expression2>...... <expression_n>	<expression>	Returns the first instance of the input expressions that evaluate to a non-NULL value.
CONVERT	data_type [(length)] , expression [,style]	<expression>	Explicitly converts one data type into another data type. Behaves similar to the CAST function.
CURRENT_TIMESTAMP	None	<timestamp>	Returns the current system date and time.
CURRENT_USER	None	<expression>	Returns the current session user. Similar to the USER function.
DATALENGTH	<expression>	INTEGER	Returns the number of bytes in an expression.
@@ERROR	None	NUMBER	Returns the error number of the last Transact-SQL statement.
HOST_ID	None	Char(8)	Returns the current workstation identification number.
HOST_NAME	None	<expression>	Returns the current workstation name.
@@IDENTITY	None	NUMBER	Returns the last inserted identity value.
IDENTITY	<data_type> [,<seed>, <increment>]	<expression>	Used to insert into an identity column.

Table continued on following page

Function Name	Input	Output	Description
ISDATE	`<expression>`	`INTEGER`	Determines whether an expression is a valid date type (or could be converted into one).
ISNULL	`<expression>`	`INTEGER`	Determines whether the expression is `NULL`.
ISNUMERIC	`<expression>`	`INTEGER`	Determines whether the expression is numeric. Returns 1 (`TRUE`) or 0 (`FALSE`).
NEWID	N/A	`UNIQUEIDENTIFIER`	Returns a unique value for the `UNIQUEIDENTIFIER` data type.
PERMISSIONS	`<objected>`, `<column name>`	32-bit bitmap	Returns a bitmap that indicates the object or column permissions for the current user.
@@ROWCOUNT	N/A	`INTEGER`	Returns the number of rows affected by the last statement.
ROWCOUNT_BIG	N/A	`BIG_INTEGER`	Returns the rows affected by the last statement as a `BIG_INTEGER`.
@@TRANCOUNT	N/A	`INTEGER`	Returns the number of active transactions for the current session.
COLLATIONPROPERTY	`<collation_name>`, `<property_name>`	SQL VARIANT	Returns the property of a given collation.
SCOPE_IDENTITY	N/A	SQL VARIANT	Returns the last identity value inserted in the identity column for the current scope.

APP_NAME()

Syntax:

```
APP_NAME()
```

The APP_NAME() function is used to return the application name of the current session. The return type of the function is NVARCHAR(128). In the following example, the function is used to show that a session was started by the Microsoft SQL Query Analyzer:

```
begin
declare @MYAPP varchar(128)
set @MYAPP = APP_NAME()
select @MYAPP as This_Application
end

This_Application
--------------------
SQL Query Analyzer
```

The APP_NAME() function does not have a direct equivalent in the other RDBMS implementations discussed in this book.

CASE

Syntax:

```
CASE input
WHEN expression  THEN result_set
.
.
.
.
ELSE else_result_set
END
```

The CASE function is used to evaluate a set of conditional WHEN statements and return a result based upon the evaluation of the input value with those conditions. This function is extremely useful in returning a fixed set of results for a column, such as deciphering a code type value. The following example demonstrates using the CASE function to evaluate a simple input value:

```
BEGIN
declare @MYCOLOR varchar(128)
set @MYCOLOR = 'Green'
SELECT CASE @MYCOLOR
WHEN 'Green' then 'Go'
WHEN 'Yellow' then 'Caution'
ELSE 'Stop!'
end as My_Command
```

```
END

My_Command
----------
Go
```

The CASE function is available in all of the RDBMS implementations discussed in this book. Oracle also supports the DECODE function, which provides similar functionality.

CAST() and CONVERT()

Syntax:

```
CAST(<expression> AS <data_type>)
CONVERT(data_type [ ( length ) ] , expression [ , style ] )
```

Both of these functions are utilized to convert one data type into another. The CAST() function is defined in the SQL 99 standard, while CONVERT() is more of a legacy construct. In Microsoft SQL Server, they provide similar functionality.

The data conversion has many minute details that you must take into consideration to avoid surprises. The information included in this chapter provides only the basics. See the vendor's documentation for more details.

The <expression> can be any valid expression. The <data_type> is any of the valid SQL Server data types (user-defined data types are not allowed).

The CAST() function is the most versatile of the two. It accepts only two arguments—<expression> and the <data_type> to which this <expression> will be converted. For example, to concatenate strings and numbers in Microsoft SQL Server, the following query could be used:

```
SELECT
    '$ ' + CAST (100 AS VARCHAR(10)) AS one_hundred_dollars

one_hundred_dollars
-------------------
$100
```

Without the CAST() function, the server would try to implicitly convert the dollar sign into INTEGER, and an error would result. Not every data type can be converted into any other data type. For the implicit and explicit conversions rules, see the following table.

From:	To:										
	binary	varbinary	char	varchar	nchar	nvarchar	datetime	smalldatetime	decimal	numeric	float	real
Binary		I	I	I	I	I	I	I	I	I	N	N
varbinary	I		I	I	I	I	I	I	I	I	N	N
Char	E	E		I	I	I	I	I	I	I	I	I
varchar	E	E	I		I	I	I	I	I	I	I	I
Nchar	E	E	I	I		I	I	I	I	I	I	I
nvarchar	E	E	I	I	I		I	I	I	I	I	I
Datetime	E	E	I	I	I	I		I	E	E	E	E
smalldatetime	E	E	I	I	I	I	I		E	E	E	E
Decimal	I	I	I	I	I	I	I	I	*	*	I	I
Numeric	I	I	I	I	I	I	I	I	*	*	I	I
Float	I	I	I	I	I	I	I	I	I	I		I
Real	I	I	I	I	I	I	I	I	I	I	I	
Bigint	I	I	I	I	I	I	I	I	I	I	I	I
int(INT 4)	I	I	I	I	I	I	I	I	I	I	I	I
smallint(INT 2)	I	I	I	I	I	I	I	I	I	I	I	I
tinyint(INT 1)	I	I	I	I	I	I	I	I	I	I	I	I
Money	I	I	E	E	E	E	I	I	I	I	I	I
smallmoney	I	I	E	E	E	E	I	I	I	I	I	I
Bit	I	I	I	I	I	I	I	I	I	I	I	I
timestamp	I	I	I	I	N	N	I	I	I	I	N	N
uniqueidentifier	I	I	I	I	I	I	N	N	N	N	N	N
Image	I	I	N	N	N	N	N	N	N	N	N	N
Ntext	N	N	E	E	I	I	N	N	N	N	N	N
Text	N	N	I	I	E	E	N	N	N	N	N	N
sql_variant	E	E	E	E	E	E	E	E	E	E	E	E

From:	To:												
	bigint	int(INT 4)	smallint(INT 2)	tinyint(INT 1)	money	smallmoney	bit	timestamp	uniqueidentifier	image	ntext	text	sql_variant
Binary	I	I	I	I	I	I	I	I	I	I	N	N	I
varbinary	I	I	I	I	I	I	I	I	I	I	N	N	I
Char	I	I	I	I	E	E	I	E	I	I	I	I	I
varchar	I	I	I	I	E	E	I	E	I	I	I	I	I
Nchar	I	I	I	I	E	E	I	E	I	N	I	I	I
nvarchar	I	I	I	I	E	E	I	E	I	N	I	I	I
Datetime	E	E	E	E	E	E	E	E	N	N	N	N	I
smalldatetime	E	E	E	E	E	E	E	E	N	N	N	N	I
Decimal	I	I	I	I	I	I	I	I	N	N	N	N	I
Numeric	I	I	I	I	I	I	I	I	N	N	N	N	I
Float	I	I	I	I	I	I	I	N	N	N	N	N	I
Real	I	I	I	I	I	I	I	N	N	N	N	N	I
Bigint		I	I	I	I	I	I	I	N	N	N	N	I
int(INT 4)	I		I	I	I	I	I	I	N	N	N	N	I
smallint(INT 2)	I	I		I	I	I	I	I	N	N	N	N	I
tinyint(INT 1)	I	I	I		I	I	I	I	N	N	N	N	I
Money	I	I	I	I		I	I	I	N	N	N	N	I
smallmoney	I	I	I	I	I		I	I	N	N	N	N	I
Bit	I	I	I	I	I	I		I	N	N	N	N	I
timestamp	I	I	I	I	I	I	I		N	I	N	N	N
uniqueidentifier	N	N	N	N	N	N	N	N		N	N	N	I
Image	N	N	N	N	N	N	N	I	N		N	N	N
Ntext	N	N	N	N	N	N	N	N	N	N		I	N
Text	N	N	N	N	N	N	N	N	N	I	N		N
sql_variant	E	E	E	E	E	E	E	N	E	N	N	N	

Legend: E = Explicit conversion, I = Implicit conversion, N = Not allowed, * = Requires an explicit CAST ( ) to prevent loss of precision or scale that might occur in an implicit conversion

Automatic data type conversion is not supported for the text and image data types. You can explicitly convert text data to character data, and image data to BINARY or VARBINARY; the maximum length is 8,000 in this case.

To use this table, you must find the data type that you are converting from in the leftmost column and match it up with the data type that you want to convert to in the topmost row. Following the row and column matches to their intersection will tell you what kind of conversion will take place.

The CONVERT() function not only converts data types, it also formats the result with optional parameters <length> and <style>. The range of values for the date and time data is shown in the following table.

Without Century	With Century	Standard	Input/Output
—	0 or 100	Default	mon dd yyyy hh:miAM (or PM)
1	101	USA	mm/dd/yy
2	102	ANSI	yy.mm.dd
3	103	British/French	dd/mm/yy
4	104	German	dd.mm.yy
5	105	Italian	dd-mm-yy
6	106	—	dd mon yy
7	107	—	Mon dd, yy
8	108	—	hh:mm:ss
-	9 or 109	Default + milliseconds	mon dd yyyy hh:mi:ss:mmmAM (or PM)
10	110	USA	mm-dd-yy
11	111	Japan	yy/mm/dd
12	112	ISO	yymmdd
—	13 or 113	Europe default + milliseconds	dd mon yyyy hh:mm:ss:mmm(24h)
14	114	—	hh:mi:ss:mmm(24h)
—	20 or 120	ODBC canonical	yyyy-mm-dd hh:mi:ss(24h)
—	21 or 121	ODBC canonical (with milliseconds)	yyyy-mm-dd hh:mi:ss.mmm(24h)
—	126 (designed for XML use)	ISO8601	yyyy-mm-dd Thh:mm:ss:mmm(no spaces)
—	130	Kuwaiti	dd mon yyyy hh:mi:ss:mmmAM
—	131	Kuwaiti	dd/mm/yy hh:mi:ss:mmmAM

The range of values for FLOAT and REAL data type conversion into character data is shown in the following table.

Value	Output
0	Six digits maximum; scientific notation, when appropriate.
1	Always eight digits; use in scientific notation.
2	Always sixteen digits; use in scientific notation.

This last table lists the styles necessary for conversion of MONEY and SMALLMONEY data types into character data types.

Value	Output
0	No commas to the left of the decimal point, and two digits to the right of the decimal point (e.g., 1000.00)
1	Commas every three digits to the left of the decimal point, and two digits to the right of the decimal point (e.g., 1,000.00)
2	No commas to the left of the decimal point, and four digits to the right of the decimal point (e.g., 1000.0000)

Here are some examples of the CONVERT() function usage—converting DATETIME data type (obtained with the use of GETDATE() function):

```
SELECT
    CONVERT(VARCHAR(25),GETDATE(),111) AS japanese_style,
    CONVERT(VARCHAR(25),GETDATE(),104) AS german_style,
    CONVERT(VARCHAR(25),GETDATE(),126) AS ISO8601_style

japanese_style      german_style        ISO8601_style
------------------- ------------------  ------------------------
2004/07/10          10.07.2004          2004-07-10T02:20:06.240
```

If the output of CAST() or CONVERT() is a character string, and the input is a character string, the output has the same collation and collation label as the input. In case the input is not a character string, the output has the default collation of the database.

The CAST() function is used almost identically across all six RDBMS implementations discussed in this book (with the exception of Sybase, which does not support CAST()). CONVERT(), however, is used for conversion from one character set to another only in Oracle and Microsoft SQL Server; in the latter, it is almost a synonym for the function CAST().

COALESCE()

Syntax:

```
COALESCE(<exp1>,<exp2> . . . <expN>)
```

The COALESCE() function returns the first non-null expression in the expression list. At least one expression must not be the literal NULL. If all expressions evaluate to NULL, then the function returns NULL. Consider the following example:

```
SELECT
    COALESCE (NULL, NULL, 'NOT NULL', NULL) test

TEST
------------
NOT NULL
```

The COALESCE() function is the most generic version of the NVL() function, and can be used instead of it. The syntax and usage is identical across all RDBMS implementations discussed in this book.

CURRENT_TIMESTAMP

Syntax:

```
CURRENT_TIMESTAMP
```

The CURRENT_TIMESTAMP function is used to return the current date and time of the database instance. It is synonymous with the GETDATE() function. The following example demonstrates the use of both functions:

```
SELECT
    CURRENT_TIMESTAMP as TIME_NOW_TIMESTAMP,
    GETDATE() AS TIME_NOW_GETDATE

TIME_NOW_TIMESTAMP                    TIME_NOW_GETDATE
-----------------------               -----------------------
2004-10-03 20:49:33.280               2004-10-03 20:49:33.280
```

The GETDATE() function is available in the Sybase ASE implementation. IBM uses the special register CURRENT_DATE. Oracle uses the SYSDATE pseudo-column to achieve similar functionality.

CURRENT_USER

Syntax:

```
CURRENT_USER
```

The CURRENT_USER function is used to return the current session user. Its functionality is similar to that of the USER function. The following example shows the use of the CURRENT_USER function to return the user of the current session:

```
SELECT
    CURRENT_USER AS CURRENTUSER_FUNCTION,
    USER AS USER_FUNCTION

CURRENTUSER_FUNCTION                  USER_FUNCTION
-----------------------               -----------------------
dbo                                   dbo
```

The CURRENT_USER functionality can be gained by using the USER function in the other RDBMS imple-mentations discussed in this book.

DATALENGTH()

Syntax:

```
DATALENGTH(<expression>)
```

The DATALENGTH() function returns the actual length of the expression, in bytes rather than in charac-ters. The expression can be of any data type, and is especially useful with variable-length fields. For example, using the tblTEST table created earlier in the chapter (see the COL_LENGTH() function dis-cussed in the section "Metadata Functions"), we could insert some records in the table as follows:

```
INSERT INTO tblTEST Values('ABC','ABCD', 1, 2,0)
GO
SELECT
    DATALENGTH(field1) AS char_10,
    DATALENGTH(field2) AS varchar_25,
    DATALENGTH(field3) AS int_field,
    DATALENGTH(field4) AS money_field,
    DATALENGTH(field5) AS bit_field,
    DATALENGTH(NULL)   AS null_field
FROM tblTEST

char_10    varchar_25  int_field  money_field bit_field  null_field
---------- ----------- ---------- ----------- ---------- -----------
10         4           4          8           1          NULL
```

As you can see, fixed-length fields display their defined length, even though actual meaningful data is shorter (CHAR_10 field). This happens because the entered value is padded with blanks (spaces) up to the length of the field. In the case of a variable-length field (VARCHAR_25), the DATALENGTH() function returns exactly 4—the number of entered characters—even though the field itself can accommodate up to 25 characters. When the input expression is NULL, the function returns NULL.

The DATALENGTH() function is also available in the Sybase ASE implementation.

@@ERROR

Syntax:

```
@@ERROR
```

The @@ERROR function is used to return the error status of the last Transact-SQL statement that was executed. At the conclusion of the Transact-SQL statement, the @@ERROR function will return 0 if the statement has executed successfully. However, if there was an error, then the @@ERROR function will return the error code of the error that occurred. The corresponding text for this number can be found by querying the sysmessages table. Normally, the @@ERROR function value is saved to a variable and then checked later in the transaction for a possible ROLLBACK because it is erased immediately after the next statement is executed. The following example demonstrates a simple method of using the @@ERROR func-tion to detect the violation of a check constraint:

```
USE NORTHWIND

UPDATE EMPLOYEES SET BIRTHDATE = DATEADD(M,3,GETDATE())
WHERE EMPLOYEEID=2
IF @@ERROR=547
PRINT 'THE BIRTHDATE CANNOT BE GREATER THAN TODAY!'

Server: Msg 547, Level 16, State 1, Line 3
UPDATE statement conflicted with COLUMN CHECK constraint 'CK_Birthdate'. The
conflict occurred in database 'Northwind', table 'Employees', column 'BirthDate'.
The statement has been terminated.
THE BIRTHDATE CANNOT BE GREATER THAN TODAY!
```

The @@ERROR statement is also available in the Sybase ASE, although its functionality is a little different. Additionally, every RDBMS implementation provides some level of error-checking support, even though the syntax may vary.

HOST_ID()

Syntax:

```
HOST_ID()
```

The HOST_ID() function is used to return the workstation identification number of the current user session. Often, this is used to insert this value into a table via an INSERT statement as a means of tracking transactions. The following example will return the current workstation ID:

```
SELECT
    HOST_ID() as MY_HOST_ID

MY_HOST_ID
----------
1892
```

The HOST_ID() function is also available in the Sybase ASE implementation.

HOST_NAME()

Syntax:

```
HOST_NAME()
```

The HOST_NAME() function is used to return the current workstation name of the current user session. Often it is used to insert this value into a table via an INSERT statement as a means of tracking transactions. The following example will return the current workstation name:

```
SELECT
    HOST_NAME() as MY_HOST_NAME

MY_HOST_NAME
-------------------
BISHOP-SERVER-04
```

The HOST_NAME() function is also available in the Sybase ASE implementation.

@@IDENTITY

Syntax:

```
SELECT @@IDENTITY
```

This function returns the last inserted identity value. If no actions that involve identity columns were performed, the function would return NULL. @@IDENTITY, SCOPE_IDENTITY, and IDENT_CURRENT are similar functions in that they return the last value inserted into the IDENTITY column of a table. However @@IDENTITY is not limited to a scope; it is global for the session, and IDENT_CURRENT is tied to a specific table. It is much more likely as a developer that you will use the SCOPE_IDENTITY function to ensure that the identity object is related to the specific instance in which it is called. We can find the last inserted identity value for Northwind's Shippers table, insert a new entry, and then check the @@IDENTITY function to see the change in the global value, as shown in the following example.

```
DECLARE @CURRENTID INT

SELECT @CURRENTID = IDENT_CURRENT('SHIPPERS')
SELECT @CURRENTID AS STARTING_ID

INSERT INTO [Northwind].[dbo].[Shippers]([CompanyName], [Phone])
VALUES('BIG SQL DEVELOPER','555-555-5555')

select @@IDENTITY AS ENDING_ID

STARTING_ID
-----------
5

(1 row(s) affected)


(1 row(s) affected)

ENDING_ID
----------------------------------------
6

(1 row(s) affected)
```

The identity concept (and its functions) corresponds to the SEQUENCE object found in many RDBMS implementations used to generate sequential numbers.

IDENTITY()

Syntax:

```
IDENTITY(<data_type> [,<seed>,<increment> ])
```

This function is used only in a SELECT statement with an INTO table clause to insert an identity column into a new table. It essentially performs the same function as the IDENTITY property, without being attached to a table. We can use the IDENTITY() function to copy our Shippers table with new values in the identity column, in the following example incremented by 10s. The following code details how this would be implemented:

```
SELECT IDENTITY(INT,1,10) AS SHIPPERID, COMPANYNAME, PHONE
INTO COPY_SHIPPERS
FROM SHIPPERS


SELECT * FROM COPY_SHIPPERS

SHIPPERID   COMPANYNAME                                   PHONE
----------- --------------------------------------------- ------------------------
1           Speedy Express                                (503) 555-9831
11          United Package                                (503) 555-3199
21          Federal Shipping                              (503) 555-9931
31          Federal Shipping                              (555)555-9931
41          BIG SQL DEVELOPER                             555-555-5555
```

There are no equivalent functions in the other RDBMS implementations discussed in this book.

ISDATE()

Syntax:

```
ISDATE()
```

This function determines whether an expression is a valid date type (or could be converted into one). Consider the following example:

```
SELECT
    ISDATE(GETDATE()) AS  getdate_value,
    ISDATE ('07/18/2004') AS date_value,
    ISDATE('67/56/07') AS not_a_date

getdate_value date_value  not_a_date
------------- ----------- -----------
1             1           0
```

ISDATE() returns 1 if the input expression is a valid date; otherwise, it returns 0.

There are no equivalent functions in the other RDBMS implementations discussed in this book.

ISNULL()

Syntax:

```
ISNULL(<check_expression>,<replacement_value>)
```

This function determines whether the expression is NULL, and if it is, replaces it with the specified replacement value. Consider the following example:

```
SELECT
    ISNULL(NULL, 'it is NULL')    AS null_value,
    ISNULL('not NULL', 'it is NULL')    AS not_null

null_value          not_null
----------          --------
it is NULL          not NULL
```

The `<replacement_expression>` must be of the same data type as `<check_expression>`.

This function is present in Sybase ASE, while Oracle's equivalent is NVL().

ISNUMERIC()

Syntax:

```
ISNUMERIC()
```

This function determines whether the expression is numeric, and returns 0 (FALSE) or 1 (TRUE). Consider the following example:

```
SELECT
    ISNUMERIC('12345') AS num_value,
    ISNUMERIC('12@345') AS not_num_value

num_value    not_num_value
-----------  -------------
1                   0
```

A returned value of 1 guarantees that the value could be converted into any of the numeric data types.

There are no equivalent functions in the other RDBMS implementations discussed in this book.

NEWID()

Syntax:

```
NEWID()
```

This function returns a unique value for the UNIQUEIDENTIFIER data type. Consider the following example, which simply produces a unique string value when executed:

```
SELECT
    NEWID() AS unique_string

unique_string
------------------------------------
ED8B0B94-EBBB-4B40-ACC6-4AF2C381B729
```

Similar functionality is obtained in other RDBMS implementations by using the UNIQUEIDENTIFIER data type for the identity column of a table. However, SQL Server is the only implementation discussed in this book that has the NEWID() function.

PERMISSIONS()

Syntax:

```
SELECT PERMISSIONS(objectID, [column])
```

The PERMISSIONS() function is a value containing a bitmap that indicates the statement, object, or column permissions for the current user. The function uses the objectID of the object in the database on which to report. The objectID can always be obtained using the OBJECT_ID() function, The column parameter is optional, and can be used to return permission information for a valid column within a table specified by the objectID. The following shows a simple example of the use of the PERMISSIONS() function to get information on the EMPLOYEES table:

```
SELECT PERMISSIONS(OBJECT_ID('EMPLOYEES')) AS BIT_MAP

BIT_MAP
-----------
1881108543
```

The corresponding bitmap can be deciphered by using the following table.

Bit(dec)	Statement Permission
1	SELECT ALL
2	UPDATE ALL
4	REFERENCES ALL
8	INSERT
16	DELETE
32	EXECUTE (PROCEDURES ONLY)
4096	SELECT ANY (AT LEAST ONE COLUMN)
8192	UPDATE ANY
16384	REFERENCES ANY

This function is only available in the Microsoft SQL Server RDBMS implementation.

ROWCOUNT_BIG and @@ROWCOUNT

Syntax:

```
SELECT ROWCOUNT_BIG()
SELECT @@ROWCOUNT
```

Both of these functions return the number of rows affected by the last statement executed. Both functions operate in exactly the same manner, except that the return type of ROWCOUNT_BIG is BIGINT data type, and that of @@ROWCOUNT is INTEGER. These are mostly useful in procedural environments.

After a SELECT statement, these functions return the number of rows returned by the SELECT statement. After an INSERT, UPDATE, or DELETE statement, they return the number of rows affected by the data modification statement. This can be extremely useful as one way in which to determine if a statement has produced the desired result. The following code could be used with the Northwind database as a check to see if an INSERT statement has correctly executed.

```
INSERT INTO
SHIPPERS(CompanyName, Phone)
VALUES('Federal Shipping','(555)555-9931')

IF @@ROWCOUNT<>0 THEN
SELECT 'INSERTED SUCCESSFULLY' AS RESULT
ELSE
SELECT 'INSERT FAILED!' AS RESULT

RESULT
--------------------
INSERTED SUCCESSFULLY
```

The @@ROWCOUNT function is available in the Sybase ASE implementation.

@@TRANCOUNT

Syntax:

```
@@TRANCOUNT
```

The @@TRANCOUNT function returns the number of pending transactions for the current session. The function is not especially useful outside of the Transact-SQL context because it requires at least two statements to be executed (that is, BEGIN TRAN being first). Each BEGIN TRAN statement increments the counter by one; a COMMIT statement sets the counter to zero. The following example demonstrates the basic principle of the @@TRANCOUNT function:

```
BEGIN TRAN T1
SELECT @@TRANCOUNT AS FIRST
BEGIN TRAN T2
SELECT @@TRANCOUNT AS SECOND
BEGIN TRAN T3
SELECT @@TRANCOUNT AS THIRD
COMMIT TRAN T3
COMMIT TRAN T2
COMMIT TRAN T1

FIRST
-----------
1

(1 row(s) affected)

SECOND
-----------
2
```

```
(1 row(s) affected)

THIRD
-----------
3

(1 row(s) affected)
```

The @@TRANCOUNT function is also available in the Sybase ASE implementation.

COLLATIONPROPERTY()

Syntax:

```
SELECT COLLATIONPROPERTY(<collation_name>,<property_name>)
```

This function returns the property of a given collation when passed a collation name (VARCHAR(128)), and a requested property. Following is an example for Croatian, case-sensitive, accent-sensitive, kanatype-insensitive, and width-insensitive for Unicode Data, SQL Server Sort Order 91 on Code Page 1250 for non-Unicode Data:

```
SELECT
    COLLATIONPROPERTY('SQL_Croatian_CP1250_CS_AS', 'CodePage') AS code_page

Code_page
-----------------
1250
```

The following table lists the properties of a collation that can be used as the second argument.

Property Name	Description
CodePage	The non-UNICODE code page of the collation.
LCID	The Windows locale ID (LCID) of the collation.
ComparisonStyle	The Windows comparison style of the collation. Returns NULL for binary or SQL collations.

*You could use a table-valued function fn_helpcollation to return the list of the supported collations (that is, select * from ::fn_helpcollations()). The returned result set displays more than 700 different collations.*

There are no direct corresponding functions in the other RDBMS implementations discussed in this book.

SCOPE_IDENTITY()

Syntax:

```
SELECT SCOPE_IDENTITY()
```

This function returns the last identity value inserted in the identity column for the current scope; the return data type is SQL_VARIANT.

A *scope* is defined as a module—a stored procedure, function, or batch. The difference between the SCOPE_IDENTITY() function and @@IDENTITY is that the latter is not limited by the scope, so its value could reflect changes made by other sessions. The function IDENT_CURRENT is limited to one specific table.

As mentioned earlier in the discussion of the @@IDENTITY function, it is usually more accurate to use the SCOPE_IDENTITY() function in order to get the IDENTITY value of the current transaction. This is extremely important in a transactional environment such as an ordering system in which multiple users may be inserting orders into a particular table at one time. In the following example, we use the Northwind database to insert a customer order into the ORDERS table and return a message to indicate what the order number is:

```
INSERT INTO
ORDERS(CustomerID, EmployeeID, OrderDate, RequiredDate,
ShippedDate, ShipVia, Freight, ShipName, ShipAddress,
ShipCity, ShipRegion, ShipPostalCode, ShipCountry)
VALUES('VINET',5,'7/4/1996','8/11/1996','7/16/1996',
3,32.38,'Vins et alcool','59 Rue de Pari','Reims','RJ',
51100,'France')

SELECT 'Your order number is: #' + CONVERT(VARCHAR(10),SCOPE_IDENTITY()) AS
ORDER_RESULT

ORDER_RESULT
--------------------
Your order number is: #11080
```

In a real-world environment, something similar to this example could be used to return the identity value (an order number) to an ASP.NET page, which would display a confirmation page to the user.

The SCOPE_IDENTITY() function is also available in the Sybase ASE implementation.

System Statistical Functions

This group of functions returns statistical information about the system. The functions discussed in this section are detailed in the following table.

Function Name	Description
@@CPU_BUSY	Returns the time (in milliseconds) since the start of the SQL Server instance.
@@IDLE	Returns idle time (in milliseconds) since the start of the SQL Server instance.
@@IO_BUSY	Returns the time (in milliseconds) since the start of the SQL Server instance, when it was busy with I/O operations.

Function Name	Description
@@TIMETICKS	Returns the number of milliseconds per CPU tick.
@@TOTAL_ERRORS	Returns the number of disk write/read errors since the start of the SQL Server instance.
@@TOTAL_READ	Returns the number of physical disk reads since the start of the SQL Server instance.
@@TOTAL_WRITE	Returns the number of physical disk writes since the start of the SQL Server instance.
fn_virtualfilestats	Returns I/O statistics for the database files.

@@CPU_BUSY

Syntax:

```
SELECT @@CPU_BUSY
```

This function returns the time (in milliseconds) that the CPU has spent working (not idling) since the start of the SQL Server instance. Consider the following example:

```
SELECT
@@CPU_BUSY AS busy

busy
-----------
49
```

This function is also present in Sybase ASE.

@@IDLE

Syntax:

```
SELECT @@IDLE
```

This function returns idle time (in milliseconds) since the start of the SQL Server instance. Consider the following example, which would display the current amount of idle time on your SQL Server implementation:

```
SELECT
    @@IDLE as doing_nothing

doing_nothing
-------------
2316701
```

The @@IDLE function is also available in the Sybase ASE implementation.

@@IO_BUSY

Syntax:

```
SELECT @@IO_BUSY
```

This function returns the time (in milliseconds) since the start of the SQL Server instance, when it was busy with I/O operations. Consider the following example, which would display the I/O operations wait time for your SQL Server instance:

```
SELECT
    @@IO_BUSY as doing

doing
-------------
14
```

The @@IO_BUSY function is also available in the Sybase ASE implementation.

@@TIMETICKS

Syntax:

```
SELECT @@TIMETICKS
```

This function returns the number of milliseconds per CPU tick. Each tick on the operating system is 31.25 milliseconds, or one-thirty-second of a second. Consider the following example:

```
SELECT
    @@TIMETICKS AS microsec_ticks

microsec_ticks
-------------
31250
```

The result translates into 1,000 milliseconds, or 1,000,000 microseconds (1 ms = 1,000 microseconds).

The @@TIMETICKS function is also available in the Sybase ASE implementation.

@@TOTAL_ERRORS

Syntax:

```
SELECT @@TOTAL_ERRORS
```

This function returns the number of disk write/read errors since the start of the SQL Server instance, while performing reading and writing (I/O operations). This function is not to be confused with the @@ERROR function, which reports an exception thrown in Transact-SQL code. If our SQL Server instance was recently restarted, we could run the following code and get the result of 0:

```
SELECT @@TOTAL_ERRORS

-----------
0

(1 row(s) affected)
```

This is because the count for the @@TOTAL_ERRORS function is reset whenever the database instance is started.

The @@TOTAL_ERRORS function is also available in the Sybase ASE implementation.

@@TOTAL_READ

Syntax:

```
SELECT @@TOTAL_READ
```

This function returns the number of physical disk reads since the start of the SQL Server instance. The information returned could be useful in identifying bottlenecks and improving the system's performance. Consider the following example:

```
SELECT
    @@TOTAL_READ AS reads
reads
-----------
426
```

Our result shows 426 reads since the start of the SQL Server instance. Once the instance is shut down and then restarted this value is reset to 0.

The @@TOTAL_READ function is also available in the Sybase ASE implementation.

@@TOTAL_WRITE

Syntax:

```
SELECT @@TOTAL_WRITE
```

This function returns the number of physical disk writes since the start of the SQL Server instance. The information returned could be useful in identifying bottlenecks and improving the system's performance. Consider the following example:

```
SELECT
    @@TOTAL_WRITE AS writes
writes
-----------
238
```

You could use the previous statement and input the value into a table to analyze your daily physical disk writes. Higher-than-normal writes versus reads on your system could indicate the need to reconfigure some aspects of your database (such as indexes) in order to accommodate the change.

The @@TOTAL_WRITE function is also available in the Sybase ASE implementation.

fn_virtualfilestats()

Syntax:

```
fn_virtualfilestats(<database_ID>,<file_ID>)
```

This function returns I/O statistics for the database files. It accepts two arguments (the database ID and the file ID) and returns a table. For example, for the database ID 1 (MASTER database), and file ID 2 (MASTLOG file), the results may be the following:

```
SELECT   *
FROM ::fn_virtualfilestats(1,2)

DbId   FileId TimeStamp NumberReads NumberWrites BytesRead  BytesWritten IoStallMS
----   ------ --------- ----------- ------------ ---------- ------------ ---------
1      2      596468646 19          93           228864     132096       30
```

The description of the returned columns for the table-valued function is listed in the following table. The database ID and file ID information can be obtained using the built-in SQL functions DB_ID and FILE_ID, respectively.

Column	Description
DBID	Database ID.
FILEID	File ID.
TIMESTAMP	Time at which the data was returned.
NUMBERREADS	Number of reads performed on the file.
NUMBERWRITES	Number of writes performed on the file.
BYTESREAD	Number of bytes read from the file.
BYTESWRITTEN	Number of bytes written to the file.
IOSTALLMS	Total amount of time, in milliseconds, that users waited for the I/Os to complete on the file.

You cannot substitute the output of the functions DB_ID and FILE_ID for the required integer values.

This function is unique to the MS SQL Server platform although similar types of information can be obtained using various system views.

Undocumented Functions

It is never a good idea to use any undocumented "feature" in any of the environments discussed in this book. You would be better off using a UDF instead, or coding the functionality in some other way. Nevertheless, some of these functions stand a good chance to enter the legitimate toolset list in the future. As such, currently these functions are only available within the MS SQL Server context and are provided simply for information purposes. The following table lists some of the functions.

Function Name	Input	Output	Description
ENCRYPT	<char_expression>	<hexadecimal_string>	Returns an encrypted string in hexadecimal format; there is *no* corresponding built-in function to decrypt the data.
fn_get_sql	<process_id>	<table>	Returns the full text of a query executed within the particular session.
@@MICROSOFTVERSION	None	INTEGER	Returns Microsoft internal tracking number (for example, 134217422).
PWDCOMPARE	<password_string>, <encrypted_password>	INTEGER	Compares a string with an encrypted password; 1 indicates that the passwords match and 0 indicates that they do not.
PWDENCRYPT	<password_string>	<hexadecimal_string>	Encrypts a string (password) using SQL Server's internal password-encryption algorithm.
TSEQUAL	<timestamp1>, <timestamp2>	INTEGER	Compares two timestamps. If they are equal, 1 is returned; otherwise, an error is raised: the timestamp shows that row has been updated by another user.

ENCRYPT()

Syntax:

```
SELECT ENCRYPT(<string_expression>)
```

This returns a string encrypted in hexadecimal format. Consider the following example:

```
SELECT
    ENCRYPT('easy') AS easy_encryption

easy_encryption
------------------
0x6500610073007900
```

There is *no* corresponding built-in function to decrypt the data, but this should not be significant, because the "encryption" simply replaces characters with their hexadecimal values. The above hexadecimal string could easily be decrypted with the following query:

```
SELECT
(
    CHAR(ASCII(0x6500))   +
    CHAR(ASCII(0x6100))   +
    CHAR(ASCII(0x7300))   +
    CHAR(ASCII(0x7900))
) AS easy_decryption

easy_decryption
---------------
Easy
```

This example converts hexadecimals into ASCII codes (101, 97, 115, 121, respectively), and then uses the CHAR() function to get the characters. The ENCRYPT() function provides a very weak defense against prying eyes, but it is a rather handy tool for getting hexadecimal values of the characters.

FN_GET_SQL()

Syntax:

```
SELECT text FROM ::FN_GET_SQL(<process_handle>)
```

This function was "sneaked" into SQL Server 2000 with the Service Pack 3. It returns the full text of a query executed within a particular session based on the process handle. The process handle can be obtained from the table SYSPROCESSES of the MASTER database, in the column SQL_HANDLE; the process ID can be supplied by the unary function @@SPID. The following is an example of code that could be used to find the SQL code being executed by a SPID. Of course, this example won't return a value unless you are running a query on a separate Query Analyzer screen under the same SPID at the time it is executed.

```
DECLARE @HANDLE BINARY(20)
SELECT @HANDLE = SQL_HANDLE FROM MASTER.DBO.SYSPROCESSES
WHERE SPID=@@SPID
SELECT text FROM ::FN_GET_SQL(@HANDLE)
```

Only members of the SYSADMIN fixed server role can execute the function, and before the data returned can contain any meaningful information, the trace flag 2861 must be turned on.

@@MICROSOFTVERSION

Syntax:

```
SELECT @@MICROSOFTVERSION
```

This function returns the Microsoft internal tracking number. Consider the following example:

```
SELECT
    @@MICROSOFTVERSION AS internal_version

internal_version
----------------
134218488
```

Of course, there is no direct correspondence to this function in any of the other RDBMS implementations discussed in the book, though some equivalents could be found.

PWDCOMPARE()

Syntax:

```
SELECT PWDCOMPARE(<password_string>,<encrypted_password>)
```

This compares a string password with an encrypted password; a result of 1 indicates that the passwords match, and 0 indicates that they do not. Consider the following example:

```
SELECT
PWDENCRYPT('password')  AS encrypted_password

encrypted_password
--------------------
0x0100EA10A30107189B2E0C82A000293C5CCD74F235D72
EC39F2E791CC422DD30B01B03B2C3B3F04C9B3A35280F1A

SELECT
    PWDCOMPARE('password',

0x0100EA10A30107189B2E0C82A000293C5CCD74F235D72EC39F2E791CC422DD30B01B03B2C3B3F04C9
B3A35280F1A) AS compare

compare
----------
1
```

You cannot compare two encrypted passwords, nor can you easily decrypt the hexadecimal hash string. See the following discussion of the PWDENCRYPT() function for more information.

PWDENCRYPT()

Syntax:

```
PWDENCRYPT()
```

This function encrypts a string (password) using SQL Server's internal password-encryption algorithm. The returned unwieldy hexadecimal is hardly human-readable. Consider the following example:

```
SELECT
    PWDENCRYPT('simple') AS encrypted_password

encrypted_password
--------------------------------------------------------------------
0x0100BE07BA153FD0288D4107408C1032FEA98B5F1B1C5B45A4FF31A2DA7AB3DD8848A38510DDB41D4
8082ACB34C9
```

The output of the PWDENCRYPT() function cannot be decrypted using another SQL Server function, and is useful as input for the PWDCOMPARE() function, discussed earlier in the chapter. The produced encrypted value can change every time you call the function. Nevertheless, the PWDCOMPARE() function will have no problems recognizing it.

Calling the PWDENCRYPT() function within the same transactional unit would yield identical results. Moreover, the function executed from different queries one after another would still yield the same hexadecimal string. Only introducing a delay between the executions would modify the output (which points to the use of the timer as one of the algorithm components). Consider the following example, which demonstrates using a delay in order to create two different encryption strings:

```
SELECT PWDENCRYPT('password') AS encrypted_pwd
GO
WAITFOR DELAY '000:00:01'
GO
SELECT PWDENCRYPT('password') AS encrypted_pwd
GO

encrypted_pwd
--------------------------------------------------------------------
0x0100CE19DA514031B37635E05DA52E49AC1EE622738544DA36B004FD51325E565395458C6AC4A6182
61CE9524F1A

(1 row(s) affected)

encrypted_pwd
--------------------------------------------------------------------
0x0100D119D67B240BC8C732F31DEA617A4351A085B6D72F6C942AC46318300DB336DDD47A6A4E716AC
A36E4A71D28

(1 row(s) affected)
```

TSEQUAL()

Syntax:

```
WHERE TSEQUAL(<timestamp1>,<timestamp2>)
```

This compares two timestamps. If there are equal, 1 is returned; otherwise an error is raised (the timestamp shows that row has been updated by another user). The function cannot be used in a SELECT clause, being mostly of the Transact-SQL domain. Nevertheless, you can use it in a WHERE clause. The following example uses the WAITFOR DELAY function to allow us to populate two timestamp values with differing results. Then we can use the TSEQUAL() function to compare the values. Also, notice that, even though we use the CURRENT_TIMESTAMP function, we still must explicitly call the CONVERT() function to convert the value to a TIMESTAMP. This is because CURRENT_TIMESTAMP returns a DATETIME value.

```
DECLARE @CURTIME TIMESTAMP
DECLARE @LATERTIME TIMESTAMP
SET @CURTIME = CONVERT(TIMESTAMP,CURRENT_TIMESTAMP)
WAITFOR DELAY '000:00:30'
SET @LATERTIME = CONVERT(TIMESTAMP,CURRENT_TIMESTAMP)

SELECT 'EQUAL' AS RESULT WHERE TSEQUAL(@CURTIME,@CURTIME)

SELECT 'NOT EQUAL' AS RESULT WHERE TSEQUAL(@CURTIME,@LATERTIME)

RESULT
------
EQUAL

(1 row(s) affected)

Server: Msg 532, Level 16, State 1, Line 9
The timestamp (changed to 0x000095d5016e6c79) shows that the row has been updated
by another user.
```

This is a direct import from Sybase ASE, but Microsoft prefers to keep the function off the charts. While you can use it with Microsoft SQL Server 2000, the documentation only tells you that TSEQUAL is a reserved keyword.

Summary

In this chapter, we presented the various built-in functions available on the MS SQL Server 2000 platform. Different groups of functions were discussed, including string, date and time, metadata, configuration, security, system, and undocumented functions. The grouping of the functions should make the material easier for you to relate to the other RDBMS implementations discussed in this book. Remember, however, that common functional names do not guarantee portability to other systems. You should also remember that the undocumented functions are merely for reference, because they may be discarded in future releases of the product.

In the next chapter, we will discuss the built-in functions available for the Sybase platform of RDBMS implementations. Since the Sybase and SQL Server platforms have a common ancestral link, you should notice a wide array of similarities between the two chapters.

9

Sybase ASE SQL Built-In Functions

Built-in SQL functions have been part of the Transact-SQL implementation since the earliest version of Sybase. The RDBMS was originally created for UNIX platforms in 1987, and was ported to IBM's OS/2 for PC a year later as a result of a partnership between Sybase, Microsoft, and Ashton-Tate companies. After the dissolution of the Microsoft-IBM partnership, because of IBM's desire to develop a new operating system (OS/2) and the Ashton-Tate fallout, Microsoft became the distributor of Sybase's product on Windows NT. The Sybase-Microsoft partnership (and a shared code base between Sybase SQL Server and Microsoft SQL Server) started with version 4.21 and continued until 1993, when the licensing agreement and cooperation between the companies ended. While their common origins are still evident in many parts of the respective RDBMS implementations, the products went their separate ways. The Sybase SQL Server has been rebranded as Adaptive Server Enterprise (ASE) since version 11.5. (The current version is ASE 12.5.)

Unlike Oracle, the line between SQL proper and its Transact-SQL extension is somewhat blurred. While there are Oracle functions that can be used in SQL but not in PL/SQL, every built-in function supported by Transact-SQL can be used in the SQL statements, and vice versa. Therefore, SQL functions and Transact-SQL functions are virtually interchangeable.

Transact-SQL, which was identical between the two RDBMS implementations up to the split in 1993, is still recognizable as a single language, though dialects are becoming ever more divergent. The number of SQL functions supported in each dialect is different (with Microsoft leading the way), and some of the functions that appear to be identical are implemented differently now. Microsoft supports Transact-SQL UDFs (since version 7.0), while Sybase ASE uses Java for this purpose.

Despite all the similarities, you should never assume that Transact-SQL code written for one RDBMS will be compiled in another. A user-friendly editor, SQL Advantage, is available to help solve this problem. SQL Advantage aids the SQL programmer in the creation of syntactically correct Transact-SQL statements. Code examples in this chapter were created using SQL Advantage.

This chapter presents some of Sybase's most useful built-in functions, and, in doing so, maintains the accepted vendor's classification, which is more or less consistent with the classifications applied to other vendors' RDBMS implementations discussed in this book.

Sybase Query Syntax

In many ways, queries are the heart of the SQL language. The SELECT statement, which is used to express SQL queries, is the most powerful and complex of the SQL statements. The basis of the Sybase Adaptive Server's SELECT statement is the same as the ANSI standard discussed in Chapter 5 and is shown once again here. The full form of the SELECT statement consists of six clauses. The SELECT and FROM clauses are required, and the next four are optional.

```
select [ all | distinct ] select_list
[ INTO new_table ]
FROM table_source
[ WHERE search_condition ]
[ GROUP BY group_by_expression ]
[ HAVING search_condition ]
[ ORDER BY order_expression [ ASC | DESC ]
```

For simple queries, the English-language request and the SQL SELECT statement are very similar. However, when requests become more complex, more features of the SELECT statement must be used to specify the query precisely, as shown here:

```
SELECT statement
    < query_expression >
    [ ORDER BY { order_by_expression | column_position [ ASC | DESC ] }    [ ,...n
]   ]
    [ COMPUTE
        { { AVG | COUNT | MAX | MIN | SUM } ( expression ) } [ ,...n ]
[ BY expression [ ,...n ] ]        ]
[ FOR { BROWSE | READ ONLY | UPDATE [ column_name_list ] } ]
```

Like MS SQL Server, the <query expression> is the basis of the SELECT statement, and we will go into more detail on it, shortly. The next statement is the optional ORDER BY clause. The purpose of this clause is to determine what columns of data are sorted and how the sort is accomplished. The columns can be column names, aliases, or a non-negative number specifying the column's location in the result set. The way in which the columns are sorted is specified by either the ASC (ascending) or DESC (descending) operator; otherwise, they are sorted as ascending by default. Ordering of the columns is important because it determines the hierarchy of what gets listed first. In addition, ordering columns need not appear in the select_list unless a UNION operator or SELECT DISTINCT is used.

The next area is the optional COMPUTE clause. Its purpose is to provide additional summary columns at the end of the result set. These can be grouped into sets by using the BY clause (similar to the GROUP BY clause), which adds in breaks and subtotals to your result set. You may use any of the following aggregate functions to provide the summary information. (See the section, "Aggregate Functions," later in this chapter for a detailed account of their functionality.)

If you use the COMPUTE BY clause, then you must also use ORDER BY in your statement. In fact, your ORDER BY statement must include all the objects in the COMPUTE clause, or at least a subset of those.

The FOR clause is used to relate the use of the BROWSE, READ ONLY, or UPDATE options. The BROWSE option must be added to the end of an SQL statement sent to the Sybase Adaptive Server in a DB-Library browse application. The READ ONLY | UPDATE option specifies whether a cursor result set is read-only or updatable. You can use this option only within a stored procedure and only when the procedure defines a query for a cursor. In this case, SELECT is the only statement allowed in the procedure.

Lastly, we will look at the `<query expression>`, which can be made up of one or more `<query specifications>` joined by the union operator, as indicated here. You will notice that this is identical to the basic `SELECT` statement discussed in Chapter 5.

```
SELECT [ ALL | DISTINCT ]
        < select_list >
[ INTO new_table ]
[ FROM { < table_source > } [ ,...n ] ]
[ WHERE < search_condition > ]
[ GROUP BY [ ALL ] group_by_expression [ ,...n ]
[ HAVING < search_condition > ]
```

Now you should have a good understanding of the basics of the Sybase Adaptive Server query structure. This will be the basis for understanding the use of the different functions and will provide you with the ability to interpret the examples provided throughout this chapter.

The following table shows types of functions discussed in this book.

Type of Function	Description
String Functions	Operate on binary data, character strings, and expressions.
Date and Time Functions	Do computations on `datetime` and `smalldatetime` values and their components and date parts.
Data Type Conversion Functions	Change expressions from one data type to another and specify new display formats for date-time information.
Security Functions	Return security-related information.
Aggregate Functions	Generate summary values that appear as new columns or as additional rows in query results.
Mathematical Functions	Return values commonly needed for operations on mathematical data.
Text and Image Functions	Supply values commonly needed for operations on text and image data.
System Functions	Return special information from the database.
Unary System Functions	Niladic (argumentless) functions that could fall in any of the preceding categories (also referred to as "global variables").

String Functions

String functions manipulate character data. There is not much difference in the manner of implementation of these functions compared with other RDBMS implementations discussed in this book. Sybase ASE will attempt to implicitly convert any compatible input argument into the expected one; if conversion cannot be done implicitly, an error will be generated. Consult the conversion table matrix in the "Conversion Functions" section later in this chapter to see which data types are compatible. When a string function accepts several character expressions but only one expression is UNICHAR, the other expressions will be internally converted to UNICHAR; this follows existing rules for mixed-mode expressions.

Input arguments for the string functions that are character string constants should be enclosed in single or double quotation marks.

The following table shows string functions discussed in this book.

Function Name	Input	Output	Description
CHARINDEX	`<char_expression1>`, `<char_expression2>`	INTEGER	Returns an integer representing the starting position of an expression.
CHAR_LENGTH	`<char_expression>`	INTEGER	The number of characters in an expression.
COMPARE	`<char_expression1>`, `<char_expression2>` `[<collation_ID> or <collation_name ]`	INTEGER	Compares two character expressions and returns integer values, based on the collation rules that you choose: 1 indicates that char_expression1 is greater than char_expression2; 0 indicates that char_expression1 is equal to char_expression2; -1 indicates that char_expression1 is less than char_expression2.
DIFFERENCE	`<char_expression1>`, `<char_expression2>`		Returns the difference between two SOUNDEX values.
LEFT	`<char_expression>`, `<length_integer>`	`<char_expression>`	Returns the leftmost part of the expression with the specified number of characters.
LTRIM	`<char_expression>`	`<char_expression>`	Returns the specified expression, trimmed of leading blanks.
PATINDEX	`'%pattern_string%'`, `<char_expression>` `[,using bytes	<or> characters]`	INTEGER	Returns the starting position of the first occurrence of a specified pattern.
REPLICATE	`<char_expression>`, `<times_integer>`	`<char_exptression>`	Returns a string consisting of the specified expression repeated a given number of times.
REVERSE	`<char_expression>`	`<char_expression>`	Returns the specified string with characters listed in reverse order.
RIGHT	`<char_expression>`, `<length_integer>`	`<char_expression>`	Returns the rightmost part of the expression with the specified number of characters.

Function Name	Input	Output	Description
RTRIM	<char_expression>	<char_expression>	Returns the specified expression, trimmed of trailing blanks.
SORTKEY	[<collation_ID> or <collation_name]	VARBINARY	Generates values that can be used to order results based on collation behavior, which allows you to work with character collation behaviors beyond the default set of Latin character–based dictionary sort orders and case or accent sensitivity.
SOUNDEX	<char_expression>	<char_expression>	Returns a four-character code representing the way an expression sounds.
SPACE	INTEGER	<char_expression>	Returns a string consisting of the specified number of single-byte spaces.
STR	(<number> [,<length_integer> [,decimal_integer]]	<char_expression>	Returns the character equivalent of the specified number.
STUFF	<char_expression1>, <start_position>, <length_integer>, <char_expression2>	<char_expression>	Returns the string formed by deleting a specified number of characters from one string and replacing them with another string.
SUBSTRING	<char_expression> , <start_integer>, <length_integer>	<char_expression>	Returns the string formed by extracting the specified number of characters from another string.
USCALAR	<unichar_expression>	INTEGER	Returns the Unicode scalar value for the first Unicode character in an expression.

CHARINDEX()

Syntax:

```
CHARINDEX(<expression1>, <expression2>)
```

The CHARINDEX() function will search <expression2> for the first occurrence of <expression1> and return an integer specifying the beginning position of the occurrence. Both expressions can be any of the character data types. Consider the following example:

```
SELECT
        CHARINDEX('E', 'ABCDEFG') AS position
     position
    ---------
           5
```

The function does not allow the use of wildcards commonly used in regular expressions or a LIKE statement; CHARINDEX() treats all wildcards as literals. An implicit conversion will be performed for character data types, with possible truncation (that is, CHAR to UNICHAR).

The CHARINDEX() function is also available in the Microsoft SQL Server implementation.

CHAR_LENGTH()

Syntax:

```
CHAR_LENGTH(<char_expression>)
```

The CHAR_LENGTH() expression returns the length of the expression, which can be of any character data type (CHAR, VARCHAR, NVARCHAR, UNICHAR, UNIVARCHAR, and so on). Both the leading and trailing blanks are included in the calculation. For example, the following query returns 8, taking into consideration four trailing blanks:

```
SELECT CHAR_LENGTH('ABCD    ') AS total_length

total_length
------------
          8
```

The number returned is the number of characters in the string, not bytes. So, Unicode and ASCII expressions will return exactly the same value, even though the latter might occupy two times less space.

The Sybase ASE also supports the legacy function LEN(), which is synonym for CHAR_LENGTH(). For example, if you call the LEN() function and pass a wrong type of argument, the error message will complain about invalid arguments passed to the CHAR_LENGTH() function. Microsoft SQL Server also has the LEN() function, but it misses the CHAR_LENGTH() function.

Oracle provides a family of equivalent LENGTH() functions. IBM DB2 UDB also supports the LENGTH() function. MySQL has the CHAR_LENGTH() and CHARACTER_LENGTH() functions, while PostgreSQL supports both the LENGTH() and CHAR_LENGTH() functions.

COMPARE()

Syntax:

```
COMPARE (<expression1>, <expression2>, [<collation_name>|<collationID>])
```

The COMPARE() function allows you to compare two strings based either on the server-default binary sort collation or specified collation rules. The supported collations are listed in the following table:

Collation ID	Collation Name	Description
50	binary	Binary sort
0	default	Default Unicode multilingual
1	thaidict	Thai dictionary
39	alnoacc	Alternative no accent
45	altdict	Alternative lowercase first
46	alnocsp	Alternative, no case preference
47	scandict	Scandinavian dictionary
48	scannocp	Scandinavian, no case preference
-	gbpinyin	GB Pinyin
51	dict	Latin-1 English, French, German dictionary
52	nocase	Latin-1 English, French, German, no case
53	nocasep	Latin-1 English, French, German, no case preference
54	noaccent	Latin-1 English, French, German, no accent
55	espdict	Latin-1 Spanish dictionary
56	espnocs	Latin-1 Spanish, no case
57	espnoac	Latin-1 Spanish, no accent
58	rusdict	Russian dictionary
63	cyrdict	Cyrillic dictionary
72	turdict	Turkish dictionary
259	sjisbin	Shift-JIS binary order

The returned result is 1 when <expression1> is greater than <expression2>, 0 when <expression1> is equal <expression2>, or –1 when <expression1> is less than <expression2>. For example, to compare two strings, you could use the following:

```
SELECT
        COMPARE('ABC',' ABC ')      as equal_default
      , COMPARE('ABC','abc')        as first_greater
      , COMPARE('abc','ABC')      as first_less
      , COMPARE('ABC','ABC',1)     as thai_dict
 equal_default first_greater first_less  thai_dict
 ------------- ------------- ----------- -----------
            0            -1           1           0
```

Here is the interpretation of these results. The first comparison has determined that the strings are equal and returned zero. The second field found that the uppercase "ABC" is less than the lowercase "abc" (because the assigned ASCII code values of the uppercase letters are less than that of the lowercase). The third field correctly identified the lowercase string as being greater than its uppercase counterpart, and the last case tried to compare the string according to Thai collation. Since none of these letters is found in Thai alphabet, the strings were compared again as ASCII and found to be equal.

The COMPARE() function does not consider empty strings to be equal to strings that contain spaces because the function relies on another built-in function, SORTKEY(), to generate collation keys for comparison.

This function is not supported in the other RDBMS implementations discussed in this book.

DIFFERENCE()

Syntax:

```
DIFFERENCE(<expression1>, <expression2>)
```

The DIFFERENCE() function returns the difference between two SOUNDEX values. These values represent four-character code corresponding to the phonetic equivalence of the string. For more information on SOUNDEX values, refer to the discussion of the SOUNDEX() function later in this section. For example, to find out how close the pronunciations of "time" and "tyme" are, you could use the following query:

```
SELECT
       SOUNDEX('time')           as time
      ,SOUNDEX('tyme')           as tyme
    ,DIFFERENCE('time', 'tyme')      as diff

time   tyme   diff
----   ----   -----------
T500   T500             4
```

As you can see, the SOUNDEX values are a perfect match, and the DIFFERENCE() function yields 4—the best match possible (0 being the lowest). As always in Sybase, if one of the expressions passed into the function is of a UNICHAR (UNIVARCHAR, and so on) data type, the other will be implicitly converted into the same data type; a truncation is possible in this scenario.

The DIFFERENCE() function is found in IBM DB2 UDB, Microsoft SQL Server, and MySQL (version 3.2 and later). Oracle provides the SOUNDEX() function, but not the DIFFERENCE() function, and, as of version 7.4.2, PostgreSQL did not have either the SOUNDEX() or the DIFFERENCE() functions implemented.

LTRIM() and RTRIM()

Syntax:

```
LTRIM(<char_expression>)
RTRIM(<char_expression>)
```

Both the LTRIM() and RTRIM() functions return the specified expression with trimmed leading or trailing blanks, respectively. Only characters that correspond to the space (blank) character in the current character set will be removed. (For Unicode, a blank is defined as the value U+0020.) The input parameter could be of any character data type or its Unicode equivalent. The returned result will be of the same data type. For Unicode expressions, the function returns the lowercase Unicode equivalent of the specified expression. Characters in the expression that have no lowercase equivalent will be left unchanged. Here is an example where the trimmed string is padded by three blanks on each side:

```
      SELECT
              ( '*' + LTRIM ('   ABC   ') + '*') AS left_trimmed
             ,( '*' + RTRIM ('   ABC   ') + '*')  AS right_trimmed

  left_trimmed right_trimed
  ------------ ------------
  *ABC   *       *   ABC*
```

Asterisk markers were added to both sides of each result to make the trim results visible.

These functions have their equivalents in every RDBMS implementation discussed in this book.

PATINDEX()

Syntax:

```
  PATINDEX('%pattern%', char_expression [,using {bytes | characters})
```

The PATINDEX() function returns the starting position of the first occurrence of the specified pattern. The main difference between PATINDEX() and CHARINDEX() is that the latter does not allow searches with wildcard characters. The wildcard search characters are listed in the following table:

Character	Description
%	Matches any string of zero or more characters.
_ (underscore)	Matches any single character within the search string.
[a-z]	Matches any single character within the specified range or set of characters.
[^]	Matches any single character that is *not* within the specified range or set of characters.

The <char_expression> can be of the CHAR or VARCHAR data types or their Unicode equivalents (including the TEXT and IMAGE data types), and the using statement refers to the format for the starting position specifying offset in either bytes (for a multibyte character string) or characters, the latter being the default.

The PATINDEX() function returns an integer representing the starting position of the specified pattern, or zero if such pattern is not found. Consider the following example:

```
  SELECT
          PATINDEX('%DE%', 'ABCDEF')        AS first_occurrence
         ,PATINDEX('%[^A]%', 'ABCDEF') AS anything_but_A
         ,PATINDEX('AB%', 'ABCDEF')        AS first_chars
         ,PATINDEX('%F', 'ABCDEFGF', using characters) AS last_chars

  first_occurrence anything_but_A first_chars last_chars
  --------------- -------------- ----------- -----------
              4              2           1           8
```

The first field returns the start position of the very first occurrence of the character combination "DE." The second is requested to find anything except "A" in the character expression. The result is predictably 2, the position of "B" in the string. The third instructs the function to search only the first characters of the string (by omitting the leading "%"), and the last field is looking for the matching last characters (because the trailing "%" is omitted).

The wildcard search characters are the same as those used in the LIKE operator. They are supported by virtually every RDBMS implementation discussed in this book, though Oracle and IBM DB2 UDB do not support range searches.

REPLICATE()

Syntax:

```
REPLICATE(<char_expression>, <times_integer>)
```

The REPLICATE() function returns a string consisting of the specified expression repeated a given number of times. The character expression can be of the CHAR, NCHAR, VARCHAR, and NVARCHAR data types, or their Unicode equivalents. The <times_integer> parameter could be of the INTEGER data type, or any of its subtypes. Consider the following example:

```
SELECT
        REPLICATE('A',5)      AS five_a
      , REPLICATE('',5)       AS five_blanks
, REPLICATE(5,2)      AS two_times_five

five_a five_blanks two_times_five
------ ----------- --------------
AAAAA              0x0500000005000000
```

The results of this query require some explanation. Uppercase "A" is repeated five times, a blank space character is repeated five times (interestingly enough, an empty string "" and a space character " " are treated the same as a blank character), and a VARBINARY representation of the number 5 is repeated two times. The last result is surprising. Sybase has converted the integer supplied in place of the CHAR or UNICHAR expression into the VARBINARY data type prior to replication. This is an undocumented behavior.

The upper limit for the resulting replicated string is 64K. The function returns NULL if a NULL was passed as the first parameter.

This function is also found in the Microsoft SQL Server implementation, although its behavior is a little different.

REVERSE()

Syntax:

```
REVERSE(<expression>)
```

The REVERSE() function returns the string passed into it with the characters in reverse order. The expression could be of the CHAR, VARCHAR, NCHAR, NVARCHAR, BINARY, or VARBINARY data types. It also could be of the UNICHAR or UNIVARCHAR data types. Consider the following example:

```
SELECT
         REVERSE('ABCD')                      AS backwards_char
, REVERSE(0x00680065006c006c006f)    AS backwards_binary


backwards_char backwards_binary
-------------- ----------------
DCBA           0x6f006c006c0065006800
```

As you can see, the function recognizes the data type passed to it and takes care to reverse it appropriately. A character expression must be placed in quotation marks (double or single). If the <expression> is NULL, a NULL will be returned.

This function is also available on the Microsoft SQL Server implementation, although it behaves slightly differently.

RIGHT() and LEFT()

Syntax:

```
RIGHT(<char_expression>,<length_integer>)
LEFT(<char_expression>,<length_integer>)
```

The RIGHT() function returns the rightmost part of the expression up to the specified length of the characters. For example, the following query returns the three rightmost characters of the string "ABCDEF":

```
SELECT
    RIGHT('ABCDEF', 3) AS three_last,
    LEFT('ABCDEF', 3)  AS three_first


three_last     three_first
----------     -----------
 DEF           ABC
```

The second result of the code executed here provides an example of the LEFT() function. The LEFT() function returns the leftmost number of characters determined by the <length_integer> from the <char_expression>. In this example, the string 'ABCDEF' is fed into the LEFT() function and the three leftmost characters, ABC, are returned.

These functions are special cases of the more generic SUBSTRING() function, which is available in Microsoft SQL server, MySQL, and PostgreSQL. The equivalent SUBSTR() function is also available in the IBM DB2 platform. The same functions are found on the Microsoft SQL Server platform.

SORTKEY()

Syntax:

```
SORTKEY(<char_expression> [,<collation_name> | <collation_id>])
```

The SORTKEY() function generates values that can be used to order results based on collation behavior. The main idea is to employ a sorting order based on collations other than the default setup for the server. The return value is of the VARBINARY data type and contains coded collation information (hardly useful by itself) for ordering the result set. The function accepts two parameters, one of which (either `<collation_name>` or `<collation_id>`) is optional (when omitted, binary collation is assumed). Consider the following example:

```
SELECT
    SORTKEY('hello') AS binary_sort
   ,SORTKEY('hello', 58) AS Russian_sort

binary_sort                   russian_sort
---------------------         ---------------------
0x00680065006c006c006f        0x090508b1094f094f0997
```

As you can see, the returned information is hardly readable by humans and is more suitable for computers. The following query shows a typical scenario where the SORTKEY() function could be used (in addition to being used by other built-in functions, such as COMPARE()), where you would like to sort information about your Turkish customers using Turkish collating order:

```
SELECT *
    FROM   customers
    WHERE  country = 'Turkey'
    ORDER BY SORTKEY(cust_name, 'turdict')
```

The first parameter passed into the function must consist of characters coded in the default character set of the server; otherwise, use data conversion functions. The parameter can be an empty string; a zero-length blank is returned and stored for comparison purposes. If the parameter is NULL, a NULL will be returned.

An empty string has a different collation value than a NULL string from a database column.

To perform multilingual sorting, Sybase ASE employs two strategies. The first (and recommended) method is available for ASE versions 11.5.1 or higher. It involves a built-in collation table that is specified by the collation ID or collation name passed into the function. The second method utilizes the Unilib library sorting functions, and a collation name is used to specify the external table found in $SYBASE/collate/Unicode on UNIX machines, or the /Sybase/collate/unicode directory on Windows.

The SORTKEY() function can generate up to six bytes of collation information for each input character. Therefore, the result from using the function may potentially exceed the length limit of the VARBINARY data type. When the limit is exceeded, the results are truncated, and a warning message is issued; the statement is allowed to run nevertheless. This truncation limit is dependent on the logical page size of your server. Consult the vendor's documentation for more information.

The in-line (that is, used directly in a SQL query) SORTKEY() function might not perform at the optimum speed because it must generate keys and sort at the same time. One of the techniques to improve performance would be creating an additional VARBINARY column that would store the SORTKEY values for a record at the time it is added to the database. These values could be later used to perform sorting, since there is no key-generation required; the operation would then execute at a much greater speed.

The list of available collations can be retrieved by executing the system stored procedure sp_helpsort, or by going directly against the SYSCHARSETS system table.

This function is not supported in the other RDBMS implementations discussed in this book.

SOUNDEX()

Syntax:

```
SOUNDEX(<char_expression>)
```

This function returns a four-character code to evaluate similarity between the sounds of two character expressions. SOUNDEX() evaluates an alpha string and returns a four-character code to find similar-sounding words or names. The first character of the code is the first character of <char_expression>, and the second through fourth characters of the code are numbers. Vowels in <char_expression> are ignored unless they are the first letter of the string. The function could be used to specify search criteria for similar-sounding words, and is, of course, case insensitive. For example, the following query finds all three words to be similarly sounding:

```
SELECT
    SOUNDEX('GOOD') AS upper_case,
    SOUNDEX('good') AS lower_case,
    SOUNDEX('GUT')  AS something_else

upper_case lower_case something_else
---------- ---------- --------------
G300       G300       G300
```

The SOUNDEX() function is found in every database discussed in the book.

SPACE()

Syntax:

```
SPACE(<number_of_spaces>)
```

The SPACE() function returns a string consisting of blanks and a specified number of single-byte space characters. The accepted input parameters can be of any integer type (INTEGER and it subtypes). The following example uses the CHAR_LENGTH function to count the number of spaces produced:

```
SELECT
    CHAR_LENGTH(SPACE(5)) AS five_spaces

five_spaces
-----------
5
```

This function is also available on the Microsoft SQL Server and IBM DB2 implementations.

STR()

Syntax:

```
STR(<number> [,<length> [,decimal]])
```

The STR() function returns the character equivalent of the specified number. It accepts three arguments, specifying the numeric value to be converted into a string, the number of the resulting characters to be returned, and the number of decimal places (the default is zero). The last two parameters are optional and can never be negative. If all the optional parameters are omitted, the result will be the rounded up or truncated integer portion of the number. Consider the following example:

```
SELECT
      STR(1234.5678, 4)          AS four_chars
     ,STR(1234.5678, 7,2)         AS seven_chars
     ,STR(1234.5678, 3,1)      AS not_enough_space

four_chars  seven_chars  not_enough_space
----------  -----------  ----------------
1235         1234.57      ***
```

Since no decimals were specified for the <four_chars> field, none were returned. In addition, the result was rounded up to fit within the specified length. In the case of the <seven_chars> field, the returned string contains seven characters (a decimal point is included in the count, as is a negative sign), and exactly two decimals (which are rounded up because the remainder of the decimal values is closer to the ceiling than to the floor; otherwise the number will be truncated). The last field displays three asterisks because the specified length (also 3) could not accommodate the five-digit integer portion of the number; the length must at the very least be equal the integer portion of the number.

This function is also available in the Microsoft SQL Server implementation.

STUFF()

Syntax:

```
STUFF(<string_expression1>, <start_position>,<length_integer>,<string_expression2>)
```

The STUFF() function returns the string created by deleting a specified number of characters from <string_expression1> and replacing them with another <string_expression2>. If the <start_integer> is negative or the <length_integer> value exceeds <string_expression1>, a NULL will be returned. Consider the following example:

```
SELECT
     STUFF('ABCDABCD',5,4,'EFG') as alphabet

alphabet
---------
ABCDEFG
```

In the this example, the function was supplied arguments to replace four characters in the first argument string with the fourth argument string, starting with the fifth character. The function could be used to delete characters inside a string or to replace them with blank spaces. Consider the following example:

```
SELECT
     STUFF('ABCDABCD',5,4,NULL)  as remove4
    ,STUFF('ABCDABCD',5,3,'')    as blank

remove4     blank
-------     -------
ABCD        ABCD D
```

In the first instance of the example, the string `'ABCDABCD'` is passed to the STUFF() function. Starting at position 5, the next four characters are replaced with the NULL value. In the second instance, the characters `'ABC'`, the first three characters starting at position 5, are replaced with a blank.

This function is present in Microsoft SQL Server.

SUBSTRING()

Syntax:

```
SUBSTRING(<expression>,<start_position>,<length_integer>)
```

The SUBSTRING() function returns part of a string defined by the beginning position and the length. The acceptable data types for the expression are CHAR, NCHAR, UNICHAR, VARCHAR, UNIVARCHAR, NVARCHAR, BINARY, or VARBINARY. For example, to extract the first three characters of an expression, the following query could be used:

```
    SELECT
SUBSTRING('ABCDEFG',1,3) AS first_three

first_three
-----------
ABC
```

The example takes the substring of `'ABCDEFG'`, which begins at the first character (denoted by the second parameter), and extracts the next three characters (denoted by the third parameter).

This function is present in Microsoft SQL Server, PostgreSQL, and MySQL. Both Oracle and IBM DB2 UDB have implemented the SUBSTR() function, which has identical behavior.

USCALAR()

Syntax:

```
USCALAR(unichar_expression)
```

The USCALAR() function returns the Unicode scalar value for the first Unicode character in an expression; it is the Unicode equivalent of the ASCII function. Consider the following example:

```
SELECT USCALAR('ABCD') as scalar

scalar
-----------
         65
```

Not surprisingly, the return value is ASCII code for the uppercase "A" since the supplied literal is not in Unicode. If the input parameter is null, the return value will be NULL. An error will be returned if a value outside the Unicode values range is supplied.

The UNICODE() function in the Microsoft SQL Server implementation provides similar functionality to the USCALAR() function.

Date and Time Functions

The date and time functions manipulate values of the data types DATETIME and SMALLDATETIME. They can be used anywhere in the SELECT statement. The limitation of the DATETIME data type is that it has a lower limit of January 1, 1753; we recommend that you use CHAR, NCHAR, VARCHAR, or NVARCHAR for earlier dates.

The following table shows the date and time functions discussed in this section:

Function Name	Input	Output	Description
DATEADD	DATE PART STRING, INTEGER, DATE	DATETIME (SMALLDATETIME)	Returns the date produced by adding a given number of years, quarters, hours, or other date parts to the specified date.
DATEDIFF	DATETIME, DATETIME	INTEGER	Returns the date part difference between two dates.
DATENAME	DATEPART STRING, DATE	CHARACTER STRING	Returns the name of the specified part of a DATETIME value.
DATEPART	DATEPART STRING, DATE	INTEGER	Returns the integer value of the specified part of a DATETIME value.
GETDATE	N/A	DATETIME	Returns the current system date and time.

In every date-time function that requires a date part as an input parameter, the full name of the part or an abbreviation can be used. Date-part abbreviations recognized by Sybase Adaptive Server are listed in the following table.

Date Part	Abbreviation	Values
YEAR	YY	1753–9999 (2079 for SMALLDATETIME)
QUARTER	QQ	1–4
MONTH	MM	1–12
WEEK	WK	1–54
DAY	DD	1–31
DAYOFYEAR	DY	1–366
WEEKDAY	DW	1–7 (Sun.–Sat.)
HOUR	HH	0–23
MINUTE	MI	0–59

Date Part	Abbreviation	Values
SECOND	SS	0–59
MILLISECOND	MS	0–999
CALWEEKOFYEAR (for use with `DATEPART` only)	CWK	1–53
CALYEAROFWEEK (for use with `DATEPART` only)	CYR	1753–9999
CALDAYOFWEEK (for use with `DATEPART` only)	CDW	1–7

When the year is entered as two characters (*YY* format), Sybase follows these rules:

❑ For numbers less than 50, the year will be interpreted as 20*YY* (for example, 15 will be considered 2015).

❑ For Numbers equal to or greater than 50 the year will be interpreted as 19*YY* (for example, 50 will be considered 1950).

DATEADD()

Syntax:

```
DATEADD(<date_part_string>,<how_many_integer>, <add_to_date>)
```

The `DATEADD()` function returns the results of adding a given number of years, quarters, hours, or other date parts to the specified date. For example, to add four days to today's date, you could use the following query:

```
SELECT DATEADD(day, 4, GETDATE()) as four_days_ahead

four_days_ahead
------------------
Jun 6 2004 10:53PM
```

This example uses the `GETDATE()` function to supply the current date and time as a third argument. Sybase will also accept a character representation of a date and will implicitly convert it into the `DATETIME` data type. For example, the query could be rewritten as follows:

```
SELECT DATEADD(day, 4, 'Jun 2 2004 10:53PM') as four_days_ahead
four_days_ahead
------------------
Jun 6 2004 10:53PM
```

The date format must be one of the Sybase-recognized formats to be accepted.

This function has a direct equivalent in the Microsoft SQL Server implementation.

DATEDIFF()

Syntax:

```
DATEDIFF(<datepart_string>, <date1>, <date2>)
```

The DATEDIFF() function returns the specified date-part difference between two dates. The calculation always involves the DATETIME data type. Even if SMALLDATETIME arguments are supplied, Sybase will convert them implicitly into DATETIME, with seconds and milliseconds set to 0.

For example, to find out how many days are between today and, say, June 26, 1965, the following query could be used:

```
SELECT DATEDIFF (day, 'Jun 26 1965', GETDATE()) as days

days
--------------
         14247
```

If <date2> is earlier than <date1>, the result will be negative.

In the previous example, Sybase calculated the number of midnights between the two specified dates.

The return parameter is of the INTEGER data type; therefore, it cannot exceed the value of 2,147,483,647, be it days, months, minutes, or seconds. This means that the function cannot be used to calculate the number of seconds passed since (in our case) June 15, 1936.

The results of the DATEDIFF() function are always truncated, not rounded. In the following example, the difference in hours between June 6, 2004 10:53PM and June 7, 2004 10:52PM, would be 23 hours, even though the second date is only 1 minute shy of being equal to the first date:

```
SELECT DATEDIFF(hour,'Jun 6, 2004 10:53PM','June 7, 2004 10:52PM') as diff

diff
-----------
         23
```

When the date part specified is MONTH, the function will count the number of "firsts of the month" between the two dates; for the WEEK date part, it is the number of Sundays between the two dates. (If the first date begins on Sunday, it is not counted.)

This function is also available in the Microsoft SQL Server implementation.

DATENAME()

Syntax:

```
DATENAME(<datepart_string>,<date>)
```

The DATENAME() function returns the full name of the specified date part extracted from the date. For example, to find the name of the current month, the following query could be used:

```
     SELECT
          GETDATE()                    as full_date
          ,DATENAME( month, GETDATE())    as month_name
  Full_date              month_name
  ---------------        -------------------
  Jun 2 2004 11:37AM     June
```

The first field supplies the current date using the GETDATE() function, while the second extracts the name of the month from the same date.

The numeric results, such as the day part name, will be returned as character data.

This function is also available on the Microsoft SQL Server platform.

DATEPART()

Syntax:

```
  DATEPART(<datepart_string>, <date>)
```

The DATEPART() function returns the integer value of the specified part of the date. For example to find a week of the year, the query could look like this:

```
  SELECT
       GETDATE()       as  today,
       DATEPART(week, GETDATE()) as week

  today                 week
  -------------------   ------------
  Jul 2 2004 2:18AM     27
```

The function returns a number (INTEGER) that follows the ISO 8601 standard. This standard defines the first day of a week and the first day of a year. If ASE is configured to use default U.S. English, some discrepancies will occur. Consider the following example:

```
  SELECT
       DATEPART(YY,  '01/01/1999')   as us_english
       ,DATEPART(CYR, '01/01/1999')  as iso_standard

  us_english      iso_standard
  -----------     ------------
  1999            1998
```

This happens because ISO defines the first week of the year as one that begins with a Monday and includes a Thursday. U.S. English defines the first week of the year as one that begins with a Sunday and contains January 4. The same goes for the rest of the identifiers prefixed with CAL that are listed in the table at the beginning of this section. ISO will produce Monday as the first day of the week, while U.S. English will insist on Sunday.

This function has a direct equivalent on the Microsoft SQL Server platform, although some of the rules differ. Oracle and MySQL both support the EXTRACT() function, which can be used for similar functionality.

GETDATE()

Syntax:

```
GETDATE()
```

The GETDATE() function accepts no input parameters and returns the current date and time of the system. Consider the following example:

```
SELECT GETDATE() as current_date

current_date
-----------------------
Jun 2 2004 10:47 PM
```

This function is also found in Microsoft SQL Server. Oracle has the analogous function SYSDATE, while IBM DB2 UDB uses the special register CURRENT DATE. MySQL sports the CURRENT_DATE() function (in addition to its synonyms NOW() and SYSDATE()), and PostgreSQL has CURRENT_DATE() and NOW(). The dates returned by these functions might or might not include the time.

Conversion Functions

Conversions are the staple of database programming: converting numeric money to printable characters (and vice versa) and converting between different numeric types (integer to money to FLOAT to HEX, just to mention a few) for a variety of reasons. Unlike its counterparts in the RDBMS business, Sybase ASE does not offer much variety; it has only three data-type conversion functions. One of them, CONVERT(), is a universal, SQL92-mandated concept that fulfills the role of the more data-type–bound functions found in Oracle or IBM DB2 UDB.

Data-type conversion happens either explicitly (using a conversion function) or implicitly (where the RDBMS does it behind the scenes). The decision of where to use implicit or explicit conversion is totally vendor dependent. For example, Oracle allows you to concatenate numbers and strings by implicitly converting the former into character data. In Microsoft SQL Server and Sybase, though, you have to use explicit conversion to achieve the same result.

The following table represents the conversion grid that shows which data types are converted into the other built-in data types implicitly (I), explicitly (E), or cannot be converted at all (X). In cases where both explicit and implicit conversions are allowed, the (I) stands for both.

	Tinyint	Smallint	Int	Decimal	Numeric	Real	Float	Char, nchar	Varchar, nvarchar	Text	Smallmoney	Money	Bit	Smalldatetime	Datetime	Binary	Varbinary	Image
Tinyint	I	I	I	I	I	I	I	E	E	X	I	I	I	X	X	I	I	X
Smallint	I	I	I	I	I	I	I	E	E	X	I	I	I	X	X	I	I	X
Int	I	I	I	I	I	I	I	E	E	X	I	I	I	X	X	I	I	X
Decimal	I	I	I	I	I	I	I	E	E	X	I	I	I	X	X	I	I	X
Numeric	I	I	I	I	I	I	I	E	E	X	I	I	I	X	X	I	I	X
Real	I	I	I	I	I	I	I	E	E	X	I	I	I	X	X	I	I	X
Float	I	I	I	I	I	I	I	E	E	X	I	I	I	X	X	I	I	X
Char, Nchar	E	E	E	E	E	E	E	I	I	I	E	E	E	I	I	I	I	I
varchar, nvarchar	E	E	E	E	E	E	E	I	I	I	E	E	E	I	I	I	I	I
Text	X	X	X	X	X	X	X	E	E	X	X	X	X	X	X	X	X	X
Smallmoney	I	I	I	I	I	I	I	I	I	X	I	I	I	X	X	I	I	X
Money	I	I	I	I	I	I	I	I	I	X	I	I	I	X	X	I	I	X
Bit	I	I	I	I	I	I	I	I	I	X	I	I	I	X	X	I	I	X
Smalldatetime	X	X	X	X	X	X	X	E	E	X	X	X	X	I	I	I	I	X
Datetime	X	X	X	X	X	X	X	E	E	X	X	X	X	I	I	I	I	X
Binary	I	I	I	I	I	I	I	I	I	X	I	I	I	I	I	I	I	I
Varbinary	I	I	I	I	I	I	I	I	I	X	I	I	I	I	I	I	I	I
image	X	X	X	X	X	X	X	X	X	X	X	X	X	X	X	I	I	X

Adaptive Server Enterprise does not allow you to convert certain data types to certain other data types, either implicitly or explicitly. Unsupported conversions result in error messages.

The data type conversion functions can be used anywhere in the select_list, in the WHERE clause, and everywhere an expression is allowed.

The following table shows the conversion functions discussed in this section.

Function Name	Input	Output	Description
CONVERT	\<convert to data_type>,\<convert from expression>	Single value of \<convert to data_type>,	Returns the specified value, converted to another data type (or a different display format, for DATETIME and character data types).
INTTOHEX	INTEGER	HEX	Returns the platform-independent hexadecimal equivalent of the specified integer.
HEXTOINT	HEX	INTEGER	Returns the platform-independent integer equivalent of a hexadecimal string.

CONVERT()

Syntax:

```
CONVERT(<data type> [(length)|(precision [,scale])]
        [NULL | NOT NULL]<convert_expression> [,style])
```

The CONVERT() function is used to perform conversion between different data types. The \<data_type> specifies the target data type, while \<convert_expression> supplies the source data to be converted; the number of optional parameters is discussed later in this section.

The basic conversion is fairly simple. For example, to allow for concatenation of the character and numeric data, the following statement could be used:

```
SELECT 'final price: $'  + CONVERT(varchar(10), 10) as PRICE

PRICE
----------------
final price: $10
```

A failure to use the CONVERT() function in this example would result in an error message such as the following:

```
Server Message:  Number 257, Severity 16
Line 1:
 Implicit conversion from datatype 'VARCHAR' to 'INT' is not allowed.
Use the CONVERT function to run this query.
```

In addition to the required \<data type> and \<convert_expression>, the CONVERT() function accepts a number of optional input parameters, which allow for more control over conversion output:

❑   [LENGTH]—An optional parameter used mostly with character data (CHAR, NCHAR, UNICHAR, UNIVARCHAR, VARCHAR, and NVARCHAR). It is also applicable to BINARY and VARBINARY data types. If the [LENGTH] parameter is not supplied, the ASE will truncate the result to 30 characters (for character data) or 30 bytes (for binary data). The maximum allowable length for either character or binary expressions is 64K.

❑ [PRECISION]—Specifies the number of significant digits in NUMERIC or DECIMAL data types; if the parameter is not supplied, ASE uses the default precision of 18.

❑ [SCALE]—Specifies the number of digits to the right of the decimal point for NUMERIC and DECIMAL data types. When the scale is not supplied, the default value of 0 is used.

❑ [NULL | NOT NULL]—Signifies the nullability of the <convert_expression>. If it is omitted, the nullability of the resulting expression will be the same as that of the source expression.

❑ [STYLE]—Specifies the display format for the converted data. For example, when converting MONEY data into character data, specifying style 1 would result in a comma separator for the hundredth digits. The following table provides accepted style values for data for DATETIME conversion formatting:

Without Century (YY)	With Century (YYYY)	Output Format
n/a	0 /100	Mon dd yyyy hh:mi AM/PM
1	101	MM/DD/YY
2	102	YY.MM.DD
3	103	DD/MM/YY
4	104	YY.MM.DD
5	105	DD-MM-YY
6	106	DD MON YY
7	107	MON DD, YY
8	108	HH:MM:SS
n/a	9/109	MON DD YYYY HH:MI:SS:MMM AM/PM
10	110	DD-MM-YY
11	111	YY/MM/DD
12	112	YYMMDD

The following example uses Sybase's built-in GETDATE() function as an input for the CONVERT() function (with output formatted according to the style formats listed in the previous table):

```
    SELECT
          CONVERT (varchar(25), GETDATE(), 1)      as YY
         ,CONVERT (varchar(25), GETDATE(), 101)    as YYYY
         ,CONVERT (varchar(25), GETDATE(), 108)    as TIME

YY      YYYY         TIME
-------- ----------- ---------
07/01/04 07/01/2004  19:53:07
```

When selecting the "convert to" data type, be sure that the allocated space is sufficient enough to hold the converted value. In the previous example, specifying VARCHAR(5) as a target data type would result in an "Insufficient result space for explicit conversion" error.

One of the foremost concerns of converting numeric data types is loss of precision. Consider the following example:

```
CREATE TABLE tblTest
  (
           field1 smallint
         ,field2 numeric
         ,field3 money
    )
INSERT INTO tblTest
         VALUES (1, 2, 3)
GO

SELECT * FROM tblTEST

field1      field2       field3
-------     -------      -------
1           2            3.00
```

As you can see, the last field has a value that was implicitly converted into the MONEY data type. Now, an attempt to insert data types that require explicit conversion would result in an error:

```
INSERT INTO tblTest VALUES (1.5, 2.5, 3.5)
Server Message:  Number  241, Severity  16
Line 1:
Scale error during implicit conversion of NUMERIC value '1.5' to a SMALLINT field.
Server Message:  Number  241, Severity  16
Line 1:
Scale error during implicit conversion of NUMERIC value '2.5' to a NUMERIC field.
```

Interestingly enough, even though Sybase ASE recognizes supplied values of NUMERIC data types, it fails to convert then implicitly (even in the case of the NUMERIC data type field). To make the previous statement succeed, an explicit conversion is required, but there is a price to pay—loss of precision. Sybase does not warn you about this, so you must know what you are doing when converting data types, as shown here:

```
INSERT INTO tblTest
           VALUES (
                CONVERT(smallint, 1.5)
               ,CONVERT(numeric, 2.5)
               ,CONVERT(money,3.5)
               )
GO

SELECT * FROM tblTEST

field1      field2       field3
-------     -------      -------
1           2            3.00
1           2            3.50
```

The following table summarizes the most common pitfalls for the CONVERT() function for the different data types:

Conversion Scenario	Things to Watch Out For
Converting character data to a noncharacter type	Leading blanks are ignored; expressions containing blanks only are converted into "Jan 1, 1900" DATETIME. Incompatible characters (for example, commas in INTEGER converted data, misspelled date parts, and so on) will result in an error.
Converting from one character type to another	When converting from a multibyte character set to a single-byte character set, characters with no single-byte equivalent are converted to question marks. When no LENGTH is specified, the output is limited to 30 characters; when specified, the limit is set by the data type's maximum limit.
Converting numbers to a character type	The character data type must provide sufficient space to accommodate the data (that is, a three-digit number cannot be converted into one character string). For the FLOAT data type, provide at least a 25-character buffer.
Conversion to and from MONEY / SMALLMONEY types	The MONEY and SMALLMONEY types store four digits to the right of the decimal point, but round up to the nearest hundredth (.01) for display purposes. When data is converted to a money type, it is rounded up to four places. This behavior holds true for reverse conversion (to character from MONEY).
Converting date and time information	Dates outside the acceptable range for the data type lead to arithmetic overflow errors. When DATETIME values are converted to SMALLDATETIME, they are rounded to the nearest minute.
Converting between numeric types	If the new type is an exact numeric whose precision or scale is not sufficient to hold the data, errors can occur. There are certain options (ARITHABORT and ARITHIGNORE) that can be set at the server level to affect the default behavior. Arithmetic overflow errors occur when the new type has too few decimal places to accommodate the results. When an explicit conversion results in a loss of scale, the results are truncated without warning; implicit conversion does produce an error. A domain error is generated when the function's argument falls outside the range over which the function is defined.

Table continued on following page

Conversion Scenario	Things to Watch Out For
Conversions between binary and integer types	The conversion is platform-dependent (for example, the string "0x0000100" represents 65536 on machines that consider byte 0 most significant and 256 on machines that consider byte 0 least significant). You should use the specific HEXTOINT/ INTTOHEX function to make it conversion-independent.
Converting between binary and NUMERIC or DECIMAL types	A conversion of BINARY or VARBINARY type to NUMERIC or DECIMAL, the "00" or "01" values must be specified after the "0x" digit.
Converting IMAGE columns to binary types	Conversion of the IMAGE data type into BINARY or VARBINARY is limited by to the maximum length of the target data types (which are, in their turn, defined by the server settings); the default value is 30.
Converting other types to BIT	The bit equivalent of 0 is 0. The bit equivalent of any other number is 1. When converting character data, the only acceptable characters are digits, a decimal point, plus or minus signs, and a currency symbol.

The CONVERT() function relies on the underlying hardware for processing and is susceptible to big-endian/little-endian treatment. For example, Macintosh computers use the PowerPC processor, which stores 2-byte integers as big-endians (that is, with the most significant byte first); the Intel x86 processors store 2-byte integers with the least significant byte first.

The terms "big-endian" and "little-endian" derive from Jonathan Swift's famous classic satire, Gulliver's Travels, where all subjects of the Blefuscu empire were divided into two fractions— big-endians and little-endians—depending on the preference from which end one starts eating an egg.

The CONVERT() function is found virtually in every RDBMS implementation discussed in this book, with the notable exception of IBM DB2 UDB. While basic functionality is very similar between these functions, the rules and advanced formatting are not. Refer to the vendor-specific documentation for details on using the CONVERT() function in the respective RDBMS environments.

INTTOHEX()

Syntax:

```
INTTOHEX(<integer>)
```

This function returns the platform-independent hexadecimal equivalent of an integer. The INTTOHEX() function is platform-independent. The following example converts the integer argument of 256 into its hexadecimal equivalent:

```
        SELECT INTTOHEX (256) gimme_256_asHex

gimme_256_asHex
----------------
0x00000100
```

Most databases handle the conversion of integers to hexadecimal data type through the use of the CAST() and CONVERT() functions.

HEXTOINT()

Syntax:

```
HEXTOINT(<char_expression>)
```

This function returns the platform-independent integer equivalent of a hexadecimal string, effectively reversing the action of the INTTOHEX() function. It is also platform-independent. The following example converts an integer into a hexadecimal number:

```
SELECT HEXTOINT ("0x00000100") gimme_256

gimme_256
----------------
  256
```

It seems that other databases provide correct platform-independent hexadecimal-to-integer conversion through their implementations of the CONVERT() and CAST() functions, in addition to specialized conversion functions.

Security Functions

There are only two functions listed in this category. This reflects deficiencies of classification rather then security in the Sybase ASE because many more functions could be found that deal with security issues. The two security functions return information about security features setup. There are no direct equivalents for the functions in any of the RDBMS implementations discussed in this book.

The following table shows these security functions:

Function Name	Input	Output	Description
IS_SEC_SERVICE_ON	Character string	INTEGER	Returns 1 if the security service is active and 0 if it is not.
SHOW_SEC_SERVICES	n/a	List of available services; if none of the services are ctivated, NULL is returned.	Lists the security services that are active for the session.

IS_SEC_SERVICE_ON()

Syntax:

```
SELECT IS_SEC_SERVICE_ON(security_service_name)
```

The `IS_SEC_SERVICE_ON()` function is used to determine whether a particular security service is enabled for the session. A result of 0 means that the service is not in use, while a result of 1 indicates that the service is enabled. Normally, you could use the following query to list all of the available security mechanisms supported by Adaptive Server:

```
SELECT * FROM SYSSECMECHS
```

This `SELECT` statement will create a virtual table for the security mechanisms and services. Once you have the service name (from the `Available_service` columns), you will be able to use the name in the `IS_SEC_SERVICE_ON()` function. One such possible value is the `"mutualauth"` service, which the following example attempts to see and finds is inactive:

```
SELECT IS_SEC_SERVICE_ON("mutualauth")

-----------------
     1
```

SHOW_SEC_SERVICES()

Syntax:

```
SELECT SHOW_SEC_SERVICES()
```

The `SHOW_SEC_SERVICES()` function is used much like the `IS_SEC_SERVICE_ON()` function, but instead of checking on a particular security service, it returns a list of all of the services that are enabled. The following example demonstrates a use of the function that returns `NULL`, which means that the Sybase server is not currently running any security services:

```
SELECT SHOW_SEC_SERVICES() AS CURRENT_SERVICES

CURRENT_SERVICES
------------------------
NULL
```

Aggregate Functions

Aggregate functions generate summary values that appear as new columns in the query results. Aggregate functions can be used in the `select_list` or `HAVING` clause of a `SELECT` statement or subquery, but they cannot be used in a `WHERE` clause. Each aggregate in a query requires its own worktable. Therefore, a query using aggregates cannot exceed the maximum number of worktables (12) allowed in a query.

Aggregates are often used with the `GROUP BY` clause. With `GROUP BY`, the table is divided into groups. Aggregates produce a single value for each group. Without `GROUP BY`, an aggregate function in the `select_list` produces a single value as the result, whether it is operating on all rows in a table or on a subset of rows defined by a WHERE clause.

Aggregate functions calculate the summary values of the non-null values in a particular column. If the ansinull option is set to off (the default), there is no warning when an aggregate function encounters a null. If ansinull is set to on, a query returns the SQLSTATE warning "Warning – null value eliminated in set function" when an aggregate function encounters a null.

Aggregate functions can be applied to all rows in a table, in which case they produce a single value, a *scalar aggregate*. They can also be applied to all the rows that have the same value in a specified column or expression (using the GROUP BY and, optionally, the HAVING clause), in which case they produce a value for each group, a *vector aggregate*.

The following table shows aggregate functions discussed in this book:

Function Name	Input	Output	Description
AVG	[all | distinct] expression	INTEGER	Returns the numeric of all distinct values.
COUNT	[all | distinct] expression	INTEGER	Returns the number of distinct non-null values.
MAX	expression	INTEGER or CHARACTER STRING	Returns the highest value in a column.
MIN	expression	INTEGER or CHARACTER STRING	Returns the lowest value in a column.
SUM	[all | distinct] expression	INTEGER	Returns the total of the values.

AVG()

Syntax:

```
avg([all | distinct] <expression>)
```

The AVG() function returns the numeric average of all (distinct) values. The all parameter applies AVG() to all values (this is the default), and distinct eliminates duplicate values before AVG() is applied. The expression may include a column name; constant; function; any combination of column names, constants, and functions connected by arithmetic or bitwise operators; or a subquery. With aggregates, an expression is usually a column. The following example will average all of the values in the advance column from a table called titles:

```
SELECT avg(advance) as "Average Advance" from titles

Average Advance
---------------
       6,281.25
```

The AVG() function is available in all of the database implementations discussed in this book.

COUNT()

Syntax:

```
count([all | distinct] <expression>)
```

The COUNT() function returns the number of (distinct) non-null values or the number of selected rows. The ALL parameter applies COUNT() to all values (this is the default) and distinctly eliminates duplicate values before COUNT() is applied. The expression may include a column name; constant; function; any combination of column names, constants, and functions connected by arithmetic or bitwise operators; or a subquery. With aggregates, an expression is usually a column. The following example will count all of the rows in the titles table:

```
SELECT count(*) as "Number of Rows" from titles

Number of Rows
--------------
          2701
```

The next example will count all of the distinct city names from the city column within the titles table:

```
SELECT count(distinct city) as "Number of Distinct Cities" from authors


Number of Distinct Cities
-------------------------
                       36
```

The COUNT() function is available in all the RDBMS implementations discussed in this book.

MAX()

Syntax:

```
max(<expression>)
```

The MAX() function returns the highest value in an expression. The expression may include a column name; constant; function; any combination of column names, constants, and functions connected by arithmetic or bitwise operators; or a subquery. The MAX() function can be used with exact and approximate numeric, character, and DATETIME columns. It cannot be used with bit columns. With character columns, MAX() finds the highest value in the collating sequence. The MAX() function implicitly converts CHAR data types to VARCHAR and UNICHAR data types to UNIVARCHAR, stripping all trailing blanks. The following example returns the maximum value in the discount column of the discounts table:

```
SELECT max(discount) as "Max Discount" from discounts

Max Discount
------------
       10.50
```

The MAX() function is available in all of the RDBMS implementations discussed in this book.

MIN()

Syntax:

```
min(<expression>)
```

The MIN() function returns the lowest value in an expression. The expression may include a column name; constant; function; any combination of column names, constants, and functions connected by arithmetic or bitwise operators; or a subquery. The MAX() function can be used with exact and approximate numeric, character, and DATETIME columns. It cannot be used with bit columns. With character columns, MIN() finds the lowest value in the sort sequence. The MAX() function implicitly converts CHAR data types to VARCHAR and UNICHAR data types to UNIVARCHAR, stripping all trailing blanks. The following example returns the minimum value in the discount column of the discounts table:

```
SELECT min(discount) as "Min Discount" from discounts

Min Discount
------------
        5.00
```

The MIN() function is available in all of the RDBMS implementations discussed in this book.

SUM()

Syntax:

```
sum([all | distinct] <expression>)
```

The SUM() function returns the total of all (distinct) values. The all parameter applies SUM() to all values (this is the default) and distinctly eliminates duplicate values before AVG() is applied. The expression may include a column name; constant; function; any combination of column names, constants, and functions connected by arithmetic or bitwise operators; or a subquery. The SUM() function finds the sum of all the values in a column and can be used only on numeric (integer, floating point, or money) data types. The following example returns the minimum value in the discount column of the discounts table:

```
SELECT sum(ytdsales) as "Sum of Year-to-Date Sales" from titles

Sum of Year-to-Date Sales
-------------------------
                    99751
```

The SUM() function is available in all of the RDBMS implementations discussed in this book.

Mathematical Functions

Mathematical functions return values commonly needed for operations on mathematical data. Mathematical function names are not keywords. Each function also accepts arguments that can be implicitly converted to the specified type. For example, functions that accept approximate numeric values also accept integer types. Sybase ASE automatically converts the argument to the desired type.

Error traps are provided to handle any domain or range errors with these functions. Users can set the `arithabort` and `arithignore` options to determine how domain errors are handled. The `arithabort arith_overflow` option specifies behavior following a divide-by-zero error or a loss of precision. The default setting, `arithabort arith_overflow` on, rolls back the entire transaction or aborts the batch in which the error occurs. If you set `arithabort arith_overflow` off, Sybase ASE aborts the statement that causes the error but continues to process other statements in the transaction or batch. The `arithabort numeric_truncation` option specifies behavior following a loss of scale by an exact numeric type during an implicit data-type conversion. (When an explicit conversion results in a loss of scale, the results are truncated without warning.) The default setting `arithabort numeric_truncation` on aborts the statement that causes the error but continues to process other statements in the transaction or batch. If you set `arithabort numeric_truncation` off, Sybase ASE truncates the query results and continues processing. By default, the `arithignore arith_overflow` option is turned off, causing Sybase ASE to display a warning message after any query that results in numeric overflow. Set this option to on to ignore overflow errors.

The following table shows mathematical functions discussed in this book:

Function Name	Input	Output	Description
ABS	INTEGER or expression	INTEGER	Returns the absolute value of an expression.
ACOS	cosine INTEGER	angle INTEGER	Returns the angle (in radians) whose cosine is specified.
ASIN	sine INTEGER	angle INTEGER	Returns the angle (in radians) whose sine is specified.
ATAN	tangent INTEGER	angle INTEGER	Returns the angle (in radians) whose tangent is specified.
ATN2	sine INTEGER, cosine INTEGER	INTEGER	Returns the angle (in radians) whose sine and cosine are specified.
CEILING	INTEGER or expression	INTEGER	Returns the smallest integer greater than or equal to the specified value.
COS	angle INTEGER	cosine INTEGER	Returns the cosine of the specified angle (in radians).
COT	angle INTEGER	tangent INTEGER	Returns the cotangent of the specified angle (in radians).
DEGREES	INTEGER	INTEGER	Returns the size (in degrees) of an angle with the specified number of radians.
EXP	INTEGER	INTEGER	Returns the exponential value that results from raising the constant to the specified power.

Function Name	Input	Output	Description
FLOOR	INTEGER	INTEGER	Returns the largest integer that is less than or equal to the specified value.
LOG	INTEGER	logarithm INTEGER	Returns the natural logarithm of the specified number.
LOG10	INTEGER	base 10 logarithm INTEGER	Returns the base 10 logarithm of the specified number.
PI	NONE	pi INTEGER	Returns constant value 3.1415926535897931.
POWER	INTEGER, power INTEGER	INTEGER	Returns the value that results from raising the specified number to a given power.
RADIANS	degrees INTEGER	angle INTEGER	Returns the size (in radians) of an angle with the specified number of degrees.
RAND	[INTEGER]	INTEGER	Returns a random float value between 0 and 1, which is generated using the optional input seed parameter.
ROUND	INTEGER, number of decimal places INTEGER	INTEGER	Returns the value of the specified number rounded to a given number of decimal places.
SIGN	INTEGER	INTEGER	Returns the sign (+1 for positive, 0, or –1 for negative) of the specified value.
SIN	angle INTEGER	sine INTEGER	Returns the sine of the specified angle (in radians).
SQRT	INTEGER	INTEGER	Returns the square root of the specified number.
TAN	angle INTEGER	tangent INTEGER	Returns the tangent of the specified angle (in radians).

ABS()

Syntax:

```
abs (<numeric expression>)
```

The ABS() function returns the absolute value of an expression. The <numeric expression> is a column name, variable, or expression whose data type is an exact numeric, approximate numeric, money, or any type that can be implicitly converted to one of these types. The following example returns the absolute value of –1:

```
SELECT abs(-1)

-------------
            1
```

The ABS() function is available in all of the RDBMS implementations discussed in this book.

ACOS()

Syntax:

```
acos(<cosine numeric value>)
```

The ACOS() function returns the angle (in radians) whose cosine is specified. The parameter is the cosine of the angle, expressed as a column name, variable, or constant (of type FLOAT, REAL, or DOUBLE PRECISION), or any data type that can be implicitly converted to one of these types. The following example returns the angle whose cosine is 0.52:

```
SELECT acos(0.52)

------------------------
       1.0239453760989525
```

The ACOS() function is available in all of the RDBMS implementations discussed in this book.

ASIN()

Syntax:

```
asin(<sine numeric value>)
```

The ASIN() function returns the angle (in radians) whose sine is specified. The parameter is the sine of the angle, expressed as a column name, variable, or constant (of type FLOAT, REAL, or DOUBLE PRECISION), or any data type that can be implicitly converted to one of these types. The following example returns the angle whose sine is 0.52:

```
SELECT asin(0.52)

-----------------------
     .54685095069594414
```

The ASIN() function is available in all of the RDBMS implementations discussed in this book.

ATAN()

Syntax:

```
atan(<tangent numeric value>)
```

The ATAN() function returns the angle (in radians) whose tangent is specified. The parameter is the tangent of the angle, expressed as a column name, variable, or constant (of type FLOAT, REAL, or DOUBLE PRECISION), or any data type that can be implicitly converted to one of these types. The following example returns the angle whose tangent is 0.50:

```
SELECT atan(0.50)

 --------------------------
         .46364760900080609
```

The ATAN() function is available in all of the RDBMS implementations discussed in this book.

ATN2()

Syntax:

```
atn2(<sine numeric value>, <cosine numeric value>)
```

The ATN2() function returns the angle (in radians) whose sine and cosine is specified. The parameters are the sine and cosine of the angle, expressed as a column name, variable, or constant (of type FLOAT, REAL, or DOUBLE PRECISION), or any data type that can be implicitly converted to one of these types. The following example returns the angle whose sine is 0.50 and cosine is 0.48:

```
SELECT atn2(0.50, 0.48)

 --------------------------
         .80580349408398644
```

MS SQL Server also has the ATN2() function available. Oracle, IBM DB2, MySQL, and PostgreSQL all use the equivalent ATAN2() function.

CEILING()

Syntax:

```
ceiling(<numeric value> | <expression>)
```

The CEILING() function returns the smallest integer greater than or equal to the specified value. The parameter is a column name, variable, or expression whose data type is an exact numeric, approximate numeric, money, or any type that can be implicitly converted to one of these types. The following example returns the discount price and ceiling for title_id PS3333 in the discount column on table salesdeteail:

```
SELECT discount Discounts, ceiling(discount) Rounded_Up from salesdetail
WHERE title_id = "PS3333"

Discount            Rounded_Up
---------------     -------------
45.10000            46.00000
46.70000            47.00000
50.00000            50.00000
```

All of the RDBMS implementations discussed in this book support either the CEILING() or shorthand CEIL() functions.

COS()

Syntax:

```
cos(<angle numeric value>)
```

The COS() function returns the cosine of the specified angle in radians. The parameter is any approximate numeric (FLOAT, REAL, or DOUBLE PRECISION), column name, or constant expression. The following example returns the cosine whose angle is 44:

```
SELECT cos (44)

-------------------------
        .99984330864769122
```

The COS() function is supported by all of the RDBMS implementations discussed in this book.

COT()

Syntax:

```
cot(<angle numeric value>)
```

The COT() function returns the cotangent of the specified angle in radians. The parameter is any approximate numeric (FLOAT, REAL, or DOUBLE PRECISION), column name, variable, or constant expression. The following example returns the cotangent whose angle is 90:

```
SELECT cot (90)

-------------------------
-0.50120278338015323
```

The COT() function is available in all of the RDBMS implementations discussed in this book, except for the Oracle platform.

DEGREES()

Syntax:

```
degrees(<radians numeric value>)
```

The DEGREES() function returns the size, in degrees, of an angle with the specified number of radians. The result is of the same type as the numeric expression input parameter. The following example returns the number of radians whose angle is 45:

```
SELECT degrees (45)

 -------------------------
                     2578
```

The DEGREES() function is available in all of the RDBMS implementations discussed in this book except for the Oracle platform.

EXP()

Syntax:

```
exp(<numeric value>)
```

The EXP() function returns the value that results from raising the constant to the specified value. The parameter is any approximate numeric (FLOAT, REAL, or DOUBLE PRECISION), column name, variable, or constant expression. The following example returns the exponential value of 3:

```
SELECT exp (3)

 -------------------------
           20.085536923187668
```

The EXP() function is available in all of the RDBMS implementations discussed in this book.

FLOOR()

Syntax:

```
floor(<numeric value>)
```

The FLOOR() function returns the largest integer that is less than or equal to the specified value. The parameter is any exact numeric (NUMERIC, DEC, DECIMAL, TINYINT, SMALLINT, or INT), approximate numeric (FLOAT, REAL, or DOUBLE PRECISION), column name, variable, or constant expression. The following example returns the floor value of 123.85:

```
SELECT floor (123.85)

 ----------
         123
```

The FLOOR() function is available in all of the RDBMS implementations discussed in this book.

LOG()

Syntax:

```
log(<numeric value>)
```

The LOG() function returns the natural logarithm of the specified number. The parameter is any approximate numeric (FLOAT, REAL, or DOUBLE PRECISION), column name, variable, or constant expression. The following example returns the natural logarithm of 20:

```
SELECT log (20)

-------------------------
          2.9957322735539909
```

The LOG() function is available in all of the RDBMS implementations discussed in this book.

LOG10()

Syntax:

```
Log10(<numeric value>)
```

The LOG10() function returns the base-10 logarithm of the specified number. The parameter is any approximate numeric (FLOAT, REAL, or DOUBLE PRECISION), column name, variable, or constant expression. The following example returns the base-10 logarithm of 20:

```
SELECT log10 (20)

-------------------------
          1.3010299956639813
```

The LOG10() function is available in all of the RDBMS implementations discussed in this book, except for the Oracle platform.

PI()

Syntax:

```
pi()
```

The PI() function returns the constant value 3.1415926535897931. It requires no input parameters. The following example returns the value of pi (3.1415926535897931):

```
SELECT pi()

-------------------------
          3.1415926535897931
```

The PI() function is available in the MS SQL Server, PostgreSQL, and MySQL RDBMS implementations.

POWER()

Syntax:

```
power(<numeric value>, <power numeric value>)
```

The POWER() function returns the value that results from raising the specified number to a given power. The parameters are a numeric value and a power, which can be an exact numeric, approximate numeric, or money value. The following example returns the power of 4 of the value of 3:

```
SELECT power (3,4)

---------
        81
```

The POWER() function is available in the MS SQL Server, PostgreSQL, and MySQL RDBMS implementations.

RADIANS()

Syntax:

```
radians(<angle numeric value in degrees>)
```

The RADIANS() function returns the size, in radians, of an angle with the specified number of degrees. The parameter is any exact numeric (NUMERIC, DEC, DECIMAL, TINYINT, SMALLINT, or INT), approximate numeric (FLOAT, REAL, or DOUBLE PRECISION), money column, variable, constant expression, or any combination of these. The following example returns the radians whose angle is 2,578 degrees:

```
SELECT radians (2578)

---------
        44
```

The RADIANS() function is available in all of the RDBMS implementations discussed in this book, except for the Oracle platform.

RAND()

Syntax:

```
rand( [ <numeric value> ] )
```

The RAND() function returns a random value between 0 and 1, which is generated using the specified seed value. The input parameter is optional and can be any integer (TINYINT, SMALLINT, or INT), column name, variable, constant expression, or any combination of these. The following example returns a random value using no seed value:

```
SELECT rand()

-----------------------
      .67097022555348007
```

The following example returns a random value using 10 as the seed value:

```
declare @seed int
select @seed=10
select rand (@seed)
----------------------
        .59575983444031322
```

The RAND() function uses the output of a 32-bit pseudo-random integer generator. The integer is divided by the maximum 32-bit integer to give a double value between 0.0 and 1.0. The RAND() function is seeded randomly at server start-up, so getting the same sequence of random numbers is unlikely, unless the user first initializes this function with a constant seed value. The RAND() function is a global resource. Multiple users calling the RAND() function progress along a single stream of pseudo-random values. If a repeatable series of random numbers is needed, the user must ensure that the function is seeded with the same value initially (like the previous example) and that no user calls RAND() while the repeatable sequence is desired.

Every RDBMS implementation discussed in this book supports either the RAND() or RANDOM() functions.

ROUND()

Syntax:

```
round(<numeric value>, <decimal places numeric value>)
```

The ROUND() function returns the value of the specified number rounded to a given number of decimal places. The input parameter is any exact numeric (NUMERIC, DEC, DECIMAL, TINYINT, SMALLINT, or INT), approximate numeric (FLOAT, REAL, or DOUBLE PRECISION), money column, variable, constant expression, or any combination of these. The following example returns the rounded value of 123.4545 rounded to two decimal places:

```
SELECT round (123.4545, 2)

----------------------
              123.4500
```

The following example returns the rounded value of 123.4545 rounded to –2 decimal places:

```
SELECT round (123.45, -2)

----------------------
              100.00
```

With the ROUND() function, a positive decimal place input parameter rounds the number of significant digits to the right of the decimal point, and a negative decimal place input parameter rounds the number of significant digits to the left of the decimal point, like the previous example displays.

The ROUND() function is supported in all of the RDBMS implementations discussed in this book.

SIGN()

Syntax:

```
sign( <numeric value> )
```

The SIGN() function returns the sign (+1 for positive, 0, or –1 for negative) of the specified value. The input parameter is any exact numeric (NUMERIC, DEC, DECIMAL, TINYINT, SMALLINT, or INT), approximate numeric (FLOAT, REAL, or DOUBLE PRECISION), or money column, variable, constant expression, or any combination of these. The following example returns the sign of 123:

```
SELECT sign (123)

---------------
              1
```

The following example returns the sign of 0:

```
SELECT sign (0)

---------------
              0
```

The following example returns the sign of –123:

```
SELECT sign (-123)

---------------
             -1
```

The SIGN() function is available in all of the RDBMS implementations discussed in this book.

SIN()

Syntax:

```
sin( <angle numeric value> )
```

The SIN() function returns the sin of the specified angle in radians. The input parameter is any approximate numeric (FLOAT, REAL, or DOUBLE PRECISION), column name, variable, or constant expression. The following example returns the sin of 45:

```
SELECT sin (45)

--------------------
   .85090352453411844
```

The SIN() function is available in all of the RDBMS implementations discussed in this book.

SQRT()

Syntax:

```
sqrt ( <numeric value> )
```

The SQRT() function returns the square root of the specified number. The input parameter is any approximate numeric (FLOAT, REAL, or DOUBLE PRECISION), column name, variable, or constant expression that evaluates to a positive number. The following example returns the square root of 8:

```
SELECT sqrt (8)

-------------------
    2.8284271247461903
```

If you attempt to select the square root of a negative number, Sybase ASE will return the error message "Domain error occurred."

The SQRT() function is supported by all of the RDBMS implementations discussed in this book.

TAN()

Syntax:

```
tan(<angle numeric value>)
```

The TAN() function returns the tangent of the specified angle in radians. The parameter is the tangent of the angle, expressed as a column name, variable, or constant (of type FLOAT, REAL, or DOUBLE PRECISION), or any data type that can be implicitly converted to one of these types. The following example returns the tangent whose angle is 60:

```
SELECT tan(60)

--------------
.32004038937956297
```

The TAN() function is supported by all of the RDBMS implementations discussed in this book.

Text and Image Functions

The text and image functions operate on text and image data. Text and image functions are not keywords. You can set the textsize option to limit the amount of text or image data that is retrieved by a SELECT statement. The patindex string function can be used on text and image columns, and can also be considered a text and image function. Use the DATALENGTH() function to get the length of data in text and image columns. Text and image columns cannot be used as parameters to stored procedures; as values passed to stored procedures; as local variables; in ORDER BY, COMPUTE, or GROUP BY clauses; in an index; in a WHERE clause (except with the keyword like); in joins; or in triggers.

The following table shows the text and image functions discussed in this section:

Function Name	Input	Output	Description
TEXTPTR	Column_name	VARBINARY	Returns a pointer to the first page of a text or image column.
TEXTVALID	Column_name	INTEGER	Returns 1 if the pointer to the specified text column is valid and 0 if it is not valid.

TEXTPTR()

Syntax:

```
textptr(<column_name>)
```

The TEXTPTR() function returns a pointer to the first page of a text or image column. The parameter is any text or image column name, and the function returns the text pointer value (a 16-byte VERBINARY value). The following example uses the TEXTPTR() function to locate the text column, copy, associated with au_id 486-29-1786 in the blurbs table. The text pointer is put into a local variable, @VAL, and supplied as a parameter to the READTEXT command, which returns 5 bytes, starting at the second byte (offset of 1).

```
DECLARE @val binary(16)
SELECT @val = textptr(copy) from titles
WHERE au_id = "486-29-1786"
READTEXT title.copy @val 1 5
```

The following example selects the au_id column and the 16-byte text pointer of the copy column from the title table:

```
SELECT au_id, textptr(copy) from title
```

If a text or an image column has not been initialized by a non-null insert or by any UPDATE statement, TEXTPTR() returns a NULL pointer. Use TEXTVALID (explained next) to check whether a text pointer exists. You cannot use WRITETEXT or READTEXT without a valid text pointer.

The TEXTPTR() function is also available in the MS SQL Server implementation.

TEXTVALID()

Syntax:

```
textvalid(<table_name>.<column_name>, <textpointer value>)
```

The TEXTVALID() function returns 1 if the pointer to the specified text column is valid and 0 if it is not. The parameter is any text or image table name.column name and text pointer value. The following example reports whether a valid text pointer exists for each value in the au_id column of the titles table:

```
SELECT textvalid ("titles.au_id", textptr(copy)) from titles
```

The TEXTVALID() function is also available in the MS SQL Server implementation.

System Functions

The system functions return special information from the database. System functions can be used in a select_list, in a WHERE clause, and anywhere an expression is allowed.

When the argument to a system function is optional, the current database, host computer, server user, or database user is assumed.

The following table shows the system functions discussed in this section:

Function Name	Input	Output	Description
COL_LENGTH	<object_name>, <column_name>	INTEGER	Returns the defined length of a column.
COL_NAME	<object_id>, <column_id> [, <database_id>]	<char_ expression>	Returns the name of the column whose table and column IDs are specified.
DATALENGTH	<expression>	INTEGER	Returns the actual length (in bytes) of the specified column or string.
DB_ID	[db_name]	INTEGER	Returns the ID number of the specified database.
DB_NAME	[db_id]	<char_ expression>	Returns the name of the database whose ID number is specified.
OBJECT_ID	<object_name>	<char_ xpression>	Returns the ID of the specified valid database object from a valid object name.
OBJECT_NAME	<object_id> [, <database_id>)]	INTEGER	Returns the name of a database object after being given the object's ID. The ID could be further qualified with the database ID, in case the object resides in a database other than the current database.
RAND	[<seed_integer>]	FLOAT	Returns a pseudo-random number between 0.0 and 1.0.
SUSER_ID	[server_user_ name]	INTEGER	Returns the server user's ID number from the SYSLOGINS table.
SUSER_NAME	[<server_ user_id>]	<char_ expression>	Returns the name of the current server user or the user whose server ID is specified.

Function Name	Input	Output	Description
TSEQUAL	<browsed_row_ timestamp>, <stored_row_ timestamp>	TRUE or FALSE	Compares timestamp values to prevent updates to a row that has been modified since it was selected for browsing. It cannot appear in SELECT clauses.
USER	N/A	<char_ expression>	Returns the name of the current user.
USER_ID	[user_name]	INTEGER	Returns the ID number of the specified user or of the current user in the database.
USER_NAME	[user_id]	<char_ expression>	Returns the name within the database of the specified user or of the current user.
VALID_NAME	<name_ identifier>	INTEGER	Returns 0 if the specified string is not a valid identifier, or a number other than 0 if the string is a valid identifier.
VALID_USER	<server_user_id>	INTEGER	Returns 1 if the specified ID is a valid user or alias in at least one database on this Adaptive Server.

COL_LENGTH()

Syntax:

```
COL_LENGTH(<object_name>, <column_name>)
```

The COL_LENGTH() function returns the length defined for a given column in a given table, view, default, or rule. It also triggers a procedure's arguments. The names must be enclosed in quotation marks, and fully qualified names are accepted (that is, the name could be in the format <server>. <database>.<database_owner>.<object>). For the columns defined as nonvariable data types (INTEGER, BINARY, and so on), the length returned will be that of the data type. For example, the following table is created to contain columns of several built-in data types:

```
CREATE TABLE tblTEST
(
        field1          CHAR(10)
        ,field2              VARCHAR(25)
        ,field3         INTEGER
        ,field4              MONEY
        ,field5         BIT
)
```

The query against this table would yield the following results:

```
SELECT
      COL_LENGTH('tblTEST', 'field1') AS char10
     ,COL_LENGTH('tblTEST', 'field2') AS varchar25
     ,COL_LENGTH('tblTEST', 'field3') AS integer4
     ,COL_LENGTH('tblTEST', 'field4') AS money8
     ,COL_LENGTH('tblTEST', 'field5') AS bit1
   ,COL_LENGTH('tblTEST', 'field6') AS bit1


char10     varchar25    integer4     money8       bit1         invalid
---------  -----------  -----------  -----------  -----------  -----------
       10           25            4            8            1          NULL
```

Each column reported its defined length, and the last column ("field6"), which was never defined in the table tblTEST, returned NULL. For the columns of TEXT or IMAGE data types, the length will always be BINARY(16), which is the length of a pointer to an actual storage; for Unicode character data types, the length will be defined by the number of characters specified for the type, not the number of bytes.

> *This function returns the length of the column, not the length of the data it stores. To find the actual data length, use the DATALENGTH() function.*

This function is also available in the Microsoft SQL Server implementation.

COL_NAME()

Syntax:

```
COL_NAME(<objct_id>, <column_id> [,<database_id>])
```

This function returns the name of the column given the table and optional database ID(s). The object ID(s) are stored in the SYSOBJECTS system table, while column information is stored in SYSCOLUMNS table. To find the ID of an object, you could use the built-in OBJECT_ID function (see the "OBJECT_ID" section later in this chapter). Another way would be querying the SYSOBJECTS table directly.

> *It is considered best practice not to query the system objects directly because they might change without notice, breaking the application. You should use the vendor-supplied interfaces like built-in functions and procedures.*

Once you've found your object ID, you could return name of the first, second, or whatever column this object contains. The following example uses the tblTEST table created earlier in the chapter:

```
SELECT
      COL_NAME(736002622,1) AS first_field
     ,COL_NAME(736002622,2) AS second_field
   ,COL_NAME(736002622,25) AS invalid_field


first_field     second_field     invalid_field
-----------     ------------     -------------
field1          field2           NULL
```

The third field in the query has yielded NULL because no such column exists in the table tblTEST definition.

This function is not available on the other RBDMS implementations discussed in this book.

DATALENGTH()

Syntax:

```
DATALENGTH(<expression>)
```

The DATALENGTH() function returns the actual length of the expression in bytes rather than in characters. The expression can be of any data type, and is especially useful with variable-length fields. For example, using the tblTEST table created earlier in the chapter (see the COL_LENGTH function), you could insert the following records into the table:

```
INSERT INTO tblTEST VAlues('ABC','ABCD', 1, 2,0)
GO
SELECT
    DATALENGTH(field1) AS char_10
    ,DATALENGTH(field2) AS varchar_25
    ,DATALENGTH(field3) AS int_field
    ,DATALENGTH(field4) AS money_field
    ,DATALENGTH(field5) AS bit_field
    ,DATALENGTH(NULL)   AS null_field
FROM tblTEST

    char_10    varchar_25  int_field   money_field bit_field   null_field
----------- ----------- ----------- ----------- ----------- -----------
         10           4           4           8           1        NULL
```

As you can see, fixed-length fields display their defined length even though the actual meaningful data they contain is shorter (CHAR_10 field). This happens because the entered value is padded with blanks (spaces) up to the length of the field. In the case of the variable field (VARCHAR_25), the DATALENGTH() function returns exactly 4—by the number of entered characters, even though the field itself could accommodate up to 25 characters. When the input expression is NULL, the function returns NULL.

This function is also available in the Microsoft SQL Server implementation.

DB_ID()

Syntax:

```
DB_ID([db_name])
```

The DB_ID() function returns the ID number for the specified database name. If no name is specified, the ID of the current database is returned. If the name is invalid, the function returns NULL. Consider the following example:

```
USE tempdb
SELECT
        DB_ID('master')     AS master_id
        ,DB_ID()            AS current_db
        ,DB_ID('nosuchthing') AS invalid_db
master_id   current_db  invalid_db
----------- ----------- -----------
          1           2        NULL
```

This batch switches context to TEMPDB and then executes the query. The ID of the master database is always 1, while the current database has an ID of 2. For the nonexistent database name, the function returns NULL.

This function is also available in the Microsoft SQL Server implementation.

DB_NAME()

Syntax:

```
DB_NAME([db_id])
```

The DB_NAME() function returns a database name after being passed a valid database ID. Consider the following example:

```
SELECT DB_NAME (1) AS db
db
------
master
```

The numeric ID for the master database is 1, and that is what the function returned. To find out valid ID(s) for a database, you might query the SYSDATABASES system table, which is located in the master database, as shown here:

```
SELECT
name      AS database_name
, dbid  AS database_id
FROM sysdatabases

database_name                database_id
-------------                -----------
master                                 1
model                                  3
sybsystemdb                        31513
sybsystemprocs                     31514
tempdb                                 2
```

If no database ID is supplied, the function returns the name of the current database.

This function is also available in the Microsoft SQL Server implementation.

OBJECT_ID()

Syntax:

```
BJECT_ID(<object_name>)
```

The OBJECT_ID() function returns the ID of the specified valid database object from a valid object name. The database object can be a table, a stored procedure, a view, a trigger, a default, or a rule. The name can be fully qualified (that is, <server>.<database>.<dbo>.<object_name>), and must be enclosed into single or double quotation marks. Consider the following example, which shows the object ID of the tblTest table:

```
    SELECT
OBJECT_ID('tblTEST') AS table_id
table_id
-----------
    736002622
```

Of course, the output of this example will vary from machine to machine because the ID numbers given to objects are dependant upon many factors.

All information about objects is stored in the SYSOBJECTS system table and can be extracted from there. This function is tied to the Sybase architecture and is found nowhere else, except for Microsoft SQL Server.

OBJECT_NAME()

Syntax:

```
OBJECT_NAME(<object_id> [,<database_id>)])
```

The OBJECT_NAME() function returns the name of a database object after being given the object's ID. The ID can be further qualified with the database ID, in case the object resides in a database other than the current database. Consider the following example, which uses the object ID you obtained in the previous example to obtain the name of your object:

```
    SELECT
OBJECT_NAME(736002622) as table_name

table_name
-----------
 tblTEST
```

All information about objects is stored in the SYSOBJECTS system table and can be extracted from there. This function is tied to the Sybase architecture and is found nowhere else, except for Microsoft SQL Server.

RAND()

Syntax:

```
RAND([seed_integer])
```

The RAND() function returns a pseudo-random number between 0 and 1. It accepts an optional parameter as a seed value, and returns a FLOAT data type number. The RAND() function uses the 32-bit pseudo-random integer generator output, which is then divided by the maximum 32-bit integer. The result is a double value between 0.0 and 1.0. Consider the following example:

```
    SELECT
        RAND() AS first
        ,RAND() AS second

 first                second
-------------------- --------------------
 .90519488551895833   .83822619441814072
```

The RAND() function is a global resource. This means that the same function is called by any users who happen to be connected to your instance of the ASE, and the pseudo-random numbers are generated in a sequence. If a repeatable series is needed, you must ensure that no one else is calling the function while the series is being generated.

When the function is invoked without a seed value, it uses a seed generated randomly at server start-up. If it is initialized to a specific seed, the function will return exactly the same number unless seed is changed. Consider the following example:

```
    SELECT
            RAND(1) AS first
            ,RAND(1) AS second

first                   second
--------------------    --------------------
  .34595759834440315     .34595759834440315
```

To receive random numbers in a range other than 0 and 1, you may use a combination of built-in functions and operators. For example, to produce a pseudo-random number in a range between 0 and 100, the following statement could be used:

```
SELECT
    ROUND(RAND()*100,0) AS first
    ,ROUND(RAND()*100,0) AS second

first                   second
--------------------    --------------------
67.0                    23.0
```

Encapsulating this functionality in a user-defined function would be a logical solution to this deficiency.

The RAND() function is present in every RDBMS implementation discussed in this book, except PostgreSQL, which implements the RANDOM() function.

SUSER_ID()

Syntax:

```
SUSER_ID([server_user_name])
```

The SUSER_ID() function returns the server user's ID from the SYSLOGINS system table. The server users are different from the database users; for example the user ID 2 is reserved for the "probe" server user but corresponds to the "guest" database user (see the "VALID_USER" section later in this chapter). The following example illustrates this:

```
SELECT
    SUSER_ID() AS default_user
    ,SUSER_ID('probe') AS probe_user
    ,SUSER_ID('guest') AS guest_user

default_user probe_user  guest_user
------------ -----------  -----------
1            2            NULL
```

The last field is NULL because there is no "guest" user defined for the server.

This function is not available in any of the other RDBMS implementations discussed in this book.

SUSER_NAME()

Syntax:

```
SUSER_NAME()
```

The SUSER_NAME() function returns the name of the server user by its ID. If the user_id is omitted, the current server username is returned. Consider the following example:

```
SELECT
          SUSER_NAME()       AS default_user
,SUSER_NAME(2) AS probe_user
          ,SUSER_NAME(4) AS invalid_user

default_user    probe_user    invalid_user
------------    ----------    ------------
sa              probe         NULL
```

This function is not available in the other RDBMS implementations discussed in this book.

TSEQUAL()

Syntax:

```
TSEQUAL(browsed_row_timestamp, stored_row_timestamp)
```

The TSEQUAL() function compares two timestamp values. The result can be used to uniquely identify records using the timestamp column. This function compares the timestamp column values to prevent an update to a row that has been modified since it was selected for browsing. The function cannot be used as a stand-alone, and it cannot appear in the SELECT part of a statement. It is valid only in the context of a table that has timestamp column, or for browsing through a client application using DB-Library for connectivity. Consult Sybase documentation for more information.

The following example uses the WAITFOR DELAY() function to allow you to populate two timestamp values with differing results. Then you can use the TSEQUAL() function to compare the values. Also notice that even though you use the CURRENT_TIMESTAMP() function, you still must explicitly call the CONVERT() function to convert the value to a TIMESTAMP. This is because CURRENT_TIMESTAMP() returns a DATETIME value.

```
DECLARE @CURTIME TIMESTAMP
DECLARE @LATERTIME TIMESTAMP
SET @CURTIME = CONVERT(TIMESTAMP,CURRENT_TIMESTAMP)
WAITFOR DELAY '000:00:30'
SET @LATERTIME = CONVERT(TIMESTAMP,CURRENT_TIMESTAMP)

SELECT 'EQUAL' AS RESULT WHERE TSEQUAL(@CURTIME,@CURTIME)
```

```
SELECT 'NOT EQUAL' AS RESULT WHERE TSEQUAL(@CURTIME,@LATERTIME)

RESULT
------
EQUAL

(1 row(s) affected)

Server: Msg 532, Level 16, State 1, Line 9
The timestamp (changed to 0x000095d5016e6c79) shows that the row has been updated
by another user.
```

This function is present only in Sybase and Microsoft SQL Server, reflecting their architectural peculiarities and common heritage. It should be noted, however, that the Microsoft version is an undocumented addition.

USER()

Syntax:

```
USER()
```

The USER() function returns the name of the current user. It accepts no input arguments. If the sa_role is active, the returned value will always be dbo. Consider the following example:

```
SELECT
      USER AS current_user

current_user
-------------
dbo
```

Note that, unlike in other functions, the USER() function does not require brackets to identify it as a function.

This function is also available in the IBM DB2 and MySQL implementations.

USER_ID()

Syntax:

```
USER_ID([user_name])
```

The USER_ID() function returns the ID number of the specified user, or that of the current user in the current database. Consider the following example:

```
      SELECT
USER_ID()             AS default_id
,USER_ID('guest')      AS guest_id
,USER_ID('invalid')     AS invalid_id

default_id  guest_id    invalid_id
```

```
----------- ----------- -----------
          1           2        NULL
```

Inside the database, the user_id of the database owner is always 1, while "guest' has an ID of 2. An invalid username makes the USER_ID() function return NULL. (If sa_role is set to off, an error will be returned in this case.)

> *The default for the database owner will always be 1 if the sa_role is enabled; to get your actual userID, the sa_role should be turned off.*

This function is not available in any of the other RDBMS implementations discussed in this book.

USER_NAME()

Syntax:

```
USER_NAME([<user_id>])
```

This function returns a valid username based on a valid user ID. Called without arguments, it returns the current username. It is doing a reverse operation of the USER_ID() function. Consider the following example:

```
SELECT
        USER_NAME()         AS default_user
      ,USER_NAME(2)          AS guest_user
      ,USER_NAME(125)     AS invalid_user

default_user  guest_user    invalid_user
------------  ----------    ------------
dbo           guest         NULL
```

If the sa_role is active in the database you are running the query against, the default user will be the database owner (dbo). Inside the database, the USER_NAME() function will always identify you as the dbo. User ID 2 is reserved for "guest," while user ID 125 does not exist.

This function is not available in any of the other RDBMS implementations discussed in this book.

VALID_NAME()

Syntax:

```
VALID_NAME(<name_identifier>)
```

The VALID_NAME() function returns 1 if the given name is a valid identifier, and 0 otherwise. The function accepts the name input parameter in any of the character data types (that is, CHAR, VARCHAR, and so on).

A valid identifier is defined as one that is a maximum of 30 bytes in length, whether single-byte or multibyte characters are used. The first character must be either an alphabetic character (as defined in the current character set) or the underscore ("_") character; it cannot be any of the reserved keywords or contain blanks. Consider the following example:

```
        SELECT
              VALID_NAME('justname')      AS valid_name
           ,VALID_NAME ('table')       AS keyword
           ,VALID_NAME ('$money')      AS invalid_prefix
           ,VALID_NAME ('@variable')       AS valid_invalid

  valid_name  keyword      invalid_prefix valid_invalid
  ----------- ----------- -------------- -------------
            1           0              0             0
```

The results are predictable. The first field reports a valid name, while second is a reserved keyword TABLE; the third name starts with an invalid character, a dollar sign ("$"), and the last name (@variable) is flagged as invalid, even though it can be used for local variables.

The only characters that are excepted from this rule are the pound sign ("#") and the at sign ("@") because they have special meanings in ASE. The former is a prefix for temporary tables (either local or global), and the latter is a prefix for local variables and procedure arguments. Even though the names beginning with these characters are valid, the VALID_NAME() function will still return zero for these names. As such, you cannot use names that start with these characters for anything but for what they were intended for—namely, temporary tables and local variables. For example, an attempt to add a field that begins with "@" to a table would result in an error.

This function is not available in any of the other RDBMS implementations discussed in this book.

VALID_USER()

Syntax:

```
VALID_USER(<server_userID>)
```

This function verifies the server user ID. It returns 1 if the ID is a valid user (or alias) for any of the databases on the ASE server. The valid ID(s) and descriptions are stored in the SYSLOGINS system table. Here is an example how the data might look on a freshly installed server with no custom users added:

```
SELECT
 name AS user_name
, suid AS user_ID
FROM syslogins

User_name     user_id
---------     --------
sa            1
probe         2
mon_user      3
```

Any of these IDs is valid, while anything else, which is not yet defined on the system, would be invalid. For example, using the system that produced the results in this example, you may test the validity of the user ID(s) as follows:

```
        SELECT
              VALID_USER(1)      AS valid
           ,VALID_USER(5) AS invalid
```

```
valid       invalid
----------- -----------
          1           0
```

The system functions can be used in a `select_` *list, in a* `WHERE` *clause, and anywhere an expression is allowed.*

This function is not available in any of the other RDBMS implementations discussed in this book.

Unary System Functions

This classification includes a wide range of functions that could fall in any of the categories previously discussed. The main difference is that the following functions belong to the *niladic* type of functions (that is, argumentless functions), and are referred to as "global variables" in the vendor's documentation.

The following table shows the unary system functions ("global variables") discussed in this book.

Function Name	Description
@@BOOTTIME	Returns the date and time since the last reboot of the Adaptive Server server.
@@CLIENT_CSID	Returns a client's character set ID for the connection. A list of valid IDs is stored in `master.dbo.syscharsets` table. If no character set was ever initialized, a value of –1 is returned.
@@CLIENT_CSNAME	Returns a client's character set name. If no character set was ever initialized, a value of `NULL` is returned.
@@CONNECTIONS	Returns the number of user logins attempted for the Adaptive Server server.
@@CPU_BUSY	Number of seconds in CPU time the ASE has been busy doing CPU work.
@@ERROR	Returns the error number most recently generated by the system. Because of its global nature, it cannot be reliably used within a session to determine whether an error occurred.
@@ERRORLOG	Returns a full path to the errorlog file for ASE, relative to `$SYBASE` directory (`%SYBASE%` on Windows).
@@IDENTITY	Returns the latest generated `IDENTITY` column value.
@@IDLE	Returns the CPU time (in seconds) when the ASE was idle.
@@IO_BUSY	Returns the number of seconds the CPU spent doing Adaptive Server input/output operations.
@@LANGID	Returns an ID assigned to the current language of the server (for example, 0 for `us_english`) from the `syslanguage.langid` table.

Table continued on following page

Function Name	Description
@@LANGUAGE	Returns the language description assigned to a particular language ID (for example, us_english) from the table syslanguages.name.
@@MAXCHARLEN	Returns the maximum length (in bytes) of a character in the default character set of the ASE.
@@MAX_CONNECTIONS	Returns the number of simultaneous connections that is configured for the given environment.
@@NCHARSIZE	Returns the maximum length (in bytes) for the default character set.
@@NESTLEVEL	Returns the current nesting level for the procedure.
@@OPTIONS	Returns a bit mask for the current session options (hexadecimal format).
@@PROBESUID	Returns a value of 2 for the probe User ID.
@@ROWCOUNT	Returns the number of rows affected by the current query (SELECT). Also used with cursors (running total of the rows fetched into the cursor. Is set to 0 by any SQL command that does not return rows in Sybase (that is, UPDATE or DELETE).
@@SPID	Returns the ASE server process ID for the current process (active session).
@@SQLSTATUS	Returns the status information of a cursor after execution of a fetch statement (0 for success, 1 for an error, and 2 for "no more data").
@@TIMETICKS	Returns the number of microseconds per CPU tick. This amount is machine (CPU) dependent.
@@TOTAL_ERRORS	Returns the number of errors detected by ASE Server while reading and writing.
@@TOTAL_READ	Returns the number of disk reads performed by ASE Server since startup.
@@TOTAL_WRITE	Returns the number of disk writes performed by ASE Server since startup.
@@TRANCHAINED	Returns the status of the T-SQL program transactional mode: 0 if it is unchained and 1 for chained. Chained mode is SQL92 standard–compatible, which requires implicit transaction before any of the data modifying the SQL statement can be executed (for example, DELETE, INSERT, UPDATE, FETCH, and so on); an explicit COMMIT or ROLLBACK is required to complete the transaction. Unchained mode requires an explicit BEGIN TRANSACTION function in addition to the COMMIT or ROLLBACK statements (SET CHAINED ON/OFF).
@@TRANCOUNT	Returns the nesting level of transactions in the current session.
@@TRANSTATE	Returns the current state of a transaction after a statement executes in the current user session: 0 = transaction is in progress; 1 = transaction is completed and committed; 2 = previous statement is aborted, but transaction is still active; and 3 = transaction is aborted and rolled back.

Function Name	Description
@@UNICHARSIZE	Returns the size of a Unicode character (value of 2).
@@VERSION	Returns the date, version string, OS build, and so on for the current release of the ASE Server.
@@VERSION_AS_INTEGER	Returns the version of the ASE Server as an integer (for example, 12500 for Adaptive Server Enterprise/12.5.1/Beta).

@@BOOTTIME

Syntax:

```
SELECT @@BOOTTIME
```

This returns the date and time since the last reboot of the RDBMS server. Consider the following example:

```
      SELECT
            @@BOOTTIME as since_when
  since_when
  --------------------------
  Jun 3 2004    1:23 AM
```

This function is not available in any of the other RDBMS implementations discussed in this book.

@@CLIENT_CSID

Syntax:

```
SELECT @@CLIENT_CSID
```

This returns client's character set ID for the connection. A list of valid IDs is stored in the MASTER.DBO.SYSCHARSETS table. If no character set was ever initialized, a value of –1 is returned. Some of the character set values are shown in the following table.

CSID	Character Set Name	Description
0	ascii_8 iso_1 cp850	ASCII, for use with unspecified 8-bit data; ISO 8859-1 (Latin-1); Western European 8-bit character set; Code Page 850 (Multilingual) character set
1	bin_iso_1	Binary ordering, for the ISO 8859/1 or Latin-1 character set (iso_1)
2	bin_cp850	Binary ordering, for use with Code Page 850 (cp850)
190	defaultml	Default Unicode multilingual ordering

Table continued on following page

CSID	Character Set Name	Description
190	utf8bin	Ordering for UTF-16 that matches the binary ordering of UTF-8
190	binary	Binary ordering for UTF-16
190	dict	General-purpose dictionary ordering
190	nocase	General-purpose case-insensitive dictionary ordering
190	cyrnocs	Common Cyrillic case-insensitive dictionary ordering
190	dynix	Chinese phonetic ordering
190	eucjisbn	Ordering that matches the binary ordering of the EUCJIS character set

The following example shows what the character set ID is set to for your current section:

```
SELECT @@CLIENT_CSID

-----------------
       1
```

This function is not available in any of the other RDBMS implementations discussed in this book.

@@CLIENT_CSNAME

Syntax:

```
SELECT @@CLIENT_CSNAME
```

This returns the client's character set name. If no character set was ever initialized, a value of NULL is returned. For example, the SQL Advantage client uses the ISO_1 character set, as shown here:

```
SELECT
        @@CLIENT_CSNAME client_charset

client_charset
------------------
iso_1
```

This function is not available in any of the other RDBMS implementations discussed in this book.

@@CONNECTIONS

Syntax:

```
SELECT @@CONNECTIONS
```

This returns the number of user logins attempted for the RDBMS server. The number includes all connections, not only active ones. Consider the following example:

```
SELECT
     @@CONNECTIONS as total_connections

total_connections
-----------------
                2
```

This function is also found in Microsoft SQL Server.

@@CPU_BUSY

Syntax:

```
SELECT @@CPU_BUSY
```

This returns the number of seconds in CPU time that ASE has been busy doing CPU work for the query. Consider the following example:

```
SELECT
@@CPU_BUSY AS busy

busy
-----------
         44
```

This function is also found in Microsoft SQL Server.

@@ERROR

Syntax:

```
SELECT @@ERROR
```

This returns the error number most recently generated by the system. Because of its global nature, it cannot be reliably used within a session to determine whether an error occurred because it could be set by any of the sessions. Consider the following example:

```
SELECT
        @@ERROR as error
error
----------
        0
```

This function is also found in Microsoft SQL Server.

@@ERRORLOG

Syntax:

```
SELECT @@ERRORLOG
```

This returns the full path to the errorlog file for the ASE, relative to the $SYBASE directory (%SYBASE% on Microsoft Windows). Consider the following example:

```
SELECT
      @@ERRORLOG as err_path

err_path
-------------------------------------
C:\sybase\ASE-12_5\install\sqlfunc.log
```

This function is not available in any of the other RDBMS implementations discussed in this book.

@@IDENTITY

Syntax:

```
SELECT @@IDENTITY
```

This returns the latest generated IDENTITY column value. If no table accessed within the session has the identity column, zero will be returned. On the other hand, if you have several tables with identity columns where you have inserted records (within the same session), only the last IDENTITY value will be returned. For example, create a table with an IDENTITY column (for simplicity's sake, assume all the defaults) and insert at least one value into it, as shown here:

```
SELECT
@@IDENTITY as new_identity
GO
new_identity
------------
   0

CREATE TABLE  identity_test
           (
 field1      NUMERIC IDENTITY NOT NULL
         ,field2      INTEGER
)
GO
INSERT INTO identity_test (field2) VALUES (1)
GO

SELECT
@@IDENTITY as new_identity
GO
new_identity
------------
           1
```

In the first iteration of the example, the @@IDENTITY function returns 0 because you have not accessed a table yet. Once you create your table and insert a value, you can see that the @@IDENTITY value returns the last value of the IDENTITY column in your table.

This function is also found in Microsoft SQL Server.

@@IDLE

Syntax:

```
SELECT @@IDLE
```

This returns the CPU time (in seconds) that the ASE spent idle since the last boot. In the following example, the test server was idle most of the time and was only rebooted:

```
     SELECT
@@IDLE as doing_nothing

  doing_nothing
  -------------
        2316701
```

This function is also found in Microsoft SQL Server.

@@IO_BUSY

Syntax:

```
SELECT @@IO_BUSY
```

This returns the number of seconds the CPU spent doing RDBMS input/output (I/O) operations (writing from or reading to or from a disk). This could be a valuable metric for tuning up your server and application to pinpoint the I/O-intensive operations. Consider the following example, which shows the idle time on our database since the last startup:

```
SELECT
@@IDLE as doing

  doing
  -------------
  43
```

This function is also found in Microsoft SQL Server.

@@LANGID

Syntax:

```
SELECT @@LANGID
```

This returns the ID assigned to the current language of the server (for example, 0 for us_english) from the SYSLANGUAGES table. The following example shows how to find the current language ID assigned to your database:

```
LECT @@LANGID AS DB_LANGUAGE

DB_LANGUAGE
-----------------
0
```

As you can see, the current language ID is 0, which corresponds to `us_english`.

This function is also found in Microsoft SQL Server.

@@LANGUAGE

Syntax:

```
SELECT @@LANGUAGE
```

This returns a language description assigned to a particular language ID (for example, `us_english`) from the SYSLANGUAGES table. Consider the following example:

```
SELECT
            @@LANGUAGE AS server_language

server_language
---------------
us_english
```

This function is also found in Microsoft SQL Server.

@@MAXCHARLEN

Syntax:

```
SELECT @@MAXCHARLEN
```

This returns the maximum length (in bytes) of a character in the default character set of the ASE. Consider the following example:

```
SELECT
            @@MAXCHARLEN AS character_length

character_length
----------------
               1
```

The result returned means that every character in the default server's language occupies exactly one byte. For Unicode or some of national languages, it might be 2 bytes per character.

This function is not available in any of the other RDBMS implementations discussed in this book.

@@MAX_CONNECTIONS

Syntax:

```
SELECT @@MAX_CONNECTIONS
```

This returns the number of simultaneous connections that is configured for the given environment. The number depends on the type of licenses you have purchased. Consider the following example:

```
SELECT
    @@MAX_CONNECTIONS AS max_out

max_out
-----------
99992
```

This number is unlikely for a production server because of licensing and performance issues.

This function is also found in Microsoft SQL Server.

@@NCHARSIZE

Syntax:

```
@@NCHARSIZE
```

This returns the maximum length (in bytes) for the default character set. Consider the following example:

```
SELECT
            @@MAXCHARLEN AS nchar_length

nchar_length
--------------
             1
```

Since the default is US_ENGLISH, it also returns 1 byte.

This function is not available in any of the other RDBMS implementations discussed in this book.

@@NESTLEVEL

Syntax:

```
SELECT @@NESTLEVEL
```

This returns the current nesting level for the procedure. The maximum allowable value is 32. Once the level is exceeded, the transaction terminates. The function is hardly useful in a SQL statement other than to check that a trigger being fired does not exceed a certain predefined level. The following example demonstrates the usage of the statement to return your current level of 0, which means that this SQL statement is being executed from the base level:

```
SELECT @@NESTLEVEL AS THIS_LEVEL

THIS_LEVEL
--------------
0
```

This function is also found in Microsoft SQL Server.

@@OPTIONS

Syntax:

```
SELECT @@OPTIONS
```

This returns a bit mask for the current session options (in hexadecimal format). Consider the following example:

```
SELECT
@@OPTIONS AS options_bitmask

options_bitmask
-------------------
0x80210000000f014403
```

The function could be useful to check the options set up for a specific session. The bitwise operator, &, is used to verify the presence of a specific value in a bitmask.

This function is also found in Microsoft SQL Server.

@@PROBESUID

Syntax:

```
SELECT @@PROBESUID
```

This function is used merely to return the user ID of the probe user instance. This number is always 2. The following example demonstrates the output of the function:

```
SELECT @@PROBESUID

----------------
        2
```

This function is not available in any of the other RDBMS implementations discussed in this book.

@@ROWCOUNT

Syntax:

```
SELECT @@ROWCOUNT
```

This returns a number of rows affected by the current query (SELECT); it is also used with cursors (returning the running total of the rows fetched into the cursor). This is set to 0 by any SQL command that does not return rows in Sybase (for example, UPDATE and DELETE). The function is global (that is, every session reads the same value).

```
CREATE TABLE TEST_TABLE( ITEM     VARCHAR(20))

INSERT INTO TEST_TABLE VALUES('APPLE')
INSERT INTO TEST_TABLE VALUES('PEACH')
```

```
INSERT INTO TEST_TABLE VALUES('APRICOT')

SELECT ITEM AS FRUIT FROM TEST_TABLE

FRUIT
---------
APPLE
PEACH
APRICOT

SELECT @@ROWCOUNT AS NUM_OF_ROWS_COUNTED

NUM_OF_ROWS_COUNTED
-------------------
3
```

This function is also found in Microsoft SQL Server.

@@SPID

Syntax:

```
SELECT @@SPID
```

This returns the ASE server process ID for the current process (active session). This uniquely identifies every active connection. Consider the following example:

```
SELECT
@@SPID AS process_id
process_id
-----------
         19
```

This function is also found in Microsoft SQL Server.

@@SQLSTATUS

Syntax:

```
SELECT @@SQLSTATUS
```

This returns the status information of a cursor after execution of a fetch statement (0 for success, 1 for an error, and 2 for "no more data"). While you are able to call the function from an SQL statement, this function is useful only in procedural processing. The following example shows a cursor and how the @@SQLSTATUS function returns a successful result:

```
declare csr1 cursor
for select * from TEST_TABLE
for read only
open csr1
begin
declare @xyz varchar(255)
fetch csr1 into @xyz
```

```
select error = @@error select sqlstatus = @@sqlstatus
end
close csr1
deallocate cursor csr1

error
--------
0

sqlstatus
---------
0
```

Note that, since you are creating a cursor, you must run the creation statement for the cursor separately from the main body of the function in Sybase.

You can achieve similar functionality by using the @@STATUS function in MS SQL Server.

@@TIMETICKS

Syntax:

```
SELECT @@TIMETICKS
```

This returns the number of microseconds per CPU tick. This amount is machine (CPU) dependent. On an x86 server, the result is as follows:

```
SELECT
@@TIMETICKS AS microsec_tick

microsec_ticks
-------------
        100000
```

This function is also found in Microsoft SQL Server (though returned results will be presented differently).

@@TOTAL_ERRORS

Syntax:

```
SELECT @@TOTAL_ERRORS
```

This returns the number of errors detected by the ASE Server while reading and writing (that is, during I/O operations). The server usually recovers by itself whenever the error occurs (because of contention, locking, and so on). The following example demonstrates the syntax and output of the @@TOTAL_ERRORS function in our database:

```
SELECT @@TOTAL_ERRORS

---------
0
```

This function is also found in Microsoft SQL Server.

@@TOTAL_READ

Syntax:

```
SELECT @@TOTAL_READ
```

This returns the number of disk reads performed by the ASE Server since startup. This can be useful for analyzing the server performance and for load balancing. The following example demonstrates the use of the @@TOTAL_READS function to return the total number of reads from our database since it last started:

```
SELECT @@TOTAL_READS

    ---------
    15456
```

This function is also found in Microsoft SQL Server.

@@TOTAL_WRITE

Syntax:

```
SELECT @@TOTAL_WRITE
```

This returns the number of disk writes performed by the ASE Server since startup. This can be useful for analyzing the server performance and for load balancing. The following example demonstrates the use of the @@TOTAL_WRITE function to return the total number of writes that have occurred on our database since it last started:

```
SELECT @@TOTAL_WRITE

    ---------
    151
```

This function is also found in Microsoft SQL Server.

@@TRANCHAINED

Syntax:

```
SELECT @@TRANCHAINED
```

This returns the status of the T-SQL program transactional mode: 0 if it is unchained and 1 for chained. The following example gives the output of the function on our generic database setup:

```
SELECT @@TRANCHAINED

    -----------
    0
```

Chained mode is SQL92 standard–compatible, which requires an implicit transaction before any of the data-modifying SQL statements (for example, DELETE, INSERT, UPDATE, FETCH, and so on) can be executed. An explicit COMMIT or ROLLBACK is required to complete the transaction. *Unchained mode* requires an explicit BEGIN TRANSACTION in addition to the COMMIT and ROLLBACK statements. The behavior is controlled by the SET CHAINED {ON|OFF} command for the batch of procedural statements. Mostly, this function is used from Transact-SQL to gather information about the execution environment settings.

This function is not available in any of the other RDBMS implementations discussed in this book.

@@TRANCOUNT

Syntax:

```
SELECT @@TRANCOUNT
```

This returns the nesting level of transactions in the current session. This is most useful within a stored procedure or an anonymous block, rather than a single SQL statement, where it usually returns zero. The following example demonstrates this:

```
SELECT
            @@TRANCOUNT as transactions

transactions
------------
            0

BEGIN TRAN
SELECT
            @@TRANCOUNT as transactions

transactions
------------
            1
```

After the BEGIN TRAN statement was issued, the number of transactions was incremented by one. It will be counted until the COMMIT TRAN statement is executed for each corresponding BEGIN TRAN statement.

This function is also found in Microsoft SQL Server.

@@TRANSTATE

Syntax:

```
SELECT @@TRANSTATE
```

This returns the current state of a transaction after a statement executes in the current user session:

❑ 0—Transaction is in progress.

❑ 1—Transaction is completed and committed.

❏ 2—Previous statement is aborted; transaction is still active.

❏ 3—Transaction is aborted and rolled back.

You can use your TEST_TABLE from a previous example to insert another item into it in the form of a transaction. In this example, you will check the @@TRANSTATE function both inside and outside of the transaction to verify that it was committed:

```
BEGIN TRANSACTION
SELECT @@TRANSTATE AS FIRST_STATE
INSERT INTO TEST_TABLE VALUES("ORANGE")
COMMIT
SELECT @@TRANSTATE AS SECOND_STATE


FIRST_STATE
-----------
          0


SECOND_STATE
------------
           1
```

Similar functionality can be achieved using the @@ERROR function in MS SQL Server.

@@UNICHARSIZE

Syntax:

```
SELECT @@UNICHARSIZE
```

This returns the size of a Unicode character. It usually returns 2 (the number of bytes required to represent a Unicode character). Consider the following example, where you verify that your database is set to return the default size of a Unicode character:

```
SELECT @@UNICHARSIZE

-----------
          2
```

This function is not available in any of the other RDBMS implementations discussed in this book.

@@VERSION

Syntax:

```
SELECT @@VERSION
```

This returns the date, full version string, OS build, platform, and so on for the current release of the ASE Server. Here is an example that displays the current version information on our instance of Sybase:

```
SELECT
        @@VERSION as my_ase_version

my_ase_version
-------------------------------------------------------------------------
Adaptive Server Enterprise/12.5.1/EBF 11522/P/NT (IX86)/OS 4.0/ase1251/1824/32-
bit/OPT/Mon Sep 29 21:41:30 2003
```

This function is also found in Microsoft SQL Server, though it returns information in a different format.

@@VERSION_AS_INTEGER

Syntax:

```
SELECT @@VERSION_AS_INTEGER
```

This returns the version of the ASE Server as an integer. The following examples demonstrate retrieving the current numeric version of our instance of Sybase:

```
SELECT
    @@VERSION_AS_INTEGER as numeric_version

numeric_version
---------------
12500
```

The `@@MICROSOFTVERSION` function in MS SQL Server provides similar functionality for that platform.

Summary

In this chapter, we detailed the various built-in functions available on the Sybase ASE platform. We covered a diverse range of function classes: string, date and time, conversion, security, aggregate, mathematical, text and image, system, and unary system functions. You should now have a good grasp of the concepts and techniques needed to use the vast array of functionality presented by the Sybase ASE platform. Additionally, by reading Chapter 8, you will have a clearer understanding of the common heritage and baseline that the MS SQL Server and Sybase ASE implementations share, as well as their differences.

In Chapter 10, we will discuss the functions available in the MySQL implementation. The MySQL platform is the largest Open Source implementation used throughout the world, and learning its syntax can be a valuable tool to tuck away in the aspiring developer's toolbox.

10

MySQL Functions

MySQL is one of the most widely used Open Source RDBMS implementations in use today. The developers of this platform pride themselves on remaining within the ANSI SQL standard, more so than any other major RDBMS implementation. This chapter discusses functions within the MySQL environment.

First, we will look at the specifics of the MySQL query syntax to give the developer a better sense of the syntax differences in this particular platform. Next, we will discuss the different types of built-in functions available to the MySQL developer. After reading this chapter, the developer should have a better understanding of the possibilities that can be achieved by using this particular system.

MySQL Query Syntax

The MySQL SELECT statement is based upon the ANSI SQL standard discussed in Chapter 5. However, there are many unique features of its syntax that are not shown in the basic syntax of the ANSI standard. Therefore, we will break down the syntax of the statement and give a brief explanation of each of its parts to give you a better understanding of the nuances of the language. The following code details the MySQL SELECT statement syntax:

```
SELECT
    [ALL | DISTINCT | DISTINCTROW]
    [HIGH PRIORITY]
    [STRAIGHT_JOIN]
    [SQL_SMALL_RESULT] [SQL_BIG_RESULT] [SQL_BUFFER_RESULT]
    [SQL_CACHE | SQL_NO_CACHE] [SQL_CALC_FOUND_ROWS]
  select_expression......
  [INTO OUTFILE 'file_name' export_options
     | INTO DUMPFILE 'file_name']
  [FROM table_references]
    [WHERE where_definition]
    [GROUP BY {col_name | expression | position}
      [ASC | DESC], ....... [WITH ROLLUP]
    [HAVING where_definition]
    [ORDER BY {col_name | expression | position}
      [ASC | DESC], ..........]
    [LIMIT {[offset,] row_count | row_count OFFSET offset}]
```

The first portion of the SELECT syntax lets you specify the ALL, DISTINCT, and DISTINCTROW options. The three options determine whether or not duplicate rows should be included in the result set. DISTINCT and DISTINCTROW are actually synonyms for one another and specify that duplicate rows should be removed. ALL returns all rows and is the default if nothing is specified, so it is rarely used.

The next section deals with the statements HIGH PRIORITY, STRAIGHT_JOIN, and the series of SQL-* statements. All of these are extensions that are specific to MySQL. SELECT HIGH PRIORITY tells the RDBMS that the SELECT statement is to be given a higher priority than any updates on the table. This ensures that the SELECT statement will run even when the table is waiting to be updated by an UPDATE statement. As such, its use should be limited to those queries that can be executed quickly and must be executed at once. The STRAIGHT_JOIN statement forces the optimizer to join the tables in your SELECT statement in the order that they are listed. This is used primarily in the rare instance that the optimizer picks a nonoptimal ordering of the joins between your tables.

SQL_BIG_RESULT can be used with either GROUP BY or DISTINCT to let the optimizer know that the result set will be very large. SQL_BUFFER_RESULT forces the optimizer to place the result set into a temporary table so that it can speed up the rate at which locks are released on the query tables. SQL_SMALL_RESULT is the opposite of SQL_BIG_RESULT and will use temporary tables to speed up the processing of the query. SQL_CALC_FOUND_ROWS will allow MySQL to count the number of rows in the result set so that they may be retrieved later with SELECT FOUND_ROWS(). The count that is collected is the same regardless of any LIMIT clause, including LIMIT 0. SQL_CACHE lets MySQL store the query result in the query cache. This is used if you have query_cache_type set to 2 or DEMAND. Finally, SQL_NO_CACHE is the opposite of SQL_CACHE and tells MySQL not to cache the results in the query results.

The select_expression is a column that you want returned in the result set. There can be multiple select_expressions that are separated by commas and can even be aliased by using the AS alias_name syntax. The AS keyword is optional and the developer must be sure to include the commas between each of the select_expressions or they will be interpreted as aliases.

The INTO OUTFILE and INTO DUMPFILE clauses are used to export the result set of the query to a file on the server's hard drive. To successfully export the result set, the user must have the FILE privilege. If you are using the INTO OUTFILE clause, then the complete result set will be exported into the file. If the INTO DUMPFILE clause is specified, then it outputs only one row to the file without the use of columns, line terminators, or escape processing. This is particularly efficient if you must output BLOB data into a file. The files created by either of these clauses are writable by anyone on the system, but cannot already exist. This prevents system files from being overwritten.

The FROM table_reference is the portion of the SELECT statement that tells it where to get the information from. It specifies a list of tables and can be referenced with an alias, just as the columns in the select_expression were.

The WHERE clause is used to restrict the data that is returned by the first part of the SELECT statement. This is done by following the WHERE keyword with a series of clauses that are joined by AND/OR keywords. These clauses can be statements relating table objects to one another, thus creating natural joins, or restricting table objects by a certain value or range of values.

The GROUP BY and HAVING clauses are related to producing summary row information in the result set. These grouping elements can be column names, aliases, or column positions, and the groups will be ordered in the order that the GROUP BY elements are declared. The HAVING clause is used to restrict the groups that are sent to the result set, unlike the WHERE clause that restricts the data placed into the groups. It should be noted that the HAVING clause is not optimized. Therefore, you should strive not to include items in the HAVING clause that should be in the WHERE clause. In addition, the HAVING clause may refer to aggregate functions, which is something that the WHERE clause cannot do.

The ORDER BY clause is used to order the select_expressions in the SELECT statement. The ordering is hierarchical, based on the order in which the items are expressed in the ORDER BY clause. The ordering can even be performed on columns not returned in the result set. The default ordering is set to ascending, but it may be specifically defined as either ascending (ASC) or descending (DESC).

Lastly, the LIMIT clause is used to limit the number of rows returned by the result set. This is normally specified with a specific row_count. Alternatively, you may use the OFFSET clause to offset to the place where the row count would begin. The rows that are returned are based on the order in which they are placed in the result set. Therefore, if a ORDER BY clause is used, then the rows that are returned are based on the ordered set. In a query that does not use one, the order is arbitrary.

Now you should have a good understanding of the basics of the MySQL platform. This will be used as a basis upon which to gain a better understanding of the use of the different functions as well as decipher the examples given herein.

Aggregate Functions

An aggregate SQL function summarizes the results of an expression for the group of rows (selected from a table, view, or table-valued function) and returns a single value for that group.

The following table contains the list of aggregate functions that are available on the MySQL platform.

Function Name	Input	Output	Description
AVG	<expression>	<expression>	Returns the average value of <expression>.
COUNT	<expression>	<num_expression>	Returns a count of the non-NULL values in <expression>. This function can also be used with the DISTINCT keyword to return a count of only the distinct values.
MAX	<expression>		Returns the maximum value of <expression>. If <expression> is a string value, then the maximum value of the string is returned.
MIN	<expression>		Returns the minimum value of <expression>. If <expression> is a string, then the minimum value of the string is returned.
SUM	<expression>	<num_expression>	Returns the sum of <expression>. If the return set has no rows, it will return NULL.

Before we begin, let's create a small sample table within the default test database that is created in the MySQL implementation. For this we are using the CARS database to keep a common thread between this chapter and Chapter 5. This also provides a rather simple set of data for the beginning MySQL developer to work from. The code for creating the table is as follows:

```
CREATE TABLE cars
(
  MAKER   VARCHAR (25),
  MODEL   VARCHAR (25),
  PRICE   NUMERIC
)

INSERT INTO CARS VALUES('CHRYSLER','CROSSFIRE',33620);
INSERT INTO CARS VALUES('CHRYSLER','300M',29185);
INSERT INTO CARS VALUES('HONDA','CIVIC',15610);
INSERT INTO CARS VALUES('HONDA','ACCORD',19300);
INSERT INTO CARS VALUES('FORD','MUSTANG',15610);
INSERT INTO CARS VALUES('FORD','LATESTnGREATEST',NULL);
INSERT INTO CARS VALUES('FORD','FOCUS',13005);
```

AVG()

Syntax:

```
AVG(expression)
```

This aggregate function will return the average of expression. Consider the following example:

```
SELECT AVG(PRICE) FROM CARS;
-> 21055.0000
```

The AVG() function is available in all of the RDBMS implementations discussed in this book.

COUNT()

Syntax:

```
COUNT(expression)
```

This function returns the count of the items in expression. Most often it is used with * to get a row count of the rows in a table. Consider the following example:

```
SELECT COUNT(*) AS NUM_OF_CARS
    FROM CARS

NUM_OF_CARS
----------------
7
```

The COUNT() function is available in all of the RDBMS implementations discussed in this book.

MAX() and MIN()

Syntax:

```
MAX(expression)
MIN(expression)
```

The MIN() and MAX() functions return the minimum and maximum values, respectively, of the set of values in expression. Consider the following example:

```
SELECT
    MIN(PRICE) AS MIN_PRICE,
    MAX(PRICE) AS MAX_PRICE
FROM CARS;

MIN_PRICE      MAX_PRICE
----------     ----------
13005          33620
```

The MAX() and MIN() functions are available in all of the RDBMS implementations discussed in this book.

SUM()

Syntax:

```
SUM(expression)
```

This function returns the sum of the values in expression. It returns NULL if there are no rows in the result set. Consider the following example:

```
SELECT
    SUM(PRICE) AS SUM_PRICE
FROM CARS;

SUM_PRICE
-------------------
125330
```

The SUM() function is available in all of the RDBMS implementations discussed in this book.

Numeric Functions

MySQL numeric functions are used primarily for numeric manipulation and/or mathematical calculations. As always, the MySQL implementation tries to stick as closely as possible to the ANSI standard for built-in functions. The following table details the numeric functions that are available in the MySQL implementation.

Function Name	Input	Output	Description
ABS	<num_expression>		Returns the absolute value of <num_expression>.
ACOS	<num_expression>		Returns the arccosine of <num_expression>. Returns NULL if the value is not in the range −1 to 1.
ASIN	<num_expression>		Returns the arcsine of <num_expression>. Returns NULL if value is not in the range 1 to 1
ATAN	<num_expression>		Returns the arctangent of <num_expression>.
ATAN2	<num_expression1>, <num_expression2>		Returns the arctangent of the two variables passed to it.
BIT_AND	<expression>		Returns the bitwise AND all the bits in expression.
BIT_COUNT	<BIGINT>		Returns the string representation of the binary value of <BIGINT>.
BIT_OR	<expression>		Returns the bitwise OR of all the bits in <expression>.
CEIL or CEILING	<num_expression>	INTEGER	Returns the smallest integer value that is not less than <num_expression>.
CONV	<num_expression>, <from_base>, <to_base>	STRING	Coverts <num_expression> between different bases. Returns a string representation of <num_expression> converted from <from_base> to <to_base>. Will return NULL if any of the values are NULL.
COS	<num_expression>		Returns the cosine of <num_expression>. The numeric expression should be expressed in radians.
COT	<num_expression>		Returns the cotangent of <num_expression>.
DEGREES	<num_expression>		Returns <num_expression> converted from radians to degrees.
EXP	<num_expression>		Returns the base of the natural logarithm (e) raised to the power of <num_expression>.

Function Name	Input	Output	Description
FLOOR	<num_expression>	INTEGER	Returns the largest integer value that is not greater than <num_expression>.
FORMAT	<num_expression1>, <num_expression2>		Returns <num_expression1> rounded to <num_expression2> number of decimal places. If <num_expression2> is zero, then the result has no decimal point.
GREATEST	<num_expression1>, <num_expression2>		Returns the largest value of the input expressions.
INTERVAL	<num_expression1>, <num_expression2>	INTEGER	Returns 0 if <num_expression1> is less than <num_expression2>, 1 if <num_expression1> is less than <num_expression3>, and so on. All arguments are treated as integers. It is required that all input values <num_expression2> and higher be in ascending order for the function to work correctly.
LEAST	<num_expression1>, <num_expression2>		Returns the minimum-valued input when given two or more.
LOG	<num_expression>		Returns the natural logarithm of <num_expression>.
LOG10	<num_expression>		Returns the base-10 logarithm of <num_expression>.
MOD	<num_expression1>, <num_expression2>		Returns the remainder of <num_expression1> divided by <num_expression2>.
OCT	<num_expression>		Returns the string representation of the octal value of <num_expression>. Returns NULL if <num_expression> is NULL.
PI			Returns the value of pi (π).
POW or POWER	<num_expression1>, <num_expression2>		Returns the value of <num_expression1> raised to the power of <num_expression2>.
RADIANS	<num_expression>		Returns the value of <num_expression> converted from degrees to radians.

Table continued on following page

Function Name	Input	Output	Description
RAND	<num_expression>		If no input parameter is specified, then the function returns a random floating point value between 0 and 1. If an input parameter is specified, then the integer argument <num_expression> is used as a seed value.
ROUND	<num_expression>	INTEGER	Returns <num_expression> rounded to an integer.
ROUND	<num_expression1>, <num_expression2>	DECIMAL	Returns <num_expression1> rounded to <num_expression2> number of decimal places. If <num_expression2> is 0, then the result has no decimal point.
SIGN	<num_expression>	INTEGER	Returns the sign of <num_expression> as –1, 0, or 1 (negative, zero, or positive).
SIN	<num_expression>		Returns the sine of <num_expression> given in radians.
SQRT	<num_expression>		Returns the non-negative square root of <num_expression>.
STD or STDDEV	<num_expression>		Returns the standard deviation of <num_expression>.
TAN	<num_expression>		Returns the tangent of <num_expression> expressed in radians.
TRUNCATE	<num_expression1>, <num_expression2>		Returns <num_expression1> truncated to <num_expression2> decimal places. If <num_expression2> is 0, then the result will have no decimal point.

ABS()

Syntax:

```
ABS(X)
```

The ABS() function returns the absolute value of X. Consider the following example:

```
SELECT ABS(2);
-> 2
SELECT ABS(-2);
-> 2
```

This function is available in all of the RDBMS implementations discussed in this book.

ACOS()

Syntax:

```
ACOS(X)
```

This function returns the arccosine of X. The value of X must range between –1 and 1 or NULL will be returned. Consider the following example:

```
SELECT ACOS(1);
      0.000000
```

This function is available in all of the RDBMS implementations discussed in this book.

ASIN()

Syntax:

```
ASIN(X)
```

The ASIN() function returns the arcsine of X. The value of X must be in the range of –1 to 1 or NULL is returned. Consider the following example:

```
SELECT ASIN(1);
-> 1.5707963267949
```

This function is available in all of the RDBMS implementations discussed in this book.

ATAN()

Syntax:

```
ATAN(X)
```

This function returns the arctangent of X. Consider the following example:

```
SELECT ATAN(1)
-> 0.78539816339745
```

This function is available in all of the RDBMS implementations discussed in this book.

ATAN2()

Syntax:

```
SELECT ATAN2(Y,X)
```

This function returns the arctangent of the two arguments: X and Y. It is similar to the arctangent of Y/X, except that the signs of both are used to find the quadrant of the result. Consider the following example:

```
SELECT ATAN2(3,6)
-> 0.46364760900081
```

This function is also available in the Microsoft SQL Server implementation. In the other RDBMS implementations discussed in this book, the equivalent function is ATN2.

BIT_AND()

Syntax:

```
BIT_AND(expression)
```

The BIT_AND function returns the bitwise AND of all bits in expression. The basic premise is that if two corresponding bits are the same, then a bitwise AND operation will return 1, while if they are different, a bitwise AND operation will return 0. The function itself returns a 64-bit integer value. If there are no matches, then it will return 18446744073709551615. The following example performs the BIT_AND function on the PRICE column grouped by the MAKER of the car:

```
SELECT
     MAKER, BIT_AND(PRICE)  BITS
     FROM CARS
     GROUP BY MAKER;

MAKER                      BITS
----------------           ----------------
CHRYSLER                   512
FORD                       12488
HONDA                      2144
```

This function is also available in the Oracle RDBMS implementation.

BIT_COUNT()

Syntax:

```
BIT_COUNT(numeric_value)
```

The BIT_COUNT() function returns the number of bits that are active in numeric_value. The following example demonstrates using the BIT_COUNT() function to return the number of active bits for a range of numbers:

```
SELECT
     BIT_COUNT(2)  AS TWO,
     BIT_COUNT(4)  AS FOUR,
     BIT_COUNT(7)  AS SEVEN

TWO          FOUR           SEVEN
------       -------        --------
1            1              3
```

The BIT_COUNT() function is not available in any of the other RDBMS implementations discussed in this book.

BIT_OR()

Syntax:

```
BIT_OR(expression)
```

The BIT_OR() function returns the bitwise OR of all the bits in expression. The basic premise of the bitwise OR function is that it returns 0 if the corresponding bits match, and 1 if they do not. The function returns a 64-bit integer, and, if there are no matching rows, then it returns 0. The following example performs the BIT_OR() function on the PRICE column of the CARS table, grouped by the MAKER:

```
SELECT
    MAKER, BIT_OR(PRICE)  BITS
    FROM CARS
    GROUP BY MAKER;

MAKER                       BITS
----------------            ---------------
CHRYSLER                    62293
FORD                        16127
HONDA                       32766
```

The BIT_OR() function is not available in any of the other RDBMS implementations discussed in this book.

CEIL() or CEILING()

Syntax:

```
CEILING(X)
CEIL(X)
```

This function returns the smallest integer value that is not smaller than X. Consider the following example:

```
SELECT CEILING(3.46);
-> 4
SELECT CEILING(-6.43);
-> -6
```

This function is available either as CEIL() or CEILING() in all of the RDBMS implementations discussed in this book.

CONV()

Syntax:

```
CONV(N,from_base,to_base)
```

The purpose of the CONV() function is to convert numbers between different number bases. The function returns a string of the value N converted from from_base to to_base. The minimum base value is 2 and the maximum is 36. If any of the arguments are NULL, then the function returns NULL. Consider the following example, which converts the number 5 from base 16 to base 2:

```
SELECT
    CONV(5,16,2) AS CONVERSION

CONVERSION
----------------
101
```

This function is not available in any of the other RBDMS implementations discussed in this book.

COS()

Syntax:

```
COS(X)
```

This function returns the cosine of X. The value of X is given in radians. Consider the following example:

```
SELECT COS(90)
-> 0.44807361612917
```

This function is available in all of the RDBMS implementations discussed in this book.

COT()

Syntax:

```
COT(X)
```

This function returns the cotangent of X. Consider the following example:

```
SELECT COT(1)
-> 0.64209261593433
```

This function is available in all of the RDBMS implementations discussed in this book, except for the Oracle implementation.

DEGREES()

Syntax:

```
DEGREES(X)
```

This function returns the value of X converted from radians to degrees. Consider the following example:

```
SELECT DEGREES(PI());
-> 180.000000
```

This function is available in all of the RDBMS implementations discussed in this book, except for the Oracle implementation.

EXP()

Syntax:

```
EXP(X)
```

This function returns the value of *e* (the base of the natural logarithm) raised to the power of X. Consider the following example:

```
SELECT EXP(3)
-> 20.085537
```

This function is available in all of the RDBMS implementations discussed in this book.

FLOOR()

Syntax:

```
FLOOR(X)
```

This function returns the largest integer value that is not greater than X. Consider the following example:

```
SELECT FLOOR(7.55);
-> 7
```

This function is available in all of the RDBMS implementations discussed in this book.

FORMAT()

Syntax:

```
FORMAT(X,D)
```

The FORMAT() function is used to format the number X in the following format: ###,###,###.## truncated to D decimal places. The following example demonstrates the use and output of the FORMAT() function:

```
SELECT
      FORMAT(423423234.65434453,2) AS BIG_NUMBER

BIG_NUMBER
-----------------
423,423,234.65
```

The FORMAT() function is not available in any of the other RDBMS implementations discussed in this book.

GREATEST()

Syntax:

```
GREATEST(n1,n2,n3,..........)
```

The GREATEST() function returns the greatest value in the set of input parameters (n1, n2, n3, and so on). The following example uses the GREATEST() function to return the largest number from a set of numeric values:

```
SELECT
     GREATEST(3,5,1,8,33,99,34,55,67,43) AS WINNER

WINNER
--------------
99
```

The GREATEST() function is also available in the Oracle RDBMS implementation.

INTERVAL()

Syntax:

```
INTERVAL(N,N1,N2,N3,..........)
```

The INTERVAL() function compares the value of N to the value list (N1, N2, N3, and so on). The function returns 0 if N < N1, 1 if N < N2, 2 if N < N3, and so on. It will return –1 if N is NULL. The value list must be in the form N1 < N2 < N3 in order to work properly. The following code is a simple example of how the INTERVAL() function works:

```
SELECT
     INTERVAL(6,1,2,3,4,5,6,7,8,9,10) AS WINNER

WINNER
----------
6
```

Remember that 6 is the zero-based index in the value list of the first value that was greater than N. In our case, 7 was the offending value and is located in the sixth index slot.

This function is not available in any of the other RDBMS implementations discussed in this book.

LEAST()

Syntax:

```
LEAST(N1,N2,N3,N4,......)
```

The LEAST() function is the opposite of the GREATEST() function. Its purpose is to return the least-valued item from the value list (N1, N2, N3, and so on). The following example shows the proper usage and output for the LEAST() function:

```
SELECT
    LEAST(3,5,1,8,33,99,34,55,67,43) AS WINNER

WINNER
--------------
1
```

The LEAST() function is only available in the MySQL RDBMS implementation.

LOG()

Syntax:

```
LOG(X)
LOG(B,X)
```

The single argument version of the function will return the natural logarithm of X. If it is called with two arguments, it returns the logarithm of X for an arbitrary base B. Consider the following example:

```
SELECT LOG(45)
-> 3.806662
SELECT LOG(2,65536)
-> 16.000000
```

This function is available in all of the RDBMS implementations discussed in this book, except for the Microsoft SQL Server.

LOG10()

Syntax:

```
LOG10(X)
```

This function returns the base-10 logarithm of X. Consider the following example:

```
SELECT LOG10(100);
-> 2.000000
```

This function is available in all of the RDBMS implementations discussed in this book, except for the PostgreSQL implementation.

MOD()

Syntax:

```
MOD(N,M)
```

This function returns the remainder of N divided by M. Consider the following example:

```
SELECT MOD(29,3);
-> 2
```

This function is available in all of the RDBMS implementations discussed in this book, except for Microsoft SQL Server and Sybase ASE. These two implementations use the modulo symbol "%."

OCT()

Syntax:

```
OCT(N)
```

The OCT() function returns the string representation of the octal number N. This is equivalent to using CONV(N,10,8). The following code demonstrates the use of the OCT() function:

```
SELECT
    OCT(12) AS OCTAL

OCTAL
---------
14
```

The OCT() function is not available in any of the other RDBMS implementations discussed in this book.

PI()

Syntax:

```
PI()
```

This function simply returns the value of pi. MySQL internally stores the full double-precision value of pi. Consider the following example:

```
SELECT PI();
-> 3.141593
```

This function is available in all of the RDBMS implementations discussed in this book, except for the Oracle and IBM DB2 implementations.

POW() or POWER()

Syntax:

```
POW(X,Y)
POWER(X,Y)
```

These two functions return the value of X raised to the power of Y. Consider the following example:

```
SELECT POWER(3,3);
-> 27
```

This function is available in all of the RDBMS implementations discussed in this book.

RADIANS()

Syntax:

```
RADIANS(X)
```

This function returns the value of X, converted from degrees to radians. Consider the following example:

```
SELECT RADIANS(90);
-> 1.570796
```

This function is available in all of the RDBMS implementations discussed in this book.

RAND()

Syntax:

```
RAND()
RAND(X)
```

This function returns a random floating-point value in the range from 0.0 to 1.0. If an argument is used, then it is used as a seed value to produce a repeatable sequence. You may also use RAND() in the ORDER BY clause of a query in conjunction with the LIMIT clause to select a random sample of rows. The following is an example of this syntax:

```
SELECT * FROM CARS ORDER BY RAND() LIMIT 3;
```

This function is available in all of the RDBMS implementations discussed in this book.

ROUND()

Syntax:

```
ROUND(X)
ROUND(X,D)
```

This function returns X rounded to the nearest integer. If a second argument, D, is supplied, then the function returns X rounded to D decimal places. D must be positive or all digits to the right of the decimal point will be removed. Consider the following example:

```
SELECT ROUND(5.693893)
-> 6
SELECT ROUND(5.693893,2)
-> 5.69
```

This function is available in all of the RDBMS implementations discussed in this book.

SIGN()

Syntax:

```
SIGN(X)
```

This function returns the sign of X (negative, zero, or positive) as –1, 0, or 1. Consider the following example:

```
SELECT SIGN(-4.65);
-> -1

SELECT SIGN(0);
-> 0

SELECT SIGN(4.65);
-> 1
```

This function is available in all of the RDBMS implementations discussed in this book.

SIN()

Syntax:

```
SIN(X)
```

This function returns the sine of X. Consider the following example:

```
SELECT SIN(90);
-> 0.893997
```

This function is also available in the Sybase ASE and PostgreSQL implementations.

SQRT()

Syntax:

```
SQRT(X)
```

This function returns the non-negative square root of X. Consider the following example:

```
SELECT SQRT(49);
-> 7
```

This function is available in all of the RDBMS implementations discussed in this book.

STD() or STDDEV()

Syntax:

```
STD(expression)
STDDEV(expression)
```

The STD() function is used to return the standard deviation of expression. This is equivalent to taking the square root of the VARIANCE() of expression. The following example computes the standard deviation of the PRICE column in our CARS table:

```
SELECT
      STD(PRICE) STD_DEVIATION
      FROM CARS;

STD_DEVIATION
---------------
7650.2146
```

The STDDEV() version of the function is available in the Oracle RDBMS implementation.

TAN()

Syntax:

```
TAN(X)
```

This function returns the tangent of the argument X, which is expressed in radians. Consider the following example:

```
SELECT TAN(45);
-> 1.619775
```

This function is available in all of the RDBMS implementations discussed in this book.

TRUNCATE()

Syntax:

```
TRUNCATE(X,D)
```

This function is used to return the value of X truncated to D number of decimal places. If D is 0, then the decimal point is removed. If D is negative, then D number of values in the integer part of the value is truncated. Consider the following example:

```
SELECT TRUNCATE(7.536432,2);
-> 7.53
```

This function is also available in the IBM DB2 implementation. The TRUNC() function provides similar functionality in the Oracle and PostgreSQL implementations.

String Functions

MySQL has a number of string functions available to the developer. These functions are primarily involved in the manipulation and transformation of character data. The following table details the string functions that are available on the MySQL platform.

Function Name	Input	Output	Description
ASCII	`<char_expression>`	INTEGER	Returns the ASCII value of the leftmost character of `<char_expression>`. If `<char_expression>` is NULL, then it returns NULL. If `<char_expression>` is an empty string, then it returns 0.
BIN	`<num_expression>`		Returns the string representation of the binary value of `<num_expression>`, which must be of type BIGINT.
CHAR	`<num_expression1>`, `<num_expression2>`		Interprets `<num_expression1>` and `<num_expression2>` as integers and returns a string of the characters of the ASCII values of those inputs. If any of the input expression is NULL, then it is skipped.
COMPRESS	`<char_expression>`		Returns a compressed version of `<char_expression>`.
CONCAT	`<char_expression1>`, `<char_expression2>`		Returns the string result of concatenating `<char_expression1>` and `<char_expression2>`.
CONCAT_WS	`<separator_char>`, `<char_expression1>`, `<char_expression2>`		Returns the same result as the CONCAT function except that the expressions are separated by `<separator_char>`. If this character is NULL, then the result is NULL. Any expression that is NULL is skipped.
ELT	`<num_expression>`, `<char_expression1>`, `<char_expression2>`		This function pulls the `<num_expression>` indexed `<char_expression>` and returns it. It returns NULL if `<num_expression>` is less than 1 or greater than the number of `<char_expression>`s. This function complements the FIELD function.
FIELD	`<match_expression>`, `<char_expression1>`, `<char_expression2>`	INTEGER	Returns the index value of the occurrence of `<match_expression>` in the `<char_expression>` arguments. Returns 0 if it does not find a match. This function complements the ELT function.

Function Name	Input	Output	Description
FIND_IN_SET	<char_expression>, <list>	INTEGER	Returns the index/indices of <char_expression> found in the <list> argument. The <list> argument is a string list of comma-separated elements. Returns 0 if either <char_expression> is not found in <list>, or <list> is an empty string. Returns NULL if either of the two arguments is NULL. Also, the first item in <list> cannot contain a comma.
HEX	<num_expression>		Returns the string representation of the hexadecimal value <num_expression>. The argument <num_expression> must be of type BIGINT. Returns NULL if <num_expression> is NULL.
INSERT	<char_expression>, <num_length>, <new_expression>		Returns the string <char_expression> with a substring added at position <num_position> with length <num_length> replaced by <new_expression>.
INSTR	<char_expression>, <match_expression>	INTEGER	Returns the position of the first occurrence of <match_expression> in <char_expression>.
ISNULL	<expression>	INTEGER	Returns 1 if <expression> is NULL, otherwise it returns 0.
LCASE or LOWER	<char_expression>		Returns <char_expression> with all characters changed to lowercase according to whatever the current character-set mapping is set to.
LEFT	<char_expression>, <num_expression>		Returns the leftmost <num_expression> number of characters from <char_expression>.
LENGTH, CHAR_LENGTH, and CHARACTER_LENGTH	<char_expression>		These functions return the length of the <char_expression> string.

Table continued on following page

Function Name	Input	Output	Description
LOCATE	\<match_expression\>, \<char_expression\>		Returns the position of the first occurrence of \<match_expression\> in \<char_expression\>. Returns 0 if \<match_expression\> is not found. This function is similar to the POSITION function.
LOCATE	\<match_expression\>, \<char_expression\>, \<num_position\>	INTEGER	Returns the position of the first occurrence of \<match_expression\> in \<char_expression\>, starting at position \<num_position\>. Returns 0 if no match is found.
LPAD	\<char_expression\>, \<num_length\>, \<pad_expression\>		Returns the string \<char_expression\>, left-padded with the string \<pad_expression\> until the expression is \<num_length\> long.
LTRIM	\<char_expression\>		Returns \<char_expression\> with leading space characters removed.
MAKE_SET	\<bit set\>, \<char_expression1\>, \<char_expression2\>		Returns a string of comma-delimited substrings. This set consists of \<char_expression\>s that have corresponding bits in \<bit set\>. NULL values are not appended to the result set. Please note that \<char_expression1\> corresponds to bit 0, \<char_expression2\> corresponds to bit 1, and so on.
NULLIF	\<expression1\>, \<expression2\>	\<expression1\> or NULL	Returns NULL if \<expression1\> = \<expression2\>; otherwise, it returns \<expression1\>.
OCT	\<num_expression\>	STRING	Returns the string representation of the octal value of \<num_expression\>.

Function Name	Input	Output	Description
ORD	`<char_expression>`	`INTEGER`	Returns the value of the left-most character in ASCII using this formula if the character is a multibyte character: [(first byte ASCII code)*256 + (second byte ASCII code)*256 + (third byte ASCII code)*256 + ...]. Otherwise, this function returns the same values as the `ASCII()` function does.
REPEAT	`<char_expression>`, `<num_count>`	`<char_expression>`	Returns `<char_expression>` repeated `<num_count>` times. If `<num_count>` <= 0, then the function returns the empty string. If `<char_expression>` or `<num_count>` is `NULL`, then the function returns `NULL`.
REPLACE	`<string_expression>`, `<from_string>`, `<to_string>`	`<char_expression>`	Returns `<string_expression>` with all occurrences of `<from_string>` replaced with `<to_string>`.
REVERSE	`<string_expression>`	`<char_expression>`	Returns `<string_expression>` with the characters in reverse order.
RIGHT	`<string_expression>`, `<num_length>`	`<char_expression>`	Returns the rightmost `<num_length>` of characters from `<string_expression>`.
RPAD	`<string_expression>`, `<num_length>`, `<pad_string>`	`<char_expression>`	Returns `<string_expression>`, right-padded with `<pad_string>` until the string is `<num_length>` long.
RTRIM	`<string_expression>`	`<char_expression>`	Returns `<string_expression>` with the trailing spaces removed.
SOUNDEX	`<string_expression>`	`<char_expression>`	Returns the SOUNDEX string from `<string_expression>`. A generic SOUNDEX string consists of four characters, but this function returns a string that is arbitrarily long. All non-alphanumeric characters are ignored.

Table continued on following page

Function Name	Input	Output	Description
SUBSTRING	`<string_expression>`, `<num_position>`, `<num_length>`	`<char_expression>`	Returns the substring `<num_length>` long from `<string_expression>` starting at position `<num_position>`.
SUBSTRING_INDEX	`<string_expression>`, `<char_delimiter>`, `<num_count>`	`<char_expression>`	Returns the substring from `<string_expression>` after `<num_count>` occurrences of `<char_delimeter>`. If `<num_count>` is positive, then everything to the left of the final delimiter is returned. If it is negative, then everything to the right of the final delimiter is returned.
TRIM	`<string_expression>`	`<char_expression>`	Removes both leading and trailing spaces from `<string_expression>`.
UCASE	`<string_expression>`	`<char_expression>`	Returns `<string_expression>` with all characters changed to uppercase according to the current character-set mapping.
UNCOMPRESS	`<compressed_string>`	`<uncompressed_string>`	Returns the uncompressed version of a string from the compressed string.
UNCOMPRESSED_LENGTH	`<compressed_string>`	INTEGER	Returns the length of the uncompressed version of the compressed string argument.

ASCII()

Syntax:

```
ASCII(str)
```

The ASCII() function returns the numeric value of the leftmost character in the string passed to it. It will not evaluate anything past the first character. It will return 0 if the string is an empty string and NULL if the string is NULL. This function will work with characters whose numeric values range from 0 to 255. Some examples of how this function works follow:

```
SELECT ASCII('A') AS BIG_A,
       ASCII('a') AS SMALL_A,
       ASCII(7) AS SEVEN;

BIG_A     SMALL_A     SEVEN
-----     -------     -----
65        97          55
```

.This function is available in all of the RDBMS implementations discussed in this book.

BIN()

Syntax:

```
BIN(N)
```

The `BIN()` function returns a string representation of the binary value of `N`. `N` must be of type `BIGINT`. If the value of `N` is `NULL`, then the function returns `NULL` Consider the following example:

```
SELECT BIN(48) AS BIT_VALUE;

BIT_VALUE
---------
110000
```

This function is not available in any of the other RDBMS implementations discussed in this book.

CHAR()

Syntax:

```
CHAR(N,.......)
```

The `CHAR()` function uses the arguments as `INTEGERS` and returns an ASCII character string determined by the values of the `INTEGERS`. All arguments are interpreted as `INTEGERS` and `NULL` values are skipped. Consider the following example:

```
SELECT
     CHAR(72,69,76,76,79) AS GREETING

GREETING
----------
HELLO
```

Microsoft SQL Server and Sybase ASE also support this function, while Oracle, IBM DB2, and PostgreSQL all use the `CHR()` function (which is equivalent).

COMPRESS()

Syntax:

```
COMPRESS(string)
```

The `COMPRESS()` function is used to compress the contents of a string. The compressed string can be uncompressed using the function `UNCOMPRESS()`. To use this function, MySQL must be compiled with a compression library such as *zlib*. If not, then the return value is always `NULL`. Consider the following example which compresses a small phrase and then we use the `UNCOMPRESS()` function to uncompress it:

```
SELECT
     COMPRESS('MARY HAD A LITTLE LAMB, WHOSE FLEECE WAS WHITE AS SNOW') AS
          COMPRESSED,
     UNCOMPRESS(COMPRESS('MARY HAD A LITTLE LAMB, WHOSE FLEECE WAS WHITE
          AS SNOW')) AS UNCOMPRESSED

COMPRESSED        UNCOMPRESSED
----------        --------------------------------------------
6                 MARY HAD A LITTLE LAMB, WHOSE FLEECE WAS WHITE AS SNOW
```

This function is not available in any of the other RDBMS implementations discussed in this book.

CONCAT()

Syntax:

```
CONCAT(str1,str2,.........)
```

The CONCAT() function takes any number of string arguments and returns a string of their concatenated values. Any numeric argument is converted to a string equivalent, while any NULL value will result in the return string being NULL. A few examples of this function can be found below.

```
SELECT CONCAT('SMITH',', ','JOHN',NULL) AS NULL_NAME;

FULL_NAME
--------------------
SMITH, JOHN


SELECT CONCAT('SMITH',' , ','JOHN',NULL) AS NULL_NAME;

NULL_NAME
------------
NULL
```

This function is available in all of the RDBMS implementations discussed in this book.

CONCAT_WS()

Syntax:

```
CONCAT_WS(separator,str1,str2,.......)
```

The CONCAT_WS() function is used to concatenate multiple string values together with a separator between the values. It behaves exactly as the CONCAT() function does, except that it skips any NULL values. If the separator is NULL, however, the result will be returned as NULL. Consider the following example, which uses a comma as the separator to concatenate the first and last names together:

```
SELECT CONCAT_WS(',','SMITH','JOHN') AS SKIP_NULL;

FULL_NAME
--------------------
SMITH,JOHN


SELECT CONCAT_WS(',','SMITH','JOHN',NULL) AS SKIP_NULL;

SKIP_NULL
-------------
SMITH,JOHN
```

This function is not available in any of the other RDBMS implementations discussed in this book.

ELT()

Syntax:

```
ELT(N,str1,str2,......)
```

The ELT() function returns str1 if N = 1, str2 if N = 2, and so on. The value of N must be greater than 1 and less than the number of arguments in the function, or it will return NULL. The ELT() function is helpful in instances in which you must convert numbers to a predetermined set of values, as shown in the following example:

```
SELECT ELT(1,'First','Second','Third',Fourth') as PLACING;

PLACING
-------------
First
```

This function is not available in any of the other RDBMS implementations discussed in this book.

FIELD()

Syntax:

```
FIELD(str,str1,str2,str3,.......)
```

The FIELD() function complements the ELT() function. Its purpose is to return the index of the string value(str) passed to it in the str1, str2, str3,..... set. If str is not found in the list, then 0 is returned. Consider the following example, which demonstrates the particular differences between this function and ELT():

```
SELECT FIELD('Third','First','Second','Third',Fourth') as PLACING;

PLACING
-------------
3
```

This function is not available in any of the other RDBMS implementations discussed in this book.

FIND_IN_SET()

Syntax:

```
FIND_IN_SET(str,string_list)
```

The FIND_IN_SET() function returns the index of str within string_list, which consists of a list of comma-delimited strings. If the string (str) is not found, or string_list is an empty string, then 0 is returned. If either argument is NULL, then NULL is returned. Also, it will not work if the first argument contains a comma. Consider the following example, which demonstrates this function's similarity to the FIELD() function:

```
SELECT FIELD_IN_SET('Third','First,Second,Third,Fourth') as PLACING;

PLACING
-------------
3
```

This function is not available in any of the other RDBMS implementations discussed in this book.

HEX()

Syntax:

```
HEX(N or Str)
```

If N_or_Str is a number, then the HEX() function returns a string representation of the hexadecimal value of N_or_Str. If the argument is a string, then the function returns a string in which each character in the argument is converted into two hexadecimal digits. Consider the following example, which shows how to convert a simple numeric into hexadecimal:

```
SELECT
    HEX(1234) AS FROM_NUMBER

FROM_NUMBER
-----------
D2040000
```

This function is also available in the IBM DB2 implementation.

INSERT()

Syntax:

```
INSERT(str,pos,len,newstr)
```

The INSERT() function returns the base string str, with the substring beginning at position pos and of length len replaced by the new string newstr. Consider the following example:

```
SELECT INSERT('Newfoundland',4,5,' Eng') WHERE_AM_I;

WHERE_AM_I
---------------
New England
```

This function is not available in any of the other RDBMS implementations discussed in this book.

INSTR()

Syntax:

```
INSTR(str,substr)
```

The INSTR() function returns the position of the first occurrence of substr in str. This function is similar to the LOCATE() function. If substr is not located, then the function will return 0. Consider the following example:

```
SELECT INSTR('foobar','bar') AS HERE_IT_IS;

HERE_IT_IS
-----------
4

SELECT INSTR('foobarbarbarbarbarbarbarbar','bar') as HERE_IT_IS;

HERE_IT_IS
-----------
4
```

This function is not available in any of the other RDBMS implementations discussed in this book.

ISNULL()

Syntax:

```
ISNULL(expr1)
```

The ISNULL() function determines whether expr1 is a NULL value or not. If expr1 is NULL, then 1 is returned, otherwise it will return 0. The ISNULL() function is useful for placing a default value in place of a NULL value in your queries. The following example demonstrates using the ISNULL() function if the PRICE field is NULL:

```
SELECT MODEL,ISNULL(PRICE) AS IS_NULL
FROM CARS;

MODEL             IS_NULL
--------------    ---------
CROSSFIRE         0
300M              0
```

```
CIVIC               0
ACCORD              0
MUSTANG             0
LATESTNGREATEST     1
FOCUS               0
```

This function is not available in any of the other RDBMS implementations discussed in this book.

LCASE() or LOWER()

```
LCASE(str)
LOWER(str)
```

These functions simply return the string `str` with all of its characters converted to their lowercase equivalents based upon the current character-set mapping. Consider the following example:

```
SELECT LOWER('UPPER CASE') AS LOWER_CASE;

LOWER_CASE
----------
upper case
```

The `LCASE()` function is also available in the IBM DB2 implementation. The `LOWER()` function is available in the Oracle, Microsoft SQL Server, and Sybase ASE implementations.

LEFT()

Syntax:

```
LEFT(str,len)
```

The `LEFT()` function return the leftmost `len` characters from the string `str`. Consider the following example:

```
SELECT LEFT('Mississippi is a long name',11) as LEFT_STRING;

LEFT_STRING
------------
Mississippi
```

This function is also available in the IBM DB2, Microsoft SQL Server, and Sybase ASE implementations.

LENGTH(), CHAR_LENGTH(), and CHARACTER_LENGTH()

Syntax:

```
LENGTH(str)
CHAR_LENGTH(str)
CHARACTER_LENGTH(str)
```

The LENGTH() function returns the length of the string str measured in bytes. This means that a multi-byte character counts as multiple bytes.

The other two functions, CHAR_LENGTH() and CHARACTER_LENGTH(), return the length of the string measured in characters. Multibyte characters only count as a single character. Therefore, a string containing two 2-byte characters would return 4 for LENGTH() and 2 for both CHAR_LENGTH() and CHARACTER_LENGTH().

Consider the following example, which calculates the length for the model name in the CARS table:

```
SELECT MODEL,LENGTH(MODEL) AS MODEL_LENGTH
FROM CARS;

MODEL                   MODEL_LENGTH
---------------         ------------
CROSSFIRE               9
300M                    4
CIVIC                   5
ACCORD                  6
MUSTANG                 7
LATESTNGREATEST         15
FOCUS                   5
```

Each of the RDBMS implementations uses the LENGTH() or LEN() functions.

LOCATE()

Syntax:

```
LOCATE(substr,str)
LOCATE(substr,str,pos)
```

The first version of the LOCATE() function returns the position of the first occurrence of the substring substr in the string str. The second does the same, except that it starts at position pos within the string str. If the substring is not found, then the function returns 0. This function is similar to the INSTR() function, but with the arguments in reverse. Consider the following example:

```
SELECT LOCATE('bar','foobar') AS HERE_IT_IS;

HERE_IT_IS
-----------
4

SELECT LOCATE('bar','foobarbarbarbarbarbarbar') as HERE_IT_IS;

HERE_IT_IS
-----------
4

SELECT LOCATE('bar','foobarbarbarbarbarbarbar',10) as HERE_IT_IS;

HERE_IT_IS
-----------
10
```

This function is also available in the IBM DB2 implementation.

LPAD()

Syntax:

```
LPAD(str,len,padstr)
```

The `LPAD()` function returns the string `str` padded with the characters in `padstr` until the length of the string `str` reaches length `len`. If the length of `str` is longer than the length `len`, then the string is shortened to `len` characters. Consider the following example:

```
SELECT LPAD('FOOBAR',10,'*') AS RESULT;

RESULT
-----------
****FOOBAR
```

This function is also available in both the IBM DB2 and PostgreSQL implementations.

LTRIM()

Syntax:

```
LTRIM(str)
```

The `LTRIM()` function returns the argument `str` with the leading spaces removed. Consider the following example:

```
SELECT LTRIM('          JONES') AS RESULT;

RESULT
------------
JONES
```

This function is available in all of the RDBMS implementations discussed in this book.

MAKE_SET()

Syntax:

```
MAKE_SET(bits,str1,str2,.........)
```

The `MAKE_SET()` function returns a comma-delimited string, a set, consisting of the strings that have the corresponding bit in the `bits` set. In the `bits` set, `str1` corresponds to bit 0, `str2` to bit 1, and so on. `NULL` values in the string are not appended to the result set. Consider the following example:

```
SELECT
    MAKE_SET(1|8,'GOOD','SO-SO','LOUSY',' MORNING',' AFTERNOON',' DAY');
-> GOOD, MORNING
```

This function is not available in any of the other RDBMS implementations discussed in this book.

NULLIF()

Syntax:

```
NULLIF(expr1,expr2)
```

The NULLIF() function returns NULL if expr1 = expr2; otherwise it returns expr1. This is the same as using the following CASE statement:

```
CASE
WHEN expr1 = expr2
THEN NULL
ELSE expr1
END;
```

Consider the following example where we compare two sets of numbers:

```
SELECT NULLIF(1,1) AS SAME,
       NULLIF(1,2) AS DIFFERENT

SAME            DIFFERENT
--------        -------------
NULL            1
```

As you can see from the first column, the two input arguments were the same and the function returned NULL. In the second column, the two input arguments were different and the function returned the first value (which was 1).

This function is available in all of the RDBMS implementations discussed in this book.

OCT()

Syntax:

```
OCT(N)
```

The OCT() function returns the string representation of the octal number N. This is equivalent to using CONV(N,10,8). The following code demonstrates a simple example of how to use the OCT() function.

```
SELECT
    OCT(12) AS OCTAL

OCTAL
----------
14
```

The OCT() function is not available in any of the other RDBMS implementations discussed in this book.

ORD()

Syntax:

```
ORD(str)
```

If the leftmost character in `str` is not a multibyte character, then this function returns the same value as the `ASCII()` function. If the leftmost character is a multibyte character, then a code is returned for that character, calculated from its bytes by using the following formula:

```
(1st byte code)
+ (2nd byte code * 256)
+ (3rd byte code * 256)
```

This function is not available in any of the other RDBMS implementations discussed in this book.

REPEAT()

Syntax:

```
REPEAT(str,count)
```

The `REPEAT()` function returns a string value consisting of the string `str` repeated `count` number of times. If `count` is less than 1, then an empty string is returned. If either input argument is `NULL`, then `NULL` is returned. Consider the following example:

```
SELECT REPEAT('YADDA!',5) AS YAKKADY;

YAKKADY
------------
YADDA!YADDA!YADDA!YADDA!YADDA!
```

This function is also available in the IBM DB2 and PostgreSQL implementations.

REPLACE()

Syntax:

```
REPLACE(str,from_string,to_string)
```

The `REPLACE()` function returns a string that consists of the base string `str` with all occurrences of `from_string` replaced with `to_string`. Consider the following example:

```
SELECT REPLACE ('Misispi','s','ss') AS PLACE;

PLACE
---------
Mississippi
```

This function is available in all of the RDBMS implementations discussed in this book, except for Sybase ASE, which uses the `STR_REPLACE()` function.

REVERSE()

Syntax:

```
REVERSE(str)
```

The REVERSE() function simply returns the base string str with all of the characters in reverse order. Consider the following example:

```
SELECT REVERSE('FORWARD') AS BACKWARD;

BACKWARD
---------
DRAWROF
```

This function is also available in the Microsoft SQL Server and Sybase ASE implementations.

RIGHT()

Syntax:

```
RIGHT(str,len)
```

The RIGHT() function simply returns len number of rightmost characters from the base string str. Consider the following example:

```
SELECT RIGHT('Soup or Sandwich',8) AS YOUR_ORDER;

YOUR_ORDER
----------
Sandwich
```

This function is also available in the IBM DB2, Microsoft SQL Server, and Sybase ASE implementations.

RPAD()

Syntax:

```
RPAD(str,len,padstr)
```

The RPAD() function returns the string str, right-padded with the string padstr up to a total length of len characters. If the length of str is greater than len, then the string is shortened to len characters. Consider the following example:

```
SELECT RPAD('HELLO',8,'!') AS SALUTATIONS;

SALUTATIONS
-----------
HELLO!!!
```

This function is also available in the Oracle and PostgreSQL implementations.

RTRIM()

Syntax:

```
RTRIM(str)
```

This function returns the base string `str` with all the trailing spaces removed. Consider the following example:

```
SELECT RTRIM('Barber Shop                    ') AS RESULT;

RESULT
----------
Barber Shop
```

This function is available in all of the RDBMS implementations discussed in this book.

SOUNDEX()

Syntax:

```
SOUNDEX(str)
```

The `SOUNDEX()` function returns the `SOUNDEX()` string from the base string `str`. Two strings that sound the same should have the same `SOUNDEX()` value. All non-alphabetic characters are ignored, and all international alphabetic characters that are outside of the range of A–Z are treated as vowels. This is commonly used to check if two strings sound the same. It can be used in the form of the following function syntax:

```
Expr1 SOUNDS LIKE Expr2
```

The following example demonstrates the output of several words to their respective `SOUNDEX()` values:

```
SELECT
    SOUNDEX('COW') AS COW,
    SOUNDEX('BOW') AS BOW,
    SOUNDEX('YOW') AS YOW,
    SOUNDEX('BROWN') AS BROWN

COW         BOW         YOW         BROWN
-------     -------     -------     -------
C000        B000        Y000        B650
```

This function is available in all of the RDBMS implementations discussed in this book, except for the PostgreSQL implementation.

SUBSTRING()

Syntax:

```
SUBSTRING(str,pos)
SUBSTRING(str FROM pos)    --variant
```

```
SUBSTRING(str,pos,len)
SUBSTRING(str FROM pos FOR len)  --variant
```

This syntax shows the two main versions of the SUBSTRING() function with corresponding variants. The first version of the function takes two arguments, str and pos. This function returns the substring of the base string str starting at position pos. The second format includes the len argument. This version of the function returns the substring of the base string str, starting at position pos, and continuing len characters in length. Consider the following example:

```
SELECT SUBSTRING('RedBlueGreenYellow',4) AS COLORS;

COLORS
----------
BlueGreenYellow

SELECT SUBSTRING('RedBlueGreenYellow',4,9) AS COLORS;

COLORS
----------
BlueGreen
```

This function is also available in the Microsoft SQL Server, Sybase ASE, and PostgreSQL implementations.

SUBSTRING_INDEX()

Syntax:

```
SUBSTRING_INDEX(str,delim,count)
```

The SUBSTRING_INDEX() function returns a substring from str before count number of delimiters (delim) is reached. If count is positive, then everything to the left of the final delimiter is returned. If count if negative, then everything to the right of the final delimiter is returned, and the function starts counting delimiters from the right. Consider the following example:

```
SELECT SUBSTRING_INDEX('www.mydomainname.com','.',1) AS BASE;

BASE
------
www

SELECT SUBSTRING_INDEX('www.mydomainname.com','.',-2) AS DOMAIN;

DOMAIN
-------
mydomainname.com
```

This function is not available in any of the other RDBMS implementations discussed in this book.

TRIM()

Syntax:

```
TRIM([{BOTH | LEADING | TRAILING} [remstr] FROM] str)
TRIM([remstr FROM] str)
```

The TRIM() function has several different options that may be invoked. BOTH is the default and specifies that prefixes and suffixes are to be removed. LEADING specifies that only prefixes should be removed. TRAILING specifies that only suffixes should be removed. The remstr argument is also optional and specifies that a specific string prefix or suffix should be removed from the base string. If remstr is not used, then spaces are removed by default. Consider the following example:

```
SELECT TRIM('     foobar      ');
-> foobar
SELECT TRIM(LEADING 'x' FROM 'xxxxxfoobarxxxxx');
-> foobarxxxxx
SELECT TRIM(TRAILING 'x' FROM 'xxxxxfoobarxxxxx');
-> xxxxxfoobar
```

This function is also available in both the Oracle and PostgreSQL implementations.

UCASE() or UPPER()

Syntax:

```
UCASE(str)
UPPER(str)
```

The UCASE() function simply returns the str argument with all of the characters converted to upper-case in correspondence with the current-character set mapping. Consider the following example:

```
SELECT UCASE('lowercase') AS UPPER_CASE;

UPPER_CASE
-----------
LOWERCASE
```

These functions are available in all of the RDBMS implementations discussed in this book.

UNCOMPRESS()

Syntax:

```
UNCOMPRESS(str)
```

The UNCOMPRESS() function is used to uncompress a string that was compressed by the COMPRESS() function. If the argument is not a compressed value, then NULL is returned. Like the COMPRESS() function, this function requires that MySQL be compiled with a compression library or it will always return NULL. Consider the following example, which compresses a small phrase and uses the UNCOMPRESS() function to uncompress it:

```
SELECT
      COMPRESS('MARY HAD A LITTLE LAMB, WHOSE FLEECE WAS WHITE AS SNOW') AS
            COMPRESSED,
      UNCOMPRESS(COMPRESS('MARY HAD A LITTLE LAMB, WHOSE FLEECE WAS WHITE
            AS SNOW')) AS UNCOMPRESSED

COMPRESSED        UNCOMPRESSED
----------        -------------------------------------------
6                 MARY HAD A LITTLE LAMB, WHOSE FLEECE WAS WHITE AS SNOW
```

This function is not available in any of the other RDBMS implementations discussed in this book.

UNCOMPRESSED_LENGTH()

Syntax:

```
UNCOMPRESSED_LENGTH(compressed_string)
```

This function returns the original length of compressed string before it was compressed. Consider the following example, which compares the uncompressed length of a compressed string with the length of the original string:

```
SELECT
    UNCOMPRESSED_LENGTH(COMPRESS('MARY HAD A LITTLE LAMB, WHOSE FLEECE WAS WHITE AS
SNOW')) AS COMP_LENGTH,
    LENGTH('MARY HAD A LITTLE LAMB, WHOSE FLEECE WAS WHITE AS SNOW') AS
UNCOMP_LENGTH

COMP_LENGTH              UNCOMP_LENGTH
---------------          -----------------
54                       54
```

This function is not available in any of the other RDBMS implementations discussed in this book.

Date-Time Functions

MySQL actually has one of the larger collections of date-time functions available. These functions are primarily involved in the reporting, manipulation, and transformation of date-time and/or timestamp values. The following table details the various date-time functions available on this platform.

Function Name	Input	Output	Description
CURDATE	<char_expression> or <num_expression>		Returns the current date as either *YYYY-MM-DD* if used in a string context, or *YYYYMMDD* if used in a numeric context.
CURTIME	<char_expression> or <num_expression>		Returns the current time as either *HH:MM:SS* if used in a string context, or *HHMMSS* format if used in a numeric context.
DATE_ADD or DATE_SUB	<date expression>, <char_interval>, <type>	DATE	Returns a date or date-time depending on <date_expression>. The <char_interval> argument specifies what interval value should be added or subtracted, and <type> indicates the type of data (year, month, day, etc.) the interval should be applied to.
DATE_FORMAT	<date_expression>, <char_format>	<date_expression>	Formats <date_expression> according to the value of <char_format>.
DAYNAME	<date_expression>	<char_expression>	Returns the name of the weekday for the specified <date_expression>.
DAYOFMONTH	<date_expression>	INTEGER	Returns the day of the month (from 1 to 31) for the specified <date_expression>.
DAYOFYEAR	<date_expression>	INTEGER	Returns the day of the year (from 1 to 366) for the specified <date_expression>.
FROM_DAYS	<num_expression>	DATE	Given a number greater than 1582, it returns a date value. The value 1582 is significant because it marks the start of the Gregorian calendar in which some days were lost when the calendar was changed.
FROM_UNIXTIME	<unix_timestamp>	<char_expression> or <num_expression>	Returns a value in the format *YYYY-MM-DD HH:MM:SS* or *YYYYMMDDHHMMSS*, depending on whether it is used in a character or numeric context.

Function Name	Input	Output	Description
HOUR	<time_expression>	INTEGER	Returns the hour of <time_expression> (from 0 to 23).
MINUTE	<time_expression>	INTEGER	Returns the minute value for <time_expression> (from 0 to 59).
MONTH	<date_expression>	INTEGER	Returns the month value for <date_expression> (from 1 to 12).
MONTHNAME	<date_expression>	<char_expression>	Returns the name of the month from <date_expression>.
NOW or SYSDATE		<char_expression>	Returns the current date and time as *YYYY-MM-DD HH:MM:SS* or *YYYYMMDDHH-MMSS*, depending on whether it is used in a character or numeric context.
PERIOD_ADD	<char_period>, <num_expression>	<num_expression>	Returns a numeric value in the format *YYYYMM* by adding <num_expression> number of months to <char_period>, which is in the format *YYMM* or *YYYYMM*. It should be noted that <char_period> is not a date value.
PERIOD_DIFF	<char_period1>, <char_period2>	INTEGER	Returns the number of months between the two period values. Each of the periods is expressed as *YYMM* or *YYYYMM*.
SECOND	<time_expression>	INTEGER	Returns the value of <time_expression> in seconds (from 0 to 59).
SEC_TO_TIME	<num_expression>	<char_expression> or <num_expression>	Returns the <num_expression>, which is a value in seconds, as either *HH:MM:SS* or *HHMMSS*, depending onf whether it is used in a character or numeric context.

Table continued on following page

Function Name	Input	Output	Description
TIME_FORMAT	`<time_expression>`, `<format_expression>`	`<date_expression>`	It is similar to the DATE_FORMAT() function, but `<format_expression>` may only contain values related to time. Specifying anything else will result in either a 0 or a NULL value.
TIME_TO_SEC	`<time_expression>`	`<num_expression>`	Returns `<time_expression>` converted into seconds.
TO_DAYS	`<date_expression>`	`<num_expression>`	Returns the number of days from year 0 to `<date_expression>`.
UNIX_TIMESTAMP	`<date_expression>`	`<unix_timestamp>`	Returns a UNIX timestamp (the number of seconds since 1970-01-01 00:00:00 GMT). If `<date_expression>` is used, then it returns the number of seconds to the argument from 1970-01-01 00:00:00 GMT.

CURDATE()

Syntax:

```
CURDATE()
```

This function returns the current date as either *YYYY-MM-DD* or *YYYYMMDD*. The format of the result depends upon whether the function is used in a string or numeric context. Consider the following example:

```
SELECT CURDATE();
-> '2004-09-08'
```

This function is not available in any of the other RDBMS implementations discussed in this book. Even though some implementations have similar functions (such as SYSDATE and GETDATE), this function has unique characteristics.

CURTIME()

Syntax:

```
CURTIME()
```

This function returns the current time either as *HH:MM:SS* or *HHMMSS*. The format returned is dependent upon whether the function is used in a string or a numeric context. Consider the following example:

```
SELECT CURTIME();
-> 20:05:36
```

This function is not available in any of the other RDBMS implementations discussed in this book.

DATE_ADD() or DATE_SUB()

Syntax:

```
DATE_ADD(date,INTERVAL expr type)
DATE_SUB(date,INTERVAL expr type)
```

These functions perform date arithmetic on date, and date is a DATE or DATETIME value that specifies the starting date to be used. The expr argument is an expression that specifies the interval value that is to be added/subtracted from the base date. It is allowable to use a negative value to specify a negative interval. The keyword type indicates how the expression should be interpreted. The following table details the link between the type value and the expression format.

Type Value	Expression Format
MICROSECOND	MICROSECONDS
SECOND	SECONDS
MINUTE	MINUTES
HOUR	HOURS
DAY	DAYS
WEEK	WEEKS
MONTH	MONTHS
QUARTER	QUARTERS
YEAR	YEARS
SECOND_MICROSECOND	SECONDS.MICROSECONDS
MINUTE_MICROSECOND	MINUTES.MICROSECONDS
MINUTE_SECOND	MINUTES:SECONDS
HOUR_MICROSECOND	HOURS.MICROSECONDS
HOUR_SECOND	HOURS:MINUTES:SECONDS
HOUR_MINUTE	HOURS.MINUTES
DAY_MICROSECOND	DAYS.MICROSECONDS
DAY_SECOND	DAYS HOURS:MINUTES:SECONDS
DAY_MINUTE	DAYS HOURS:MINUTES
DAY_HOUR	DAYS HOURS
YEAR_MONTH	YEARS-MONTHS

The following example adds five years to the current date value.

```
SELECT
    DATE_ADD(CURDATE(),INTERVAL 5 YEAR) AS NEW_DATE

NEW_DATE
------------
2009-10-13
```

A similar function, DATEADD(), is available in both the Microsoft SQL Server and Sybase ASE implementations.

DATE_FORMAT()

Syntax:

```
DATE_FORMAT(date,format)
```

This function formats date according to the format string. The following table specifies which objects can be used in the format string.

Specifier	Description
%a	Abbreviated weekday name (Mon...Sun)
%b	Abbreviated month name (Jan...Dec)
%c	Month, numeric (0...12)
%D	Day of month with English suffix (0th ,1st,2nd...)
%d	Day of month, numeric (00...31)
%e	Day of month, numeric (0...31)
%f	Microseconds (000000...999999)
%H	Hour (00...23)
%h	Hour (01...12)
%I	Hour (01...12)
%i	Minutes, numeric (00...59)
%j	Day of Year (001...366)
%k	Hour (0...23)
%l	Hour (1...12)
%M	Month name (January...December)
%m	Month, numeric (00...12)
%p	AM or PM

Specifier	Description
%r	Time, 12-hour (hh:mm:ss followed by AM or PM)
%S	Seconds (00...59)
%s	Seconds (00...59)
%T	Time, 24-hour (hh:mm:ss)
%U	Week (00...53), Sunday is first day of Week
%u	Week (00...53), Monday is first day of Week
%V	Week (01...52), Sunday is first day of Week
%v	Week (01...52), Monday is first day of Week
%W	Weekday name (Sunday...Saturday)
%w	Day of the Week (0...6), Sunday first day of week
%X	Year numeric, four-digits, Sunday first day of week
%x	Year numeric, four-digits, Monday first day of week
%Y	Year, numeric, four-digits
%y	Year, numeric, two-digits
%%	A literal '%'

Consider the following example:

```
SELECT
    DATE_FORMAT(CURDATE(),'%a %e %M,%X') AS NEW_DATE

NEW_DATE
---------------------
Thu 13 January,2005
```

This function is not available in any of the other RDBMS implementations discussed in this book.

DAYNAME()

Syntax:

```
DAYNAME(date)
```

This function returns the name of the weekday for the respective date value. Consider the following example:

```
SELECT DAYNAME('2004-02-23');
-> Monday
```

This function is also available in the IBM DB2 and Sybase ASE implementations.

DAYOFMONTH()

Syntax:

```
DAYMONTH(date)
```

This function returns the day of the month for the date with a numeric range of 1 to 31. Consider the following example:

```
SELECT DAYOFMONTH('2001-04-09');
-> 9
```

This function is not available in any of the other RDBMS implementations discussed in this book.

DAYOFYEAR()

Syntax:

```
DAYOFYEAR(date)
```

This function returns the day of the year for the date value with a range of 1 to 366. Consider the following example:

```
SELECT DAYOFYEAR('1998-02-25');
-> 56
```

This function is also available on the IBM DB2 implementation.

FROM_DAYS()

Syntax:

```
FROM_DAYS(N)
```

This function returns a date value based on the value of N. The date is based on the number of days since January 1, 4712 B.C. (the start of the Julian date calendar). It is not reliable for values that precede the Gregorian calendar (1582). Consider the following example:

```
SELECT FROM_DAYS(710325) AS OLD_DATE;

OLD_DATE
---------------
1944-10-21
```

This function is not available in any of the other RDBMS implementations discussed in this book.

FROM_UNIXTIME()

Syntax:

```
FROM_UNIXTIME(unix_timestamp)
FROM_UNIXTIME(unix_timestamp,format)
```

This function returns a string representation of the `unix_timestamp` argument as either *YYYY-MM-DD HH:MM:SS* or *YYYYMMDDHHMMSS*. The format is dependent upon whether the function is used in a string or numeric context. If `format` is given as an input argument, then the result is formatted according to the `format` string. Consider the following example:

```
SELECT FROM_UNIXTIME(871723980) AS OLD_DATE;

OLD_DATE
--------------------
1997-08-16 04:33:00
```

This function is not available in any of the other RDBMS implementations discussed in this book.

HOUR()

Syntax:

```
HOUR(time)
```

This function returns the hour for the given `time` value. The range of the value returned is from 0 to 23 for time of day values, even though it can return values much larger. Consider the following example:

```
SELECT HOUR('14:32:33');
-> 14
```

This function is also available in the IBM DB2 implementation.

MINUTE()

Syntax:

```
MINUTE(time)
```

This function returns the minute portion of the given `time` value. The value returned is in the range of 0 to 59. Consider the following example:

```
SELECT MINUTE('14:32:33');
-> 32
```

This function is also available in the IBM DB2 implementation.

MONTH()

Syntax:

```
MONTH(date)
```

This function returns the month portion of the `date` value. The value returned is in the range of 1 to 12. Consider the following example:

```
SELECT MONTH('2001-04-03');
-> 4
```

This function is also available in both the IBM DB2 and Microsoft SQL Server implementations.

MONTHNAME()

Syntax:

```
MONTHNAME(date)
```

This function returns the full name of the month in the `date` value. Consider the following example:

```
SELECT MONTHNAME('2003-10-01');
-> October
```

This function is also available in the IBM DB2 implementation.

NOW() or SYSDATE()

Syntax:

```
NOW()
SYSDATE()
```

This function returns the current date and time as either *YYYY-MM-DD HH:MM:SS* or *YYYYMMDD HHMMSS*. The format of the return value is determined by the context that the function is used in. Consider the following example:

```
SELECT NOW();
-> 2004-10-10 12:32:33
```

The `NOW()` function is also available in the IBM DB2 implementation, while the `SYSDATE()` function is available in the Oracle implementation.

PERIOD_ADD()

Syntax:

```
PERIOD_ADD(P,N)
```

This function will add N months to the period P, formatted as *YYMM* or *YYYYMM*. It returns a value in the format *YYYYMM*. P is not a date value. Consider the following example:

```
SELECT PERIOD_ADD(200405,4);
-> 200409
```

This function is not available in any of the other RDBMS implementation discussed in this book.

PERIOD_DIFF()

Syntax:

```
PERIOD_DIFF(P1,P2)
```

This function returns the number of months between the periods P1 and P2. These are in the format *YYMM* or *YYYYMM* and are not date values. Consider the following example:

```
SELECT PERIOD_DIFF(200110,200102);
-> 8
```

This function is not available in any of the other RDBMS implementations discussed in this book.

SECOND()

Syntax:

```
SECOND(time)
```

This function returns the second value from the `time` value in a range of 0 to 59. Consider the following example, which will grab the current second value on the internal clock:

```
SELECT SECOND(CURTIME()) AS CUR_SECOND;

CUR_SECOND
---------------
9
```

This function is also available in the IBM DB2 implementation.

SEC_TO_TIME()

Syntax:

```
SEC_TO_TIME(seconds)
```

This function returns the `seconds` argument converted to hours, minutes, and seconds. The format is either *HH:MM:SS* or *HHMMSS*, depending on whether the function is used in a character or a numeric context. Consider the following example:

```
SELECT SEC_TO_TIME(48753);
-> 13:32:33
```

This function is not available in any of the other RDBMS implementations discussed in this book.

TIME_FORMAT()

Syntax:

```
TIME_FORMAT(time,format)
```

This function is used like the DATE_FORMAT() function. However, the format string may only contain those format specifiers that handle time values. If the hours value is greater than 23, you must use either %H or %h; otherwise, the result will be returned with the value *modulo 12*. Consider the following example, which formats the current time:

```
SELECT TIME_FORMAT(CURTIME(), '%H %k %h %I %l') AS FORMATTED_TIME;

FORMATTED_TIME
----------------------------
23 23 11 11 11
```

This function is not available in any of the other RDBMS implementations discussed in this book.

TIME_TO_SEC()

Syntax:

```
TIME_TO_SEC(time)
```

This function is the reverse of the SEc_TO_TIME() function. It returns the time value converted to seconds. Consider the following example:

```
SELECT TIME_TO_SEC('16:17:42');
-> 58662
```

This function is not available in any of the other RDBMS implementations discussed in this book.

TO_DAYS()

Syntax:

```
TO_DAYS(date)
```

This function is the opposite of the FROM_DAYS() function. Given a date value, this function returns the number of days since year 0. As with the FROM_DAYS() function, it is not very helpful for time periods prior to the advent of the Gregorian calendar (1582). Consider the following example, which calculates the number of days from today:

```
SELECT TO_DAYS(CURDATE()) AS NO_OF_DAYS

NO_OF_DAYS
--------------
732324
```

This function is not available in any of the other RDBMS implementations discussed in this book.

UNIX_TIMESTAMP()

Syntax:

```
UNIX_TIMESTAMP()
UNIX_TIMESTAMP(date)
```

This function, if called with no arguments, returns a UNIX timestamp as an unsigned integer. The UNIX timestamp is the number of seconds since 1970-01-01 00:00:00 GMT. If a `date` argument is used, then it returns the number of seconds since 1970-01-01 00:00:00 GMT. The `date` value cannot be earlier than 1970. Consider the following example, which returns the current UNIX timestamp value:

```
SELECT UNIX_TIMESTAMP(CURDATE()) AS UNIX_TIME

UNIX_TIME
---------------
1105592400
```

This function is not available in any of the other RDBMS implementations discussed in this book.

Miscellaneous Functions

As always, there are some functions that do not fit very neatly into any one category. MySQL is no different, so the following table details some of the various miscellaneous functions that are available on the MySQL platform.

Function Name	Input	Output	Description
BENCHMARK	<count>, <expression>		This function is used to execute the <expression> statement <count> number of times. It is useful in timing expressions.
COALESCE	<list>		Returns the first non-NULL value in the list argument.
CONNECTION_ID		<num_expression>	Returns the thread_id for the current connection (it is unique for every connection).
DATABASE		<char_expression>	Returns the current database name.
LOAD_FILE	<file_name>	<char_expression>	Returns the string value <char_expression> of the contents of the file that is read from <file_name> which is (the full pathname to the file). In order to work, the file must exist and the user must have the FILE privilege to read it.

BENCHMARK()

Syntax:

```
BENCHMARK(count,expr)
```

This function can be used to execute the `expr` statement `count` number of times. It is mainly used in the MySQL client to time the execution speed of an expression. The output of the `BENCHMARK()` function is always 0 and the execution speed of the `expr` statement. Consider the following example in which we use the `BENCHMARK()` function to time the execution of a simple `ENCODE` statement:

```
SELECT BENCHMARK(100000, ENCODE('Hello', 'World') );
-> 0
   1 row in set (2.37 sec)
```

This function is not available in any of the other RDBMS implementations discussed in this book.

COALESCE()

Syntax:

```
COALESCE(value,.........)
```

The `COALESCE()` function returns the first non-`NULL` value in the arguments list. Consider the following example:

```
SELECT COALESCE(NULL,NULL,'Chicken','Beef','Pork');
-> Chicken
```

This function is supported in all of the other RDBMS implementations discussed in this book.

CONNECTION_ID()

Syntax:

```
CONNECTION_ID()
```

This function returns the unique connection ID for the current thread. Consider the following example, which will return your current connection ID:

```
SELECT CONNECTION_ID() AS YOUR_ID

YOUR_ID
-------------
162
```

This function is not supported in any of the other RDBMS implementations discussed in this book.

DATABASE()

Syntax:

```
DATABASE()
```

This function returns the current database name. Consider the following example:

```
SELECT DATABASE();
-> HUMAN_RESOURCES
```

This function is not available in any of the other RDBMS implementations discussed in this book.

LOAD_FILE()

Syntax:

```
LOAD_FILE(filename)
```

This function reads the file associated with file_name and returns the contents as a string. In order for this function to work, the file must be located on the server, you must specify the full pathname, and you must have the FILE privilege. If the file cannot be read, then the function will return NULL. Consider the following example, which reads a small text file located on the computer's C drive:

```
SELECT LOAD_FILE('C:\SQL.txt') AS FILE_CONTENTS

FILE_CONTENTS
------------------------
Testing.....
1...2...3
Testing.....
```

This function is not available in any of the other RDBMS implementations discussed in this book.

Summary

In this chapter, we discussed in great detail the functions available on the MySQL RDBMS implementation. By now, you should have a very good understanding of the capabilities and limitations of the system and its built-in functions. Specifically, we discussed a wide range of functions to broaden your knowledge of MySQL syntax and to give you a foundation upon which other RDBMS systems can be judged.

In the next chapter, we will look at the other Open Source RDBMS solution that we discuss in this book, PostgreSQL. After combining the knowledge gleaned from both chapters, you should see a clear contrast between the styles of the two systems.

PostgreSQL Functions

The PostgreSQL platform was first created to incorporate all of the functionality that a database should have on the operating side. This tended to leave its available SQL arsenal rather depleted for the power-hungry developer. However, in recent years, that trend has shifted and more built-in functions and coding functionality have been incorporated. Now, PostgreSQL sports a decent array of built-in functions for the developer, as well as some unique ones that you will not find in any other database implementation that we discuss in this book. In this chapter, we will concentrate on enlightening the developer as to what built-in functions PostgreSQL has to offer. First, however, we will discuss the PostgreSQL brand of query syntax so that the reader may contemplate the differences between this system and the other RDBMS systems discussed in previous chapters.

PostgreSQL Query Syntax

The basis of the PostgreSQL query syntax is the SELECT statement, which is based upon the ANSI SQL standard discussed in Chapter 5. To gain a better understanding of the particulars of the PostgreSQL SELECT statement, we will examine each of the sections of the statement in turn. The complete syntax for the SELECT statement is as follows:

```
SELECT
    [ ALL | DISTINCT [ ON ( expression [, ....] )]]
    * | expression [ AS output_name ] [, ...]
    [ FROM from_item [, ...]]
    [ WHERE condition ]
    [ GROUP BY expression [, ...]]
    [ HAVING condition [, ...]]
    [ { UNION | INTERSECT | EXCEPT } [ ALL ] select ]
    [ ORDER BY expression [ ASC | DESC | USING operator ] [,....]]
    [ LIMIT { count | ALL } ]
    [ OFFSET start ]
    [ FOR UPDATE [ OF table_name [, ...]]]
```

The first clause of the SELECT statement is often referred to as the DISTINCT clause. The ALL keyword specifies that all rows from the result set should be returned, even if they are duplicates. This is the default for all queries, and so this syntax is rarely used. If DISTINCT is used, then duplicate rows are removed from the result set and only one row is kept for each group of duplicates. DISTINCT may also be used with the ON syntax. This option allows the query to keep only the first rows in which the expression(s) evaluate to true. It can use multiple expressions, and all of them are governed by the same rules as the ORDER BY clause.

The next section of the SELECT statement is the select list. It contains the columns or items that will be returned from the query in the result set. If the "*" syntax is used, then all the rows from the items in the FROM clause will be returned. The "*" may also be prefixed with a table name in order to return all the columns from just that table. Column names and expressions may also be used to better define the results that are desired. The items in the select list may also be given an alias by using the AN output_name syntax.

The FROM clause determines from what sources the SELECT statement will draw its data. These sources can include tables, functions, and subqueries. These items may also be given aliases by using the AS alias_name syntax to improve readability. Additionally, items in the FROM clause may also be bound together using joins.

The WHERE clause specifies what limitations should be placed upon the data being returned to the result set. The clause contains a condition or sets of conditions that are joined together by AND/OR statements. The conditions can be equality/inequality constraints between two items in the FROM clause, or they can be constraints put upon items in the FROM clause.

The GROUP BY and HAVING clauses are responsible for producing summary information rows to be returned in the result set. The expressions in the GROUP BY clause can be an input column name, an output column name, the ordinal number of an output column, or an expression that is formed from input column values. The GROUP BY expressions are hierarchal and are ranked in the order that they appear in the list. If any aggregate functions are used in the select list, then their values are computed across the range of group items in which they appear. The HAVING clause is used for restraining the groups that are created with the GROUP BY clause. In contrast, the WHERE clause restricts the rows that are returned in the result set. The conditions in the WHERE clause should be the same as those specified in the GROUP BY clause.

The UNION, INTERSECT, and EXCEPT clauses are all meant to join together SELECT statements to produce a master result set. The UNION operator returns the complete set of results of both SELECT statements. Duplicate rows are disregarded unless you specify the ALL operator as well. In order for the UNION operator to work, both SELECT statements must produce the same output columns with compatible data types. The INTERSECT operator computes the intersection set of both result sets. Rows are returned in the intersection set if they appear in both of the base result sets. If the ALL operator is specified, then duplicate rows are returned. However, only the minimum number of rows is returned. This is based upon whichever result set has the minimum number of the duplicate row in question. The EXCEPT operator will return only those rows in the left-hand SELECT statement that are not in the right-hand SELECT statement.

The ORDER BY clause determines in which order the result set values will appear. The expressions that can appear in the ORDER BY clause can be column names, ordinal output column numbers, or expression that are formed with input column values. The order in which the columns are sorted is hierarchal and determined by the order in which they appear in the list. Additionally, while the default column ordering is ascending, the ordering can be specified as either ascending (ASC) or descending (DESC) for each item in the ORDER BY clause.

The LIMIT clause it used to specify the maximum number of rows to be returned in the result set. It is always recommended that you use the ORDER BY clause when using the LIMIT statement. Otherwise, an arbitrary resultant set of rows will be returned. The OFFSET clause may also be used to specify a certain offset at which the LIMIT statement is supposed to execute. So, you may use the following syntax to return rows 10 through 20:

```
LIMIT 11
OFFSET 10
```

Of course, remember that you should also specify the ORDER BY clause beforehand to ensure that the query will return the desired results.

The FOR UPDATE clause is used to cause the rows retrieved by the SELECT statement to be locked as though they were being updated. This is helpful when you want to lock the resultant rows from being UPDATED until the current transaction ends. You may also specify specific table names in the clause. If this is done, then only those rows within the named tables will be locked. The only limitation to this clause is that it cannot be used in queries for which the returned rows are not clearly identifiable (such as aggregate functions).

Now you should have a good understanding of the basics of the PostgreSQL platform. This will be a basis on which to build a better understanding of the use of the different functions as well as the ability to decipher the examples provided throughout this chapter.

Aggregate Functions

An aggregate SQL function summarizes the results of an expression for the group of rows (selected from a table, view, or table-valuated function) and returns a single value for that group. The following table details the few aggregate functions that are available in the PostgreSQL implementation.

SQL Function	Input Arguments	Return Arguments	Notes
AVG	Numeric Expression	Numeric or Double Precision	Calculates the average of the set of numbers; NULL values are ignored.
COUNT	Any	BigInt	Returns the number of records in the set.
MAX	Numeric Expression, String, or Date-Time	Same as Input	Returns a single maximum value in a given set.
MIN	Numeric Expression, String, or Date-Time	Same as Input	Returns a single minimum value in a given set.
STDDEV	SmallInt, Integer, BigInt, Real, Double Precision	Numeric or Double Precision	Returns a standard deviation value for the set of numerical values.
SUM	Numeric Expression	BigInt, SmallInt, Integer, Numeric or Double Precision	Returns the sum of the values in a set.
VARIANCE(X)	Numeric Expression	Numeric or Double Precision	Returns the sample variance of the input values X.

Again we will be using our CARS table (introduced in Chapter 5) to demonstrate some of the functions:

```
CREATE TABLE cars
(
  MAKER   VARCHAR (25),
  MODEL   VARCHAR (25),
  PRICE   INTEGER
)
INSERT INTO CARS VALUES('CHRYSLER','CROSSFIRE',33620);
INSERT INTO CARS VALUES('CHRYSLER','300M',29185);
INSERT INTO CARS VALUES('HONDA','CIVIC',15610);
INSERT INTO CARS VALUES('HONDA','ACCORD',19300);
INSERT INTO CARS VALUES('FORD','MUSTANG',15610);
INSERT INTO CARS VALUES('FORD','LATESTnGREATEST',NULL);
INSERT INTO CARS VALUES('FORD','FOCUS',13005);
```

AVG()

Syntax:

```
AVG(expression)
```

The AVG() function returns the average of the expression passed to it. Normally, this is used to get the average of a set of numeric values. Consider the following example:

```
SELECT
    AVG(price) AS average_price
FROM cars;
average_price
--------------------
21055
```

To find the models of cars that are below the average price of the group, we would place our previous statement in a subquery, as shown here:

```
// Now an example of an aggregate function in a subquery to retrieve the // model
that are below the average price.

SELECT
Model
FROM cars
WHERE price < (SELECT AVG(price) FROM cars);

Model
----------
CIVIC
ACCORD
MUSTANG
FOCUS
```

The AVG() function is available in all of the RDBMS implementations discussed in this book.

COUNT()

Syntax:

```
COUNT(*)
COUNT(expression)
```

The COUNT() function can be used to get a count of all the resultant rows. To see how many cars we have within our table, we would use a simple query like this:

```
SELECT COUNT(*) AS CAR_COUNT FROM CARS;

CAR_COUNT
---------
7
```

We can also use COUNT() to count only a specific column in our SELECT query:

```
SELECT COUNT(price) AS CAR_COUNT_PRICE FROM CARS;

CAR_COUNT_PRICE
---------------
6
```

The result shows the fundamental difference in the two versions of the COUNT syntax. The COUNT() function will skip over those items that have a NULL value. So, in retrospect, you can see that the COUNT(*) syntax is in actuality a row count of the result set, while the COUNT() function with an argument is a count of all items in the column that are not NULL.

The COUNT() function is available in all of the RDBMS implementations discussed in this book.

MAX()

Syntax:

```
MAX(expression)
```

The MAX() function returns the maximum value in the expression set. To find the maximum value of the price of our CARS table, we would use the following simple query:

```
SELECT
    MAX(PRICE)  AS EXPENSIVE
FROM CARS;

EXPENSIVE
-----------------
33620
```

It should also be noted that when using aggregate functions that are applied across an entire table, PostgreSQL will use a sequential scan. This is somewhat different from other RDBMS systems that may use an index to improve performance.

The MAX() function is available in all of the RDBMS implementations discussed in this book.

MIN()

Syntax:

```
MIN(expression)
```

The MIN() function is the opposite of the MAX() function. Its purpose is to return the minimum value of the expression argument. The expression argument need only contain a reference to a column in the FROM clause. For example, we could find out the least amount of sales tax that we would owe when buying a car using a 5 percent rate:

```
SELECT
    MIN(PRICE*0.05) AS MINIMUM_TAX
FROM CARS;

MINIMUM_TAX
-----------------------
650.25
```

The MIN() function is available in all of the RDBMS implementations discussed in this book.

STDDEV()

Syntax:

```
STDDEV(expression)
```

The STDDEV() function returns the standard deviation of the expression argument. The following example shows how to use the STDDEV() function to get the standard deviation of the PRICE column in the CARS table:

```
SELECT
    STDDEV(PRICE) AS STANDARD_DEV
FROM CARS;

STANDARD_DEV
-----------------------
8380.390205
```

The STDDEV() function is also available in the Oracle and MySQL implementations.

SUM()

Syntax:

```
SUM(expression)
```

The SUM() function returns the sum of the expression argument passed to it. The following could be used to get the total cash worth of inventory on hand:

```
SELECT
    SUM(PRICE) AS INVENTORY_VALUE
FROM CARS;

INVENTORY_VALUE
------------------------------
126330
```

It should be noted that all the aggregate functions, except for COUNT(), will return NULL if no rows are selected. You might expect that the COUNT() function would return 0 if no rows are returned but it will surprisingly return NULL.

The SUM() function is available in all of the RDBMS implementations discussed in this book.

VARIANCE()

Syntax:

```
VARIANCE(expression)
```

This function returns the variance of the input arguments. The *variance* is defined as the square of the sample's standard deviation. We could use the following to find the variance of the price of cars in our sample table:

```
SELECT
    VARIANCE(PRICE) AS INVENTORY_VALUE
FROM CARS;
INVENTORY_VALUE
------------------------------
70230940.0
```

The VARIANCE() function in not available in any of the other RDBMS implementations discussed in this book.

String Functions

PostgreSQL string functions are mainly used in the manipulation and conversion of character data. Although their scope is limited compared to the vast array of functions available on other system, PostegreSQL does provide a decent amount of functionality for the developer. The following table details the built-in string functions available on the PostgreSQL platform.

SQL Function	Input Arguments	Return Arguments	Notes
ASCII(X)	String	Integer	Returns the ASCII code of the first character of the string X.
BTRIM(X,Y)	String, String	String	Returns the string X with the longest string consisting of the characters in the string Y removed from the beginning and end of the base string.

Table continued on following page

SQL Function	Input Arguments	Return Arguments	Notes
`BIT_LENGTH (X)`	String	Integer	Returns the number of bits in the character string X.
`CHAR_LENGTH (X)`	String	Integer	Returns the number of charac ters in the string X.
`CHR(X)`	Integer	String	Returns the character for the given ASCII value of X.
`CONVERT (X USING Y)`	String and Conversion Name	String	Returns the String value X con verted into the specified encod- ing type.
`DECODE(X,Y)`	String, String	Bytea	Returns the binary data that was previously encoded using the `ENCODE()` function.
`ENCODE(X,Y)`	Byte, String	String	Encodes the binary data string X using a supported type Y.
`INITCAP(X)`	String	String	Converts the first character of each word to uppercase.
`LENGTH(X)`	String	Integer	Returns the number of charac- ters in the string X.
`LOWER(X)`	String	String	Returns the string X with all the characters converted to lowercase.
`LPAD(X,Y,Z)`	String, Integer, and Fill String	String	Pads the string X up to a length Y with the fill string Z.
`LTRIM(X,Y)`	String	String	Returns the string X with the longest string made from the characters in Y removed from the beginning of the string.
`MD5(X)`	String	String	Returns the MD5 hash of the string X returning the result in hexadecimal.
`OCTET_LENGTH (X)`	String	Integer	Returns the number of bytes contained in the string X.
`OVERLAY(X placing Y from a to b)`	String, String, Integer, and Integer	String	Returns the string X replaced with Y in positions a to b.
`POSITION(X in Y)`	String and String	Integer	Returns the position of X within the string Y.

SQL Function	Input Arguments	Return Arguments	Notes
QUOTE_IDENT (X)	String	String	Returns the string X, quoted sufficiently to be used as an identifier in a SQL statement.
QUOTE_LITERAL (X)	String	String	Returns the string X, quoted sufficiently to be used as a string literal in a SQL statement.
REPEAT(X,Y)	String, Integer	String	Returns the string X repeated Y number of times.
REPLACE (X,Y,Z)	String	String	Returns the string X with all occurrences of substring Y replaced by Z.
RPAD(X,Y,Z)	String, Integer, and Fill String	String	Returns the string X padded to Y number of characters that are filled with Z.
RTRIM(X,Y)	String and Character String	String	Returns the string X with the longest string consisting of characters in Y removed from the right side of the string.
SUBSTRING(X from a to b)	String, Integer, Integer	String	Returns the substring of X starting at position a to position b.
SUBSTRING(X from Y)	String and Pattern String	String	Returns the substring of X that matches the POSIX expression Y.
SUBSTRING(X from Y for E)	String, Pattern String, And Escape String	String	Returns the substring of X that matches the SQL regular expression given as Y for E (with Y being the pattern string and E being the escape character).
TRIM ([LEADING | TRAILING | BOTH] X from Y)	String	String	Returns the string Y with the character string X removed from the LEADING, TRAILING, or BOTH ends.
UPPER(X)	String	String	Returns the string X with all of the characters converted to uppercase.

ASCII()

Syntax:

```
ASCII(text)
```

The ASCII() function returns the ASCII character code for the leftmost character of the argument string passed to it. Consider the following example in which we use the ASCII() function to return the character code for the leftmost character:

```
SELECT ASCII('a') AS LITTLE_A,
       ASCII('A') AS BIG_A,
       ASCII('A cow jumped over the moon.') AS SENTENCE
LITTLE_A       BIG_A     SENTENCE
---------      ------    --------
97             65        65
```

The ASCII() function is available in all of the RDBMS implementations discussed in this book.

BTRIM()

Syntax:

```
BTRIM(string, characters)
```

This function removes the longest string made from the characters in the characters argument from the beginning and end of the string argument. Consider the following example:

```
SELECT BTRIM('ABCABCABCABThis is a test.ABCABCABCA',
             'ABC') TEST_STRING;

TEST_STRING
--------------
This is a test.
```

The BTRIM() function is not available in any of the other RDBMS implementations discussed in this book.

BIT_LENGTH()

Syntax:

```
BIT_LENGTH(string)
```

This function returns the number of bits in the argument string. Consider the following example:

```
SELECT BIT_LENGTH('Arie5')AS USERNAME_LENGTH

USERNAME_LENGTH
---------------
40
```

The BIT_LENGTH() function is also available in the MySQL RDBMS implementation.

CHAR_LENGTH()

Syntax:

```
CHAR_LENGTH(string)
CHARACTER_LENGTH(string)
```

The CHAR_LENGTH() function returns the number of characters in the argument string. Consider the following example:

```
SELECT CHAR_LENGTH('Mississippi') as THIS_LENGTH;

THIS_LENGTH
-----------
11
```

The CHAR_LENGTH() function is also available in the Sybase ASE and MySQL RDBMS implementations.

CHR()

Syntax:

```
CHR(integer)
```

This function is the opposite of the ASCII() function. The CHR() function returns the character that is associated with the ASCII code that is passed as the argument. Consider the following example:

```
SELECT CHR(65) AS GIMME_AN_A;

GIMME_AN_A
-----------
A
```

The CHR() function is also available in the Oracle and IBM DB2 implementations. The CHAR() function is an equivalent function available in the Microsoft SQL Server, Sybase ASE, and MySQL implementations.

CONVERT()

Syntax:

```
CONVERT(string, source_encoding, dest_encoding)
```

This function converts the string argument from source_encoding to dest_encoding. The passing of a source_encoding argument is optional and, if not used, then the current database encoding is assumed. The following example is a simple example of the proper syntax usage of the CONVERT() function:

```
SELECT
    CONVERT('This_sentence_is_in_unicode','UNICODE','LATIN1') as RESULT;

RESULT
---------------
This_sentence_is_in_unicode
```

The CONVERT() function is also available in the Oracle and Sybase ASE implementations.

DECODE()

Syntax:

```
DECODE(string, type)
```

The DECODE() function decodes the binary data from the string argument that was previously encoded using the ENCODE() function. The type argument is one of the supported types of the database. The available types are base64, escape, and hex. Consider the following example in which we will decode a string encoded with the hexadecimal type:

```
SELECT DECODE('4d415259204841442041204c4954544c45204c414d42','HEX') AS UNCODED;

UNCODED
----------------------------
MARY HAD A LITTLE LAMB
```

The DECODE() function is also available in the Oracle RDBMS implementation.

ENCODE()

Syntax:

```
ENCODE(data, type)
```

The ENCODE() function encodes the binary data argument to an ASCII-only format. The type argument is one of the three supported types of the database: base64, escape, and hex. Consider the following example, which encodes the phrase using the hexadecimal type:

```
SELECT ENCODE('MARY HAD A LITTLE LAMB','HEX') AS ENCODED;

ENCODED
-------------------------------------------------------------
4d415259204841442041204c4954544c45204c414d42
```

The ENCODE() function is not available in any of the other RDBMS implementations discussed in this book.

INITCAP()

Syntax:

```
INITCAP(text)
```

The INITCAP() function works as an in-between for the UPPER() and LOWER() functions. Its purpose is to return the text argument with the initial character of each word capitalized. Word boundaries are determined by white space. Consider the following example:

```
SELECT INITCAP('hello, world!') AS GREETING;

GREETING
-------------
Hello, World!
```

The `INITCAP()` function is also available in the Oracle RBDMS implementation.

LENGTH()

Syntax:

```
LENGTH(string)
```

The `LENGTH()` function is a synonym for the `CHAR_LENGTH()` function. It returns the number of characters in the string argument. Consider the following example, which returns the character length of the string argument passed to it:

```
SELECT LENGTH('Mississippi') as THIS_LENGTH;

THIS_LENGTH
-----------
11
```

The `LENGTH()` function is available in the IBM DB2, Oracle, MS SQL Server, and Sybase implementations. The MySQL implementation uses the `CHAR_LENGTH()` function for this purpose.

LOWER()

Syntax:

```
LOWER(string)
```

The `LOWER()` function returns the argument string with all the characters converted to their lowercase equivalents. Consider the following example, which returns the lowercase version of the word `'STRING'`:

```
SELECT
    LOWER('STRING') lowercase

LOWERCASE
------------
string
```

The `LOWER()` function is available in the Oracle, MS SQL Server, and Sybase RDBMS implementations. The IBM DB2 and MySQL implementations use the equivalent `LCASE()` function.

LPAD()

Syntax:

```
LPAD(string, length, fill)
```

The `LPAD()` function returns the string argument padded to the `length` number of characters with the `fill` text. If no `fill` argument is supplied, then the string is padded with blanks. If the `length` argument is smaller than the character length of the string argument, then the `string` argument is truncated to `length` number of characters. Consider the following example:

```
SELECT
    LPAD('PASSWORD:',20,'*') AS RESULT;

RESULT
---------------
***********PASSWORD:
```

The `LPAD()` function is also available in the Oracle and MySQL RDBMS implementations.

LTRIM()

Syntax:

```
LTRIM(string, char_string)
```

This function returns the `string` argument with the longest string containing the characters in the `char_string` argument removed from the start of the string. Consider the following example:

```
SELECT
    LTRIM('ZZZZZZZZZTRIMMED STRING','Z') AS TRIMMED_STRING;

TRIMMED_STRING
--------------
TRIMMED STRING
```

The `LTRIM()` function is available in all of the RDBMS implementations discussed in this book.

MD5()

Syntax:

```
MD5(string)
```

The `MD5()` function calculates the MD5 hash of the string argument and returns the result in hexadecimal format. Consider the following example in which we encode a simple string value:

```
SELECT MD5('MARY HAD A LITTLE LAMB') AS CODED;

CODED
------------------------------------------
e3d5d73d35512534611e06352c06d626
```

The `MD5()` function is not available in any of the other RDBMS implementations discussed in this book.

OCTET_LENGTH()

Syntax:

```
OCTET_LENGTH(string)
```

The OCTET_LENGTH() function is similar to the BIT_LENGTH() function except that it returns the number of bytes in the string argument. Consider the following example, in which we return the number of bytes contained in a simple string:

```
SELECT OCTET_LENGTH('MARY HAD A LITTLE LAMB') AS BYTES;

BYTES
--------
22
```

The OCTET_LENGTH() function is not available in any of the other RDBMS implementations discussed in this book.

OVERLAY()

Syntax:

```
OVERLAY(string PLACING substring FROM index TO num_places)
```

The OVERLAY() function replaces the substring of the string argument defined by the index and num_places arguments with the substring value. Consider the following example:

```
SELECT
    OVERLAY('xxxxxxENGLAND' PLACING 'NEW ' FROM 1 FOR 6) AS NEW_VALUE;

NEW_VALUE
------------
NEW ENGLAND
```

The OVERLAY() function is not available in any of the other RDBMS implementations discussed in this book.

POSITION()

Syntax:

```
POSITION(substring IN string)
```

The POSITION() function is used to find the position of the substring argument within the string argument. Consider the following example:

```
SELECT
    POSITION('COW' IN 'THE COW JUMPED OVER THE MOON') AS POS_NUMBER;

POS_NUMBER
----------------
5
```

The POSITION() function is not available in any of the other RDBMS implementations discussed in this book.

QUOTE_IDENT()

Syntax:

```
QUOTE_IDENT(string)
```

This function returns the `string` argument sufficiently quoted to be used as an identifier in a SQL statement. Embedded quotation marks are properly doubled and quotation marks are only added if necessary. Consider the following example, in which we modify a string to contain quotation marks and use this function to safely modify it for a SQL statement:

```
SELECT QUOTE_IDENT('MARY HAD A LITTLE LAMB WHO SAID,"BAH!"') AS QUOTED;

QUOTED
----------------------------------------
"MARY HAD A LITTLE LAMB WHO SAID,""BAH!"""
```

The QUOTE_IDENT() function is not available in any of the other RDBMS implementations discussed in this book.

QUOTE_LITERAL()

Syntax:

```
QUOTE_LITERAL(string)
```

This is similar to the QUOTE_IDENT() function, except that this function returns the argument `string` sufficiently quoted to be used as a literal in a SQL statement. Embedded quotation marks and backslashes are properly doubled. Consider the following example in which we perform a similar action to that taken in the QUOTE_IDENT() function example:

```
SELECT QUOTE_LITERAL('MARY HAD A LITTLE LAMB WHO SAID,"BAH!"') AS QUOTED;

QUOTED
----------------------------------------
'MARY HAD A LITTLE LAMB WHO SAID,"BAH!"'
```

This function is not available in any of the other RDBMS implementations discussed in this book.

REPEAT()

Syntax:

```
REPEAT(string, integer)
```

The REPEAT() function returns a text value made of the `string` argument repeated `integer` number of times. Consider the following example:

```
SELECT REPEAT('YADDA',5) AS BIG_TALK;

BIG_TALK
--------------------
YADDAYADDAYADDAYADDAYADDA
```

The REPEAT() function is also available in the IBM DB2 and MySQL RDBMS implementations.

REPLACE()

Syntax:

```
REPLACE(string, from, to)
```

The REPLACE() function replaces all occurrences of the from argument with the to argument in the string argument.

The following example replaces an uppercase "A" from a string with an asterisk ("*") in the first field. The second field, where the third argument is omitted, returns a string with all occurrences of "A" removed.

```
SELECT
    REPLACE ('ABCDA', 'A','*') AS replace_A,
    REPLACE ('ABCDA', 'A','') AS remove_A

REPLACE_A    REMOVE_A
---------    --------
*BCD*        BCD
```

The REPLACE() function is available in all of the other RDBMS implementations discussed in this book, except for the Sybase ASE platform, which uses the STR_REPLACE() function.

RPAD()

Syntax:

```
RPAD(string, length, fill)
```

This function pads the string argument to a length number of characters with the fill characters appended on the end. If no fill characters are provided, then the string argument is padded with blanks. If the length argument is less than the length of the string argument, then the string argument is truncated. Consider the following example:

```
SELECT
    RPAD('PASSWORD:',20,'*') AS RESULT;

RESULT
----------------
PASSWORD: **********
```

The RPAD() function is also available in the Oracle and MySQL RDBMS implementations.

RTRIM()

Syntax:

```
RTRIM(string, char_string)
```

The RTRIM() function removes the longest string containing characters of the char_string argument from the trailing end of the string argument. Consider the following example:

```
SELECT
    RTRIM('TRIMMED STRINGZZZZZZZZZZZZ','Z') AS TRIMMED_STRING;

TRIMMED_STRING
--------------
TRIMMED STRING
```

The RTRIM() function is available in all of the RDBMS implementations discussed in this book.

SUBSTRING()

Syntax:

```
SUBSTRING(string, from, to)
SUBSTRING(string FROM pattern)
SUBSTRING(string FROM pattern FOR escape)
```

The SUBSTRING() function has three different versions that are used to extract substrings from the string argument. The first version of the function extracts the substring from the string argument using the from and to arguments to determine from which index span to extract. The from and to arguments do not have to be used together. If the from argument is used alone then the substring is taken starting at the from index and traversing to the end of the string. If the to argument is used alone, then the substring is taken from the start of the string to the index identified by the to argument.

The second version of the function uses a POSIX regular expression pattern to extract the substring from the string argument. Finally, the last version of the function uses the SQL regular expression pattern to return the substring from the string argument.

Consider the following example:

```
SELECT SUBSTRING('MISSISSIPPPI',2,8) AS FIRST_VER,
       SUBSTRING('ALASKA' FROM '....$') AS SECOND_VER,
       SUBSTRING('OKLAHOMA' FROM '%#"O_A#"%' FOR '#') AS THIRD_VER;

FIRST_VER       SECOND_VER      THIRD_VER
-----------     -----------     -----------
ISSISSIP        ASKA            OMA
```

The SUBSTRING() function is also available in the MS SQL Server, Sybase ASE, and MySQL RDBMS implementations. The IBM DB2 implementation uses the SUBSTR() function.

TRIM()

Syntax:

```
TRIM( [ LEADING | TRAILING | BOTH ] characters FROM string)
```

The TRIM() function removes unwanted characters from the beginning and end of a string argument. The LEADING option will remove the longest string of characters within the characters argument from the leading end of the string argument. The TRAILING argument removes the largest string of characters within the characters argument from the trailing end of the string argument. If the BOTH option is chosen, then the largest string of characters from the characters argument is removed from both ends of the string argument. BOTH is the default, and the characters argument defaults to the space character.

Consider the following example, which shows the different forms of the TRIM() function:

```
SELECT
    TRIM('A' FROM 'ABCA') AS both,
    TRIM(LEADING  'A' FROM 'ABCA') AS lead,
    TRIM(TRAILING 'A' FROM 'ABCA') AS trail;

BOTH     LEAD     TRAIL
-------  -------  ------
BC       BCA      ABC
```

The TRIM() function is also available in the Oracle and MySQL RDBMS implementations.

UPPER()

Syntax:

```
UPPER(string)
```

The UPPER() function returns the string argument with all its characters converted to their uppercase equivalents. Consider the following example, which converts the word 'string' into its uppercase equivalent:

```
SELECT
    UPPER('string') uppercase

UPPERCASE
-------------
STRING
```

The UPPER() function is also available in the Oracle, MS SQL Server, and Sybase ASE RDBMS implementations. The Oracle and MySQL implementations use the equivalent UCASE() function.

Mathematical Functions

PostgreSQL provides a large number of mathematical functions for the developer. These mathematical functions are mainly involved in the manipulation of numeric data and calculations based upon numeric values. The following table details the various mathematical functions we will be discussing.

SQL Function	Input Arguments	Return Arguments	Notes
ABS(X)	Numeric value	Numeric value	Returns the absolute value of the argument X.
ACOS(X)	Numeric or Double Precision	Double Precision	Returns the arccosine of the value of X.
ASIN(X)	Numeric or Double Precision	Double Precision	Returns the arcsine of the value of X.
ATAN(X)	Numeric or Double Precision	Double Precision	Returns the arctangent of the value of X.
ATAN2(X, Y)	Numeric or Double Precision	Double Precision	Returns the arctangent of X/Y.
CBRT(X)	Double Precision	Double Precision	Returns the cube root of the argument X.
CEIL(X)	Numeric or Double Precision	Numeric or Double Precision	Returns the smallest integer that is not less than the value of X.
COS(X)	Numeric or Double Precision	Double Precision	Returns the cosine of X.
COT(X)	Numeric or Double Precision	Double Precision	Returns the cotangent of X.
DEGREES(X)	Double Precision	Double Precision	Returns the value of X converted from radians to degrees.
EXP(X)	Numeric or Double Precision	Numeric or Double Precision	Returns the exponential value of the argument X (that is, e to the power of X).
FLOOR(X)	Numeric or Double Precision	Numeric or Double Precision	Returns the largest integer value that is not larger than X.
LN(X)	Numeric or Double Precision	Numeric or Double Precision	Returns the natural logarithm of the argument X.
LOG(X)	Numeric or Double Precision	Numeric or Double Precision	Returns the base-10 logarithm of X.
LOG(B,X)	Numeric	Numeric	Returns the logarithm of X to the base of B.

SQL Function	Input Arguments	Return Arguments	Notes
MOD(Y,X)	Numeric or Double Precision	Numeric or Double Precision	Returns the remainder of Y/X.
PI()	None	Double Precision	Returns the value of pi (π).
POW(X,Y)	Numeric or Double Precision	Numeric or Double Precision	Returns the value of X raised to the power of Y.
RADIANS(X)	Double Precision	Double Precision	Returns the value of X converted from degrees to radians.
RANDOM()	None	Double Precision	Returns a random value that is between 0 and 1.
ROUND(X)	Numeric or Double Precision	Numeric or Double Precision	Returns the value of X rounded to the nearest integer.
SETSEED(X)	Double Precision	Integer	Sets the seed value for the next iteration of the RANDOM() function.
SIGN(X)	Numeric or Double Precision	Numeric or Double Precision	Returns –1, 0, or 1, if X is negative, zero, or positive, respectively.
SIN(X)	Numeric or Double Precision	Double Precision	Returns the sine of X.
SQRT(X)	Numeric or Double Precision	Numeric or Double Precision	Returns the square root of the value of X.
TRUNC(X,N)	Numeric or Double Precision	Numeric or Double Precision	Returns the value of X truncated to N number of decimal places.

ABS()

Syntax:

```
ABS(X)
```

The ABS() function returns the absolute value of the argument X. Consider the following example:

```
SELECT ABS(-345.45) AS ABSOLUTE;

ABSOLUTE
---------
345.45
```

The ABS() function is available in all of the RDBMS implementations discussed in this book.

ACOS()

Syntax:

```
ACOS(X)
```

The `ACOS()` function returns the arccosine of the argument *X*. The following code gives an example of the use of the `ACOS()` function:

```
SELECT
    ROUND(DEGREES(ACOS(.5)),0) as FIRST_ANGLE,
    ROUND(DEGREES(ACOS(.75)),0) as SECOND_ANGLE,
    ROUND(DEGREES(ACOS(1.0)),0) as THIRD_ANGLE

FIRST_ANGLE     SECOND_ANGLE     THIRD_ANGLE
------------    ------------     -----------
60.0            41.0             0.0
```

The `ACOS()` function is available in all of the RDBMS implementations discussed in this book.

ASIN()

Syntax:

```
ASIN(X)
```

The `ASIN()` function returns the arcsine of the argument *X*. Consider the following example, which shows the `ASIN()` function being used with various angles:

```
SELECT
    ROUND(DEGREES(ASIN(.5)),0) as FIRST_ANGLE,
    ROUND(DEGREES(ASIN(.75)),0) as SECOND_ANGLE,
    ROUND(DEGREES(ASIN(1.0)),0) as THIRD_ANGLE

FIRST_ANGLE     SECOND_ANGLE     THIRD_ANGLE
------------    -------------    ------------
30.0            49.0             90.0
```

The `ASIN()` function is available in all of the RDBMS implementations discussed in this book.

ATAN()

Syntax:

```
ATAN(X)
```

The `ATAN()` function returns the arctangent of the argument *X*. Consider the following example, which shows the arctangent of .5:

```
SELECT
    ATAN(.5) AS FIRST_RESULT;


FIRST_RESULT
------------
  .463647609
```

This function is available in all of the RDBMS implementations discussed in this book.

ATAN2()

Syntax:

```
ATAN2(X,Y)
```

The ATAN2() function returns the arctangent of X/Y. Consider the following example, which shows the use of the ATAN2 function:

```
SELECT
    ATAN2(.5,1.0) AS RESULT;


RESULT
------------
  .463647609
```

The ATAN2() function is available in all of the RDBMS implementations in this book, except for the MS SQL Server and Sybase ASE platforms. These two use the equivalent ATN2() function.

CBRT()

Syntax:

```
CBRT(X)
```

The CBRT() function returns the cube root of the argument X. Consider the following example:

```
SELECT CBRT(27) AS CUBED_BASE;

CUBED_BASE
----------
3
```

The CBRT() function is not available in any of the other RDBMS implementations discussed in this book.

CEIL()

Syntax:

```
CEIL(X)
```

The CEIL() function returns the lowest integer value that is not less than the argument X. Consider the following example:

```
SELECT CEIL(12.25) AS CEILING;

CEILING
--------
13
```

The CEIL() function is available in all of the RDBMS implementations discussed in this book.

COS()

Syntax:

```
COS(X)
```

The COS() function returns the cosine of the argument X. Consider the following example, which shows some simple uses of the COS() function:

```
SELECT
    COS(RADIANS(0)) AS FIRST_ANGLE,
    COS(RADIANS(45)) AS SECOND_ANGLE,
    COS(RADIANS(90)) AS THIRD_ANGLE

FIRST_ANGLE          SECOND_ANGLE          THIRD_ANGLE
-------------        ---------------       --------------
1.0                  1.0                   0.54030230586813977
```

The COS() function is available in all of the RDBMS implementations discussed in this book.

COT()

Syntax:

```
COT(X)
```

The COT() function returns the cotangent of the argument X. Consider the following simple example of the use of the COT() function:

```
SELECT
    COT(RADIANS(90)) AS ANGLE

ANGLE
-----------------------
0.64209261593433076
```

The COT() function is available in all of the RDBMS implementations discussed in this book.

DEGREES()

Syntax:

```
DEGREES(X)
```

The `DEGREES()` function returns the argument *X* converted from radians to degrees. Consider the following example, which shows how to code a simple conversion technique:

```
SELECT
    CEIL(DEGREES (0.7853981633)) AS DEGREE

DEGREE
------------
45
```

The `DEGREES()` function is available in all of the RDBMS implementations discussed in this book, except for Oracle.

EXP()

Syntax:

```
EXP(X)
```

The `EXP()` function returns the exponential value of *X*. Consider the following example, which returns the exponential value of 10:

```
SELECT
    EXP(10) AS EXPONENT

EXPONENT
--------------------
22026.465794806718
```

There are no restrictions on the use of zero, fractional, or negative values as input arguments for the `EXP()` function and the function is available in all of the RDBMS implementations discussed in this book.

FLOOR()

Syntax:

```
FLOOR(X)
```

The `FLOOR()` function returns the largest integer value that is not larger than *X*. Consider the following example:

```
SELECT FLOOR(34.65) AS FLOORING;

FLOORING
---------
34
```

The FLOOR() function is available in all of the RDBMS implementations discussed in this book.

LN()

Syntax:

```
LN(X)
```

The LN() function returns the natural logarithm of the argument X. The natural logarithm is LN() in mathematical notation. Its base is a number that equals approximately 2.71828183. Essentially, LN equals a standard logarithm with base 2.71828183. The natural logarithm is especially useful in calculus because of its simple derivative (as opposed to the derivative of logarithms with any other base). Consider the following example, which calculates the natural logarithm of 5:

```
SELECT LOG(45) AS LOG_OF_FIVE;

LOG_OF_FIVE
-------------
3.806662
```

The LN() function is available in all of the other RDBMS implementations discussed in this book, with the exception of the MS SQL Server and Sybase platforms.

LOG()

Syntax:

```
LOG(X)
LOG(B,X)
```

The first version of the LOG() function will return the base-10 logarithm of the argument X. The B argument is the log base that you want the logarithm function to use if you do not wish to use the default base-10. So, LOG(2,15) would return the base-2 logarithm of 15. Consider the following example:

```
SELECT LOG(45) AS BASE_TWO,
       LOG(2,65536) AS BASE_TEN;

BASE_TWO          BASE_TEN
-------------     -------------
3.806662          16.000000
```

The LOG() function is available in all of the other RDBMS implementations discussed in this book.

MOD()

Syntax:

```
MOD(X,Y)
```

The MOD() function returns the remainder of X/Y. Consider the following example:

```
SELECT MOD(26,4) AS REMAINDER;

REMAINDER
---------
2
```

The MOD() function is available in all of the RDBMS implementations discussed in this book, except for MS SQL Server and Sybase (which use the modulo syntax "%").

PI()

Syntax:

```
PI()
```

The PI() function returns the constant pi (π). Normally this is used in mathematical equations such as the circumference of a circle. Consider the following example:

```
SELECT
    PI() AS RESULT_OF_PI

RESULT OF PI
-----------------------
3.1415926535897931
```

The PI() function is available in the SQL Server, Sybase, MySQL, and PostgreSQL platforms. Oracle and IBM DB2 do not support its use.

POW()

Syntax:

```
POW(X,Y)
```

The POW() function returns the argument X raised to the power Y. Consider the following example:

```
SELECT POW(3,3) AS RESULT;

RESULT
-------
27
```

The POW() function is available in all of the other RDBMS systems under the name POWER().

RADIANS()

Syntax:

```
RADIANS(X)
```

The RADIANS() function returns the argument *X* converted from degrees to radians. Consider the following example simple example:

```
SELECT radians (2578)

---------
       44
```

The RADIANS() function is available in all of the RDBMS implementations discussed in this book, except for the Oracle platform.

RANDOM()

Syntax:

```
RANDOM()
```

The RANDOM() function generates a random value with the range of 0 to 1. Consider the following example:

```
SELECT rand()

----------------------
     .42767894555348007
```

This function is available in every RDBMS implementation discussed in this book as either RANDOM() or its shorter form, RAND().

ROUND()

Syntax:

```
ROUND(Numeric, Integer)
```

The ROUND() function returns the numeric argument rounded to the integer number of decimal places. If the integer argument is zero then no decimal places or fractional equivalents are returned, and the value is rounded to the closest integer. If the integer argument is negative then the rounding is to the left of the decimal location. Consider the following example, which rounds the number to a single decimal place:

```
SELECT
    ROUND(109.09 ,1) rounded

ROUNDED
------------
109.10
```

The ROUND() function is available in every RDBMS implementation discussed in this book.

SETSEED()

Syntax:

```
SETSEED(X)
```

The SETSEED() function is used to set a seed value for the next call of the RANDOM() function. Consider the following example, which sets the seed of the random-number generator:

```
SETSEED(0.435434);
SELECT RANDOM() AS NEW_NUMBER;

NEW_NUMBER
---------------
.75384959
```

This function is only found in the PostgreSQL implementation.

SIGN()

Syntax:

```
SIGN(X)
```

The SIGN() function returns –1, 0, or 1, depending on whether the argument X is a negative, zero, or positive value. Consider the following example:

```
SELECT SIGN(-34.56) AS RESULT;

RESULT
------
-1
```

The SIGN() function is available in all of the other RDBMS implementations discussed in this book.

SIN()

Syntax:

```
SIN(X)
```

The SIN() function returns the sine of the argument X. Consider the following example:

```
SELECT SIN(90);

----------
0.893997
```

The SIN() function is also available in the Sybase ASE and MySQL implementations.

SQRT()

Syntax:

```
SQRT(X)
```

The SQRT() function returns the square root of the argument X. Consider the following example:

```
SELECT SQRT(64) AS ROOT;

ROOT
-----
8
```

The SQRT() function is available in all of the RDBMS implementations discussed in this book.

TRUNC()

Syntax:

```
TRUNC(Numeric)
TRUN(Numeric, Integer)
```

The TRUNC() function is used to truncate the Numeric value to a specific number of decimal places. If the Integer value is 0 or nonexistent, then the Numeric value will not have any decimal or fractional part to it. If the Integer value is negative, the Numeric value is truncated at the corresponding number of places to the left of the decimal location. Consider the following example, which truncates the number to a single decimal place:

```
SELECT
    TRUNC(109.29, 1) AS TRUNCATED

TRUNCATED
------------
109.20
```

The TRUNC() function is also available in the Oracle and IBM DB2 implementations, while the MySQL platform uses the TRUNCATE() syntax to perform comparable operations.

Date-Time Functions

Date-time functions are those functions primarily dealing with manipulation and calculations of date and timestamp values. PostgreSQL provides a limited number of functions for the developer, which are detailed in the following table.

SQL Function	Input Arguments	Return Arguments	Notes
AGE(X)	Timestamp	Interval	Returns the interval value that corresponds to the difference in time between today and the value of X.
AGE(X,X)	Timestamp, Timestamp	Interval	Returns the interval between the two timestamp input values.
CURRENT_DATE	None	Date	Returns today's date.
CURRENT_TIME	None	Time	Returns the current time.
DATE_PART(X,Y)	String, Timestamp	Double Precision	Retrieves the subfield X of the timestamp argument Y.
DATE_TRUNC (X,Y)	String, Timestamp	Timestamp	Returns the timestamp Y truncated to the precision of X.
EXTRACT (X from Y)	String, Timestamp or Interval	Double Precision	Retrieves the subfield X from the timestamp or interval value Y.
ISFINITE(X)	Timestamp or Interval	Boolean	Returns true or false based upon whether the timestamp or interval is finite.
LOCALTIME	None	Time	Returns the current time of day.
LOCALTIMESTAMP	None	Timestamp	Returns the current date and time.
NOW()	None	Timestamp with Time zone	Returns the current date and time.
TIMEOFDAY()	None	String	Returns the current date and time.

AGE()

Syntax:

```
AGE(timestamp)
AGE(timestamp, timestamp)
```

The AGE() function returns the interval of how much time has passed from the timestamp argument until today. If both timestamp arguments are supplied, then the interval is the period between the two arguments. Consider the following example:

```
SELECT AGE(TIMESTAMP '2004-07-29') AS TIME_PASSED;

TIME_PASSED
--------------------
0 years 3 months 13 days
```

The AGE() function is unique to PostgreSQL.

CURRENT_DATE()

Syntax:

```
CURRENT_DATE
```

The CURRENT_DATE function returns the current date. Consider the following example, which simply returns the current date:

```
SELECT CURRENT_DATE;

-------------
2004-11-14
```

The CURRENT_DATE function is also available in the IBM DB2 RDBMS implementation.

CURRENT_TIME()

Syntax:

```
CURRENT_TIME
```

This function simply returns the current time with the time zone data. Consider the following example, which simply returns the current system time:

```
SELECT CURRENT_TIME;

------------------
01:20:57.0070-05
```

The CURRENT_TIME function is unique to the PostgreSQL platform.

DATE_PART()

Syntax:

```
DATE_PART(subfield, timestamp)
DATE_PART(subfield, interval)
```

The DATE_PART() function extracts pieces of date-time information from timestamp and interval arguments passed to it. Consider the following example:

```
SELECT
    DATE_PART('month',timestamp '1996-10-03 13:34:45') AS MONTH_PART;

MONTH_PART
----------
10
```

The DATE_PART() function is unique to the PostgreSQL implementation.

DATE_TRUNC()

Syntax:

```
DATE_TRUNC(subfield, timestamp)
```

The DATE_TRUNC() function truncates the timestamp argument to the precision that is defined in the subfield argument. Consider the following example:

```
SELECT
    DATE_TRUNC('hour',timestamp '1995-08-02 14:33:12') AS TRUNCED;

TRUNCED
--------------
1995-08-02 14:00:00
```

The DATE_TRUNC() function is unique to the PostgreSQL implementation.

EXTRACT()

Syntax:

```
EXTRACT(field FROM timestamp)
EXTRACT(field FROM interval)
```

The EXTRACT() function is used to extract a particular field from the timestamp or interval value argument. Consider the following example:

```
SELECT
 EXTRACT('month' FROM timestamp '2002-10-12 09:22:13') AS THIS_MONTH;

THIS_MONTH
----------
10
```

The EXTRACT() function is also available in the Oracle implementation.

ISFINITE()

Syntax:

```
ISFINTITE(timestamp)
ISFINITE(interval)
```

The `ISFINITE()` function returns a true or false evaluation of whether the `timestamp` or `interval` argument is a finite element. This corresponds to the value not being equal to infinity. Consider the following example, in which we use the `LOCALTIMESTAMP` function to test this function:

```
SELECT ISFINITE(LOCALTIMESTAMP);

-------
t
```

The `ISFINITE()` function is unique to the PostgreSQL implementation.

LOCALTIME()

Syntax:

```
LOCALTIME
```

This function returns the time of day without the time zone data. Consider the following example, which returns the current local time value of the system:

```
SELECT LOCALTIME;

---------------
01:24:45.0540
```

The `LOCALTIME` function is unique to the PostgreSQL implementation.

LOCALTIMESTAMP

Syntax:

```
LOCALTIMESTAMP
```

This function returns the current date and time value without the corresponding time zone information. Consider the following example, in which we find the current local timestamp value:

```
SELECT LOCALTIMESTAMP;

-------------------------------------
2004-11-14 01:25:49.335
```

The LOCALTIMESTAMP function is unique to the PostgreSQL implementation.

NOW()

Syntax:

```
NOW()
```

The NOW() function is the traditional PostgreSQL equivalent to the CURRENT_TIMESTAMP function. The function is meant to return the current time with the time zone data. Consider the following example:

```
SELECT NOW();

-------------------------------------
2005-01-14 01:27:11.538-05
```

The NOW() function is also available in the MySQL implementation.

TIMEOFDAY()

Syntax:

```
TIMEOFDAY()
```

This function returns the current date and time as a text string value. Consider the following example, which we use to return the string value of the current time of day:

```
SELECT TIMEOFDAY();

-----------------------------------------
Fri Jan 14 01:29:16.835000 2005 EST
```

The TIMEOFDAY() function is unique to the PostgreSQL implementation.

Geometric Functions

Geometric functions are PostgreSQL's high point as far as functions are concerned. You will not be able to find these types of calculations and manipulative functions in any of the other RDBMS implementations discussed in this book. The following table details the various geometric functions that we will be discussing.

SQL Function	Input Arguments	Return Arguments	Notes
AREA(X)	Object	Double Precision	Returns the area of the object X.
BOX_INTERSECT (X,Y)	Box	Box	Returns the intersection of the boxes X and Y.
CENTER(X)	Object	Point	Returns the center of the object X.
DIAMETER(X)	Circle	Double Precision	Returns the diameter of the circle X.
HEIGHT(X)	Box	Double Precision	Returns of the vertical size of the box X.
ISCLOSED(X)	Path	Boolean	Returns either true or false depending on whether X is a closed path or not.
ISOPEN(X)	Path	Boolean	Returns either true or false depending on whether X is an open path or not.
LENGTH(X)	Object	Double Precision	Returns the length of the object path X.
NPOINTS(X)	Path	Integer	Returns the number of points on the path X.
NPOINTS(X)	Polygon	Integer	Returns the number of points on the polygon X.
PCLOSE(X)	Path	Path	Returns the path X converted into a closed path.
POPEN(X)	Path	Path	Returns the path X converted into an open path.
RADIUS(X)	Circle	Double Precision	Returns the radius of the circle X.
WIDTH(X)	Box	Double Precision	Returns the horizontal size of the box X.

AREA()

Syntax:

```
AREA(object)
```

The AREA() function returns the area of the object argument. Consider the following example:

```
SELECT AREA(box '((0,0),(2,2))') AS BOX_AREA;

BOX_AREA
---------
4
```

The AREA() function is unique to the PostgreSQL implementation.

BOX_INTERSECT()

Syntax:

```
BOX_INTERSECT(box1, box2)
```

The BOX_INTERSECT() function returns the intersect of the two box arguments. Consider the following example, which finds the points of intersection for our two box objects:

```
SELECT BOX_INTERSECT(box '((0,0),(2,2))',box '((1,1),(2,2))') AS INTERSECTION;

INTERSECTION
--------------------
(2,2),(1,1)
```

The BOX_INTERSECT() function is unique to the PostgreSQL implementation.

CENTER()

Syntax:

```
CENTER(object)
```

The CENTER() function returns the point object that is the center of the object argument. Consider the following example:

```
SELECT CENTER(box '((0,0),(1,2))') AS BOX_CENTER;

BOX_CENTER
-----------
(0.5,1)
```

The CENTER() function is unique to the PostgreSQL implementation.

DIAMETER()

Syntax:

```
DIAMETER(circle)
```

The DIAMETER() function returns the diameter of the circle argument passed to it. Consider the following example, which figures the diameter of a circle of radius 4:

```
SELECT DIAMETER('((0,0),4)'::CIRCLE) AS ACROSS;

ACROSS
--------
8
```

The DIAMETER() function is unique to the PostgreSQL implementation.

HEIGHT()

Syntax:

```
HEIGHT(box)
```

The HEIGHT() function returns the vertical size of the box argument. Consider the following example, which calculates the height of a box object:

```
SELECT HEIGHT(box '((0,0),(2,2))') AS BOX_HEIGHT;

BOX_HEIGHT
----------
2
```

The HEIGHT() function is unique to the PostgreSQL implementation.

ISCLOSED()

Syntax:

```
ISCLOSED(path)
```

The ISCLOSED() function returns true or false, depending upon whether the path object is a closed path. Consider the following example, which shows the result when the input is a closed path:

```
SELECT isclosed('((0,0),(2,1),(5,3))'::path) AS A_CLOSED_PATH;

A_CLOSED_PATH
---------------
t
```

The ISCLOSED() function is unique to the PostgreSQL implementation.

ISOPEN()

Syntax:

```
ISOPEN(path)
```

The ISOPEN() function is the opposite of the ISCLOSED() function. It returns true or false, depending upon whether the path object is an open path. Consider the following example, which shows an open version of the same path used in the previous example:

```
SELECT isopen('[(0,0),(2,1),(5,3)]'::path) AS AN_OPEN_PATH;

AN_OPEN_PATH
----------------
t
```

The ISOPEN() function is unique to the PostgreSQL implementation.

LENGTH()

Syntax:

```
LENGTH(object)
```

The LENGTH() function returns the length of the object such as a path object. Consider the following example, which returns the length of our previous path:

```
SELECT LENGTH('[(0,0),(2,1),(5,3)]'::path) AS PATH;

PATH
--------------------
5.84161925296378
```

This particular use of the LENGTH() function is unique to the PostgreSQL implementation.

NPOINTS()

Syntax:

```
NPOINTS(path)
NPOINTS(polygon)
```

The NPOINTS() function is used to determine either the number of points along a path or the number of points (corners) on a polygon. Consider the following example, which returns the correct number of points along a path:

```
SELECT NPOINTS('[(0,0),(2,1),(5,3)]'::path) AS NO_OF_POINTS;

NO_OF_POINTS
--------------
3
```

The NPOINTS() function is unique to the PostgreSQL implementation.

PCLOSE()

Syntax:

```
PCLOSE(path)
```

The PCLOSE() function is used to convert an open path object to a closed path object. Consider the following example in which we transform an open path to a closed one:

```
SELECT PCLOSE('[(0,0),(2,1),(5,3)]'::path) AS CLOSED;

CLOSED
--------------------
((0,0),(2,1),(5,3))
```

The PCLOSE() function is unique to the PostgreSQL implementations.

POPEN()

Syntax:

```
POPEN(path)
```

The POPEN() function is used to convert a closed path object to an open path object. Consider the following example in which we take the closed path from the previous example and convert it back to an open path:

```
SELECT POPEN('((0,0),(2,1),(5,3))'::path) AS OPENED;

OPENED
-------------
[(0,0),(2,1),(5,3)]
```

The POPEN() function is unique to the PostgreSQL implementation.

RADIUS()

Syntax:

```
RADIUS(circle)
```

The RADIUS() function is used to determine the radius of a circle object. Consider the following example, in which we return the radius of a circle object:

```
SELECT RADIUS('((0,0),4)'::CIRCLE) AS MY_RADIUS;

MY_RADIUS
-------------
4
```

The RADIUS() function is unique to the PostgreSQL implementation.

WIDTH()

Syntax:

```
WIDTH(box)
```

The WIDTH() function returns the horizontal size of the box argument. Consider the following example, in which we return the width from our previous box example:

```
SELECT WIDTH(box '((0,0),(2,2))') AS BOX_WIDTH;

BOX_WIDTH
-----------
2
```

The WIDTH() function is unique to the PostgreSQL implementation.

Miscellaneous Functions

These PostgreSQL functions do not fit neatly into any of the other categories previously discussed, so they are relegated to the miscellaneous container. The following table details the various miscellaneous functions that we will be discussing in this section.

SQL Function	Input Arguments	Return Arguments	Notes
COALESCE (X, ...)	Any	Any	Returns the first of the set of arguments X that is not NULL.
CURRENT_ DATABASE()	None	String	Returns the name of the current database.
CURRENT_SCHEMA()	None	String	Returns the name of the current database schema.
CURRENT_ SCHEMAS(X)	Boolean	Array of Strings	Returns the names of the schemas in the search path.
CURRENT_USER	None	String	Returns the username of the current context.
NULLIF(X,Y)	Any	Any or Null	Returns NULL if X=Y otherwise returns X.
SESSION_USER	None	String	Returns the session username.
USER	None	String	Equivalent to the current user.
VERSION()	None	String	Returns the PostgreSQL version information.

COALESCE()

Syntax:

```
COALESCE( value1, value2,......)
```

This function returns the first of its arguments that is not NULL. Often, this is used to substitute default values for database fields when they are NULL. The only time that this function would return NULL is when all of the arguments passed to it are NULL. The following example shows how to use a simple COALASCE() function to return a default value for objects that do not have a price defined explicitly:

```
CREATE TABLE SOFTWARE(SOFTWARE_NAME      VARCHAR(30),
                      DEVELOPER          VARCHAR(30),
                      PRICE              MONEY
                      );

INSERT INTO SOFTWARE(SOFTWARE_NAME,DEVELOPER,PRICE)
     VALUES('GIGAPIXAR ver 2.0','JONES',30.00);
INSERT INTO SOFTWARE(SOFTWARE_NAME,DEVELOPER,PRICE)
     VALUES('BIGCOPY ver 3.5','SMITH',19.95);
INSERT INTO SOFTWARE(SOFTWARE_NAME,DEVELOPER)
     VALUES('SECURESTUFF v1.0','CHAMBERS');
INSERT INTO SOFTWARE(SOFTWARE_NAME,DEVELOPER)
     VALUES('ITSFREEMAN v 8.5','CRAIG');

SELECT
     SOFTWARE_NAME, DEVELOPER, COALASCE(PRICE,'FREEWARE') AS COST
FROM SOFTWARE;

SOFWARE_NAME            DEVELOPER       COST
----------------       ------------    ---------
GIGAPIXAR ver 2.0      JONES           30.00
BIGCOPY ver 3.5        SMITH           19.95
SECURESTUFF v1.0       CHAMBERS        FREEWARE
ITSFREEMAN v 8.5       CRAIG           FREEWARE
```

The COALESCE() function is available in all of the other RDBMS implementations discussed in this book.

CURRENT_DATABASE

Syntax:

```
CURRENT_DATABASE
```

The CURRENT_DATABASE function returns the name of the current database. Consider the following example, in which we find the current database we are working within:

```
SELECT CURRENT_DATABASE();

----------
Test
```

The CURRENT_DATABASE function is not available in any of the other RDBMS implementations discussed in this book. However, the DB_NAME function provides a similar function in the MS SQL Server and Sybase ASE implementations.

CURRENT_SCHEMA

Syntax:

```
CURRENT_SCHEMA
```

This function returns the schema name of the schema that is in the front of the search path. Normally, this would be the schema that would be used as the default when creating tables or other objects and not specifying one. Consider the following example:

```
SELECT CURRENT_SCHEMA();


----------
public
```

The CURRENT_SCHEMA is not available in any of the other RDBMS implementations discussed in this book.

CURRENT_USER

Syntax:

```
CURRENT_USER
```

This function returns current_user for the database queried. The value of current_user is the user ID that is used currently for permission checking. The function output is normally the same as the session_user and can be changed during the execution of functions by using the SECURITY DEFINER attribute. Consider the following example:

```
SELECT CURRENT_USER;


----------
postgres
```

The CURRENT_USER function is unique to the PostgreSQL implementation. The USER function provides similar functionality in the IBM DB2, MS SQL Server, and Sybase platforms.

NULLIF()

Syntax:

```
NULLIF(X,Y)
```

The NULLIF() function is used to compare the two input parameters and return NULL if $X = Y$, or X otherwise. The following code could be used to weed out undesirable results in our CARS table:

```
UPDATE CARS SET PRICE=0 WHERE MODEL='LATESTnGREATEST';

SELECT MAKER,MODEL,CASE WHEN NULLIF(PRICE,0) IS NULL
THEN 'FREE!' ELSE TO_CHAR(PRICE) END AS PRICE FROM CARS;

MAKER                MODEL                    PRICE
--------------       ---------------------    ----------
CHRYSLER             CROSSFIRE                33620
CHRYSLER             300M                     29185
HONDA                CIVIC                    15610
HONDA                ACCORD                   19300
FORD                 MUSTANG                  15610
FORD                 LATESTnGREATEST          FREE!
FORD                 FOCUS                    13005
```

This function is available in all of the RDBMS implementations discussed in this book.

SESSION_USER

Syntax:

```
SESSION_USER
```

The `SESSION_USER` function returns `session_user` for the current connection. The value of `session_user` is fixed for the duration of the connection that is being used and cannot be altered. Consider the following example:

```
SELECT SESSION_USER;

----------
postgres
```

The `SESSION_USER` function is unique to the PostgreSQL implementation. The `USER` function provides similar functionality in the IBM DB2, MS SQL Server, and Sybase platforms.

USER

Syntax:

```
USER
```

The `USER` function returns the `current_user` identifier, and is the same as the `CURRENT_USER` function. Consider the following example:

```
SELECT USER;

-------------
postgres
```

The `USER` function is also available in the IBM DB2, MS SQL Server, and Sybase ASE implementations.

VERSION

Syntax:

```
VERSION
```

The `VERSION` function returns information on the version of PostgreSQL that is currently running on the machine.

Consider the following example, which shows the current version information of the PostgreSQL instance running on my server:

```
SELECT VERSION();

------------------------------------------------------------------
PostgreSQL 8.0.0rc5 on i686-pc-mingw32, compiled by GCC gcc.exe (GCC) 3.4.2 (mingw-
special)
```

Microsoft SQL Server and Sybase ASE provide a similar function called @@VERSION.

Summary

In this chapter, we reviewed the syntax and built-in functions of the PostgreSQL implementation. The dedication of the creators of PostgreSQL to provide a fully functional RDBMS implementation has produced some unique built-in functions for you to use that will not be found in other platforms. Specifically, we discussed the various function classes: aggregate, string, mathematical, date-time, geometrical, and miscellaneous. By reviewing these functions and comparing them to the ones in the previous chapter, you will be able to more fully understand the fundamental differences between the MySQL and PostgreSQL platforms.

In the next chapter, we will shift the focus to creating your own functions, user-defined functions (UDFs). We will begin with a look at what the ANSI standard defines or outlines for UDFs in order to get a good base from which to work.

12

ANSI SQL User-Defined Functions

As discussed in Chapter 1, the ANSI SQL standard, currently SQL:2003, is the foundation upon which the various RDMS implementations base their SQL language syntax. To understand how the RDMS implementations comply with the ANSI SQL standard, it is important to see where they are derived from. The developer will be hard-pressed to find references to user-defined functions (UDFs) in the massive SQL standard modules. Instead, you will find that UDFs are thinly veiled in references to SQL routines and Persistent Stored Modules (PSM). In fact, most of the information can be found in Module 2 (SQL Foundation) and Module 4 (PSM). This chapter examines the basics of the UDF as outlined in the ANSI standard.

User-Defined Functions or SQL Routines?

So, are SQL routines the ANSI equivalent to the UDF? Well, yes and no. A SQL routine consists of, at the very least, a `<schema qualified routine name>`, `<SQL parameter declarations>`, and a `<routine body>`. The syntax format is as follows:

```
<routine invocation> ::= <routine name> <SQL argument list> <routine body>

<routine name> ::= [ <schema name> .] <qualified identifier>

<SQL argument list> ::=
    ( [ <value expression>|<generalized expression>|<target specification>
    [,<SQL argument>,............] ] )
```

As you can see from this syntax, the routine is not required to have an argument list. If the routine has no such list of parameters, then it is referred to as an *invocable routine.*

In order for the routine to be considered an *executable routine* (or one that can be executed via a SQL statement), the current privilege set must contain the EXECUTE permission for the routine. This is no different from any other object in the SQL hierarchy. You must have permissions to perform an action before you take it.

Functions versus Procedures

A SQL routine is actually either a SQL-invoked *function* or a SQL-invoked *procedure*. There is a difference between the two, albeit relatively syntactic, but a rather large difference nonetheless. A SQL-invoked procedure is a SQL-invoked routine that takes parameters, but does not return a value. This means that its primary invocation is via the CALL statement. Since it does not directly return a value, it cannot be used within a SQL statement. This is because, since the procedure returns no value, it depends on the SQL parameters, which can be IN, OUT, or INOUT. The following code shows an example of such a stored procedure as used in SQL Server. The procedure get_account_balance uses the input parameter @account_id and returns the output parameter @account_balance. There is no way to get the return value without specifically declaring and returning the output parameter.

```
CREATE TABLE bank_accounts(
        Account_id      bigint,
        Account_balance decimal(15,2)
                         );

INSERT INTO bank_accounts(account_id,account_balance) VALUES(37446643,123.32);
INSERT INTO bank_accounts(account_id,account_balance) VALUES(43234433,5677.78);
INSERT INTO bank_accounts(account_id,account_balance) VALUES(83478339,232.56);

CREATE PROCEDURE get_account_balance
@account_id bigint   -- This is the input parameter.
@account_balance decimal(15,2) OUTPUT -- This is the output parameter.
AS

--Get the account balance for the specified account_id and
--stuff it into the output parameter.

SELECT @account_balance = account_balance,
FROM bank_accounts
WHERE account_id = @account_id

RETURN
GO

DECLARE @balance_total  decimal(15,2)

EXECUTE get_account_balance
            3744643,@account_balance=@balance_total OUTPUT

SELECT @balance_total as Your_Account_Balance
Your_Account_Balance
--------------------
123.32
```

A function, on the other hand, only accepts input parameters and then returns a single value. The following example shows our previous procedure get_account_balance written as a function. Notice how, since the invoked function returns the value rather than an output parameter, we are able to use it in a SELECT statement. This one small issue is able to provide us with a greater degree of flexibility and ease of use over the invoked procedure version just presented.

```
CREATE FUNCTION get_account_balance
(@account_id  bigint)   -- This is the input parameter.
RETURNS decimal(15,2) -- This is type of value that is returned.
AS
BEGIN
DECLARE @account_balance  decimal(15,2)
--Get the account balance for the specified account_id and
--stuff it into the output parameter.

SELECT @account_balance = account_balance
FROM bank_accounts
WHERE account_id = @account_id

RETURN @account_balance
END
GO

SELECT get_account_balance(3744643) as Your_Account_Balance


Your_Account_Balance
--------------------
123.32
```

Internal versus External Functions

In addition to the function/procedure division, routines (and, therefore, functions) can be further subdivided into *SQL routines* and *external routines*. The SQL routine is one in which the body of the routine statement consists of a series of SQL queries or statements. There are limitations to this, however, such as disallowing the use of SQL connection statements and any transactions statements other than savepoints and rollbacks. These SQL statements are all executed in the same manner as any other SQL statement in the system, and are run under the same session as that which invoked the routine.

An external routine is one in which the body of the routine is written not in SQL, but in some programming language such as C, C++, or Java. The body of the routine is merely a reference to a program written in the desired language. It is executed in whatever manner is relevant to the programming language in which it was written. Furthermore, it has the same restrictions as the SQL routine (that is, it is not allowed to execute SQL connection statements or transaction statements other than savepoints and rollbacks).

Creating UDFs

The CREATE FUNCTION syntax is used to create a function. The following code specifies the syntax for the ANSI SQL:2003 version of the CREATE FUNCTION syntax:

```
CREATE FUNCTION  function_name
(
[ { parameter_name parameter_datatype
    [AS LOCATOR] [RESULT] } .......]
)
RETURNS datatype [AS LOCATOR][CAST FROM datatype [AS LOCATOR]]
```

```
[LANGUAGE  ADA | C | FORTRAN | JAVA | PASCAL | PLI | SQL]
[PARAMETER STYLE SQL | GENERAL]
[SPECIFIC name ]
[DETERMINISTIC | NONDETERMINISTIC]
[NO SQL | CONTAINS SQL | READS SQL DATA | MODIFIES SQL DATA]
[RETURN NULL ON NULL INPUT | CALL ON NULL INPUT]
[STATIC DISPATCH]
code ...
```

To gain a better understanding of the functionality of the ANSI SQL:2003 version of the CREATE FUNCTION statement, we will examine each of the sections in turn. The first section of code after the first line handles the creation of the parameter list for the function. This list declares one or more parameters that can be used. You will notice that we only use the parameter_name and the datatype and leave off the declaration of whether the parameters are IN, OUT, or INOUT. Remember (from the previous discussion) that functions only accept input parameters. The output value is handled by the next section with the RETURNS clause, which is used to specify what data type is to be returned by the function.

The LANGUAGE clause declares the language in which the function is written. The preceding list is by no means exclusive. Some RDBMS implementations will not support all of these languages, while others will support ones not on the list. An example of this would be Microsoft's new SQL Server 2005 platform, which will strongly integrate with their .NET language platform. If this clause is not used, then the default is always SQL.

The PARAMETER STYLE clause is exclusive to external routines such as those discussed in the previous section. It specifies whether certain parameters are passed with either the SQL or the GENERAL style. The SQL style passes automatic parameters, while the GENERAL style does not. The default is always SQL.

The nature of the SPECIFIC clause is to uniquely identity the function. It is normally used in conjunction with user-defined types, which are beyond the scope of this book.

Next, we can specify whether the function is DETERMINISTIC or NONDETERMINISTIC. A DETERMINISTIC function returns the same value every time when given the same input parameters. A NONDETERMINISTIC function can return varying results even when given the same input parameters. (See Chapter 2 for a more complete discussion of this issue.)

The next clause, NO SQL | CONTAINS SQL | READS SQL DATA | MODIFIES SQL DATA, is used in conjunction with the LANGUAGE clause to specify what kind (if any) of SQL is contained within the function. NO SQL indicates that the function contains no SQL whatsoever and is used with non-SQL LANGUAGE clauses. CONTAINS SQL is the default for the clause and indicates that there may be SQL statements that are other than the general SELECT, INSERT, UPDATE, and DELETE. READS SQL DATA specifies that the code contains only SELECT or FETCH statements. MODIFIES SQL DATA indicates that the function contains modification statements such as INSERT, UPDATE, and DELETE.

The RETURN NULL ON NULL INPUT and CALL ON NULL INPUT clauses are used for those LANGUAGE clause languages that do not support null values. The RETURN NULL ON NULL INPUT tells the function that it is to return a null value if it is passed a null value in its parameter set. CALL ON NULL INPUT is used when you want the function to null according to standard rules.

The last clause is the STATIC DISPATCH. It specifies that the function is to return the static values of an ARRAY or a user-defined type. It is required if you have a non-SQL function that uses either of the two previous data types as parameters.

Altering UDFs

The ALTER FUNCTION syntax is used to alter existing functions within the RDBMS. Its layout is similar to the CREATE FUNCTION syntax discussed in the previous section. The following code presents the syntax for the statement. For a detailed explanation of the different clauses contained in the syntax, refer to the discussion in the previous section. The only new clauses are the CASCADE and RESTRICT clauses. These enable the developer to either CASCADE changes down to dependent functions, or to RESTRICT the changes from occurring if the function has dependent objects.

```
ALTER FUNCTION  function_name
( [ { parameter_name parameter_datatype } .......] )
[NAME new_function_name]
[LANGUAGE  ADA | C | FORTRAN | JAVA | PASCAL | PLI | SQL]
[PARAMETER STYLE SQL | GENERAL]
[NO SQL | CONTAINS SQL | READS SQL DATA | MODIFIES SQL DATA]
[RETURN NULL ON NULL INPUT | CALL ON NULL INPUT]
[CASCADE | RESTRICT]
```

Removing UDFs

To remove an existing UDF, you must use the DROP FUNCTION syntax. This is a fairly simple statement and is outlined in the following code line:

```
DROP FUNCTION function_name {RESTRICT | CASCADE}
```

The CASCADE and RESTRICT clauses provide the same functionality as they do with the ALTER FUNCTION statement. CASCADE allows all the objects that are dependent upon the function to be dropped as well. RESTRICT prevents the function from being dropped if it has dependent objects.

Summary

You should now have a general understanding of the nature of the ANSI SQL:2003 standard for UDFs. Additionally, we have covered how to CREATE, ALTER, and DROP UDFs and the syntax involved. This will be a valuable building block for the chapters ahead, since we will be delving into the specific RDBMS implementations and their many varying versions of the standard. Keep this standard syntax in mind when trying to decipher just how closely compliant the differing RDBMS implementations are to the ANSI standard.

Now that we have discussed the general properties of UDFs as they apply to the ANSI standard, we will move on to discussions of the six specific RDBMS implementations. In the next chapter, we will specifically be dealing with creating UDFs in the Oracle platform.

13

Creating User-Defined Functions in Oracle

The ability to create PL/SQL user-defined functions (UDFs) has existed since release 2.1 of the PL/SQL compiler (Oracle 7.1). Its latest incarnation is built into Oracle 10g. It boasts vast improvement in raw computational speed because of a complete redesign of the PL/SQL compiler/interpreter. Let's take a closer look at the PL/SQL inner workings.

PL/SQL Compiler

Unlike many of its competitors, Oracle provides quite a bit of information on implementing its built-in procedural language. The PL/SQL compiler can be conditionally separated into two parts: *front-end* and *back-end* (also known as the *code generator*).

The front-end module ensures semantic and syntactic correctness of the PL/SQL source code. Syntactic correctness includes checking for commas, correct spelling of the keywords, and so on. Semantic correctness means that the program makes practical sense. All the procedures and functions are where the program says they are and are accessible, and the user has enough privileges to execute them. Whenever a syntactic or semantic error is found, the whole compilation process is aborted and error information is sent to the output console. This might be Oracle's own SQL*Plus interface, or one of the dozens of third-party integrated development environments (IDEs), such as TOAD or SQL Station.

If no errors are found in the source code of your PL/SQL program, an internal representation of the code is created. The internal representation is an error-free, semantically and syntactically correct, ready-to-compile intermediate code. PL/SQL uses Descriptive Intermediate Attributed Notation for Ada (DIANA) for its internal representation. DIANA is a high-level, tree-structured intermediate language for Ada that provides communication internal to compilers and other tools. It uses the abstract syntax tree of the formal specification and has many attributes based on ADA and TCOL-ADA (initial standards used in Ada compiler development).

The DIANA intermediate code is then fed into the back-end compiler, which generates the final executable code, targeting the operating system (OS) for which it was compiled. Prior to the release of Oracle9i, this code was usually byte-code for the PL/SQL Virtual Machine (PVM) to interpret and execute (which made PL/SQL an interpreted language). This machine is a software abstraction of the real hardware, similar to Java Virtual Machine (JVM), as well as the .NET Framework and its Common Runtime Library (CLR).

Oracle9i introduced a *native compilation* option, which allows the DIANA code to be compiled to a machine code for any given OS — UNIX, Linux, or Windows. Native compilation is covered in much more detail later in this chapter when we discuss creating UDFs.

When the back-end compiles, it produces executable code for PVM — the code is stored internally in Oracle's system-managed tables of the SYS schema. The code is loaded upon request, and executed, in interpreted mode. The mode of execution (either interpreted or native) is resolved at this time. The m-code is loaded and executed in Oracle's SGA memory, while natively compiled code is loaded and executed in the OS memory. While inter-process communications certainly would exact their toll, it opens a potential for faster execution and throughput.

In general, when compiled to native code, PL/SQL executes faster than its interpreted equivalent. Nevertheless, this might not be the case where the SQL UDFs are concerned. While two compilation modes are fully compatible (that is, native code can call interpreted, and vice versa), there is a performance price to pay for switching the context from one to another. For a SQL function that is called from within a SQL statement (an interpreted environment, by definition), advantages of faster execution might be greatly reduced (or even eliminated altogether) when the function is compiled into native code.

Oracle 10g Compiler Optimization

The changes introduced in Oracle 10g have been tested for some time now in the 8i and 9i versions without drawing much attention. However, some changes are truly revolutionary, like code generation optimization. This essentially means that the compiler sees the big picture (the whole procedure execution rather than going line-by-line) and is able to find shortcuts that can speed up the execution without altering the logic of the procedure. The new instance parameter plsql_optimize_level allows you to specify the degree of the smart optimization. The allowed parameters are 0, 1, and 2, the latter being the default, resulting in the most optimized code. Choosing the highest level of optimization will result in the slowest compilation process, though rewarded with faster execution time; setting the parameter to 0 or 1 would mean doing the compilation the "old," pre-10g way.

While the parameter is exposed to the customers for the first time in 10g, the new code generator was included with previous releases, where it was running alongside the existing one. Oracle claims that this allowed them to conduct exhaustive testing of the new features prior to releasing them to the public. It also claims that the optimized PL/SQL compiled under 10g runs two times faster than the old one.

Acquiring Permissions

Before you can do anything with the Oracle RDBMS, you must acquire sufficient privileges. In addition to CONNECT and RESOURCE roles needed to connect to Oracle and execute SQL queries, you must have one or more of the privileges listed in the following table.

Privilege	Description
ALTER ANY PROCEDURE	Allows the user to modify a procedure/function in any schema in the given Oracle database.
CREATE ANY PROCEDURE	Allows the user to create a procedure/function in any schema in the given Oracle database.
CREATE ANY OPERATOR	Allows the user to create any operator in any schema in the given Oracle database.
CREATE PROCEDURE	Assigned through RESOURCE role, allows the user to create procedures/functions in his or her schema.
CREATE OPERATOR	Assigned through RESOURCE role, allows user to create operators in his or her schema.
DROP ANY OPERATOR	Allows the user to drop any operator in any schema in the given Oracle database.
DROP ANY PROCEDURE	Allows the user to drop any procedure/function in any schema in the given Oracle database.
EXECUTE ANY OPERATOR	Allows the user to execute any operator in any schema in the given Oracle database.
EXECUTE ANY PROCEDURE	Allows the user to execute any procedure/function in any schema in the given Oracle database.

Normally, each user will have CONNECT and RESOURCE roles assigned, which allows for creating, dropping, and altering stored procedures and UDFs in his or her own schema.

Before PL/SQL can be used at all, a special script DBMSSTDX.SQL must be run by user SYS. Normally, this is part of the standard scripts run during the creation of an Oracle database.

This also precludes using any of the procedures located in different schemas, since the procedures (and functions) have local and global scopes. To call a function or procedure located in a different schema, you must have the EXECUTE ANY PROCEDURE privilege, and the calling syntax must include the schema name (as well as some optional keywords), as shown here:

```
[[schema.]package.]function_name[@dblink][(param_1..param_n)]
```

@DBLINK is a schema object in the local database that enables you to access objects on a remote database. It is created with the CREATE DATABASE LINK statement, and requires an identically named system privilege on a local database, as well as a CREATE SESSION privilege on the remote database. The remote database does not have to be an Oracle system, which opens another can of worms—heterogeneous environment operations.

Granting of the DBA role automatically passes to the grantee all the system privileges listed in the previous table.

Creating UDFs

In general, Oracle follows the ANSI/ISO standard for creating a UDF with PL/SQL. The ability to create the UDFs had existed since version 2.0 (shipped with the Oracle 7.0 database server), and the ability to use these functions in SQL statements was added in Oracle 7.1 a year later. (Prior to that, the UDF could only be used from within other functions and stored procedures.) A stored function (or a UDF) is nothing more than a set of PL/SQL statements, compiled under a single name, and callable from a SQL and/or PL/SQL statement by that name.

The function can be created either as stand-alone or as part of a package. One advantage to making the function part of a package is that doing so allows for overloading the function. The penalty for using a function from a package is exacted in terms of computer memory. Even though you might be using only one function in your SQL statement, the whole package must be loaded on that account.

A user must have sufficient privileges to be able to create, drop, or alter functions. (Permissions were discussed in the previous section.)

The basic syntax (which you are most likely to use) is as follows:

```
CREATE [OR REPLACE] FUNCTION [schema.]function_name
(
    <argument> [IN]|[OUT]|[IN OUT][NOCOPY] <datatype>
)
RETURN <datatype>
[DETERMINISTIC][IS]|[AS]
<PL/SQL function body>;
```

The optional clause [OR REPLACE] means just that—a function with such a name exists, and must be dropped prior to compiling the new function. Oracle handles this behind the scenes, without you having to worry about dropping the object beforehand. This is different from MS SQL Server, Sybase, or IBM DB2, which have no REPLACE clause in the CREATE FUNCTION statement.

Using the OR REPLACE clause when no such function exists might result in the error "ORA_04043: object <function_name> does not exist" in some front-end tools like TOAD. The function will be created nevertheless.

The function's name can be qualified with the schema name prefix. If none is specified, the current schema is assumed. This is important for establishing scope of the function (function SCHEMA_1.FOO is not the same as function SCHEMA_2.FOO), as well as for an additional security level.

This chapter deals with the creation of UDFs utilizing PL/SQL. Oracle RDBMS, version 8i or later, also allows for creating the UDFs in Java or C general-purpose programming languages.

A function can have zero or more arguments, which are defined as IN (incoming) or OUT (outgoing). There is a combined type IN OUT that defines an argument containing values sent to the function and values returned from the function upon completion of execution. The IN OUT argument must not be confused with the return value of the function. The former is an argument passed to the function and returns the value BY REFERENCE (see Chapter 1), while the latter is returning the data BY VALUE. The IN clause for the argument is implied for every argument in the function signature. Furthermore, the arguments of the function can be assigned default values in the signature of the function.

> The function with an argument defined as **OUT** or **IN OUT** cannot be used in a SQL query. The Oracle error "ORA-06572: Function <function_name> has out arguments" will be returned on an attempt to call such a function from a SQL statement.

The NOCOPY clause means passing the pointer to the argument BY REFERENCE instead of passing it BY VALUE (see Chapter 1). This may result in significantly improved performance when OUT and IN OUT parameters are complex structures (such as a record, index-by table, or array). The IN argument is always passed as NOCOPY. You must understand the ramifications of passing arguments by reference. Any changes made to the argument will be immediately visible both in the calling procedure, and the called one, because the change is made to the single memory location to which both functions keep pointers.

Since the emphasis of this book is on SQL-callable functions, we are using a DUAL table to select from. Please see Chapter 5 for more information on DUAL tables.

A data type must be specified for the incoming, outgoing, and return arguments. Data types are discussed in greater detail in Appendix C.

It is important to note that the arguments' data types must *not* be sized. In other words, an argument could be declared as VARCHAR2, but never as VARCHAR2(10).

Consider the following example:

```
CREATE OR REPLACE FUNCTION fn_helloworld
    (arg1 IN VARCHAR2)
RETURN VARCHAR2
IS
BEGIN
    RETURN arg1 || ' world!';
END fn_helloworld;
```

This function would happily compile, and here are the results of calling it from within a SQL statement executed from the SQL*Plus Oracle utility:

```
SQL> SELECT fn_helloworld ('Hello') FROM DUAL;

FN_HELLOWORLD('HELLO')
--------------------------------
Hello world!
```

At the same time, the following function would never compile, while complaining about "PLS-00103: Encountered the symbol...," or issuing warnings of the "Warning: Function created with compilation errors" type:

```
CREATE OR REPLACE FUNCTION fn_helloworld
    (arg1 IN VARCHAR2(10))
RETURN VARCHAR2
IS
```

```
BEGIN
    RETURN arg1 || ' world!';
END fn_helloworld;
```

To specify a default for the function's argument, you could use the following syntax:

```
CREATE OR REPLACE FUNCTION fn_helloworld
    (arg1 IN VARCHAR2 DEFAULT 'Hello')
RETURN VARCHAR2
IS
BEGIN
    RETURN arg1 || ' world!';
END fn_helloworld;
```

Now, if you accidentally did not supply a parameter, the "Hello, world" would still be returned, while the "normal" functionality will be preserved:

```
SQL> SELECT
    fn_helloworld () result1,
    fn_helloworld ('Down with the') result2
FROM DUAL;
RESULT1            RESULT2
--------------     ----------------
Hello world!       Down with the world!
```

The extended syntax, which you might never encounter, adds a ton of complexity.

```
CREATE [OR REPLACE] FUNCTION [schema.]function_name
(
    <argument> [IN]|[OUT]|[INOUT]  [NOCOPY] <datatype>
)
RETURN <datatype> [DETERMINISTIC]|[ AUTHID [CURRENT_USER] | [DEFINER]]|[{PARRALEL
ENABLE clause}] [AGGREGATE]|[PIPELINED]
USING [schema.]<implementation type>]|[[PIPELINED]
[IS]|[AS]
[PRAGMA AUTONOMOUS_TRANSACTION;]
[<pl/sql function body>]|[call spec]];
```

Following is an explanation of the parts of this syntax:

❑   DETERMINISTIC — Initially meant as an optimization hint, this clause specifies that the function returns exactly the same results when passed precisely the same arguments. PL/SQL functions used in function-based indexes must be compiled with this clause. Deterministic functions can reside in a package. In this case, the clause should be used in the package specification; no private function can be declared with this clause. See more about deterministic versus non-deterministic functions in Chapter 1.

❑   AUTHID [CURRENT_USER] | [DEFINER] — This clause allows you to specify where it is going to be executed and what privileges are needed to do so. CURRENT_USER means that the function is to be executed with the privileges of the current user, in the current user's schema. It also limits the scope for name resolution: Oracle will look for the function by name in the current user's schema. DEFINER means that the function is to be executed with the privileges assigned to the owner of the schema the function resides in, and that all external names are to be resolved within the same schema.

❏   PARALLEL ENABLE — This clause is an optimization hint, instructing Oracle to execute it in parallel whenever called from within a SQL query. The processing would be split between parallel processes (UNIX), or threads (Windows). It could result in a speed improvement on multiprocessor machines. The clause itself has additional complexity:

```
PARALLEL ENABLE [(PARTITION <argument> BY [ANY] | [[HASH] | [RANGE]
(<column1>,<column2>,...)] ) [ORDER] | [CLUSTER] BY (<column1>,<column2>,...)
```

   ❏   ORDER BY — This indicates that the rows on the parallel execution server must be locally ordered.

   ❏   CLUSTER BY — This specifies that the rows on the parallel execution server must have exactly the same key values as on the <column> list.

❏   AGGREGATE USING — This clause identifies the function as an aggregate type (that is, one that returns a single row based on the evaluation of a group of rows). These functions could be used with a GROUP BY clause, a HAVING clause, and so on. If a function is defined as aggregate, only one input argument is allowed. An aggregate function cannot be directly implemented in PL/SQL; see more details on the subject later in this chapter.

A user-defined aggregate function can be used as an analytic function in a SQL query. Oracle has the OVER <analytic_clause> *syntax for this scenario.*

❏   PIPELINED — This clause specifies that the function is a table function (that is, it returns a table), and that its results should be returned iteratively via PIPE ROW. Such a function returns a collection of the table type and can be used in the FROM clause of the SELECT statement. PIPELINED USING <implementation_type> is useful when the body of the function is implemented in some external language (such as C or Java).

❏   PRAGMA AUTONOMOUS_TRANSACTION — This instructs the PL/SQL compiler to mark the function as independent, which allows the function to suspend the main transaction (the one from which the function was invoked), and roll back or commit its own SQL operations.

The function body syntax is identical to that of the stored procedures, with an important exception: it must return a value of the type specified in the function declaration, as shown here:

```
BEGIN
executable statements
RETURN <value>|<expression>
[EXCEPTION
exception handlers]
END [name];
```

Unlike stored procedures, the RETURN statement of a function can include expressions (or even other functions), and a function can have one or more RETURN states, with only one being executed. The return data type is specified in the header of the function, and the assigned value must be of the exact same data type. Upon execution of this statement, the function is terminated, and the result is returned to the calling procedure.

An ability to call a function as a part of the RETURN *statement opens yet another way to create a recursive function.*

A call specification (call spec) is used to map a C or Java function name and signature in conjunction with the CREATE LABRARY statement.

When calling UDFs, it is beneficial to understand how Oracle resolves the name. For example, if your SQL statement calls `my_package.fn_my_function`,*Oracle first checks for the package* `MY_PACKAGE` *in the current schema. If the package is found, Oracle proceeds to locate the entry point in* `FN_MY_FUNCTION`. *If such a function is not found, the error message is returned. If a* `MY_PACKAGE` *package is not found, then Oracle looks for a schema named* `MY_PACKAGE` *that contains a top-level* `FN_MY_FUNCTION` *function. If the* `FN_MY_FUNCTION` *function is not found in the* `MY_PACKAGE` *schema, then an error message is returned. A* `@DBLINK` *clause would direct the search (and execution) to be conducted on the remote database.*

Creating a Recursive UDF

A *recursive function* is a function that calls itself to perform calculations iteratively. The most obvious example of such a function is for calculating the factorial of a number. A factorial is defined for a positive integer *N* as follows:

```
N! = N x (N-1) . . . 2 x 1
```

For example, 5! = 5 x 4 x 3 x 2 x 1 = 120. A PL/SQL function calculating a factorial could be implemented as follows (no recursion involved):

```
CREATE OR REPLACE FUNCTION
    fn_FACTORIAL(arg1 NUMBER)
    RETURN NUMBER
IS
l_result NUMBER  := 1;
l_counter NUMBER := arg1;
BEGIN
   WHILE l_counter > 1
   LOOP
      l_result := l_result * l_counter;
      l_counter := l_counter - 1;
   END LOOP;
   RETURN l_result;
END;
```

Here is the result of the `SELECT` statement:

```
SQL> select fn_factorial(5) result from dual;

RESULT
--------
120
```

To use this algorithm, we had to declare an additional variable, `l_counter`, because no assignment is allowed to the `arg1` declared as an `IN` argument. This is the only type allowed; no `OUT` or `IN OUT` parameters are allowed in the PL/SQL functions if you intend to call them from SQL.

If we are going to use recursion, the algorithm might be somehow more concise:

```
CREATE OR REPLACE FUNCTION
    fn_RECURSIVE_FACTORIAL(arg NUMBER)
    RETURN NUMBER
```

```
IS
BEGIN
   RETURN arg*fn_RECURSIVE_FACTORIAL(arg-1);
END;
```

Unfortunately, execution of this function would inevitably result in the following error:

```
ORA-04030: out of process memory when trying to allocate 8204 bytes
```

```
(PLS non-lib hp, PL/SQL Stack);
```

```
Lklk
```

Here is the catch: unlike the harmless WHILE loop that assigns the values to the same memory allocation unit (variables l_result and l_counter), the recursive function allocates it on the memory stack. The error was thrown because this function has no restraints upon itself — it will consume all available stack memory and could potentially crash your computer.

To remedy the situation, we must monitor the bottom value and interrupt the execution once the critical level is reached:

```
CREATE OR REPLACE FUNCTION
   fn_RECURSIVE_FACTORIAL(arg NUMBER)
   RETURN NUMBER
IS
BEGIN
   IF arg > 1 THEN
      RETURN arg*fn_RECURSIVE_FACTORIAL(arg - 1);
   ELSE
      RETURN 1;
   END IF;
END;
```

The result of the SELECT statement is predictable:

```
SQL> select fn_RECURSIVE_FACTORIAL(5) result from dual;

RESULT
--------
120
```

If there are any performance gains of the recursive algorithm over a non-recursive one, they ought to be negligible for all practical purposes. Let's analyze what is happening here:

1. The function fn_RECURSIVE_FACTORIAL is called for the first time; the initial value of the argument is 5.

2. The value is checked against the condition arg > 1, which evaluates to TRUE, and the function is called again with an argument of (arg – 1).

3. Steps 1 and 2 are repeated until condition arg > 1 evaluates to FALSE. This terminates the execution and unwinds the stack, eventually returning the product of all levels (because of multiplication sign). The last multiplier is supplied by the RETURN 1 statement.

The moral: when using recursion, always think of the memory stack management.

429

Creating an Aggregate UDF

User-defined aggregate functions are part of the SQL3 specification (and were, before that, in the Informix RDBMS). There are also attempts to implement a special language to create user-defined aggregates like the SQL-AG proposal, Logic Database Language (LDL)++5.1, Simple Aggregate Definition Language (SADL), and Aggregate eXtension Language (AXL).

While it is possible to simulate an aggregate function using PL/SQL procedures, that falls outside the scope of this book. The recommended way to create a custom aggregate UDF in Oracle is to use external C or Java code.

Creating a Table-Valuated, Pipelined UDF

A *table-valuated function* is the only type of function you can actually use in the FROM clause. This is especially useful for returning a large amount of data. The data returned from a pipelined function that produces it is consumed immediately — row by row, without being staged in tables or a cache before being input into the next transformation. A *pipelined table function* can return the table function's result collection in subsets. The returned collection behaves like a stream that can be fetched from on demand. This makes it possible to use a table function like a virtual table.

Pipelining enables a table function to return rows faster and can reduce the memory required to cache a table function's results. Since the producer and consumer processes run on separate threads, this speeds up the transformation process considerably.

To create such a function, you must use the PIPELINED AS clause for PL/SQL (PIPELINED USING implementation_type for external C- and Java-implemented functions). Here is a step-by-step example of creating such a function:

1. Create and populate a table SCOUTS:

```
CREATE TABLE SCOUTS
 (
     FIRST_NAME  VARCHAR2 (25),
     LAST_NAME   VARCHAR2 (25)
 );
 INSERT INTO scouts VALUES ('Alex', 'Kriegel');
 INSERT INTO scouts VALUES ('Phillip', 'Windsor');
 INSERT INTO scouts VALUES ('Michael', 'DeVry');
```

2. Create a user-defined type PERSON:

```
CREATE OR REPLACE TYPE person AS OBJECT
 (
     first_name   VARCHAR2(25),
     last_name    VARCHAR2(25),
     description  VARCHAR2(25)
 );
```

3. Create a table type of the type PERSON:

```
CREATE TYPE scout_pack AS TABLE OF person;
```

4. Create a package spec for the return cursor of the table SCOUTS row type:

```
CREATE PACKAGE pkg_cursor IS
    TYPE cur_scouts IS REF CURSOR RETURN scouts%ROWTYPE;
END pkg_cursor;
```

5. Create a table-valued function:

```
CREATE OR REPLACE FUNCTION get_names(p_c        pkg_cursor.cur_scouts)
RETURN scout_pack
PIPELINED AS
    ret_record person := person(NULL,NULL,NULL);
    in_record p_c%ROWTYPE;
BEGIN
    LOOP
        FETCH p_c INTO in_record;
        EXIT WHEN p_c%NOTFOUND;
        ret_record.last_name  := in_record.last_name;
        ret_record.first_name := in_record.first_name;
        ret_record.description := 'FUNCTION VALUE';
        PIPE ROW(ret_record);
    END LOOP;
        CLOSE p_c;
        RETURN;
    END;
```

6. Execute a SQL query that returns the values from the function:

```
SELECT *
    FROM TABLE(get_names(CURSOR(SELECT * FROM scouts)));

FIRST_NAME      LAST_NAME              DESCRIPTION
-------------   ------------------     --------------------------
Alex            Kriegel                FUNCTION VALUE
Phillip         Windsor                FUNCTION VALUE
Michael         DeVry                  FUNCTION VALUE
```

The DESCRIPTION field contains a value that is not in the underlying table, which was the purpose of this exercise. Note that while table SCOUTS in this example is populated, that is not necessarily a requirement. The data assigned to the fields of the RET_RECORD could be fetched from anywhere and then pipelined to the calling procedure.

A pipelined function must include an empty RETURN statement; PIPE ROW is optional, and could be omitted if the function returns no rows. See Oracle's documentation for more information on pipelined functions.

Altering UDFs

Once the function is compiled, it could become invalid for a variety of reasons, the most common of which is some change in the objects referenced by the function. ALTER FUNCTION statement is used to recompile any invalid stand-alone function. The syntax is simple:

```
ALTER FUNCTION [schema.]function_name COMPILE [DEBUG] [REUSE SETTINGS];
```

The COMPILE keyword is required. If any errors are generated during compilation, you can list the errors by issuing the SHOW ERRORS command from the SQL*Plus interface (or by querying view USER_ERRORS).

The DEBUG clause is optional and is used to instruct the compiler to generate and store the code for the PL/SQL debugger.

REUSE SETTINGS instructs Oracle to use current PL/SQL compiler settings; otherwise, the settings will be dropped and reacquired from the system.

Specifying both DEBUG and REUSE SETTINGS would result in setting the system's PLSQL_COMPILER_FLAGS parameter to INTERPRETED, DEBUG. (See the section, "Error Handling in PL/SL Functions," later in this chapter.)

You cannot alter and recompile a built-in SQL function.

Dropping UDFs

A PL/SQL function can be dropped as any other Oracle object, as long as the user has sufficient privileges. The following syntax is all you need:

```
DROP FUNCTION [schema.]function_name;
```

If there are any user-defined statistics associated with the function, Oracle would drop the statistics as well. All objects within Oracle that reference the function would become invalid.

Removing a function from a package requires a bit more work. You will have to remove the definition of the function from the SPEC part of the package, and the body of the function from the BODY part of it. The package must then be recompiled with the OR REPLACE option. Alternatively, the whole package could be dropped and re-created.

Debugging PL/SQL Functions

The debugging of PL/SQL functions is hardly different from any PL/SQL stored procedure, and general guidelines of the unit debugging also apply. A PL/SQL procedure can be debugged either locally or remotely.

You have to make sure that you have sufficient privileges to conduct debugging. For Oracle 9i Release 1 or earlier, you should have the CREATE ANY PROCEDURE privilege. For Oracle 9i Release 2 and higher, you should have DEBUG ANY PROCEDURE and DEBUG CONNECT SESSION privileges.

The PL/SQL code must be compiled into INTERPRETED mode. Debugging in the NATIVE mode is not supported. The switch between the modes is set in the INIT.ORA configuration file.

The most effective way to debug a procedure is from within a PL/SQL IDE, such as TOAD (from Quest), SQL Station (from Computer Associates), RapidSQL (from Embarcadero Technologies), or PL/SQL Developer (from Allround Automation), to name just a few. These will allow you to set breakpoints and execute the procedure line by line while watching the changing values of your variables. You also could use Oracle's very own JDeveloper to do the job. If you are serious about PL/SQL development, you should get one of these tools.

If you prefer to do things the hard way, and the only tool you have at your disposal is SQL*Plus, there are two ways to debug from SQL*Plus: DBMS_OUTPUT and DBMS_DEBUG.

DBMS_OUTPUT

The easiest (and most time-consuming) way to debug your procedures is using Oracle's built-in DBMS_OUTPUT package.

Oracle's built-in packages were introduced in PL/SQL Version 2. They contain routines and functions implemented by Oracle Corporation. They are usually written in C and provide functionality that is hard (or impossible) to achieve with SQL or PL/SQL alone (writing/reading files, for example). There are virtually dozens of different packages, catering to developers and DBAs, and the number continues to grow with each new release.

From SQL*Plus, issue the following command:

```
SQL> set serveroutput on;
```

This would instruct the Oracle server to direct all the output to the SQL*Plus console. Next, you should embed the debugging statements into your PL/SQL code:

```
CREATE OR REPLACE FUNCTION fn_helloworld
    (arg1 IN VARCHAR2) RETURN VARCHAR2
IS
BEGIN
    DBMS_OUTPUT.ENABLE(10000);
    /* load DBMS_OUTPUT, set buffer to 10000 characters*/
    DBMS_OUTPUT.PUT_LINE('output from the procedure');
    RETURN arg1 || ' world!';
END fn_helloworld;
```

Here, the DBMS_OUTPUT.ENABLE command loads the package and reserves the output buffer of 10,000 characters. The DBMS_OUTPUT.PUT_LINE will output the string in the brackets into the output buffer. Now, let's test it in the SQL*Plus console:

```
declare
v_sentence VARCHAR(15);
begin
select
fn_helloworld('hello')into v_sentence
FROM dual;
end;
/

output from the procedure

PL/SQL procedure successfully completed.
```

You must use a PL/SQL anonymous block to test your function; the regular SQL SELECT statement will produce no DBMS_OUTPUT information.

If you accidentally forget to turn the serveroutput parameter on, the DBMS_OUTPUT will be accumulated in the buffer, and no output will be produced. The output will be displayed all at once as soon as the option is turned on, and a DBMS_OUTPUT.PUT_LINE command is executed.

DBMS_DEBUG

A more programmer-like way to debug PL/SQL stored procedures from SQL*Plus would be to use the DBMS_DEBUG package. To debug your code with this package, you would need two sessions: a *debugger* session and a *debugee* session. The former would run the PL/SQL code and the latter would set breakpoints, query variables, and so on.

You must set the PLSQL_DEBUG parameter to TRUE in the debugee session and then initialize the debugging session through the INITIALIZE function of the DBMS_DEBUG package. This function returns a unique debugging session ID that you feed into the ATTACH_SESSION function of the same package executed in the separate *debugger* session. You're ready to roll! You can set a breakpoint, print the value of the variables in the executing code, step to the next line, dump the program tack, and more.

There are a number of user custom packages that encapsulate the functionality of Oracle's built-in package DBMS_DEBUG, or you could come up with your own; and yet, in terms of developer productivity, you would be in the Stone Age compared to the users of the IDE.

The key to a successful debugging is repeatability of the error. This allows you to identify the source of an error and eventually understand the root cause. When you need to catch an intermittent error, it is very beneficial to know the exact values of all variables declared in the package at the time when the error occurred. To do this, you would need a dump for the function to capture the context; numerous commercial solutions exist, or you could devise your own.

Error Handling in PL/SQL Functions

There is not much difference in error handling inside the functions in comparison to procedures: you write an exception handler as a part of the function's body. There are a number of predefined exceptions supplied by Oracle, or you could declare your own. The following table lists some of the most common predefined exceptions.

PL/SQL Exception	Description
NO_DATA_FOUND	Most of the time, this error refers to the absence of data in a SELECT INTO query. There are other cases when this error could be encountered, such as reading past the end-of-file using a UTL_FILE package.
PROGRAM_ERROR	This error reports an internal PL/SQL problem. Your chances are slim to solve it by yourself; you may want to call Oracle support.
TOO_MANY_ROWS	Your SELECT INTO statement had returned more than one row. You may either rewrite the query or use a cursor instead.

PL/SQL Exception	Description
ZERO_DIVIDE	This error flags the illegal mathematical operation of division by zero.
OTHERS	This error category encompasses everything else. Use SQLERRM and SQLCODE to return a meaningful message to the calling routine.

Here is an example of predefined exception handling by a UDF:

```
CREATE OR REPLACE FUNCTION fn_dividebyzero
    (arg1 IN NUMBER) RETURN VARCHAR2
IS
BEGIN
    RETURN 5/arg1;
    EXCEPTION WHEN OTHERS THEN
    RETURN SQLERRM;
END fn_dividebyzero;
```

In this example the exception (if any) is handled, and the error message is returned as a field in the result set of the SQL query; the query completes successfully. In case the handling routine was not included with your function, the error message would be returned to the client application, and the query would fail.

Ensure that the RETURN clause is included in your exception-handling routine; otherwise, the SQL query fails, and the following error will be returned:

```
ORA-06503: PL/SQL: Function returned without value
```

Here is result of the execution:

```
SQL>select
fn_dividebyzero(0) result
from dual;

RESULT
-----------------------------------------------
ORA-01476: divisor is equal to zero
```

Within PL/SQL, you can define your very own exceptions that, for all practical purposes, would behave identically to the predefined ones. To define your exception, you must declare it in the body of your function and then order the PL/SQL compiler to initialize the exception with a PRAGMA EXCEPTION_ INIT directive. The error number assigned to the custom exception must be greater than minus 10,000,000; it cannot be a 0 or any positive number (except 1), and it should not use reserved numbers (such as 1403 for NO_DATA_FOUND).

Consider the following example:

```
CREATE OR REPLACE FUNCTION fn_dividebyzero
    (arg1 IN NUMBER) RETURN VARCHAR2
IS
divide_by_5 EXCEPTION;
PRAGMA EXCEPTION_INIT (divide_by_5, - 50000);
```

```
BEGIN
   IF arg1=5 THEN
   RAISE divide_by_5;
   END IF;
   RETURN 5/arg1;
   EXCEPTION
      WHEN divide_by_5 THEN
      RETURN 'divide by 5 error';
      WHEN OTHERS THEN
      RETURN SQLERRM;
END fn_dividebyzero;
```

Let's try it now with an input parameter of 5:

```
SQL> select
fn_dividebyzero(5) response
from dual;

RESPONSE
----------------------------------------
divide by 5 error
```

If, instead of handling the exception and returning your custom message, you decide to use predefined SQLERRM, you would get the following error:

```
SQL> select fn_dividebyzero(4) response from dual;

RESPONSE
-------------------------------------------------------------
ORA-50000:Message 50000 not found;product=RDBMS;facility=ORA
```

Alternatively, you could use the RAISE_APPLICATION_ERROR function in the calling application:

```
RAISE_APPLICATION_ERROR (error_number, message[, {TRUE | FALSE}]);
```

The error_number is a negative integer in the range –20,000 to 20,999, and message is a character string up to 2,048 bytes long. The third parameter is optional: TRUE means that the error is added to the stack of all previous errors, FALSE (the default value) specifies that the error should replace the stack. Here is our function, fn_dividebyzero, modified for this situation:

```
CREATE OR REPLACE FUNCTION fn_dividebyzero
(
   arg1 IN NUMBER
   ,arg2 IN NUMBER
)
RETURN VARCHAR2
IS
BEGIN
   IF arg1=0 THEN
      RAISE_APPLICATION_ERROR
         (- 20100,'divide by 0 error', TRUE);
   END IF;
   RETURN arg2/arg1;
   EXCEPTION
```

```
        WHEN OTHERS THEN
          RETURN SQLERRM;
    END fn_dividebyzero;
```

You would get the following error when executing the function:

```
SQL> select fn_dividebyzero(0,1) response from dual;

RESPONSE
----------------------------------------
ORA-20100: divide by 0 error
```

Either way, the handled exception will be returned as part of the result set of your SQL query, so you could handle it on the calling application side.

You also may choose to raise the exception to the calling routine and let it handle it. Or, you could simply raise an error when some of your very own conditions are met. In this case you would use a RAISE statement (for example, RAISE NO_DATA_FOUND).

Adding PL/SQL Functions to an Oracle Package

An Oracle package provides a convenient way to group functions and procedures into a single object, which could be easier to maintain. In addition, there are important features that can be exploited from within a package only.

We assume that you are already familiar with the concept and will discuss issues pertaining to the focus of this book. It is generally recommended to avoid using stand-alone procedures and functions.

Here is an example of a simple package, wrapping up our sample functions:

```
CREATE OR REPLACE PACKAGE pkg_functions
AUTHID CURRENT_USER
AS
FUNCTION fn_dividebyzero
(
    arg1 IN NUMBER, arg2 IN NUMBER
)
RETURN VARCHAR2;

FUNCTION fn_helloworld
(
    arg1 IN VARCHAR2
)
RETURN VARCHAR2;

PRAGMA RESTRICT_REFERENCES (fn_dividebyzero, WNDS);
divide_by_0 EXCEPTION;

PRAGMA EXCEPTION_INIT (divide_by_0, - 50000);
```

```
END pkg_functions;


CREATE OR REPLACE PACKAGE BODY pkg_functions AS
FUNCTION fn_dividebyzero
    (arg1 IN NUMBER, arg2 IN NUMBER) RETURN VARCHAR2
IS
BEGIN
 IF arg1=0 THEN
    RAISE divide_by_0;
 END IF;
 RETURN arg2/arg1;
EXCEPTION
      WHEN divide_by_0 THEN
          RETURN 'divide by 0 error';
      WHEN OTHERS THEN
          RETURN SQLERRM;
END fn_dividebyzero;

FUNCTION fn_helloworld
   (arg1 IN VARCHAR2)
RETURN VARCHAR2
IS
BEGIN
RETURN arg1 || ' world!';
END;
END pkg_functions;
```

So, now we have a single package, `pkg_functions`, that contains two functions we've used as examples throughout this chapter. Note that the PRAGMA function and variable declarations could be placed in the package spec; doing so would give them a global scope within the package. (They will not be accessible from outside the package.)

The calling conventions are the same, except that the package name must appear in front of the function name, as shown here:

```
SQL> select pkg_functions.fn_dividebyzero(5,2) response from dual;
RESPONSE
----------------
2.5
```

If the package resides in a schema other than your own, you must specify the schema name.

PL/SQL packages are loaded into the user global area (UGA) memory corresponding to the number of package variables and cursors in the package. This might cause potential problems because the memory increases linearly with the number of users. Oracle alleviates the negative impact of the packages loaded into a different UGA by introducing a PRAGMA SERIALLY_REUSABLE declaration in the package spec. For serially reusable packages the package global memory is kept in a small pool and reused for different users, rather than loading many different copies of the package variables, cursors, and so on.

Overloading

Oracle packages provide the only way to create an overloaded, stored function in Oracle RDBMS. (Another way would be declaring it in a PL/SQL anonymous block, but that would not be a reusable, *stored* function.) Consider the following example:

```
CREATE OR REPLACE PACKAGE pkg_functions
AS
    FUNCTION fn_helloworld(arg1 IN VARCHAR2)
        RETURN VARCHAR2;
    FUNCTION fn_helloworld
        (arg1 IN VARCHAR2, arg2 IN VARCHAR2)
        RETURN VARCHAR2;
END pkg_functions;
/
CREATE OR REPLACE PACKAGE BODY pkg_functions AS
FUNCTION fn_helloworld
    (arg1 IN VARCHAR2)
RETURN VARCHAR2
IS
BEGIN
 RETURN arg1 || ' world!';
END;

/* overloaded function, same name */
FUNCTION fn_helloworld
    (arg1 IN VARCHAR2, arg2 IN VARCHAR2)
RETURN VARCHAR2
IS
BEGIN
RETURN arg1 || ' world! ' || arg2;
END;

END pkg_functions;
```

The call to an overloaded function will be resolved based on the supplied arguments' data types and quantity:

```
SQL> SELECT
        pkg_functions.fn_helloworld ('Hello') response
     FROM DUAL;

RESPONSE
-------------------------------
Hello world!
```

Called again with different arguments, the function produces a quite different result:

```
SQL> SELECT
        pkg_functions.fn_helloworld ('Hello', '... Again') response
     FROM DUAL;

RESPONSE
-------------------------------
Hello world!...Again
```

As you can see, Oracle resolved the correct function based on the arguments passed to it, even though the package contains two functions with identical names.

There are certain restrictions for overloading the functions:

❑ The overloading is allowed only in packages; no stand-alone function or procedure can be overloaded.

❑ The functions (procedures) can differ by the mode of their arguments (that is, one is IN, and the other functions are OUT).

❑ The arguments of the overloaded functions can also be different in the data type only, and both data types are in the same family. (For example, one is REAL and another is INTEGER; they are both of the NUMBER family.)

❑ The arguments of one of the functions can be a subtype of another; or both are subtypes of the same type.

❑ If overloaded functions differ in RETURN argument data type only the following Note applies:

If you leave the signatures of the functions alone (i.e., their quantity and data types) but change the RETURN data type, Oracle will compile the package. Nevertheless, invoking the function would produce the following error: ORA-06553:PLS-307:too many declarations of 'FN_HELLOWORLD' match this call. This is rather confusing because Oracle should not have allowed the compiling of this package in the first place.

Using PL/SQL UDF in Transactions

The built-in SQL functions used in the context of transactions are subject to the same conditions as the SQL query within which they are used. With PL/SQL functions, the situation is slightly different: a SELECT statement executed within a PL/SQL function would be able to see changes to the schema committed from the beginning of the execution of the main SQL query that includes the function, while the main SQL query would not. This could lead to inconsistency issues in the heavy-load, multiuser environment and is something to keep in mind when debugging your PL/SQL functions.

Compiling PL/SQL Modules into Machine Code

Oracle introduced the capability to compile PL/SQL code into native machine code in its RDBMS version 9i. The PL/SQL code is translated into C code, which is then compiled using an external C-compiler, and Oracle supplies the make file.

Beginning with version 10g, all Oracle-supplied packages (that is, DBMS_OUTPUT) will be compiled into native code.

You may use any C compiler; though, obviously, your choice would be influenced by the platform on which you are running your Oracle RDBMS. The most popular compilers include gcc from GNU Foundation, Microsoft Visual C++, and Borland C++ Builder.

First, you must set up the compilation environment. Start by modifying the make file, spnc_makfile.mk, found in your $ORACLE_HOME/plsql directory, to adjust it to your computer configuration. The parameters within the make file that you need to change are shown in the following table.

Make File Parameter	Description
PLSQLHOME	$(ORACLE_HOME)/plsql/
PLSQLINCLUDE	$(PLSQLHOME)include/
PLSQLPUBLIC	$(PLSQLHOME)public/
CC	Native C compiler (for example, /usr/local/bin/gcc for UNIX)
LD	Native linker

The next step is setting PLSQL_COMPILER_FLAGS to NATIVE; the default value is INTERPRETED. These settings affect the entire Oracle database, so it must be set by DBA, and all the ramifications must be thoroughly pondered. Once the parameter is set to NATIVE, all new procedures created after this will be compiled into native code. The PL/SQL procedures compiled into interpretive mode will continue to run through PL/SQL VM.

```
SQL> connect sys/<password> as sysdba
Connected.
SQL> show parameter plsql_compiler_flags
NAME                                  TYPE        VALUE
------------------------------------- ----------- ----------------------
plsql_compiler_flags                  string      INTERPRETED, NON-DEBUG

SQL> ALTER SYSTEM SET plsql_compiler_flags = NATIVE SCOPE = both;
System altered.
SQL> show parameter plsql_compiler_flags
NAME                                  TYPE        VALUE
------------------------------------- ----------- ------------------
plsql_compiler_flags                  string      NATIVE, NON-DEBUG
```

There are a number of other parameters you may want to modify, some of which are listed in the following table:

Parameter	Description	Comments
PLSQL_NATIVE_LIBRARY_DIR	Provides the output directory where compiled objects will be stored.	
PLSQL_NATIVE_C_COMPILER	Provides the fully qualified path to the native C compiler; overrides the 'CC' entry in the spnc_makefile.mk makefile, which will be used if the parameter is not set.	Do not use any optimization hints for your compiler because doing so would greatly increase compilation time, while providing minuscule performance gains.

Table continued on following page

Parameter	Description	Comments
PLSQL_NATIVE_ LIBRARY_SUBDIR_ COUNT	Specifies the number of subdirectories for compiled objects output; helps to reduce the performance impact when compiling a large number of objects all at once.	The names of the subdirectories must start with [d]. A sequential numeric value will be added upon creating the directory (for example, d100, d324).
PLSQL_NATIVE_ LINKER	Provides the name of the linker to use. Overrides the 'LD' entry of the spnc_makefile.mk make file.	Default linker in the make file; the file contains platform-dependent entries.
PLSQL_NATIVE_ MAKE_FILE_NAME	Provides the fully qualified path to the spnc_makefile.mk make file.	Located in $ORACLE_HOME/ plsql/spnc_makefile.mk.
PLSQL_NATIVE_ MAKE_UTILITY	Provides the fully qualified path to a make utility.	Usually, /usr/bin/gmake.

To check your environment on UNIX/Linux OS, you may run the following command from the SQL*Plus utility:

```
SQL> show parameter native
NAME                                TYPE    VALUE
----------------------------------- ------  --------------------
plsql_native_c_compiler             string
plsql_native_library_dir            string  /u01/app/oracle2/test/9.2/plsql/lib
plsql_native_library_subdir_count   integer 0
plsql_native_linker                 string
plsql_native_make_file_name         string
/u01/app/oracle2/test/9.2/plsql/spnc_makefile.mk
plsql_native_make_utility           string /usr/bin/gmake
```

Now, assuming that all parameters are set correctly, we can compile our function into the native C code:

```
SQL> CREATE OR REPLACE FUNCTION fn_helloworld
        (arg1 IN VARCHAR2) RETURN VARCHAR2
2  IS
3  BEGIN
4     RETURN arg1 || ' world!';
5  END;
6  /
Function created.
```

Finally, we can execute it:

```
SQL> select fn_helloworld('hello') sentence from dual;

SENTENCE
----------------------------------
hello world!
```

If you have PL/SQL-stored procedures and functions compiled into INTERPRETED mode, you could convert them into NATIVE mode by issuing the following command: ALTER FUNCTION [schema.] function_name COMPILE. You cannot do the same for the natively compiled procedures and functions, as the DIANA tree (and the source code) for the natively compiled functions is discarded.

Native compilation on a Windows system could be tricky. Be sure you understand the internals of the make file and your particular compiler switches. You may need to install Cygwin utilities to make it work.

To check whether our function is INTERPRETED or NATIVE, we could execute the following query:

```
SQL>select param_value from user_stored_settings
        where param_name = 'plsql_compiler_flags'
        and object_name = 'FN_HELLOWORLD'
        and object_type = 'FUNCTION'

PARAM_VALUE
---------------------------
NATIVE, NON-DEBUG
```

When compiling the function (procedure, package) from a SQL*Plus interface you may take a look at the errors produced (if any) by issuing the SHOW ERRORS command at the SQL prompt.

As a note of caution, remember that compiling your functions and stored procedures into native machine code would not necessarily make them faster. Only computationally intensive processes would benefit from the native compilation, and even this advantage could be further hindered by context switching between native code and interpreted SQL.

Finding Information about UDFs in the RDBMS

The standard way of accessing this information is through an ISO/ANSI-mandated INFORMATION_SCHEMA. This schema is supposed to provide all metadata information about database objects like tables, views, procedures, and UDFs. A UDF is a database object. The database contains all the information that describes the function, its location, assigned privileges, and sometimes even the source code.

Oracle maintains a similar (at least in spirit) set of views, called the *Data Dictionary*. They are split into three broad categories: all objects, user objects, and DBA objects. Oracle conveniently prefixes the views' names with ALL_, USER_, and DBA_, respectively. The following table lists the Dictionary Views relevant to our purposes.

Data Dictionary View	Fields	
ALL_PROCEDURES	OWNER	VARCHAR2(30)
	OBJECT_NAME	VARCHAR2(30)
	PROCEDURE_NAME	VARCHAR2(30)
	AGGREGATE	VARCHAR2(3)
	PIPELINED	VARCHAR2(3)
	IMPLTYPEOWNER	VARCHAR2(30)
	IMPLTYPENAME	VARCHAR2(30)
	PARALLEL	VARCHAR2(3)
	INTERFACE	VARCHAR2(3)
	DETERMINISTIC	VARCHAR2(3)
	AUTHID	VARCHAR2(12)
DBA_PROCEDURES	OWNER	VARCHAR2(30)
	OBJECT_NAME	VARCHAR2(30)
	PROCEDURE_NAME	VARCHAR2(30)
	AGGREGATE	VARCHAR2(3)
	PIPELINED	VARCHAR2(3)
	IMPLTYPEOWNER	VARCHAR2(30)
	IMPLTYPENAME	VARCHAR2(30)
	PARALLEL	VARCHAR2(3)
	INTERFACE	VARCHAR2(3)
	DETERMINISTIC	VARCHAR2(3)
	AUTHID	VARCHAR2(12)
USER_PROCEDURES	OBJECT_NAME	VARCHAR2(30)
	PROCEDURE_NAME	VARCHAR2(30)
	AGGREGATE	VARCHAR2(3)
	PIPELINED	VARCHAR2(3)
	IMPLTYPEOWNER	VARCHAR2(30)
	IMPLTYPENAME	VARCHAR2(30)
	PARALLEL	VARCHAR2(3)
	INTERFACE	VARCHAR2(3)
	DETERMINISTIC	VARCHAR2(3)
	AUTHID	VARCHAR2(12)
ALL_SOURCE	OWNER	VARCHAR2(30)
	NAME	VARCHAR2(30)
	TYPE	VARCHAR2(12)
	LINE	NUMBER
	TEXT	VARCHAR2(4000)
DBA_SOURCE	OWNER	VARCHAR2(30)
	NAME	VARCHAR2(30)
	TYPE	VARCHAR2(12)
	LINE	NUMBER
	TEXT	VARCHAR2(4000)
USER_SOURCE	NAME	VARCHAR2(30)
	TYPE	VARCHAR2(12)
	LINE	NUMBER
	TEXT	VARCHAR2(4000)

Information about UDFs is stored in system tables and can be viewed either directly or through Data Dictionary views. For example, to see your `fn_helloworld` function's source code, you could use the following query:

```
SQL> select * from USER_SOURCE where name = 'FN_HELLOWORLD';

NAME              TYPE           LINE    TEXT
-------------     ---------      ----    -------------------------
FN_HELLOWORLD     FUNCTION       1       FUNCTION fn_helloworld
FN_HELLOWORLD     FUNCTION       2       (arg1 IN VARCHAR2) RETURN VARCHAR2 IS
FN_HELLOWORLD     FUNCTION       3       BEGIN
FN_HELLOWORLD     FUNCTION       4       RETURN  arg1 || ' world!';
FN_HELLOWORLD     FUNCTION       5       END;

5 rows selected.
```

The other views could yield insights into the type of the function (that is, whether it is DETERMINSTIC), ownership, and so on. Keep in mind that to query these views, you must have sufficient privileges.

One can easily spot similarities between the views, and for a good reason. They are extracting the data from the same base tables: OBJ\$, USER\$, and PROCEDUREINFO\$. To query these tables directly would be against Oracle recommendations, accepted programming practices, and common sense since there is no written or implied guarantee that the tables and their structures would remain constant. Also, giving the user permission to query these tables would constitute a potential security threat. These are for internal Oracle purposes and should be left alone for your own good.

Restrictions on Calling PL/SQL UDFs from SQL

Although using PL/SQL-coded functions from within PL/SQ code is simple, calling UDFs from a SQL query can be a tricky business. A custom function must adhere to a certain set of rules to be used with SQL.

We briefly discussed restrictions imposed by RDBMS vendors on UDFs in Chapter 1

If your function performs any Data Manipulation Language (DML) operations such as INSERT, UPDATE, or DELETE inside its body, it cannot be used within a SQL query. Consider the following function, fn_helloworld, introduced earlier in the chapter, and modified here, to illustrate this point:

```
CREATE TABLE TEST(ARGS VARCHAR2(50));

CREATE OR REPLACE FUNCTION fn_helloworld
    (arg1 IN VARCHAR2) RETURN VARCHAR2
IS
BEGIN
    INSERT INTO TEST VALUES(arg1);
    COMMIT;
    RETURN arg1 || ' world!';
END fn_helloworld;
```

There would be no complaints should the function be used from within a stored procedure or PL/SQL anonymous block, and everything would work as intended. Invoking the function from within a SQL statement, however, would result in an error, as shown here:

```
SELECT fn_helloworld('HELLO') FROM dual;
ERROR at line 1:
ORA-14552: cannot perform a DDL, commit or rollback inside a query or DML
```

Prior to Oracle 8i, it was a requirement to specify *Purity Level* using PRAGMA RESTRICT_REFERENCES shown in the following table.

Specification	Description
RNDS	Reads no database state.
RNSP	Reads no package state.
WNDS	Writes no database state.
WNPS	Writes no package state.
TRUST	Delays verification until run-time.

Omitting this instruction in your code would result in Oracle checking the function for compliance each and every time it is called from SQL statements. We strongly recommend using this PRAGMA, as it allows you to catch potential inconsistencies at debug time rather than having a surprise in your production environment.

> PRAGMA *identifies an instruction for the PL/SQL compiler within the PL/SQL code. For example* PRAGMA RESTRICT_REFERENCES *specifies the purity level, or* PRAGMA EXCEPTION_INIT *initializes custom exceptions.*

Here is the function fn_helloworld compiled as a part of a package:

```
CREATE OR REPLACE PACKAGE my_package AS
    FUNCTION fn_helloworld(arg1 VARCHAR2) RETURN VARCHAR2;
    PRAGMA RESTRICT_REFERENCES (fn_helloworld,WNDS);
END my_package;
/
CREATE OR REPLACE PACKAGE BODY my_package AS
FUNCTION fn_helloworld
    (arg1 IN VARCHAR2) RETURN VARCHAR2
IS
BEGIN
 INSERT INTO TEST VALUES(arg1);
 COMMIT;
    RETURN arg1 || ' world!';
END fn_helloworld;
END my_package;
```

Then, the following error would be reported during compile time:

```
PLS-00452: Subprogram 'FN_HELLOWORLD' violates its associated pragma.
```

To be called from SQL, a UDF must declare at least the WNDS purity level.

> *PRAGMA can only be used in Oracle packages — one more reason to consider packaging even custom functions and procedures.*

While specifying the purity level is no longer required, it is no longer needed. Rather, Oracle moved on to trusting the developers to implement the functions in a way that would allow their use within a SQL query. This does not mean that a rogue function will be allowed to be executed; an error will be returned if the function does not behave properly.

While a PL/SQL function must observe certain restrictions when called from a SQL query, there are no limitations on their usage in user-defined types, views, tables, other PL/SQL functions, and procedures. The restrictions are also lifted on the possible data types the function can return.

The PRAGMA RESTRICT_REFERENCES requirement was lifted because of the capability to call procedures written in Java or C, first introduced in version 8i. Oracle had no mechanisms checking the C or Java source code for PRAGMA compliance, and to ensure compatibility with the existing PRAGMA, a new keyword, TRUST, was introduced. It can be used for your PL/SQL functions and C or Java functions alike. Essentially, it turns off the RESTRICT_REFERENCES PRAGMA and is used for backward compatibility.

There are several other restrictions concerning PL/SQL functions called from a SQL query or a DML statement:

- ❑ The function must be a stored function, not one declared by a PL/SQL block.

- ❑ A UDF cannot issue COMMIT or ROLLBACK statements or create a SAVEPOINT.

- ❑ A UDF cannot issue ALTER SYSTEM or ALTER SESSION statements.

- ❑ A UDF must use standard SQL data types. PL/SQL data types (such as VARRAY, RECORD, and so on) are not allowed.

- ❑ A UDF called from a query (SELECT) statement or from a parallelized DML statement may not execute a DML statement or otherwise modify the database.

- ❑ A UDF called from a DML statement may not read or modify the particular table being modified by that DML statement.

Summary

By now you should have a good idea of the general concepts of creating UDFs on the Oracle RDBMS platform. A brief overview of the Oracle PL/SQL and 10g compilers was presented in order to give you a better idea of the workings of the native compilers upon which the UDFs will be created.

The connect and resource roles for work were touched upon in order to gain a better understanding of the permissions required to create a UDF. The basic UDF, as well as three specific types of hybrid functions (recursive, aggregate, and table-valued pipelined), were detailed. Additionally, we discussed in detail the steps and syntax required to create, alter, execute, and drop the UDFs onto the Oracle platform. To build on this knowledge, the concepts of debugging and error handling were explored, as well as packages, such as DBMS_OUTPUT and DBMS_DEBUG, that provide the developer with the tools necessary to create more robust and complete applications. Lastly, we discussed how to overload existing UDFs and also how to compile UDFs into machine code to provide a better understanding of the "total concept" of function development.

In Chapter 14 we will discuss the different aspects of creating functions within the IBM DB2 product line.

14

Creating User-Defined Functions with IBM DB2 UDB

IBM database users have had the ability to create custom functions since time immemorial (the mainframe days, that is). The stored procedures were introduced in the IBM DB2 390 V4 Release 4 back in 1994 with very basic rudimentary capabilities and no user-defined functions (UDFs). They were further enhanced in versions 5 and 6 (where the UDF first appeared). The IBM flagship database for Linux, UNIX, and Windows (also known as DB2 LUW) featured this capability as early as version 5, with quite a few restrictions (for example, it could not contain SQL statements). Version 7 added an ability to return a value with a SELECT statement, and 7.2 allowed for use of the compound statement. The latest incarnation (version 8.1 as of the writing of this book) added a number of significant improvements.

The stored routines started as C routines (also COBOL, REXX, ASSEMBLE, COMPJAVA, to name just a few) and evolved into SQL PL implementation, with a number of limitations significantly reduced and more options made available. A UDF is registered with the DB2 database in the SYSCAT. FUNCTIONS table through the execution of the CREATE FUNCTION statement. The UDFs are never part of SYSIBM schema and reside either in the SYSFUN schema, the SYSPROC schema, or in any custom schema created in the database.

For iSeries, the UDFs are registered with QSYS2.SYSFUNCS, and for z/OS they are registered in SYSIBM.SYSROUTINES.

While Oracle's (and Microsoft's) stored procedures and UDFs are virtually identical in their implementation, this is not the case for IBM DB2 UDB.

A stored procedure within an IBM database will always be translated into a C shared library with an additional component (DB2 bind file) that contains information about the actual executable library. When the procedure is executed, IBM DB2 UDB finds the package (the BIND component), loads the library, and executes it.

On the AS/400, the CREATE FUNCTION statement is interpreted into a C program with embedded SQL and located in the QTEMP library of the current, active job. The Create Structure Query Language ILE C (CRTSSQLCI) compiler produces an AS/400 service program object, which is then converted into a named library component. The entries are made into SYSROUTINES and SYSPARAMS catalog tables of the QSYS2 library.

A SQL UDF is purely a SQL PL construct; it is stored, compiled and executed within the SQL engine. As such, a UDF within IBM DB2 UDB is a purely database object, while a stored procedure (being part of the IBM DB2 since its mainframe days) could be considered an external object. Only so-called *external* functions are similar to the stored procedures in the DB2 UDB domain.

Using SQL PL it is possible to create perfectly valid functions for use within stored procedures and/or other functions that cannot be used within a SQL statement. For example, a reference data type or structured data type cannot be used as an input parameter data type or a return data type in a UDF prior to DB2 Version 7.1. Though it became possible to do so with the current version 8.1, such data types still cannot be used in the UDF invoked from a SQL statement.

Acquiring Permissions

Before you can create a function within an IBM DB2 UDB schema, some privileges must be granted. Having SYSADM or DBADM authority would do the job, though it gives the user many more privileges than the ordinary developer would require.

Granting CONTROL and SELECT privileges on any object (table, view, alias, functions in other schemas, and so on) used in the body of the UDF will allow for the proper compilation of the body of the function. Additionally, the developer must have the CREATEIN privilege on the schema where the function is to be created.

If the implicit or explicit schema does not exist, the user would need IMPLICIT_SCHEMA authority.

Access privileges assigned through a group would not be considered (unless it is a PUBLIC group). The access privileges for an aliased view or table are checked the moment the function is invoked. (It is also checked when the function is compiled.) Whenever the system detects insufficient privileges an error (SQLSTATE 42502) will be returned.

> It is possible to map a connection ID to an existing authorization ID to avoid the hassle of granting all these privileges separately.

Permissions also are required to execute UDFs. Anyone with DBADM authority is able to execute a function by default; for the rest of the users (with the exception of the function's definer) an EXECUTE privilege is required. The privilege is granted through the GRANT statement, and is revoked through the REVOKE statement. Just like the rest of the database objects, the WITH GRANT modifier also applies. Here is the syntax for the GRANT statement:

```
GRANT EXECUTE ON FUNCTION
      <schema_name>.<function_name> TO
      <group_name>|[PUBLIC]|[USER <user_name>]
[WITH GRANT OPTION]
```

Consider the following example:

```
GRANT EXECUTE ON FUNCTION db2admin.my_func() TO PUBLIC;
DB20000I  The SQL command completed successfully.
```

The REVOKE statement contains several additional keywords:

```
REVOKE EXECUTE ON FUNCTION
       <schema_name>.<function_name> TO
       <group_name>|[PUBLIC]|[USER <user_name>
[BY ALL] RESTRICT
```

Specifying BY ALL would result in revoking privileges from all named users who were explicitly granted this privilege, regardless of who had granted it. This constitutes the default behavior.

The RESTRICT keyword specifies that the operation must be aborted if there are dependent objects of the function (for example, tables, views, or other functions), and the loss of the privilege would prevent the definer (owner) of these objects from invoking the function. This keyword is required.

To revoke the privilege, the following command might be executed:

```
REVOKE EXECUTE ON FUNCTION db2admin.my_func()
FROM USER db2admin RESTRICT;
DB20000I  The SQL command completed successfully.
```

Alternatively, you may use the visual interface of the IBM DB2 UDB Control Center for the purpose of granting and revoking privileges.

Creating UDFs

IBM uses the SQL standard statement for creating its UDFs: CREATE FUNCTION. The statement could be used to create any of the seven different types of functions:

❑ *SQL Scalar UDF* — The function returns a single scalar value. Both the signature and the body of the function are implemented in pure SQL PL. Such a function is compiled, stored, and executed within a database. In a SQL query, it would be used in the SELECT clause.

❑ *SQL Table UDF* — The function returns a table and is used in the FROM clause of the regular SQL query. Its implementation follows the same rules as the SQL scalar UDF.

❑ *SQL Row UDF* — The function returns a single row. This type of function can only be used for transformation of structured data types. (That is, it accepts as an incoming parameter a structured, user-defined data type and returns its base types.) This type of function cannot be called from a SQL query.

❑ *External Scalar UDF* — The function returns a single scalar value. The body of the function is written in some general programming language (usually C/C++) and compiled for the host operating system (UNIX, Windows). It is then registered with the database alongside supplemental information: path to the executable function's signature (data types, quantity and order of parameters, and so on).

❑ *External Table UDF* — This, essentially, follows the same rules as the external scalar UDF, with the exception that it returns a table (so it should be used in the FROM clause).

❑ *OLE DB External Table UDF* — The data for the returned table is pumped from some OLE DB provider.

❑ *Sourced or Template UDF* — The body of the function is based on some other function (built-in, external, SQL or sourced) already registered with the database. The template function is essentially a signature, defining arguments to be passed and returned, but containing no executable code. The signature is then mapped to some source function within a federated (distributed) database. As such, it can only be registered with an application server designated as a main, federated server. While we are going to discuss this type of function in some detail, full coverage is beyond the scope of this book.

Creating Scalar UDFs

The syntax for creating the UDF in SQL PL is fairly standard, though some IBM-specific features can be confusing. Let's take a closer look at it:

```
CREATE FUNCTION <function_name>
          (arg1, arg2... argN)
          RETURNS [param <datatype>]
[SPECIFIC <specific_name>]
[LANGUAGE SQL]
[DETERMINISTIC][NOT DETERMINISTIC]
[NO EXTERNAL ACTION][EXTERNAL ACTION]
[READS SQL][CONTAINS SQL][NO SQL]
[STATIC DISPATCH]
[CALLED ON NULL INPUT]
[FEDERATED][NOT FEDERATED]
[INHERIT SPECIAL REGISTERS]
[PREDICATES <specification>]
     <function body>
RETURN <expression>
```

The signature of the function is in line with all the other vendors, with the notable absence of IN/OUT modifiers for parameters. All arguments for the DB2 UDB functions are IN by default.

IBM DB2 UDB stored procedures have IN, OUT, and INOUT modifiers for the arguments passed into the procedures.

The SPECIFIC keyword refers to overloading features in the IBM DB2 UDB. A function can be overloaded. That is, two or more functions with exactly the same name (but not signatures!) can peacefully co-exist within the same schema, as long as they have different specific names. The specific name can be up to 18 characters long, and cannot be used to invoke the function either from a SQL query or otherwise (though a specific name can be the same as the function name). Its only purpose is to uniquely identify a function within the current schema (for example, it must be used when dropping an overloaded UDF). See more on overloading in the section, "Overloading," later in this chapter. If the SPECIFIC keyword is omitted, the IBM DB2 UDB Database Manager automatically generates a unique identifier for the function in the format SQLyymmddhhmmssxxx (the "SQL" keyword, followed by a datestamp).

LANGUAGE SQL indicates that the procedure is written in SQL PL. This is the default option, to satisfy SQL99 requirements.

The DETERMINISTIC (or NOT DETERMINISTIC) clause refers to whether the function will return exactly the same results when fed identical input parameters. For more information on a function's determinism, see Chapter 2.

The clause NO EXTERNAL ACTION (or EXTERNAL ACTION) specifies whether the function can change the database state of an object not managed by the IBM DB2 UDF database manager (for example, writing/reading a file in the OS managed folders). Specifying NO EXTERNAL ACTION allows the RDBMS to perform some additional optimization to increase a function's performance.

The READS SQL and CONTAINS SQL optional clauses (compare to PRAGMA keyword of Oracle) restrict the UDF with regard to the type of the SQL statement. The first specifies that only SQL statements that do not modify data be allowed (that is, SELECT only; no UPDATE or DELETE statements are allowed). The CONTAINS SQL clause that says only statements that neither read nor modify SQL data can be executed within the function's Data Definition Language (DDL) and/or Data Control Language (DCL) statements is an example.

> **A function or method that contains SQL statements cannot be used in a parallel environment. The NO SQL option will prevent run-time errors.**

The STATIC DISPATCH clause specifies that, during invocation time, the function's name be resolved based on the static (declared) data types of the arguments. Not all editions of DB2 support this feature. Consult the vendor documentation for more information.

The CALLED ON NULL INPUT clause specifies that the function be called regardless of whether any of the input arguments is NULL. This implies that the function will be responsible for testing for NULL argument values.

The FEDERATED or NON FEDERATED clauses refer to the capability of the function to use federated objects inside its body. If the clause is omitted, the compiler determines whether the function contains federated objects, and marks it as FEDERATED or NOT FEDERATED, accordingly. A warning will be issued if any federated objects were employed.

Statements within the function that access federated objects may require additional authorization privileges.

The INHERITS SPECIAL REGISTERS clause indicates that the function will inherit all the special registers (also called "global variables" in Microsoft/Sybase lingo) from the invoking statement. For example, CURRENT SCHEMA of the SQL statement would be different from that of a UDF residing in a different schema. Inheriting the value from the invoking statement would make the values identical. For the function invoked from a SELECT statement, the values will be inherited from the environment at the moment the cursor was open.

The values of these special registers (changed inside the function) never get propagated back to the calling statement. Some special registers are never inherited because they reflect properties of the currently executed statements (for example, if the function resides on a remote server, its CURRENT TIME register would contain the time of that server, even though the calling statement resides in a different time zone).

The PREDICATES clause indicates that any predicate using this function could exploit the index extensions and can use the optional SELECTIVITY clause for its search conditions. The list of the predicate specification is {"=", "<", ">", ">=", "<=", "<>"}. If the clause is specified, the function also must include DETERMINISTIC and NO EXTERNAL ACTION clauses.

Let's try some examples of creating UDFs in SQL PL. The function `fn_helloworld` from Chapter 13 could be implemented, as follows, in the IBM DB2 UDB:

```
db2=> CREATE FUNCTION fn_helloworld
          (arg1 VARCHAR(15))
RETURNS VARCHAR(50)
     RETURN arg1 || ' world!'
DB20000I The SQL command completed successfully.
```

To try this function, you could issue the following statement from DB Command Line Processor:

```
Db2=> VALUES fn_helloworld('Hello ')
1
-----------------------------------
Hello world!
1 record(s) selected.
```

Alternatively, you could execute `SELECT fn_helloworld ('Hello') from SYSIBM.SYSDUMMY1` because the results would be identical.

> There is no such thing as a recursive function in DB2 UDB. The official explanation is because "such a function could not exist to be called." Neither Oracle nor Microsoft SQL Server 2000 has such a restriction.

DB2 UDB supports multiple `RETURN` statements that could be used for returning conditional values. If more than a single statement is used within the body of the function, `BEGIN ATOMIC` becomes a required clause to ensure that the function executes as a single unit.

For example, if the function detects that the parameter passed is `NULL`, then it returns an error. Otherwise, it returns the value, as shown here:

```
db2=> CREATE FUNCTION fn_helloworld
    (arg1 VARCHAR(15))
RETURNS VARCHAR(50)
DETERMINISTIC NO EXTERNAL ACTION
BEGIN ATOMIC
IF arg1 IS NULL
THEN
     RETURN 'IS NULL error!;
ELSE
     RETURN arg1 || ' world!';
END IF;
END
DB20000I The SQL command completed successfully.
```

Error handling is discussed in more detail in the section "Error Handling in UDFs," later in this chapter.

Creating Table UDFs

The basic syntax of the creating a table-valued function is the same as for the scalar UDFs with the exception of the return type, which is a table structure. The table function is the only type of function that can be used in the `FROM` clause of the SQL statement. Consider the following example:

```
CREATE FUNCTION <function_name>
          (arg1, arg2... argN)
          RETURNS [table]
[SPECIFIC <specific_name>]
[LANGUAGE SQL]
[DETERMINISTIC][NOT DETERMINISTIC]
[NO EXTERNAL ACTION][EXTERNAL ACTION]
[READS SQL][CONTAINS SQL]
[STATIC DISPATCH]
[CALLED ON NULL INPUT]
[FEDERATED][NOT FEDERATED]
[INHERIT SPECIAL REGISTERS]
     <function body>
RETURN <expression>
```

The table UDFs in IBM DB2 UDB (and Microsoft SQL Server 2000, for that matter) are more transparent than in Oracle and behave more like a regular table for the selection purposes. Here is the example we used while creating a table UDF in Oracle RDBMS:

```
CREATE TABLE SCOUTS
(
        FIRST_NAME  VARCHAR (25),
        LAST_NAME   VARCHAR (25)
);
INSERT INTO scouts VALUES ('Alex', 'Kriegel');
INSERT INTO scouts VALUES ('Phillip', 'Windsor');
INSERT INTO scouts VALUES ('Michael', 'DeVry');
```

To use this table with a table UDF, we could create the following function:

```
CREATE FUNCTION get_names ()
    RETURNS TABLE
          (first_name VARCHAR(25)
          , last_name VARCHAR(25))
SPECIFIC get_all_names
RETURN
    SELECT * FROM scouts

DB20000I The SQL command completed successfully.
```

Now, we can call upon this function using the following syntax:

```
db2=> SELECT * FROM TABLE(get_names()) as ALL_NAMES

FIRST_NAME          LAST_NAME
-----------------   ----------------------
Alex                Kriegel
Phillip             Windsor
Michael             DeVry

     3 record(s) selected.
```

Note that the alias (ALL_NAMES) is required for the query to work properly. Also, the parentheses must be specified with the function's name, even though the function does not accept any arguments. The return result of the function must be explicitly cast to the TABLE type (even though the return type of the function is a TABLE).

Now, DB2 UDB allows you to specify input parameters that could make the returned table much more selective. Let's say that we would like our function to perform a search and return only records satisfying our criteria. Here is one way to do it:

```
CREATE FUNCTION get_names(fname VARCHAR(25))
    RETURNS TABLE
        (first_name VARCHAR(25)
        , last_name VARCHAR(25))
SPECIFIC get_specific_name
RETURN
    SELECT * FROM scouts
        WHERE first_name = fname

DB20000I The SQL command completed successfully.
```

This function would return only records from the SCOUTS table where the FIRST_NAME column is equal to the one passed in as an argument. Let's check it:

```
db2=> SELECT * FROM TABLE(get_names('Alex')) as ALL_NAMES
FIRST_NAME          LAST_NAME
-----------------   ----------------------
Alex                Kriegel

    1 record(s) selected.
```

As we expected, only matching records are returned.

The table UDF acts as a view, with an additional advantage of the ability to use procedural SQL PL inside (views could use pure SQL only, though a UDF could alleviate the deficiency to a certain extent).

You may have noticed that the two table functions just created have exactly the same name. Nevertheless, IBM DB2 UDB has no difficulties differentiating between them and calling the correct version. This is because IBM DB2 UDB supports overloading. See the section "Overloading" later in this chapter.

Creating Sourced UDFs

Now we are going to take a closer look at the uniquely IBM feature of sourced functions. The syntax for creating sourced functions is fairly straightforward:

```
CREATE FUNCTION [schema_name.]function_name
    ([argument_name] data_type)
    RETURNS data_type
[SPECIFIC] name
SOURCE [schema_name]
    [function_name]
    [specific_name]
    [function_name (data_type)]
```

The only difference in the standard UDF is that the function signature does not have to specify named parameters, only their data types. The input must be compatible with the source function input parameters — both in the count and the data types.

The RETURNS clause must specify the return data type that is compatible with the return data type of the function in the SOURCE clause. For example, if the source function's return data type is DOUBLE, you cannot specify VARCHAR for your UDF, though the INTEGER data type is acceptable.

The SOURCE clause refers to the actual function that implements the logic. You must define the source function either by name (must be unique), by specific name (unique by default), or by name and input argument data types.

If a nonexistent schema is specified as a part of the CREATE FUNCTION statement, the schema will be created, provided that you have an IMPLICIT_SCHEMA authority.

The definer of the UDF must have authority to execute the source function; the source function must reside in the current schema or any schema accessible to the definer.

For example, you've decided to create an improved built-in function for the calculation of the square root of a number that would accept an integer only, as shown here:

```
CREATE FUNCTION int_sqrt(INTEGER)
     RETURNS INTEGER
     SOURCE SQRT
DB20000I  The SQL command completed successfully.
```

Here is the result of the query:

```
db2 => SELECT
          SQRT(9.5) AS SOURCE_SQRT
          ,INT_SQRT(9) AS NEW_SQRT
FROM SYSIBM.SYSDUMMY1

SOURCE_SQRT                 NEW_SQRT
------------------------ -----------
  +3.08220700148449E+000          3

  1 record(s) selected.
```

Calling this function with a DOUBLE input argument would result in an error:

```
SQL0440N No authorized routine named "INT_SQRT" of type "FUNCTION" having
compatible arguments was found. SQLSTATE=42884
```

Because the new UDF will inherit all of its attributes from the source function, any clause you would normally use with the CREATE FUNCTION statement (for example, LANGUAGE..., EXTERNAL, DETERMINISTIC, and so on) will be invalid, and an error will be generated upon violation of this rule.

The data types of the arguments supplied for the UDF must be compatible with the source data types; this refers both to the input and return parameters. The IBM DB2 UDB will attempt an implicit conversion of the data types, and would return an error at compile time if they were found incompatible.

Creating Template UDFs

One of the most intriguing features of the IBMDB2 UDB is the ability to create a template function that is mapped on a remote function residing in a federated heterogeneous database (such as Oracle or Microsoft SQL Server). You cannot use this in a non-federated database installation. The template serves as a stub that relegates the call to the source function in the remote database, while making it appear to be a locally defined function for all practical purposes.

The syntax is similar to that of a regular, sourced function:

```
CREATE FUNCTION [schema_name.]function_name
           ([argument_name] data_type)
          RETURNS data_type
[SPECIFIC] name
AS TEMPLATE
[DETERMINISTIC]|[NOT DETERMINISTIC]
[NO EXTERNAL ACTION]|[EXTERNAL ACTION]
```

A UDF created as a template must be mapped before it could ever be invoked either from a SQL statement or some other function. The CREATE FUNCTION MAPPING statement is used to create a mapping between the template and the source (the actual implementation in the federated database).

A detailed discussion of the UDFs in federated database systems is beyond the scope of this book.

Overriding with Sourced UDFs

It is also possible to override the existing built-in function through creating a *sourced* UDF. Overriding would create a function with exactly the same name and signature as an existing built-in function, but the logic could be different.

For example, we could create a new function called COUNT. Normally, this is a built-in function that accepts a column name (or single integer)and returns the count of the rows in a SELECT statement. Here we are going to force this function to return a DOUBLE value that is the square root of the number of rows:

```
db2=> CREATE FUNCTION COUNT
          (INTEGER)
      RETURNS DOUBLE
      SOURCE SQRT(DOUBLE)

DB20000I  The SQL command completed successfully.
```

Now, we have two COUNT functions: one built-in and another just a moniker for the SQRT function (a built-in function that calculates the square root of the argument).

To be absolutely sure what version you are calling, you must use a fully qualified path. Assuming that you have created the overriding version of COUNT (admittedly, of limited use), you could execute the following query against the IBM DB2 UDB database:

```
SELECT
          count(1)              as ROWS_COUNT
          ,db2admin.COUNT(100) as SQUARE_ROOT
FROM sysibm.sysdummy1

ROWS_COUNT      SQUARE_ROOT
----------      ---------------
         1                   10
1 record(s) selected.
```

The same statement called without the schema would return 1 for both functions because the original built-in version will be called. This might not be the behavior you would see on your system. The IBM DB2 UDB manager resolves the name of a function in a sequence specified in the database SQL path parameter. If the schema where the overriding function resides comes before the system schemas, the database manager will choose the UDF over the built-in one. Any application that uses an unqualified name of the function will be utilizing the overridden version, even though the original one was required. This affects both dynamic statements and the rebound statements.

The CURRENT PATH special register will return information about the SQL path set for the session. Usually, you'll see something like this: SYSIBM, SYSFUNC, SYSPROC, <your_schema>.

Altering UDFs

Altering a function in IBM DB2 UDB means changing the attributes of the existing function. This is quite unlike Oracle's or Microsoft SQL Server's ALTER FUNCTION statement, which alters the body of the function or its signature. The attributes changed with this statement pertain to the way the function is treated in the IBM DB2 UDB environment.

Here is the syntax:

```
ALTER FUNCTION <function_name>
[EXTERNAL NAME <function_name>|<identifier>]
[FENCED][NOT FENCED]
[THREADSAFE][NOT THREADSAFE]
```

This statement is relevant only for functions created in a language other than SQL and is inapplicable to the subject of this chapter. Trying to execute ALTER FUNCTION for any SQL-coded UDF would result in an error:

```
SQL0658N The object <schema>.<function_name> cannot be explicitly dropped or
altered. SQLSTATE=42917
```

Instead of the function's name, you also could use its specific name.

Dropping UDFs

Virtually every object created in an RDBMS could be dropped with a universal DROP statement followed by the object's type. In the case of the UDFs, the statement would look like the following:

```
DROP FUNCTION [schema].<function_name>
```

Without the [SCHEMA] qualifier, the IBM DB2 UDB would search for the specified function within the current schema (actually, within schemas specified in the SQL PATH environmental variable). Of course, whoever issues the DROP command must have sufficient privileges to do so; the definer of the function has this privilege by default.

To drop a function by name, you should specify an unambiguous name. If the function is unique and has no objects relying on it, the following syntax would do the job:

```
db2 => drop function fn_helloworld
DB20000I  The SQL command completed successfully.
```

When there are objects in the database that depend on your function, it becomes harder to drop the function—the dependent objects must be altered or dropped first. Consider the following example:

```
db2=> CREATE FUNCTION fn_helloagain
         (arg1 VARCHAR(25))
         RETURNS VARCHAR(50)
         SPECIFIC helloagain
         RETURN fn_helloworld('Hello') || arg1

DB20000I  The SQL command completed successfully.
db2=> VALUES fn_helloagain(' Again')
1
--------------------
Hello, world Again
db2 => drop function fn_helloworld
SQL0478N  DROP or REVOKE on object type "FUNCTION" cannot be processed because
there is an object "DB2ADMIN.HELLOAGAIN", of type "FUNCTION", which
depends on it.  SQLSTATE=42893
```

The function fn_helloagain must be dropped first in order for this statement to succeed. The same process is applicable to the sourced functions.

You could always drop the function (assuming that you have sufficient authority and that the function has no dependencies) using the specific name of the function. The syntax is very simple:

```
db2 => drop specific function SQL040322145500200
DB20000I  The SQL command completed successfully.
```

If you did not include the SPECIFIC clause when creating your function, or simply forgot the name, you could query the catalog view SYSCAT.ROUTINES to find it. Refer to the section "Finding Information about UDFs in the Database" later in this chapter.

Dropping overloaded functions could be somewhat tricky. If you do not use a specific name, the DB2 would not know which version of the identically named function to drop. Specifying input argument data types would help in this case. To drop the UDF COUNT (created earlier in this chapter), you could use the following syntax:

```
db2=> DROP FUNCTION COUNT(INTEGER)
DB20000I  The SQL command completed successfully.
```

You cannot DROP a built-in function. This example was successful only because we created an over-loaded, sourced version earlier.

Debugging UDFs

You can debug your functions the old-fashioned way—by inserting dozens of debug messages inside your function's body and either displaying them or writing them into some debug log.

The more effective way, though, would be using some tool like IBM's very own DB2 Development Center, or third-party utilities such as Quest Central from Quest Software.

The IBM DB2 Development Center provides an integrated environment for building, testing, and deploying IBM DB2 UDB solutions. The built-in SQL Debugger (IBM-Distributed Debugger for Java) allows you to set up breakpoints, step through the code line-by-line while monitoring call stack and variables values.

Here is a brief tutorial on using the IBM DB2 UDB Development Center for UDF debugging using the Wizard. (Of course, you could choose to edit an existing project or create your function manually.) After starting the application (and, being written in Java, its GUI will be virtually identical for every platform on which you choose to run it), you would be asked to create/open a project, add a database connection, and select the type of object to create (see Figure 14-1).

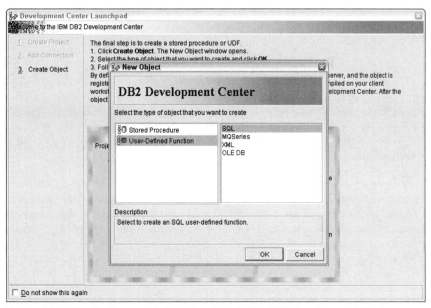

Figure 14-1. Creating a user-defined function in the DB2 Development Center.

For the purposes of this chapter, we are going to select UDF for SQL (other types will be discussed later in the book). Click OK. The Wizard will prompt you for the name. Supply the name of your future function, and click Next. The Wizard will display the function definition screen (see Figure 14-2). Select all

461

appropriate options and click Next. The SQL Assist screen displayed next will help you assemble the SQL statements for your function. Once you're satisfied with your main SELECT statement, click OK and select values for your return data type.

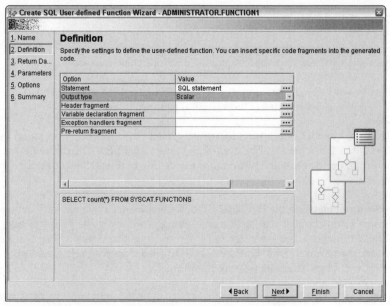

Figure 14-2. Developing the initial framework of your UDF.

The next screen will ask for input parameters and their properties (see Figure 14-3). Click Next.

The next screen will prompt you to add a specific name by which the function will be known across your schema and database (see information earlier in the chapter). After you click the Finish button, you will be presented with the Project view, which would now include your function. If a function with the same name and signature were already in the database, the IBM DB2 UDB would ask whether you wish to drop the existing function.

Debugger views provide you with Breakpoint View, Call Stack View, and Variables View. Before the function can be debugged it must be built for debugging. Use the Build For Debug toolbar button. After that you can run the function/procedure in debug mode, set the breakpoint, watch/change local variables, and monitor the program stack. (See Chapter 2 for information on the program stack.)

The IBM DB2 Development Center is one of the most advanced integrated environments among the RDBMS vendors, comparable only to the Microsoft SQL Server Query Analyzer. Both Oracle and Sybase rely mostly on third-party tools for development and debugging. The same goes for MySQL and PostgreSQL.

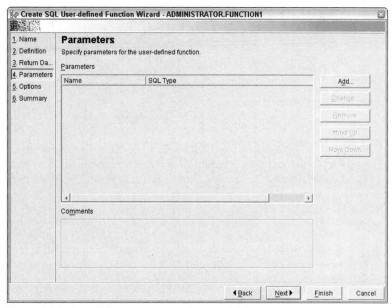

Figure 14-3. Specifying parameters for your UDF.

Error Handling in UDFs

Every error that occurred while a stored procedure is executed must be handled; this goes double for the UDFs. IBM DB2 UDB provides a framework of conditions and predefined exception handlers for this purpose, somewhat similar to Oracle's EXCEPTION handlers. Unfortunately, in the current release of IBM DB2 UDB (also known as DB2 LUW — DB2 for Linux, UNIX, and Windows), they can only be used with the SQL PL-stored procedures. This leaves the only option of anticipating the exception and handling it with custom error handling.

Unlike its LUW cousin, the IBM DB2 for AS/400 can make full use of the exception handlers.

IBM DB2 UDB provides two special registers, SQLCODE and SQLSTATE, which are returned after the execution of a routine. These might or might not represent errors. In a stored procedure you could declare and use variables that would contain respective values and use them to create a structured error handler. This is not so in the UDF; the SQLSTATE and SQLCODE will be set (and returned to the calling procedure), but you cannot access them within the function itself.

Here is an IBM DB2 UDB version of a "Divide By Zero" function that relies on the IBM DB2 UDB to return a predefined error message to the calling routine without any attempt to handle it:

```
db2=> CREATE FUNCTION fn_dividebyzero
        (
              arg1 INTEGER
            ,arg2 INTEGER
        )
        RETURNS INTEGER
DETERMINISTIC NO EXTERNAL ACTION
```

```
BEGIN ATOMIC
     RETURN arg1/arg2;
END

DB20000I The SQL command completed successfully.
db2=> VALUES fn_dividebyzero(5,0)
1
-------------------
SQL0801N Division by zero was attempted. SQLSTATE=22012
```

In many cases this is what is needed, and the client application that calls this function will handle the error by itself. If you decide to handle the error inside the function itself, you may want to raise a custom error, or handle the condition yourself without raising an error. The following example raises a custom error:

```
db2=> CREATE FUNCTION fn_dividebyzero
          (
                  arg1 INTEGER
                 ,arg2 INTEGER
          )
          RETURNS INTEGER
DETERMINISTIC NO EXTERNAL ACTION
BEGIN ATOMIC
     IF arg2 = 0 THEN
     SIGNAL SQLSTATE '90000'
     SET MESSAGE_TEXT = 'Error: Invalid data for second argument';
   END IF;
     RETURN arg1/arg2
END
DB20000I The SQL command completed successfully.
db2=> VALUES fn_dividebyzero(5,0)
1
-------------------
SQL0438N Application raised error with diagnostic text
"Error: Invalid data for second argument'.
SQLSTATE=90000
```

The SQLCODE = SQL0438N signifies that the error is a custom one, raised through the RAISE_ERROR function (an internal function called by the SIGNAL statement).

> The length of your custom error message set in the **MESSAGE_TEXT** should not exceed 70 characters. If it does, the message will be truncated to be exactly 70 characters in length.

Receiving SQLSTATE= 90000 (your own custom number, as opposed to the system-defined one) will indicate that some specific action should be taken to correct the error. This allows you to add your own custom definitions to validate data in the UDF.

SQLCODE and SQLSTATE

Every function or procedure executed by IBM DB2 UDB server sets two important values: SQLCODE and SQLSTATE. The first represents an integer value. It follows certain rules, though: a 0 means successful completion, positive numbers mean a warning, and negative numbers indicate an error. The messages associated with the SQLCODE numbers are always vendor-specific.

The second value is a five-digit numeric string that is defined in the ISO/ANSI SQL92 standard. It is a structured flag, where each position has significance. The first two digits (also known as SQLSTATE class code) indicate the status of the procedure (function) completion: 00 for success, 01 for a warning, and 02 indicates the "not found" condition. Everything else is considered an error.

These two values are set after each statement execution and must be accessed immediately for relevant information because each subsequent statement will change the values.

For greater portability of your code, it is recommended to use SQLSTATE instead of SQLCODE, which is vendor-specific (with some rare exceptions).

Using Error Messages

Every error and/or warning returned by IBM DB2 UDB is accompanied by a unique identifier, which is three letters (indicating the source of the error), followed by a four- or five-digit number and a suffix. The prefixes are listed in the following table, along with a brief description.

Message Prefix	Description
ADM	Denotes messages generated by many DB2 components. These messages are written in the Administration Notification log file.
AMI	Denotes messages generated by the MQ Application Messaging Interface.
ASN	Denotes messages generated by DB2 replication.
AUD	Denotes messages generated by the DB2 Audit facility.
CCA	Denotes messages generated by the Client Configuration Assistant.
CLI	Denotes messages generated by Call Level Interface.
DBA	Denotes messages generated by the Database Administration tools.
DBI	Denotes messages generated by installation and configuration.
DBT	Denotes messages generated by the Database tools.
DB2	Denotes messages generated by the command-line processor.
DIA	Denotes messages generated by many DB2 components. These messages are written in the diagnostics log file db2diag.log.
DLFM	Denotes messages generated by the Data Links File Manager.
DQP	Denotes messages generated by the Query Patroller.

Table continued on following page

Message Prefix	Description
DWC	Denotes messages generated by the Data Warehouse Center.
GOV	Denotes messages generated by the DB2 governor utility.
GSE	Denotes messages generated by the DB2 Spatial Extender.
ICC	Denotes messages generated by the Information Catalog Center.
MQL	Denotes messages generated by the MQ Listener.
SAT	Denotes messages generated in a satellite environment.
SPM	Denotes messages generated by the sync point manager.
SQL	Denotes messages generated by the database manager when a warning or error condition has been detected.

The suffix adds some overtones to the message code:

❑   The letter "C" indicates a severe message (such as a server crash).

❑   The letter "E" indicates an urgent message.

❑   The letter "N" indicates an error.

❑   The letter "W" indicates a warning.

❑   The letter "I" indicates an informational message.

Although the preceding table lists the most common message prefixes, it does not list all possible ones. Refer to IBM documentation whenever in doubt.

The help for a specific error message could be accessed through a command-line prompt as follows:

```
db2 => ? SQL0000
SQL0000W Statement processing was successful.
Explanation:
The SQL statement executed successfully, unless a warning
condition occurred.
User Response:
Check SQLWARN0 to ensure that it is blank.  If it is blank, the statement executed
successfully.  If it is not blank, a warning condition exists. Check the other
warning indicators to determine the particular warning condition.  For example, if
SQLWARN1 is not blank, a string was truncated.
Refer to the Application Development Guide .
sqlcode :  0
sqlstate : 00000,01003,01004,01503,01504,01506,1509,01517
```

In general, the format for querying is <blank><message identifier>. The query is case-insensitive, and a suffix is not required. Some of the messages you are most likely to encounter while developing UDFs are listed in the following table:

Message Identifier	SQLCODE	SQLSTATE	Message Description	Resolution
SQL0017N	-17	42632	The SQL function or method either does not contain a RETURN statement, or the function or method did not end with the execution of a RETURN statement.	Ensure that your function has a RETURN statement, and that this statement is executed.
SQL0057N	-57	42631	A RETURN statement is specified in the SQL function or method without a value to return.	Ensure that the RETURN statement is followed by a value of the specified function's signature data type.
SQL0097N	-97	42601	SQL functions do not support variables or parameters of LONG VARCHAR or LONGVARGRAPHIC data types.	Do not use any of these in your function's body or signature. Sized VARGRAPHIC and sized VARCHAR data type can be substituted for LONG VARGRAPHIC and LONG VARCHAR, respectively.
SQL0123N	-123	42601	One or more of the input parameters of the function is defined as a constant, but a variable (for example, the output of a function) is supplied.	Ensure that you use constants where they are required.
SQL0138N	-138	22011	The second or third argument of the SUBSTR function is out of range.	If you use the built-in SUBST function in the body (or signature) of your UDF, ensure that you supply all of the right arguments.
SQL0158N	-158	42811	The number of columns specified for the TABLE function is not the same as the number of columns in the resulting table.	Ensure that the returned table's columns match those of the table defined in the signature of the UDF.

Table continued on following page

Message Identifier	SQLCODE	SQLSTATE	Message Description	Resolution
SQL0170N	-170	42605	The number of arguments for the scalar function is wrong.	Supply the correct number of input arguments.
SQL0172N	-172	42601	The function name used in your SQL statement is either misspelled, requires additional qualifiers (like a schema name), or does not exist.	Ensure that the function is registered within the database and that you supply a fully qualified name for it.
SQL0191N	-191	22504	The database detected a fragmented multi-byte character (a solution for non-Latin characters in the pre-Unicode era). In the Unicode database, a common cause of this could be that the start or length of a UTF-8 string is incorrect.	It could happen with built-in functions (like SUBSTR or TRANSLATE); for your own functions ensure that you handle your data properly.
SQL0208N	-208	42707	The ORDER BY clause is not valid because the column name is not part of the resulting table.	Columns specified in the SELECT and ORDER BY lists of the query must match.
SQL0348N	-348	428F9	A sequence expression cannot be used in the UDF signature.	Remove CURRVAL, NEXTVAL, and such for the default values of your input parameters.
SQL0370N	-370	42601	You have attempted to create a UDF with an unnamed parameter in the signature of the function.	All parameters for functions defined as LANGUAGE SQL must be named.

Message Identifier	SQLCODE	SQLSTATE	Message Description	Resolution
SQL0374N	−374	428C2	Some of the optional clauses were required because the function's body attempt undertake some specific action.	The following situations may be the cause of this error. NOT DETERMINISTIC must be specified if either of the following conditions apply within the body of the function: a function that has the NOT DETERMINISTIC property is called or a special register (unary function) is accessed. READS SQL DATA must be specified if the body of the function defined with LANGUAGE SQL contains a subselect or if it calls a function that can read SQL data. EXTERNAL ACTION must be specified if the body of the function defined with LANGUAGE SQL calls a function that has the EXTERNAL ACTION property.
SQL0430N	−430	38503	A UDF has abnormally terminated.	There is something wrong with the function. More debugging is required.
SQL0431N	−431	38504	Client application has interrupted the UDF's execution.	Could indicate some problem with the function or with the client application.
SQL0439N	−439	428A0	A source function (that is, one that provides implementation for the SOURCED function) has returned an error.	Examine the error message for clues. The error might be with the source UDF, or, in case of a built-in, with the environment setup.

Table continued on following page

Message Identifier	SQLCODE	SQLSTATE	Message Description	Resolution
SQL0448N	–448	54023	A maximum number of 90 input parameters was exceeded for the UDF.	Reduce the number of input parameters.
SQL0457N	–457	42939	You have attempted to use a reserved word or character for your function name	Ensure that you do *not* use any of the following in your function's name: "=","<",">",">=","<=","&=","&>","&<", "!=","!>","!<","<>"; SOME, ANY, ALL, NOT, AND, OR, BETWEEN, NULL, LIKE, EXISTS, IN, UNIQUE, OVERLAPS, SIMILAR, or MATCH.
SQL0465N	–465	58032	Indicates an internal error.	You have a problem not specifically related to DB2 UDB: memory glitch, hard-drive, file system corruption, nuclear explosion— all could produce this error. If everything else fails, try calling IBM.
SQL0586N	–586	42907	The length of the data contained in a special CURRENT FUNCTION PATH register has exceeded 254 characters.	Move the function to a different schema, or consider shorter names for your database objects.
SQL1022C	–1022	57011	There was not enough memory on the server to load your function.	The memory size allocated to the UDF is controlled by udf_mem_sz parameter; it needs to be adjusted.

Message Identifier	SQLCODE	SQLSTATE	Message Description	Resolution
SQL1180N	−1180	42724	The function has caused an OLE (ActiveX) error.	This is a MS Windows-specific problem. OLE objects could be utilized by external functions, and they may throw errors. Analyze the error message and the returned OLE code for possible problems. You may, for example, encounter an `0x80020005` error which is "`Type Mismatch,`" or an `0x80020006` error which is "`specified method name does not exist.`"

If your application returns a `SQLCODE` of -30081, it means that a communications error has been detected. This refers to communication between client and server (even if both reside on the same computer). It is not your SQL PL code.

Overloading

IBM DB2 UDB supports overloading for its UDFs. Unlike in Oracle, the functions can only be overloaded based on differences in the signature (that is, only input parameters count).

It may seem that the `SPECIFIC` clause specified at the time the UDF is created could provide some overloading solution. This is not the case. A specific name is nothing more that a unique label to identify the object in the schema (if the `SPECIFIC` clause is not used, the database manager assigns its own unique identifier). You can neither invoke the function by its specific name nor pass any parameters to it. The specific name is only useful for dropping, altering, sourcing, or commenting on the function.

Consider the example of the simple scalar function from earlier in this chapter. It accepts one argument of `VARCHAR(15)` type and returns a value of the `VARCHAR(50)` type. It is possible to create a function with the identical name that accepts `INTEGER` and returns `VARCHAR`, but any attempt to create an additional function with exactly the same name that accepts `VARCHAR(15)` and returns `INTEGER` would fail with the following error message:

```
db2=> CREATE FUNCTION fn_helloworld
        (arg1 VARCHAR(15))
RETURNS INTEGER
    RETURN LENGTH(LTRIM(RTRIM(arg1)))
```

```
SQL0454N The signature provided in the definition for routine"DB2ADMIN.FUNC1"
matches the signature of some other routine that already exists in the schema or
for the type.
LINE NUMBER=1. SQLSTATE=42723
```

However, the number of input parameters does count toward determining the uniqueness of the function. The following function will be compiled with IBM DB2 UDB without any complaints:

```
db2=> CREATE FUNCTION fn_helloworld
            (
                arg1 VARCHAR(15)
              ,arg2 VARCHAR(15)
            )
RETURNS VARCHAR(30)
      RETURN arg1 || ' ' || arg2

DB20000I The SQL command completed successfully.
```

The maximum number of input arguments allowed for the UDFs in IBM DB2 UDB v8.1 is 90. An attempt to add more than this number would result in the following SQL error being returned:

```
SQL0448N Error in defining routine"DB2ADMIN.FN_HELLOWORLD". The maximum number of
allowable parameters (90 for user defined functions, 32767 for stored procedures)
has been exceeded.  LINE NUMBER=101. SQLSTATE=54023
```

When resolving the overloaded function's name, the database manager compares the data types of the arguments with which the function was called to those in the signature of the function in the database. It does *not* consider any length, precision, or scale attributes of the argument. Synonymous and inherited data types are considered identical. For example, REAL and FLOAT, and DOUBLE and FLOAT are considered a match; CHAR (5) and CHAR (25) are considered to be the same, but CHAR (25) and VARCHAR (25) are treated as different data types. The precision of numeric data types also does not matter; DECIMAL (1, 2), and DECIMAL (10, 3) are treated as identical. To add to the confusion, the character and graphic types are considered to be the same. For example, the following are considered to be the same type: CHAR and GRAPHIC, VARCHAR and VARGRAPHIC, and CLOB and DBCLOB.

> *If the function has more than 30 parameters, IBM DB2 UDB for z/OS and GOS/390 only considers the first 30 parameters to determine whether the function is unique.*

A function name and signature must be unique within the schema it resides in, which means that it is possible to have two identical functions with exactly the same name and signature as long as they reside in their own schemas. The actual function is resolved during invocation. If just the function's name is specified, the current schema is assumed (unless the function resides in one of the system schemas: SYSIBM, SYSFUNC, or SYSPROC). You must specify a fully qualified name (<schema_name>.<function_name>) to make it totally unambiguous.

It is possible to overload an existing built-in function, as long as you provide different data types for the input arguments. Consider the following example. The built-in function CONCAT accepts two character strings and returns a result of their concatenation. It does not support implicit conversion, so if you call this function with the numeric type of arguments, it will throw in an error.

```
db2=> VALUES CONCAT(1,2)
SQL0440N No authorized routine named "CONCAT" of type "FUNCTION" having compatible
arguments was found. SQLSTATE=42884
```

Let's create an overloaded version of the function that will accept numeric values, explicitly convert them into characters, and return the concatenated string:

```
db2 => CREATE FUNCTION CONCAT
           (
            first FLOAT
           ,second FLOAT
           )
       RETURNS VARCHAR(50)
       RETURN RTRIM(LTRIM(CHAR(first))) ||
       RTRIM(LTRIM(CHAR(second)))

DB20000I  The SQL command completed successfully.
```

To test our new CONCAT function, we could use the following query:

```
db2 => SELECT
           CONCAT(1.5,2.5)          as NUMBERS,
           CONCAT('one','two')      as STRINGS
       FROM sysibm.sysdummy1

NUMBERS                 STRINGS
--------------------    -------
1.5E02.5E0              onetwo

1 record(s) selected.
```

IBM DB2 UDB provides a capability to create an overloaded version of a function based on the original function through so-called *source functions*. For example, if later we decide that we need yet another version of our overloaded function CONCAT that accepts only integers as its input parameters, instead of retyping all the code we have put into our function CONCAT from the previous example, we could create a sourced CONCAT function:

```
db2=> CREATE FUNCTION CONCAT
          (INTEGER
          ,INTEGER)
      RETURNS VARCHAR(50)
      SOURCE db2admin.CONCAT(FLOAT,FLOAT)

DB20000I  The SQL command completed successfully.
```

Now, within your schema, you could call the function CONCAT with the integer values that will be converted into float data type, and a VARCHAR result will be returned. More information on sourced functions was provided earlier in this chapter in the section, "Overriding with Sourced UDFs."

Overloading of the function is a useful programming technique, but it should be exercised with caution, and the cause for the employment of overloading should be well documented.

Using SQL PL UDF in Transactions

A UDF in IBM DB2 UDB represents a single transaction (see the section, "Restrictions on UDFs," later in this chapter). If used within a SQL statement that also executes in the context of some transaction, all the nested transaction rules apply. You cannot use SAVEPOINT or ROLLBACK statements within UDFs

Finding Information about UDFs in the Database

The information about all databases can be found in the catalog views provided in compliance with the SQL standard INFORMATION_SCHEMA concept. Most of the views are defined in the SYSCAT schema.

The main views to query for information on the UDFs are SYSCAT.ROUTINES and SYSSTAT.ROUTINES. Both views are fairly large, and should be approached with caution. The first one, defined in SYSCAT schema, will provide most information about all routines (stored procedures, triggers, UDFs) registered with your DB2 database, while the second one, defined in SYSSTAT, would omit built-in functions, and contains a subset of the larger SYSCAT.ROUTINES columns.

Beginning with version 7.2, the SYSCAT.ROUTINES view supersedes previously used SYSCAT.FUNC-TIONS and SYSCAT.PROCEDURES views (which are still supplied for compatibility purposes). This view contains more than 70 columns and could be intimidating. It deals with every possible routine type, including external procedures and functions created in C, Java, or COBOL. The following table provides a subset of the view's columns that contain the most commonly used information.

Column Name	Data Type	Description
ROUTINESCHEMA	VARCHAR(128)	Contains a qualified schema name where the function resides.
ROUTINENAME	VARCHAR(128)	Contains the actual name of the function (procedure, method, trigger).
ROUTINETYPE	CHAR(1)	Specifies the type of routine: "F" for functions; "M" for methods; "P" for procedures.
DEFINER	VARCHAR(128)	Authorization ID of the routine definer.
SPECIFICNAME	VARCHAR(128)	The name of the specific routine instance (either user-defined or system-generated).
RETURNTYPENAME	VARCHAR(128)	The name of the type (built-in or UDF).
ORIGIN	CHAR(1)	Specifies the origin of the routine: "B" is for built-in; "E" is for user-defined, external; "M" is for template; "Q" is for user-defined, SQL; "U" is for user-defined, sourced; "S" is for system-generated; "T" is for system-generated transform.
FUNCTIONTYPE	CHAR(1)	Specifies the type of the function: "C" is for column function; "R" is for row function; "S" is for scalar function; "T" is for table function; and a blank signifies a procedure.
LANGUAGE	CHAR(8)	Specifies the language of implementation. If ORIGIN has values other than "E" or "Q," it shows blank. The valid values are C, COBOL, JAVA, OLE, SQL.
DETERMINISTIC	CHAR(1)	Contains either "Y" (for DETERMINISTIC functions), or "N" (for NOT DETERMINISTIC"). The value is blank for routines not defined as E or Q in ORIGIN column.

Column Name	Data Type	Description
SQL_DATA_ACCESS	CHAR(1)	"C" is for CONTAINS SQL (only SQL statements that do not read or modify data are allowed); "M" is for MODIFIES SQL (any type of SQL statements is allowed, cannot be used with UDFs); "N" is for NO SQL (no SQL statements are allowed); and "R" is for READS SQL (only SQL statements that read data are allowed).
SPEC_REG	CHAR(1)	"I" is for INHERIT SPECIAL REGISTERS (invoking routine will set the value of the registers for the function; value is blank if ORIGIN is not "E" or "Q").
CREATE_TIME	TIMESTAMP	Set to 0 when the function is created.
ALTER_TIME	TIMESTAMP	Timestamp of the most recent routine alteration.
FUNCT_PATH	VARCHAR(254)	SQL PATH at the time the routine was created.
QUALIFIER	VARCHAR(128)	Value of the default schema where object was defined.
REMARKS	VARCHAR(254)	User-specified comments for the object.
TEXT	CLOB(2M)	If LANGUAGE is SQL, then it contains the full text of the routine's code.

Here is an example of the query to retrieve some information about our UDFs from earlier sections of the chapter:

```
Db2=> SELECT
         definer
        ,specificname
        ,origin
        ,functiontype
    FROM SYSCAT.ROUTINES
    WHERE routinename = 'FN_HELLOWORLD'

DEFINER      SPECIFICNAME        ORIGIN   FUNCTIONTYPE
---------    -----------         -------  ------------
DB2ADMIN     SQL040322145500202  Q        S

1 record(s) selected.
```

Note that the data is uppercase. The comparison results might not be what you are expecting if you use lowercase or mixed case for the character data.

Restriction on UDFs

There are a number of restrictions on the UDFs created in IBM DB2 UDB, and those called from within SQL statements are subject to even more stringent conditions:

❑ Data modifying SQL statements inside the UDF body is not supported.

❑ A UDF cannot make a call to a stored procedure.

- ❏ PREPARE, EXECUTE, and EXECUTE IMMEDIATE statements are not supported in UDFs.

- ❏ Exception handlers (either predefined or custom-defined) are not supported within a UDF.

- ❏ A UDF invoked from a SQL statement is restricted to utilizing basic SQL data types; no user-defined types are allowed.

- ❏ A UDF is executed as a single transactional unit. If a UDF contains more than one statement, the BEGIN ATOMIC clause is required.

- ❏ The body of a SQL function cannot contain a recursive call to itself.

- ❏ If a UDF is defined as READS SQL DATA, no statement in the function can access data that is being modified by the same statement that invoked the function.

Some more restrictions concerning use of UDFs created either as DETERMINISTIC or NOT DETERMINISTIC are listed in the Chapter 2.

Summary

IBM DB2 UDP is one of the oldest RDBMS platforms to provide UDFs to its developers. By now, you should have a good understanding of the basics of the IBM DB2 UDP platform in creating your own UDFs. Once again, we discussed the proper usage of permissions to ensure that you, as the developer, can successfully create your own UDFs.

We were particularly concerned with the four main types of UDFs within the IBM DB2 UDB platform: scalar UDFs, table UDFs, sourced UDFs, and template UDFs. In this context, we also discussed the user's ability to overload his or her own existing, and also predefined, UDFs. SQLCODE and SQLSTATE were discussed as ways to implement error checking and debugging within the UDFs structure. Adhering to these concepts can provide a robust platform from which the developer can create solutions to particular business problems.

In the next chapter, we will discuss the specifics of creating UDFs in the SQL Server 2000 platform. Although the Microsoft implementation has several differences from the previous RDBMS implementations, you should readily recognize the similarities. This should be used as the basis to begin your learning curve for this system.

15

Creating User-Defined Functions Using Microsoft SQL Server

The ability to create user-defined functions (UDFs) was introduced in Microsoft SQL Server version 2000. Despite this lack of vintage, the UDF support and features are surprisingly robust and rich, respectively.

The Transact-SQL UDFs enhance the programmer's toolset. But, as usual, the power comes with a price. Anyone who ever tried programming in SQL Server was warned against using cursors code because of its drag on resources. Using a UDF within your SQL statement replaces optimized set-based logic with procedural cursor logic, and, therefore, should be done judiciously.

> *Cursors are implemented differently in Oracle and IBM DB2 UDB and pose somewhat less of a resource challenge in those implementations.*

Nevertheless, in our opinion, the advantages of UDFs outweigh their drawbacks. UDFs (as with the stored procedures before them) bring in the structural programming features with their ability to reuse code. The price exacted in terms of performance and, to a certain extent, portability of the code seems to be worth it.

Acquiring Permissions

Before you can create a UDF in Microsoft SQL Server 2000, you must have the CREATE FUNCTION permission. This permission is granted by default to the members of the SYSADMIN predefined server role, as well as to the DB_OWNER and DB_DLLADMIN roles. The members of these roles can, in turn, grant the permission to a user or a role using the standard GRANT statement, as shown here:

```
GRANT CREATE FUNCTION TO [<USER>]|[<GROUP>]
```

Once the function is created, only users who have an EXECUTE permission (in addition to access to the database) are able to execute the function. Only the owner of the function has this privilege by default, as well as members of the predefined roles mentioned previously. Consider the following example:

```
GRANT EXECUTE ON dbo.<function_name> TO [<USER>]|[<GROUP>]
```

To create or alter objects that reference the function (for example, a computed column in a view), you must also have REFERENCES permission to the function.

If any of these permissions is granted to a group or a role, it could be further fine-tuned through the DENY statement to some of the members of the group. The DENY statement has higher precedence than GRANT and will be considered first when any overlapping permissions are detected. The DENY keyword is unique to MS SQL Server, and is not a part of the SQL standard.

Creating UDFs

Out of the three big RDBMS vendors discussed in this book, Microsoft has, arguably, the simplest syntax:

```
CREATE  FUNCTION [ owner_name. ] function_name
(
    [{ @parameter_name [AS] parameter_data_type [ = default ] } [ ,...n ] ]
 )
RETURNS <return_data_type definition>
[WITH [ENCRYPTION | SCHEMABINDING]]
[ AS ]
BEGIN
   [function_body]
   RETURN return_expression
END
```

Nevertheless, the syntax has a lot to offer if you bother to delve into the details. The CREATE FUNCTION statement is a common thread among all RDBMS implementations that provide the capability to create UDFs.

The owner_name is optional and specifies the existing user who will own the function. If this modifier is omitted, the dbo (database owner) becomes the owner of the function. When a function is invoked, either from a SQL query or stored procedure, it must have this owner_name qualifier in front of itself; see further in the chapter for the usage examples.

The function name must be specified, and it must be unique. Since the function's name comprises two parts (the optional <owner_name> and the <function_name>), specifying different owners and identical function names will yield two different functions. The UDFs dbo.udf_helloworld and acme.udf_helloworld would peacefully coexist within the same Microsoft database. To create a function, you must be in the context of the database where you wish the function to reside. You *cannot* qualify a name as <database_name>.<owner_name>.<function_name>.

The @parameter_name means that the function could accept none, one, or more parameters. The maximum number of parameters is currently set at 1,024 (compare to 90 accepted by IBM DB2 UDB and to virtually no practical limits on the number of arguments passed to a PL/SQL function). The "at" sign (@) denotes a variable in Transact-SQL and is, therefore, required.

> As a rule of thumb, if you find yourself defining more than 20 arguments for your UDF, you should ask yourself about the validity of your design.

A parameter's name is always preceded by the "at" sign (@), and the name itself must conform to the general rules for the Transact-SQL identifiers (see the section, "Rules for Naming Identifiers," later in this chapter).

Only constants can take the place of the parameters. You cannot pass in, say, a database object or a reference type.

A default value could be specified for the input argument. However, when calling the function, you must still fill in every place in the signature. Unlike with the stored procedures (where you could simply omit the argument), a DEFAULT keyword must be specified in the place of the missing argument. This feature is consistent with the SQL99 standard and is implemented in Oracle, but not in IBM DB2 UDB.

The parameter parameter_data_type can be of any *scalar* data type. You cannot specify user-defined types (UDTs) or even some built-in ones like TEXT, NTEXT, IMAGE, and TIMESTAMP. This restriction applies not only to UDFs you could call from a SQL query, but any UDF that could be created with Transact-SQL within Microsoft SQL Server. (You cannot create a Transact-SQL UDF in Sybase. You must use Java for this purpose.)

Rules for Naming Identifiers

The first character must be one of the following:

- ❏ A letter, as defined by the Unicode Standard 2.0. The Unicode definition of letters includes Latin characters from "a" through "z" and from "A" through "Z," in addition to letter characters from other languages.

- ❏ The underscore (_), "at" sign (@), or number sign (#). Certain symbols at the beginning of an identifier have special meaning in SQL Server. An identifier beginning with the "at" sign (@) denotes a local variable or parameter. An identifier beginning with a number sign (#) denotes a temporary table or procedure. An identifier beginning with double number signs (##) denotes a global temporary object.

- ❏ Some Transact-SQL functions have names that start with double "at" signs (@@). Although it is possible, it is recommended that you not use names that start with @@, to avoid confusion with these functions.

Subsequent characters can be the following:

- ❏ Letters as defined in the Unicode Standard 2.0.

- ❏ Decimal numbers from either Basic Latin or other national scripts.

- ❏ The "at" sign (@), dollar sign ($), number sign (#), or underscore (_).

- ❏ Embedded spaces and special characters are not allowed. By definition, the first character of the parameter in the UDF, or a declared variable, is the "at" sign @, but the function name is subject to the same rules that apply to the first character. For many identifiers used within SQL Server, it is mandated that the identifier not be a Transact-SQL-reserved word (both the uppercase and lowercase versions). However, the "at" sign (@), with which a UDF parameter (and declared variable) starts in Transact-SQL, shields you from most of these restrictions. It is quite possible to have identifiers such as `@$@@@` or to name your variable `@DATABASE`. (Whether it would be a smart decision is a completely different matter.)

The return-data-type definition hides a lot inside itself and will be dealt with separately. Microsoft classifies its UDFs into three categories:

❏ Scalar-valued UDFs

❏ Multistatement table-valued UDFs

❏ Inline table-valued UDFs

The return data type definition varies depending on what type of function you create. For the scalar-valued function, it will be a built-in data type (except for TEXT, NTEXT, IMAGE, and TIMESTAMP). For a table-valued function, it will be some table definition. Note that for scalar functions, the return data type must be sized (like in IBM DB2 UDB and unlike in Oracle's UDF).

The `WITH [ENCRYPTION | SCHEMABINDING]` clause deserves a more detailed discussion. The first option refers to the ability to encrypt the function's body to hide it from prying eyes (including yours). Once encrypted, the source code of the function's body will be undecipherable; for any future modifications you must maintain the source code in a separate place.

> **Do not assume that encryption will secure your function. It might serve as the first line of defense against the curious, but it would do nothing to deter a knowledgeable and determined hacker.**

The SCHEMABINDING option ties the function to the database. A function created with this option is bound to the database objects it references (that is, they cannot be dropped or modified). However, if the function itself is dropped or modified with the SCHEMABINDING option removed, this restriction is lifted.

Using ENCRYPTION prevents the function from being published as part of a SQL Server replication.

Before the option can be used a number of conditions must be satisfied:

❏ All UDFs and views referenced by the function must also be schema-bound.

❏ The objects referenced by the function must be referenced by using their fully qualified two-part name (that is, if a function queries some table, that table must appear as `<user>.<table_name>`).

❏ The function and the objects it references must belong to the same database.

❏ The user who creates the function must have REFERENCES permission on all the database objects used in the function.

Only two objects in the Microsoft SQL Server can be created with SCHEMABINDING option: views and UDFs. The two work in tandem whenever indexed views (a new feature of SQL Server 2000, which is comparable to Oracle's materialized views) make use of the UDFs. Only schema-bound UDFs are allowed in the indexed views.

As discussed in Chapter 2, these types could be either DETERMINISTIC or NON-DETERMINISTIC. Unlike Oracle and IBM DB2 UDB, Microsoft does not provide a declarative keyword to define a function as being of either type. Instead, it relies on circumstantial evidence—the logic implemented in the function's body. It is not easy to create a non-deterministic UDF using Transact-SQL because Microsoft explicitly disallowed the use of any built-in, non-deterministic functions within your very own UDF. A list of the functions you cannot use within your UDF is given in the following table.

Built-In SQL Function	Description
@@CONNECTIONS	Returns the number of attempted connections since the start of SQL Server.
@@CPU_BUSY	Returns the time (in milliseconds) since SQL Server was started.
@@IDLE	Returns the idle time (in milliseconds) since SQL Server was started.
@@IO_BUSY	Returns the time (in milliseconds) spent on I/O operations since SQL Server was started.
@@MAX_CONNECTIONS	Returns the maximum number of concurrent user connections.
@@PACK_RECEIVED	Returns the number of inbound packets since SQL Server was started.
@@PACK_SENT	Returns the number of outbound packets since SQL Server was started.
@@PACKET_ERRORS	Returns the number of the errors in packets transmissions occurred since SQL Server was started.
@@TIMETICKS	Returns the number of microseconds per CPU tick.
@@TOTAL_ERRORS	Returns the number of disk read/write errors since SQL Server was started.
@@TOTAL_READ	Returns the number of physical disk reads since SQL Server was started.
@@TOTAL_WRITE	Returns the number of physical disk writes since SQL Server was started.
GETDATE	Returns the system's current date and time.
GETUTCDATE	Returns the system's current UTC date and time.
NEWID	Returns a unique value as the UNIQUEIDENTIFIER data type.
RAND	Returns the random number (float) in the 0 to 1 range.
TEXTPTR	Returns the text pointer value corresponding to a text, NTEXT, or an IMAGE in VARBINARY format.

There are several workarounds for the restriction on using non-deterministic, built-in functions in a UDF. One of them is utilizing the ability to perform the SELECT operation from a table or view. If a view is set up to return a value of a non-deterministic function in one of its columns, you could assign the returned value to an internal variable of the UDF and return it. Here is an example of a function that returns values of the non-deterministic functions as a VARCHAR through a view:

```
CREATE VIEW vw_workaround
    AS
    SELECT
          v_getdate = GETDATE()
         ,v_connections = @@CONNECTIONS
         ,v_total_write = @@TOTAL_WRITE
GO

CREATE FUNCTION udf_get(@switch INT)
    RETURNS VARCHAR(20)
AS
BEGIN
DECLARE @return VARCHAR(20)
    IF @switch = 1
        SELECT @return = CAST(v_getdate AS VARCHAR(20))
            FROM vw_workaround
    IF @switch = 2
        SELECT @return = CAST(v_connections AS VARCHAR(20))
FROM vw_workaround
    IF @switch = 3
        SELECT @return = CAST(v_total_write AS VARCHAR(20))
FROM vw_workaround
    IF @switch > 3
        SELECT @return = 'unknown'
    RETURN @return
END

The command(s) completed successfully.

SELECT dbo.udf_get(1) AS result
GO
result
--------------------
Apr 27 2004  8:33PM

(1 row(s) affected)
```

This workaround has its own drawbacks and limitations, one of which is a necessity to create and manage yet another object in the database. Another way to work around this limitation is to use the non-deterministic value as an input parameter for the function.

Creating Scalar-Valued UDFs

This type of function is probably the most commonly used one to augment deficiencies of the SQL non-procedural nature. Here is an example of the Transact-SQL version of the `udf_helloworld` function:

```
CREATE FUNCTION
          udf_helloworld(@arg1 VARCHAR(5))
    RETURNS VARCHAR(20)
AS
BEGIN
    RETURN @arg1 + ' ,world!'
END
GO
```

```
The command(s) completed successfully.

SELECT dbo.udf_helloworld('Hello') AS result
GO
result
--------------------
Hello ,world!

(1 row(s) affected)
```

The dbo prefix is required when calling a UDF in SQL Server. If the function does not reside in the current database, the remote database name must be specified, alongside with the dbo (or current user) prefix (the table-valued functions are exempt from the rule). For example, assuming that udf_helloworld resides in database DB1 and the user was granted access privileges, you would call it from database DB2 with the following syntax (the first line of the example switches context to DB2):

```
USE DB2
GO
SELECT DB1.dbo.udf_helloworld('Hello') AS result
GO

result
--------------------
Hello ,world!

(1 row(s) affected)
```

You can specify default values for the parameters passed into the function. Here is an example of using the default values (compare to Oracle DEFAULT keyword):

```
CREATE FUNCTION
        udf_helloworld(@arg1 VARCHAR(5) = 'HELLO')
    RETURNS VARCHAR(20)
AS
BEGIN
    RETURN @arg1 + ' ,world!'
END
GO
The command(s) completed successfully.
```

To call this function with its default value, you must use the DEFAULT keyword. You cannot just omit the argument as in Oracle.

```
SELECT dbo.udf_helloworld(DEFAULT) AS result
GO

result
--------------------
Hello ,world!

(1 row(s) affected)
```

The scalar functions do not have to be as simple as our examples. You are free to use almost every tool available in the Transact-SQL programming environment.

It is possible to create a UDT and bind a user-defined default to it, and then use this type as input/return parameters in a UDF. Refer to vendor's documentation for more information.

Microsoft SQL Server allows for use of the UDT as either input arguments and/or return parameters for the UDFs. The UDT in MS SQL Server is essentially an extension (a subset) of some system data type (for example, VARCHAR, INTEGER, BIGINT, and so on). The only difference is that you can name it, bind a rule or a default to it, and specify whether it allows NULL(s). For some data types, you can also restrict length. A new UDT is created either through a system-stored procedure, sp_addtype, or through SQL Server Enterprise Manager Console. (It is also possible to use SQL-DMO interface, but details are beyond the scope of this book.)

Creating Inline, Table-Valued UDFs

The inline, table-valued UDF syntax is similar to that of the scalar UDF, with a notable exception that only SQL could be used in the function's body (similar to PostgreSQL UDF discussed in Chapter 18). The return data type is TABLE, and the RETURN statement must contain the SELECT statement. The SELECT statement is not limited to selecting data from a table, but could be a Transact-SQL assignment statement. Here is an example of the udf_helloworld function rewritten as an inline, table-valued function:

```
CREATE FUNCTION
        udf_helloworld(@arg1 VARCHAR(5) = 'HELLO')
    RETURNS TABLE
AS
    RETURN (SELECT @arg1 + ' ,world!' AS result)

GO
The command(s) completed successfully.

SELECT * FROM udf_helloworld(DEFAULT)
result
-------------
HELLO ,world!

(1 row(s) affected)
```

Normally, you would create an inline, table-valued function to select data from an existing regular table, based on some input parameter.

A Transact-SQL UDF function can neither access (SELECT) a temporary table nor create one. Any Data Definition Language (DDL) statements, as well as INSERT and DELETE, are disallowed. The only exception is made for table *variables* within the scope of the function.

To illustrate the point, we are going to utilize our scouts table example created earlier in Chapter 13:

```
    CREATE TABLE scouts
    (
    FIRST_NAME  VARCHAR (25)
    ,LAST_NAME   VARCHAR (25)
       ,CAMP_ID      INTEGER
    )
GO
  The command(s) completed successfully.
```

```
        INSERT INTO scouts VALUES ('Alex', 'Kriegel',1)
        INSERT INTO scouts VALUES ('Phillip', 'Windsor',1)
        INSERT INTO scouts VALUES ('Michael', 'DeVry', 2)
     GO
```

Now, we are going to create an inline, table-valued function to extract information from the table based on some condition. The following function returns all records from the `scouts` table where the first letter of the first name matches a passed argument:

```
CREATE FUNCTION
    udf_getnames_only(@arg1 VARCHAR(1))
RETURNS TABLE
AS
RETURN (
    SELECT * FROM scouts
    WHERE first_name LIKE @arg1 + '%')
GO
The command(s) completed successfully.

SELECT * FROM udf_getnames_only ('A')
GO

FIRST_NAME        LAST_NAME        CAMP_ID
----------------  ------------     --------
Alex              Kriegel          1

(1 row(s) affected)
```

Note that, unlike with the scalar functions, you do not have to specify the `dbo` (or `current_user`) prefix. The rest of the invocation conventions are exactly the same as with scalar UDFs.

Virtually any valid SELECT statement could be used in the RETURN clause of the inline, table-valued function. This includes subqueries, as well as GROUP BY and ORDER BY queries. The ORDER BY clause is invalid in inline functions unless TOP is also specified; the same restriction applies to views, derived tables, and subqueries.

The table-valued functions can be used for JOIN queries just as a regular table. For example, to find which camp a scout will attend, we could use the JOIN function from the previous example and a table CAMPS, as follows:

```
CREATE TABLE CAMPS
    (
    CAMP_ID    INTEGER
    ,CAMP_NAME VARCHAR (25)
    )
GO
  The command(s) completed successfully
INSERT INTO camps VALUES  (1, 'Meriwether')
INSERT INTO camps VALUES (2, 'Gilbert Ranch')
INSERT INTO camps VALUES (3, 'Ireland')
GO

SELECT
    CAMP_NAME FROM CAMPS c
```

```
    INNER JOIN udf_getnames_only ('A') sc
    ON c.CAMP_ID = sc.CAMP_ID

CAMP_NAME
------------------------
Meriwether
(1 row(s) affected)
```

Creating Multistatement, Table-Valued UDFs

The inline UDFs are limited to one and only one SELECT statement. This effectively means that you are limited to the SQL functionality only (including the use of built-in and user-defined functions). All procedural logic is lost. To overcome this particular deficiency, you are allowed to create multistatement, table-valued UDFs.

Since the returned table structure is not inferred from the single SELECT statement, the table structure must be explicitly declared in the RETURNS statement of the UDF definition. The following example constructs the table variable on the fly inside the function (it is assumed that the previous CAMPS table was created and populated):

```
CREATE FUNCTION
        udf_getnames(@arg1 INTEGER, @arg2 VARCHAR(15))
     RETURNS  @scout_camp TABLE
        (
               first_name VARCHAR(25)
              ,last_name  VARCHAR(25)
              ,camp_name  VARCHAR(25)
        )
AS
BEGIN
IF LEN(LTRIM(RTRIM(@arg2))) = 0
    INSERT @scout_camp
        SELECT
 s.first_name
            ,s.last_name
,c.CAMP_NAME FROM scouts s
        INNER JOIN camps c
ON s.CAMP_ID = c.CAMP_ID
            WHERE c.CAMP_ID = @arg1
ELSE
    INSERT @scout_camp
        SELECT
             s.first_name
            ,s.last_name
            ,c.CAMP_NAME
        FROM scouts s
        INNER JOIN camps c
ON s.CAMP_ID = c.CAMP_ID
            WHERE s.first_name LIKE @arg2 + '%'
            AND c.CAMP_ID = @arg1
RETURN
END
```

Calling the newly created function with the input parameter of 1 would retrieve all scouts going to the camp with ID 1 (Merriwether). Since Transact-SQL does not support optional parameters, both input parameters must be supplied, as shown here:

```
select * from udf_getnames(1,'')
GO

first_name            last_name                camp_name
--------------------  -----------------------  ---------
Alex                  Kriegel                  Merriwether
Phillip               Windsor                  Merriwether

(2 row(s) affected)
```

Now, if we want to retrieve all scouts attending the Merriwether camp whose first name starts with "A," we would supply some non-empty value for the second parameter, as shown here:

```
select * from udf_getnames(1,'A')
GO

first_name            last_name                camp_name
--------------------  -----------------------  ---------
Alex                  Kriegel                  Merriwether

(1 row(s) affected)
```

Generally, it is considered bad practice to overload variables with more than one purpose. In this example, we are using the length of @arg2 as a flag and @arg2 as a parameter for a SELECT query at the same time. It might be a valid solution for simple cases, but things are bound to get out of the control when complex logic is involved. Use your best judgment when planning functions.

Schema-Bound UDFs

The requirements for creating schema-bound UDFs were described earlier in the chapter when discussing the rules for naming identifiers. Here we look at some examples of such functions.

A function created WITH SCHEMABINDING prevents the schema objects to which it is bound to be modified or dropped. For example, if we create the function UDF_GETNAMES_ONLY (from the earlier example) with this option, the table SCOUTS can not be dropped or modified until we either un-bind the function (using ALTER FUNCTION statement) or drop the function altogether. We must also modify the function as "*" (meaning ALL fields). This is just not allowed in schema-bound functions. Moreover, the table SCOUTS must be referenced as a two-part name—for example, dbo.scouts (or prefixed with current_user).

```
-- drop the function if it already exists
IF EXISTS (SELECT * FROM dbo.sysobjects
           WHERE id = object_id(N'[dbo].[udf_getnames]')
           AND xtype in (N'FN', N'IF', N'TF'))
DROP FUNCTION [dbo].[udf_getnames1]
GO
-- create new version of the function WITH SCHEMABINDING option
CREATE FUNCTION
        udf_getnames_only(@arg1 VARCHAR(1))
```

```
        RETURNS TABLE
        WITH SCHEMABINDING
AS
        RETURN (
            SELECT
                    first_name
                  ,last_name
                  ,camp_id
            FROM dbo.scouts
                  WHERE first_name LIKE @arg1 + '%')
The command(s) completed successfully.
```

From now on, an attempt to drop the table SCOUTS would result in the following error message:

```
DROP TABLE scouts
GO
Server: Msg 3729, Level 16, State 1, Line 1
Cannot DROP TABLE 'scouts' because it is being referenced by object
'udf_getnames_only'.
```

Dropping a schema-bound function instead poses no such problem and releases the SCOUTS table from the "bondage."

The advantage of using schema-bound objects (and there are only two kinds of objects that can be created with this option: views and UDFs) is that the relational structure is fixed and cannot be accidentally disrupted. The disadvantage is that it makes any change to the referenced object a real pain (which might not be for the best at early stages of development).

The objects referenced in schema-bound functions must be in two-part format, and they cannot reference themselves (meaning no schema-bound recursive functions).

Encrypting Transact-SQL Functions

Specifying the WITH ENCRYPTION option in the CREATE FUNCTION or ALTER FUNCTION statements encrypts the body of your function, hiding it from prying eyes. Any attempt to extract this information using common means (see the section "Finding Information about UDFs" later in this chapter) would result in the following message:

```
/****** Encrypted object is not transferable, and script can not be generated.
******/
```

Essentially, this means that you cannot modify the function unless you have the source code on hand. This might make sense when distributing your code to the client site, but it creates more problems than it solves during the development and maintenance stages.

Moreover, the encryption algorithm used by Microsoft SQL Server was cracked and is now in public domain. So, your protection is rather illusory anyway.

Recursive Functions

So far, only Oracle and Microsoft-SQL server are providing support for the recursive UDFs. Here is the possible implementation of the udf_RECURSIVE_FACTORIAL function:

```
CREATE  FUNCTION dbo.udf_RECURSIVE_FACTORIAL(@arg BIGINT)
RETURNS INT
AS
BEGIN
DECLARE @result INT
     IF @arg = 1
   SET @result = @arg
 ELSE
SET @result = @arg * dbo.udf_RECURSIVE_FACTORIAL(@arg - 1)

  RETURN @result
END
```

The function works perfectly until you try to calculate the factorial of 13. Then the following message is displayed:

```
SELECT dbo.udf_RECURSIVE_FACTORIAL(13)

Server: Msg 8115, Level 16, State 2, Procedure udf_RECURSIVE_FACTORIAL,
Line 9 Arithmetic overflow error converting expression to data type int.
```

Why is that? There is no such restriction in Oracle. The error was produced because the returned data type is INTEGER, and the value of 87,178,291,200 (factorial of 14) is greater than this data type could hold (the INTEGER data type has a length of 4 bytes, and stores numbers from –2,147,483,648 through 2,147,483,647). Switching to the BIGINT data type (it can hold integers in the range of –9,223,372,036,854,775,808 through 9,223,372,036,854,775,807) would allow us to calculate the factorial of 20, and using the FLOAT data type would allow us to calculate the factorial of 32. After that, a new error message will be displayed:

```
Server: Msg 217, Level 16, State 1, Procedure udf_RECURSIVE_FACTORIAL, Line 10
Maximum stored procedure, function, trigger, or view nesting level exceeded
(limit 32).
```

The reason is the limit imposed by SQL Server on the nesting levels depth. It can go as deep as 32 levels, after which this particular error is raised. A recursion could be an elegant and simple solution, but must be used with caution. In our example, a loop organized within the function would be a more robust solution, as the nesting limit restriction would be lifted.

Creating Template UDFs

Microsoft supplies a set of predefined templates for most common database objects. In the case of UDFs, there are templates loaded from the scripts found in the Tools/Templates/SQL Query Analyzer/Create Function directory. There are three separate scripts, one for each type of UDF: Create Scalar Function.tql, Create Inline Function.tql, and Create Table Function.tql. They can be accessed from the SQL Query Analyzer's menu with Edit ➪ Insert Template (or press Ctrl+Shift+Ins while in the Templates tab of the SQL Query Analyzer). Alternatively, you could select an appropriate node from the Templates tab.

The selected template script appears in the Query pane as CREATE FUNCTION. You could further utilize the Replace Template Parameters tool as a convenient way to customize the function. It is invoked from the Edit ➪ Replace Template Parameters... Menu option (or by pressing Ctrl+Shift+M while the focus is in the relevant query pane).

Creating UDFs with Extended Stored Procedures

Object Linking and Embedding (OLE) Automation has been around for almost 10 years and, admittedly, is going out of fashion. It is being replaced by .NET in the Microsoft world. Nevertheless, using OLE Automation provides your function with the capability to plug into a rich functionality of complex programs, such as Microsoft Office (like Word or Excel), or any client compliant with the Component Object Model (COM). In order to use any of these extended stored procedures, you must be a member of the SYSADMIN fixed server role.

The list of the extended stored procedures used to manipulate the OLE objects from within the SQL Server 2000 environment is shown in the following table.

Stored Procedure Name	Description
sp_OACreate	Creates an instance of the OLE object.
sp_OADestrroy	Destroys an OLE object (watch out for circular references—a known problem in the COM world).
sp_OAGetErrorInfo	Gets information about all possible exceptions thrown in the OLE object during execution.
sp_OAGetProperty	Obtains the value of the public property of the OLE object.
sp_OAMethod	Calls a public method within an OLE object.
sp_OASetProperty	Assigns a value to the property of an OLE object.
sp_OAStop	Stops the server-wide OLE Automation stored procedure execution environment.

This chapter is not intended to be an exhaustive introduction to OLE Automation. The stated goal is to make you aware of the possibilities and show you how to get started. Things could easily get more complicated as you proceed to debugging and optimization.

Here is an example of using OLE Automation procedures inside of a UDF. The following example utilizes Microsoft Word OLE Automation to save some text into a Word document. The example assumes that you have Microsoft Word installed (a version that supports OLE Automation—Word 97 or later).

```
CREATE FUNCTION udf_SaveToWord
(
    @text VARCHAR(255)
    ,@file VARCHAR(255)
)
RETURNS INT
AS
BEGIN
    DECLARE @document    INT
    DECLARE @app         INT
    DECLARE @content     INT
    DECLARE @hresult     INT
    DECLARE @return          INT

    -- the function will return 0 (success) or 1 (failure)
```

```
        SET @return = 1
        EXEC @hresult = sp_OACreate
                            'Word.Document'
                            ,@document OUT
    IF @hresult = 0
    -- success, OLE Automation object is created
    -- get handle to the Application OLE object
    EXEC @hresult = sp_OAGetProperty
                                @document
                                ,'application'
                                ,@app OUT

        -- if @hresult is not zero, then object creation fails
        -- use sp_OAGetErrorInfo to retrieve detailed error information

        -- get handle to Content OLE object
        IF @hresult = 0
        -- success, OLE Automation object is created
    EXEC @hresult = sp_OAGetProperty
                                @document
                                ,'Content'
                                ,@content OUT

        -- assign the @send_text to the Text property of the Content object
        IF @hresult = 0
    EXEC @hresult = sp_OASetProperty
                                @content
                                ,'text'
                                ,@text

-- it might be a good idea to suspend the execution
-- for some 10 - 25 seconds to give the object enough time to initialize
-- unfortunately, you cannot use WAITFOR DELASY within a UDF
-- you could use some LOOP though

    IF @hresult = 0
    EXEC @hresult = sp_OAMethod
                                @document
                                , 'SaveAs'
                                , NULL
                                , @file

    SET @return = @hresult
    -- again, this is the place sp_OAGetErrorInfo to retrieve detailed error
information
    -- which could be returned as a part of the RETURN statement
    -- clean up
    EXEC @hresult = sp_OADestroy @content
    EXEC @hresult = sp_OADestroy @app
    EXEC @hresult = sp_OADestroy @document
    -- return state
    RETURN @return
END
```

You can then call the function just like any other UDF:

```
SELECT dbo.udf_SaveToWord
(
    'OLE Automation UDF example'
    ,'C:\temp\OA_test.doc'
)
AS result
GO

result
-----------
0
(1 row(s) affected)
```

An examination of your C:\temp\directory should reveal file OA_test.doc, which is just like any other Microsoft Word-created file.

This function lacks the robustness you would expect from a production-quality function. There are many ways it could be improved with proper error handling: checking for disk space prior to saving the file, checking whether the file already exists, and maybe opening it, to mention just a few.

The rich functionality of the COM object comes at a price. COM objects are notoriously resource-hungry—both in terms of memory and CPU usage. It might not be a good idea to utilize them where the resources are scarce and the workload is high.

Built-in System UDFs

There are about 30 built-in system UDFs in MS SQL Server 2000, depending on the installation option selected. The system UDFs have a global scope and, for all practical purposes, behave the same as all the other built-in functions. The only exception is the calling syntax for a table returning functions, which requires a double colon prefix (see examples later in this chapter).

The Microsoft-supplied system UDFs can be split into two broad categories: documented functions and undocumented ones. Information on the functions falling into the former category can be found in "Books Online," which is installed with every SQL Server installation. Information about the latter-category functions can only be guessed at or inferred. This is why it might not be such a good idea to use them at all. Microsoft makes no warranties that the undocumented functions will be present in future releases. In fact, Microsoft explicitly discourages their use.

The following table lists some of the documented system UDFs.

System Function	Description
fn_get_sql	Returns the last statement executed within the current SQL connection (passed in as a binary handle). It was introduced with Service Pack 3.
fn_helpcollations	Returns a list of all the collations supported by Microsoft SQL Server 2000.
fn_listextendedproperty	Returns extended property values of database objects as a table.

System Function	Description
fn_servershareddrive	Returns the names of shared drives used by the clustered server.
fn_trace_getinfo	Returns information about a specified trace or existing traces.
fn_virtualfilestats	Returns I/O statistics for database files, including log files.
fn_virtualservernodes	Returns the list of nodes on which the virtual server can run. Such information is useful in failover clustering environments.

All system functions are defined in the MASTER database and belong to the SYSTEM_FUNCTION_SCHEMA user; they all start with fn_ and ought to be spelled in lowercase characters. They may include numbers and underscores.

> The characters in a system UDF name are supposed to be all lowercase. This is mandatory when trying to create a system UDF using SYSTEM_FUNCTION_SCHEMA. Creating a function as dbo and then changing the ownership allows you to bypass this requirement.

A close examination of the Microsoft-supplied system UDFs reveals that some of them are using unorthodox syntax that is reserved for the system functions and procedures only.

A brief look at the MASTER database in the Enterprise Manager Console would give you a list of all system UDFs installed on your system. The exact count would differ, depending on the installation options selected and service packs applied, but it should be somewhere around 30. These functions are installed by running SQL scripts, which still can be found on your system in the subdirectory \Microsoft SQL Server\MSSQL\Install. Investigating the system functions source code might give you an insight into the inner workings of the system, but do not make assumptions about their functionality. Using undocumented functions in your own code is a sure way to non-portable, non-upgradeable code, because the functionality might change with every new service pack release, not to mention new version release.

Creating a System UDF

There is no reason why your very own UDF cannot become a system UDF, as long as it complies with the following rules:

❑ It resides in the MASTER database.

❑ The function must start with the fn_ prefix.

❑ The special user SYSTEM_FUNCTION_SCHEMA must own it.

The following example makes the UDF udf_helloworld a system function:

```
USE master
GO

CREATE FUNCTION
  dbo.fn_helloworld(@arg1 VARCHAR(5) = 'HELLO')
```

```
        RETURNS VARCHAR(20)
AS
BEGIN
        RETURN @arg1 + ' ,world!'
END
GO

EXEC sp_ChangeObjectOwner
            'dbo.fn_helloworld','system_function_schema'
```

In this example, we have created the function as `dbo` and then have changed the object's ownership. There is nothing to prevent you from creating the `SYSTEM_FUNCTION_SCHEMA.fn_helloworld` function in the first place.

Once a UDF is made into a system function, it can be called as any of the built-in or system functions (there is no need to qualify it with the `dbo/user` prefix), and it is accessible throughout the SQL Server databases:

```
USE pubs
GO

SELECT fn_helloworld('Hello') AS result
result
--------------------
Hello ,world!

(1 row(s) affected)
```

The new system function is protected as any other system function—you cannot easily drop the function, or even see its source code from the Enterprise Manager. The only way to see your system function's (or any system function's) source code would be by querying either system catalogs or `INFORMATION_SCHEMA` views.

Now you can see why this `dbo/user` prefix is made a requirement—there will no conflict between the `fn_helloworld` function and the `dbo.fn_helloworld` one. But what about our table-valued functions? While a table-valued UDF does not have to have the prefix, its system version must have a double colon in front of it. If we create a system version of the inline, table-valued `udf_helloworld` created earlier in the chapter (to demonstrate the point it has to be called `fn_helloworld` both in the local database and in the MASTER database), we would call it as follows:

```
-- switch context to a database other than master
USE pubs
-- calling system table-valued UDF
select * from ::fn_helloworld('Hello')
result
-------------
Hello ,world!
(1 row(s) affected)

-- calling local table-valued UDF
select * from fn_helloworld('Hello')
result
```

```
-------------
Hello ,world!
(1 row(s) affected)
```

This is as close as you can get to overloading in Microsoft SQL Server 2000, as none of the overloading features found in Oracle, IBM DB2 UDB, and PostgreSQL are supported.

To drop a system version of your system UDF using Transact-SQL, you must first enable updates for the system table (this, of course, requires administrative privileges):

```
USE master
GO
-- Enable updates for system tables
EXEC sp_configure 'allow updates', 1
GO
RECONFIGURE WITH OVERRIDE
GO


-- Drop the system UDF
IF EXISTS (SELECT * FROM sysobjects WHERE type =
'fn' AND
    name='fn_helloworld' and uid = 4)
BEGIN
    DROP FUNCTION
        system_function_schema.fn_helloworld
END
GO

-- Disable updates for system table
EXEC sp_configure 'allow updates', 0
GO
RECONFIGURE WITH OVERRIDE
GO
```

Alternatively, you could use Enterprise Manager Console, which makes this procedure much easier; though it might not always work properly because of some SQL-DMO idiosyncrasies.

Altering UDFs

Once a UDF is created, it can be altered using the ALTER FUNCTION statement.

To execute this statement, you must have the ALTER FUNCTION privilege. As with other privileges pertaining to UDFs, this one cannot be granted to a user unless he or she is a member of the sysadmin, db_owner or db_dlladmin database roles.

The syntax is identical to the CREATE FUNCTION statement, with the exception of the opening keyword:

```
ALTER FUNCTION [schema.] function_name
        [standard syntax from CREATE FUNCTION statement]
```

When altering the function, any of the options appearing on the CREATE FUNCTION list could be modified. At the same time, this statement cannot be used to change the name of the function or to change a scalar-valued function to a table-valued function (or vice versa). Also, ALTER FUNCTION cannot be used to change an inline function to a multistatement function, or vice versa.

Here is an example of modifying the udf_helloworld function through Query Analyzer window (note the additional statements added by the Query Analyzer template):

```
DROP FUNCTION udf_helloworld
SET QUOTED_IDENTIFIER OFF
GO
SET ANSI_NULLS ON
GO

CREATE FUNCTION
 udf_helloworld(@arg1 VARCHAR(5) = 'HELLO')
     RETURNS VARCHAR(25)
AS
BEGIN
     RETURN @arg1 + ' ,Transact-SQL!'
END

GO
SET QUOTED_IDENTIFIER OFF
GO
SET ANSI_NULLS ON
GO
```

We need to DROP the function first in the example above and re-CREATE it because we are changing the type of the function from TABLE to VARCHAR(25). If we were to try to use the ALTER FUNCTION statement here, SQL Server would complain about the type mismatch.

Normally, any object created in a SQL Server database could be renamed using the sp_rename system stored procedure. It could be used to rename a UDF, but there is a catch: the source code of the function still would maintain the old name. Even though, for all practical purposes, the function was renamed, the syscomments table would still display the old name. Whenever you need to rename your function in SQL Server, we recommend dropping it altogether and re-creating anew.

Dropping UDFs

UDFs in SQL Server 2000 are dropped just like any other user object, using fairly standard SQL syntax:

```
DROP FUNCTION [owner_name.]<function_name>
```

The DROP FUNCTION permission defaults to the function's owner and cannot be granted. However, members of the sysadmin, db_owner or db_dlladmin database roles could drop it any time by referring to it by the fully qualified name: <owner_name>.<function_name>.

It is possible to drop several functions at once by supplying the comma-separated function names list.

For example, an owner could drop the udf_helloworld function by using the following syntax:

```
DROP FUNCTION udf_helloworld
The command(s) completed successfully.
```

A sysadmin would have to add the dbo (or user) prefix:

```
DROP FUNCTION dbo.udf_helloworld
The command(s) completed successfully.
```

Since there is no overloading in SQL Server 2000, you do not have to specify the function's signature (like in Oracle or IBM DB2 UDB). Doing so would result in an error.

Debugging Transact-SQL UDFs

There is no direct support for debugging Transact-SQL UDFs in SQL Server 2000. You must create a stored procedure to do this. You can debug all types of the UDF described, each in its own way.

The scalar and multistatement UDFs are the ones that make the most sense to debug. Debugging inline functions doesn't do much—except provide an opportunity to step through any other UDF it might reference.

Here is an example of debugging udf_RECURSIVE_FACTORIAL UDF. First we must create a calling stored procedure:

```
CREATE PROCEDURE usp_debug(@arg INT)
AS
BEGIN
DECLARE @result INT
     SELECT @result = dbo.udf_RECURSIVE_FACTORIAL(@arg)
END
```

The debugging tool is integrated into Microsoft SQL Server Query Analyzer, which is included with every SQL Server installation. Start up the Query Analyzer and select Tools ➪ Object Browser ➪ Show / Hide menu option. (Alternatively, you could press the F8 key.) Figure 15-1 shows the expanded node of Stored Procedures in our UDF_TEST database. The very last option in the pop-up menu is Debug. (This option is disabled for UDFs.)

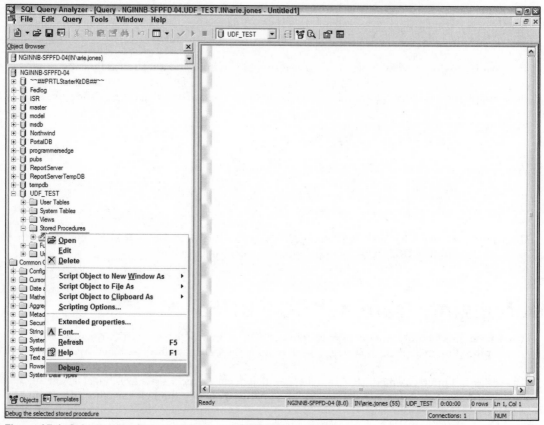

Figure 15-1. Selecting the Debug option in the Object Viewer window.

Selecting this option brings up the Debug Procedure dialog (Figure 15-2), which allows you to specify some options, as well as set up the input parameters.

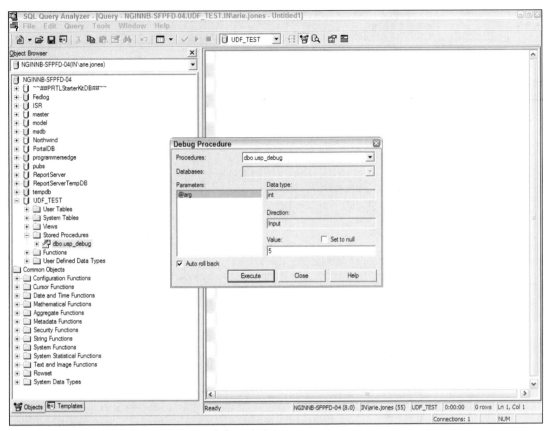

Figure 15-2. The Debug Procedure user dialog window.

Clicking the Execute button on the dialog window brings up the debug pane with the stored procedure source code, with the first executable statement highlighted, as shown in Figure 15-3.

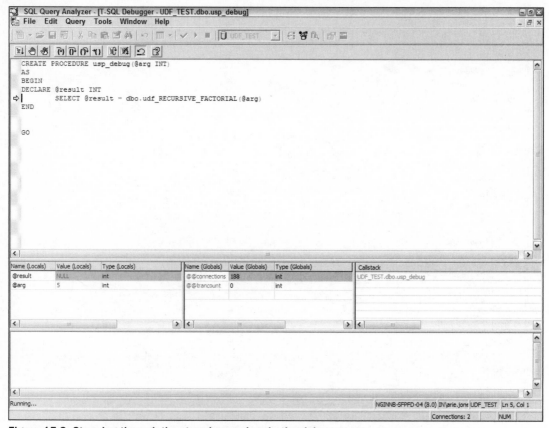

Figure 15-3. Stepping through the stored procedure in the debug pane.

When setting the debugging options, it would be a good idea to leave the Auto-Rollback checkbox checked; it will roll back any changes your procedures might inflict upon your database.

The lower part of the screen contains three smaller panes, representing Local Variables, Global Variables, and Callstack, respectively.

As you step through the procedure (by using either the F11 key, or the control buttons {}), you will see that different parts of the code are loaded into the source code pane, eventually coming to the udf_RECURSIVE_FACTORIAL. Stepping through the function's source code, you can see how all the values in the Local Variables, Global Variables, and Callstack change according to the dataflow. (It is especially interesting to watch the Callstack for the recursive function unwinding.) Finally, the variables acquire their final values, and the debugger stops. Had our stored procedure contained one more executable line we would have returned to the stored procedure. Now, the debugger stops displaying the function's source code in the pane (Figure 15-4).

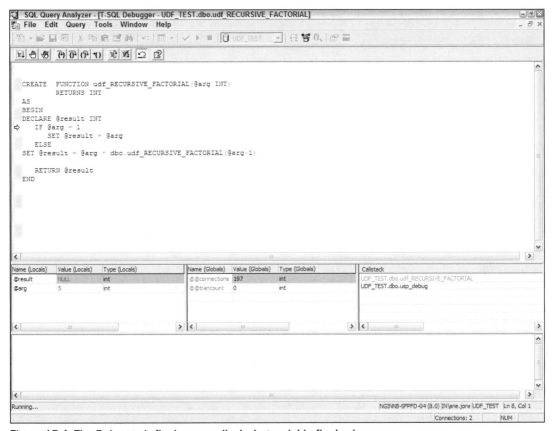

Figure 15-4. The Debugger's final screen, displaying variable final values.

The Query Analyzer is not the only tool available for debugging Transact-SQL stored procedures. There are some third-party tools, and you could even use Visual studio.NET for this purpose.

Microsoft supplies a tool to be used in analyzing the performance of the SQL Server, which is a great tool for tracing UDFs. When it comes to the tracing of UDFs, they are treated as stored procedures, and all the traceable events would be found under the Stored Procedures node on the Events tab of the Trace Properties dialog. The events you may want to trace are SP: Completed *(raised when a UDF completes),* SP: Starting *(raised each time a UDF is started), and* SP:Recompiled *(raised when a UDF is recompiled). Since SQL Profiler events are geared toward stored procedures, you would find many other events that have no meaning in the UDF context. While MS SQL Server 2000 includes the system-stored procedure* sp_trace_generateevent *to raise your own events to the SQL Profiler, it cannot be utilized within a UDF, only within a stored procedure.*

Error Handling in Transact-SQL UDFs

The support for handling run-time errors in UDFs is rather limited. Almost none of the error-handling arsenal available in stored procedures is applicable to UDFs.

To demonstrate the error-handling capabilities of a UDF, we are going to create a SQL Server analog of the FN_DIVIDEBYZERO function:

```
CREATE FUNCTION udf_dividebyzero
    (@arg1 INT, @arg2 INT) RETURNS INT
AS
BEGIN
DECLARE @result INT
DECLARE @error_value INT
    SET @result = @arg1/@arg2
-- check for errors
    SET @error_value = @@ERROR
    IF @error_value > 0
-- try returning an error value
    SET @result= @error_value

 RETURN @result
END
```

The logic of this function is rather simple: divide the first input parameter by the second input parameter; if division by zero occurs, return an error code; otherwise, return the result. Executing this function shows that the function is terminated as soon as the error occurs, leaving you no means to handle the error within the function.

```
select dbo.udf_dividebyzero(5,0)
select @@ERROR as error
GO
Server: Msg 8134, Level 16, State 1, Procedure udf_dividebyzero, Line 6
Divide by zero error encountered.

error
-----------
0

(1 row(s) affected)
```

As you can see, the @@ERROR value is available inside the udf_dividebyzero, but not to the next statement in the batch, which makes post-fact error handling virtually impossible. You must anticipate the error and handle it *before* it occurs.

Essentially, this leaves you with two complementing options:

❑　First, to anticipate all possible errors by carefully checking input parameters and intermediate results for the allowable range/type.

❑　Second, handle the unexpected errors within the calling client (which, unfortunately, cannot be a Transact-SQL stored procedure).

SQL Server will return the error to the client, and it will be up to the client to handle the error. When an exception is thrown from a UDF called from within a stored procedure, the statement that contains the function is terminated, but the stored procedure continues to be executed. Of course, the @@ERROR function called right after that returns zero as if nothing happened.

There is a way to report an error condition from a UDF—before it happens, of course. You may consider using an extended stored procedure xp_logevent to report the event to the Windows NT system log.

If your function makes extended stored procedures, the errors generated in these procedures are to be handled just like they would be in stored procedures.

Using Transact-SQL UDFs in Transactions

A UDF executes within the transaction space of the calling routine and cannot start a transaction of its own. Both BEGIN TRANSACTION and COMMIT TRANSACTION are invalid within the context of a UDF.

MS SQL Server allows you to execute another function or an extended stored procedure from within itself. Surprisingly enough, a UDF would compile even if the EXEC statement has a "regular" stored procedure specified. Executing such a function would result in the following error message, though:

```
Server: Msg 557, Level 16, State 2, Procedure udf_run_procedure, Line 13
```

Only functions and extended stored procedures can be executed from within a function.

Interesting possibilities are offered by the ability of the UDF to execute an extended stored procedure that *can* start a transaction from outside, but exploring this functionality is beyond the scope of this book.

> *Microsoft provides a way to document every object you create in your database through extended properties. Three system-stored procedures, sp_addextendedproperty, sp_updateextendedproperty, and sp_dropextendedproperty, allow for adding, modifying, and deleting custom properties of the objects, respectively. The same could be done from the graphical user interface of the Query Analyzer. To retrieve information added through these procedures, use the system function fn_listextendedproperty. Storing the metadata information about database objects inside the database itself has its advantages and disadvantages, which ought to be considered.*

Finding Information about UDFs

Following the Sybase legacy, Microsoft SQL Server provides system-stored procedures to obtain information about UDFs. The system-stored procedure sp_help reports information about UDFs (but is useless against system UDFs). It is complemented by the sp_helptext system-stored procedure, which returns the source of the UDF. To find information about dependent objects, a stored procedure sp_depends could be used. It will list the name and type of the objects dependent on the UDF and/or referenced by the UDF.

The procedures are still supported for backward compatibility, and are the recommended means for obtaining this information about database objects in MS SQL Server version 6.5 or earlier. They will not work for system UDFs, though. Of course, there were no UDFs back then.

Ever since the release of the SQL Server version 7.0, Microsoft also provided INFORMATION_SCHEMA views, which is the SQL standard way of obtaining system information. The three following views report information about UDFs: ROUTINES, PARAMETERS, and ROUTINE_COLUMNS.

The following table lists some of the most useful columns from the ROUTINES view.

Column	Data Type	Description
ROUTINE_CATALOG	nvarchar(128)	Catalog name of the function.
ROUTINE_SCHEMA	nvarchar(128)	Owner name of the function.
ROUTINE_NAME	nvarchar(128)	Name of the function.
ROUTINE_TYPE	nvarchar(20)	Returns PROCEDURE for stored procedures, and FUNCTION for functions.
ROUTINE_BODY	nvarchar(30)	Returns SQL for a Transact-SQL function, and EXTERNAL for an externally written function. In SQL Server 2000, functions will always be SQL.
ROUTINE_DEFINITION	nvarchar(4000)	Returns the definition text of the function or stored procedure if the function or stored procedure is not encrypted. Otherwise, returns NULL.
CREATED	datetime	The time the routine was created.
LAST_ALTERED	datetime	The last time the function was modified.

The ROUTINES view contains more than 50 columns, most of which are reserved for future use. The view is queried just as any other view or table in the database. Here is an example using SQL Query Analyzer:

```
SELECT
    routine_body
    ,routine_name
    FROM INFORMATION_SCHEMA.ROUTINES
WHERE routine_type = 'FUNCTION'
routine_body                routine_name
---------------------- ----------------------------
SQL                         fn_listextendedproperty
. . .              . . .
SQL                         udf_RECURSIVE_FACTORIAL
(43 row(s) affected)
```

Querying the INFORMATION_SCHEMA views (or system catalog tables) is the only way to access the source of the system functions coded in Transact-SQL. This is true for both user-defined and built-in functions. To retrieve the source code for, say, the system UDF fn_helloworld, the following query could be executed:

```
SELECT
    ROUTINE_DEFINITION
FROM INFORMATION_SCHEMA.ROUTINES
WHERE ROUTINE_NAME = 'fn_helloworld'
ROUTINE_DEFINITION
--------------------------------------------------------------
CREATE FUNCTION
    dbo.fn_helloworld(@arg1 VARCHAR(5) = 'HELLO')
    RETURNS VARCHAR(20)
AS
BEGIN
    RETURN @arg1 + ' ,world!'
END
(1 row(s) affected)
```

The contents of the ROUTINE_DEFINITION are subject to the 4,000-character length limit. Everything beyond that will be truncated. Querying the underlying SYSCOMMENTS table is subject to the same constraint.

> *If you are running these statements from SQL Query Analyzer, make sure you change the "Maximum Characters per column" setting to 8,192 (the maximum allowable value). With the default set at 256, you are guaranteed to have truncated results for most of the system UDFs, even those whose length is less than 4,000.*

The INFORMATION_SCHEMA view ROUTINE_COLUMNS, listed in the following table, contains one row for each column returned by the table-valued functions accessible to the current user in the database. A table-valued function returning two columns will have two records in the view.

Column	Data Type	Description
TABLE_NAME	nvarchar(128)	Name of the table-valued function
COLUMN_NAME	nvarchar(128)	Column name
COLUMN_DEFAULT	nvarchar(4000)	Default value for the column
IS_NULLABLE	varchar(3)	If this column allows NULL, returns YES; otherwise, NO
DATA_TYPE	nvarchar(128)	System-supplied

The third way of obtaining the information would be SQL Server system tables. This is not a recommended way, and Microsoft makes it clear that the structure and names of the tables are subject to change any moment. Some of the relevant system tables are listed in the following table.

System Table	Information Contained
sysobjects	Includes one row of information per UDF. The TYPE column of the table specifies the type of the object: C—CHECK constraint

Table continued on following page

System Table	Information Contained
	D—Default or DEFAULT constraint
	F—FOREIGN KEY constraint
	FN—Scalar function
	IF—Inline table function
	K—PRIMARY KEY or UNIQUE constraint
	L—Log
	P—Stored procedure
	R—Rule
	RF—Replication filter stored procedure
	S—System table
	TF—Table function
	TR—Trigger
	U—User table
	V—View
	X—Extended stored procedure
	Only three object types, FN, IF, and TF, refer to the UDFs.
sysdepends	Shows dependencies: database objects referenced in a UDF and UDF definitions used with database objects (tables, views, procedures, other UDFs).
sysconstraints	Used when UDFs are specified as CONSTRAINT(s) on tables
syscomments	The source code of the UDF created with the CREATE FUNCTION statement is stored there. The fields are CTEXT of the VARBINARY(8000) data type, and TEXT of the NVARCHAR(4000) data type. The latter stores the source in a human-readable format. It contains information about permissions granted and denied to users, groups, and roles in the database. It contains GRANT and DENY information for system objects, including UDFs. The column ACTION (of the TINYINT data type) contains the permissions for a specific object or user/group. The allowable values are as follows:
	26—REFERENCES
	178—CREATE FUNCTION
	193—SELECT
	195—INSERT
	196—DELETE

System Table	Information Contained
	197—UPDATE
	198—CREATE TABLE
	203—CREATE DATABASE
	207—CREATE VIEW
	222—CREATE PROCEDURE
	224—EXECUTE
	228—BACKUP DATABASE
	233—CREATE DEFAULT
	235—BACKUP LOG
	236—CREATE RULE

It is recommended to use these tables only to retrieve information that is not available through INFORMATION_SCHEMA or system-stored procedures.

Beginning with the SQL Server version 7.0, Microsoft is providing an additional interface to its RDBMS: SQL-Distributed Management Objects (SQL-DMO). This interface is essentially a COM wrapper on top of the SQL Server. It comes in really handy when an external client (and even an internal one, such as a stored procedure/function, through the sp_OA* family of system-stored procedures) must access some information about SQL Server.

The full coverage of the SQL-DMO is outside the scope of this book. The DMO model contains more than 80 objects, with hundreds of properties each.

> *Because of some Microsoft marketing tricks, the COM standard is also known as OLE and ActiveX standards. They all point to the same thing.*

Restrictions on Transact-SQL UDFs

While the UDFs could be used virtually anywhere in your Transact-SQL code, there are certain situations when you cannot (or should not) use them. You cannot do any of the following:

❑ Invoke non-deterministic functions from a UDF.

❑ Modify data in the database using an INSERT, UPDATE, or DELETE statement (though it is possible to circumvent this restriction through custom-extended stored procedures).

❑ Start or commit a transaction.

❑ Execute dynamic SQL.

❑ Execute a stored procedure (with the exception of extended stored procedures).

- ❑ Execute extended stored procedures that return rowsets of data.

- ❑ Access, create, modify, or drop temporary tables.

- ❑ Return messages other than through a RETURN statement.

- ❑ Use RAISEERROR to raise a custom error/message.

- ❑ Use SET [OPTION] or SET [COMMAND]. (UDF inherits the option settings in effect at the time of the function's creation.)

The User-Defined Data types in SQL server are always derived from a built-in system data type. Therefore, there is no restriction on using them in a SQL statement (though you might need to cast them to the required data type).

Summary

Microsoft SQL Server is one of the largest RDMS systems on the market. You should now have a better grasp of the steps and resources available to create your own UDFs. First, we discussed the proper usage of permissions to ensure that the developer can successfully create UDFs. It cannot be stressed enough that one of the most frustrating instances is when the developer cannot get productive results because of a permission restriction. Additionally, you must pay careful attention to the naming conventions that you implement and realize the limitation of which built-in functions cannot be used in your UDFs.

In general, we discussed how to create, alter, and remove the different forms of UDFs, how to handle debugging and error checking, and how to transform your UDFs into system functions. By paying close attention to the inherent rules of the SQL Server platform, you can provide a rich database architecture in which to provide business solutions.

In the next chapter, we will take a look at creating UDFs in the Sybase implementation. Since the two database platforms are nearly identical, you should notice a lot of similarity. For the seasoned developer, the transition from SQL Server to Sybase (and vice versa) should be a trivial matter at best.

16

Creating User-Defined Functions in Sybase SQL

Although Sybase and Microsoft SQL Server share (to a certain extent) the procedural Transact-SQL language, their respective dialects began to diverge when Microsoft introduced SQL Server 7.0. Microsoft had chosen to overhaul the language and add the features that would put it on the level of more robust and mature players like Oracle's PL/SQL. Even with the upcoming Yukon version (which will allow you to create procedures and functions in .NET-family languages), it is explicitly stated that Transact-SQL offers superior performance (though not flexibility) because of its closer relationship to SQL Server's engine.

Starting with Sybase ASE version 12.0, Sybase started supporting user-defined functions (UDFs) that can be used in SQL statements. These UDFs must be implemented in Java and are executed in a dedicated Java Virtual Machine (JVM) inside the Sybase ASE server. The only way to add a UDF to a Sybase database nowadays implies using Java programming language (SQLJ). Using Java within Sybase Adaptive Server requires a separate license for the ASE_JAVA option. (It is included in the developer edition of ASE free of charge, though.) Using Java classes inside ASE has opened up an enormous range of functionality that cannot be implemented in pure T-SQL. Using Java allows the developer to leverage the power of the RDBMS implementation with the flexibility of the Java programming language. Now you can access functionality that includes everything from file I/O, Web services, XML, and e-mail.

Acquiring Privileges

Only a database owner or user with assigned SA (system administrator) role has the ability to create a function (and drop function, for that matter). This privilege cannot be granted and comes only with the database ownership or SA role.

Permission to execute the SQLJ functions is granted to PUBLIC implicitly, but, in addition, the user must have access privileges for all of the objects in the RDBMS that this function references.

Creating UDFs

To add a custom function to ASE, you still use `create` function syntax, but all it does is create a stub (a SQL wrapper for a Java static method) within the Sybase database to call an external library. The SQLJ syntax for the `create` function is as follows:

```
create function [owner].sql_function_name
([sql_parameter_name sql_datatype
[( length)| (precision[, scale])]
[, sql_parameter_name sql_datatype
[( length ) | ( precision[, scale]) ]]
...])
returns sql_datatype
[( length)| (precision[, scale])]
[modifies sql data]
[returns null on null input |
called on null input]
[deterministic | not deterministic]
[exportable]
language java
parameter style java
external name 'java_method_name
[([java_datatype[ {, java_datatype }
...]])]'
```

Following is an explanation of the `create` function parameters:

❑ `sql_function_name`—This is the Transact-SQL name of the function. It must conform to the rules for identifiers and cannot be a variable.

❑ `sql_parameter_name`—This is the name of an argument to the function. The value of each input parameter is supplied when the function is executed. Parameters are optional; a SQLJ function need not take arguments. Parameter names must conform to the rules for identifiers. If the value of a parameter contains non-alphanumeric characters, it must be enclosed in quotation marks. This includes object names qualified by a database name or owner name, since they include a period. If the value of the parameter begins with a numeric character, it also must be enclosed in quotation marks.

❑ `sql_data type [(length) | ( precision [, scale])]`—This is the Transact-SQL data type of the parameter.

❑ `sql_data type`—This is the SQL procedure signature.

❑ `returns sql_data type`—This specifies the result data type of the function.

❑ `modifies sql data`—This indicates that the Java method invokes SQL operations, reads, and modifies SQL data in the database. This is the default and only implementation. It is included for syntactic compatibility with the ANSI standard.

❑ `deterministic | not deterministic`—These are supported for syntactic compatibility with the ANSI standard. They are not implemented.

❑ `Exportable`—This specifies that the procedure is to be run on a remote server using the Adaptive Server OmniConnect feature. Both the procedure and the method it is built on must reside on the remote server.

❑   `language java`—This specifies that the external routine is written in Java. This is a required clause for SQLJ functions.

❑   `parameter style java`—This specifies that the parameters passed to the external routine at run-time are Java parameters. This is a required clause for SQLJ functions.

❑   `External`—This indicates that the `create` function defines a SQL name for an external routine written in a programming language other than SQL.

❑   `Name`—This specifies the name of the external routine (Java method). The specified name— `'java_method_name [ java_data type[{, java_data type} ...]]'`—is a character-string literal and must be enclosed in single quotation marks.

❑   `java_method_name`—This specifies the name of the external Java method.

❑   `java_data type`—This specifies a Java data type that is mappable or result-set mappable. This is the Java method signature.

Here is an example of the simplified syntax:

```
CREATE FUNCTION fn_helloworld(arg1 varchar(15))
        RETURNS java.lang.String
        LANGUAGE JAVA
        PARAMETER STYLE JAVA
EXTERNAL NAME "javaExample.fn_helloworld"
```

All the logic will be implemented in Java class `"javaExample"`, and this statement just registers the function with Sybase server, allowing it to be called just like any built-in SQL function. You cannot create a SQLJ function with the same name as an ASE built-in function. You can create UDFs (based on Java static methods) and SQLJ functions with the same class. A maximum of 31 parameters can be included in a create function statement.

When creating a SQLJ function, keep the following in mind:

❑   The SQL function signature is the SQL data type `sql_data type` of each function parameter.

❑   To comply with the ANSI standard, do not include an "at" sign (@) before parameter names. Sybase adds an "at" sign internally to support parameter name binding. You will see the "at" sign when using `sp_help` to print out information about the SQLJ function.

❑   When creating a SQLJ function, you must include the parentheses that surround the `sql_parameter_name` and `sql_data type` information—even if you do not include that information. Consider the following example:

```
create function sqlj_fc()
    language java
    parameter style java
external name 'SQLJExamples.fn.method'
```

❑   The `modifies sql data` clause specifies that the method invokes SQL operations and reads and modifies SQL data. This is the default value. You do not need to include it, except for syntactic compatibility with the SQLJ Part 1 standard.

❑ returns null on null input and called on null input specify how Adaptive Server handles NULL arguments of a function call. returns null on null input specifies that if the value of any argument is NULL at run-time, the return value of the function is set to NULL and the function body is not invoked. called on null input is the default. It specifies that the function be invoked regardless of NULL argument values.

❑ You can include the deterministic or not deterministic keywords, but Adaptive Server does not use them. They are included for syntactic compatibility with the SQLJ Part 1 standard.

❑ The exportable keyword specifies that the function is to run on a remote server using Sybase OmniConnect capabilities. Both the function and the method on which it is based must be installed on the remote server.

❑ Clauses language java and parameter style java specify that the referenced method is written in Java and that the parameters are Java parameters. You must include these phrases when creating a SQLJ function.

❑ The external name clause specifies that the routine is not written in SQL and identifies the Java method, class, and package name (if any).

❑ The Java method signature specifies the Java data type java_data type of each method parameter. The Java method signature is optional. If it is not specified, Adaptive Server infers the Java method signature from the SQL function signature. Sybase recommends that you include the method signature because this practice handles all data-type translations.

❑ You can define different SQL names for the same Java method using the create function and then use them in the same way.

Before you can create a SQLJ function, you must write the Java method that it references, compile the method class, and install it in the database. In the following example, SQLJExamples.region() maps a state code to a region number and returns that number to the user:

```
public static int region(String s)
     throws SQLException {
  s = s.trim();
  if (s.equals("MN") || s.equals("VT") ||
       s.equals("NH") ) return 1;
  if (s.equals("FL") || s.equals("GA") ||
       s.equals("AL") ) return 2;
  if (s.equals("CA") || s.equals("AZ") ||
       s.equals("NV") ) return 3;
   else throw new SQLException
      ("Invalid state code", "X2001");
}
```

After writing and installing the method, you can create the SQLJ function as shown in the following example:

```
create function region_of(state char(20))
     returns integer
language java parameter style java
external name
     'SQLJExamples.region(java.lang.String)'
```

The SQLJ `create function` statement specifies an input parameter (`state char(20)`) and an `integer` return value. The SQL function signature is `char(20)`. The Java method signature is `java.lang.String`. You can call a SQLJ function directly, as if it were a built-in function, as shown in the following example:

```
select name, region_of(state) as region
    from sales_emps
where region_of(state)=3
```

The search sequence for functions in ASE is as follows:

1. Built-in functions

2. SQLJ functions

3. Java-SQL functions that are called directly

Handling NULL Argument Values

Java class data types and Java primitive data types handle NULL argument values in different ways:

❑ Java object data types that are classes (such as `java.lang.Integer`, `java.lang.String`, `java.lang.byte[]`, and `java.sql.Timestamp`) can hold both actual values and NULL reference values.

❑ Java primitive data types (such as `boolean`, `byte`, `short`, and `int`) have no representation for a NULL value. They can hold only non-NULL values.

When a Java method is invoked, and causes a SQL NULL value to be passed as an argument to a Java parameter whose data type is a Java class, it is passed as a Java NULL reference value. When a SQL NULL value is passed as an argument to a Java parameter of a Java primitive data type, however, an exception is raised because the Java primitive data type has no representation for a NULL value.

Typically, you will write Java methods that specify Java parameter data types that are classes. In this case, NULLs are handled without raising an exception. If you choose to write Java functions that use Java parameters that cannot handle NULL values, you can either:

❑ Include the `returns null on null input` clause when you create the SQLJ function.

❑ Invoke the SQLJ function using a `case` or other conditional expression to test for NULL values and call the SQLJ function only for the non-NULL values.

You can handle expected NULLs when you create the SQLJ function or when you call it. The following sections describe both scenarios and reference this method:

```
public static String job(int jc)
    throws SQLException {
if (jc==1) return "Admin";
else if (jc==2) return "Sales";
else if (jc==3) return "Clerk";
else return "unknown jobcode";
}
```

Handling NULLS When Creating the Function

If NULL values are expected, you can include the returns null on null input clause when you create the function. Consider the following example:

```
create function job_of(jc integer)
    returns varchar(20)
returns null on null input
language java parameter style java
external name 'SQLJExamples.job(int)'
```

You can then call job_of in this way:

```
select name, job_of(jobcode)
    from sales_emps
where job_of(jobcode) <> "Admin"
```

When the SQL system evaluates the call job_of(jobcode) for a row of sales_emps in which the jobcode column is NULL, the value of the call is set to NULL without actually calling the Java method QLJExamples.job. For rows with non-NULL values of the jobcode column, the call is performed normally.

Thus, when a SQLJ function created using the returns null on null input clause encounters a NULL argument, the result of the function call is set to NULL, and the function is not invoked.

If you include the returns null on null input clause when creating a SQLJ function, the returns null on null input clause applies to all function parameters, including nullable parameters.

If you include the called on null input clause (the default), NULL arguments for non-nullable parameters generate an exception.

Mapping Java and SQL Data Types

When you create a function that references a Java method, the data types of input and output parameters or result sets must not conflict when values are converted from the SQL environment to the Java environment and back again. The rules for how this mapping takes place are consistent with the Java Database Connectivity (JDBC) standard implementation. JDBC will be discussed in depth in Chapter 24.

Each SQL parameter and its corresponding Java parameter must be mappable. SQL and Java data types are mappable in the following ways:

❏   A SQL data type and a primitive Java data type are *simply mappable* if so specified in the table that follows.

❏   A SQL data type and a non-primitive Java data type are *object mappable* if so specified in the table that follows.

- ❏ A SQL abstract data type (ADT) and a non-primitive Java data type are *ADT mappable* if both are the same class or interface.

- ❏ A SQL data type and a Java data type are *output mappable* if the Java data type is an array and the SQL data type is simply mappable, object mappable, or ADT mappable to the Java data type (for example, character and string [ ] are output mappable).

- ❏ A Java data type is *result set mappable* if it is an array of the result set–oriented class `java.sql.ResultSet`.

In general, a Java method is mappable to SQL if each of its parameters is mappable to SQL and its result-set parameters are result-set mappable and the return type is mappable. The following table shows the SQL data types and corresponding Java simply mappable and object mappable data types:

SQL Data Type	Java Simply Mappable	Java Object Mappable
char/unichar		java.lang.String
Nchar		java.lang.String
varchar/univarchar		java.lang.String
nvarchar		java.lang.String
Text		java.lang.String
Numeric		java.math.BigDecimal
Decimal		java.math.BigDecimal
Money		java.math.BigDecimal
smallmoney		java.math.BigDecimal
Bit	Boolean	Boolean
Tinyint	Byte	Integer
Smallint	Short	Integer
Integer	Int	Integer
Real	Float	Float
Float	Double	Double
double precision	Double	Double
Binary		byte [ ]
varbinary		byte [ ]
Datetime		java.sql.Timestamp
smalldatetime		java.sql.Timestamp

When you create a SQLJ function, you typically specify a Java method signature. You can also allow ASE to infer the Java method signature from the routine's SQL signature according to standard JDBC data type correspondence rules described in the preceding table. Sybase recommends that you include the Java method signature because this practice ensures that all data type translations are handled as specified.

You must explicitly specify the Java method signature for data types that are object mappable. Otherwise, ASE infers the primitive, simply mappable data type. For example, the SQLJExamples.job method contains a parameter of type int. When creating a function referencing that method, ASE infers a Java signature of int, and you need not specify it. However, suppose the parameter of SQLJExamples.job were Java Integer, which is the object mappable type. Consider the following example:

```
public class SQLJExamples {
    public static String job(Integer jc)
        throws SQLException ...
```

Then, you must specify the Java method signature when you create a function that references it:

```
create function job_of(jc integer)
...
external name
    'SQLJExamples.job(java.lang.Integer)'
```

If an installed class has been modified, ASE checks to make sure that the method signature is valid when you invoke a SQLJ function that references that class. If the signature of a modified method is still valid, the execution of the SQLJ routine succeeds.

Altering UDFs

Once the function has been created with the CREATE FUNCTION statement it can be modified using the ALTER FUNCTION statement. The ALTER FUNCTION syntax is the same as the CREATE FUNCTION syntax and is as follows:

```
ALTER FUNCTION [owner.]function_name
    Function_definition
```

It is important to note that the full function definition must be given with the statement and that any permissions are maintained. This is preferable in a production environment, as the DBA wants to incur as little interference as possible.

Of course, by using Java UDFs you also have the option of updating the java methods that are used. Normally, this is accomplished by recoding some part of the java method, recompiling, and loading the method into the database. Updating a java method within the database is a simple task of using the update switch within the INSTALL JAVA syntax. The following is the syntax for this method:

```
INSTALL JAVA UPDATE
[ JAR 'jarname' ]
FROM FILE 'filename'
```

This is assuming that the function method prototype does not change. Any change in the function name, input parameters, or return type forces the use of the ALTER FUNCTION statement so that the database will accurately reflect the changes made.

Dropping UDFs

Dropping functions from the database is a relatively simple matter of using the appropriate DROP FUNCTION call. The syntax for the DROP statement is as follows:

```
DROP FUNCTION 'function_name'
```

Dropping a function also removes any of the permissions that the function had assigned to it unlike the ALTER FUNCTION statement. This is important for the DBA to remember, as dropping and re-creating a function also entails reassigning all of the existing permissions back to the function.

Additionally, removing a function statement in this manner does not automatically de-reference the associated JAR or class file. In order to take care of this "cleanup" task, you will need to use the following REMOVE JAVA statement.

```
REMOVE JAVA PACKAGE "class_name"
```

Of course, you can retain the classes internally and just remove their association with a specific JAR. This is often used when you want to reconfigure and/or consolidate several JARs into a new, single one. In order to accomplish this you would use the RETAIN CLASSES option as shown in this example:

```
REMOVE JAVA PACKAGE "class name" RETAIN CLASSES
```

Debugging UDFs

Sybase ASE's debugging support for UDFs is about on par with its cohort, MS SQL Server. Natively, there is no debugging menu within ASE itself. The main amount of debugging is taken care of with the context of SQL Advantage. Even so, this is still limited at best because it requires that you debug the body of your functions separately from the shell. Any error messages are displayed in the output window to prompt the developer to fix his or her code.

There are some bright spots in the future, as Sybase's SQL Server Anywhere has a fairly decent debugging environment from which to work. No doubt this will be converted and placed in with the ASE framework so that the same functionality can be had by both systems.

Error Handling in UDFs

Error handling within UDFs in Sybase has many of the same limitations as its counterpart, Microsoft SQL Server. Errors within the SQL code are handled through the use of the @@ERROR function. The caveat is that any error handling must be performed within the space of the UDF's lifetime, because error information is not automatically handed off to the next accompanying statement. This often causes headaches for developers if they want to maintain consistency when checking within their UDFs. Consider the following example of creating a simple SQL function DIVIDEBYZERO:

```
CREATE FUNCTION udf_dividebyzero
    (@arg1 INT, @arg2 INT) RETURNS INT
AS
BEGIN
DECLARE @result INT
DECLARE @error_value INT
    SET @result = @arg1/@arg2
-- check for errors
    SET @error_value = @@ERROR
    IF @error_value > 0
-- try returning an error value
  SET @result= @error_value

 RETURN @result
END
```

The purpose of this function is to simply divide the first argument by the second argument and, if any error occurs, to then return the error code as the result. While the system will normally return a valid value, if we place a zero as the second argument the function will return the appropriate error code. However, let's see what actually happens when we try to read the error number when using the @@ERROR syntax.

```
select dbo.udf_dividebyzero(5,0)
select @@ERROR as error
GO
Server: Msg 8134, Level 16, State 1, Procedure udf_dividebyzero, Line 6
Divide by zero error encountered.

error
-----------
0

(1 row(s) affected)
```

As you can see, the error is returned by the function properly, but we are not able to view it on the other end with the @@ERROR statement.

Finding Information about UDFs

The Sybase way (shared by Microsoft SQL Server, and to a certain extent by MySQL) of accessing system information is through system-stored procedures. The latest version of Sybase Adaptive Server added the INFORMATION_SCHEMA views to comply with the SQL standard.

The system-stored procedures that can help you to obtain information about SQLJ functions are listed in the following table.

System Stored Procedure	Description
sp_depends	Lists all database objects referenced by a SQLJ function, as well as database objects that reference the SQLJ function.
sp_help	Lists each parameter name, type, length, precision, scale, parameter order, parameter mode, and return type of the SQLJ routine.
sp_helpjava	Lists information about Java classes and Java archives (JARs) installed in the database. The depends parameter lists dependencies of specified classes that are named in the external name clause of the SQLJ create function or SQLJ create procedure statement.
sp_helpprotect	Lists the permissions for SQLJ stored procedures and SQLJ functions.

The other way to extract the information about UDFs would be querying the system tables (for example, sysprocedures) directly. This approach is not recommended because it relies on the table structure to be there in future releases. This is not always the case.

Summary

As you have seen in this chapter, Sybase and Microsoft SQL Server share the procedural language of Transact-SQL, although individual characteristics of each vendor's implementation began to diverge with SQL Server 7.0. As of Sybase ASE version 12.0, Sybase began supporting UDFs that are used in conjunction with SQL statements. UDFs in Sybase ASE are implemented in Java and are executed in a dedicated JVM inside the Sybase ASE server. Although the only way to add a UDF to a Sybase database is with the Java programming language (SQLJ), along with the fact that Sybase Adaptive Server requires a separate license for the ASE_JAVA option, a great deal of robustness and flexibility is now available for Sybase users who want to create UDFs to empower their SQL database environments.

Chapter 17 will detail the creation of UDFs in the MySQL platform. You will come to notice that the MySQL platform does not prove as robust an environment in which to create your UDFs as some of the other implementations. This goes back to the creation of the MySQL platform as a fast database rather than one focusing on robustness. However, in recent years, some strides have been made, and the MySQL implementation is slowly starting to adopt more of the versatility of some of the other systems.

Creating User-Defined Functions in MySQL

The Open Source movement has gained momentum in recent years, and the MySQL RDBMS is at the top of the popularity list. It is now deployed in thousands of locations around the world. The database measures up to its entrenched rivals quite impressively. However, it lacks many of the more advanced features (such as internal transactional support, integrity constraint, and so on). An ability to create user-defined functions (UDFs) using a built-in procedural language is one of the deficiencies in the current release. The upcoming MySQL version 5.0 adds support for stored procedures, functions, and triggers to the developer's toolkit.

Acquiring Permissions

To add a function to the database, all you need is the INSERT privilege. Also, the DELETE privilege is needed to execute the DROP FUNCTION statement successfully. This reflects the underlying mechanism employed for keeping track of the privileges, namely system tables, where a record is inserted the moment a UDF is added, and deleted once the function is dropped.

It would be reasonable to assume that CREATE, ALTER, DROP, and EXECUTE privileges would extend to the UDFs, but as of the writing of this book, none of these options had been implemented.

Creating UDFs

The syntax for creating a UDF in the new MySQL is based on the existing one that is used to employ external shared libraries, with some modifications:

```
CREATE FUNCTION <function_name>
          (arg1 data_type,... ,n)
RETURNS data_type
[LANGUAGE SQL]
[[NOT] DETERMINISTIC]
[SQL SECURITY (DEFINER | INVOKER)]
```

```
[COMMENT string]
[BEGIN]
     <function_body>
[END]
```

The syntax resembles that of IBM DB2 UDB, and comes very close to compliance with the SQL3 standard.

The signature of the function includes a list of the named input arguments together with their data types, which can be any valid MySQL data type.

The RETURN data type can be any of the valid MySQL data types <***>. This includes the ones that cannot be returned as a part of a SELECT statement, and are intended for use with stored procedures only.

The arguments further can be marked with IN, OUT, or INOUT modifiers specifying the intended use. The IN argument (being default) is used to pass the data into the function by value, OUT arguments are used for returning data (by reference), and INOUT has the best attributes of both—it can be used to get the data in, as well as to return it. These modifiers cannot be used within a function, and are valid for stored procedures only.

LANGUAGE SQL is optional. It implies that more languages will be supported in the future. MySQL hints at the possibility of including PHP (an Open Source hypertext processor) as one of the first for this purpose.

The DETERMINISTIC and NOT DETERMINISTIC clauses specify the respective type of the function. MySQL states that these are not currently used by the optimizer, and are reserved for future use.

The SQL SECURITY characteristic can be used to specify whether the routine should be executed using the permissions of the user who creates the routine, or the user who invokes it. The default is DEFINER. This is as close as MySQL got to the privilege system implemented by its more mature counterparts. There is no GRANT/REVOKE EXECUTE privilege.

The COMMENT clause allows you to insert in-line comments for the function. This information is displayed with the SHOW CREATE FUNCTION command.

The BEGIN...END compound statement allows you to create multiple-statement functions. It also supports *labeling*, which means that you could have multiple named compound statements inside your function's body.

There is no transactional support inside the body of the function (that is, BEGIN ATOMIC, using the IBM SQL PL terminology), meaning that it can be executed as a part of the invoking transaction only.

> **MySQL does not support overloading for its functions and stored procedures.**

Here is an example of a user-defined function, FN_HELLOWORLD, implemented within MySQL:

```
mysql> CREATE FUNCTION fn_helloworld(arg1 char(15))
    -> RETURNS CHAR(30)
    -> LANGUAGE SQL
    -> COMMENT 'example of MySQL user defined function'
    -> RETURN CONCAT(arg1,', ', 'world!');
Query OK, 0 rows affected (0.01 sec)
```

To invoke the function, the following statement could be used:

```
mysql> select fn_helloworld('Hello') as result;
+----------------+
| result         |
+----------------+
| Hello ,world!  |
+----------------+
1 row in set (0.00 sec)
```

The UDFs (but not stored procedures) in MySQL 5.0 Alpha may not contain references to tables. This limitation excludes some SELECT statements. In addition, some SET statements are subject to the same limitations. Any attempt to use them would result in the following error message:

```
ERROR 1298 (0A000): Statements like SELECT, INSERT, UPDATE (and others) are not
allowed in a FUNCTION
```

This effectively precludes any operations involving data tables within UDFs.

MySQL UDFs support simple cursors, loops, conditional execution, and other programming constructs. Here is an example of factorial calculation using a WHILE loop (the first command changes the default delimiter from semicolon to double slash to allow for inclusion of the semicolons in the function's body):

```
mysql>  delimiter //
mysql>  CREATE FUNCTION fn_factorial(arg1 INTEGER)
    ->    RETURNS INTEGER
    ->    BEGIN
    ->    DECLARE l_result INT default 1;
    ->        DECLARE l_counter INT;
    ->      SET l_counter = arg1;
    ->      WHILE l_counter > 1 DO
    ->      SET l_result = l_result * l_counter;
    ->      SET l_counter = l_counter - 1;
    ->      END WHILE;
    ->      RETURN l_result;
    -> END;
    -> //
Query OK, 0 rows affected (0.00 sec)
mysql> select fn_factorial(5) as result;
    -> //
+------------------+
| result           |
+------------------+
|              120 |
+------------------+
1 row in set (0.00 sec)
```

There is no way to create a recursive version of the function. The reason is not that MySQL procedural language does not support recursion, but rather that you cannot refer to the object that has yet to be created. This behavior is very similar to that displayed by IBM DB2 UDB.

The upper limit for our version of the recursive function is determined by the data type used to hold the value.

MySQL supports multiple return statements for UDFs, functionality similar to that of Oracle. The function implemented in this way works similarly to the SWITCH statement:

```
mysql>  delimiter //
mysql> CREATE FUNCTION fn_evaluate(arg INTEGER)
           RETURNS VARCHAR(25)
    -> BEGIN
    -> IF arg > 10 AND arg < 20 THEN
    ->    RETURN 'small';
    ->        ELSEIF arg > 20 AND arg < 80 THEN
    ->        RETURN 'medium';
    ->        ELSEIF arg > 80 then
    ->        RETURN 'pretty big';
    ->        END IF;
    -> END;
    -> //
Query OK, 0 rows affected (0.00 sec)

mysql> select fn_evaluate(25);
    -> //
+-----------------+
| fn_evaluate(25) |
+-----------------+
| medium          |
+-----------------+
1 row in set (0.01 sec)
```

Now, the function FN_EVALUATE contains an error that might not be quite obvious: what if the value is *less* than 10?

```
mysql> select fn_evaluate(8);
    -> //
ERROR 1305 (2F005): FUNCTION fn_evaluate ended without RETURN
```

The moral: a UDF must have a RETURN clause for any execution path that the flow-control algorithm allows. In the previous example, an addition of the default ELSE case would solve the problem:

```
mysql> CREATE FUNCTION fn_evaluate(arg INTEGER)
           RETURNS VARCHAR(25)
    -> BEGIN
    -> IF arg > 10 AND arg < 20 THEN
    ->    RETURN 'small';
    ->        ELSEIF arg > 20 AND arg < 80 THEN
    ->        RETURN 'medium';
    ->        ELSEIF arg > 80 then
    ->        RETURN 'pretty big';
    ->    ELSE
    ->        RETURN 'too small'
    ->        END IF;
    -> END;
    -> //
Query OK, 0 rows affected (0.00 sec)
```

Creating External Functions

You can still create a UDF in MySQL the hard way, using the C/C++ programming language. There are two ways to add new functions to your MySQL environment: it could be either an external UDF registered with the database through a CREATE FUNCTION statement, or a built-in function added to the server's source code and compiled into the MySQL executable.

The external and internal SQL functions share the same namespace. Since no overloading is supported, the functions will be considered identical based on the function's name alone (regardless of the signature of the function—which is the case for IBM and Oracle). Error 1288 (42000): FUNCTION <function_name> already exists will be returned upon an attempt to create another function with exactly the same name.

The syntax for adding a new UDF is simple:

```
CREATE [AGGREGATE]FUNCTION <function_name> (arg1...,n)
        RETURNS <STRING|REAL|INTEGER>
SONAME <shared_library_name>
```

As you can see, only three data types are allowed for the RETURN statement. The shared_library_name is the name of the actual executable implementing the function's logic.

You can compare this to TEMPLATE functions of IBM DB2 UDB, or Sybase's (and Oracle's) functions implemented in Java.

To add a function through a CREATE FUNCTION statement, your operating system must support dynamic loading. Most modern operating systems do.

Altering UDFs

To alter an existing user-defined function, you would use the ALTER FUNCTION statement, as shown here:

```
ALTER FUNCTION <function_name>
[NAME <new_function_name>]
[SQL SECURITY (DEFINER | INVOKER)]
[COMMENT string]
```

The statement can only be used to alter characteristics of the function, not the actual body. The following example alters the FN_FACTORIAL function:

```
mysql> alter function fn_factorial COMMENT 'calculates factorial';
    -> //
Query OK, 0 rows affected (0.02 sec)
```

You can specify more than one change when altering a function. To change the function signature or body definition, you must drop and re-create the function.

Dropping UDFs

The standard DROP FUNCTION (with an optional MySQL-specific clause) statement can be used to remove a function from the database, as shown here:

```
DROP  FUNCTION [IF EXISTS] <function_name>
```

For example, to drop the FN_FACTORIAL function, we could use the following command:

```
mysql> DROP FUNCTION IF EXISTS fn_factorial;
    -> //
Query OK, 0 rows affected (0.00 sec)
```

The IF EXISTS clause is optional, aimed at preventing the server from returning errors. If it is specified, the query would execute without an error, indicating that the warning was issued (you could use the SHOW WARNINGS command to retrieve the set of warnings); otherwise, ERROR 1289 (42000): FUNCTION <function_name> does not exist will be returned.

In the case of an external function, this syntax will de-register the function, but it will not remove the executable from the system.

Error Handling and Debugging

MySQL introduces conditions and handlers modeled after IBM DB2 UDB. The similarity does not end there. Like IBM DB2 UDB, there is no way to use conditions and handlers to handle the exceptions in UDFs, only in stored procedures.

Debugging the new MySQL functions is rather primitive: no stepping through, breakpoint, or other features you get used to with more mature environments are available in MySQL. For external functions, use the debugger supplied with your particular compiler.

Since MySQL is an Open Source project, you might try to add custom debugging by recompiling the source and configuring the server for debugging. This is definitely not for the faint-hearted, and requires a thorough understanding of C/C++ programming on the platform you are targeting. Refer to the MySQL AB documentation for more details.

The new stored routines feature was only introduced recently, and is still in alpha release version as of the writing of this book. Some bugs still must be ironed out before it could become a stable and reliable tool in the MySQL programmer's toolset.

Finding Information about UDFs

MySQL does not implement standard INFORMATION_SCHEMA views. To obtain information about database objects, you must use MySQL extension commands.

To retrieve information about a UDF, you would execute the SHOW CREATE FUNCTION statement:

```
mysql> SHOW CREATE FUNCTION fn_factorial;
+---------------+-----------------------------------------+
| Function      | Create Function                         |
+---------------+-----------------------------------------+
| fn_factorial  | CREATE FUNCTION fn_factorial            |
|               |                     (arg1 INTEGER)      |
|               | RETURNS INTEGER                         |
|               | BEGIN                                   |
|               | DECLARE l_result INT default 1;         |
|               | DECLARE l_counter INT;                  |
|               | SET l_counter = arg1;                   |
|               | WHILE l_counter > 1 DO                  |
|               |   SET l_result = l_result * l_counter;  |
|               |   SET l_counter = l_counter - 1;        |
|               | END WHILE;                              |
|               | RETURN l_result;                        |
|               | END;                                    |
+---------------+-----------------------------------------+
1 row in set (0.00 sec)
```

The command returns the statements that were used to create the function, and little more. To display information about the creation date, modification history, and so on, the command SHOW FUNCTION STATUS can be used:

```
mysql> show function status LIKE 'fn_factorial';
   -> //
```

The returned information is presented in the following table.

Column Name	Description	Data
Name	Name of the object	fn_factorial
Type	Type of the object	FUNCTION
Definer	Name of user who created the object on local machine	@localhost
Modified	The modification date and time; if there have been no modifications, shows [0000-00-00 00:00:00]	2004-04-12 23:17:44
Created	Date the function was created	2004-04-12 19:09:53
Security_type	The security type specified at the time of creation; could be DEFINER or INVOKER	DEFINER
Comment	The string added with a COMMENT clause in the CREATE FUNCTION statement	Calculates factorial

Information about external UDFs (but not the functions created with LANGUAGE SQL clause) is also added to the mysql.func system table. MySQL 5.0 adds a new table, mysql.proc, to maintain the information about the new UDFs. The following table shows the structure of the PROC system table. The table contains one more column ([Extra]), which contains no values, and is reserved for future use.

Field Name	Type	Null	Key	Default
Db	varchar(64)	N	PRI	FUNCTION
Name	varchar(64)	N	PRI	
Type	enum('FUNCTION','PROCEDURE')	N	PRI	
Specific_name	varchar(64)	N		
language	enum('SQL')	N		SQL
sql_data_access	enum('CONTAINS_SQL')	N		CONTAINS_SQL
is_deterministic	enum('YES','NO')	N		NO
Security_type	enum('INVOKER','DEFINER')	N		DEFINER
param_list	Blob	N		
Returns	varchar(64)	N		
Body	blob	N		
Definer	varchar(77)	N		
Created	timestamp	Y		NULL
Modified	timestamp	Y		NULL
sql_mode	set(REAL_AS_FLOAT,PIPES_AS_CONCAT,ANSI_QUOTES,IGNORE_SPACE,NOT_USED,ONLY_FULL_GROUP_BY,NO_UNSIGNED_SUBTRACTION,NO_DIR_IN_CREATE,POSTGRESQL,ORACLE,MSSQL,DB2,MAXDB,NO_KEY_OPTIONS,NO_TABLE_OPTIONS,NO_FIELD_OPTIONS,MYSQL323,MYSQL40,ANSI,NO_AUTO_VALUE_ON_ZERO)	N		
comment	varchar(64)	N		

You can select any subset of the data from the PROC table to suit your needs. Here are the results produced by querying this table when using the mysql database:

```
mysql> SELECT
          name
         ,language
         ,security_type
```

```
         ,definer
FROM proc;
+--------------+----------+---------------+------------+
| name         | language | security_type | definer    |
+--------------+----------+---------------+------------+
|fn_factorial  | SQL      | DEFINER       | @localhost |
+--------------+----------+---------------+------------+
1 row in set (0.00 sec)
```

The SHOW CREATE FUNCTION command is based on this new PROC table, and shows a subset of the information contained in it.

All active external functions are reloaded each time the server starts, unless you start mysqld with the '--skip-grant-tables' option. The new SQL functions are loaded and are available by default.

Summary

The MySQL platform is based on the premise of creating a fast RDBMS. Consequently, it lacks many features that are now being built in to accommodate user demand. The purpose of this chapter was to inform you as a developer of the upcoming functionality of UDFs in the newest release of the MySQL platform (currently 5.0). The limited functionality for creating, altering, and dropping UDFs was addressed, and also the primitive debugging capabilities available to the developer. Rest assured that, as the MySQL platform progresses, more features will be added to create a more robust platform in terms of functionality.

In the next chapter, we will detail the creation of UDFs using the PostgreSQL platform. The MySQL and PostgreSQL implementations are the quintessential yin and yang of Open Source database platforms. While MySQL is more concerned with speed, the PostgreSQL platform was developed as a full-blown functional solution and is just now starting to concern itself with overall speed of use. You will be able to readily see the vast differences in implementation between the two platforms after reading the next chapter.

Creating User-Defined Functions in PostgreSQL

PostgreSQL is arguably the most SQL3-compliant noncommercial database in active use today. Although it does not have a full-fledged built-in procedural SQL extension language, it provides four different mechanisms for adding a user-defined function (UDF) to the environment:

❑   Query functions written in SQL (this is correct, in SQL; there is no built-in procedural extension similar to PL/SQL or Transact-SQL here).

❑   Procedural functions, written in PL/Tcl or PL/pgSQL. Unlike the internal PL/SQL or Transact-SQL, these are languages loadable into the PostgreSQL environment. Currently, PostgreSQL distributes four such languages (PL/pgSQL, PL/Tcl, PL/Perl, and PL/Python), although a custom language could also be added, provided that it complies with the requirements.

❑   Internal built-in functions (added to the PostgreSQL source code).

❑   External functions built with C/C++.

PostgreSQL allows not only base data types to be sent to and returned from the UDFs but also composite ones. The syntax of the function created with SQL is similar to that of the rest of the RDBMS implementations discussed in this book:

```
CREATE FUNCTION function_name (data_type1, ...n)
    RETURNS <data_type>
    AS ' <SQL statements>; [AS RESULT]'
LANGUAGE SQL
[WITH (ISSTRICT | ISCACHABLE)];
```

The list of the function's arguments contains only data types, no names. The sizable data types (that is, VARCHAR) could be sized (that is, VARCHAR(25)) or not; this applies to both input and output parameters.

The function could return a singular scalar value or a composite data type or a set (table-valuated functions). In the case in which no return is expected, the VOID must be specified; of course, this defies the purpose of the SQL function as it is discussed in this book.

Note that the body of the function is SQL statements only. There are no procedural language constructs such as variables, loops, or control-of-flow statements. This effectively precludes use or recursion, cursors, and other programming constructs. The statements are separated by semicolons and enclosed in single quotation marks.

Use the escape character \ or two single quotation marks (") to include special characters in your function's body. An explicit data type cast is required by PostgreSQL to determine the data type of the resulting expression; see the following table for the most common special characters and for the usage examples throughout this chapter.

Character	Name	Description
*	Asterisk	Used in the SELECT command to specify the return of all columns in the table. Used with the COUNT() aggregate function to specify all rows in a table.
()	Parentheses	Used to specify group expressions, enforce operator precedence, and denote function calls.
[]	Brackets	Used in conjunction with array functionality.
;	Semicolon	Used to terminate a SQL command.
,	Comma	Used to separate elements within a list.
.	Period	Used in user-defined types to signify attributes (in floating-point constants).
:	Colon	Used to select slices from arrays.
$	Dollar sign	Used in the body of a function definition to represent a positional parameter or argument.

The optional WITH clause has two possible settings: ISSTRICT and ISCACHABLE. The former instructs the function to return NULL if any of the arguments are null, and the latter specifies that the function is deterministic — that is, always returns the same results after having been given the same input parameters.

Acquiring Permissions

PostgreSQL closely follows the SQL standard syntax for granting the permissions to the EXECUTE user function. Only the database owner and the superuser (see the following note) have the privilege to CREATE a function.

```
GRANT { EXECUTE | ALL [ PRIVILEGES ] }
ON FUNCTION <function_name> ([type, ...]) [, ...]
TO { username | GROUP groupname | PUBLIC } [, ...]
```

The EXECUTE privilege allows the use of the specified function and the use of any operators that are implemented on top of the function. This is the only type of privilege that is applicable to functions.

The privilege can be granted to individual users and groups. Thus, every user will have all the privileges granted to the group to which the user belongs, as well as all the privileges granted to the PUBLIC group, in addition to the privileges granted to the user directly.

> *It should be noted that database* superusers *can access all objects regardless of object privilege settings. This is comparable to the rights of* root *in a UNIX system. As with* root, *it's unwise to operate as a* superuser *except when absolutely necessary.*

The privilege is revoked by using standard REVOKE syntax, as shown here:

```
REVOKE { EXECUTE | ALL [ PRIVILEGES ] }
ON FUNCTION funcname ([type, ...]) [, ...]
FROM { username | GROUP groupname | PUBLIC } [, ...]
```

If the revoked privilege (and, in the case of UDFs, it can only be EXECUTE) was granted to the user directly, and also through a group the user belongs to, it must be revoked from both; otherwise, the user will still have the privilege.

Information about privileges can be found through INFORMATION_SCHEMA views. See the section entitled "Finding Information about UDFs" later in this chapter.

Query SQL Functions

These functions are created in pure SQL — only Data Query Language (DQL), Data Manipulation Language (DML), and Data Definition Language (DDL) statements are allowed here (SELECT, UPDATE, DELETE, INSERT, CREATE, and so on). This is more than any of the "big league" RDBMSs are ready to offer, wherein DDL statements are explicitly banned from the SQL functions domain (admittedly, for a reason).

This power comes with more responsibility being placed on the user, because it is quite possible to create a function that drops a table, creates a new one, and returns a result — all at the same time!

The body of the function comprises a set of the SQL statements, the last of which must be a SELECT, returning results of the type declared in the functions signature. If the SELECT returns multirow results, the first row will be returned as the functions output (for information on multirow returning functions, see the section entitled "SQL Row and Table Functions" later in this chapter). The order of the returned rows is random, unless an ORDER BY clause was used.

Here is a PostgreSQL version of the FN_HELLOWORLD:

```
test_db=# CREATE FUNCTION
            fn_helloworld(VARCHAR)
        RETURNS VARCHAR
        AS
            'SELECT $1 || \',world!\';'
        LANGUAGE SQL;
```

In order to return a literal 'world', we had to enclose it in single quotation marks. Since the single quotation marks have a special meaning in the context, we had to add escape characters.

All example statements are executed from the PostgreSQL command-line utility PSQL. The line following the statement is an acknowledgment that the statement executed successfully; otherwise, an error message will be displayed

The arguments passed to the functions could be referred to in the body of the function as $1, $2, and so on, the number signifying the order in which the arguments are listed in the function's signature. In the previous example, the passed argument is concatenated with a literal, and a combined string is returned.

For user-defined types (*composite types* in PostgreSQL lingo), the format would include attributes (for example, $1.attribute1). PostgreSQL's ability to use user-defined types either as parameters or return values is unparalleled among RDBMS implementations.

Here are the results of the execution of the previous function:

```
test_db=# SELECT fn_helloworld('Hello')as hello;
    hello
-------------
Hello ,world!
(1 row)
```

Let's take a look at how to use DDL statements inside UDFs. The following function FN_ADDTABLE creates a table:

```
CREATE FUNCTION fn_addtable()
RETURNS VOID
AS
    'CREATE TABLE new_table (
            field1 VARCHAR(10)
            , field2 VARCHAR(10)
            );'
LANGUAGE SQL;
```

You cannot refer to the newly created table within the same function's body, because the table itself did not exist at the time the function was parsed and compiled (this means no SELECT, INSERT, DELETE, and so on, until the function is executed). Once the function is executed, it creates a table. Each subsequent call to the same function will result in an error. The name of the database object created in this way must be a literal. You cannot, for example, substitute the name of the table created inside the function with a variable passed into it as an argument.

Using Composite Types with PostgreSQL Functions

Unlike most of its competitors, PostgreSQL's functions allow for non-conventional data types to be passed into and returned from, such as composite types (similar to anchored types in Oracle).

When the composite type based on a table is passed into the function, the SELECT statement that uses the function must also include the table. The syntax for accessing the attributes of the composite types follows the standard notation, <type>.<attribute> (for example $1.description).

Consider the following example:

```
test_db=# CREATE TABLE products
        (
        description VARCHAR(50)
        ,price          NUMERIC
        ,units          CHAR(5)
        );
test_db=# INSERT INTO TABLE products
     VALUES ('apples', 1.25, 'lb');
test_db=# INSERT INTO TABLE products
     VALUES ('oranges', 1.50, 'lb');

test_db=# CREATE FUNCTION adjust_price
              (
                products
               ,VARCHAR(25)
               ,NUMERIC)
          RETURNS NUMERIC
           AS
           'SELECT $1.price * $3 AS new_price
            FROM products
            WHERE $1.description = $2;'
          LANGUAGE SQL;
test_db=# SELECT
              description
             ,price
             ,adjust_price(products, 'apples', 1.25)
          FROM products;

description  | price | adjust_price
-------------+-------+--------------
 apples      | 1.25  |     1.5625
 oranges     | 1.50  |
(2 rows)
```

As you can see, the function returned an adjusted price for the specified product. The required values for the SELECT statement in the function's body were substituted with the properties of the composite data type—a row of the PRODUCTS table.

To return a composite type from a UDF, you could make the following adjustments to the previous example:

```
test_db=# CREATE FUNCTION adjust_price
              (
                products
               ,VARCHAR(25)
               ,NUMERIC)
          RETURNS products
           AS
           'SELECT
               $1.description
             , $1.price * $3 AS new_price
             , $1.units
            FROM products
            WHERE $1.description = $2;'
          LANGUAGE SQL;
```

It is important to understand that the return type is a RECORD, not a table. An attempt to call the function from a SQL statement directly would result in the following error:

```
test_db=# SELECT
            adjust_price(products,'apples',1.25)
      FROM products;
ERROR:  Cannot display a value of type RECORD
```

Here is the proper syntax for invoking the function:

```
test_db=# SELECT
                description
                ,price
            ,(adjust_price(products, 'apples', 1.25)).price
            FROM products;

description  | price |    price
-------------+-------+------------
  apples     | 1.25  |    1.5625
  oranges    | 1.50  |
(2 rows)
```

Even though we have aliased the name as 'new_price', we cannot refer to this attribute by that name. The record is a record of the PRODUCTS type and it must specify exact attributes.

You also could extract the attribute from the function by using the following syntax:

```
price(adjust_price(products, 'apples', 1.25))
```

The results would be identical to these shown in the previous example. The <table>.<attribute> and the <attribute>(<table>) notations are interchangeable.

It is also possible to create a function that returns a record of the specified type by constructing it inside the function's body, without even mentioning the base table. In this case, all the attributes corresponding to the table's type fields must be listed in the exact order and be explicitly cast to the exact type of the field.

SQL Row and Table Functions

Although the composite type function in the previous examples returned a row, it cannot be used in the FROM clause because it relies on the composite table type being passed as the first argument, and the table type itself had to be in the query. If we modify the ADJUST_PRICE function not to use the table as an argument, we could create a PostgreSQL row function:

```
test_db=# CREATE FUNCTION get_record
                (
                    VARCHAR(25)
                )
            RETURNS products
            AS
            'SELECT * FROM products
            WHERE description = $1;'
```

```
            LANGUAGE SQL;
test_db=# SELECT * FROM get_record('apples')
description | price | units
------------+-------+---------
 apples     |  1.25 | lb
 (1 row)
```

No matter how many matching rows in the PRODUCTS table we have, the function GET_RECORD would return exactly one record from the top of the selected set. To return all matching rows, a SETOF clause must be used in the return type specification. The following example adds additional rows to the PRODUCTS table and then creates a function to return the rowset of products:

```
test_db=# INSERT INTO products
     VALUES ('fuji apples', 1.95, 'lb');
test_db=# INSERT INTO TABLE products
     VALUES ('golden apples', 1.45, 'lb');
test_db=# CREATE FUNCTION get_products
                (
                     VARCHAR(25)
                )
RETURNS SETOF products
AS
'SELECT * FROM products
        WHERE description LIKE \'%\' || $1 || \'%\';'
LANGUAGE SQL;
test_db=# SELECT * FROM get_products('app');
description           | price |    price
---------------------+-------+------------
 apples              |  1.25 | lb
 fuji apples         |  1.95 | lb
 golden apples       |  1.45 | lb

(3 rows)
```

Here, we used the LIKE predicate to return all the records where the description includes an 'app' character sequence without regard to its location.

The current version of PostgreSQL also allows for returning hierarchical data sets where each row returned through the function would call the function again. However, this feature is deprecated and might not be supported in future releases.

Dropping UDFs

The syntax for dropping a function within PostgreSQL is fairly standard:

```
DROP FUNCTION [schema_name.]<function_name>
        ([datatype1],...,[datatypeN])
    [CASCADE]|[RESTRICT];
```

You must supply the correct data types of the input arguments in the correct order. The server would not be able to differentiate between overloaded versions of the function. (See the section entitled "Overloading UDFs" later in this chapter.)

The CASCADE clause specifies that all objects dependent on the function must be dropped as well (see later).

The RESTRICT clause instructs the server *not* to drop the function if any dependent objects exist within the database. The RESTRICT clause is the default.

The CASCADE and RESTRICT clauses do work with operators and triggers. At the same time, if your function references a table or other function, these clauses would do nothing. You will be able to drop these referenced objects, without much fuss, from the RDBMS.

The ALTER FUNCTION statement is not supported in PostgreSQL. The only way to alter the function is to drop it and re-create it again.

Debugging PostgreSQL UDFs

The debugging of the UDFs created with LANGUAGE SQL in PostgreSQL is mostly a manual process of adjusting the logic of your SQL statements in the body of the function until it works. Debugging externally created functions belongs to the domain of the procedural languages with which the function is created.

Error Handling

There is no structured error handling in the PostgreSQL UDFs (similar to MS SQL Server and MySQL, in this regard) except for that provided by the RDBMS itself. The error message will invariably be returned to the client, because there is no way you could handle it within your SQL function body.

Overloading UDFs

PostgreSQL supports overloading for its UDFs (SQL standard section T322). A UDF is uniquely identified by its name and the number and data types of its inbound arguments; the return parameter is not taken into consideration. This behavior is illustrated by the following examples:

```
test_db=# CREATE FUNCTION foo(VARCHAR)
               RETURNS VARCHAR
            AS 'SELECT $1;'
            LANGUAGE SQL;
```

The preceding example produces a very simple function that returns the argument passed into it unchanged. The following example is a modification. The passed-in argument's data type is changed to INTEGER. As you can see, an overloaded version of the function FOO is created:

```
test_db=# CREATE FUNCTION foo(INTEGER)
              RETURNS VARCHAR
           AS 'SELECT CAST($1 AS VARCHAR);'
           LANGUAGE SQL;
```

An attempt to create yet another FOO function that accepts INTEGER and returns INTEGER will fail:

```
test_db=# CREATE FUNCTION foo(INTEGER)
              RETURNS INTEGER
           AS 'SELECT $1;'
           LANGUAGE SQL;
  ERROR: function foo exists with the same argument types
```

Changing the number of the arguments would render the new function FOO different from all its overloaded versions:

```
test_db=# CREATE FUNCTION foo(INTEGER, INTEGER)
              RETURNS VARCHAR
           AS 'SELECT CAST($1 + $2 AS VARCHAR);'
           LANGUAGE SQL;
```

PostgreSQL will resolve a call to an overloaded function based on the type and number of the input arguments. Each version of such a function would have a separate entry in the system catalog tables.

Finding Information about UDFs

Beginning with version 7.4, PostgreSQL includes SQL3-compliant INFORMATION_SCHEMA views to provide the metadata information about database objects. Before that, you could find the information in system catalogs.

Once you know the fields containing information you are looking for, the querying of both system catalog tables and INFORMATION_SCHEMA views is no different from querying any other view or table in the PostgreSQL server.

The system catalogs still exist in the new version of PostgreSQL, but use of INFORMATION_SCHEMA views is recommended for obtaining information about RDBMS objects. This is because the former represents proprietary PostgreSQL structures (which could be changed from release to release), whereas the latter are the standard views on top of the system catalogs (and will be maintained in accordance with the SQL standard).

PG_PROC Functions

The PG_PROC catalog stores the information about functions (and procedures, in the future) defined in the current installation. The following table shows the structure of the catalog.

Field Name	Description
Proname	Name of the function.
Pronamespace	Object ID (OID) of the namespace that contains this function. Object IDs are used internally as primary keys for some system tables.
Proowner	Owner of the function.
prolong	Implementation language or call interface of this function.
Proisagg	Function is an aggregate function.
Prosecdef	Function is a security definer (that is, a "setuid" function).
Proisstrict	Function returns NULL if any call argument is null. In that case, the function won't actually be called at all. Functions that are not "strict" must be prepared to handle NULL inputs.
Proretset	Function returns a set (that is, multiple values of the specified data type).
Provolatile	This tells whether the function's result depends only on its input arguments or is affected by outside factors. It is i for "immutable" functions, which always deliver the same result for the same inputs. It is s for "stable" functions, whose results (for fixed inputs) do not change within a scan. It is v for "volatile" functions, whose results may change at any time. (Use v also for functions with side effects, so that calls to them cannot get optimized away.)
Pronargs	Number of arguments.
Prorettype	Data type of the return value.
Proargtypes	An array with the data types of the function arguments.
Prosrc	This tells the function handler how to invoke the function. It might be the actual source code of the function for interpreted languages, a link symbol, a filename, or just about anything else, depending on the implementation language/call convention.
Probin	Additional information about how to invoke the function. Again, the interpretation is language-specific.
Proacl	Access privileges.

ROUTINES Functions

The ROUTINES view contains information about all the functions defined in the current database. The functions shown are those for which the user has access. The following table lists the columns in the view. Since the view is mandated by the SQL standard, some of the columns defined in the view are applicable to some features not available in PostgreSQL; such columns (numbering more than 30) are not listed.

Field Name	Description
specific_catalog	Name of the database containing the function (always the current database).
specific_schema	Name of the schema containing the function.
specific_name	The "specific name" of the function. This is a name that uniquely identifies the function in the schema, even if the real name of the function is overloaded. The format of the specific name is not defined. It should only be used to compare it to other instances of specific routine names.
routine_catalog	Name of the database containing the function (always the current database).
routine_schema	Name of the schema containing the function.
routine_name	Name of the function (may be duplicated in case of overloading).
routine_type	Always FUNCTION. (In the future, there might be other types of routines.)
data_type	Return data type of the function if it is a built-in type, or ARRAY if it is some array (in that case, see the view element_types), else USER-DEFINED (in that case, the type is identified in type_udt_name and associated columns).
dtd_identifier	An identifier of the data type descriptor of the return data type of this function, unique among the data type descriptors pertaining to the function. This is mainly useful for joining with other instances of such identifiers. (The specific format of the identifier is not defined and not guaranteed to remain the same in future versions.)
type_udt_catalog	Name of the database in which the return data type of the function is defined (always the current database).
type_udt_schema	Name of the schema in which the return data type of the function is defined.
type_udt_name	Name of the return data type of the function.
routine_body	If the function is a SQL function, then SQL; else EXTERNAL.
routine_definition	The source text of the function (NULL if the current user is not the owner of the function). (According to the SQL standard, this column is only applicable if routine_body is SQL, but in PostgreSQL it will contain whatever source text was specified when the function was created.)
external_name	If this function is a C function, then the external name (link symbol) of the function; else NULL. (This works out to be the same value that is shown in routine_definition.)
external_language	The language in which the function is written.

Table continued on following page

Field Name	Description
parameter_style	Always GENERAL. (The SQL standard defines other parameter styles, which are not available in PostgreSQL.)
is_deterministic	If the function is declared immutable (called *deterministic* in the SQL standard), then YES; else NO. (You cannot query the other volatility levels available in PostgreSQL through the information schema.)
sql_data_access	Always MODIFIES, meaning that the function possibly modifies SQL data. This information is not useful for PostgreSQL.
is_null_call	If the function automatically returns NULL if any of its arguments are null, then YES; else NO.
schema_level_routine	Always YES. (The opposite would be a method of a user-defined type, which is a feature not available in PostgreSQL.)
security_type	If the function runs with the privileges of the current user, then INVOKER. If the function runs with the privileges of the user who defined it, then DEFINER.

ROUTINE PRIVILEGES Functions

The information about the privileges for the UDF assigned to a group or a user could be obtained from the ROUTINE_PRIVILEGES view of the INFORMATION_SCHEMA. The structure of the view is shown in the following table.

Field Name	Description
Grantor	Name of the user who granted the privilege.
Grantee	Name of the user or group to whom the privilege was granted.
specific_catalog	Name of the database containing the function (always the current database).
specific_schema	Name of the schema containing the function.
specific_name	The "specific name" of the function.
routine_catalog	Name of the database containing the function (always the current database).
routine_schema	Name of the schema containing the function.
routine_name	Name of the function (may be duplicated in case of overloading).
privilege_type	Always EXECUTE (the only privilege type for functions).
is_grantable	YES if the privilege is grantable; NO if not.

Restrictions on Calling UDFs from SQL

PostgreSQL assumes a *laissez-faire* approach to UDFs, summarized by "if it is not explicitly prohibited, then it is probably allowed." Since PostgreSQL allows DDL statements in the body of the function, you must exercise caution when invoking such a function from a SELECT statement. Changing database structure might not be the desired outcome. Common sense would also advise against using user-defined data types as return data type for the functions used in SELECT statement. Consult the most current PostgreSQL documentation for more information.

Summary

The PostgreSQL RDBMS is one of the most SQL3-compliant database architectures in use today. It still does not provide for several things (such as a procedural extension language, error handling, or debugging). It overcomes these deficiencies, however, in the robust manner in which it supports UDFs. In general, there are four preferred methods by which to create your UDFs: query functions, procedural functions, internal built-in functions, and external functions. PostgreSQL is unlike the other RDBMS architectures discussed in this book because it allows the use of DDL statements within functions. This is a powerful feature and should be treated with caution to leverage the inherent power of this capability.

In Chapter 19, we will start to investigate instances in which we can develop UDFs to provide functionality in real-world situations. To that end, Chapter 19 deals specifically with reporting and ad hoc queries. For the most part, users want to store data in databases in order to quickly assemble reports and information from a single source. This should prove to be a valuable chapter for the DBA/developer to feel out the different aspects involved in providing reporting services to their users.

Reporting and Ad Hoc Queries

One of the basic roles of an RDBMS implementation is to provide reporting services for its clients. In this respect, you can think of the RDBMS implementation as a sort of bank. Within its structure there are accounts that either have funds or do not have funds. These accounts are managed by their owners, who can be thought of as managers. Now, it is not enough for the managers to know that they may or may not have money in the bank. They want to know details. Granted, some only want an account balance, but others want to know the transactions that occurred to bring their account to its current balance.

This is what the developer faces when trying to provide reporting solutions. What data should you pull? What format should the reports be in? What is the least-cost path to providing all of your users with all the information that they need? In this case, a monthly bank statement with account balance and detailed transaction listing is the ticket to success. However, in most business applications this might not be so clearly defined.

The main purpose of reporting is to allow your user base to gain access to the valuable information contained within your database implementation. Good reporting leads to all kinds of advantages (such as increased efficiency and quality of information). Users are able to spend less time compiling figures to see how different aspects of the business are faring. Additionally, the time taken to produce these reports is reduced, sometimes dramatically, and this improves the quality of time-sensitive information. In today's environment, this is almost paramount because management wants to have an immediate point-in-time knowledge of how aspects of the business are behaving.

Identifying Your Reporting Needs

One of the most important steps in the planning of any set of reporting services for your RDBMS implementations is to take the time to plan based on your reporting needs. Planning for your system before implementation should never be underestimated because it can save you time, money, and headaches over a quickly implemented (but poorly defined) set of reports. In trying to decipher the reporting needs of the system, the developer should try to keep three things in mind: scope, goals, and stakeholders.

Scope involves setting the basic characteristics and limitations of your reporting project. In essence, you are establishing where the boundaries of your project begin and end. Establishing these boundaries in the initial stages of your project is essential to ensuring that all the players (both developers and stakeholders) understand what is within the project and what is not. Projects without clearly defined boundaries often are plagued by what is termed *project creep*. This is when loosely defined project boundaries are constantly being expanded. Since the project boundaries are expanded, progress and an eventual end to the project are never realized.

Goals are established to clearly define what constitutes success and failure before the project is even implemented. This is important in any environment, but more so in the IT environment to clearly demonstrate the positive effects of newly implemented functionality. In addition, these goals must be as specific as possible. Explaining to your stakeholders that you are establishing reporting functionality for the database that will be able to deliver reports in a timely manner in several different media formats will lead to nothing but disappointment. Some users may expect your reporting arm to provide reports in PDF format, but it only provides them in HTML, which is seen as a failure. Another set of users may expect the reports to provide point-in-time reporting, and your system is running materialized views that are updated every 24 hours. Once again, this may be seen as a failure. Yet, even more users may expect the reports to be sent to them instead of having to surf to a company intranet site in order to pull them down.

You can see how perfectly good projects can suddenly steamroll into an undesirable failure by not establishing realistic goals. In general, it is almost always preferable to set attainable goals with the possibility of overachievement, rather than shooting for the stars and falling far short. In brief, know your limitations.

Last, knowing the *stakeholders* in your system should be the basis upon which you actually pursue your project. Who are the people who would actually benefit from the reporting aspects? What reports would they most benefit from? These are important questions that you should not rely on intuition alone to answer. Deal with the people involved to get their perspective on the process.

Creating Standardized Reports

Standardized reports are those reports that try to capture the basic essentials of the business environment in which your particular RDBMS implementation works. These reports will establish the basis on which you will create a standard set of queries, functions, and stored procedures from which to draw data. This is not to mean that these reports should produce all things for all people. If that were attainable, there would be no need to discuss ad hoc queries within this chapter. Instead, you should strive to create a set of standardized reports that fulfill the greatest number of needs and wants of your users without overreaching your established scope.

There are several things that should be taken into account when establishing what will be included in your set of standardized reports. Most important, the size, resources, and climate of your business culture will dictate what reports you will be able to provide to your users. The size and resources available to your RDBMS will dictate the size and complexity of the reports that can be drawn "safely" from the system without compromising the integrity of your system. For the most part, these standardized queries can be simple functions and views. To continue with the examples in the chapter, it is necessary to create some very basic tables in which to hold sales data. The following code demonstrates how to create the tables used in the examples for this chapter:

```
CREATE TABLE [dbo].[CurrentSales] (
    [OrderID] [int] IDENTITY (1, 1) NOT NULL ,
    [ShipperName] [nvarchar] (50) COLLATE SQL_Latin1_General_CP1_CI_AS NULL ,
    [ProductID] [int] NULL ,
    [PurchaseDate] [datetime] NULL ,
    [Total_Price] [money] NULL ,
    [Sales_RegionID] [int] NULL
) ON [PRIMARY]
GO

CREATE TABLE [dbo].[Sales2003] (
    [OrderID] [int] IDENTITY (1, 1) NOT NULL ,
    [ShipperName] [nvarchar] (50) COLLATE SQL_Latin1_General_CP1_CI_AS NULL ,
    [ProductID] [int] NULL ,
    [PurchaseDate] [datetime] NULL ,
    [Total_Price] [money] NULL ,
    [Sales_RegionID] [int] NULL
) ON [PRIMARY]
GO

CREATE TABLE [dbo].[Sales2002] (
    [OrderID] [int] IDENTITY (1, 1) NOT NULL ,
    [ShipperName] [nvarchar] (50) COLLATE SQL_Latin1_General_CP1_CI_AS NULL ,
    [ProductID] [int] NULL ,
    [PurchaseDate] [datetime] NULL ,
    [Total_Price] [money] NULL ,
    [Sales_RegionID] [int] NULL
) ON [PRIMARY]
GO

CREATE TABLE [dbo].[Sales2001] (
    [OrderID] [int] IDENTITY (1, 1) NOT NULL ,
    [ShipperName] [nvarchar] (50) COLLATE SQL_Latin1_General_CP1_CI_AS NULL ,
    [ProductID] [int] NULL ,
    [PurchaseDate] [datetime] NULL ,
    [Total_Price] [money] NULL ,
    [Sales_RegionID] [int] NULL
) ON [PRIMARY]
GO
```

The following example shows how someone can create a simple function that could possibly be used to show different variations of a report. This is often used to select information from different tables based on dates.

```
CREATE FUNCTION Sales_Report
(
    @report_year int
)
RETURNS @OrdersReport TABLE
    (
    OrderID          int,
    ShipperName      nvarchar(50),
    ProductID        int,
```

```
        PurchaseDate        datetime,
        Total_Price         money,
        Sales_RegionID      int
    )
AS
BEGIN

IF @report_year=2004
    BEGIN
        INSERT INTO @OrdersReport
            SELECT OrderID, ShipperName,ProductID,
                    PurchaseDate, Total_Price, Sales_RegionID
            FROM CurrentSales
    END
ELSE IF @report_year=2003
    BEGIN
        INSERT INTO @OrdersReport
            SELECT OrderID, ShipperName,ProductID,
                    PurchaseDate, Total_Price, Sales_RegionID
            FROM Sales2003
    END
ELSE IF @report_year=2002
    BEGIN
        INSERT INTO @OrdersReport
            SELECT OrderID, ShipperName,ProductID,
                    PurchaseDate, Total_Price, Sales_RegionID
            FROM Sales2002
    END
ELSE IF @report_year=2001
    BEGIN
        INSERT INTO @OrdersReport
            SELECT OrderID, ShipperName,ProductID,
                    PurchaseDate, Total_Price, Sales_RegionID
            FROM Sales2001
    END

    RETURN
END
```

The following query would enable the DBA to distribute older sales data into archive tables to improve the overall performance of their system. By calling the function Sales_Report() with a specified year, the DBA could control the output of a yearly sales report with the following code:

```
SELECT SUM(TOTAL_PRICE) AS TOTAL_SALES,'2004' AS FISCAL_YEAR FROM
SALES_REPORT(2004)
UNION
SELECT SUM(TOTAL_PRICE) AS TOTAL_SALES,'2003' AS FISCAL_YEAR FROM
SALES_REPORT(2003)
UNION
SELECT SUM(TOTAL_PRICE) AS TOTAL_SALES,'2002' AS FISCAL_YEAR FROM
SALES_REPORT(2002)
UNION
SELECT SUM(TOTAL_PRICE) AS TOTAL_SALES,'2001' AS FISCAL_YEAR FROM
SALES_REPORT(2001)
```

This syntax makes the DBA's life easier because when a new fiscal year comes along, he or she can extract the data from the current sales table to a read-only table `SalesXXXX`, and make changes in two parts of code to add the 2004 sales year to update the system.

Processing Ad Hoc Query Requests

Ad hoc queries are those specialized queries that are requested but are out of the scope of your current implementation of standardized reports. Often these reports are requested with a high demand and a short timeline. These "customized" reports should be considered carefully, as is the case with standardized reports, to maintain a high standard of quality in your system.

Interpreting the requirements for ad hoc reports is much like the process for determining those of the standardized reports. You may try to determine these requirements ahead of time by considering those reports that have been asked for during the standardized process but that are still out of the scope of your current reporting set. By doing this, you may be able to mitigate some of the overhead of creating reports on the spot by implementing architecture in your standardized reports that will facilitate implementing customized reports. This can easily be done by implementing your own user-defined functions (UDFs) and stressing planning and reusability in the planning stage. Let's revisit the UDF that we created earlier:

```
CREATE FUNCTION Sales_Report
(
    @report_year int
)
RETURNS @OrdersReport TABLE
    (
    OrderID         int,
    ShipperName     nvarchar(50),
    ProductID       int,
    PurchaseDate    datetime,
    Total_Price     money,
    Sales_RegionID  int
    )
AS
BEGIN

IF @report_year=2004
  BEGIN
        INSERT INTO @OrdersReport
            SELECT OrderID, ShipperName,ProductID,
                    PurchaseDate, Total_Price, Sales_RegionID
            FROM CurrentSales
  END
ELSE IF @report_year=2003
    BEGIN
        INSERT INTO @OrdersReport
            SELECT OrderID, ShipperName,ProductID,
                    PurchaseDate, Total_Price, Sales_RegionID
            FROM Sales2003
    END
ELSE IF @report_year=2002
    BEGIN
```

```
                INSERT INTO @OrdersReport
                    SELECT OrderID, ShipperName,ProductID,
                            PurchaseDate, Total_Price, Sales_RegionID
                    FROM Sales2002
        END
   ELSE IF @report_year=2001
        BEGIN
                INSERT INTO @OrdersReport
                    SELECT OrderID, ShipperName,ProductID,
                            PurchaseDate, Total_Price, Sales_RegionID
                    FROM Sales2001
        END

      RETURN
   END
```

This function is perfectly adaptable to a variety of ad hoc reporting uses. First let's create a series of tables and populate them with some random data. We will use portions of the Northwind database from the SQL Server platform to populate certain sections of our code to make it easier. We will try to stay true to the nature of the book and implement some UDFs in our loading.

```
--First we create this view as a sneaky way to get around the limitation of not
-- being able to use the random number generator or GETDATE() in a user-defined
function
-- which is an important point: Know the limitations of your system but also know
your
-- possibilities as they will take you further along.

CREATE VIEW GET_RAND AS
SELECT RAND() AS RAND_NUM

CREATE VIEW GET_TODAYS_DATE AS
SELECT GETDATE() AS THIS_DATE

-- Now create a function to get a random companyname from the Suppliers table
CREATE FUNCTION GetCompany ()
RETURNS varchar(50)
AS
BEGIN
DECLARE @THISCOMPANY  VARCHAR(50)
select @THISCOMPANY=CompanyName from Suppliers where supplierid = (select
cast(floor(RAND_NUM * 29) as int) from GET_RAND)
RETURN(@THISCOMPANY)
END

-- Now create one to produce a random date generator for a specific year.
CREATE FUNCTION GET_RAND_YEARLY_DATE(@YEAR INT)
RETURNS DATETIME
AS
BEGIN
DECLARE @RANDDATE DATETIME
SELECT @RANDDATE = THIS_DATE FROM GET_TODAYS_DATE
DECLARE @NUMOFDAYS  INT
SELECT @NUMOFDAYS= CEILING((RAND_NUM* 365) )  FROM GET_RAND
SET @RANDDATE = DATEADD(DD,@NUMOFDAYS ,@RANDDATE)
```

```
SET @RANDDATE = CAST(MONTH(@RANDDATE) AS VARCHAR(2)) + '/' + CAST(DAY(@RANDDATE) AS
VARCHAR(2)) + '/' + CAST(@YEAR AS CHAR(4))
RETURN(@RANDDATE)
END

-- Now we create the stored procedure that will use the functions and fill our
tables
BEGIN
DECLARE @NUM_COUNT INT
SET @NUM_COUNT = 0

WHILE @NUM_COUNT<=100
BEGIN
INSERT INTO [Northwind].[dbo].[CurrentSales]( [ShipperName], [ProductID],
[PurchaseDate], [Total_Price], [Sales_RegionID])
SELECT DBO.GetCompany(), CAST((RAND_NUM*1000) AS INT),
DBO.GET_RAND_YEARLY_DATE(2004), CAST(ROUND(((RAND_NUM*100000/3)-234),2) AS
MONEY),CAST((RAND_NUM*10) AS INT)
FROM GET_RAND

INSERT INTO [Northwind].[dbo].[Sales2003]( [ShipperName], [ProductID],
[PurchaseDate], [Total_Price], [Sales_RegionID])
SELECT  DBO.GetCompany(), CAST((RAND_NUM*1000) AS INT),
DBO.GET_RAND_YEARLY_DATE(2003), CAST(ROUND(((RAND_NUM*100000/3)-234),2) AS
MONEY),CAST((RAND_NUM*10) AS INT)
FROM GET_RAND

INSERT INTO [Northwind].[dbo].[Sales2002]( [ShipperName], [ProductID],
[PurchaseDate], [Total_Price], [Sales_RegionID])
SELECT DBO.GetCompany(),CAST((RAND_NUM*1000) AS INT),
DBO.GET_RAND_YEARLY_DATE(2002), CAST(ROUND(((RAND_NUM*100000/3)-234),2) AS
MONEY),CAST((RAND_NUM*10) AS INT)
FROM GET_RAND

INSERT INTO [Northwind].[dbo].[Sales2001]( [ShipperName], [ProductID],
[PurchaseDate], [Total_Price], [Sales_RegionID])
SELECT DBO.GetCompany(), CAST((RAND_NUM*1000) AS INT),
DBO.GET_RAND_YEARLY_DATE(2001), CAST(ROUND(((RAND_NUM*100000/3)-234),2) AS
MONEY),CAST((RAND_NUM*10) AS INT)
FROM GET_RAND

SET @NUM_COUNT = @NUM_COUNT + 1
END

END
```

Now that we have our tables populated, we could possibly implement a report very easily that shows gross sales for the previous four years by using the following code:

```
SELECT YEAR(PURCHASEDATE) AS [YEAR], SUM(TOTAL_PRICE) AS YEARLY_SALES
    FROM SALES_REPORT(2004)
    GROUP BY YEAR(PURCHASEDATE)
UNION
SELECT YEAR(PURCHASEDATE) AS [YEAR], SUM(TOTAL_PRICE) AS YEARLY_SALES
    FROM SALES_REPORT(2003)
```

```
        GROUP BY YEAR(PURCHASEDATE)
UNION
SELECT YEAR(PURCHASEDATE) AS [YEAR], SUM(TOTAL_PRICE) AS YEARLY_SALES
    FROM SALES_REPORT(2002)
        GROUP BY YEAR(PURCHASEDATE)
UNION
SELECT YEAR(PURCHASEDATE) AS [YEAR], SUM(TOTAL_PRICE) AS YEARLY_SALES
    FROM SALES_REPORT(2001)
        GROUP BY YEAR(PURCHASEDATE)

YEAR        YEARLY_SALES
----------- --------------------
2001        490347.1433
2002        457594.6663
2003        483689.4349
2004        1682265.0545

(4 row(s) affected)
```

On the other hand, the manager who requested the previous report may now decide that the report needs to be further subjugated into only years 2004 and 2003, with the totals grouped by the shipper's name so that the manager can decide with whom to place more sales resources in order to boost sales. Possibly, the manager needs only the 10 lowest companies out of each year. This is not really a problem since our system is flexible. The following query will cover these requirements by using the last two without major modifications:

```
SELECT TOP 10 YEAR(PURCHASEDATE) AS [YEAR], SHIPPERNAME,
    SUM(TOTAL_PRICE) AS YEARLY_SALES
FROM SALES_REPORT(2004)
    WHERE SHIPPERNAME IS NOT NULL
    GROUP BY YEAR(PURCHASEDATE), SHIPPERNAME
UNION
SELECT TOP 10 YEAR(PURCHASEDATE) AS [YEAR], SHIPPERNAME,
    SUM(TOTAL_PRICE) AS YEARLY_SALES
FROM SALES_REPORT(2003)
    WHERE SHIPPERNAME IS NOT NULL
    GROUP BY YEAR(PURCHASEDATE), SHIPPERNAME
ORDER BY YEAR DESC,YEARLY_SALES ASC

YEAR        SHIPPERNAME                                         YEARLY_SALES
----------- --------------------------------------------------- ---------
2004        Exotic Liquids                                      10618.8976
2004        Bigfoot Breweries                                   17599.3701
2004        Gai pâturage                                        52388.6951
2004        G'day, Mate                                         55429.4919
2004        Heli Süßwaren GmbH & Co. KG                         55914.4113
2004        Grandma Kelly's Homestead                           57425.9869
2004        Cooperativa de Quesos 'Las Cabras'                  70018.7848
2004        Formaggi Fortini s.r.l.                             86007.4525
2004        Escargots Nouveaux                                  116413.7229
2004        Aux joyeux ecclésiastiques                          129196.9942
2003        Heli Süßwaren GmbH & Co. KG                         3749.0021
2003        Aux joyeux ecclésiastiques                          3815.5478
2003        Bigfoot Breweries                                   7204.3594
2003        Grandma Kelly's Homestead                           11020.0012
2003        Exotic Liquids                                      13391.3189
```

```
2003        Formaggi Fortini s.r.l.               13885.0101
2003        Cooperativa de Quesos 'Las Cabras'    14871.0433
2003        Gai pâturage                          25586.9502
2003        Escargots Nouveaux                    27541.2298
2003        G'day, Mate                           54857.1043

(20 row(s) affected)
```

Our system is able to reduce the amount of time and money invested because of careful planning up front and realizing that reusability plays an important part in making your reporting system robust.

Effectively Delivering Data to the Requestor

Delivering your reports to your stakeholders who rely upon them is the second most important step (next to actually being able to generate the report). You will normally determine this during the initial planning stages of your reporting implementation. In general, there are two main areas in which you need to concentrate your efforts: method and format.

Method refers to the method of report delivery, or how your users actually obtain their reports. There are three main methods that are generally available to any RDBMS reporting implementation: push, pull, and subscription.

The *push method* is used to systematically push any number of reports out to your user base on some sort of schedule. This is usually done as an all-encompassing effort in which users receive the reports even if they are not actively seeking them. There are parameters such as who actually gets the reports, and the schedule is usually determined by a general consensus of the group of individuals to whom the report is sent.

The *pull method* is the counterpart to the push method. In essence, the user goes out to a reporting engine and actively makes a request for the report, which is fulfilled at that time. It is up to the users to take the time to go out and have the report generated for them. This method is often employed to reduce administrative overhead of setting up schedules on which to send various reports for the users.

Last, the *subscription method* has come into the fold recently. It basically strikes a balance between the push and pull methods. The users determine whether a report is important enough for them to receive on a regular basis. Then the users "subscribe" to the particular report, determining at what time and in what manner they would like to receive the report. Nothing stops the users from pulling the report off of the regular schedule or one that they have not subscribed to. An example of this method can be seen with Microsoft's SQL Server Reporting Services.

Formatting details in what form the reports will be distributed to the base of users. This can consist of everything from simple text-based reports to complicated PDF formats that contain such things as drill-down capability and content bars. What is tantamount in deciding what format or formats to support is the resource level of your users. You surely would not distribute reports to your company or organization in PDF format if they did not have access to a PDF viewer. Always keep in mind that you must work within the limitations not only of your hardware and software, but also the limitations of those of your users. There is always a solution that can be found to work best. If the user base can't view PDFs, but they have an Internet browser, then maybe the reporting solution should be centered on web-based HTML reports. Maybe the solution, to reduce the users' need for ad hoc queries of the database, is to provide their data in a spreadsheet so that they may perform calculations on the data. Being creative in the solutions delivered to your users will pay big dividends.

Summary

You should now have a general idea of how reporting and ad hoc queries can be planned, created, and managed. It cannot be stressed enough that proper planning is the key to a successful reporting implementation. Functions can and should be a part of that implementation. With properly chosen UDFs, the developer can not only make the transition to the new reporting environment easier, but also provide the template for processing ad hoc query requests.

In addition, we discussed the methods and formats in which reports can be distributed to the stakeholders. A good reporting solution is useless unless the users can receive their reports in a timely manner and in a format that they can use. All of these concepts will be in the background in later chapters as we discuss such things as data warehousing that rely upon good reporting implementation.

The next chapter deals with using functions with respect to assisting the DBA/developer in migrating data from one platform to another. This is a very important chapter to pay attention to, because at least once in your career as a DBA you will be tasked with moving your data from one place to another. Understanding how functions can assist with making the transition a smooth one may preclude the necessity of having to spend a couple of long nights at the office.

20

Using Functions for Migrating Data

Migrating data and databases has come a long way since the first days of the systems in the early 1980s. In those days, when a DBA or developer had to move a database or data from one machine to another, the transfer consisted of using a language such as COBOL to export all the information from the database into a flat file. This file would then be transported to another machine, where another COBOL program would "reassemble" the database on the other end. Those developers who can remember these days would probably agree that the process was rather asset-intensive and was prone to error. Also, to move a database from one platform to another was, at best, a major operation in intellectual ingenuity and testing the limits of your patience.

One of your major goals in developing a migration project is a good understanding of the basics of what data migration entails. Without a firm foothold on the basics of the current state of data migration within the industry, you will be (at best) stumbling around in the dark looking for answers.

Understanding Migration of Data

Luckily for us, with time come major improvements. All of the six major platforms discussed in this book either have built-in migration tools or have third-party programs that will handle the transition for you. There is nothing like using a system in which moving a production database from one machine to another involves the click of a mouse to transfer the database, its data, objects, users, and permissions. However, it is rarely this easy in real life because databases reside on different networks, different domains, and even different operating systems. Moreover, the migration may not even be to the same database platform. This is where the knowledge of a particular RDBMS implementation and ingenuity in the use of user-defined functions (UDFs) can reduce the burden of the migration.

In addition, you will want to know both the causes and the effects that influence the need for migration. Migration for migration's sake is often a painstaking activity with little improvement in either performance or scalability. In the next section, we will discuss some of the major influencing factors and effects that migration entails.

Causes and Effects of Migrating

There are many possible reasons for having to migrate your RDBMS implementation. Generally, these can be reduced to either a decision based on equipment or an application lifecycle. Equipment lifecycle can mean that, because of age, equipment is outdated and must be moved to another platform. A lifecycle-based migration could also be required because of database capacity. The database may have grown to such an extent that it cannot support its current load of users and queries. Sometimes it is less expensive to upgrade the equipment than to spend the time and resources to squeeze efficiency out of an RDBMS implementation.

Application lifecycle also plays an important role in determining when it is time to migrate the database implementation. The current implementation may not have the functionality desired, or a newer version of the database platform may now be available. An example would be a database implementation of an older version of MySQL, possibly 3.0. The IT department decides that it is time to implement MySQL 5.0 so that we can take advantage of things like cursors. This will require us to migrate the database from the older version to the newer one. If we are lucky, there may be an upsizing wizard that will take care of most of the migration for us. However, if there is not such a life preserver hanging out there, then it is up to us to ensure that all of the objects and data end up in the right place. Other times, we may find that our current RDBMS platform just does not suit our needs, and we find ourselves migrating across different platforms. You can understand, from reading the previous chapters on the syntactic differences between the different systems, that these moves are often tricky.

With all of this in mind, there are still some major benefits that can result from the effects of migrating your database and data. The first benefit, of course, is realized as a consequence of the reasons that you are migrating in the first place: added functionality or capacity. By moving to bigger or better systems, we strive to increase either the functionality of the system or the capacity that the system can handle. Beyond these obvious reasons for migration, there are some secondary effects that can be utilized, which can be summed up as a "chance to change." Since the migration process inherently demands that you look closely at your RDBMS implementation to ensure migration success, it also gives you the chance to make changes to be carried over to the next system. This could be something like the partitioning of tables to streamline the workload of your queries and functions. It could also be the opportunity to cleanse incorrect, inconsistent, or unneeded data from your system. You are taking the time to examine your system, so why not use it wisely and work smarter, not harder.

Databases Migrating Databases

The foundation of your database system must be in place in order to have a place for your data to reside. In that respect, you must systematically move your database implementation (or some subset) from one area to another. Migrating the initial framework of your database requires moving these three things:

❑ Schema or database

❑ Tables

❑ Views, procedures, functions, and UDFs

Following this list, the first thing you must move is the schema or the underlying database framework that holds all of the objects (tables, views, and so on). Once the basic framework of the new database is in place, you would move on to reproducing the table structure of your RDBMS implementation. Last, you would rebuild all the miscellaneous views, procedures, functions, and user-defined types. You must do these things in the particular order in which they were given. You cannot have tables without a schema in which to place them. Likewise, you cannot have views and functions without the underlying tables that support them.

In almost all RDBMS implementations, these items can be automatically scripted out. For custom solutions, you could write your own stored procedure or function to take care of the scripting by querying system tables and views on the parent database. These tables vary across the different RDBMS implementations, and you will have to check your vendor-specific documentation for a better idea of what you will have to use.

Migrating Data

Now that we have migrated our database structure, it is time to turn our attention to the data. To ensure that our data retains its consistency, we must take the time to detail the data types and sizes that will be moved onto the new database implementation. If the type or size is inconsistent with the destination database, then a conversion may have to be made. Carefully checking the documentation of your RDBMS platform is the key. Do not assume that because two data types have the same name that they are automatically interchangeable. You might also consider writing custom functions and queries that would handle scripting out the data as a series of INSERT statements that can be run against the destination database to populate the tables. If your tables are very large, you may consider writing custom functions to extract your data into something like XML, which can then be imported into the destination database.

Migrating Other Database-Related Components

Now that the framework and data are in place on the destination database implementation, it is time to turn our attention to the other various database-related components. Namely, we are talking about the following:

- ❑ User accounts
- ❑ Account permissions
- ❑ Cursors, constraints, indexes, and relationships

We leave these items until the end of the migration process to keep them from interfering with the loading of the data into the system during our second phase of migrating the database. If we were to have scripted and built these items when we assembled the tables and views, we may have seriously corrupted our data. INSERT triggers may have been present that would have fired upon every INSERT into the affected table. Likewise, having constraints and relationships (or keys) created before we input our data would possibly prevent us from entering data into tables that have foreign key values. It is always best to logically plan your migration, which we will discuss in the next section.

Understanding the Data Migration Process

Understanding the migration process will help you as a DBA or developer gain a better understanding of the aspects and time involved in ensuring a successful migration. In short, the migration process consists of four very distinct phases: planning, testing, implementing, and validation.

Planning Migration

By now, you can safely assume that this phase is where you will spend most of your time. There is no substitute for the time spent on the planning phase. Your main objective in planning is to mitigate any problems that may occur and come up with contingency plans for those issues that arise even with the most thorough plan. This is often referred to as Murphy's Law, which states "Anything that can go wrong, probably will...." This is not very comforting, but although you may not be able to eliminate all problems, you can reduce their effect on your migration outcome. In addition, you must think about time and cost estimates. Time is money, and you must plan your migration accordingly.

What you should be most concerned about is solidifying your plans. It is best to write out your plan, detailing each of the steps that you will take to migrate the three different areas of the database detailed previously. These plans will be used as your checklist for the test and actual migration, so they must be as detailed as possible.

Last, you will want to set up realistic goals for the success of your migration project. What are you looking to accomplish? Are there time limitations that must be met? Will there be the possibility of data loss and what amount of loss is acceptable? All of these questions and more must be addressed for everyone involved in the migration project to have a clear idea of what the outcome is expected to be.

Testing the Migration Plan

Your plan is in place and you have outlined our plan in a detailed migration checklist. Now is the time to test our migration plan to ensure that everything will work according to plan. You should run through the plan in the same scenario in which you will be executing the real migration, ensuring that you have proper backups of any systems that will be accessed during the test. The closer you model your test to the actual migration environment, the more chances you have to catch any shortfalls. With this in mind, you must ensure that you stay with the format of your checklist. If any deviations are made from the checklist, they must be annotated to take them into consideration when evaluating the plan.

After completing the test migration, you must examine the results and make changes to your plan and subsequent execution checklist. If needed, you may run one or more tests until you become comfortable with the plan. Remember, you are spending your learning time during this phase. You do not want to do that when the production database is down and the company is actively waiting for you to complete the migration.

Implementing the Migration Plan

We have finally, after much planning and testing, reached the implementation stage. This is the phase in which all of your hard work should pay off. The first thing you should consider for this phase is the element of time. When will the migration occur? How long will it take? These generally need to be thoroughly considered to present the least amount of impact to the system and the users who access it. Some of the time limits will have been established in the testing phase, but overestimating is usually a good plan, because you will undoubtedly move a little more cautiously when working with the live data.

Second, you must pool the resources that are available to you. Bring other people in to assist in the implementation of the migration plan. They will be there to double-check what you are doing with respect to the checklist. Also, if any problems arise, it is always good to have more than one person thinking about a solution. This is especially true because, most of the time, your migration will occur in the middle of the night when your mind may tend to wander as to why you are not in bed at a critical part of the migration.

Last, stick to the plan! What will ruin a good plan for migration more often than not is a deviation (deliberate or accidental) from the checklist. A lot of time and effort has been put into the creation and verification of the checklist and, as such, it should be followed. If all goes well, you will end up with as successful a transfer as you did in the trial runs.

Validating a Successful Migration

Once the migration process of actually transferring the objects and data to the destination database is complete, you must verify that the data is consistent across the two platforms. You have several different avenues of approach when dealing with the verification process:

- ❑ Third-party utilities
- ❑ User applications and reporting systems
- ❑ Queries, custom functions, and stored procedures

Third-party utilities exist that are used to test database integrity across any number of platforms. Most of these generate reports highlighting the conformance or non-conformance of the new database implementation in relation to the source database. Some are better than others, and you will have to do your own research as to which would most likely fit your needs.

Of course, your own applications and reporting systems could be used to confirm the integrity of your new database. You can test applications to ensure that the proper access permissions are there, run reports to ensure that the initial data is present, and run some test transactions to ensure that your stored procedures and trigger are all functioning properly.

If you have the wherewithal, you may decide that it is best to implement your own validation strategy, consisting of custom queries, functions, and stored procedures. As discussed earlier in this chapter, every RDBMS implementation has system tables that can be queried to ascertain what is within the database. Once you understand where this data is stored and in what format, it is a trivial account to write a function to return a table of all unlike objects. Data can be checked in one of two ways. You can write a series of queries against both databases to locate dissimilar rows and output them for scrutiny. Otherwise, most RDBMS implementations provide some form of function or stored procedure that will produce a checksum value of a table. You can have the names of the tables output into a list for further scrutiny, or combine the two methods by checking the checksum values first and then using the query method second if the first one fails.

SQL Function's Role in Data Migration

Developers write functions for several reasons. Some write them to add functionality to their systems. Others write them to perform some kind of function outside of the main scope of their application (such as in a reporting system). However, they are all written to make the DBA or developer's life easier. In no other place is that more relevant than in the processes of migrating data.

Common Functions Used

Normally, the lifeblood of any migration functions that you have within your development arsenal for migration will consist of transformational functions. In turn, these transformational UDFs will contain built-in functions such as DECODE, COALESCE, CAST, CONVERT, CASE, and TO_DATE, just to name a few. Of course, we could probably produce the same type of object by using a stored procedure, but why would we? Can you imagine how you would go about converting a single column to another type or format within a table that contains several million records? The inherent power of functions comes to full light when we realize that we can use them literally as part of our SQL query syntax as part of our migration. The following discussion demonstrates several useful user-defined functions (UDFs) that will give you an outline of the types of things that you could produce to use in your migration efforts. For clarity and conciseness, all of the examples are written in Microsoft SQL Server throughout.

Examples

A simple example of a UDF would be an instance in which, during the migration process, it is necessary to convert an INT field for a phone number into a specific character string on a SQL Server 2000 system, as shown here:

```
Create function convert_phone (@phone int)
returns varchar(14)
as
begin

-- This function will convert the int to the format ###-###-####

declare @new_phone varchar(14)
declare @old_phone varchar(10)
set @old_phone = CAST(@phone AS VARCHAR(14))
set @new_phone = LEFT(@old_phone,3) + '-' + SUBSTRING(@old_phone,4,3)
                + '-' + RIGHT(@old_phone,4)
return(@new_phone)
end
go

-- An Example of using the function

select dbo.convert_phone(555555555)

Output should produce '555-555-5555'
```

Although the previous function would be helpful in some situations, we would like to also have functions that would work with every data migration that we did. Another example would be a simple type conversion function that could be used when possibly outputting scripts used to migrate database structure to another implementation. The following code shows a simple function to perform a really simple mapping of data type from SQL Server to Oracle:

```
 CREATE FUNCTION SQLColumns_to_OracleColumns(@TABLEID varchar(100))
RETURNS  @CODE_TABLE TABLE(COLUMN_ROW varchar(2000) )
AS
BEGIN

DECLARE @CURRENTCOLUMN  VARCHAR(50)
DECLARE @BEGINTYPE  VARCHAR(50)
DECLARE @ENDTYPE VARCHAR(50)
DECLARE @NUM_TYPE INT
DECLARE @COLUMN_LIST  VARCHAR(2000)
SET @COLUMN_LIST='('

--CREATE CURSOR TO GO THROUGH THE VARIOUS COLUMNS AND EVALUATE

DECLARE COLUMN_CURSOR CURSOR FOR
```

```
SELECT C.NAME,T.NAME,C.LENGTH FROM SYSCOLUMNS C
INNER JOIN SYSTYPES T ON C.XTYPE=T.XTYPE  AND T.NAME<>'sysname'
WHERE C.ID=(SELECT ID FROM SYSOBJECTS WHERE NAME=@TABLEID AND XTYPE='U')
ORDER BY C.COLID

OPEN COLUMN_CURSOR

FETCH NEXT FROM COLUMN_CURSOR
     INTO @CURRENTCOLUMN,@BEGINTYPE,@NUM_TYPE

WHILE @@FETCH_STATUS=0
BEGIN

SELECT @ENDTYPE =
CASE @BEGINTYPE
WHEN 'nchar' THEN 'char(' + CAST(@NUM_TYPE AS VARCHAR(10)) + ')'
WHEN 'text' THEN 'varchar2(' +  CAST(@NUM_TYPE AS VARCHAR(10))  + ')'
WHEN 'nvarchar' THEN 'varchar2(' +  CAST(@NUM_TYPE AS VARCHAR(10))  + ')'
WHEN 'tinyint' THEN 'number(' +  CAST(@NUM_TYPE AS VARCHAR(10))  + ')'
WHEN 'int' THEN 'number(' +  CAST(@NUM_TYPE AS VARCHAR(10))  + ')'
WHEN 'bigint' THEN 'number(' +  CAST(@NUM_TYPE AS VARCHAR(10))  + ')'
WHEN 'datetime' THEN 'date'
END

SET @COLUMN_LIST =@COLUMN_LIST + @CURRENTCOLUMN + '  ' + @ENDTYPE

FETCH NEXT FROM COLUMN_CURSOR
     INTO @CURRENTCOLUMN,@BEGINTYPE,@NUM_TYPE

IF @@FETCH_STATUS=0
SET @COLUMN_LIST = @COLUMN_LIST +','
ELSE
SET @COLUMN_LIST = @COLUMN_LIST +')'

END
CLOSE COLUMN_CURSOR
DEALLOCATE COLUMN_CURSOR

INSERT INTO @CODE_TABLE(COLUMN_ROW) VALUES (@COLUMN_LIST)

RETURN
END
```

Now, we can add onto this function by building a function to use it to run through the tables of the database and output for us a set of SQL statements to re-create the database tables in an Oracle system where an empty database instance named Northwind already exists:

```
CREATE FUNCTION fn_script_tables (@SCHEMA VARCHAR(20))
RETURNS  @tables_table TABLE(
                             TABLE_SCRIPT    NVARCHAR(2000)
                             )
AS
BEGIN

DECLARE table_cursor CURSOR FOR
```

561

```
select DISTINCT TABLE_NAME = convert(nvarchar(134),o.name)
   from
      sysobjects o
   where
      o.type in ('U')    /* Object type for User Table */


OPEN table_cursor
DECLARE @TABLENAME  NVARCHAR(134)

-- Check @@FETCH_STATUS to see if there are any more rows to fetch.
WHILE @@FETCH_STATUS = 0
BEGIN
-- This is executed as long as the previous fetch succeeds.

FETCH NEXT FROM table_cursor into @TABLENAME

insert into @tables_table
select ' CREATE TABLE ' + @SCHEMA + '.' + @TABLENAME + COLUMN_ROW FROM
SQLColumns_to_OracleColumns(@TABLENAME)

END

CLOSE table_cursor
DEALLOCATE table_cursor

RETURN
END
```

Now, we can pass this function a string value to indicate what schema we would be creating the tables on the Oracle implementation, and we would receive output like this:

```
SELECT * from FN_SCRIPT_TABLES('Northwind')
TABLE_SCRIPT
 CREATE TABLE Northwind.Categories(CategoryID  number(4),CategoryName
varchar2(30),Description  varchar2(16),Picture  varchar2(16))
 CREATE TABLE Northwind.CustomerCustomerDemo(CustomerID  char(10),CustomerTypeID
char(20))
 CREATE TABLE Northwind.CustomerDemographics(CustomerTypeID  char(20),CustomerDesc
varchar2(16))
 CREATE TABLE Northwind.Customers(CustomerID  char(10),CompanyName
varchar2(80),ContactName  varchar2(60),ContactTitle  varchar2(60),Address
varchar2(120),City  varchar2(30),Region  varchar2(30),PostalCode
varchar2(20),Country  varchar2(30),Phone  varchar2(48),Fax  varchar2(48))
 CREATE TABLE Northwind.dtproperties(id  number(4),objectid  number(4),property
varchar2(64),value  varchar2(255),uvalue  varchar2(510),lvalue
varchar2(16),version  number(4))
 CREATE TABLE Northwind.Employees(EmployeeID  number(4),LastName
varchar2(40),FirstName  varchar2(20),Title  varchar2(60),TitleOfCourtesy
varchar2(50),BirthDate  date,HireDate  date,Address  varchar2(120),City
varchar2(30),Region  varchar2(30),PostalCode  varchar2(20),Country
varchar2(30),HomePhone  varchar2(48),Extension  varchar2(8),Photo
varchar2(16),Notes  varchar2(16),ReportsTo  number(4),PhotoPath  varchar2(510))
 CREATE TABLE Northwind.EmployeeTerritories(EmployeeID  number(4),TerritoryID
varchar2(40))
```

```
  CREATE TABLE Northwind.Order Details(OrderID  number(4),ProductID
number(4),UnitPrice  varchar2(8),Quantity  varchar2(2),Discount  varchar2(4))
  CREATE TABLE Northwind.Orders(OrderID  number(4),CustomerID  char(10),EmployeeID
number(4),OrderDate  date,RequiredDate  date,ShippedDate  date,ShipVia
number(4),Freight  varchar2(8),ShipName  varchar2(80),ShipAddress
varchar2(120),ShipCity  varchar2(30),ShipRegion  varchar2(30),ShipPostalCode
varchar2(20),ShipCountry  varchar2(30))
  CREATE TABLE Northwind.Products(ProductID  number(4),ProductName
varchar2(80),SupplierID  number(4),CategoryID  number(4),QuantityPerUnit
varchar2(40),UnitPrice  varchar2(8),UnitsInStock  varchar2(2),UnitsOnOrder
varchar2(2),ReorderLevel  varchar2(2),Discontinued  varchar2(1))
  CREATE TABLE Northwind.Region(RegionID  number(4),RegionDescription  char(100))
  CREATE TABLE Northwind.Shippers(ShipperID  number(4),CompanyName
varchar2(80),Phone  varchar2(48))
  CREATE TABLE Northwind.Suppliers(SupplierID  number(4),CompanyName
varchar2(80),ContactName  varchar2(60),ContactTitle  varchar2(60),Address
varchar2(120),City  varchar2(30),Region  varchar2(30),PostalCode
varchar2(20),Country  varchar2(30),Phone  varchar2(48),Fax  varchar2(48),HomePage
varchar2(16))
  CREATE TABLE Northwind.Territories(TerritoryID  varchar2(40),TerritoryDescription
char(100),RegionID  number(4))
  CREATE TABLE Northwind.Territories(TerritoryID  varchar2(40),TerritoryDescription
char(100),RegionID  number(4))

(15 row(s) affected)
```

Of course, it should be understood that this script is not all-encompassing, and you could add as much functionality as you wish. Of course, almost anything is possible because you could tie these various functions into stored procedures to push the functionality even further. This is because of the limitation discussed earlier, that UDFs cannot execute DDL syntax that would manipulate database structure or content.

An especially helpful function would be one that would verify the rowcounts for the various tables in our database. In the verification process, this could be one of our initial verification techniques to determine if the data transferred correctly.

```
create function check_rowcount(@TABLES_LIKE  varchar(50))
RETURNS @TABLE_ROWCOUNT TABLE(
                             TABLE_NAME VARCHAR(50),
                             ROW_COUNT  BIGINT
                             )


BEGIN


SET @TABLES_LIKE = @TABLES_LIKE + '%'

INSERT INTO @TABLE_ROWCOUNT(TABLE_NAME,ROW_COUNT)
SELECT     o.name, i.[rows]
FROM       sysobjects o
     INNER JOIN  sysindexes i
ON         o.id = i.id
WHERE      (o.type = 'u') AND (i.indid = 1) AND O.NAME LIKE (@TABLES_LIKE)
ORDER BY i.[rows] desc


RETURN
```

```
END
SELECT * FROM CHECK_ROWCOUNT('') ORDER BY TABLE_NAME

TABLE_NAME                                          ROW_COUNT
--------------------------------------------------- --------------------
Categories                                          8
Customers                                           91
dtproperties                                        0
Employees                                           9
Order Details                                       2155
Orders                                              830
Products                                            77
Shippers                                            3
Suppliers                                           29

(9 row(s) affected)
```

You could further expand upon this idea to dynamically create a query in which you would also output the checksum value of the table. By having both of these items available to check against the similar values of the parent database, you now have a great validation tool to use for your migration efforts.

Summary

Now you should have a general working knowledge of the processes behind the migration of data and databases. We have discussed a wide range of topics dealing with migration in this chapter, ranging from the causes and effects of migration to actually implementing a plan. Database migration should always be approached with caution and a certain amount of respect. It only takes one bad migration to leave a bad taste in your mouth. Similarly, you should always save everything that you write (as far as functions) someplace where they are readily available. Migration functions are usually a little more sophisticated than the usual lot, and you can always go back and add more functionality to them later. Next, we will examine the idea of data warehousing and some of the roles that functions can play within them.

In the next chapter, we will delve into the interesting topic of data warehousing. This is a conceptual buzzword that almost every DBA and developer has heard recently, and we will attempt to show you some areas of data warehousing in which functions can assist you in feeding, querying, and maintaining its structure.

Using Functions to Feed a Data Warehouse

Data warehousing was developed out of the enormous expansion of computing power and the need to effectively develop reports from legacy data systems. Data warehouses were developed as a way to provide a layer between the reporting needs of the users and the computational cost to the production database environment. In general, the data warehouse's main mission is to provide three things:

❑ Bring data from many sources into a central area in an effective manner.

❑ Protect your production environment from excessive load.

❑ Separate the data that is used in the user environment from the production environment.

Mainly, these systems are derived to provide information to key decision makers in an efficient and timely manner. This is often achieved through a series of reporting analysis services that deliver reports based on the information contained within the system. By separating the layers between the production environment and the user running these queries, you protect the integrity of the production environment and free up resources. The main effort of the system is in the extracting, transforming, and loading of the data from the parent systems. However, data warehousing does provide the following important benefits:

❑ Better management of the data required for reporting and analysis services.

❑ Better decision making by those in decision-making positions by providing all data in a centralized location.

❑ Reduction in the computing cost by separating from the production layer.

❑ Better access for the users for data that may have been spread across several RDBMS implementations.

The purpose of this chapter is to familiarize you with the common concepts of what is needed to operate a data warehouse and where functions fit into that role. Unless otherwise noted, all of these examples were implemented on a SQL Server 2000 RDBMS platform by using a portion of the Northwind database, which is normally installed by default on the system. Most of the examples can be modified to create the same functionality on other RDBMS implementations as well.

Architecture of a Data Warehouse

The typical structures for a data warehouse are an E/R schema, the star schema, or a combination of both. The *E/R schema* is mainly used to show entities and relationships and as a way of easily mapping data from legacy systems.

The *star schema* is named as such because it has one centralized table that houses the majority of the information with subtables hanging off of the main table (which provide supporting data). This is normally the design used for a data warehouse because it is easy to manage and deploy.

Last, you may decide to use a combination of the two previous methods to establish what is commonly referred to as a "snowflake" schema. The *snowflake schema* is a hybrid of the E/R and star schema in that it maintains a centralized main table in which subsets of supporting tables diverge off. The difference is that it extends further by allowing these subsets of information to be detailed relationship combinations (as in the E/R schema).

SQL Function's Role in Data Warehouse Processing

From the previous discussion, you have probably deduced that the data warehousing environment is a complex animal. To help it perform its role optimally it needs help, and that help can come in a variety of ways by using user-defined functions (UDFs). The most important thing to remember because of the complexity of the base systems involved is that sometimes it is required to "think outside of the box" to get the results that you want.

Feeding a Data Warehouse

Feeding the data warehouse is one of the most time-consuming aspects of creating your own warehousing environment. The main objective is to pool your data resources from multiple objects, which could include multiple instances of RDBMS implementations that may or may not be of the same type. If they are of the same type, then the problem may be that the data is housed in multiple database objects that could be storing the data differently. Your objective in feeding the data warehouse is to pull this data from multiple locations into your warehouse, and make it standardized. Generally, this is no small task when you are talking about pulling information from multiple sources and trying to fit it into the same table.

Another problem that you may often encounter is inconsistent data entry between different systems. Consider the case of a large-scale warehousing corporation consisting of sales, accounting, and warehouse departments. This means having three database implementations that are all on the same platform but that work independently of one another to track the various sales, billing, and warehouse activities. You are commissioned to create a data warehouse so that the decision makers of the company can produce aggregate reports and analysis over the three departments simultaneously. After your initial investigation of the data you come across their biggest client, Worldwide Stuff Corporation. This normally wouldn't be a problem except that in the sales database, they are entered as `'WSCorp'`, the warehouse department has them as `'Worldwide Stuff'`, and the Accounting department uses the full name `'Worldwide Stuff Corporation'`. You would not want to have to account for the various names in the different departments in every query across the database, so you decide that it is time to create a standard. You create a table called `Standard_Naming` with the columns `Naming_Varation`, and

Standard_Name. Then you create the following function in SQL Server 2000 so that you can use the standard naming convention across a multitude of areas:

```
CREATE FUNCTION STANDARD_NAME(@NAME VARCHAR(100))
RETURNS VARCHAR(100)
AS
BEGIN

DECLARE @STANDARD_NAME VARCHAR(100)

-- First check to see if the name exists.
IF EXISTS (
SELECT * FROM STANDARD_NAMING
    WHERE NAMING_VARIATION=@NAME
)
    BEGIN
    -- Set the name equal to the standard name in the database.
        SELECT @STANDARD_NAME = STANDARD_NAME
            FROM STANDARD_NAMING
        WHERE NAMING_VARIATION=@NAME
    END
ELSE
    SET @STANDARD_NAME = @NAME

RETURN @STANDARD_NAME
END
```

Now, we have a very robust standard naming convention to use to feed the database. It is not tied to any one particular insertion point, so it can be used across multiple instances. Now, all we have to do to insert the names from the separate systems into ours is to use something similar to the pseudocode that follows:

```
INSERT INTO WAREHOUSE(NAME,.............)
SELECT STANDARD_NAME(NAME),......................
    FROM ACCOUNTING
UNION
SELECT STANDARD_NAME(NAME),................
    FROM SALES
UNION
SELECT STANDARD_NAME(NAME),............
    FROM WAREHOUSE
```

The true beauty of the UDF is that this is not tied to any one instance of a name now. It doesn't necessarily have to be a company name. It could be anything that had a naming variance across any of your database (such as product_name, distributing_company, salesman, and so on). In fact, some of the same principles could be used to create a functional table of conversion types for the different database implementations.

Querying a Data Warehouse

Querying your warehouse by using ad hoc queries from the decision makers needing the data is the lifeblood of the day-to-day operation of your system. Giving them the tools to effectively get that data, considering that they might not be as fluent in SQL as you, is paramount in providing a real cost valuation for the system. To ensure this "ease of use" doctrine, you may provide them with several UDFs to help them out.

A good example would be that of a national investment firm that analyzes portfolios via the data warehouse that you administer. The warehouse produces a small series of standardized reports, but the brokers are more interested in ad hoc queries because each has a particular formula to determine when to buy and sell stocks from the different funds. You have a table named Funds that contains the Stock_ Symbol and Fund_Name columns. Another table, Daily_Rate, keeps track of the stocks process at the close of business via the Stock_Symbol, Shares, Price, and Trade_Date columns. The main table, Brokers, houses the broker information, which funds they currently own, and how much via Broker_ ID and Fund. Unfortunately for you, the brokers can't figure out the intricacies of JOINs in SQL and can only use a few basic commands. They would like a way to easily grab the account information over a certain time period. You decide to implement the following UDF:

```
CREATE FUNCTION ACCOUNT_STATUS(
@BROKER        VARCHAR(50),
@STARTDATE     DATE,
@ENDDATE       DATE
)
RETURNS @BROKER_STATUS TABLE(
                        STOCK_SYM      VARCHAR(10),
                        FUND_NAME      VARCHAR(50),
                        SHARES         INT,
                        PRICE          MONEY,
                        TRADE_DATE     DATE
                        )
AS
BEGIN

INSERT INTO @BROKER_STATUS(STOCK_SYM,FUND_NAME,SHARES,PRICE,TRADE_DATE)
SELECT B.STOCK_SYMBOL, A.FUND_NAME, C.SHARES,
       C.PRICE, C.TRADE_DATE
FROM BROKERS A, FUNDS B, DAILY_RATE C
WHERE A.BROKER_ID = @BROKER
   AND A.FUND = B.FUND_NAME
   AND B.STOCK_SYMBOL = C.STOCK_SYMBOL
   AND C.TRADE_DATE BETWEEN @STARTDATE AND @ENDDATE


RETURN
END
```

Now, our brokers can happily perform any calculations on their own without having to write all of the JOIN clauses between the three tables. All they must use is a SELECT statement similar to the following:

```
SELECT FUND_NAME, SUM(SHARES*PRICE) AS TOTAL_FUND_COST,TRADE_DATE
    FROM ACCOUNT_STATUS('LARRY','5/1/2004','6/1/2004')
    GROUP BY FUND_NAME,TRADE_DATE
    ORDER BY FUND_NAME ASC;
```

If we wanted to, we could also produce other UDFs so that they could use multiple UDFs in one query. In the prior query, what if our broker, Larry, wanted to grab the average weekly price of the funds that he manages. Perhaps we could produce for him a UDF that would look similar to the following:

```
CREATE FUNCTION WEEKOFMONTH(
@THIS_DATE   DATETIME
)
RETURNS INT
AS
BEGIN
DECLARE @WEEK INT



RETURN (@WEEK)
END
```

Maintaining a Data Warehouse

The data warehouse is not, in and of itself, a self-maintaining operation. It is the administrator's job to ensure the accuracy and consistency of the data contained within its tables. You might wonder why we need to worry about the data within the warehouse application because it comes from the proprietary database implementations. Wouldn't that make the data incorrect? This is not a bad question to ask. Why do we need to constantly monitor and maintain the data in the warehouse? Once we set up the schedules on which it is fed so that it is consistently updated, what is there to do? Consider an example of a major distribution company that conducts most of its business via an online ordering system. The back end of the system is what the salespeople use to confirm orders and payments on the invoice. A few of the customers with larger accounts receive bulk discounts for several items they order on a continuing basis. The sales database is not able to handle these discounts, however, and they are tracked mainly by the accounting department to keep the books straight. In this situation, if you relied only on the database from the production sales system, any reports that were generated detailing gross sales and equivalent profit for the company would be incorrect. You would have to devise a method to draw in the data from the accounting division, by which you could update the information in the system to give a true accounting of the cash flow of the company.

Feeding and Using the Data Warehouse

To give you a better idea of the different actions involved in the operations of the data warehouse, we will go over several examples of tasks that can be used to create your own UDFs. This is not an all-encompassing list, but it should serve as a good basis for you to start realizing the different areas in which UDFs can be useful.

Data Scrubbing

Data scrubbing is usually a process that is used in the feeding of data from the component database implementations to the data warehouse. In general, data scrubbing can mean anything that has to do with a variety of subtopics. However, for our purposes, we will limit our definition to the filtering of individual data columns on their way to the data warehouse environment.

For this example, let's create a true filtering mechanism that we use to parse down the data from the source implementation into a data warehouse that handles the reporting aspect of the sales of the company. The data will be drawn from the Accounting database and placed into our data warehouse arena, but the owner does not want any of the Expenses to be fed into the warehouse other than refunds to customers. We know that employee payroll information would be tied to the EmployeeID number in the Employees table, and that the Transaction_Type would be EFT for Electronic Funds Transfer. Customers, on the other hand, would be reimbursed by check and they would be recorded by their CustomerID in the Customers table.

You might think that this is a fairly simple matter that can be handled through a few SQL statements. However, what if the same owner comes back next week and asks that the refunds not be shown because it will depress the sales staff? Of course, the owner may decide to show an employee salary (by mistake, of course) to spur competition among the sales staff. Wouldn't it be easier to encapsulate the logic into generalized functions and stored procedures to reuse it later? By now, you should understand the answer is "yes."

Let's discuss what would be needed to implement such a routine. First, let's take a look at the structure of the different tables involved. Remember, we are only extracting information from the Accounting table and are using the Employees and Customers tables to filter the data.

Standardizing Data from Multiple Database Environments

To understand possible instances in which you may have to standardize data coming from multiple database instances, let's revisit our previous discussion. It would be nice if we could ensure that things such as company names, personnel names, and possibly product names were all standardized across all of our database implementations. Unfortunately, this is often not the case, and what may be stored as 'ABC Company Inc.' in one system may be stored as merely 'ABC' in another. Although it might not be important that each one of these independent systems store exactly the same name, it is of paramount importance in the data warehouse environment (especially when the data is centrally located and could possibly be grouped by the naming context). So, let's expand upon our original thought of having a standard naming function that can be used to input the name and retrieve the standardized version. Here is our original code for the function:

```
CREATE FUNCTION STANDARD_NAME(@NAME VARCHAR(100))
RETURNS VARCHAR(100)
AS
BEGIN

DECLARE @STANDARD_NAME VARCHAR(100)

-- First check to see if the name exists.
IF EXISTS (
SELECT * FROM STANDARD_NAMING
    WHERE NAMING_VARIATION=@NAME
)
   BEGIN
   -- Set the name equal to the standard name in the database.
      SELECT @STANDARD_NAME = STANDARD_NAME
           FROM STANDARD_NAMING
      WHERE NAMING_VARIATION=@NAME
   END
ELSE
   SET @STANDARD_NAME = @NAME

RETURN @STANDARD_NAME
END
```

Now, let's use our sales tables from Chapter 19 to test our hypothesis and ensure that the function will perform as desired. We will first create the STANDARD_NAMING table and fill it with an abbreviated syntax of the company names and what company they correspond to. Then we will be using CurrentSales and Sales2003 to test the function with the company names truncated in the latter table. Then we will see if the CurrentSales table will give us the names without having an entry in the table, and the names from the Sales2003 table should now come back as the full company name instead of the abbreviation.

```
CREATE TABLE STANDARD_NAMING(
                        NAMING_VARIATION VARCHAR(100),
                        STANDARD_NAME     VARCHAR(100)
                        )
INSERT INTO STANDARD_NAMING(STANDARD_NAME,NAMING_VARIATION)
SELECT SHIPPERNAME ,SUBSTRING(SHIPPERNAME,1,5) FROM SALES2003

UPDATE SALES2003 SET SHIPPERNAME = SUBSTRING(SHIPPERNAME,1,5)

(101 row(s) affected)
(101 row(s) affected)

SELECT top 10 orderid,shippername FROM SALES2003

orderid     shippername
----------- ----------------------------
1           Leka
2           Zaans
3           New O
4           Plutz
5           G'day
6           Plutz
7           Svens
8           Svens
9           Heli
10          Karkk

(10 row(s) affected)
```

Now that we have ensured that our tables are correct, we can try a couple of queries to ensure that our UDF operates properly.

```
SELECT SHIPPERNAME,SUM(TOTAL_PRICE)AS [YEARLY SALES],[YEAR]
FROM
(SELECT TOP 10 DBO.STANDARD_NAME(SHIPPERNAME) AS SHIPPERNAME,TOTAL_PRICE,2004 AS
[YEAR] FROM CURRENTSALES WHERE SHIPPERNAME IS NOT NULL
 UNION
 SELECT TOP 10 DBO.STANDARD_NAME(SHIPPERNAME) AS SHIPPERNAME,TOTAL_PRICE,2003 AS
[YEAR] FROM SALES2003 WHERE SHIPPERNAME IS NOT NULL)A
GROUP BY [YEAR],SHIPPERNAME
ORDER BY [YEAR] DESC, SHIPPERNAME


SHIPPERNAME                       YEARLY SALES          YEAR
------------------------------    --------------------  -----------
Bigfoot Breweries                 18315.9700            2004
```

Formaggi Fortini s.r.l.	6945.0800	2004
Grandma Kelly's Homestead	17737.4800	2004
Karkki Oy	21792.4100	2004
New Orleans Cajun Delights	2233.5800	2004
Pavlova, Ltd.	19010.2600	2004
PB Knäckebröd AB	14215.5200	2004
Plutzer Lebensmittelgroßmärkte	31454.1900	2004
Refrescos Americanas LTDA	5707.5600	2004
G'day, Mate	10539.5700	2003
Heli Süßwaren GmbH & Co. KG	19430.2800	2003
Karkki Oy	645.3300	2003
Leka Trading	1735.6400	2003
New Orleans Cajun Delights	26744.6800	2003
Plutzer Lebensmittelgroßmärkte	45442.3800	2003
Svensk Sjöföda AB	37035.5300	2003
Zaanse Snoepfabriek	7678.9000	2003

```
(17 row(s) affected)
```

As you can see, our function works just as designed. Values that are not in our STANDARD_NAMING table are left alone, and those that are have been converted to the standard form. Using this same format, you could devise a standards section for almost any data type.

Summarizing Data

Often it is the case that you do not want to see the details of what is in your database, but would rather work in generalized terms with summations. Normally, this would all be handled by the built-in functions MAX, MIN, and AVG. However, what if we need a custom solution for our business environment? Suppose we are using the CurrentSales table that we used in the previous example. Modify the Fill_Tables procedure to place several thousand rows into the CurrentSales table. If management wants the company with the most or least number of purchases per year, finding them involves mainly running through the motions of using MAX, MIN, and COUNT functions. For various reasons, however, we may want to get the company with the middle-of-the-road sales or the company that is at the three-quarters mark. We may want to put this reasoning into a function so that other users who are querying the database can more easily implement it. Let's create the following function and give it a run-through:

```
ALTER FUNCTION GET_COMPANY_ATLEVEL(@LEVEL INT)
RETURNS VARCHAR(100)
AS
BEGIN
DECLARE @COMPANYNAME VARCHAR(100)
DECLARE @TOTAL_COMP INT
DECLARE @CURSOR_PICK INT
DECLARE @COMP_TABLE TABLE( COMPANY_NAME VARCHAR(100),
                           COMP_COUNT    INT
                         )

INSERT INTO @COMP_TABLE(COMPANY_NAME,COMP_COUNT)
SELECT SHIPPERNAME,COUNT(*)
    FROM CURRENTSALES
    WHERE SHIPPERNAME IS NOT NULL
    GROUP BY SHIPPERNAME
```

```
     ORDER BY COUNT(*) DESC


SELECT @TOTAL_COMP = COUNT(*) FROM @COMP_TABLE

SET @CURSOR_PICK = (CAST(@LEVEL AS DECIMAL)/100) * @TOTAL_COMP

DECLARE COMPANY_CURSOR CURSOR SCROLL FOR
SELECT COMPANY_NAME FROM @COMP_TABLE ORDER BY COMP_COUNT DESC

OPEN COMPANY_CURSOR
FETCH RELATIVE @CURSOR_PICK FROM COMPANY_CURSOR INTO @COMPANYNAME
CLOSE COMPANY_CURSOR
DEALLOCATE COMPANY_CURSOR

RETURN(@COMPANYNAME)
END

-- Let's look at the regular list of sales count

SELECT SHIPPERNAME,COUNT(*)
   FROM CURRENTSALES
   WHERE SHIPPERNAME IS NOT NULL
   GROUP BY SHIPPERNAME
   ORDER BY COUNT(*) DESC

SHIPPERNAME
------------------------------------------------- -----------
Formaggi Fortini s.r.l.                           242
Pavlova, Ltd.                                     234
Exotic Liquids                                    232
Grandma Kelly's Homestead                         229
New Orleans Cajun Delights                        227
Escargots Nouveaux                                226
Leka Trading                                      226
Pasta Buttini s.r.l.                              219
Svensk Sjöföda AB                                 218
Norske Meierier                                   218
G'day, Mate                                       216
Aux joyeux ecclésiastiques                        213
Tokyo Traders                                     213
Gai pâturage                                      212
Heli Süßwaren GmbH & Co. KG                       211
Plutzer Lebensmittelgroßmärkte AG                 210
PB Knäckebröd AB                                  209
Nord-Ost-Fisch Handelsgesellschaft mbH            208
Mayumi's                                          206
Specialty Biscuits, Ltd.                          198
Lyngbysild                                        197
Karkki Oy                                         197
Zaanse Snoepfabriek                               196
Refrescos Americanas LTDA                         193
Bigfoot Breweries                                 187
Ma Maison                                         186
New England Seafood Cannery                       184
```

```
Cooperativa de Quesos 'Las Cabras'                      174

(28 row(s) affected)

-- Now let's look at a couple of examples of our function
-- We pass an integer to the function representing the % mark we want

SELECT DBO.GET_COMPANY_ATLEVEL(25)
SELECT DBO.GET_COMPANY_ATLEVEL(50)
SELECT DBO.GET_COMPANY_ATLEVEL(75)
SELECT DBO.GET_COMPANY_ATLEVEL(100)


-----------------------------------
Leka Trading

(1 row(s) affected)


-----------------------------------
Gai pâturage

(1 row(s) affected)


-----------------------------------
Lyngbysild

(1 row(s) affected)


-----------------------------------
Cooperativa de Quesos 'Las Cabras'

(1 row(s) affected)
```

While this is a trivial problem, it goes to the heart of the matter in showing what great flexibility you have when using UDFs.

Concatenating Data

Sometimes it is necessary to map several columns of data into a single column in the data warehouse. This is usually the case when you have something like an address block. In component systems, this may be a derived set of columns, for example, Street, City, Region, Zip, and possibly Country. However, it may be desirable or even required to place this data into the warehouse in one block for Address. The code for such a function is outlined as follows:

```
CREATE FUNCTION MERGE_ADDRESS(
                    @STREET VARCHAR(50),
                    @CITY   VARCHAR(50),
                    @REGION VARCHAR(50),
                    @COUNTRY VARCHAR(50),
                    @ZIP    VARCHAR(10)
```

```
                                     )
RETURNS VARCHAR(210)
AS
BEGIN
DECLARE @BIG_ADDRESS VARCHAR(210)

SET @BIG_ADDRESS = @STREET + ' ' + @CITY + ', ' + @REGION
                   + ', ' + @COUNTRY + ' ' + @ZIP

RETURN(@BIG_ADDRESS)
END

SELECT DBO.MERGE_ADDRESS('2003 South Stephenson' ,'Indianapolis',
      'Indiana','United States','54543-4565') AS NEW_ADDRESS

NEW_ADDRESS
-----------------------------------------------------------------
2003 South Stephenson Indianapolis, Indiana, United States 54543-4565

(1 row(s) affected)
```

Although this is a rather simplistic example, it can be expanded to create almost any form of concatenation that you can think of—names, addresses, company information, identification numbers, and so on.

Breaking Data Apart and Putting It Back Together

Sometimes it is necessary for you to break data apart and then immediately put it back together. This may be necessary to format a certain section of your data in different manners. Another example is one in which we want to migrate datetime data types from a SQL Server or Sybase database to an Oracle data warehouse. The datetime in the former and the date data type in Oracle have different precision and can lead to complications. You may decide to grab the date information, split it apart, and then recombine it into the desired Oracle format to be inserted into the data warehouse. Following is an example of such a function:

```
CREATE FUNCTION TO_ORACLE_DATE(@OLDDATE DATETIME)
RETURNS VARCHAR(10)
AS
BEGIN
DECLARE @NEWDATE VARCHAR(12)
DECLARE @DAY VARCHAR(2)
DECLARE @MONTH VARCHAR(2)
DECLARE @YEAR  VARCHAR(4)

-- First we break the date apart and format each part
SET @DAY = CAST(DAY(@OLDDATE) AS VARCHAR(2))
SET @MONTH = CAST(MONTH(@OLDDATE) AS VARCHAR(2))
SET @YEAR = CAST(YEAR(@OLDDATE) AS VARCHAR(4))

-- Now we put it back together in the proper format
SET @NEWDATE = @YEAR + '-' + @MONTH + '-' + @DAY

RETURN(@NEWDATE)
```

```
END

SELECT DBO.TO_ORACLE_DATE(GETDATE()) AS TODAY

TODAY
----------
2004-09-18

(1 row(s) affected)
```

Once again, this is a simplistic example, but one that can be built upon to create a truly robust function to use in converting date values. Consider that you could expand the function header to accept an additional parameter, @CONV_TYPE INT, where the number would correspond to the type of conversion that is to take place. For one instance, it could be an Oracle conversion, and in another, it may be to just format in the current system as 18 September 2004.

Summary

We have covered most aspects of using UDFs within the concept of data warehousing. A data warehouse is a database layer that separates the component database processing layer from the reporting layer used by the users. Since this is a separate layer from the processing layer, that data warehouse must be fed and maintained by data from the various component database sources. This opens the data warehouse implementation, which is ripe with areas in which the power and flexibility of UDFs can be harnessed. Specifically, we looked at the different areas of feeding, querying, and maintaining your data within the warehouse environment.

Now that we have covered the main uses of UDFs in various aspects created within the database context, in the next chapters we will turn our attention to embedding functions in different instances.

22

Embedded Functions and Advanced Uses

Embedded functions refer to functions written in a supported third-generation language (3GL), such as C. *Embedded SQL* (ESQL) and includes SQL statements that are embedded directly in the source code of an application. ESQL is used to provide direct interaction between the data within the database and the program components. The language that the ESQL interacts with is mainly determined by the particular RDBMS implementation. Some of the various languages supported by the different RDBMS implementations are detailed in the following table.

RDBMS	Supported Languages
Oracle	C, COBOL, FORTRAN, JAVA, PL\I
IBM DB2 UDB	Assembler, COBOL, FORTRAN, JAVA, PL\I
Sybase	C, COBOL
MS SQL Server	C
MySQL	None
PostgreSQL	C

Since the SQL code is not recognized by the compiler of the language within which it is written, it is necessary to first run the code through a *precompiler*. The job of the precompiler is to separate the SQL commands from the base programming implementation, compile, and bind them to the RDBMS. Since the precompiler is what compiles the ESQL into a form that can be used by the RDBMS, the level of compatibility with the RDBMS implementation will be determined by it. To find out what your specific implementation supports, check the product documentation for the RDBMS, and also possibly for the precompiler (because some implementations can use more than one).

> Each RDBMS implementation has documentation on compiling and linking the programs. For example, if you are using MS SQL Server, you would run the compiler CI.exe and then the linker Linker.exe. Check the product documentation for more information.

Consider the concept that everything in the programming world should be compartmentalized into nice, neat bundles. Now, consider these bundles to actually be functions that provide the basis for understanding the difference between a user-defined function (UDF) and an embedded one. The embedded UDF is one in which the code is compiled separately from the database implementation. Therefore, it is actually considered an external element that is linked to the RDBMS implementation. This is a fundamental difference from the UDFs that have been discussed previously. However, this does provide us with several unique advantages:

- ❑ The application is precompiled and is, thus, transferable. The developer can move the executable file and the database request module to another implementation and rebind them to the new database.

- ❑ Since the application is precompiled, it removes the necessity of parsing and determining an execution plan at run time. This makes the program very efficient as far as utilizing computing resources.

- ❑ Since you are using ESQL in a 3GL language, the developer must only have an understanding of the basic SQL language. Since variables, flow-control syntax, input/output routines, and structure are handled by the 3GL, the developer does not need to be concerned with extended language constructs of the different implementations.

ESQL Statements

ESQL statements are a rather simple concept to understand once you have the semantics down. In their most simplistic form, they can be individual, self-contained objects that do not return any values. Borrowing from some of our examples in Chapter 19, consider the `Sales` tables that we created. We used a stored procedure called `Fill_Tables()` to populate the tables with up to a thousand random rows each time it executed. For the purpose of our example, suppose we coded the stored procedure incorrectly and we have introduced incorrect data into our `Sales2003` table. We could have a small program that, when executed, would remove the incorrect data from that table. The following code details such a solution to our problem:

```
main()
{

exec sql include sqlca;
/* Execute the sql statement to delete the rows from the table */
exec sql delete from sales2003
     where year(purchasedate)<>2003;

/* Output a simple message */
printf("You just deleted the bad stuff! \n");

/* Exit the routine */
exit();

}
```

The preceding code was produced in C and, although it seems intellectually boring, it does provide us with a first glance at ESQL. You will see that the EXEC SQL is what introduces the parts of the application that contain SQL. Also, you may notice that the terminator for the SQL statement and the line continuation for the delete statement both mirror that of the C language. This strikes at the heart of the third bullet from the previous section. The SQL code only handles the connecting to the database and gathering of data. Everything else is handled by the rules of the 3GL that it is being embedded in. This provides that extra degree of productivity for the C developer who doesn't have to be bogged down with learning all the specifics of a SQL extension language.

Static versus Dynamic Querying

The preceding was a good example of what is known as *static SQL*. This is ESQL that has a predetermined pattern with which to access the database. So, no matter how many times you run the simple application, it will still only remove those entries in the `Sales2003` table that do not correspond to having been purchased in 2003. Of course, the parameters of the ESQL standard allow some flexibility by using *host variables*. These are variables that are declared and used for a means of input and output between the SQL code and the code in which it resides. The data type that is declared in your code must match the corresponding SQL data type that is to be referenced in the ESQL statements, as well as its size. The following table shows you the corresponding data types to use when using C, COBOL, or PL\I.

SQL	C	COBOL	PL\I
BIT	char x[1]	PIC X(1)	BIT
SMALLINT	Short	PIC S9(4) COMP	FIXED BIN(15)
INTEGER	Long	PIC S9(9) COMP	FIXED BIN(31)
DOUBLE	double	COMP-2	BIN FLOAT(53)
NUMERIC	double	COMP-3	FIXED DEC
CHAR	char x	PIC X	CHAR
VARCHAR	char x	None	CHAR (N) VAR
DATE	None	None	None
INTERVAL	None	None	None
TIME	None	None	None
TIMSTAMP	None	None	None

From the preceding table, you can see that some data types do not have a corresponding data type in the embedded language. Most notably are the VARCHAR and date data types. COBOL has no corresponding variable-length data types, so these must be converted into fixed-length strings to be passed to the embedded function. In addition, the embedded languages do not support date, time, or date/time data types. These must be converted into their string representation equivalents.

We could modify our previous example to delete various years from a combined `Sales` table, possibly for purging old data from the system:

```
main()
{

exec sql include sqlca;
/* We declare our variables in the next section */
```

```
exec sql begin declare section;
    int     old_year;      /* Year from which to base removal */
exec sql end declare section

/* Ask for a year to be input */
printf("Please enter a year: ");
scanf("%d", &old_year);
/* We write this number to the variable */

/* Execute the sql statement to delete the rows from the table */
exec sql delete from sales2003
    where year(purchasedate)< :old_year;

/* Output a simple message */
printf("You just deleted the bad stuff! \n");

/* Exit the routine */
exit();

}
```

So, the static SQL does not keep us necessarily from creating what could be called a *semidynamic statement*. However, what if we wanted to purge information from any number of different tables? What if we needed to alter the name of a current table to archive it, and then build a table in its place? This is where *dynamic SQL* would come in quite handy.

Dynamic SQL is similar to static SQL except that it allows the program to build the query statement and then pass that onto the RDBMS on-the-fly. This is less efficient than static SQL and relies on the EXCUTE IMMEDIATE and the separate PREPARE and EXECUTE statements for database access. The EXECUTE IMMEDIATE syntax is the simplest because you just have to pass the query execution string to be run against the database to it. The query execution string can be constructed any way you please, as long as the end result is a valid SQL statement. This allows you to give as much freedom as you like to the user or system that is accessing your particular function.

The following example shows a simple update function for our Sales tables. We have constrained the SQL statement so that the user can enter in a table and a surcharge to add onto each sales total. This is normally the pattern that you will use for your embedded functions because allowing the users to define the complete SQL statement leads to a lot of headaches every time they enter Drop Table tablename.

```
main()
{

/* Update a sales table in the database with a special sales surcharge */

exec sql include sqlca;
exec sql begin declare section;
    char output_buffer[300];  /* SQL string */
exec sql end declare section;

char tablename[100];
char surcharge[10];

/* We first start building the header for the update statement */
```

```
/* with the c strcpy (string copy) statement */
strcpy(output_buffer,"update ");

/* Now we request the table from the user */
printf("Please enter a table name to place the surcharge upon:");
gets(tablename);
strcat(output_buffer,tablename);

/* Now we can put in the middle section of our statement */
strcat(output_buffer, " set total_price = total_price + ");

/* Now we prompt for the surcharge */
printf("Please enter the surcharge amount:");
gets(surcharge);
strcat(output_buffer,surcharge);

/* Now we can execute our statement against the RDBMS */
exec sql execute immediate :output_buffer;

/* Check to see if there were any errors in updating the table */
if (sqlca.sqlcode < 0 )
    printf("SQL error in updating the table: %ld\n", sqlca.sqlcode);
else
    printf("The surcharge has been applied successfully to %s.\n",tablename);

/* Now exit the routine

exit();

}
```

The preceding code is, again, fairly straightforward; it is up to you to flesh it out to perform whatever operations you see fit. It is good, however, to show the basic concepts of using dynamic ESQL in your code. It also outlines another important syntax that will be used within your code: incorporating error handing with the SQLCODE syntax. The SQLCODE syntax is a variable within the SQL communications area (SQLCA). Check the include statement at the top of the code. Its purpose is to give us feedback on the completion status of the current statement that has executed. The SQLCODE value can be decoded as follows:

❑ A negative value indicates that a serious error has occurred in the execution of the statement and it did not execute correctly. There are separate run-time errors that correspond to the negative value assigned to SQLCODE.

❑ Zero indicates successful completion.

❑ A positive value indicates that a warning has been issued. A separate run-time warning is assigned to each value given. The most common is an error of 100+, which indicates that there are no more rows left to retrieve from the query results. However, the codes vary somewhat from implementation to implementation, and you should check your vendor-specific documentation.

Common Uses of Embedded Functions

Since embedded functions are written mainly in the context of the 3GL language that is supported by the database implementation, it stands to reason that this adds another layer of flexibility to development, since the 3GL languages can perform tasks that the SQL language cannot (such as file I/O and system interoperability). The next few subsections detail some of the various instances in which you can expand upon the use of the SQL language by using embedded functions.

Single-Row Functions

Single-row functions are normally used to return a single row of data based on certain inputs from the user or the system. These are most often used in transaction-processing applications in which the function will return a certain user's account information or information about a particular sale. In our previous example, we used host variables to store the information that the user input in order to form our UPDATE statement. We use the same syntax when performing single-row operations, except that the variables are actually considered output host variables since they are used to store output information. Every output variable corresponds to a column from the result set that we want to have returned. As mentioned before, these must match a corresponding column in both type and number. The following example shows the retrieval of account balance information when entering customer information:

```
Get_Account_Balance()
{

exec sql include sqlca;
exec sql begin declare section;
    int  customerid;     /* customer identification number */
    int  accounttype;    /* customer account type 1-Checking 2-Savings */
    int accountnum;      /* customer account number(output) */
    float balance;       /* account balance(output) */
exec sql end declare section;

/* Prompt for the customers id number */
printf("Please enter the customers id number:");
scanf("%d", &customerid)

/* Prompt to check the user's checking or saving account */
printf("Please select an account type:\n");
printf("1-Checking or 2-Savings");
scanf("%d", &accounttype)

/* Use the inputs to execute the SQL statement */
exec sql select accountnum, balance
        from accounts
        where customerid = :customerid and
        account_type = :accounttype
        into :accountnum, :balance;

/* Now we can check for errors */
if (sqlca.sqlcode == 0)
{
   /* Success! Display account balance */
   printf("Account Number %d has a balance of $%f \n", accountnum,
             balance);
}
else if (sqlca.sqlcode == 100)
{
   /* No account information */
   printf("This person does not have an account.\n");
```

```
    }
    else
    {
        /* Another failure type has occurred. */
        printf("An SQL error has occurred: %ld\n", sqlca.sqlcode);
    }

    /* Exit the function */
    exit();

}
```

Sometimes, it is more advantageous to use data structures if your programming language supports them. Fortunately, C allows this, and so we can demonstrate our previous example enhanced somewhat by using a data structure. The use of data structures allows you to act as if the structure type is one composite user-defined data type when used in the SQL statement. This not only makes your code more readable for other developers, but enables you to keep better track of the various variables in your code as well.

```
Get_Structured_Account()
{

exec sql include sqlca;
exec sql begin declare section;
    int  customerid;    /* customer identification number */
    int  accounttype;   /* customer account type 1-Checking 2-Savings */
    struct {
    char  customer_name[20]  /* customer name */
    char customer_addr[50]   /* customer address */
    int accountnum;       /* customer account number(output) */
    float balance;        /* account balance(output) */
    } accountinfo;
exec sql end declare section;

/* Prompt for the customers id number */
printf("Please enter the customers id number:");
scanf("%d", &customerid)

/* Prompt to check the user's checking or saving account */
printf("Please select an account type:\n");
printf("1-Cheking or 2-Savings");
scanf("%d", &accounttype)

/* Use the inputs to execute the SQL statement */
exec sql select accountnum, balance
        from accounts
        where customerid = :customerid and
        account_type = :accounttype
        into :accountinfo;

/* Now we can check for errors */
if (sqlca.sqlcode == 0)
{
    /* Success! Display account information from structure */
    printf("Name: %s \n", accountinfo.customer_name);
    printf("Address: %s \n", accountinfo.customer_addr);
```

```
    printf("Account Number: %d \n", accountinfo.accountnum);
    if (accounttype == 1)
      printf("Account Type: Checking \n");
    else
      printf("Account Type: Savings \n");
     printf("Account Balance: %f \n, accountinfo.balance);
}
else if (sqlca.sqlcode == 100)
{
    /* No account information */
    printf("This person does not have an account.\n");
}
else
{
    /* Another failure type has occurred. */
    printf("An SQL error has occurred: %ld\n", sqlca.sqlcode);
}

/* Exit the function */
exit();

}
```

Scalar Functions

Scalar functions are used when you need a single value to be returned. Normally, these are functions that work on a single value from a single column of a result set. One possible example is using your own form of encryption to encrypt usernames into a database table. This, of course, does not have to be anything complicated and can be as novel an idea as converting the character string into a string of ASCII equivalent numbers. You could implement a more sophisticated method by using the XOR "^" operator and defining an encryption/decryption key. The following code shows one such implementation of this plan:

```
#include <stdio.h>

main()
{
/* Initialize the BLOCK_SIZE & key variables */

int BLOCK_SIZE;
char key[40];

BLOCK_SIZE = 3;
Key ="HMygHG*b6GVLLiokstRDx.aohbvwsuixzghzlqJK";

exec sql include sqlca
exec sql begin declare section;
    char  username(20);    /* user's username */
    char  password(40);    /* user's password */
exec sql end declare section;

/* Get the user to input his desired username */
fprint("Please enter a username:");
```

```
    fgets(username);

    /* Get the password for the username that will be encrypted. */
    fprint("Please enter a password that will be encrypted:");
    fgets(password);


    /* Now encrypt the password before inserting it into the database */

    for(int i = 0, y = 0; i <= strlen(password); )
    {
      for(int o = 0; o <= BLOCK_SIZE; o++) {
        if(password[i] != '') {
          password[i] ^= key[y]; }
        i++; }
      y++;
      if(key[y] == '') {
        y = 0; }
    };

    /* Now insert the values into the database */
    exec sql insert into users(username,password)
        values(:username, :password);

    if (sqlca.sqlcode == 0 )
        fprint("Your username and password have been inserted.\n");
    else
        fprint("There has been an error in inserting your info.\n");

    /* Exit the function */

    exit();

    }
```

The best part of this function is that by using a key and the XOR statement, a slight variation of the function using the same key can be used to decode the password and compare it against the entry. Of course, easy is not always best, and you should use a stricter form of encryption for your development systems.

Aggregate Functions

Aggregate functions are used to operate against a collection of values to return a single value. Since there will be multiple rows of data taken from the database call, this will be handled a little differently from the standard single-row function. Application languages are not set up to deal with the intricacies of table objects the way SQL is, so they need some way in which to read and work on the data one row at a time. To accomplish this, we implement the query to the database by creating a cursor object to read the data. The cursor achieves its objective by using a series of DECLARE, OPEN, FETCH, and CLOSE statements. The following code demonstrates how you can use the CURSOR object to effectively get one row at a time from the results set and work on the data. The code details a simple function to create the HTML code for the order list of items (or an HTML list that has numbers in front of each of the list items). The following code details the basic function:

```
main()
{

exec sql include sqlca;
ecec sql begin declare section;
     char    tag_list[1000]    /* tag list for the final output */
     char    ind_tag[20]       /* individual tag to be input into list */
exec sql end declare section;

/* Get the Shipper's Name form the Sales table */
/* For this we need to declare a cursor */
exec sql declare shippercur cursor for
          select shippername
          from sales
          order by shippername;

/* Open the cursor */
exec sql open shippercur;

/* Concatenate the beginning tag to the output list */
strcat(tag_list,"<ol>");

/* Now we loop through the cursor adding list items */
for (,,) {

/* Fetch a row */
exec sql fetch shippercur
               into :ind_tag;

/* Concatenate the individual tag to the tag_list */
strcat(tag_list,"<li>");
strcat(tag_list,ind_tag);


} /* Returns to the beginning of the loop */

/* Concatenate the ending tag */
strcat(tag_list,"</ol>");

/* Output the results */
printf("%s \n",tag_list);


/* Exit the module */
exit();

}
```

Mathematical Functions

ESQL functions can perform complex mathematical computations that may not be possible in the normal context of the SQL language. One possibility would be to create your own functions to handle factorials. The factorial of a number N is $N *$ factorial $(N–1)$, with the factorial of 1 equal to 1. So, the easiest way to implement this is with a *recursive function* (a function that calls itself part of the solution). The following code demonstrates one possible implementation of the factorial function that determines the markup of a product in a `Product` table within a sales database implementation:

```c
#Include <stdio.h>

int factorial(int num_value)
{

if (num_value == 1)
    return(1);
else
    return(num_value * factorial(num_value - 1);

}


void main(void)
{

/* We will be entering a product id. This will be used to find the
   cost of the product and then determine its markup based on the
   factorial of the markup column. */

/* initialize holding variables for later
     float markup_perc;
     float total_markup;

exec sql include sqlca;
exec sql begin declare;
     int    productid  /* Product identification number */
     float cost;    /* cost of the item */
     int    markup;  /* markup value to use */
exec sql end declare;

/* Get input from the user for the productid */
fprint("Please enter the Product ID:");
fgets(productid);

/* Now execute the sql statement to get the product information */
exec sql select cost,markup
     from products
     into :cost, :markup;

markup_perc = factorial(markup);
total_markup = (markup_perc/100) * cost;

/* Now output the results */

printf("Product Cost: $%f\n", cost);
printf("Markup Percentage: %f \n", markup_perc);
printf("Total Markup: $%f \n", total_markup);
printf("Total Retail Price: $%f \n",(cost+total_markup));

}
```

Date and Time Functions

Date and time functions embedded inside application code are tricky to deal with. As mentioned earlier, there are no standard data types that match the proprietary SQL date and time data types of the various RDBMS implementations. This means that every date or time instance that you have in your SQL statement must be converted into its equivalent string format before being placed into a variable on the application side. This is inherently a tricky concept to handle because you may be drawing and inserting date/time values several times within one function. Considering this, we will demonstrate a simple function that will be used to determine which government fiscal year the sale is made in by using the Oracle syntax for to_char in the sql statement:

```
Gov_fiscal_year()
{

exec sql include sqlca;
exec sql begin declare section;
    int    ordernum;        /* OrderID for the order */
    char   adate(8);        /* variable to hold the character year value */
    char   cmonth(2);       /* variable to hold the character month value */
    char   cyear(4);        /* variable to hold the character year value */
    int    imonth;
    int    iyear;
    int    result;
exec sql end declare section;

/* Get the OrderID for the sale from the user */
printf("Please enter an OrderID:");
fgets(ordernum);


/* Now construct the query and assign the variables */
exec sql select to_char(orderdate,'YYYYMMDD') from sales
        where ordered = :ordernum
        into :adate;

/* Now we can parse the adate string in format YYYYMMDD
   to get the month and year */

strncat(cyear, adate, 4)
iyear = atoi(cyear);

/* Now remove the year from the date before getting the month value */
strstr-rem(adate, cyear)

/* Now get the month value */
strncat(cmonth, adate, 2)
imonth = atoi(cmonth)

if (imonth>10)
    result = iyear + 1;
else
```

```
    result = iyear;

/* Return the result to the user */
printf("The

}
```

This is not the most elegant programming solution, but it works. Since there is no direct representation of the SQL date/time values in any of the embedded languages, it leaves the programming landscape ripe with opportunities in which to code your own functions to handle specific, custom date/time calculations.

String Functions

String functions perform some fundamental transformation of the string objects or objects that are passed to it. These are usually straightforward in their implementation except that 3GL languages such as C tend to treat their strings more as characters in an array rather than as succinct stand-alone objects. However, this can lead to some interesting ideas for some functions. The following example details such a function that could be used for something fun like a word scramble. Its object is to scramble each of the words passed to it.

```
main()
{

exec sql include sqlca;
exec sql begin declare section;
    char  temp_word[20];
exec sql end declare section;

/* Retrieve a list of words from table wordlist */
/* Create cursor for multiple rows */
exec sql create wordcursor cursor for
        select words
        from wordlist;

/* Open the cursor */
exec sql open wordcursor;

/* Now we loop through the cursor adding list items */
for (,,) {

/* Fetch a row */
exec sql fetch wordcursor
            into :temp_word;

/* Now start the scrambling series */
int j,k,l;            /* this holds the random number */
int N;                /* this holds the array size */
char temp_char[1]  /* temp holding character */
 N = strlen(temp_word)

For(l=0;l<100;l++) {
j=(int)N*rand()/(RAND_MAX + 1.0); /* first array slot */
```

```
k=(int)N*rand()/(RAND_MAX + 1.0); /* second array slot */
temp_char = temp_word[j];
temp_word[j] = temp_word[k];
temp_word[k] = temp_char;
}

/* We scramble the word a hundred times and then output */
printf("%s \n",temp_word);


} /* Back to beginning of loop */

/* Exit the routine */
exit()


}
```

Of course, you might remember from your C programming experience that there is also a `srand()` function that controls the seed value that starts the random-number sequence. Since you can get the same sequence of random numbers by starting with the same seed value, you could use this for other useful purposes. One instance could be a scrambling technique that involved a numerical password that was used for the seed value, which could then be used to grab the random-number sequence and unscramble the message. This is not much as far as elegant coding goes, but it does serve a valuable purpose.

Summary

By now, you should be thoroughly familiar with some of the different aspects in which you can use a 3GL language and embed your SQL code into it, and then create your own ESQL functions. The way in which static SQL and dynamic SQL are compiled and the differences in performance between the two should be one of the deciding factors in implementing embedded code into your development platform. Also, you should thoroughly consider the flexibility involved in each of the different selections. Are your users more apt to create ad hoc queries, or is this a standardized reporting system? Questions like these will help you strike a balance between system performance and the needs of your users.

Second, we touched upon different ways to create some of the different classes of functions. In addition, the difference in coding between the single-row and multirow functions was examined. This will be important in later chapters when we discuss using these ESQL functions, as well as the command-line interface (CLI), in different forms of applications.

Generating SQL with SQL and SQL Functions

One of the most common things a database administrator will have to do is to write SQL code that generates other SQL code. No one wants to type perhaps hundreds of lines of SQL code to produce some sort of desired results on the database. Instead, it is more advantageous and reliable (especially if you are a bad typist) to use SQL to generate its own SQL statements. Whether it is to move data from one platform to another, or to merely make mass changes within the database, producing code should be the staple of any good DBA/developer's toolbox.

This chapter discusses various aspects in which you can use SQL and SQL functions to generate code. These techniques can be used for a myriad of instances, some of which we have already discussed (such as migration of data and feeding of data warehouses).

Writing custom SQL code and functions to handle the creation of custom SQL code is not necessarily a hard thing to accomplish, but it does take a fair amount of imagination to accomplish it elegantly. We will look at several instances in which we could use custom SQL code to effectively generate solutions by producing more SQL code than can be executed at a later time. In most cases, you will be using these sequences to dump the resulting code into a text file that you can then run on whichever implementation is required.

Using Literal Values, Column Values, and Concatenation

A favorite resource to turn to is the ability to write SQL code that will generate SQL code to migrate data from one platform to another platform. You know that it will not be as simple as a point-and-click type of operation. The following code details a simple SQL code that you could use to generate a series of INSERT statements to migrate the contents of the Sales2003 table to another platform:

```
SELECT 'INSERT INTO NEWSALES_TABLE SET' +
   ' ORDERID=''' + CAST(ORDERID AS VARCHAR(8)) + ''', SHIPPERNAME=''' +
SHIPPERNAME + ''',
   PRODUCTID=''' + CAST(PRODUCTID AS VARCHAR(8)) + ''', PURCHASEDATE=''' +
CAST(PURCHASEDATE AS VARCHAR(30)) + ''',
```

```
        TOTAL_PRICE=''' + CAST(TOTAL_PRICE AS VARCHAR(30)) + ''', SALES_REGIONID=''' +
        CAST(SALES_REGIONID AS VARCHAR(2)) + ''';' FROM SALES2003


INSERT INTO NEWSALES_TABLE SET ORDERID='1', SHIPPERNAME='Leka ',
    PRODUCTID='59', PURCHASEDATE='May 19 2003 12:00AM',
    TOTAL_PRICE='1735.64', SALES_REGIONID='0';
INSERT INTO NEWSALES_TABLE SET ORDERID='2', SHIPPERNAME='Zaans',
    PRODUCTID='237', PURCHASEDATE='May  3 2003 12:00AM',
    TOTAL_PRICE='7678.90', SALES_REGIONID='2';
INSERT INTO NEWSALES_TABLE SET ORDERID='3', SHIPPERNAME='New O',
    PRODUCTID='809', PURCHASEDATE='Apr 16 2003 12:00AM',
    TOTAL_PRICE='26744.68', SALES_REGIONID='8';
    .
    .
    .
    .
```

This does its job, but if we are particularly savvy and know a little about the system tables, then we could possibly create a function that would automatically create this SQL code without knowing any knowledge of the underlying table structure. The following is an example of such code for the Microsoft SQL Server database:

```
CREATE FUNCTION PRODUCE_TABLE_DUMP(@NEWTABLE VARCHAR(50),@OLDTABLE VARCHAR(50))
RETURNS VARCHAR(2000)
BEGIN
DECLARE @FINAL_SQL VARCHAR(2000)
DECLARE @COLNAME    VARCHAR(50)
DECLARE @TYPE       VARCHAR(50)
DECLARE @LENGTH     INT
DECLARE @ENDTYPE    VARCHAR(100)
DECLARE @ROWSET     INT
SET @ROWSET = 0
SET @FINAL_SQL = 'SELECT ''INSERT INTO ' + @NEWTABLE + ' SET '

DECLARE COLUMN_CURSOR CURSOR FOR
SELECT C.NAME,T.NAME,C.LENGTH FROM SYSCOLUMNS C
INNER JOIN SYSTYPES T ON C.XTYPE=T.XTYPE  AND T.NAME<>'sysname'
WHERE C.ID=(SELECT ID FROM SYSOBJECTS WHERE NAME=@OLDTABLE AND XTYPE='U')
ORDER BY C.COLID

OPEN COLUMN_CURSOR

FETCH NEXT FROM COLUMN_CURSOR
    INTO @COLNAME, @TYPE, @LENGTH

WHILE @@FETCH_STATUS=0
BEGIN

IF @ROWSET <> 0
SET @FINAL_SQL = @FINAL_SQL + ', '

-- We can now make sure that the column is converted

SELECT @ENDTYPE =
CASE @TYPE
```

```
WHEN 'tinyint' THEN @COLNAME + '='''+ CAST(' + @COLNAME + ' AS ' +
    'VARCHAR(' + CAST(@LENGTH AS VARCHAR(4)) + ')) + '''' '
WHEN 'int' THEN @COLNAME + '='''+ CAST(' + @COLNAME + ' AS VARCHAR(' +
    CAST(@LENGTH AS VARCHAR(4)) + ')) + '''' '
WHEN 'bigint' THEN @COLNAME + '='''+ CAST(' + @COLNAME + ' AS VARCHAR('
    + CAST(@LENGTH AS VARCHAR(4)) + ')) + '''' '
WHEN 'datetime' THEN @COLNAME + '='''''+ CAST(' + @COLNAME + ' AS ' +
    'VARCHAR(' + CAST(@LENGTH AS VARCHAR(4)) + ')) + '''''' '
ELSE @COLNAME + '='''''+ ' + @COLNAME + ' + '''''' '
END

SET @FINAL_SQL = @FINAL_SQL + @ENDTYPE

FETCH NEXT FROM COLUMN_CURSOR
    INTO @COLNAME, @TYPE, @LENGTH
SET @ROWSET = @ROWSET + 1
END
CLOSE COLUMN_CURSOR
DEALLOCATE COLUMN_CURSOR


SET @FINAL_SQL = @FINAL_SQL + ';'' FROM ' + @OLDTABLE
RETURN (@FINAL_SQL)
END

GRANT EXECUTE ON DBO.PRODUCE_TABLE_DUMP TO PUBLIC


SELECT DBO.PRODUCE_TABLE_DUMP('NEW_TABLE','SALES2003')

-----------------------------------------------------------------
SELECT 'INSERT INTO NEW_TABLE SET OrderID=''+ CAST(OrderID AS VARCHAR(4)) + '' ,
ShipperName='''+ ShipperName + ''' , ProductID=''+ CAST(ProductID AS VARCHAR(4)) +
'' , PurchaseDate='''+ CAST(PurchaseDate AS VARCHAR(8)) + ''' , Total_Price=''+
Total_Price + '' , Sales_RegionID=''+ CAST(Sales_RegionID AS VARCHAR(4)) + '' ;'
FROM SALES2003

(1 row(s) affected)
```

Now, this is a decent start to having a good function for these purposes. It should be fleshed out a little bit to include translation for all the different data types. Yet, it does do a lot of things, like automatically drawing the column names, data types, and even length from the system tables, so it is something handy to have.

In addition, you could use functions to create SQL statements to rearrange data within the database. Consider our Customers table that contains the following columns related to the customer's address: Address, City, Region, and PostalCode. It has been decided that these fields must be combined into the common column, Customer_Address, and moved to the new Customers table in another system. You decide that the best course of action is to write some SQL that will produce the INSERT statements necessary to insert the proper data into the new table. We could implement this in a very simple SQL statement, such as the one shown here:

```
SELECT 'UPDATE CUSTOMERS SET CUSTOMER_ADDRESS=' +
    '''' + ISNULL(ADDRESS,'') + ' ' + ISNULL(CITY,'')  + ', ' +
    ISNULL(REGION,'') + ' ' + ISNULL(POSTALCODE,'') + ''' ' +
    ' WHERE CUSTOMERID=''' + ISNULL(CUSTOMERID,'') + ''';'
```

```
                FROM CUSTOMERS

                UPDATE CUSTOMERS SET CUSTOMER_ADDRESS='Obere Str. 57 Berlin,  12209'
                WHERE CUSTOMERID=ALFKI;
                UPDATE CUSTOMERS SET CUSTOMER_ADDRESS='Avda. de la Constitución 2222 México D.F.,
                05021'  WHERE CUSTOMERID=ANATR;
                UPDATE CUSTOMERS SET CUSTOMER_ADDRESS='Mataderos  2312 México D.F.,  05023'  WHERE
                CUSTOMERID=ANTON;
                UPDATE CUSTOMERS SET CUSTOMER_ADDRESS='120 Hanover Sq. London,  WA1 1DP'  WHERE
                CUSTOMERID=AROUT;
                UPDATE CUSTOMERS SET CUSTOMER_ADDRESS='Berguvsvägen  8 Luleå,  S-958 22'  WHERE
                CUSTOMERID=BERGS;
                UPDATE CUSTOMERS SET CUSTOMER_ADDRESS='Forsterstr. 57 Mannheim,  68306'  WHERE
                CUSTOMERID=BLAUS;
                UPDATE CUSTOMERS SET CUSTOMER_ADDRESS='24, place Kléber Strasbourg,  67000'  WHERE
                CUSTOMERID=BLONP;
                .
                .
                .
```

Other Functions Commonly Used to Generate SQL Code

Intricate knowledge of your particular RDBMS implementation and a good sense of imagination is all that is needed to produce some amazing results. You should strive to become what has commonly been referred to as the "lazy developer." Of course, this doesn't mean that you are really lazy. It means that you strive to use the principles of things like functional encapsulation, reuse of code, and automation of tasks to make your life easier. While other DBAs spend hours and hours coding changes and updates by hand, you use a proven set of functions, procedures, and SQL queries to effortlessly complete important tasks. Let's look at another example that will demonstrate how to automate some SQL processes. For this example, let's see how we can use functions to autopopulate our columns with a random value. We can create functions for some of the different data types to facilitate maximum flexibility in using them in the future.

```
-- First I need to set up a few views to use in these functions
CREATE VIEW GET_RAND AS
SELECT RAND() AS RAND_NUM

CREATE VIEW GET_TODAYS_DATE AS
SELECT GETDATE() AS THIS_DATE

-- Now let's create a random integer generator
CREATE FUNCTION GET_RAND_INTEGER(@CEILING INT)
RETURNS INT
AS
BEGIN
DECLARE @RANDINT INT

SELECT @RANDINT = CAST(FLOOR(RAND_NUM * @CEILING) AS INT) FROM GET_RAND

RETURN(@RANDINT)
```

```
END

-- Now let's create a random float generator
CREATE FUNCTION GET_RAND_FLOAT(@CEILING INT)
RETURNS FLOAT
AS
BEGIN
DECLARE @RANDFLOAT FLOAT

SELECT @RANDFLOAT = CAST((RAND_NUM * @CEILING) AS FLOAT) FROM GET_RAND

RETURN(@RANDFLOAT)
END

-- We will even create one to produce random character strings
CREATE FUNCTION GET_RAND_CHAR(@CEILING INT)
RETURNS VARCHAR(2000)
AS
BEGIN
DECLARE @CHARCOUNT INT
DECLARE @TEMPCHAR INT
DECLARE @CHARSTRING  VARCHAR(2000)
SET @CHARCOUNT = 1
SET @CHARSTRING = ''
WHILE @CHARCOUNT<=@CEILING
BEGIN
SELECT @TEMPCHAR = CAST(((RAND_NUM * 57)+65) AS INT) FROM GET_RAND
IF @TEMPCHAR>13
BEGIN
SET @CHARSTRING = @CHARSTRING + CHAR(@TEMPCHAR)
SET @CHARCOUNT = @CHARCOUNT + 1
END
END

RETURN(@CHARSTRING)
END

-- Now create one to produce a random date generator for a specific year.
CREATE FUNCTION GET_RAND_YEARLY_DATE(@YEAR INT)
RETURNS DATETIME
AS
BEGIN
DECLARE @RANDDATE DATETIME
SELECT @RANDDATE = THIS_DATE FROM GET_TODAYS_DATE
DECLARE @NUMOFDAYS  INT
SELECT @NUMOFDAYS= CEILING((RAND_NUM* 365) )  FROM GET_RAND
SET @RANDDATE = DATEADD(DD,@NUMOFDAYS ,@RANDDATE)
SET @RANDDATE = CAST(MONTH(@RANDDATE) AS VARCHAR(2)) + '/' + CAST(DAY(@RANDDATE) AS
VARCHAR(2)) + '/' + CAST(@YEAR AS CHAR(4))
RETURN(@RANDDATE)
```

```
END

// Now lets try them out

SELECT DBO.GET_RAND_INTEGER(100) AS MYINT

SELECT DBO.GET_RAND_FLOAT(100) AS MYFLOAT

SELECT DBO.GET_RAND_CHAR(20) AS MYSTRING

SELECT DBO.GET_RAND_YEARLY_DATE(2004) AS MYDATE

MYINT
-----------
74

(1 row(s) affected)

MYFLOAT
------------------------------
95.194095592931532

(1 row(s) affected)

MYSTRING
------------------------------
pcv_bjOQiMGdtVcTIalT

(1 row(s) affected)

MYDATE
------------------------------
2004-07-04 00:00:00.000

(1 row(s) affected)
```

Since one of the basic rules of functions is that they cannot manipulate the data or structures of objects in the database, we cannot write a function to directly populate a table. However, we could combine these with a function similar to our previous one, PRODUCE_TABLE_DUMP, to create a function that would output the SQL code we needed to populate our tables. We need only to pass the name of the table and the number of rows we need it to populate. An example of such a function is shown here:

```
CREATE FUNCTION FILL_TABLE_STRUCTURE(@NEWTABLE VARCHAR(50),@NUMROWS INT)
RETURNS @RESULTTABLE TABLE(FINAL_SQL  VARCHAR(1500))
BEGIN
DECLARE @FINAL_SQL VARCHAR(1500)
DECLARE @COLNAME   VARCHAR(50)
DECLARE @TYPE      VARCHAR(50)
DECLARE @LENGTH    INT
DECLARE @ENDTYPE   VARCHAR(100)
DECLARE @ROWSET    INT
DECLARE @STATEMENTS INT
SET @STATEMENTS = 0
```

```
SET @ROWSET = 0

WHILE @STATEMENTS<= @NUMROWS
BEGIN
SET @FINAL_SQL = 'INSERT INTO ' + @NEWTABLE + ' SET '

DECLARE COLUMN_CURSOR CURSOR FOR
SELECT C.NAME,T.NAME,C.LENGTH FROM SYSCOLUMNS C
INNER JOIN SYSTYPES T ON C.XTYPE=T.XTYPE  AND T.NAME<>'sysname'
WHERE C.ID=(SELECT ID FROM SYSOBJECTS WHERE NAME=@NEWTABLE AND XTYPE='U')
ORDER BY C.COLID

OPEN COLUMN_CURSOR

FETCH NEXT FROM COLUMN_CURSOR
    INTO @COLNAME, @TYPE, @LENGTH

WHILE @@FETCH_STATUS=0
BEGIN

IF @ROWSET <> 0
SET @FINAL_SQL = @FINAL_SQL + ', '

-- We can now make sure that the column is converted

SELECT @ENDTYPE =
CASE @TYPE
WHEN 'tinyint' THEN @COLNAME + '=' + CAST(DBO.GET_RAND_INTEGER(100) AS
      VARCHAR(4)) + ' '
WHEN 'int' THEN @COLNAME + '=' + CAST(DBO.GET_RAND_INTEGER(100) AS
      VARCHAR(4)) + '  '
WHEN 'bigint' THEN @COLNAME + '=' + CAST(DBO.GET_RAND_INTEGER(100) AS
      VARCHAR(4)) + ' '
WHEN 'money' THEN @COLNAME + '=' + CAST(DBO.GET_RAND_FLOAT(100) AS
      VARCHAR(10)) + ' '
WHEN 'datetime' THEN @COLNAME + '=''' + CAST(DBO.GET_RAND_YEARLY_DATE(2004) AS
VARCHAR(10)) + ''' '
ELSE @COLNAME + '=''' + DBO.GET_RAND_CHAR(20) + ''' '
END

SET @FINAL_SQL = @FINAL_SQL + @ENDTYPE

FETCH NEXT FROM COLUMN_CURSOR
    INTO @COLNAME, @TYPE, @LENGTH
SET @ROWSET = @ROWSET + 1
END
CLOSE COLUMN_CURSOR
DEALLOCATE COLUMN_CURSOR


SET @FINAL_SQL = @FINAL_SQL + ';'

INSERT INTO @RESULTTABLE VALUES(@FINAL_SQL)
SET @STATEMENTS = @STATEMENTS + 1
SET @ROWSET = 0
END
```

```
RETURN
END


SELECT * FROM DBO.FILL_TABLE_STRUCTURE('SALES2003',10)

FINAL_SQL
----------------------------------------------------------------------
INSERT INTO SALES2003 SET OrderID=8  , ShipperName='sANJxxkpxMf_W^ZKCO`R' ,
ProductID=53  , PurchaseDate='Nov 19 200' , Total_Price=20.6 , Sales_RegionID=25  ;
INSERT INTO SALES2003 SET OrderID=27  , ShipperName='lgxyFcS]^o^sWKIVGWPS' ,
ProductID=53  , PurchaseDate='Feb 15 200' , Total_Price=13.729 , Sales_RegionID=46
;
INSERT INTO SALES2003 SET OrderID=17  , ShipperName='dWgsKTXlAKbctSHqhMVl' ,
ProductID=92  , PurchaseDate='Dec 11 200' , Total_Price=60.8099 , Sales_RegionID=92
;
INSERT INTO SALES2003 SET OrderID=75  , ShipperName='tWllxmPNOtWxJqQY`REf' ,
ProductID=51  , PurchaseDate='Dec 20 200' , Total_Price=65.2417 , Sales_RegionID=67
;
INSERT INTO SALES2003 SET OrderID=42  , ShipperName='QOiaFcEEFbThcKxBGGgC' ,
ProductID=77  , PurchaseDate='Aug 12 200' , Total_Price=85.5714 , Sales_RegionID=22
;
INSERT INTO SALES2003 SET OrderID=27  , ShipperName='fVf_pZYu^QvJhik\XM\B' ,
ProductID=12  , PurchaseDate='Dec  9 200' , Total_Price=38.8375 , Sales_RegionID=45
;
INSERT INTO SALES2003 SET OrderID=88  , ShipperName='mehjRYX]sk[ZXEACCBwe' ,
ProductID=1  , PurchaseDate='Aug 27 200' , Total_Price=88.7844 , Sales_RegionID=43
;
INSERT INTO SALES2003 SET OrderID=75  , ShipperName='pCB`eAWKGS_caFCkGadQ' ,
ProductID=33  , PurchaseDate='Apr 14 200' , Total_Price=54.0554 , Sales_RegionID=87
;
INSERT INTO SALES2003 SET OrderID=98  , ShipperName='EYJfZDZIHameuxMeQZpu' ,
ProductID=19  , PurchaseDate='Oct  1 200' , Total_Price=93.3286 , Sales_RegionID=26
;
INSERT INTO SALES2003 SET OrderID=32  , ShipperName='hYcmhuFNFoqFuapTxpqH' ,
ProductID=0  , PurchaseDate='Nov 24 200' , Total_Price=7.55744 , Sales_RegionID=79
;
INSERT INTO SALES2003 SET OrderID=31  , ShipperName='pkTZVNWkvC`wEO_EVjNq' ,
ProductID=97  , PurchaseDate='Nov 21 200' , Total_Price=94.5217 , Sales_RegionID=91
;

(11 row(s) affected)
```

Summary

SQL code that writes other SQL code is normally written to automate certain tasks that may not be easily achieved without the use of custom code and functions. We discussed several instances in which these implementations can help with such things as migration of data. In addition, the importance or reuse and encapsulation of SQL functionality was briefly mentioned, as well as other ways in which to use this SQL spawning of code to your advantage.

The examples in this chapter should be taken as a brief introduction to the possibilities that can be achieved with the proper implementation of SQL creating code. However, you should remember that the more complex logic you code into your SQL functions, the longer these functions will take to execute. Subsequently, running any system-intensive queries should be saved for lighter system load times. Optimization of functions and their impact on queries is discussed further in Chapter 26.

In the next chapter, we will change gears a little and start talking about using SQL in applications. As any software developer knows, the "Holy Grail" of their craft is creating intricate three-tier database applications. To that end, we will discuss how SQL statements can be integrated into various applications.

SQL Functions in an Application

Creating applications that call SQL functions is more of an art form than simple programming these days. With the vast array of options for database platforms, connection protocols, and programming languages, it is up to the developers to decipher the cryptic maze of which path is the best to travel. In its essence, however, the role of SQL functions within a database application is simple. These functions provide a means by which to link the granular data within the database structure to the end user who uses a client application so the data can be displayed in some meaningful way. This is all broken down into sets of SQL calls that are most likely made to an API, which in turn encodes it into a format the database can understand. The various functions, procedures, INSERTS, UPDATES, and DELETES are run, and then a result or result set is sent back to the client for more processing.

This chapter discusses some of the basics that you must understand to embed SQL within your application architecture. We will be discussing several areas, such as prerequisites for obtaining data from an RDBMS implementation, API platforms, and development practices. In addition, we will be creating some small applications (one client-based and one Web-based) that will test user log-in information.

Calling Functions from an Application

As mentioned earlier, calling SQL functions from your applications is somewhat of an art form nowadays. There are several steps involved that you should at least attempt to go through, if not strictly adhere to. In the next few sections, we will provide a brief overview of what is needed for you to create a database connection from your application, call, and return information from one of your RDBMS implementations. In addition, we will go over some of the different types of different database connections, as well as some of their inherent strengths and weaknesses. This should be considered an introduction to these elements and, before leaping headfirst into one of them, we would highly recommend that you read the vendor-specific information on each of the connection types and programming models before implementing any of them. The worst thing that can happen to an application's development cycle is to find out midway through implementation that some of your choices will obviously not work together.

Establishing a Database Connection

There are several ways in which you can create database connections in your applications. The choice will undoubtedly be made not only by which RDBMS implementation you are trying to connect to, but also by such factors as your programming language and the type of application you are making. At its basic level, however, you must acquire the appropriate security account for access, create a connection string, and open the connection. Some methods are more difficult than others and some are faster. We will cover several different types of connections so that you can make an informed decision in your application development.

Connection Pools

Creating a connection is the most inefficient step in communicating with a database. It can take a second or more to negotiate and create a connection. One second may not seem like a significant delay, but when repeated, that second quickly becomes a nuisance. There are two ways of dealing with the connection delay:

❑   Create and reuse a single connection throughout the program.

❑   Create and maintain a connection pool.

Creating and reusing a single connection will speed an application noticeably. By sharing a single connection among all database calls in a program, the connection delay is only experienced once. Unfortunately, this method has a major drawback. A database connection can only be used for one call at a time. Therefore, all statements will be executed serially. Using this method will speed an application noticeably, but the serial execution of database statements can quickly cause a performance bottleneck. For the most efficient database operations, use a connection pool.

A *connection pool* is simply a collection of open connections to a database. Upon creation of a connection pool, a predetermined number of connections are opened. The application requests a connection from the connection pool when it needs access to the database. When the application is finished with the connection, it is returned to the pool for future use. The connections are not closed until the application quits.

Connection pools can easily be used from multiple threads and can provide a means of connecting to a database in parallel. Assuming the application is properly written, lengthy database calls will not slow the entire application.

Acquiring Permissions

Without the proper permissions, you are creating your application for naught. Depending on your specific RDBMS implementation, you must ensure that you have several different things accounted for. The first is to ensure that the user account with which you will be connecting to the database has the right to CONNECT with the database instance. Then it must be given rights to access the specific table spaces, databases, tables, and other objects that it needs to successfully perform its series of SQL calls. If you are having trouble implementing SQL embedded in application architecture, break down your database access levels and try to either confirm or deny a security problem. Can you connect to the database? Can you access a certain area of the database? Can you run your SELECT, INSERTS, UPDATES, and DELETES separately and with success? These questions and more will soon become part of your repertoire as you get more in tune with the application-building process.

ODBC Connectivity

Open Database Connectivity (ODBC) works to abstract the database from its physical location and makes it available over a network connection. The ODBC protocol works as a broker between the application program and the database transport such as SQL*NET. There are actually several levels of activity that go in between the application and the database. To obtain an ODBC connection to any database, you normally have to have a data source name set up on the computer and a data transport. In some cases, the ODBC driver is considered multitier, and you do not need the separate data transport to be loaded on the machine. Basically, the current-day version of ODBC is comprised of three layers that allow it to be used with a variety of database implementations:

❑　The *top layer* of the ODBC platform is a callable API that is packaged as a DLL. This allows the API to be used by all application programs.

❑　The *middle layer* of the platform is the driver manager. Its main purpose is to act as a switchboard for loading and unloading of the various drivers. It also ensures that API calls from the various applications accessing it get their calls routed to the proper driver.

❑　The *bottom layer* of the ODBC platform is comprised of all the collections of individual drivers for each of the different database implementations.

ODBC provides a good extended set of properties outside of the SQL/CLI standard calls. However, the implementation of those capabilities is left to the bottom layer of drivers. This is because these drivers have direct interaction with the RDBMS implementation. Of course, this is also by design because Microsoft wanted to create the ODBC API so that any number of database implementations could adopt it. The flexibility of the "take it or not" implementation provides the RDBMS implementations the ability to adopt the ODBC platform without sacrificing their native environments.

JDBC Connectivity

Java Database Connectivity (JDBC) is the standard API that is used with the Java programming language. This API was developed by a Sun Microsystems as part of their Java suite of programming APIs. The current version is 3.0 and, since its inception, it has become the official standard for SQL database access when using Java. Currently, there are no other consequential competing APIs that need to be discussed.

The JDBC platform can basically be divided into two distinct APIs: one for the core implementation functionality and the other handles an extension set. The newest version includes features of the other database APIs (such as distributed transactions and scrollable cursors). On its base level, the JDBC platform is modeled after ODBC. The drivers are not characterized by the RDBMS type that they interact with. Rather, they are scoped into four generalized types:

❑　The *Type 1 driver* transforms the JDBC class into ODBC, which is considered a vendor-neutral API, since most databases implement some form of ODBC connectivity. Once the call is handed over to the ODBC layer, it is then handled in the same manner as if using ODBC natively. This tends to have a computing overhead because the call must travel through many different layers to reach its destination.

❑　The *Type 2 driver* translates the JDBC call into the native RDBMS implementation's API. The main disadvantage to this is that the Type 2 driver is tied to a specific RDBMS implementation. So, it lacks the flexibility of the Type 1 driver in being able to connect with several different database implementations. Also, the performance gain in connecting directly with an RDBMS native API is assuming that the native API is not ODBC. If it is, then you might as well be using a Type 1 driver.

❑　The *Type 3 driver* is also known as a *network-neutral driver*. This is because the JDBC calls are translated into a vendor-neutral format and then sent across the network. On the other end of the network, calls are received at the server and translated by a middle-tier object in the RDBMS native API. The process is then reversed for the query results that are to be passed back to the client. Since this translation is vendor-neutral, it means that the application code for the client side is very portable and able to be used against many different RDBMS implementations. The only prerequisite is that the code be in Java and that it resides on a machine that supports the Java language either through the Java APIs or Java Virtual Machine (JVM). The major drawback is that, once again, using vendor-neutral coding practices limits being able to access certain aspects of your RDBMS implementation.

❏   *Type 4 drivers* operate in much the same manner as the Type 3 drivers except that the network translation is made into a RDBMS proprietary format. It preserves many of the same benefits as the Type 3 drivers (mainly client portability). However, since it translates the network messages in vendor-specific format, it is essentially tied to the RDBMS implementation for which it was written and will affect the application side's flexibility.

The methods used by all of these types are straightforward and often parallel similar routines written in C++. For these reasons, it has become the inherent connection architecture to use in Web-based applications that must be portable across a wide range of server platforms. Other languages such as C/C++ have written their own APIs, but they are less widely used than Java and, therefore, are not thoroughly discussed in this book.

Proprietary Database Networking Software

Every major implementation of an RDBMS has its own proprietary APIs that interact with its own particular brand of RDBMS. Usually, the independent vendors work very hard to ensure that their particular API works faster than any other competing brand. Although most of the features will be the same between the differing APIs, the performance gain is enough to draw high-end applications to use the vendor-specific APIs. This does have its drawbacks, because using a vendor-specific API locks the application developer into that RDBMS implementation and pigeon-holes flexibility.

Oracle's API, Oracle Call Interface (OCI), is one of the most widely used of the different brands. In part, this is because of Oracle's large share of the database market. It uses many of the same standards as the other networking APIs discussed earlier. The main difference is that, since this API is optimized for the Oracle platform, it provides the application developer with several hundred different routines from which to choose. Obviously, an in-depth discussion of these routines is beyond the scope of this book, but it's good to know what you have to work with.

Modeling the Process

One of the most important steps in application development, as in any undertaking, is planning. Before you start programming your database application, you should be able to answer several key questions:

❏   How many layers will the application have? Client? Business Layer? Data-Access Layer?

❏   What will the client application model be? PC-based? Server-based? Web-based?

❏   Where will the client application reside in relation to the RDBMS? Same machine? Different machines? Same network? Different networks?

All of these questions and more can be answered simply by modeling the processes that will be occurring in your database application. Normally, this is done before the first line of code is written and can save the developer many frustrating hours of rewriting possibly thousands of lines of code.

When modeling your process, you can use any format you want (UML diagrams, application-modeling programs, or just scratch paper). It is not the format of the model that is important; it is the processes in which it maps out. When modeling the process for your application, try to answer all of the questions just presented. However, be cautious in just haphazardly selecting a random assortment of parameters to throw into an application model. Specifically, you should try to ask more questions that better define what the correct answers are:

❑ What specifically is the application meant to do? (Remember our discussion of project scope in previous chapters.)

❑ What is the impact on computing resources (client computer, server, and network)?

❑ What is the programming language standard to be (Java, C, C++, .NET)?

❑ Is the application *transaction heavy* (many calls to the database) or is it *data heavy* (large result sets)?

❑ Will the business logic on which the system is based change frequently or infrequently?

Questions like these will help you not only to be able to diagram the processes involved in the database application, but will also give you, as a developer, a better understanding of what the expected intent of your code is. If your application will only be used by five people in one office, why would you create a four-tier Web-based application? However, what if those five people were the main decision makers within the corporation and they were housed in the New York offices while you were in L.A.? For transaction-heavy applications, you may have to think about things such as asynchronous calls to the database so as to not overburden the system with connections. On the other hand a data-heavy solution may need to work with disjointed data sets, which leads to questions of concurrency and safeguarding the integrity of the data.

In short, your process modeling should be a real effort and not some doodles on the back of a napkin. Strive to model the process as a whole. Show the interactions and calls between the various levels that will be made. Incorporate relationships between the programming objects that are making the calls to one another.

In addition, brainstorm for possible failures or shortcomings of the system. This is not meant to be a session in which you toss your initial ideas into the trash and throw your hands in the air. Put on your "black hat" for a while and objectively look at your process model. What are the shortcomings? How do you overcome them? How will things look from the client perspective? How will things look from the database perspective? This is an attempt to make your application better and stronger than it would have been initially, to reduce frustration midway through a project and get everyone on board with respect to feeling good about the implementation.

Creating or Identifying the SQL Functions

Now that we have our process model complete, and have a good understanding of what our application is going to do with respect to the database layer, we can concentrate on the functions that may or may not be involved. If your application is to be used with an existing database, the first thing that you should do is an audit of the database system. By cataloging all the functions, views, and stored procedures on the database system, you will be able to identify existing functions that can be used by your application. This turns out to be a valuable time-saving tool in your application-development timeline. Since the functions are already written, they should already be thoroughly debugged and optimized for the current system. It should be stressed that, in this instance, newer is not always better, and the previously cited advantages are all well worth the time invested in looking over the database.

If, after determining which current functions from the existing database can be used, you are still left with gaps in functionality from your process model, then it will be time to create your own. Of course, you could just implement all your SQL calls by using dynamic SQL, but that would defeat the purpose of making your application efficient. Remember, SQL functions are precompiled, which means that execution plans are already derived before the process is ever run through your application. Dynamic SQL, on the other hand, must be compiled dynamically at run time because the query is not "known" by the RDBMS until execution time. This causes a lot of overhead and will degrade performance by slowing down your queries and hogging CPU and memory.

When considering efficiency when writing your own SQL functions for the application, keep this simple thought in mind: smaller is better. Look at your process model to see if your larger processes can be broken down into smaller steps. Attempt to break each process down into a smaller set of logical operations based upon usage. The reason for this is that most RDBMS implementations only store one execution plan for each function or stored procedure. If your function class involves several different transactions that may or may not run according to certain input parameters, there is a very good chance that your function or stored procedure may be optimized for a path that you are not currently taking. By breaking up larger processes into smaller transactions, a query plan is developed for each function. This allows for the fact that one function may pass off operations to another function. However, this time the function being called has an optimized execution plan available to it.

Last, try to cover all the bases on your process model in terms of availability to use functions and procedures. Besides performance, by putting your SQL query syntax into functions, they are more readily updatable if database structure changes or client-side query information needs change. It is essentially easier to change the coding within the function block rather than having to recode portions of your application that may be using dynamic SQL to derive their results.

> *There are several tips for writing the database function/procedure. First, when using some database implementations such as Oracle, it is possible to return values one by one, or as rows in a table. When the purpose of a function or procedure is to check state, retrieve a small number of specific data points, or verify input, it is most efficient to return values one by one. When the purpose of a function or procedure is to retrieve a collection of data, it is most efficient to return values as rows in a table. This is done by returning a reference cursor.*
>
> *Also, when using Java, use database return types that require minimal processing on the Java side. Integer processing is very efficient in Java, so make use of this by returning 1 or 0 instead of true/false or "Y"/"N." String processing is not efficient in Java and adds processing overhead. Avoid using "Y" and "N" as return values.*

Coding the Application Component

Now that we have the preliminaries out of the way as far as planning is concerned, it is time to start coding our application. The way in which you do this is largely determined by the modeling processes that you undertook in the last few sections. However, the basic principle behind all of them is the same. We create a connection to the database, open the connection, execute a query, retrieve the results, and close the connections. No matter how many times you perform this operation and in no matter how fancy a manner, in the end this is the basic premise. So, let's look at some examples of making a connection and calling a SQL function, as well as processing the results that are returned to the application. For these examples, we will be using some simple Java statements to demonstrate our points.

Calling the SQL Function

Calling the SQL function is a relatively simple matter as long as you know the connection string that is to be used for your RDBMS implementation. Of course, this entails knowing certain things such as what server, what database, and permissions for access. First, you create an instance of the connection object, your SQL `querystring` object, and any other variables that you need. Then you create a connection by passing the `connection` object, the connection string, and opening the connection. This can be done several different ways depending on what type of connection architecture you have decided to use, or, in our case, with Java, which Type (1, 2, 3, or 4) we would be using. You will find, however, that most are created and opened the same way. There are only modest modifications to your code that you would have to make to switch from one to the other. The following example uses Java to open a connection to our small employees database and retrieve all the employees with the first name of Fred:

```
// This is our initialization section for our variables
Connection DBconnection;     // Our database connection object
String First_Name;           // Employees first name
String Last_Name;            // Employees last name
String Dept;                 // Employees department
Float  Sal;                  // Employees salary
String querystr = "SELECT FIRSTN,LASTN,DEPARTMENT,SALARY FROM
    GET_EMPLOYEES('Fred')";

<Here we would create our implementation specific connection and open it>

// We can create a statement object pass our query to
Statement stmt = DBconnection.createStatement();

// Now we stuff our query into the statement object
ResultSet results = stmt.executeQuery(querystr);

// Hoorah! We just managed to call an SQL function
```

Tips for calling the database function/procedure include using a database connection pool for a quicker application and ensuring that you close where applicable. For example, Java requires the `Connection`, `Statement`, *and* `ResultSet` *(where used) to be closed.*

Processing the Returned Data

Now that we have actually called the SQL statement or function, the results will be stuffed into our result set. From there, you are pretty much free to process the results in any way you see fit. Of course, there is usually a standard, logical way in which to do these things and, in this case, there is no exception. We will loop through the results object one row at a time, just like a cursor, and process the results of our query one row at a time. In this case, we will just output the results with a simple header to explain what they mean. Of paramount importance in this case is the length of time that you have the database connection open. In general, you need to open and close your connections as soon as possible. This frees up the resources that you are holding onto by having the connection open. So, now we move on to our set of code that will show you how to process that data on our company's Freds:

```
// Print out a small header to tell what the results are
System.out.println("Salaries of Fred");
System.out.println(" ");

// Now we just set up a simple loop to output all the rows.....

while (results.next())
{

First_Name = results.getString("FIRSTN");
Last_Name = results.getString("LASTN");
Dept = results.getString("DEPARTMENT");
Sal = results.getFloat("SALARY");

// Now print a line before looping
System.out.Println(Last_Name + ", " + First_Name + " from " + Dept + " $" + Sal);

}

// Now we need to close our cursor and db objects
results.close();
DBconnection.close();

// Our resources are freed and we are free to leave.
```

Sample User Login Application Using VB.Net and SQL Server

Now, let's try to create our own user login application. This is simple enough, because all we want to do is to pass a username and password to the database and have it authenticate with the server. If the connection is made, we want some kind of notification that we were successful. If not, it would be good to have a "Try Again" routine. For this section, we have decided to code both of these small applications in Visual Basic.NET to give you a taste of another programming language than what is used elsewhere in this book. We will be connecting to the Northwind database on a remote SQL Server instance.

We will start off by creating a very simple client form interface that basically contains a username textbox, a password textbox, and a submit button. Figure 24-1 shows the form.

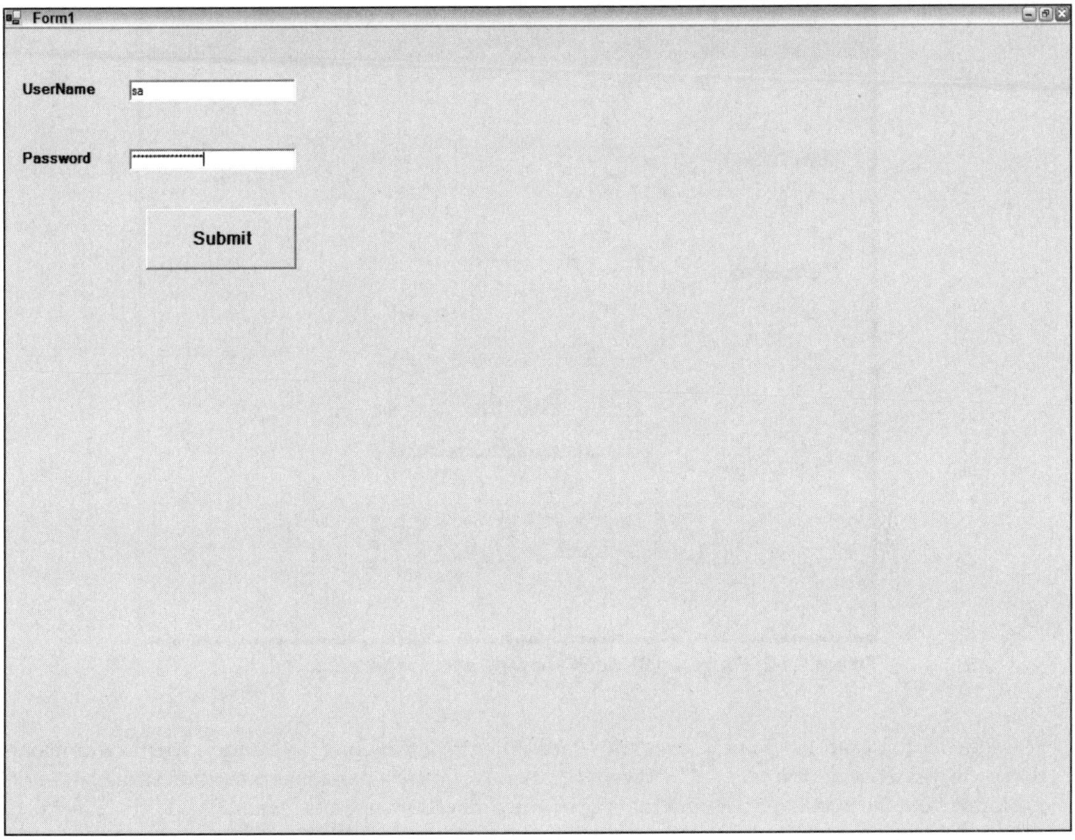

Figure 24-1. Sample forms application.

As you can see, we just have a simple form in which the user can enter a username and password and the click the Submit button. If the user enters in the correct information, the label below the submit button will say "SUCCESS!" as shown in Figure 24-2; otherwise, it will show "FAILURE!"

Figure 24-2. Forms application showing successful login.

The code for this example is fairly straightforward. After the creation of the buttons, we place our connection code inside the button's on_click event handler. We create a dynamic connection string based on the input from the two text boxes and try to open the connection. If it fails, then "FAILURE!" is set to display in the text box and it will exit the subroutine. If it does not fail, then "SUCCESS" is set to display in the text box and the subroutine is exited gracefully. The following code should be fairly self-explanatory:

```
Public Class Form1
    Inherits System.Windows.Forms.Form
.
.
.
' Bunch of System Generated Code here.
.
.
.

    Private Sub btnSubmit_Click(ByVal sender As System.Object, ByVal e As
System.EventArgs) Handles btnSubmit.Click

' Set up dynamic connection string
    Dim connectionstring As String = "server=REMOTE_WIN05;user id=" &
        txtUserName.Text & ";Password=" & txtPassword.Text &
        ";database=Northwind"

' Configure database connection object
        Dim dbconn As New SqlClient.SqlConnection(connectionstring)

' Attempt to open a connection
```

```
        Try
            dbconn.Open()
        Catch ex As Exception
            'Catch the failure, display message,and exit.
            lblResults.Text = "FAILURE!"
            Exit Sub
        End Try
' Success. Display the results.
            lblResults.Text = "SUCCESS!"
    End Sub
End Class
```

Sample User Login Application Using Java and Oracle

This example uses a login algorithm to demonstrate an Oracle function call. Note that for the sake of simplicity, a connection pool is not used. Keep in mind that connection pools increase the efficiency of database communications and are recommended for applications that use repeated database calls.

This method, `attemptLogin()`, takes a username and password as arguments. These are passed to a database function for verification. The function checks the database and returns either 0 or 1 to indicate the validity of the login credentials.

```
public boolean attemptLogin(String username, String password) {

    userid = null;
    noOfAttempts++;
Connection connection = null;
    if (password.length == 0) {
      return false;
    }
```

The database driver is dynamically installed and loaded in this `try-catch` block:

```
try {
   Class.forName(dbDriver);
}
catch (ClassNotFoundException e) {
        Logger.log(this, e);
   System.exit(0);
}
```

The connection is created in this `try-catch` block:

```
        try {
```

Oracle provides mechanisms for encrypting and verifying network data communications. These mechanisms are used by passing a preloaded `Properties` object to the `getConnection()` method, as shown here:

```
        Properties prop = new Properties();
        prop.put("oracle.net.encryption_client", "REQUESTED");
        prop.put("oracle.net.encryption_types_client", "( RC4_40 )");
        prop.put("oracle.net.crypto_checksum_client", "REQUESTED");
        prop.put("oracle.net.crypto_checksum_types_client", "(MD5)");
        prop.put ("user", Globals.username);
        prop.put ("password",Globals.password);
        prop.put ("defaultRowPrefetch","1");

    connection =
DriverManager.getConnection(Globals.connectionURL, prop);
        }
```

If an exception is thrown during the creation of the connection, it is taken care of here. This type of error could be caused by a number of things: network failure, database server failure, or database listener failure. To remedy this exception, check network connections, confirm that the database server is on, confirm that the database is running, and confirm that all applicable listeners are on. For the sake of simplicity, this method logs the exception and returns false.

```
        catch (SQLException e) {
          Logger.log(this, e);
          return false;
        }
```

The function call is dynamically created using the local variables username and password. This function call specifies one parameter (indicated by the question mark).

```
        String function = "begin {? = callUSER.verifyUserCredential('"
  + username + "','" + password + "')}; end;";
```

The statement object is created and the function call is passed to the database in this try-catch block:

```
        try {
```

The statement call is created with the contents of the string function.

```
        CallableStatement statement = conn.prepareCall(function);
```

All parameters in the statement must be registered. Parameter places are marked with question marks and are numbered from the left starting at 1.

```
        statement.registerOutParameter(1,
                              oracle.jdbc.OracleTypes.INTEGER);
        statement.execute();
```

Any return values are retrieved. Here the integer for slot 1 is retrieved.

```
        //returns 1 if the username and password are good
        int result = statement.getInt(1);
```

The statement and connection are closed.

```
        statement.close();
        conn.close();

        // Successful Login
        return (result == 1);
    }
```

During this process, many things can go wrong. SQL exceptions are thrown for a variety of different reasons. It is a good idea to handle these exceptions gracefully. The remainder of the code is shown for completeness. The dummy `return` is required by the Java compiler and must be included.

```
        catch (SQLException e) {
          Logger.log(this, e);
        }
      }
    }
    return false;
  }
```

Sample User Login Application Using ASP.NET

You will find the following Web application example quite similar to the Windows client example. The differences here are that we will be using ASP.NET to generate our pages, and our class code will be wrapped in a DLL separate from the Web page. We will be doing the exact same project this time, except connecting through a Web page, so we will give you the HTML code as well. Once again, we start off with a simple log-on Web page that is created with the following code for the .aspx page:

```
<%@ Page Language="vb" AutoEventWireup="false" Codebehind="WebForm1.aspx.vb"
Inherits="TestCon.WebForm1"%>
<!DOCTYPE HTML PUBLIC "-//W3C//DTD HTML 4.0 Transitional//EN">
<HTML>
    <HEAD>
        <title>WebForm1</title>
        <meta name="GENERATOR" content="Microsoft Visual Studio .NET 7.1">
        <meta name="CODE_LANGUAGE" content="Visual Basic .NET 7.1">
        <meta name="vs_defaultClientScript" content="JavaScript">
        <meta name="vs_targetSchema"
content="http://schemas.microsoft.com/intellisense/ie5">
    </HEAD>
    <body MS_POSITIONING="GridLayout">
        <form id="Form1" method="post" runat="server">
            <asp:Label id="label1" style="Z-INDEX: 101; LEFT: 104px; POSITION:
absolute; TOP: 48px" runat="server">UserName</asp:Label>
            <asp:Label id="label2" style="Z-INDEX: 102; LEFT: 104px; POSITION:
absolute; TOP: 88px" runat="server">Password</asp:Label> 
            <asp:Button id="btnSubmit" style="Z-INDEX: 103; LEFT: 192px;
POSITION: absolute; TOP: 136px"
                runat="server" Text="Submit" Width="106px"
Height="56px"></asp:Button>
```

```
                    <asp:TextBox id="txtUserName" style="Z-INDEX: 104; LEFT: 184px;
       POSITION: absolute; TOP: 48px"
                        runat="server"></asp:TextBox>
                    <asp:TextBox id="txtPassword" style="Z-INDEX: 105; LEFT: 184px;
       POSITION: absolute; TOP: 80px"
                        runat="server" TextMode="Password"></asp:TextBox>
                    <asp:Label id="lblResults" style="Z-INDEX: 106; LEFT: 208px;
       POSITION: absolute; TOP: 232px"
                        runat="server" Width="200px" Height="56px" ForeColor="#00C000"
       Font-Bold="True" Font-Size="X-Large"></asp:Label>
            </form>
        </body>
    </HTML>
```

The code-behind page is where all the action takes place and it is in the Submit buttons on `Click` event once again that causes a post back to the server so that the event code can be run. Once the event code is run, the ASP.NET framework then assembles the new HTML output for the page and sends it back to the client. The code from the button `Click` event is shown here so that you can see that the coding is essentially the same:

```
    Private Sub btnSubmit_Click(ByVal sender As System.Object, ByVal e As
    System.EventArgs) Handles btnSubmit.Click
        Dim connectionstring As String = "server=REMOTE_WIN05;user id=" &
    txtUserName.Text & ";Password=" & txtPassword.Text & ";database=Northwind"

        Dim dbconnection As New SqlClient.SqlConnection(connectionstring)

        Try
            dbconnection.Open()
        Catch ex As Exception
            lblResults.Text = "FAILURE!"
            Exit Sub
        End Try
        lblResults.Text = "SUCCESS!"
    End Sub
```

So, now all we have left to do is to test our application to ensure that we can indeed connect to the server. This is easy enough if we know the URL and have a Web browser. Figure 24-3 shows the output from our simple Web page.

Figure 24-3. Sample Web application in ASP.NET showing successful login.

Summary

With the last three chapters under your belt, you should now feel fairly confident in your understanding of the different aspects of using SQL functions within an application architecture. We have discussed in this chapter the various things that you need to connect to an RDBMS implementation from within your application (such as proper permissions and connection strings). We also discussed the different types of connection platforms to include, ODBC, JDBC, and native APIs, and then instructed you on some of the pros and cons with each one.

In addition, we showed you the types of planning that must occur to ensure a successful database application. This included such things as mapping the process of your application. From there, we showed how you should opt for a mixture of old and new function code for your database calls from your application. This stressed the points of reusability and also some performance tips that you can use when creating your own applications.

Last, we showed you programmatically how to connect, query, and process the query data by using some simple Java code. Also, we demonstrated some simple coding techniques using Visual Basic.NET, Java, and ASP.NET to program a simple user login application. Then we took that application and made it Web-based. So, you should now have several examples of how embedded SQL can be used in different aspects within your application.

In Chapter 25, we will detail how to get more flexibility and power from your queries by incorporating views and functions. This chapter should be extremely helpful to the developer who must program very complex queries, and it should be followed very carefully.

Empowering the Query with Functions and Views

A *view* is nothing more than a virtual table that you create within your database. Unlike a table, however, a view does not contain its own data. Instead, it is defined by a query and contains the columns and rows of data defined by the query. The data is provided by the query when it is called at run time. Otherwise, the view can be considered an abstracted layer of the table structure. This produces the illusion to the user that the view is a real data entity within the database.

This abstraction of the view from the actual data within the tables also provides another important feature of the view. The view enables you to combine and rearrange data from existing database tables. This is a valuable tool that enables the developer to simplify complex queries by encapsulating some of the data within views. In addition, the view can be given user permissions just like a table. This allows the developer or DBA the ability to simplify access to the data within the system by providing users with a customized view of the database structure so they are not interacting directly with the tables within the system. Lastly, abstraction from the data allows for a consistent presentation of the data to the end user, even if the underlying table structure is changed. If the developer must change the underlying structure of the tables, it is a simple matter to reorganize the query within the view, and the end user is none the wiser about the switch. While this does not seem to be a very important aspect on the surface, it is an important force in stabilizing the database layer in the eyes of any applications or users who access the system. By stabilizing the view of the data that is given to the outside world, you allow yourself more flexibility in your database designs and a significantly simpler application life cycle.

A view is a very simple object to create in the database. If you understand what query you need to get the data that you want, then you will have no trouble creating views. A view is created by using the simplified SQL statement detailed here:

```
CREATE VIEW view_name AS <SELECT QUERY>

// An example
CREATE VIEW VW_EMPLOYEES
AS
SELECT E.EMPID, E.EMP_NAME, D.DEPT
FROM EMPLOYEES E, DEPARTMENT D
WHERE E.DEPTID = D.DEPTID
```

This view allows us to use the basic employee data derived from the employees and department. Now, if we want to change the underlying structure of the database, we merely need to ensure that the query that fills the view is modified to produce the same result set.

This chapter examines several ways in which you can incorporate views into your development toolbox to empower your queries. Specifically, we will be looking at ways in which views are used to boost your query flexibility, readability, and longevity.

Understanding How Views Empower Queries

Views are powerful weapons in your development toolbox. Many times, developers tend not to use the full potential of views and instead use them just to add a layer of abstraction. This can often be identified by the overuse of simple views such as the following:

```
CREATE VIEW view_name AS
SELECT * FROM table_name
```

Views such as this tend to oversimplify the use of the view. In general, views can be classified into two types: horizontal and vertical.

Horizontal views are used to partition rows within a table. This is usually used to provide a unique perspective of the data to a certain individual or group of individuals. Suppose we have a table, Employees, that holds employee information for everyone in a company. Each employee would be assigned to a region within the country: North, South, East, or West. We would not necessarily want to provide access to the entire Employees table to each of the regional managers. Instead, we could create a series of views that would separate the employees into each of their respective regions. Then, we could assign permissions to the regional managers so that they had access to their respective views of their employees. Here's an example of what the coding would look like:

```
CREATE VIEW EMPLOYEES_EAST AS
SELECT *
FROM EMPLOYEES
WHERE REGION = 'East'
CREATE VIEW EMPLOYEES_WEST AS
SELECT *
FROM EMPLOYEES
WHERE REGION = 'West'
CREATE VIEW EMPLOYEES_NORTH AS
SELECT *
FROM EMPLOYEES
WHERE REGION = 'North'
CREATE VIEW EMPLOYEES_SOUTH AS
SELECT *
FROM EMPLOYEES
WHERE REGION = 'South'
// Now we can grant select rights to each of the managers.
GRANT SELECT ON EMPLOYEES_EAST TO MARK_SMITH;
GRANT SELECT ON EMPLOYEES_WEST TO STEPHEN_GRANT;
GRANT SELECT ON EMPLOYEES_NORTH TO JULIE_JONES;
GRANT SELECT ON EMPLOYEES_SOUTH TO JOE_KILWASKI;
```

Now we have effectively separated the data so it can only be viewed by those people who need to see it. In addition, this simplifies administrative control over the access to the data because we have used views to access the tables. This is effectively another way in which to assign group access to objects instead of roles.

Vertical views separate the specific columns of data for viewing by the users. One reason you may want to do this is the fact that views may be used to update data as well as just select data from it. In order for a view to be updateable, it must follow several syntax rules:

❑ The view can only access one table in the FROM clause. If the FROM clause specifies another view, then that view must also adhere to this rule.

❑ The query cannot have a GROUP BY, HAVING, or DISTINCT clause in it.

❑ The SELECT list must only contain simple columns (no expressions, calculations, or column functions).

❑ The WHERE clause cannot contain any subqueries.

Basically, these rules ensure that the view is able to find the correct row in the source table from which it is deriving information. This does not mean we cannot combine the vertical and horizontal views. For example, what if we wanted to reuse the Employees views from the previous example? The HR department in each region might want to update certain employee information, such as EmpID, Name, Address, City, State, Zip, and Phone_Num, but not Salary or Region. Such a subset of views can be created as shown in the following code:

```
CREATE VIEW HR_EAST AS
SELECT EMPID, NAME, ADDRESS, CITY, STATE, ZIP, PHONE_NUM
FROM EMPLOYEES_EAST

CREATE VIEW HR_WEST AS
SELECT EMPID, NAME, ADDRESS, CITY, STATE, ZIP, PHONE_NUM
FROM EMPLOYEES_WEST

CREATE VIEW HR_NORTH AS
SELECT EMPID, NAME, ADDRESS, CITY, STATE, ZIP, PHONE_NUM
FROM EMPLOYEES_NORTH

CREATE VIEW HR_SOUTH AS
SELECT EMPID, NAME, ADDRESS, CITY, STATE, ZIP, PHONE_NUM
FROM EMPLOYEES_SOUTH
// Now we grant access to each of the views.
GRANT SELECT, UPDATE ON HR_EAST TO EASTERN_OFFICE;
GRANT SELECT, UPDATE TO HR_WEST_TO WESTERN_OFFICE;
GRANT SELECT, UPDATE TO HR_NORTH TO NORTHERN_OFFICE;
GRANT SELECT, UPDATE TO HR_SOUTH TO SOUTHERN_OFFICE;
```

The views can now be used to update the relevant HR information for the employees in the different regions. It follows the ANSI SQL rules for creating updateable tables because it only accesses one base table, even though it is through another view. It should be noted, however, that most RDBMS systems are less restrictive than the ANSI SQL standard when it comes to updateable views. You should check your vendor-specific documentation to see what exact restrictions your RDBMS implementation will place on you.

Understanding the Role of SQL Functions in Views

Of course, horizontal and vertical views are nothing more than general categories that we use to talk about a view. You are not specifically tied to just these two types. In fact, functions can be used to expand the scope of possible uses for your views. You can use functions to create grouped views in which aggregate information is stored and can be used for further querying. For example, the CurrentSales table (from previous examples) contains information on shippers, sales totals, and regional ordering areas. We may want to create a grouped view of this information so that we can query the grouped information, making it easier to make valuable decisions about the distribution network. The following is one such example:

```
CREATE VIEW CURRENT_SALES_REGIONAL AS
SELECT SHIPPERNAME, SUM(TOTAL_PRICE) AS TOTAL_SALES,
SALES_REGIONID
FROM CURRENTSALES
GROUP BY SALES_REGIONID, SHIPPERNAME
```

This view will give us a virtual table of the summary information of how much each shipper is ordering from each of the different sales regions. You may notice that we do not have an ORDER BY clause in the view. This is because you are not allowed to have an ORDER BY clause in any view. This makes sense if you think of the view as a virtual table. The data in your tables in the database is not ordered; only the SQL queries that you run against the data will make it into an ordered set. This is the same concept that is used in making views. Now, we could use this virtual table to find the shippers that are ordering the largest quantity of goods from each region with the following simple query:

```
select * from current_sales_regional
order by sales_regionid, Total_Sales, shippername;

shippername                            Total_Sales      sales_regionid
-------------------------------------- ---------------- --------------------
New England Seafood Cannery            13336.9700       0
Mayumi's                               15058.0000       0
Ma Maison                              16277.4900       0
Leka Trading                           18218.0500       0
Formaggi Fortini s.r.l.                18841.3900       0
Pasta Buttini s.r.l.                   22605.0300       0
       .
       .
       .
       .
       .
       .
```

We could even use this view to obtain a summary of the average number of sales from each region by using the following query:

```
select avg(Total_Sales) as Average_Sales,sales_regionID
from current_sales_regional
group by sales_regionid
order by sales_regionid;


Average_Sales          sales_regionID
```

```
----------------------    --------------
27551.3517               0
105584.1853              1
178630.4357              2
245370.6492              3
307125.0332              4
372767.3096              5
411522.5957              6
554131.0907              7
586401.6985              8
636739.3282              9
```

Keep in mind that not all RDBMS systems will allow this to be done with grouped views. The base SQL standard does not allow for nested column functions such as AVG(SUM(Sales)). Check your documentation to be sure of what is allowed in the current version of your RDBMS implementation. However, this may be the place for you to use a table-valued function instead to replace the view or to encapsulate the view that you just created. Two possible table function variations that you could use with the previous example to encapsulate the logic of your view are presented below:

```
create function fn_sales_regional()
returns @Sales_Regional table( Shippername nvarchar(50),
                               Total_Sales money,
                               Sales_RegionID  int
                              )
as
BEGIN

INSERT INTO @SALES_REGIONAL(SHIPPERNAME,TOTAL_SALES,SALES_REGIONID)
select shippername,sum(total_price) as Total_Sales, sales_regionid
from currentsales
group by sales_regionid, shippername

RETURN
END


// Or you could just encapsulate your premade view.

create function fn_sales_regional()
returns @Sales_Regional table( Shippername nvarchar(50),
                               Total_Sales money,
                               Sales_RegionID  int
                              )
as
BEGIN

INSERT INTO @SALES_REGIONAL(SHIPPERNAME,TOTAL_SALES,SALES_REGIONID)
select * from current_sales_regional

RETURN
END


// Now we can use the function to select from the various regions.

select avg(A.Total_Sales) as Average_Sales,A.sales_regionID
```

```
from dbo.fn_sales_regional() A
GROUP by A.sales_regionid
order by A.sales_regionid;

Average_Sales          sales_regionID
---------------------  ---------------
27551.3517             0
105584.1853            1
178630.4357            2
245370.6492            3
307125.0332            4
372767.3096            5
411522.5957            6
554131.0907            7
586401.6985            8
636739.3282            9
```

You are able to use these because the function is actually returning a table object and is not necessarily just masking the SQL code like a view does. You can even use your functions as a way in which to decide which view to select data from. The following code expands upon the idea of the previous function and makes one that selects from several different views of the sales tables:

```
CREATE VIEW SALES_REGIONAL_CURRENT AS
SELECT SHIPPERNAME, SUM(TOTAL_PRICE) AS TOTAL_SALES,
SALES_REGIONID
FROM CURRENTSALES
GROUP BY SALES_REGIONID, SHIPPERNAME;

CREATE VIEW SALES_REGIONAL_2003 AS
SELECT SHIPPERNAME, SUM(TOTAL_PRICE) AS TOTAL_SALES,
SALES_REGIONID
FROM SALES2003
GROUP BY SALES_REGIONID, SHIPPERNAME
CREATE VIEW SALES_REGIONAL_2002 AS
SELECT SHIPPERNAME, SUM(TOTAL_PRICE) AS TOTAL_SALES,
SALES_REGIONID
FROM SALES2002
GROUP BY SALES_REGIONID, SHIPPERNAME
CREATE VIEW SALES_REGIONAL_2001 AS
SELECT SHIPPERNAME, SUM(TOTAL_PRICE) AS TOTAL_SALES,
SALES_REGIONID
FROM SALES2001
GROUP BY SALES_REGIONID, SHIPPERNAME
create function fn_sales_regional(@YEAR INT)
returns @Sales_Regional table( Shippername nvarchar(50),
                               Total_Sales money,
                               Sales_RegionID  int
                             )
as
BEGIN
IF @YEAR = 2004
INSERT INTO @SALES_REGIONAL(SHIPPERNAME,TOTAL_SALES,SALES_REGIONID)
select * from sales_regional_current
ELSE IF @YEAR = 2003
INSERT INTO @SALES_REGIONAL(SHIPPERNAME,TOTAL_SALES,SALES_REGIONID)
```

```
select * from sales_regional_2003
ELSE IF @YEAR = 2002
INSERT INTO @SALES_REGIONAL(SHIPPERNAME,TOTAL_SALES,SALES_REGIONID)
select * from sales_regional_2002
ELSE
INSERT INTO @SALES_REGIONAL(SHIPPERNAME,TOTAL_SALES,SALES_REGIONID)
select * from sales_regional_2001

RETURN
END
```

Of course, one of the main reasons to use views is to create a joined view in which the view accesses many different tables. This is common for many different third-party, normal-form databases that use a lot of ID numbers and store their informational lists in many different tables to store the data in as small a footprint as possible. Consider the previous example of the Sales_Regional_Current view. While this view is perfectly good at returning the data that is asked for, it is a little cumbersome for the end user who must know what each of the Sales_RegionIDs correspond to. A better way to display the data in an easy-to-read format would be by combining this information with the Regions table and returning the region name. An example of this is as follows:

```
CREATE VIEW SALES_REGIONAL_CURRENT AS
SELECT SHIPPERNAME, SUM(TOTAL_PRICE) AS TOTAL_SALES,
REGIONDESCRIPTION
FROM CURRENTSALES, REGION
WHERE CURRENTSALES.SALES_REGIONID = REGION.REGIONID
GROUP BY REGIONDESCRIPTION, SHIPPERNAME
SELECT * FROM SALES_REGIONAL_CURRENT ORDER BY REGIONDESCRIPTION;


SHIPPERNAME                          TOTAL_SALES          REGIONDESCRIPTION
-----------------------------------  -------------------  -----------------
Aux joyeux ecclésiastiques           466816.4300          Great Plains
Bigfoot Breweries                    635433.3200          Great Plains
Cooperativa de Quesos 'Las Cabras'   688672.8600          Great Plains
Escargots Nouveaux                   723057.0600          Great Plains
Exotic Liquids                       688238.0800          Great Plains
Formaggi Fortini s.r.l.              946235.9900          Great Plains
Gai pâturage                         441063.9200          Great Plains
G'day, Mate                          693630.2000          Great Plains
Grandma Kelly's Homestead            970853.6100          Great Plains
Heli Süßwaren GmbH & Co. KG          663357.0000          Great Plains
  .
  .
  .
  .
  .
  .
```

Now you have a much more user-friendly view for customers to use. This approach is not only helpful for making your data more readable, but it also provides a way for you to encapsulate complex definitions into a relatively simple format. Consider that your end users may want to find the average of sales receipts for each shipper by region over the previous four years. Instead of requiring your users to figure out what SQL is needed to perform such a query, you could use a view combined with built-in functions, as shown here:

```
CREATE VIEW AVG_SHIPPERS AS

SELECT SHIPPERNAME,AVG(TOTAL_PRICE) AS AVERAGE_SALES,
REGIONDESCRIPTION
FROM
(
SELECT SHIPPERNAME,TOTAL_PRICE,
REGIONDESCRIPTION
FROM CURRENTSALES, REGION
WHERE CURRENTSALES.SALES_REGIONID = REGION.REGIONID
UNION
SELECT SHIPPERNAME,TOTAL_PRICE,
REGIONDESCRIPTION
FROM SALES2003, REGION
WHERE SALES2003.SALES_REGIONID = REGION.REGIONID
UNION
SELECT SHIPPERNAME,TOTAL_PRICE,
REGIONDESCRIPTION
FROM SALES2002, REGION
WHERE SALES2002.SALES_REGIONID = REGION.REGIONID
UNION
SELECT SHIPPERNAME,TOTAL_PRICE,
REGIONDESCRIPTION
FROM SALES2001, REGION
WHERE SALES2001.SALES_REGIONID = REGION.REGIONID
) COMBINED_SALES
GROUP BY REGIONDESCRIPTION,SHIPPERNAME

SELECT * FROM AVG_SHIPPERS ORDER BY REGIONDESCRIPTION;

SHIPPERNAME                         AVERAGE_SALES        REGIONDESCRIPTION
---------------------------------   ------------------   ----------------
Aux joyeux ecclésiastiques          31409.9898            Great Plains
Bigfoot Breweries                   31473.3677            Great Plains
Cooperativa de Quesos 'Las Cabras'  31482.3298            Great Plains
Escargots Nouveaux                  31539.2911            Great Plains
Exotic Liquids                      31236.2976            Great Plains
Formaggi Fortini s.r.l.             31443.0670            Great Plains
Gai pâturage                        31543.5457            Great Plains
G'day, Mate                         31486.9377            Great Plains
.
.
.
.
```

This is a much better method for the end user to use than the compound SELECT statement that it took to create the view. This should also be seen as a way for you to eliminate some of your administration duties because it will surely cut down on the amount of phone calls that you will have to take to explain to an end user the proper way to format a subquery in SQL.

Summary

You should now have an appreciation for the flexibility and power that views provide. We have looked at the various kinds of views, both horizontal and vertical. Remember that these are only vague definitions of views that are used to give people a better understanding of views in general. In addition, we discussed using grouped and joined views to encapsulate aggregate information and information from more than one table. Lastly, we discussed using composite combinations of different forms of views to encapsulate complex logic to make it easier for end users to query information from the database.

You should be cautioned to avoid overusing views and to think about the performance costs of implementing certain types of complex logic in your system. Not all uses of functions and views should be used just because they are available. Sometimes the performance hit taken by the system will outweigh the good that implementing the view would have made. Chapter 26 discusses the performance impacts of using functions within your queries and how to minimize the effects.

Understanding the Impact of SQL Functions on Query and Database Performance

Possibly the biggest factor that you will take into account when implementing the use of functions within your database structure will be performance. More often than not, the key component within any database application is the database itself. If the queries and procedures run within the database are not optimized, then your system will suffer dramatically. System resources for the database are usually scarce, because it is often easier to add another Web server or to upgrade the client PC than to cluster databases. However, with careful planning and constant reevaluation of ways in which your database functions can be optimized, you can prevent the database from being the linchpin of your system. This chapter examines some of the factors that affect the performance of your functions and which areas are most detrimental to performance.

Prioritizing Transaction and Query Performance

Databases are generally prioritized to do one of two things: process transactions or run queries. As any DBA understands, the things that you do to improve transactional processing will undoubtedly hurt your query performance, and improving on the other end will hurt transactional processing. In a perfect world, it would be worthwhile to strike a happy medium between the two, but it is not so in the database world. Systems are often slanted toward one type of process or another. So, it is up to the developer and DBA to decide which sacrifices must be made to ensure the success of a system.

The best way to determine which way your system slants is to take an objective look not at what the system is theoretically supposed to do, but what it actually does do. Just because you are looking at optimizing a sales system does not necessarily mean that you should optimize the database for transactional processing. The sales application as a whole may be Web-based. It may have a user interface that is highly database dependent. There may be thousands of queries that are run between the time the user first accesses the application and the time that a true "transactional" query is run. If this were the case and you had optimized the database for transactional processing, you might effectively cripple the application when the first 100 concurrent users started to access your site. Therefore, it is useful to compare systems that are built to be mainly transactional in nature with those that are optimized for queries.

Transactional Database Architecture

A *transactional database* is one that is built to process INSERT, UPDATE, and DELETE statements. It is called transactional because most of these functions are wrapped within transactional statements that can be fairly long in nature if the rules involved in processing them are complex. Most often, this involves the locking of tables, rows, and even columns of data while the transactions are being processed. While these objects are locked, they cannot be accessed by other statements because this would result in what is commonly referred to as a "dirty read." Dirty reads occur when data is read that is then subsequently changed or deleted, so the end-use application or user gets a false sense of what the data is within the system. Of course, this is an unimaginable horror to a DBA and must be avoided at all costs.

To accomplish this, statements are grouped into distinct sets of actions and executed inside of a SQL transaction. The ANSI SQL standard defines the transaction as beginning with the execution of the first SQL statement. It is then ended in one of three different ways:

❑ A COMMIT statement signals to the RDBMS that the transaction has effectively ended successfully and that all changes should be made permanent. A new transaction is spawned the next time a SQL statement is executed.

❑ A ROLLBACK statement signals to the RDBMS that the transaction has failed and all changes should be backed out of the database. A new transaction is spawned as soon as the next SQL statement is executed.

❑ A successful program terminates normally, and the transaction terminates just as if a COMMIT statement had been issued. If the program terminates abnormally, then the transaction terminates just as if a ROLLBACK statement had been issued.

Some RDBMS applications (most notably Sybase and Microsoft's SQL Server) implement additional resources that allow you to run multiple nested transactions. This allows for the ROLLBACK of specific sections of the transaction and also allows you to determine where a transaction begins.

To ensure that the transaction can be rolled back to the state that the data was in before the transaction began, the RDBMS implementation locks the rows. These locks are held for as long as the transaction is being processed. This is because we do not want the other operators on the database system to read data that may be in the midst of a transaction that needs to be rolled back. Since this locking keeps other processes from obtaining access to the data, you must strive to make these transactions as fast as possible.

One possible way to do this is to commit transactions in the shortest amount of time possible. Once the transactions have been committed and the changes are made permanent, then the locks are dropped and the data can be accessed again. Another way that this can be done is by ensuring that the individual INSERT, UPDATE, and DELETE statements can be performed as quickly as possible. This involves ensuring that the indexes on the system are optimized. Indexes can allow the data to be found, and thus changed, more quickly, but they can also hinder the updating of data. This is because every time the data that is linked to an index is modified, the index must also be updated to take into account the new data. Therefore, indexes must be carefully analyzed to see if there are new indexes that would help performance or unused indexes that may be dragging the system down.

Analytical Processing Database Architecture

The *analytical database model* is one that is optimized for direct queries of the data to analyze the contents. Often, these systems are informational or reporting systems in which the data is not updated very often in comparison to the amount of time that is spent querying the contents. As such, they have much different requirements for optimization than the transactional database.

First of all, the analytical database is mainly used to process SELECT statements and, thus, does not use the SQL transactional processing statements. This eliminates much of the detriments of excessive database locking on the tables and rows of the database and enters in new considerations to be met.

Often the analytical database must process multiple complex queries in order to output result sets to the end application or user. In order to do this, the SELECT statements must be optimized so that they can gather the data in the fastest and most efficient way possible.

One of the most effective ways to do this is by implementing a carefully planned index strategy. Indexes allow the database to have intricate knowledge of where the data is held. However, in order for the index to be effective it must be placed over the proper column or columns and, in some cases, those must be in the right order. This involves carefully analyzing your queries to see which data they are accessing and where indexes could be of a benefit. In addition, you must ensure that they are accessing the right index when executing the query plan. It is often the case that there may be too many indexes on the tables being accessed and, instead of selecting the optimum index, it picks another one that has one or two of the same data columns as the SELECT statement.

Another way to effectively enhance the database performance is to ensure that your queries, procedures, and functions are optimized to their maximum level of efficiency. This can be done by removing redundant code, simplifying expressions, explicitly naming SELECT list items, and paying careful attention to such things as joins and triggers. These types of items often require your SQL processes to draw more resources (CPU, memory, and disk I/O) and, thus, are detrimental to database performance.

Of course, there are several ways in which you can optimize your procedures and functions that will pay dividends as well. The first is to look not only at the functions performance overall, but to break down the individual statements within the objects and ensure that the SQL logic is optimized.

Secondly, if your functions and procedures involve complex invocations of business logic then maybe those can be broken down into simpler methods. The reason is two-fold. First, by breaking down your procedures and functions into simpler methods, you can optimize each method individually, which is often easier. Then you also have the added benefit that it is often better in terms of query plans to have smaller methods with a lesser number of options.

Consider a function or procedure that performs one of five different blocks of SQL code based on an input value. Since the procedure is precompiled, then the query plan for the procedure is already set. However, this plan may be based upon the execution of the first block of SQL code and not the second, third, fourth, or fifth. So, when the function or procedure is then subsequently run with another input parameter, it is using a non-optimized query plan. If we take that function and break it down into one function that calls one of five other functions dependent upon the input parameter, then we now effectively ensure that an optimal path is always taken to retrieve the data.

Most RDBMS implementations also provide other ways in which to speed up query performance, and it is best to check your documentation carefully for instances in which you can reap the benefits.

Understanding the Adverse Effects of Function Performance

Even though functions aid the developer in many ways, it must be recognized that using functions can affect performance on your system. Because of this, you must not haphazardly enter into a routine of adding functions merely for the fact that you can. A poorly implemented function can adversely affect the performance of your system, sometimes more than regular SQL can. This section discusses how functions affect performance on several different levels.

Effects on Query Performance

Queries are where you will first notice any ill effects of using functions. You must remember that in your queries, depending on what kind of function it is and where it is executed, a function can be executed more than once. Consider the following query in which a function is used to format a phone number into a standard format:

```
SELECT NAME, ADDRESS, CITY, STATE, ZIP, FORMAT_PHONE(PHONE)
FROM CUSTOMERS
WHERE REGIONID = 3;
```

This seems like a relatively simple query, but it can actually become quite complicated, depending on the use of the FORMAT_PHONE function. If this function has to perform any complex calculations or transformations, then these are carried out for each iteration of the result set. So, if there are 10,000 customers from region three, then the function is carried out 10,000 times. Maybe the phone number could be formatted more efficiently on the client side.

A function could also be a table-valued function and be the object of the SELECT statement. In this instance, the function may not be performed as many times as the previous one, but may adversely affect performance, nonetheless. The following is such an example:

```
SELECT NAME, ADDRESS, CITY, STATE, ZIP, PHONE
FROM DBO.GET_ALL_CUSTOMERS()
WHERE REGIONID = 3;
```

If the GET_ALL_CUSTOMERS function returns a very large result set, then the query will be held hostage until the result set is returned. Additionally, the function may involve complex logic that may slow down the return of the result set. If you know that the result set of a table valued function will be very large, and that you will be restricting it by certain constraints in the WHERE clause, then make those built into the function to limit the set returned. Additionally, it must be understood that table-valued functions do not benefit from such things as indexing. Take a close look at these types of functions if they are hurting performance to see if they can be optimized or even eliminated.

Effects on Database Performance

Functions can have several adverse effects on the performance of your database, the worst of which is locking and blocking. This is especially true in the transactional model of databases, primarily because transactions hold locks on data until the transaction is completed or a rollback occurs. When two objects are trying to access the same piece of data at the same time, then this is considered a block because one query will be determined the winner and given access while the other is made to wait. This may lead to other locks because the function may be executed multiple times and then every query must stand in line to access the piece of data. This may cause some queries to go beyond their maximum execution time and be dropped.

Additionally, databases traditionally have a limited number of connections that they can support. This is normally kept low by a process known as *connection pooling*, in which a database process that has already been spawned is kept open to handle the next query to reduce the overhead of spawning a new process. If the functions are making the queries take an unreasonably long time to execute, then the query will hold onto the process. If this is systemic, then it will cause new queries to spawn new process threads to handle their requests. More threads mean that, to manage the database, you must not only work to make these new processes, but also to manage them. Keeping functions optimized and working efficiently will allow the initial batch of database processes to be reused more efficiently and keep this in check.

Effects on Non-database Resources

Badly performing queries can even affect performance outside of the database environment. Remember that the database is not a self-enclosed system. In order for the database to do its work, it must have certain resources from the server on which it is housed. These resources include the CPU, memory, and disk I/O.

Functions can be CPU-intensive if they use complex queries that require many computations to process a result set. When a function is CPU-intensive and hogs the processor of the system, this forces other queries to wait for free CPU time. This is equivalent to sitting in traffic. The car in front of the line either slows down or stops, causing a ripple effect that affects all the cars behind it. The best thing to do with these types of functions is to examine them to see if there are ways in which the process can be simplified either by making simpler calculations or by breaking the calculation up into smaller pieces. This should bring the CPU usage down to a manageable level.

Memory is important for storing result sets, temporary table objects, and caching query plans. If functions attempt to deal with large result sets or table objects, then they are prone to consuming more than their fair share of memory. The use of extremely large result sets is most often caused by poor planning in the development stage. Result sets can often be reduced by constraints such as those in the WHERE clause. If extremely large result sets are needed for reporting purposes, then the possibility of running such queries during non-peak hours and then caching the results should be investigated.

Lastly, functions can have an effect like any SQL statement on disk I/O depending on the type and amount of data that is being read. Logical reads against the database file result in disk I/O. There are several factors that can affect this, including how much data is retrieved. Besides the amount of data, indexes can also be a big factor, because a well-placed index can ensure that the RDBMS can find the exact location of the data it is looking for without having to scan through the majority of the data file. With that thought, the proper implementation of indexes and constraining excessive data in the result set can effectively manage the amount of disk I/O that your functions initiate.

Examining the Impact of SQL Functions in SQL Statements

The impact of functions on performance, however, are not all bad. Functions are precompiled code that have their execution plans already determined and laid out ahead of time. They can provide positive benefits if used in the right way.

SELECT Clause

Functions in the SELECT clause can provide a benefit in performance over using more complicated logic to compile results. Consider the following simple query for example:

```
SELECT SALES.EMPID, EMPLOYEES.EMPNAME, AVG(SALES.SALES)
FROM SALES, EMPLOYEES
WHERE SALES.EMPID = EMPLOYEES.EMPID
GROUP BY SALES.EMPID
ORDER BY EMPNAME;
```

In this simple statement, the built-in AVG function provides us with an easy-to-implement (and fast) way in which to calculate the average of each employee's sales. How would you implement this without the use of the AVG function? More than likely, you would have to use cursors and temporary tables to get the same aggregate information provided by the AVG function. This would not only be less efficient in terms of things like locking (because of the cursors) but would also have to be compiled by the RDBMS when executed. This would make extra overhead on the RDBMS (such as parsing, determining a query plan, and executing the excess code).

FROM Clause

Using table-valued functions or functions that return table or rowset objects in the FROM clause is almost always the place in your queries that can take the biggest hit as far as performance is concerned. This is really caused by a two-fold problem. The first part of the problem occurs when the resultant rowset is very large. Large rowsets are held in memory, and the more memory they consume, the less there is for the other queries to use. If your system does not have enough memory to hold the contents of the rowset, then it will undoubtedly use the I/O cache hand to write information to disk, which will slow the process down further. Secondly, the table objects returned by these functions have no indexes associated with them. Since indexes are what allow information within a table structure to be accessed quickly, these tables are prone to use table scans, which are a slower form of query access.

With that said, using functions in particular places can almost always improve query performance. This is usually true when replacing a subquery within a particular query. The reason that a function is normally faster than a subquery is because the function is precompiled. Therefore, its SQL code is already preparsed and its execution plan has already been determined. This is usually enough to justify the creation and use of a function to replace the subquery. This speaks to the larger issue that you should look for justified reasons to implement your functions before doing so. This is to ensure that you are not proverbially "shooting yourself in the foot" by implementing a function that, in the end, degrades performance.

WHERE Clause

Functions in the WHERE clause are generally faster at execution time than similar types of subqueries. This is once again because a function is already precompiled. This means that the SQL code has already been parsed and found well formed, and its optimal execution plan is already predetermined. However, it should be noted that these functions can fall into the same traps as those that are used in the SELECT clause.

GROUP BY Clause

The GROUP BY clause is, in itself, considered a function, and items in the GROUP BY list are determined based on the need to group them by the use of an aggregate function in the select list. Therefore, it is generally forbidden to include functions within the GROUP BY clause. This limitation does not apply to the HAVING clause, because it is a constraint device. The use of functions in the HAVING clause normally do not have as dramatic of an effect on the query as those in the WHERE clause do. This is because the WHERE clause is used to limit the number of rows returned in a query, while the HAVING clause works to restrict the number of groups. Thus, the HAVING clause is generally accessed in fewer iterations than the WHERE clause.

Comparing Built-in Functions and User-Defined Functions

User-defined functions (UDFs) provide the developer with a way to create customized functions to handle a myriad of different problems. You might be tempted to write individual versions of built-in functions. Although UDFs are flexible, they are not the fastest in implementation. Built-in functions will always be faster than any similar version of UDFs that the developer could create. These functions have been encoded in their particular RDBMS implementation and optimized to run as efficiently as possible. Therefore, the developer should use the built-in functions whenever possible. It is the developer's responsibility to implement the least obstructive path available to achieve the goals of creating or managing the database. With this in mind, you must look carefully at what functionality you are trying to implement. If this can be done using a combination of built-in functions, then use them. This is what they are there for, to make your life as a developer easier.

Even though it is always tempting for developers to believe that they can do things better and faster than the current way, this is one area in which it just cannot be. Instead, you should lean on these functions and expand your knowledge of them so that they can become an intricate part of your IT toolbox.

Creating a Balance between Security and Performance

Functions provide a great opportunity for the developer or DBA to implement another layer of security within the database model. By abstracting the layer of data access from the actual data itself, you not only restrict the people who access your data, but also essentially what they can do with the data. This is a very powerful attribute to use such things as views, procedures, and functions. In almost all cases, these processes can be optimized to outperform dynamic SQL queries because procedures and functions are precompiled and their query plans are already calculated.

You must strive to keep a balance between the need to maintain the security of the system and the performance of the system as a whole. This is sometimes a tricky situation in which the developer or DBA must determine not just what the impact of the function is on a query, but also what its overall effect is on the database as a whole. You should use the information given in the previous sections to guide your decision, as well as some constructive testing. In the end, it is your decision on whether new functionality can be brought into the system through functions or ad hoc queries (requiring table access).

Summary

This chapter dealt with the performance implications of using functions within your RDBMS implementations. We discussed different database formats that may affect the judgments you make as far as how and when to implement functions. In addition, we discussed several different factors that could cause functions to degrade your system's performance and some possible remedies for them. Lastly, we discussed some of the positive effects that functions provide to your queries and databases.

The main point of this chapter is to suggest that performance and optimization should not be an afterthought of developing a database. Instead, it should be something that is considered during the initial planning, the development, the implementation, and after the fielding. Database performance should be involved in all aspects of a database lifecycle. A database often becomes a "living entity" as it develops, grows, and functionality is both added and removed. Therefore, developers must be diligent in testing their changes to ensure that system efficiency is retained.

In the next chapter, we will look at a special set of tables called the System Catalog. These tables are maintained by the RDBMS implementation itself and contain valuable information on the database.

Useful Queries from the System Catalog

The *System Catalog* is a special collection of tables contained within a database that the RDBMS implementation maintains itself. These tables hold specific information about the database structure and the object contained therein. The use of these tables is two-fold. First, since the information is contained within tables in the database itself, the RDBMS system can use its own query routines to quickly and effectively gather needed data about itself. Second, more often than not, these tables are open for querying against by the developer. This provides an easy and accessible way for the developer to execute queries against the database to retrieve information about the structure of the database. These queries often come in handy when you want to write functions that are capable of being used across different databases without having to know a substantial amount up front about its structure.

You may remember from discussions in previous chapters that the SQL Server sysobjects table can be used in some queries to pull information on the tables, functions, and procedures of a particular database. The sysobjects table is one of the SQL Server's System Catalogs. Most System Catalogs can be readily identified because they belong to a special user such as DBA, MASTER, or SYSTEM. Access to these tables, of course, is read-only to maintain database integrity. The only way they can be modified is through direct application of Data Definition Language (DDL) statements such as CREATE, ALTER, and DROP. Even with this limitation, the System Catalog is a powerful tool for the developer.

You can imagine that, since every RDBMS implementation has its own particular version of SQL, it would also have differences in the way in which it implements its System Catalog. In this chapter we will detail some of the different intricacies of the separate RDBMS platforms' implementations of the System Catalog.

Useful System Catalog Queries for the Programmer

System Catalog queries are particularly helpful to the developer when writing functions to handle the generation of custom SQL scripts such as those discussed in Chapter 23. These types of functions can normally be easily transferred between database platforms, as long as you understand the differences in syntax of the System Catalogs. Generally, the System Catalog can be separated into the following five different areas:

- ❏ *Table catalogs* — These describe the basic properties (name, owner, size, etc.) of the tables located within the database.

- ❏ *View catalogs* — These describe each of the different views that are located within the database including the view name, owner, and SQL definition within the view.

- ❏ *Column catalogs* — These describe each of the columns within the tables of the database. These catalogs contain things such as table, column name, data type, and size.

- ❏ *Users catalog* — This describes each of the users who are authorized on the database.

- ❏ *Privileges catalog* — This describes the privileges given to the users of the Users catalog to access aspects of the database.

The following subsections will detail what some of the most important tables are and some common queries in each of the different database platforms discussed in the book.

Oracle

The Oracle platform uses two main views to provide information and access to other views within the system. These are the DICTIONARY and the DICT_COLUMNS views. The DICTIONARY view (or DICT, for short) only contains two columns: Table_Name and Comments. These two columns contain a listing and comments for each and every table and view within the system. You can use a query to pull up information from the DICTIONARY view. The following query details all the views in the system, and the accompanying table displays the results of the query in a more user-friendly format:

```
SELECT TABLE_NAME, COMMENTS
FROM DICT
WHERE TABLE_NAME LIKE '%VIEWS%';
```

Table Name	Description
ALL_MVIEW_AGGREGATES	Description of the materialized view aggregates accessible to the user
ALL_MVIEW_ANALYSIS	Description of the materialized views accessible to the user
ALL_MVIEW_DETAIL_RELATIONS	Description of the materialized view detail tables accessible to the user
ALL_MVIEW_JOINS	Description of the join between two columns in the WHERE clause of a materialized view accessible to the user
ALL_MVIEW_KEYS	Description of the columns that appear in the GROUP BY list of a materialized view accessible to the user
ALL_MVIEWS	All materialized views in the database
ALL_VIEWS	Description of the views accessible to the user

Table Name	Description
DBA_MVIEW_AGGREGATES	Description of the materialized view aggregates accessible to the DBA
DBA_MVIEW_ANALYSIS	Description of the materialized views accessible to the DBA
DBA_MVIEW_DETAIL_RELATIONS	Description of the materialized view detail tables accessible to the DBA
DBA_MVIEW_JOINS	Description of a join between two columns in the WHERE clause of a materialized view that is accessible to the DBA
DBA_MVIEW_KEYS	Description of the columns that appear in the GROUP BY list of a materialized view accessible to the DBA
DBA_MVIEWS	All materialized views in the database accessible to the DBA
DBA_VIEWS	Description of all views in the database accessible to the DBA
GV$FIXED_VIEW_DEFINITION	Synonym for GV_$FIXED_VIEW_DEFINITION
USER_MVIEW_AGGREGATES	Description of the materialized view aggregates created by the user
USER_MVIEW_ANALYSIS	Description of the materialized views created by the user
USER_MVIEW_DETAIL_RELATIONS	Description of the materialized view detail tables of the materialized views created by the user
USER_MVIEW_JOINS	Description of a join between two columns in the WHERE clause of a materialized view created by the user
USER_MVIEW_KEYS	Description of the columns that appear in the GROUP BY list of a materialized view created by the user
USER_MVIEWS	All materialized views in the database
USER_VIEWS	Description of the user's own views
V$FIXED_VIEW_DEFINITION	Synonym for V_$FIXED_VIEW_DEFINITION

The DICT_COLUMNS view is similar to the DICT view except that it consists of three columns: TABLE_NAME, COLUMN_NAME, and COMMENTS. This view is often used to determine which of the views would be most beneficial to the type of query you want to perform. For example, if we are looking for a COLUMN_NAME of USER_NAME, then we could use the following query:

```
SELECT TABLE_NAME
FROM DICT_COLUMNS
WHERE COLUMN_NAME LIKE '%USER_NAME%'
AND TABLE_NAME LIKE '%USER%';


TABLE_NAME
------------------------------
ALL_REPCAT_USER_AUTHORIZATIONS
```

```
ALL_REPCAT_USER_PARM_VALUES
DBA_REPCAT_USER_AUTHORIZATIONS
DBA_REPCAT_USER_PARM_VALUES
USER_REPCAT_TEMPLATE_SITES
USER_REPCAT_USER_AUTHORIZATION
USER_REPCAT_USER_PARM_VALUES
```

Now that we have identified the main informational views of the Oracle database, we will examine some of the views that are available for querying.

USER_CATALOG

The USER_CATALOG view contains the basic information on the tables, views, sequences, and synonyms that the user can use a SELECT statement on to get information from. The USER_CATALOG contains the columns detailed in the following table.

Column	Description
TABLE_NAME	This is the name of the table, view, sequence, or synonym.
TABLE_TYPE	This is the type of object that the table name refers to.

Consider the following example:

```
SELECT TABLE_NAME, TABLE_TYPE
FROM USER_CATALOG WHERE ROWNUM<=10;

// Return the first 9 items from the view

TABLE_NAME                       TABLE_TYPE
-------------------------------- -----------
APPLICATION                      TABLE
APP_EI                           TABLE
ARLOC_GELOC                      TABLE
ASIP_STATION                     TABLE
ASITLS                           VIEW
AUTH_MAT_ITM                     VIEW
BOIP                             VIEW
BOIPEQP                          VIEW
BOIPPERS                         VIEW

9 rows selected.
```

The USER_CATALOG view only gives general information about the object. As you can see from the previous table, it just does not do the job when you need to know the specifics of an object within the database. To gain further information on the object, you must go to the USER view that specifically identifies that type of object. The following subsections discuss the two major types in the USER_CATALOG view: the USER_TABLES and USER_VIEWS views.

USER_TABLES

The USER_TABLES view provides the DBA with much more detailed information on the tables within the system. Some of the useful columns that are available within the USER_TABLES view are detailed in the following table.

Column	Description
BACKED_UP	This column indicates whether the table has been backed up since the last modification.
NUM_ROWS	This column retrieves the number of rows from the table.
PARTITIONED	This column indicates whether the table is a partitioned table or not.
PCT_FREE	This indicates the percentage of free storage space within the table.
PCT_USED	This indicates the percentage of used storage space within the table.
TABLE_NAME	This is the name of the table.

Consider the following example:

```
SELECT TABLE_NAME, BACKED_UP, PARTITIONED,
       NUM_ROWS, PCT_FREE, PCT_USED
FROM USER_TABLES
WHERE ROWNUM<=10;

// Return information about the first 10 tables in the view.

TABLE_NAME                      B PAR   NUM_ROWS   PCT_FREE   PCT_USED
------------------------------- - ---  ---------- ---------- ----------
APPLICATION                     N NO            3         10         40
APP_EI                          N NO           12         10         40
ARLOC_                          N NO        15516         10         40
ASIP_STATION                    N NO         7152         10         40
BACKUP_ORG                      N NO            0         10         40
CIVILIAN_PERSONNEL              N NO          762         10         40
CIV_MISMATCHS                   N NO            0         10         40
CIV_MAP_CNFG                    N NO            0         10         40
CIV_ORGANIZATION                N NO            0         10         40
```

There are far more columns available than these. Check your current set of database documentation to identify which columns are currently supported.

USER_VIEWS

The USER_VIEWS view contains detailed information about the various views available to the user. The following table details each of the columns available through the USER_VIEWS view. The main columns that are used within this view are VIEW_NAME, TEXT_LENGTH, and TEXT. The other columns can still be of use, but only for object views.

Column	Description
OID_TEXT	This details the WITH OID clause.
OID_TEXT_LENGTH	This details the length of the WITH OID clause.
TEXT	This is the query that forms the body of the view statement.
TEXT_LENGTH	This is the character length of the view's base query.
TYPE_TEXT	This indicates the type clause of the typed view.
TYPE_TEXT_LENGTH	This is the length of the type clause.
VIEW_NAME	This is the name of the view.
VIEW_TYPE	This indicates the type of view.
VIEW_TYPE_OWNER	This is the owner of the view's type.

It should also be noted that this table only applies to the traditional views. If you wanted to get more information on materialized views, you would have to query the USER_MVIEWS view. The following code shows some possible queries available to you by using the USER_VIEWS view:

```
SELECT VIEW_NAME
FROM USER_VIEWS
WHERE ROWNUM <=10;

// Get a list of the first 10 views in the view.

VIEW_NAME
------------------------------
ASITLS
AUTH_MAT_ITM
BOIP
BOIPEQP
BOIPPERS
BOIP_NARR
CNTRY
CTU
DIV_BDE
DOCBOIP

10 rows selected.

// Now we can see the text in one of the views.

SELECT TEXT
FROM USER_VIEWS
WHERE VIEW_NAME='CNTRY';

TEXT
-----------------------------------------------------------------
select "CNTRY_CD","CNTRY_NM" from WORKERS.CNTRY HR with read only
```

IBM DB2

The IBM DB2 UDB platform has a single schema that provides access to all the system views for drawing information from the system tables. This schema is the SYSCAT schema, and all of the views are of the format SYSCAT.<view_name> (such as SYSCAT.TABLES). The following table details some of the more useful views that are available on the DB2 platform.

View	Description
SYSCAT.COLUMNS	This describes the columns within the tables of the database.
SYSCAT.DBAUTH	This details the database's permissions.
SYSCAT.FUNCTIONS	This describes the user-defined functions (UDFs) within the database.
SYSCAT.INDEXCOLUSE	This describes the column indexes that are within the database.
SYSCAT.PROCEDURES	This describes the stored procedures within the database.
SYSCAT.SCHEMATA	This details the various schemas that are present within the database.
SYSCAT.TABAUTH	This details the table permissions granted within the database.
SYSCAT.TABLES	This describes the tables that reside within the database.
SYSCAT.VIEWS	This describes the various views that are within the database.

The following subsections discuss some of the characteristics of the main System Catalog views. These are the ones that we have deemed to be the most important to know and understand. You can find detailed explanations of the others in the IBM DB2 documentation.

FUNCTIONS

The SYSCAT.FUNCTIONS view contains information on the UDFs within the system. The following table details some of the more important columns in the view.

Column	Description
BODY	When the LANGUAGE column is SQL, this column returns the SQL language used to construct the body of the function or method.
DEFINER	This is the authoritative ID of the person who created the function.
FUNCID	This is the internal ID of the function.
FUNCNAME	This is the fully qualified name of the function.
FUNCSCHEMA	This is the schema name of the function.
LANGUAGE	This column is blank if the ORIGIN type is not "E" or "Q." Otherwise, it returns a code defining what language is used for defining the function (C, JAVA, OLE, SQL, or OLEDB).

Table continued on following page

Column	Description
ORIGIN	This is a code based on what the origin type of the function is: "B" stands for "built"; "E" stands for "user defined — external"; "Q" stands for "user defined — SQL"; "U" stands for "user defined — based on source"; and "S" stands for "system generated."
REMARKS	This is a set of user-directed remarks.
RETURN_TYPE	This is the internal type code of the return type of the function.
TYPE	This column describes the type of function based on one of the following codes: "C" stands for "column"; "R" stands for "row"; "S" stands for "scalar"; and "T" stands for "table."

We can examine some of the basic aspects of the view by examining the USERS built-in function to view things like its ORIGIN, as shown here:

```
SELECT FUNCSCHEMA, FUNCNAME, DEFINER, ORIGIN
FROM SYSCAT.FUNCTIONS
WHERE FUNCNAME='USERS';

FUNCSCHEMA     FUNCNAME     DEFINER     ORIGIN
----------     --------     -------     ------
SYSFUN         USERS        SYSIBM      Q
```

This function is particularly helpful in discerning which functions are overloaded versions of existing functions. You can also use similar queries to parse out functions by ORIGIN type, and, if you are vigilant in posting descriptive remarks on your UDFs, then you can use the remarks to look for keywords.

SCHEMATA

The SYSCAT.SCHEMATA view contains entries for each of the schemas with the system. The following table details the columns within the view.

Column	Description
CREATE_TIME	This is the timestamp of when the schema was created.
DEFINER	This is the user who created the schema.
OWNER	This is the authoritative ID of the schema. Any implicitly created schema will have the ID of SYSIBM.
REMARKS	This contains user-provided remarks about the table.
SCHEMANAME	This is the name of the schema.

By using a SELECT statement on the IBM DB2 Sample database, you can see all of the default schema information that is initially set up for the database, as shown here:

```
SELECT * FROM SYSCAT.SCHEMATA;

SCHEMANAME      OWNER       DEFINER     CREATE_TIME               REMARKS
----------      ------      ------      -----------------------   ----------
SYSIBM          SYSIBM      SYSIBM      2004-11-25 21:16:23.429
SYSCAT          SYSIBM      SYSIBM      2004-11-25 21:16:23.429
SYSFUN          SYSIBM      SYSIBM      2004-11-25 21:16:23.429
SYSSTAT         SYSIBM      SYSIBM      2004-11-25 21:16:23.429
SYSPROC         SYSIBM      SYSIBM      2004-11-25 21:16:23.429
NULLID          SYSIBM      DB2ADMIN    2004-11-25 21:17:31.768001
DB2ADMIN        SYSIBM      DB2ADMIN    2004-11-25 21:18:45.734005
```

This would be an important view to remember when writing custom code to script out all of your personally defined schemas and objects without including things that would be in the system schemas.

TABLES

The SYSCAT.TABLES view contains entries for each table, view, alias, or nickname created in the database. This view even contains entries for each of the System Catalog tables. The SYSCAT.TABLES view contains a significant amount of information, but the following table summarizes some of the more important columns available in the view.

Column	Description
CARD	This contains the number of rows within the table.
CHILDREN	This contains the number of referential constraints of which the table is a parent.
CREATE_TIME	This contains the timestamp of when the table was created.
PARENTS	This contains the number of referential constraints of which the table is a dependent.
REMARKS	This contains user-entered remarks about the table.
SELFREFS	This contains the number of self-referencing constraints on the table.
STATS_TIME	This contains the last time when any change was made to the statistics on the table.
TABNAME	This is the name of the object (table, view, alias, or nickname).
TABSCHEMA	This is the schema name of the object (table, view, alias, or nickname).
TYPE	This describes the type of object based on the following format: "A" stands for "alias"; "H" stands for "hierarchy Table"; "N" stands for "nickname"; "S" stands for "summary table"; "T" stands for "table"; "U" stands for "untyped table"; "V" stands for "view"; and "W" stands for "typed view."

The SYSCAT.TABLES view will probably be your most often used view of the catalog views available on the IBM DB2 platform. We know that the DEFINER of the Samples database in DB2 is the DB2ADMIN, so we could create a query to define all the user tables that are in the Samples database, as shown here:

```
SELECT TABSCHEMA, TABNAME, TYPE, REMARKS
FROM SYSCAT.TABLES
WHERE DEFINER='DB2ADMIN';

TABSCHEMA        TABNAME        TYPE    REMARKS
-------------    ----------     ----    --------------
DB2ADMIN         ORG            T

DB2ADMIN         STAFF          T

DB2ADMIN         DEPARTMENT     T

DB2ADMIN         EMPLOYEE       T

DB2ADMIN         EMP_ACT        T

DB2ADMIN         PROJECT        T

DB2ADMIN         EMP_PHOTO      T

DB2ADMIN         EMP_RESUME     T

DB2ADMIN         SALES          T

DB2ADMIN         CL_SCHED       T

DB2ADMIN         IN_TRAY        T
```

VIEWS

The SYSCAT.VIEWS view contains information on the various views throughout the system. The following table details some of the more useful tables within the SYSCAT.VIEWS view.

Column	Description
DEFINER	This is the authoritative ID of the user who defined the view.
READONLY	This returns Y or N depending on whether the view is read-only.
TEXT	This contains the text of the body of the view-creation statement.
VALID	This returns a code detailing whether the view is valid or not: "Y" stands for "The definition is valid"; "X" stands for "The view is inoperative and must be re-created."
VIEWCHECK	This column returns a code that details what type of checking is enabled on the view: "N" stands for "no check option"; "L" stands for "local check option"; and "C" stands for "cascaded check option."
VIEWNAME	This is the name of the view.
VIEWSCHEMA	This is the schema name of the view.

More often than not, you will use the `SYSCAT.VIEWS` view to find out if you have any invalid view definitions that need attention, or you will be drawing from the TEXT column to write transfer scripts. The following query demonstrates the first 10 of approximately 144 entries of column data available from the view:

```
SELECT VIEWSCHEMA, VIEWNAME, DEFINER, READONLY, VALID
FROM SYSCAT.VIEWS;

VIEWSCHEMA        VIEWNAME                 DEFINER     READONLY    VALID
------------      --------------------     ---------   --------    -----
SYSIBM            CHECK_CONSTRAINTS        SYSIBM      Y           Y
SYSIBM            COLUMNS                  SYSIBM      Y           Y
SYSIBM            COLUMNS_S                SYSIBM      Y           Y
SYSIBM            REFERENTIAL_CONSTRAINTS  SYSIBM      Y           Y
SYSIBM            REF_CONSTRAINTS          SYSIBM      Y           Y
SYSIBM            TABLE_CONSTRAINTS        SYSIBM      Y           Y
SYSIBM            TABLES                   SYSIBM      Y           Y
SYSIBM            TABLES_S                 SYSIBM      Y           Y
SYSIBM            USER_DEFINED_TYPES       SYSIBM      Y           Y
SYSIBM            UDT_S                    SYSIBM      Y           Y
```

PostgreSQL

PostgreSQL has a set of System Catalog tables that provide the developer with a set of system views to access the tables in a more reliable fashion. These views are PostgreSQL-specific and augment the standard set of ANSI-compliant views that are contained within the `Information` schema. The system views available are detailed in the following table.

View	Description
Pg_indexes	This describes indexes within the database.
Pg_locks	This describes information on the currently held locks in the system.
Pg_rules	This provides information on database rules.
Pg_settings	This describes the current parameter settings.
Pg_stats	This provides information on the current planner statistics.
Pg_tables	This describes the various tables within the current database.
Pg_user	This provides information on current authorized users of the system.
Pg_views	This describes views within the database.

We will go into detail on the most often used set of these views. Where possible, we have documented what base table is related to each column in the view. This way you can use the base System Catalog tables instead of using the views. However, remember that the purpose of views is to maintain compatibility with the development layer when the base tables change. Not using the views in favor of direct table access may one day lead to a rewrite of your code.

Pg_tables

The `pg_tables` view provides you with information on the tables contained in the database, as well as their attributes. The `pg_tables` system view contains the columns detailed in the following table.

Name	Type	Base Table Ref.	Description
Hasindexes	Boolean	Pg_class.relhasindex	This object returns True if the table has indexes.
Hasrules	Boolean	Pg_class.relhasrules	This object returns True if the table has rules.
Hastriggers	Boolean	Pg_class.reltriggers	This object returns True if the table has triggers.
schemaname	Name	Pg_namespace.nspname	This is the name of the schema containing the table.
Tablename	Name	Pg_class.relname	This is the name of the table.
Tableowner	Name	Pg_shadow.usename	This is the owner of the table.

This view is useful when troubleshooting performance issues with your system. We have often run across various systems that have performance issues, and one of the first things that we check on the tables that are having issues is if they contain triggers. You can perform an expedient query such as the following on the `pg_tables` view to check which tables have triggers associated with them:

```
SELECT SCHEMANAME, TABLENAME, TABLEOWNER
    FROM PG_CATALOG.PG_TABLES
WHERE HASTRIGGERS = 'TRUE'
AND TABLEOWNER='your table owner name';
```

You can then use this information to construct queries of the tables `pg_class` and `pr_triggers` to pull out the specific trigger information from the catalogs. Then you can do a detailed analysis on the various possible problem triggers.

Pg_user

The `pg_user` view is a direct readable access to the `pg_shadow` system table. The `pg_shadow` system table contains information about the authorized database users on the system. The only difference is that the password field is blanked out by asterisks (*) in the view itself. The main columns within the view are detailed in the following table.

Name	Type	Description
Passwd	Text	This always reads ********.
Usecatupd	Bool	The user has the ability to modify the System Catalogs.
Useconfig	Text[]	This shows the default user-session values for configuration variables.
Usecreatedb	Bool	The user has the ability to create databases.
Username	Name	This is the username.

Name	Type	Description
Usesuper	Bool	The user is a superuser.
Usesysid	Int4	This is the ID number for the user. It is used in the system to reference this user.
Valuntil	Asbtime	This is the expirary time of the user ID.

This view is often handy to have because you can make some readily available queries to keep track of who has access to the system. For example, we may need to know who on the system has the ability to create databases. We could create a simple query such as the following to do the job:

```
SELECT USERNAME
FROM  PG_CATALOG.PG_USER
WHERE USECREATEDB = 'TRUE';
```

Pg_views

The pg_views view provides information about the various views that reside in the database. The pg_views view contains the columns detailed in the following table.

Name	Type	Base Table Ref.	Description
Schemaname	Name	Pg_namespace.nspname	This contains the name of the schema that contains the view.
Viewname	Name	Pg_class.relname	This contains the name of the view.
Viewowner	Name	Pg_shadow.usename	This contains the name of the view's owner.
Definition	Text		This contains the view's definition, which is basically the SELECT statement that was used to construct the view.

You can use this view to grab the definition statement for the view using this simple query:

```
SELECT definition
  FROM pg_catalog.pg_views
WHERE view_name='name of your view';
```

You should note that this query does not take into account the schema that the view is stored in. It would be useful to further constrict it to a particular schema defined by the user to only obtain the specific view you are looking for. Similarly, you could use this view to construct the SQL statements needed to reconstruct your view on a remote system by using something similar to the following:

```
SELECT 'CREATE VIEW ' + VIEWNAME + ' AS ' +
       DEFINITION
   FROM PG_CATALOG.PG_VIEWS
WHERE SCHEMANAME='your schema name';
```

Microsoft SQL Server

The Microsoft SQL Server platform is usually queried directly from the system tables. These system tables are of limited number, and the available columns for queries are limited because most of them are reserved or for internal use only. However, these limitations make the system tables within the SQL Server very user-friendly in terms of querying objects to find information on the system. The following table details some of the major system tables available on the SQL Server platform.

Table	Description
SYSCOLUMNS	This table contains information on the various columns in the tables of the database.
SYSCOMMENTS	This table contains information for all the views, stored procedures, defaults, and user-defined constraints in the database.
SYSOBJECTS	This table contains entries for every object in the database.
SYSUSERS	This table contains information on all of the user accounts in the database.

SYSCOLUMNS

The SYSCOLUMNS table contains detailed information on the columns within the tables of the system. The following table details some of the more useful columns available in the table.

Column	Description
NAME	This is the name of the column.
ID	This is the unique ID of the table that the columns belong to.
XTYPE	This is the type ID code of the data type of the column.
LENGTH	This is the length of the column.
COLID	This is the ID of the column, which is only unique within the table itself.
PREC	This is the precision of the data type of the column.
SCALE	This is the scale of the object type of the column.
ISCOMPUTABLE	This determines if the column is a computable column: 0 means No; 1 means Yes.
ISNULLABLE	This indicates whether the column can contain NULL items: 0 means No; 1 means Yes.

In the following example, we create a query using the SYSCOLUMNS tables to get column details on the Employees table within the Northwind database. You should also note that we were able to obtain the data type by joining the SYSCOLUMNS table with the SYSTYPES table.

```
SELECT C.NAME + ' ' + T.NAME + '(' +
       CAST(C.LENGTH AS VARCHAR(10)) + ')'
       AS COLUMN_DETAILS
FROM NORTHWIND.DBO.SYSCOLUMNS C INNER JOIN
NORTHWIND.DBO.SYSTYPES T ON
C.XTYPE = T.XTYPE
AND C.ID = (
SELECT ID
FROM NORTHWIND.DBO.SYSOBJECTS
WHERE NAME='EMPLOYEES'
)
ORDER BY C.COLID

COLUMN_DETAILS
------------------------------
EmployeeID  int(4)
LastName  nvarchar(40)
LastName  sysname(40)
FirstName  nvarchar(20)
FirstName  sysname(20)
Title  nvarchar(60)
Title  sysname(60)
TitleOfCourtesy  nvarchar(50)
TitleOfCourtesy  sysname(50)
BirthDate  datetime(8)
HireDate  datetime(8)
Address  nvarchar(120)
Address  sysname(120)
City  nvarchar(30)
City  sysname(30)
Region  nvarchar(30)
Region  sysname(30)
PostalCode  nvarchar(20)
PostalCode  sysname(20)
Country  nvarchar(30)
Country  sysname(30)
HomePhone  nvarchar(48)
HomePhone  sysname(48)
Extension  nvarchar(8)
Extension  sysname(8)
Photo  image(16)
Notes  ntext(16)
ReportsTo  int(4)
PhotoPath  nvarchar(510)
PhotoPath  sysname(510)

(30 row(s) affected)
```

SYSCOMMENTS

The SYSCOMMENTS table contains information for all the views, stored procedures, defaults, and user defined constraints in the database. Users may use the TEXT column to retrieve the original SQL invocation statements. The major columns of the SYSCOMMENTS table are detailed in the following table.

Column	Description
COLID	This is the row sequence number for definitions of objects that are longer than 4,000 characters, which is the maximum size of the TEXT column.
COMPRESSED	This returns a bit value indicating whether the procedure is compressed: 1 means Yes; 0 means No.
ENCRYPTED	This returns a bit value indicating whether the procedure is encrypted: 1 means Yes; 0 means No.
ID	This is the object ID to which the entry is applied.
TEXT	This is the actual definition language of the object.

The following query shows how you can query the definition of the view from SYSCOMMENTS using a subquery from the SYSOBJECTS table:

```
SELECT TEXT FROM
NORTHWIND.DBO.SYSCOMMENTS
WHERE ID = (
SELECT ID
FROM NORTHWIND.DBO.SYSOBJECTS
WHERE XTYPE='V'
AND NAME='Alphabetical list of products'
)


TEXT
------------------------------------------------------------
create view "Alphabetical list of products" AS
SELECT Products.*, Categories.CategoryName
FROM Categories INNER JOIN Products ON Categories.CategoryID = Products.CategoryID
WHERE (((Products.Discontinued)=0))

(1 row(s) affected)
```

SYSOBJECTS

The SYSOBJECTS table is the cornerstone of the SQL Server system tables. The table contains entries for every object within the database. Many of the columns are reserved and are not readily available, but the important ones are detailed in the following table.

Column	Description
ID	This is the object ID for the object and is assigned internally.
NAME	This is the name of the object.
UID	This is the user ID of the user who owns the object.

Column	Description
XTYPE or TYPE	Either of these columns returns a CHAR(2) value that indicates what type of object the entry refers to: "C" stands for "check constraint"; "D" stands for "default or default constraint"; "F" stands for "foreign key constraint"; "L" stands for "log"; "FN" stands for "scalar function"; "IF" stands for "inlined table function"; "P" stands for "stored procedure"; "PK" stands for "primary key constraint"; "RF" stands for "replication filter stored procedure"; "S" stands for "system table"; "TF" stands for "table function"; "TR" stands for "trigger"; "U" stands for "user table"; "UQ" stands for "unique constraint"; "V" stands for "view"; and "X" stands for "extended."

The following query details one of the possible uses of the SYSOBJECTS table. Here we use the table to pull the list of user tables, denoted by the XTYPE code "U" from the Northwind database.

```
SELECT NAME,ID,XTYPE
FROM NORTHWIND.DBO.SYSOBJECTS
WHERE XTYPE='U'
ORDER BY NAME

// Now we get the list of user tables

NAME                             ID            XTYPE
-------------------------------- ------------- -----
Categories                       2041058307    U
CurrentSales                     1973582069    U
CustomerCustomerDemo             853578079     U
CustomerDemographics             869578136     U
Customers                        2073058421    U
dtproperties                     1109578991    U
Employees                        1977058079    U
EmployeeTerritories              917578307     U
Order Details                    325576198     U
Orders                           21575115      U
Products                         117575457     U
Region                           82099333      U
Sales2001                        2005582183    U
Sales2002                        1989582126    U
Sales2003                        1957582012    U
Shippers                         2105058535    U
STANDARD_NAMING                  2101582525    U
Suppliers                        2137058649    U
Territories                      901578250     U

(19 row(s) affected)
```

SYSUSERS

The SYSUSERS table provides invaluable knowledge of the user accounts within the database. By studying the contents of the table closely, you will come to understand the intricacies of how the system determines whether an account is a SQL Server account or a Windows domain account. The following table details the columns available in the SYSUSERS table.

Column	Description
GID	This is the group ID that the entry belongs to. If this is the same as the UID field, then this is a group.
HASDBACCESS	This returns 1 if the user has database access.
ISALIASED	This returns 1 if the account is aliased to another user.
ISAPPROLE	This returns 1 if the account is an application role.
ISLOGIN	This returns 1 if this is a login account, either for the Windows or the SQL Server.
ISNTGROUP	This returns 1 if the account is a Windows group.
ISNTNAME	This returns 1 if the account is a Windows group or user.
ISNTUSER	This returns 1 if the account is a Windows user.
ISSQLROLE	This returns 1 if the account is a SQL Server role.
ISSQLUSER	This returns 1 if the account is a SQL user account.
NAME	This is the name of the account.
SID	This is the security identifier for this entry.
UID	This is the user ID of the account. It is always unique within the database. The UID for the system account is always 1.

This table is especially helpful in keeping tabs on what roles and users have access to your databases, as detailed in the following simple query:

```
SELECT NAME,HASDBACCESS
FROM NORTHWIND.DBO.SYSUSERS
WHERE ISLOGIN = 1
ORDER BY NAME

NAME                                   HASDBACCESS
-------------------------------------- -----------
dbo                                    1
guest                                  1

(2 row(s) affected)
```

Sybase

Since the Sybase platform and the Microsoft SQL Server platform are derived from the same base, much of their internal structure looks similar. In the following subsections, we will detail a few of the system tables available within the system. Further information on the tables is available in the database documentation.

Table	Description
SYSCOLUMNS	This table contains information for all of the columns contained in the tables of the Sybase instance.
SYSDOMAIN	This table contains information on each of the predefined data types in the Sybase instance.
SYSTABLE	This table contains information on all of the tables and views in the Sybase instance.

SYSCOLUMNS

The SYSCOLUMNS table contains information on all of the columns contained within all the tables in the Sybase instance. Most of the useful columns from the table are listed in the following table.

Column	Description
CHECK	This column contains the value for any CHECK conditions defined on the column.
COLUMN_ID	This column identifies the unique COLUMN_ID assigned to the column. The COLUMN_ID number is unique within the table, and its value indicates its ordering within the table.
COLUMN_NAME	This column indicates the name of the column associated with this row in the SYSCOLUMNS table.
DEFAULT	This column specifies the default value for the column if one is not specified within the INSERT statement.
DOMAIN_ID	This column indicates the data type that is associated with the column by the number listed in the SYSDOMAIN table.
ESTIMATE	This column contains a self-tuning parameter that is used by the optimizer.
NULLS	This is a single-character value that indicates whether the column accepts NULL values or not.
PKEY	This is a single character value that indicates whether the column is the primary key of the table.
REMARKS	These are user-defined remarks that are associated with the column.
SCALE	This is a SMALLINT value that indicates the precision scale associated with the column.
TABLE_ID	This column identifies the unique TABLE_ID number associated with the table that the column belongs to.
USER_TYPE	If the table is defined using a user-defined data type, then the data type value is placed here.
WIDTH	This column is an SMALLINT value that indicates the width of the data type within the column.

Using the SYSCOLUMNS table, you can get the list of column names from a particular table in the order that they were declared using a query similar to the example found below. This would be the basis for creating a SQL script to produce the CREATE TABLE statement to reproduce the base table.

```
SELECT COLUMN_NAME
    FROM SYSCOLUMNS, SYSTABLE
WHERE SYSCOLUMNS.TABLE_ID = SYSTABLE.TABLE_ID
AND SYSTABLE.TABLE_NAME = 'your table name'
ORDER BY COLUMN_ID
```

SYSDOMAIN

The SYSDOMAIN table contains information on each of the predefined data types in the Sybase instance. These values are never changed because the table is used as a reference table by the system. The following table provides details.

View	Description
DOMAIN_ID	This column contains the unique identifying number assigned to each of the predefined data types in the system.
DOMAIN_NAME	This column contains the name of the data type.
PRECISION	If the data type is numeric, then this column contains the number of significant digits that can be stored in this data type. If the data type is nonnumeric, then this column contains NULL.
TYPE_ID	This column indicates the corresponding ODBC data type ID that is associated with this data type. This value corresponds to a data type housed in the SYSTYPES table.

This table is normally used in conjunction with the SYSCOLUMNS table to construct a more detailed view of the columns, such as in the following example:

```
SELECT COLUMN_NAME AS COLUMN, DOMAIN_NAME AS DATA_TYPE,
       WIDTH AS SIZE, SCALE AS PRECISION
FROM SYSCOLUMNS
```

SYSTABLE

The SYSTABLE table contains information on all of the tables and views that are located within the Sybase instance. The columns associated with this table are detailed in the following table.

Column	Description
COUNT	If the associated item is a table, then this column contains the number of rows within the table. This value is updated on each successful CHECKPOINT. If the item is a view, then this column is always 0.

Column	Description
CREATOR	This column contains the user_id of the user who created the table or view. This number is associated with a value in the SYSUSERPERM table.
FILE_ID	This file ID number indicates which database file contains the table and is associated with the SYSFILE table.
FIRST_PAGE	This column indicates the first page that contains information on a table within the database. If the item is a view, then this number is always 0.
LAST_PAGE	This column indicates the last page that contains information on the table. If the item is a view, then this value is always 0.
PRIMARY_ROOT	If the table has a primary key defined, then this column contains the location of the root of the B-tree for the primary key. If the item is a view, or if there is no associated primary key, then this value is 0.
REMARKS	This column contains user-defined remarks about the table.
REPLICATE	This column indicates whether or not the table is a primary data source in a Replication Server installation.
TABLE_ID	This column contains the unique ID number that is associated with each table or view.
TABLE_NAME	This column contains the name of the table or view. This name must be unique per creator because no one creator can have two tables or views with the same name.
TABLE_TYPE	This column contains a value indicating what type of object the row describes: BASE is the base table; VIEW is the view; GBL TEMP is the global temporary table; and LCL TEMP is the local temporary table.
VIEW_DEF	If the object that the row describes is a table, then this column contains any CHECK constraints for the table. If the object is a view, then this column contains the CREATE VIEW command used to create the view.

Using the SYSTABLE table, you can gather all the definition statements for all the views in the system using a query similar to the following:

```
SELECT TABLE_NAME AS VIEW_NAME, VIEW_DEF AS DEFINITION
    FROM SYSTABLE
WHERE TABLE_TYPE='BASE'
```

MySQL

MySQL does not have a System Catalog. It does come with a separate database to control user access, but, unfortunately, support for the System Catalog architecture is one of the many features that it is lacking.

Summary

This chapter discussed System Catalogs. System Catalogs are various tables or views that are used to query the RDBMS for information pertaining to database objects and operation. The various RDBMS platforms were discussed, and we also looked at a few examples of using System Catalogs to query certain information from the various platforms.

You should now have a good understanding of System Catalog tables and views, as well as what different kinds of information can be obtained from them. These catalog tables are often the basis for many of the graphical user interfaces (GUIs) that are available for the different RDBMS implementations. By having a better understanding of the underlying implementations of the catalog tables and views, you can create your own interfaces and system-monitoring tools. For a complete listing of the various types of data that the catalog tables contain, you should check your vendor documentation.

Built-in Function Cross-Reference Table

The following table is a compilation of the various built-in functions available on the platforms discussed throughout this book. It is meant to provide you with a quick cross-reference for the various functions and their implementations on the various platforms. In looking over the table, keep the following legend in mind to locate the information you need.

❑ *Y*—This indicates that the function is implemented on the platform. The column names provide the chapter number in parentheses where information can be found on the function within that implementation.

❑ *[BLANK]*—This indicates that the function is not implemented on this particular platform.

❑ *E (#)*—This indicates that the function has an equivalent implementation on the platform. The "#" indicates which function ID number in the table relates to the equivalent function.

Function #	Function Name	ANSI (5)	Oracle (6)	IBM DB2 (7)	SQL Server (8)	Sybase (9)	MySQL (10)	Post-greSQL (11)
1	@@BOOTTIME					Y		
2	@@CLIENT_CSID					Y		
3	@@CLIENT_CSNAME					Y		
4	@@CONNECTION(S)				Y	Y		
5	@@CPU_BUSY				Y	Y		
6	@@ERROR				Y	Y		

Table continued on following page

Function #	Function Name	ANSI (5)	Oracle (6)	IBM DB2 (7)	SQL Server (8)	Sybase (9)	MySQL (10)	PostgreSQL (11)
7	@@ERRORLOG					Y		
8	@@IDENTITY				Y	Y		
9	@@IDLE				Y	Y		
10	@@IO_BUSY				Y	Y		
11	@@LANGID				Y	Y		
12	@@LANGUAGE				Y	Y		
13	@@LOCK_TIMEOUT				Y			
14	@@MAX_CHARLEN					Y		
15	@@MAX_CONNECTIONS				Y	Y		
16	@@NCHARSIZE					Y		
17	@@NESTLEVEL				Y	Y		
18	@@OPTIONS				Y	Y		
19	@@PROBESUID					Y		
20	@@ROWCOUNT				Y	Y		
21	@@SPID				Y	Y		
22	@@SQLSTATUS					Y		
23	@@TIMETICKS				Y	Y		
24	@@TOTAL_ERRORS				Y	Y		
25	@@TOTAL_READ				Y	Y		
26	@@TOTAL_WRITE				Y	Y		
27	@@TRANCHAINED					Y		
28	@@TRANCOUNT				Y	Y		
29	@@TRANSTATE					Y		
30	@@UNICHARSIZE					Y		
31	@@VERSION				Y	Y		
32	@@VERSION_AS_INTEGER					Y		
33	ABS	Y	Y	Y	Y	Y	Y	Y

Func-tion #	Function Name	ANSI (5)	Oracle (6)	IBM DB2 (7)	SQL Server (8)	Sybase (9)	MySQL (10)	Post-greSQL (11)
34	ACOS	Y	Y	Y	Y	Y	Y	Y
35	ADD_MONTHS		Y					
36	AGE							Y
37	AREA							Y
38	ASCII	Y	Y	Y	Y	Y	Y	Y
39	ASIN	Y	Y	Y	Y	Y	Y	Y
40	ATAN	Y	Y	Y	Y	Y	Y	Y
41	ATAN2	Y	Y	Y	E (42)	E (42)	Y	Y
42	ATN2	E (41)	E (41)	E (41)	Y	Y	E (41)	E (41)
43	AVG	Y	Y	Y	Y	Y	Y	Y
44	BENCHMARK						Y	
45	BIN						Y	
46	BIT_AND		Y				Y	
47	BIT_COUNT						Y	
48	BIT_LENGTH						Y	Y
49	BIT_OR						Y	
50	BOX_INTERSECT							Y
51	BTRIM							Y
52	CAST		Y					
53	CBRT							Y
54	CEIL	Y	Y	Y	Y	Y	Y	Y
55	CEILING	E (54)	Y	E (54)	E (54)	Y	Y	E (54)
56	CENTER							Y
57	CHAR	E (60)	E (60)	E (60)	Y	Y	Y	E (60)
58	CHARINDEX				Y	Y		
59	CHAR_LENGTH	Y				Y	Y	Y
60	CHR	Y	Y	Y	E (57)	E (57)	E (57)	Y
61	COALESCE	Y	Y	Y	Y	Y	Y	Y

Table continued on following page

Func-tion #	Function Name	ANSI (5)	Oracle (6)	IBM DB2 (7)	SQL Server (8)	Sybase (9)	MySQL (10)	Post-greSQL (11)
62	COL_LENGTH				Y	Y		
63	COL_NAME					Y		
64	COMPARE					Y		
65	COMPOSE		Y					
66	COMPRESS						Y	
67	CONCAT	Y	Y	Y	Y	Y	Y	Y
68	CONCAT_WS						Y	
69	CONNECTION_ID						Y	
70	CONV						Y	
71	CONVERT		Y			Y		Y
72	CORR		Y					
73	COS	Y	Y	Y	Y	Y	Y	Y
74	COSH	Y	Y	Y				
75	COT	Y		Y	Y	Y	Y	Y
76	COUNT	Y	Y	Y	Y	Y	Y	Y
77	CURDATE						Y	
78	CURRENT_ DATABASE							Y
79	CURRENT_DATE			Y				Y
80	CURRENT_ DEFAULT_ TRANSFORM_ GROUP			Y				
81	CURRENT DEGREE			Y				
82	CURRENT EXPLAIN MODE			Y				
83	CURRENT EXPLAIN SNAPSHOT			Y				
84	CURRENT NODE			Y				
85	CURRENT PATH			Y				

Func- tion #	Function Name	ANSI (5)	Oracle (6)	IBM DB2 (7)	SQL Server (8)	Sybase (9)	MySQL (10)	Post- greSQL (11)
86	CURRENT QUERY OPTIMIZATION			Y				
87	CURRENT SCHEMA			Y				
88	CURRENT_ SCHEMA							Y
89	CURRENT_ SCHEMAS							Y
90	CURRENT SERVER			Y				
91	CURRENT TIME			Y				
92	CURRENT_TIME							Y
93	CURRENT TIMESTAMP			Y				
94	CURRENT TIMEZONE			Y				
95	CURRENT_USER							Y
96	CURTIME						Y	
97	DATABASE						Y	
98	DATALENGTH				Y	Y		
99	DATE			Y				
100	DATEADD				Y	Y		
101	DATE_ADD						Y	
102	DATEDIFF				Y	Y		
103	DATE_FORMAT						Y	
104	DATENAME				Y			
105	DATEPART				Y	Y		
106	DATE_PART							Y
107	DATE_SUB						Y	
108	DATE_TRUNC							Y

Table continued on following page

Function #	Function Name	ANSI (5)	Oracle (6)	IBM DB2 (7)	SQL Server (8)	Sybase (9)	MySQL (10)	PostgreSQL (11)
109	DAY			Y	Y			
110	DAYNAME			Y		Y	Y	
111	DAYOFMONTH						Y	
112	DAYOFWEEK			Y				
113	DAYOFWEEK_ISO			Y				
114	DAYOFYEAR			Y			Y	
115	DAYS			Y				
116	DB_ID				Y	Y		
117	DB_NAME				Y	Y		
118	DBTIMEZONE		Y					
119	DEC			Y				
120	DECODE		Y					Y
121	DECOMPOSE		Y					
122	DECRYPT_BIN			Y				
123	DECRYPT_CHAR			Y				
124	DEGREES	Y		Y	Y	Y	Y	Y
125	DIAMETER							Y
126	DIFFERENCE				Y	Y		
127	DIGITS			Y				
128	DOUBLE			Y				
129	DUMP		Y					
130	ELT						Y	
131	ENCODE							Y
132	ENCRYPT			Y				
133	EXP	Y	Y	Y	Y	Y	Y	Y
134	EXTRACT		Y					Y
135	FIELD						Y	
136	FILE_ID				Y			
137	FILE_NAME				Y			

Func-tion #	Function Name	ANSI (5)	Oracle (6)	IBM DB2 (7)	SQL Server (8)	Sybase (9)	MySQL (10)	Post-greSQL (11)
138	FLOOR	Y	Y	Y	Y	Y	Y	Y
139	FN_VIRTUAL FILESTATS				Y			
140	FORMAT						Y	
141	FROM_DAYS						Y	
142	FROM_UNIXTIME						Y	
143	GENERATE_ UNIQUE			Y				
144	GETDATE				Y	Y		
145	GETHINT			Y				
146	GETUTCDATE				Y			
147	GREATEST		Y				Y	
148	GROUPING		Y					
149	HEIGHT							Y
150	HEX			Y			Y	
151	HEXTOINT					Y		
152	HOUR			Y			Y	
153	INITCAP		Y					Y
154	INSERT			Y			Y	
155	INSTR						Y	
156	INT			Y				
157	INTERVAL						Y	
158	INTTOHEX					Y		
159	ISCLOSED							Y
160	ISFINITE							Y
161	ISNULL						Y	
162	ISOPEN							Y
163	IS_SEC_ SERVICE					Y		

Table continued on following page

Func-tion #	Function Name	ANSI (5)	Oracle (6)	IBM DB2 (7)	SQL Server (8)	Sybase (9)	MySQL (10)	Post-greSQL (11)
164	JULIAN_DAY			Y				
165	LCASE	Y	E (178)	Y	E (178)	E (178)	Y	E (178)
166	LEAST						Y	
167	LEFT			Y	Y	Y		
168	LEN	Y	E (169)	E (169)	Y	Y	E (169)	E (169)
169	LENGTH	Y	Y	Y	E (168)	E (168)	E (59)	E (59)
170	LN	Y	Y	E (175)	E (175)	E (175)	Y	Y
171	LOAD_FILE						Y	
172	LOCALTIME							Y
173	LOCALTIME STAMP							Y
174	LOCATE			Y			Y	
175	LOG	Y	Y				Y	Y
176	LOG2	Y					Y	
177	LOG10	Y		Y	Y	Y	Y	
178	LOWER	Y	Y	E (165)	Y	Y	E (165)	Y
179	LPAD		Y				Y	Y
180	LTRIM		Y	Y	Y	Y	Y	Y
181	MAKE_SET						Y	
182	MAX	Y	Y	Y	Y	Y	Y	Y
183	MD5							Y
184	MICROSECONDS			Y				
185	MIDNIGHT_ SECONDS			Y				
186	MIN	Y	Y	Y	Y	Y	Y	Y
187	MINUTE			Y			Y	
188	MOD	Y	Y	Y	'%'	'%'	Y	Y
189	MONTH			Y	Y		Y	
190	MONTHNAME			Y			Y	

Func-tion #	Function Name	ANSI (5)	Oracle (6)	IBM DB2 (7)	SQL Server (8)	Sybase (9)	MySQL (10)	Post-greSQL (11)
191	MONTHS_BETWEEN		Y					
192	NCHAR				Y			
193	NEW_TIME		Y					
194	NOW						Y	Y
195	NPOINTS							Y
196	NULLIF	Y	Y	Y	Y	Y	Y	Y
197	NVL		Y					
198	NVL2		Y					
199	OBJECT_ID					Y		
200	OBJECT_NAME					Y		
201	OCT						Y	
202	OCTET_LENGTH							Y
203	ORD						Y	
204	OVERLAY							Y
205	PATINDEX					Y		
206	PCLOSE							Y
207	PERIOD_ADD						Y	
208	PERIOD_DIFF						Y	
209	PI	Y			Y	Y	Y	Y
210	POPEN							Y
211	POSITION							Y
212	POSSTR			Y				
213	POWER	Y	Y	Y	Y	Y	Y	POW
214	QUOTE_INDENT							Y
215	QUOTE_LITERAL							Y
216	QUOTENAME				Y			
217	RADIANS	Y		Y	Y	Y	Y	Y

Table continued on following page

Func-tion #	Function Name	ANSI (5)	Oracle (6)	IBM DB2 (7)	SQL Server (8)	Sybase (9)	MySQL (10)	Post-greSQL (11)
218	RADIUS							Y
219	RAND or RANDOM	Y	Y	Y	Y	Y	Y	Y
220	REPEAT			Y			Y	Y
221	REPLACE	Y	Y	Y	Y	STR_REPLACE	Y	Y
222	REPLICATE				Y	Y		
223	REVERSE				Y	Y	Y	
224	RIGHT			Y	Y	Y	Y	
225	ROUND	Y	Y	Y	Y	Y	Y	Y
226	RPAD		Y				Y	Y
227	RTRIM		Y	Y	Y	Y	Y	Y
228	SECOND			Y			Y	
229	SEC_TO_TIME						Y	
230	SESSION TIMEZONE		Y					
231	SESSION_USER							Y
232	SETSEED							Y
233	SHOW_SEC_ SERVICES					Y		
234	SIGN	Y	Y	Y	Y	Y	Y	Y
235	SIN	Y				Y	Y	Y
236	SINH	Y	Y	Y				Y
237	SMALLINT			Y				
238	SORTKEY					Y		
239	SOUNDEX		Y	Y	Y	Y	Y	
240	SPACE			Y	Y	Y		
241	SQRT	Y	Y	Y	Y	Y	Y	Y
242	SQUARE	Y			Y	Y		

Function #	Function Name	ANSI (5)	Oracle (6)	IBM DB2 (7)	SQL Server (8)	Sybase (9)	MySQL (10)	Post-greSQL (11)
243	STDDEV		Y				Y	Y
244	STR				Y	Y		
245	STUFF				Y	Y		
246	SUBSTR			Y				
247	SUBSTRING				Y	Y	Y	Y
248	SUBSTRING_ INDEX						Y	
249	SUM	Y	Y	Y	Y	Y	Y	Y
250	SUSER_ID					Y		
251	SUSER_NAME					Y		
252	SYSDATE		Y				Y	
253	TABLE_NAME			Y				
254	TAN	Y	Y	Y	Y	Y	Y	Y
255	TANH	Y	Y	Y				
256	TEXTPTR					Y		
257	TEXTVALID					Y		
258	TIME			Y				
259	TIME_FORMAT						Y	
260	TIMEOFDAY							Y
261	TIMESTAMP			Y				
262	TIMESTAMPDIFF			Y				
263	TIMESTAMP_ FORMAT			Y				
264	TIMESTAMP_ISO			Y				
265	TIME_TO_SEC						Y	
266	TO_CHAR		Y					
267	TO_DAYS						Y	
268	TRANSLATE		Y	Y				
269	TRIM		Y				Y	Y

Table continued on following page

Func-tion #	Function Name	ANSI (5)	Oracle (6)	IBM DB2 (7)	SQL Server (8)	Sybase (9)	MySQL (10)	Post-greSQL (11)
270	TRUNC	Y	Y	Y			E (271)	Y
271	TRUNCATE	Y	E (270)	Y			Y	E (270)
272	TSEQUAL					Y		
273	TYPE_ID			Y				
274	TYPE_NAME			Y				
275	UCASE	E (281)	E (281)	Y	E (281)	E (281)	Y	E (281)
276	UID		Y					
277	UNCOMPRESS						Y	
278	UNICODE				Y			
279	UNISTR		Y					
280	UNIX_TIMESTAMP						Y	
281	UPPER	Y	Y	E (275)	Y	Y	E (275)	Y
282	USCALAR					Y		
283	USER			Y		Y		Y
284	USER_ID					Y		
285	USER_NAME					Y		
286	VALID_NAME					Y		
287	VALID_USER					Y		
288	VALUE			Y				
289	VARCHAR			Y				
290	VARIANCE						Y	
291	VERSION						Y	
292	VSIZE		Y					
293	WEEK			Y				
294	WEEK_ISO			Y				
295	WIDTH						Y	
296	YEAR			Y	Y			

ANSI and Vendor Keywords

This appendix is provided for the convenience of the programmer in the identification of reserved words across the major SQL implementations. It is helpful to have a quick reference to key words to ensure that SQL names such as table names, column names, and variable names do not conflict with reserved words. The coverage in this appendix includes ANSI SQL, Oracle, DB2, SQL Server, MySQL, Sybase, and PostgreSQL (in that order).

ANSI SQL Keywords

The following table lists keywords for ANSI SQL 1992 (SQL2), ANSI SQL 1999 (SQL3), and ANSI SQL 2003.

ANSI SQL 1992 Keywords (SQL2)	ANSI SQL 1999 Keywords (SQL3)	ANSI SQL 2003 Keywords
ABSOLUTE	ABSOLUTE	
ACTION	ACTION	
ADD	ADD	ADD
	AFTER	
ALL	ALL	ALL
ALLOCATE	ALLOCATE	ALLOCATE
ALTER	ALTER	ALTER
AND	AND	AND
ANY	ANY	ANY
ARE	ARE	ARE
	ARRAY	ARRAY

ANSI SQL 1992 Keywords (SQL2)	ANSI SQL 1999 Keywords (SQL3)	ANSI SQL 2003 Keywords
AS	AS	AS
ASC	ASC	
	ASENSITIVE	ASENSITIVE
ASSERTION	ASSERTION	
	ASYMMETRIC	ASYMMETRIC
AT	AT	AT
	ATOMIC	ATOMIC
AUTHORIZATION	AUTHORIZATION	AUTHORIZATION
AVG		
	BEFORE	
BEGIN	BEGIN	BEGIN
BETWEEN	BETWEEN	BETWEEN
		BIGINT
	BINARY	BINARY
BIT	BIT	
BIT_LENGTH		
	BLOB	BLOB
	BOOLEAN	BOOLEAN
BOTH	BOTH	BOTH
	BREADTH	
BY	BY	BY
CALL	CALL	CALL
	CALLED	CALLED
CASCADE	CASCADE	
CASCADED	CASCADED	CASCADED
CASE	CASE	CASE
CAST	CAST	CAST
CATALOG	CATALOG	
CHAR	CHAR	CHAR
CHARACTER	CHARACTER	CHARACTER

ANSI SQL 1992 Keywords (SQL2)	ANSI SQL 1999 Keywords (SQL3)	ANSI SQL 2003 Keywords
CHARACTER_LENGTH		
CHAR_LENGTH		
CHECK	CHECK	CHECK
	CLOB	CLOB
CLOSE	CLOSE	CLOSE
COALESCE		
COLLATE	COLLATE	COLLATE
COLLATION	COLLATION	
COLUMN	COLUMN	COLUMN
COMMIT	COMMIT	COMMIT
CONDITION	CONDITION	CONDITION
CONNECT	CONNECT	CONNECT
CONNECTION	CONNECTION	
CONSTRAINT	CONSTRAINT	CONSTRAINT
CONSTRAINTS	CONSTRAINTS	
	CONSTRUCTOR	
CONTAINS		
CONTINUE	CONTINUE	CONTINUE
CONVERT		
CORRESPONDING	CORRESPONDING	CORRESPONDING
COUNT		
CREATE	CREATE	CREATE
CROSS	CROSS	CROSS
	CUBE	CUBE
CURRENT	CURRENT	CURRENT
CURRENT_DATE	CURRENT_DATE	CURRENT_DATE
CURRENT_PATH	CURRENT_PATH	CURRENT_PATH
	CURRENT_ROLE	CURRENT_ROLE
CURRENT_TIME	CURRENT_TIME	CURRENT_TIME
CURRENT_TIMESTAMP	CURRENT_TIMESTAMP	CURRENT_TIMESTAMP

Table continued on following page

ANSI SQL 1992 Keywords (SQL2)	ANSI SQL 1999 Keywords (SQL3)	ANSI SQL 2003 Keywords
CURRENT_USER	CURRENT_USER	CURRENT_USER
CURSOR	CURSOR	CURSOR
	CYCLE	CYCLE
	DATA	
DATE	DATE	DATE
DAY	DAY	DAY
DEALLOCATE	DEALLOCATE	DEALLOCATE
DEC	DEC	DEC
DECIMAL	DECIMAL	DECIMAL
DECLARE	DECLARE	DECLARE
DEFAULT	DEFAULT	DEFAULT
DEFERRABLE	DEFERRABLE	
DEFERRED	DEFERRED	
DELETE	DELETE	DELETE
	DEPTH	
	DEREF	DEREF
DESC	DESC	
DESCRIBE	DESCRIBE	DESCRIBE
DESCRIPTOR	DESCRIPTOR	
DETERMINISTIC	DETERMINISTIC	DETERMINISTIC
DIAGNOSTICS	DIAGNOSTICS	
DISCONNECT	DISCONNECT	DISCONNECT
DISTINCT	DISTINCT	DISTINCT
DO	DO	DO
DOMAIN	DOMAIN	
DOUBLE	DOUBLE	DOUBLE
DROP	DROP	DROP
	DYNAMIC	DYNAMIC
	EACH	EACH
		ELEMENT

ANSI SQL 1992 Keywords (SQL2)	ANSI SQL 1999 Keywords (SQL3)	ANSI SQL 2003 Keywords
ELSE	ELSE	ELSE
ELSEIF	ELSEIF	ELSEIF
END	END	END
	EQUALS	
ESCAPE	ESCAPE	ESCAPE
EXCEPT	EXCEPT	EXCEPT
EXCEPTION	EXCEPTION	
EXEC	EXEC	EXEC
EXECUTE	EXECUTE	EXECUTE
EXISTS	EXISTS	EXISTS
EXIT	EXIT	EXIT
EXTERNAL	EXTERNAL	EXTERNAL
EXTRACT		
FALSE	FALSE	FALSE
FETCH	FETCH	FETCH
	FILTER	FILTER
FIRST	FIRST	
FLOAT	FLOAT	FLOAT
FOR	FOR	FOR
FOREIGN	FOREIGN	FOREIGN
FOUND	FOUND	
	FREE	FREE
FROM	FROM	FROM
FULL	FULL	FULL
FUNCTION	FUNCTION	FUNCTION
	GENERAL	
GET	GET	GET
GLOBAL	GLOBAL	GLOBAL
GO	GO	
GOTO	GOTO	

Table continued on following page

673

ANSI SQL 1992 Keywords (SQL2)	ANSI SQL 1999 Keywords (SQL3)	ANSI SQL 2003 Keywords
GRANT	GRANT	GRANT
GROUP	GROUP	GROUP
	GROUPING	GROUPING
HANDLER	HANDLER	HANDLER
HAVING	HAVING	HAVING
	HOLD	HOLD
HOUR	HOUR	HOUR
IDENTITY	IDENTITY	IDENTITY
IF	IF	IF
IMMEDIATE	IMMEDIATE	IMMEDIATE
IN	IN	IN
INDICATOR	INDICATOR	INDICATOR
INITIALLY	INITIALLY	
INNER	INNER	INNER
INOUT	INOUT	INOUT
INPUT	INPUT	INPUT
INSENSITIVE	INSENSITIVE	INSENSITIVE
INSERT	INSERT	INSERT
INT	INT	INT
INTEGER	INTEGER	INTEGER
INTERSECT	INTERSECT	INTERSECT
INTERVAL	INTERVAL	INTERVAL
INTO	INTO	INTO
IS	IS	IS
ISOLATION	ISOLATION	
	ITERATE	ITERATE
JOIN	JOIN	JOIN
KEY	KEY	
LANGUAGE	LANGUAGE	LANGUAGE
	LARGE	LARGE

ANSI SQL 1992 Keywords (SQL2)	ANSI SQL 1999 Keywords (SQL3)	ANSI SQL 2003 Keywords
LAST	LAST	
	LATERAL	LATERAL
LEADING	LEADING	LEADING
LEAVE	LEAVE	LEAVE
LEFT	LEFT	LEFT
LEVEL	LEVEL	
LIKE	LIKE	LIKE
LOCAL	LOCAL	LOCAL
	LOCALTIME	LOCALTIME
	LOCALTIMESTAMP	LOCALTIMESTAMP
	LOCATOR	
LOOP	LOOP	LOOP
LOWER		
	MAP	
MATCH	MATCH	MATCH
MAX		
		MEMBER
		MERGE
	METHOD	METHOD
MIN		
MINUTE	MINUTE	MINUTE
	MODIFIES	MODIFIES
MODULE	MODULE	MODULE
MONTH	MONTH	MONTH
		MULTISET
NAMES	NAMES	
NATIONAL	NATIONAL	NATIONAL
NATURAL	NATURAL	NATURAL
NCHAR	NCHAR	NCHAR
	NCLOB	NCLOB

Table continued on following page

ANSI SQL 1992 Keywords (SQL2)	ANSI SQL 1999 Keywords (SQL3)	ANSI SQL 2003 Keywords
	NEW	NEW
NEXT	NEXT	
NO	NO	NO
	NONE	NONE
NOT	NOT	NOT
NULL	NULL	NULL
NULLIF		
NUMERIC	NUMERIC	NUMERIC
	OBJECT	
OCTET_LENGTH		
OF	OF	OF
	OLD	OLD
ON	ON	ON
ONLY	ONLY	ONLY
OPEN	OPEN	OPEN
OPTION	OPTION	
OR	OR	OR
ORDER	ORDER	ORDER
	ORDINALITY	
OUT	OUT	OUT
OUTER	OUTER	OUTER
OUTPUT	OUTPUT	OUTPUT
	OVER	OVER
OVERLAPS	OVERLAPS	OVERLAPS
PAD	PAD	
PARAMETER	PARAMETER	PARAMETER
PARTIAL	PARTIAL	
	PARTITION	PARTITION
PATH	PATH	
POSITION		

ANSI SQL 1992 Keywords (SQL2)	ANSI SQL 1999 Keywords (SQL3)	ANSI SQL 2003 Keywords
PRECISION	PRECISION	PRECISION
PREPARE	PREPARE	PREPARE
PRESERVE	PRESERVE	
PRIMARY	PRIMARY	PRIMARY
PRIOR	PRIOR	
PRIVILEGES	PRIVILEGES	
PROCEDURE	PROCEDURE	PROCEDURE
PUBLIC	PUBLIC	
	RANGE	RANGE
READ	READ	
	READS	READS
REAL	REAL	REAL
	RECURSIVE	RECURSIVE
	REF	REF
REFERENCES	REFERENCES	REFERENCES
	REFERENCING	REFERENCING
RELATIVE	RELATIVE	
	RELEASE	RELEASE
REPEAT	REPEAT	REPEAT
RESIGNAL	RESIGNAL	RESIGNAL
RESTRICT	RESTRICT	
	RESULT	RESULT
RETURN	RETURN	RETURN
RETURNS	RETURNS	RETURNS
REVOKE	REVOKE	REVOKE
RIGHT	RIGHT	RIGHT
	ROLE	
ROLLBACK	ROLLBACK	ROLLBACK
	ROLLUP	ROLLUP
ROUTINE	ROUTINE	

Table continued on following page

ANSI SQL 1992 Keywords (SQL2)	ANSI SQL 1999 Keywords (SQL3)	ANSI SQL 2003 Keywords
	ROW	ROW
ROWS	ROWS	ROWS
	SAVEPOINT	SAVEPOINT
SCHEMA	SCHEMA	
	SCOPE	SCOPE
SCROLL	SCROLL	SCROLL
	SEARCH	SEARCH
SECOND	SECOND	SECOND
SECTION	SECTION	
SELECT	SELECT	SELECT
	SENSITIVE	SENSITIVE
SESSION	SESSION	
SESSION_USER	SESSION_USER	SESSION_USER
SET	SET	SET
	SETS	
SIGNAL	SIGNAL	SIGNAL
	SIMILAR	SIMILAR
SIZE	SIZE	
SMALLINT	SMALLINT	SMALLINT
SOME	SOME	SOME
SPACE	SPACE	
SPECIFIC	SPECIFIC	SPECIFIC
	SPECIFICTYPE	SPECIFICTYPE
SQL	SQL	SQL
SQLCODE		
SQLERROR		
SQLEXCEPTION	SQLEXCEPTION	SQLEXCEPTION
SQLSTATE	SQLSTATE	SQLSTATE
SQLWARNING	SQLWARNING	SQLWARNING
	START	START

ANSI SQL 1992 Keywords (SQL2)	ANSI SQL 1999 Keywords (SQL3)	ANSI SQL 2003 Keywords
	STATE	
	STATIC	STATIC
		SUBMULTISET
SUBSTRING		
SUM		
	SYMMETRIC	SYMMETRIC
	SYSTEM	SYSTEM
SYSTEM_USER	SYSTEM_USER	SYSTEM_USER
TABLE	TABLE	TABLE
		TABLESAMPLE
TEMPORARY	TEMPORARY	
THEN	THEN	THEN
TIME	TIME	TIME
TIMESTAMP	TIMESTAMP	TIMESTAMP
TIMEZONE_HOUR	TIMEZONE_HOUR	TIMEZONE_HOUR
TIMEZONE_MINUTE	TIMEZONE_MINUTE	TIMEZONE_MINUTE
TO	TO	TO
TRAILING	TRAILING	TRAILING
TRANSACTION	TRANSACTION	
TRANSLATE		
TRANSLATION	TRANSLATION	TRANSLATION
	TREAT	TREAT
	TRIGGER	TRIGGER
TRIM		
TRUE	TRUE	TRUE
	UNDER	
UNDO	UNDO	UNDO
UNION	UNION	UNION
UNIQUE	UNIQUE	UNIQUE
UNKNOWN	UNKNOWN	UNKNOWN

Table continued on following page

ANSI SQL 1992 Keywords (SQL2)	ANSI SQL 1999 Keywords (SQL3)	ANSI SQL 2003 Keywords
	UNNEST	UNNEST
UNTIL	UNTIL	UNTIL
UPDATE	UPDATE	UPDATE
UPPER		
USAGE	USAGE	
USER	USER	USER
USING	USING	USING
VALUE	VALUE	VALUE
VALUES	VALUES	VALUES
VARCHAR	VARCHAR	VARCHAR
VARYING	VARYING	VARYING
VIEW	VIEW	
WHEN	WHEN	WHEN
WHENEVER	WHENEVER	WHENEVER
WHERE	WHERE	WHERE
WHILE	WHILE	WHILE
	WINDOW	WINDOW
WITH	WITH	WITH
	WITHIN	WITHIN
	WITHOUT	WITHOUT
WORK	WORK	
WRITE	WRITE	
YEAR	YEAR	YEAR
ZONE	ZONE	

Oracle Keywords

This section covers Oracle and includes keywords for both Oracle 9i and Oracle 10g. Although Oracle 10g is the latest release, many Oracle 9i installations still exist.

Oracle 9i Reserved Words and Keywords

The following table lists Oracle 9i reserved words and keywords.

ACCESS	ELSE	MLSLABEL	ROWS
ADD	EXCLUSIVE	MODE	SELECT
ALL	EXISTS	MODIFY	SESSION
ALTER	FILE	NOAUDIT	SET
AND	FLOAT	NOCOMPRESS	SHARE
ANY	FOR	NOT	SIZE
AS	FROM	NOWAIT	SMALLINT
ASC	GRANT	NULL	START
AUDIT	GROUP	NUMBER	SUCCESSFUL
BETWEEN	HAVING	OF	SYNONYM
BY	IDENTIFIED	OFFLINE	SYSDATE
CHAR	IMMEDIATE	ON	TABLE
CHECK	IN	ONLINE	THEN
CLUSTER	INCREMENT	OPTION	TO
COLUMN	INDEX	OR	TRIGGER
COMMENT	INITIAL	ORDER	UID
COMPRESS	INSERT	PCTFREE	UNION
CONNECT	INTEGER	PRIOR	UNIQUE
CREATE	INTERSECT	PRIVILEGES	UPDATE
CURRENT	INTO	PUBLIC	USER
DATE	IS	RAW	VALIDATE
DECIMAL	LEVEL	RENAME	VALUES
DEFAULT	LIKE	RESOURCE	VARCHAR
DELETE	LOCK	REVOKE	VARCHAR2
DESC	LONG	ROW	VIEW
DISTINCT	MAXEXTENTS	ROWID	WHENEVER
DROP	MINUS	ROWNUM	WHERE

Oracle 10g Reserved Words and Keywords

The following table lists Oracle 10g reserved words and keywords.

ACCESS	EXCLUSIVE	MODIFY	SET
ADD	EXISTS	NOAUDIT	SHARE
ALL	FILE	NOCOMPRESS	SIZE
ALTER	FLOAT	NOT	SMALLINT
AND	FOR	NOWAIT	START
ANY	FROM	NULL	SUCCESSFUL
AS	GRANT	NUMBER	SYNONYM
ASC	GROUP	OF	SYSDATE
AUDIT	HAVING	OFFLINE	TABLE
BETWEEN	IDENTIFIED	ON	THEN
BY	IMMEDIATE	ONLINE	TO
CHAR	IN	OPTION	TRIGGER
CHECK	INCREMENT	OR	UID
CLUSTER	INDEX	ORDER	UNION
COLUMN	INITIAL	PCTFREE	UNIQUE
COMMENT	INSERT	PRIOR	UPDATE
COMPRESS	INTEGER	PRIVILEGES	USER
CONNECT	INTERSECT	PUBLIC	VALIDATE
CREATE	INTO	RAW	VALUES
CURRENT	IS	RENAME	VARCHAR
DATE	LEVEL	RESOURCE	VARCHAR2
DECIMAL	LIKE	REVOKE	VIEW
DEFAULT	LOCK	ROW	WHENEVER
DELETE	LONG	ROWID	WHERE
DESC	MAXEXTENTS	ROWNUM	WITH
DISTINCT	MINUS	ROWS	
DROP	MLSLABEL	SELECT	
ELSE	MODE	SESSION	

DB2 Reserved Words and Keywords

The following table lists DB2 reserved words and keywords.

ACQUIRE	CURRENT_ TIMESTAMP	GOTO	NULLS	SECOND
ADD	CURRENT_ TIMEZONE	GRANT	NUMPARTS	SECONDS
AFTER	CURRENT_USER	GRAPHIC	OBID	SECQTY
ALIAS	CURSOR	GROUP	OF	SECURITY
ALL	DATA	HANDLER	ON	SELECT
ALLOCATE	DATABASE	HAVING	ONLY	SENSITIVE
ALLOW	DATE	HOUR	OPEN	SET
ALTER	DAY	HOURS	OPTIMIZATION	SHARE
AND	DAYS	IDENTIFIED	OPTIMIZE	SIMPLE
ANY	DB2GENERAL	IF	OPTION	SOME
APPLICATION	DB2SQL	IMMEDIATE	OR	SOURCE
AS	DBA	IN	ORDER	SPECIFIC
ASC	DBINFO	INDEX	OUT	SQL
ASSOCIATE	DBSPACE	INDICATOR	OUTER	STANDARD
ASUTIME	DECLARE	INNER	PACKAGE	STATIC
AUDIT	DEFAULT	INOUT	PAGE	STATISTICS
AUTHORI ZATION	DELETE	INSENSITIVE	PAGES	STAY
AUX	DESC	INSERT	PARAMETER	STOGROUP
AUXILIARY	DESCRIPTOR	INTEGRITY	PART	STORES
AVG	DETERMINISTIC	INTERSECT	PARTITION	STORPOOL
BEFORE	DISALLOW	INTO	PATH	STYLE
BEGIN	DISCONNECT	IS	PCTFREE	SUBPAGES
BETWEEN	DISTINCT	ISOBID	PCTINDEX	SUBSTRING
BINARY	DO	ISOLATION	PIECESIZE	SUM
BUFFERPOOL	DOUBLE	JAVA	PLAN	SYNONYM
BY	DROP	JOIN	POSITION	TABLE
CACHE	DSSIZE	KEY	PRECISION	TABLESPACE

Table continued on following page

CALL	DYNAMIC	LABEL	PREPARE	THEN
CALLED	EDITPROC	LANGUAGE	PRIMARY	TO
CAPTURE	ELSE	LC_CTYPE	PRIQTY	TRANSACTION
CASCADED	ELSEIF	LEAVE	PRIVATE	TRIGGER
CASE	ENCODING	LEFT	PRIVILEGES	TRIM
CAST	END	LIKE	PROCEDURE	TYPE
CCSID	END-EXEC	LINKTYPE	PROGRAM	UNDO
CHAR	ERASE	LOCAL	PSID	UNION
CHARACTER	ESCAPE	LOCALE	PUBLIC	UNIQUE
CHECK	EXCEPT	LOCATOR	QUERYNO	UNTIL
CLOSE	EXCEPTION	LOCATORS	READ	UPDATE
CLUSTER	EXCLUDING	LOCK	READS	USAGE
COLLECTION	EXCLUSIVE	LOCKMAX	RECOVERY	USER
COLLID	EXECUTE	LOCKSIZE	REFERENCES	USING
COLUMN	EXISTS	LONG	RELEASE	VALIDPROC
COMMENT	EXIT	LOOP	RENAME	VALUES
COMMIT	EXPLAIN	MAX	REPEAT	VARIABLE
CONCAT	EXTERNAL	MICROSECOND	RESET	VARIANT
CONDITION	FENCED	MICROSECONDS	RESOURCE	VCAT
CONNECT	FETCH	MIN	RESTART	VIEW
CONNECTION	FIELDPROC	MINUTE	RESTRICT	VOLUMES
CONSTRAINT	FILE	MINUTES	RESULT	WHEN
CONTAINS	FINAL	MODE	RETURN	WHERE
CONTINUE	FOR	MODIFIES	RETURNS	WHILE
COUNT	FOREIGN	MONTH	REVOKE	WITH
COUNT_BIG	FREE	MONTHS	RIGHT	WLM
CREATE	FROM	NAME	ROLLBACK	WORK
CROSS	FULL	NAMED	ROW	WRITE
CURRENT	FUNCTION	NHEADER	ROWS	YEAR
CURRENT_DATE	GENERAL	NO	RRN	YEARS

CURRENT_LC_ PATH	GENERATED	NODENAME	RUN
CURRENT_ PATH	GET	NODENUMBER	SCHEDULE
CURRENT_ SERVER	GLOBAL	NOT	SCHEMA
CURRENT_ TIME	GO	NULL	SCRATCHPAD

SQL Server Reserved Words

This section covers the SQL Server and is organized into two subsections containing reserved words for SQL Server 2000 and SQL Server ODBC.

SQL Server 2000 Reserved Words

The following table lists SQL Server 2000 reserved words.

ADD	DELETE	IS	RETURN
ALL	DENY	JOIN	REVOKE
ALTER	DESC	KEY	RIGHT
AND	DISK	KILL	ROLLBACK
ANY	DISTINCT	LEFT	ROWCOUNT
AS	DISTRIBUTED	LIKE	ROWGUIDCOL
ASC	DOUBLE	LINENO	RULE
AUTHORIZATION	DROP	LOAD	SAVE
BACKUP	DUMMY	NATIONAL	SCHEMA
BEGIN	DUMP	NOCHECK	SELECT
BETWEEN	ELSE	NONCLUSTERED	SESSION_USER
BREAK	END	NOT	SET
BROWSE	ERRLVL	NULL	SETUSER
BULK	ESCAPE	NULLIF	SHUTDOWN
BY	EXCEPT	OF	SOME
CASCADE	EXEC	OFF	STATISTICS
CASE	EXECUTE	OFFSETS	SYSTEM_USER

Table continued on following page

CHECK	EXISTS	ON	TABLE
CHECKPOINT	EXIT	OPEN	TEXTSIZE
CLOSE	FETCH	OPENDATASOURCE	THEN
CLUSTERED	FILE	OPENQUERY	TO
COALESCE	FILLFACTOR	OPENROWSET	TOP
COLLATE	FOR	OPENXML	TRAN
COLUMN	FOREIGN	OPTION	TRANSACTION
COMMIT	FREETEXT	OR	TRIGGER
COMPUTE	FREETEXTTABLE	ORDER	TRUNCATE
CONSTRAINT	FROM	OUTER	TSEQUAL
CONTAINS	FULL	OVER	UNION
CONTAINSTABLE	FUNCTION	PERCENT	UNIQUE
CONTINUE	GOTO	PLAN	UPDATE
CONVERT	GRANT	PRECISION	UPDATETEXT
CREATE	GROUP	PRIMARY	USE
CROSS	HAVING	PRINT	USER
CURRENT	HOLDLOCK	PROC	VALUES
CURRENT_DATE	IDENTITY	PROCEDURE	VARYING
CURRENT_TIME	IDENTITYCOL	PUBLIC	VIEW
CURRENT_TIMESTAMP	IDENTITY_INSERT	RAISERROR	WAITFOR
CURRENT_USER	IF	READ	WHEN
CURSOR	IN	READTEXT	WHERE
DATABASE	INDEX	RECONFIGURE	WHILE
DBCC	INNER	REFERENCES	WITH
DEALLOCATE	INSERT	REPLICATION	WRITETEXT
DECLARE	INTERSECT	RESTORE	
DEFAULT	INTO	RESTRICT	

SQL Server ODBC Reserved Words

The following table lists SQL Server ODBC reserved words.

ABSOLUTE	DECLARE	IS	ROLLBACK
ACTION	DEFAULT	ISOLATION	ROWS

ADA	DEFERRABLE	JOIN	SCHEMA
ADD	DEFERRED	KEY	SCROLL
ALL	DELETE	LANGUAGE	SECOND
ALLOCATE	DESC	LAST	SECTION
ALTER	DESCRIBE	LEADING	SELECT
AND	DESCRIPTOR	LEFT	SESSION
ANY	DIAGNOSTICS	LEVEL *	SESSION_USER
ARE	DISCONNECT	LIKE	SET
AS	DISTINCT	LOCAL	SIZE
ASC	DOMAIN	LOWER	SMALLINT
ASSERTION	DOUBLE	MATCH	SOME
AT	DROP	MAX	SPACE
AUTHORIZATION	ELSE	MIN	SQL
AVG	END	MINUTE	SQLCA
BEGIN	END-EXEC	MODULE	SQLCODE
BETWEEN	ESCAPE	MONTH	SQLERROR
BIT	EXCEPT	NAMES	SQLSTATE
BIT_LENGTH	EXCEPTION	NATIONAL	SQLWARNING
BOTH	EXEC	NATURAL	SUBSTRING
BY	EXECUTE	NCHAR	SUM
CASCADE	EXISTS	NEXT	SYSTEM_USER
CASCADED	EXTERNAL	NO	TABLE
CASE	EXTRACT	NONE	TEMPORARY
CAST	FALSE	NOT	THEN
CATALOG	FETCH	NULL	TIME
CHAR	FIRST	NULLIF	TIMESTAMP
CHARACTER	FLOAT	NUMERIC	TIMEZONE_HOUR
CHARACTER_LENGTH	FOR	OCTET_LENGTH	TIMEZONE_MINUTE
CHAR_LENGTH	FOREIGN	OF	TO
CHECK	FORTRAN	ON	TRAILING

Table continued on following page

687

CLOSE	FOUND	ONLY	TRANSACTION
COALESCE	FROM	OPEN	TRANSLATE
COLLATE	FULL	OPTION	TRANSLATION
COLLATION	GET	OR	TRIM
COLUMN	GLOBAL	ORDER	TRUE
COMMIT	GO	OUTER	UNION
CONNECT	GOTO	OUTPUT	UNIQUE
CONNECTION	GRANT	OVERLAPS	UNKNOWN
CONSTRAINT	GROUP	PAD	UPDATE
CONSTRAINTS	HAVING	PARTIAL	UPPER
CONTINUE	HOUR	PASCAL	USAGE
CONVERT	IDENTITY	POSITION	USER
CORRESPONDING	IMMEDIATE	PRECISION	USING
COUNT	IN	PREPARE	VALUE
CREATE	INCLUDE	PRESERVE	VALUES
CROSS	INDEX	PRIMARY	VARCHAR
CURRENT	INDICATOR	PRIOR	VARYING
CURRENT_DATE	INITIALLY	PRIVILEGES	VIEW
CURRENT_TIME	INNER	PROCEDURE	WHEN
CURRENT_TIMESTAMP	INPUT	PUBLIC	WHENEVER
CURRENT_USER	INSENSITIVE	READ	WHERE
CURSOR	INSERT	REAL	WITH
DATE	INT	REFERENCES	WORK
DAY	INTEGER	RELATIVE	WRITE
DEALLOCATE	INTERSECT	RESTRICT	YEAR
DEC	INTERVAL	REVOKE	ZONE
DECIMAL	INTO	RIGHT	

* LEVEL is no longer a reserved word.

MySQL Reserved Words and Keywords

The following table lists MySQL reserved words and keywords.

ALL	DELIMITER	LONGFILE	SQLID
AND	DUPLICATES	MESSAGE	SQLMODE
ANSI	EBCDIC	NOT	STAMP
APPEND	EUR	NULL	START
ASCII	EXTRACT CATALOG	NUMBER	SYSDATE
AUTOCOMMIT	EXTRACT DATA	OFF	TABLE
BINARY	EXTRACT DB	ON	TABLEEXTRACT
BOOLEAN	EXTRACT TABLE	OR	TABLELOAD
BY	FASTLOAD	ORACLE	TABLEUNLOAD
CATALOG	FILE	ORDER	TABLEUPDATE
CATALOGEXTRACT	FOR	OTHERWISE	TAPE
CATALOGLOAD	FORMATTED	OUTFILE	TERMCHARSET
CHAR	HEX	OUTFIELDS	TIME
CODESET	HILO	OUTSTREAM	TIMESTAMP
CODETYPE	IF	PACKAGE	TRUNC
COMPRESS	IGNORE	PAGES	UID
CONFIGURATION	INFILE	PIPE	UPDATE
COUNT	INSTALLATION	POS	UPDATE DATA
CURRENT	INSTREAM	REAL	UPDATE TABLE
DATA	INTEGER	RECORDS	USA
DATAEXTRACT	INTERNAL	REJECT	USAGE
DATALOAD	ISO	RELEASE	USE
DATAUPDATE	JIS	RESTART	USER
DATE	KEY	ROUND	USERGROUP
DB2	LANGUAGE	ROWS	USERKEY
DBEXTRACT	LOAD CATALOG	SCALE	VERSION
DBLOAD	LOAD DATA	SEPARATOR	WITH
DEC	LOAD DB	SEQNO	ZONED
DECIMAL	LOAD TABLE	SERVERDB	
DEFAULT	LOHI	SET	

Sybase Reserved Words and Keywords

The following table lists Sybase 12.5 reserved words and keywords.

ADD	END	MIN	RETURN
ALL	ENDTRAN	MIRROR	RETURNS
ALTER	ERRLVL	MIRROREXIT	REVOKE
AND	ERRORDATA	MODIFY	ROLE
ANY	ERROREXIT	NATIONAL	ROLLBACK
ARITH_OVERFLOW	ESCAPE	NEW	ROWCOUNT
AS	EXCEPT	NOHOLDLOCK	ROWS
ASC	EXCLUSIVE	NONCLUSTERED	RULE
AT	EXEC	NOT	SAVE
AUTHORIZATION	EXECUTE	NULL	SCHEMA
AVG	EXISTS	NULLIF	SELECT
BEGIN	EXIT	NUMERIC_TRUNCATION	SET
BETWEEN	EXP_ROW_SIZE	OF	SETUSER
BREAK	EXTERNAL	OFF	SHARED
BROWSE	FETCH	OFFSETS	SHUTDOWN
BULK	FILLFACTOR	ON	SOME
BY	FOR	ONCE	STATISTICS
CASCADE	FOREIGN	ONLINE	STRINGSIZE
CASE	FROM	ONLY	STRIPE
CHAR_CONVERT	FUNC	OPEN	SUM
CHECK	FUNCTION	OPTION	SYB_IDENTITY
CHECKPOINT	GOTO	OR	SYB_RESTREE
CLOSE	GRANT	ORDER	SYB_TERMINATE
CLUSTERED	GROUP	OUT	TABLE
COALESCE	HAVING	OUTPUT	TEMP
COMMIT	HOLDLOCK	OVER	TEMPORARY
COMPUTE	IDENTITY	PARTITION	TEXTSIZE
CONFIRM	IDENTITY_GAP	PERM	TO
CONNECT	IDENTITY_INSERT	PERMANENT	TRAN

CONSTRAINT	IDENTITY_START	PLAN	TRANSACTION
CONTINUE	IF	PRECISION	TRIGGER
CONTROLROW	IN	PREPARE	TRUNCATE
CONVERT	INDEX	PRIMARY	TSEQUAL
COUNT	INOUT	PRINT	UNION
CREATE	INSERT	PRIVILEGES	UNIQUE
CURRENT	INSTALL	PROC	UNPARTITION
CURSOR	INTERSECT	PROCEDURE	UPDATE
DATABASE	INTO	PROCESSEXIT	USE
DBCC	IS	PROXY_TABLE	USER
DEALLOCATE	ISOLATION	PUBLIC	USER_OPTION
DECLARE	JAR	QUIESCE	USING
DEFAULT	JOIN	RAISERROR	VALUES
DELETE	KEY	READ	VARYING
DESC	KILL	READPAST	VIEW
DETERMINISTIC	LEVEL	READTEXT	WAITFOR
DISK DISTINCT	LIKE	RECONFIGURE	WHEN
DOUBLE	LINENO	REFERENCES REMOVE	WHERE
DROP	LOAD	REORG	WHILE
DUMMY	LOCK	REPLACE	WITH
DUMP	MAX	REPLICATION	WORK
ELSE	MAX_ROWS_PER_PAGE	RESERVEPAGEGAP	WRITETEXT

PostgreSQL Reserved Words and Keywords

The following table lists PostgreSQL reserved words and keywords.

ABORT	DESC	MATCH	ROW
ABSOLUTE	DISTINCT	MAXVALUE	RULE
ACCESS	DO	MINUTE	SCHEMA
ACTION	DOUBLE	MINVALUE	SCROLL
ADD	DROP	MODE	SECOND

Table continued on following page

AFTER	EACH	MONTH	SELECT
AGGREGATE	ELSE	MOVE	SEQUENCE
ALL	ENCODING	NAMES	SERIAL
ALTER	END	NATIONAL	SERIALIZABLE
ANALYZE	EXCEPT	NATURAL	SESSION
AND	EXCLUSIVE	NCHAR	SESSION_USER
ANY	EXECUTE	NEW	SET
AS	EXISTS	NEXT	SETOF
ASC	EXPLAIN	NO	SHARE
AT	EXTEND	NOCREATEDB	SHOW
BACKWARD	EXTRACT	NOCREATEUSER	SOME
BEFORE	FALSE	NONE	START
BEGIN	FETCH	NOT	STATEMENT
BETWEEN	FLOAT	NOTHING	STDIN
BINARY	FOR	NOTIFY	STDOUT
BIT	FORCE	NOTNULL	SUBSTRING
BOTH	FOREIGN	NULL	SYSID
BY	FORWARD	NULLIF	TABLE
CACHE	FROM	NUMERIC	TEMP
CASCADE	FULL	OF	TEMPLATE
CASE	FUNCTION	OFF	TEMPORARY
CAST	GLOBAL	OFFSET	THEN
CHAR	GRANT	OIDS	TIME
CHARACTER	GROUP	OLD	TIMESTAMP
CHECK	HANDLER	ON	TIMEZONE_HOUR
CLOSE	HAVING	ONLY	TIMEZONE_MINUTE
CLUSTER	HOUR	OPERATOR	TO
COALESCE	IMMEDIATE	OPTION	TOAST
COLLATE	IN	OR	TRAILING
COLUMN	INCREMENT	ORDER	TRANSACTION
COMMENT	INDEX	OUTER	TRIGGER
COMMIT	INHERITS	OVERLAPS	TRIM

COMMITTED	INITIALLY	OWNER	TRUE
CONSTRAINT	INNER	PARTIAL	TRUSTED
CONSTRAINTS	INSENSITIVE	PASSWORD	TYPE
COPY	INSERT	PATH	UNION
CREATE	INSTEAD	PENDANT	UNIQUE
CREATEDB	INTERSECT	POSITION	UNLISTEN
CREATEUSER	INTERVAL	PRECISION	UNTIL
CROSS	INTO	PRIMARY	UPDATE
CURRENT	IS	PRIOR	USER
CURRENT_DATE	ISNULL	PRIVILEGES	USING
CURRENT_TIME	ISOLATION	PROCEDURAL	VACUUM
CURRENT_TIMESTAMP	JOIN	PROCEDURE	VALID
CURRENT_USER	KEY	PUBLIC	VALUES
CURSOR	LANCOMPILER	READ	VARCHAR
CYCLE	LANGUAGE	RECIPE	VARYING
DATABASE	LEADING	REFERENCES	VERBOSE
DAY	LEFT	REINDEX	VERSION
DEC	LEVEL	RELATIVE	VIEW
DECIMAL	LIKE	RENAME	WHEN
DECLARE	LIMIT	RESET	WHERE
DEFAULT	LISTEN	RESTRICT	WITH
DEFERRABLE	LOAD	RETURNS	WITHOUT
DEFERRED	LOCAL	REVOKE	WORK
DELETE	LOCATION	RIGHT	YEAR
DELIMITERS	LOCK	ROLLBACK	ZONE

C

ANSI and Vendor Data Types

This appendix provides a reference of ANSI and vendor-specific data types. ANSI data types are guidelines for vendors offering SQL implementations and represent different types of data that can be stored in a SQL database. Vendor-specific data types allow the SQL programmer to define data that is stored in specific implementations. The vendor implementations covered in this appendix are the same as those covered throughout the book (Oracle, IBM DB2 UDB, SQL Server, Sybase, MySQL, and PostgreSQL).

ANSI SQL Data Types

The following table lists ANSI SQL data types.

BINARY LARGE OBJECT	CHARACTER VARYING	INTERVAL	SMALLINT
BIT	DATE	NATIONAL CHARACTER	TIME
BIT VARYING	DECIMAL	NATIONAL CHARACTER LARGE OBJECT	TIMESTAMP
BOOLEAN	DOUBLE PRECISION	NATIONAL CHARACTER VARYING	TIMESTAMP WITH TIME ZONE
CHARACTER	FLOAT	NUMERIC	TIME WITH TIME ZONE
CHARACTER LARGE OBJECT	INTEGER	REAL	

Oracle 9i Data Types

The following table lists Oracle 9i data types.

BFILE	INTERVAL DAY TO SECOND	NCLOB	TIMESTAMP
BLOB	INTERVAL YEAR TO MONTH	NUMBER	TIMESTAMP WITH LOCAL TIME ZONE
CHAR	LONG	NVARCHAR2	TIMESTAMP WITH TIME ZONE
CLOB	LONG RAW	RAW	UROWID
DATE	NCHAR	ROWID	VARCHAR2

Oracle 10g Data Types

The following table lists Oracle 10g data types.

BFILE	DOUBLE PRECISION	NATIONAL	ROWID
BINARY_DOUBLE	FLOAT	NCHAR	TIMESTAMP
BINARY_FLOAT	INTEGER	NCLOB	TIMESTAMP WITH LOCAL TIME ZONE
BLOB	INTERVAL DAY TO SECOND	NUMBER	TIMESTAMP WITH TIME ZONE
CHAR	INTERVAL YEAR TO MONTH	NVARCHAR2	UROWID
CLOB	LONG	RAW	VARCHAR2
DATE	LONG RAW	REAL	

IBM DB2 Data Types

The following table lists IBM DB2 data types.

BIGINT	DBCLOB	LONG GRAPHIC	SMALLINT
BLOB	DECIMAL	LONG VARCHAR	TIME
CHAR	DOUBLE	LONG VARCHAR FOR BIT DATA	TIMESTAMP
CHAR FOR BIT DATA	FLOAT	NUMERIC	VARCHAR
CLOB	GRAPHIC	REAL	VARCHAR FOR BIT DATA
DATE	INTEGER	ROWID	VARGRAPHIC

SQL Server Data Types

The following table lists SQL Server data types.

BIGINT	FLOAT	NVARCHAR	TEXT
BINARY	IMAGE	REAL	TIMESTAMP
BIT	INT	SMALLDATETIME	TINYINT
CHAR	MONEY	SMALLINT	UNIQUEIDENTIFIER
CURSOR	NCHAR	SMALLMONEY	VARBINARY
DATETIME	NTEXT	SQL_VARIANT	VARCHAR
DECIMAL	NUMERIC	TABLE	

Sybase Data Types

The following table lists Sybase data types.

BINARY	IDENTITY	RAWOBJECT IN ROW	TIMESTAMP
BIT	IMAGE	REAL	TINYINT
CHAR	INT	RS_ADDRESS	UNICHAR
DATE	MONEY	SMALLDATETIME	UNIVARCHAR
DATETIME	NCHAR	SMALLINT	VARBINARY
DECIMAL	NUMERIC	SMALLMONEY	VARCHAR
DOUBLE PRECISION	NVARCHAR	TEXT	
FLOAT	RAWOBJECT	TIME	

MySQL Data Types

The following table lists MySQL data types.

BIGINT	FLOAT	MEDIUMTEXT	TIMESTAMP
BLOB	INT	NUMERIC	TINYBLOB
CHAR	INT UNSIGNED	REAL	TINYINT
DATE	LONGBLOB	SET	TINYINT UNSIGNED
DATETIME	LONGTEXT	SMALLINT	TINYTEXT

Table continued on following page

DECIMAL	MEDIUMBLOB	SMALLINT UNSIGNED	VARCHAR
DOUBLE	MEDIUMINT	TEXT	YEAR
ENUM	MEDIUMINT UNSIGNED	TIME	

PostgreSQL Data Types

The following table lists PostgreSQL data types.

BIGINT	FLOAT	LINE	SERIAL
BIT	FLOAT4	LSEG	SMALLINT
BOOL	FLOAT8	MACADDR	TEXT
BOX	INET	MONEY	TIME
CHARACTER	INT	NUMERIC	TIME WITH TIME ZONE
CIDR	INT2	OID	TIMESTAMP
CIRCLE	INT4	PATH	VARBIT
DATE	INT8	POINT	VARCHAR
DECIMAL	INTEGER	POLYGON	XID
DOUBLE PRECISION	INTERVAL	REAL	

Database Permissions by Vendor

This appendix lists database permissions for the vendor SQL implementations covered in this book. Permissions allow the SQL database user to perform certain actions within the scope of the database (such as creating tables, dropping tables, creating users, and granting users access to your tables). Depending on the implementation, database permissions are also referred to as *privileges*. There are two very basic types of permissions: *system/database level* and *object level*. Where applicable, we have separated object permissions from system/database level permission in each vendor section.

Oracle 9i Privileges

The following table lists Oracle 9i privileges.

ADMINISTER DATABASE TRIGGER	CREATE ANY DIRECTORY	CREATE TABLE	DROP TABLESPACE
ALTER ANY CLUSTER	CREATE ANY INDEX	CREATE TABLESPACE	DROP USER
ALTER ANY DIMENSION	CREATE ANY INDEXTYPE	CREATE TRIGGER	EXECUTE ANY INDEXTYPE
ALTER ANY INDEX	CREATE ANY LIBRARY	CREATE TYPE	EXECUTE ANY OPERATOR
ALTER ANY INDEXTYPE	CREATE ANY MATERIALIZED VIEW	CREATE USER	EXECUTE ANY PROCEDURE
ALTER ANY MATERIALIZED VIEW	CREATE ANY OPERATOR	CREATE VIEW	EXECUTE ANY TYPE
ALTER ANY OUTLINE	CREATE ANY OUTLINE	DELETE ANY TABLE	EXEMPT ACCESS POLICY

Table continued on following page

ALTER ANY PROCEDURE	CREATE ANY PROCEDURE	DROP ANY CLUSTER	FORCE ANY TRANSACTION
ALTER ANY ROLE	CREATE ANY SEQUENCE	DROP ANY CONTEXT	FORCE TRANSACTION
ALTER ANY SEQUENCE	CREATE ANY SYNONYM	DROP ANY DIMENSION	GLOBAL QUERY REWRITE
ALTER ANY TABLE	CREATE ANY TABLE	DROP ANY DIRECTORY	GLOBAL QUERY REWRITE
ALTER ANY TRIGGER	CREATE ANY TRIGGER	DROP ANY INDEX	GRANT ANY PRIVILEGE
ALTER ANY TYPE	CREATE ANY TYPE	DROP ANY INDEXTYPE	GRANT ANY ROLE
ALTER DATABASE	CREATE ANY VIEW	DROP ANY LIBRARY	INSERT ANY TABLE
ALTER PROFILE	CREATE CLUSTER	DROP ANY MATERIALIZED VIEW	LOCK ANY TABLE
ALTER RESOURCE COST	CREATE DATABASE LINK	DROP ANY OPERATOR	MANAGE TABLESPACE
ALTER ROLLBACK SEGMENT	CREATE DIMENSION	DROP ANY OUTLINE	ON COMMIT REFRESH
ALTER SESSION	CREATE INDEXTYPE	DROP ANY PROCEDURE	QUERY REWRITE
ALTER SYSTEM	CREATE LIBRARY	DROP ANY ROLE	RESTRICTED SESSION
ALTER TABLESPACE	CREATE MATERIALIZED VIEW	DROP ANY SEQUENCE	RESUMABLE
ALTER USER	CREATE OPERATOR	DROP ANY SYNONYM	SELECT ANY DICTIONARY
ANALYZE ANY	CREATE PROCEDURE	DROP ANY TABLE	SELECT ANY OUTLINE
AUDIT ANY	CREATE PROFILE	DROP ANY TRIGGER	SELECT ANY SEQUENCE
AUDIT SYSTEM	CREATE PUBLIC DATABASE LINK	DROP ANY TYPE	SELECT ANY TABLE
BACKUP ANY TABLE	CREATE PUBLIC SYNONYM	DROP ANY VIEW	SYSDBA
BECOME USER	CREATE ROLE	DROP LIBRARY	SYSOPER
COMMENT ANY TABLE	CREATE ROLLBACK SEGMENT	DROP PROFILE	UNDER ANY TYPE
CREATE ANY CLUSTER	CREATE SEQUENCE	DROP PUBLIC DATABASE LINK	UNDER ANY VIEW
CREATE ANY CONTEXT	CREATE SESSION	DROP PUBLIC SYNONYM	UNLIMITED TABLESPACE
CREATE ANY DIMENSION	CREATE SYNONYM	DROP ROLLBACK SEGMENT	UPDATE ANY TABLE

Oracle 9i Object Privileges

The following table lists Oracle 9i object privileges.

ALTER	READ
DELETE	REFERENCES
EXECUTE	SELECT
INDEX	UNDER
INSERT	UPDATE
ON COMMIT REFRESH	WRITE
QUERY REWRITE	

Oracle 10g Privileges

The following table lists Oracle 10g privileges.

ADMINISTER ANY SQL TUNING SET	EXECUTE ANY PROCEDURE	CREATE USER	EXECUTE ANY LIBRARY
ADMINISTER DATABASE TRIGGER	EXECUTE ANY PROGRAM	CREATE VIEW	EXECUTE ANY OPERATOR
ADMINISTER SQL TUNING SET	EXECUTE ANY RULE	DBA	EXECUTE ANY TYPE
ADVISOR	EXECUTE ANY RULE SET	DEBUG ANY PROCEDURE	EXECUTE_CATALOG_ ROLE
ALTER ANY CLUSTER	CREATE ANY INDEXTYPE	DEBUG CONNECT ANY	EXEMPT ACCESS POLICY
ALTER ANY DIMENSION	CREATE ANY JOB	DEBUG CONNECT SESSION	EXP_FULL_DATABASE
ALTER ANY INDEX	CREATE ANY LIBRARY	DELETE ANY TABLE	FLASHBACK ANY TABLE
ALTER ANY INDEXTYPE	CREATE ANY MATERIALIZED	DELETE_CATALOG_ ROLE	FLASHBACK ANY TABLE
ALTER ANY MATERIALIZED VIEW	CREATE ANY OPERATOR	DROP ANY CLUSTER	FORCE ANY TRANSACTION
ALTER ANY OPERATOR	CREATE ANY OUTLINE	DROP ANY CONTEXT	FORCE TRANSACTION

Table continued on following page

ALTER ANY OUTLINE	CREATE ANY PROCEDURE	DROP ANY DIMENSION	GLOBAL QUERY REWRITE
ALTER ANY PROCEDURE	CREATE ANY SEQUENCE	DROP ANY DIRECTORY	GRANT ANY OBJECT PRIVILEGE
ALTER ANY ROLE PROFILE	CREATE ANY SQL CONTEXT	DROP ANY EVALUATION	GRANT ANY PRIVILEGE
ALTER ANY SEQUENCE	CREATE ANY SYNONYM	DROP ANY INDEX	GRANT ANY ROLE
ALTER ANY SQL PROFILE	CREATE ANY TABLE	DROP ANY INDEXTYPE	IMP_FULL_DATABASE
ALTER ANY TABLE	CREATE ANY TRIGGER	DROP ANY LIBRARY	INSERT ANY TABLE
ALTER ANY TRIGGER	CREATE ANY TYPE	DROP ANY MATERIALIZED VIEW	LOCK ANY TABLE
ALTER ANY TYPE	CREATE ANY VIEW	DROP ANY OPERATOR	MANAGE SCHEDULER
ALTER DATABASE	CREATE CLUSTER	DROP ANY OUTLINE	MANAGE TABLESPACE
ALTER PROFILE	CREATE DATABASE LINK	DROP ANY PROCEDURE	ON COMMIT REFRESH
ALTER RESOURCE COST	CREATE DIMENSION	DROP ANY ROLE	QUERY REWRITE
ALTER ROLLBACK SEGMENT	CREATE INDEXTYPE	DROP ANY RULE	RECOVERY_ CATALOG_OWNER
ALTER SESSION	CREATE JOB	DROP ANY RULE SET	RESOURCE
ALTER SYSTEM	CREATE LIBRARY	DROP ANY SECURITY PROFILE	RESTRICTED SESSION
ALTER TABLESPACE	CREATE MATERIALIZED VIEW	DROP ANY SEQUENCE	RESUMABLE
ALTER USER	CREATE OPERATOR	DROP ANY SQL PROFILE	SELECT ANY DICTIONARY
ANALYZE ANY	CREATE PROCEDURE	DROP ANY SYNONYM	SELECT ANY SEQUENCE
AQ_ADMINISTRATOR_ ROLE	CREATE PROFILE	DROP ANY TABLE	SELECT ANY TABLE
AQ_USER_ROLE	CREATE PUBLIC DATABASE LINK	DROP ANY TRIGGER	SELECT ANY TRANSACTION
AUDIT ANY	CREATE PUBLIC SYNONYM	DROP ANY TYPE	SELECT_CATALOG_ ROLE
AUDIT SYSTEM	CREATE ROLE	DROP ANY VIEW	SNMPAGENT
BACKUP ANY TABLE	CREATE ROLLBACK SEGMENT	DROP PROFILE	SYSDBA

COMMENT ANY TABLE	CREATE SEQUENCE	DROP PUBLIC DATABASE LINK	SYSOPER
CONNECT	CREATE SESSION	DROP PUBLIC SYNONYM	UNDER ANY TYPE
CREATE ANY CLUSTER	CREATE SYNONYM	DROP ROLLBACK SEGMENT	UNDER ANY VIEW
CREATE ANY CONTEXT	CREATE TABLE	DROP TABLESPACE	UNLIMITED TABLESPACE
CREATE ANY DIMENSION	CREATE TABLESPACE	DROP USER	UPDATE ANY TABLE
CREATE ANY DIRECTORY	CREATE TRIGGER	EXECUTE ANY CLASS	
CREATE ANY INDEX	CREATE TYPE	EXECUTE ANY INDEXTYPE	

Oracle 10g Object Privileges

The following table lists Oracle 10g object privileges.

ALTER	QUERY REWRITE
DEBUG	READ
DELETE	REFERENCES
EXECUTE	SELECT
INDEX	UNDER
INSERT	UPDATE
ON COMMIT REFRESH	WRITE

IBM DB2 Database Privileges

The following table lists IBM DB2 database privileges.

BINDADD	IMPLICIT_SCHEMA
CONNECT	LOAD
CREATE_NOT_FENCED	PASSTHRU
CREATETAB	USE

IBM DB2 Privileges

The following table lists IBM DB2 privileges.

ACTIVATE DATABASE	DROP NODE VERIFY	LIST HISTORY	RESTART DATABASE
ADD NODE	ECHO	LIST INDOUBT TRANSACTIONS	RESTORE DATABASE
ATTACH	EXPORT	LIST NODE DIRECTORY	REWIND TAPE
BACKUP DATABASE	FORCE APPLICATION	LIST NODEGROUPS	ROLLFORWARD DATABASE
BIND	GET ADMIN CONFIGURATION	LIST NODES	RUNSTATS
CALL	GET AUTHORIZATIONS	LIST ODBC DATA SOURCES	SET CLIENT
CATALOG APPC NODE	GET CLI CONFIGURATION	LIST PACKAGES/ TABLES	SET RUNTIME DEGREE
CATALOG APPCLU NODE	GET CONNECTION STATE	LIST TABLESPACE CONTAINERS	SET TABLESPACE CONTAINERS
CATALOG APPN NODE	GET DATABASE CONFIGURATION	LIST TABLESPACES	SET TAPE POSITION
CATALOG DATABASE	GET DATABASE MANAGER CONFIGURATION	LOAD	START DATABASE MANAGER
CATALOG DCS DATABASE	GET DATABASE MANAGER MONITOR SWITCHES	LOAD QUERY	STOP DATABASE MANAGER
CATALOG GLOBAL DATABASE	GET INSTANCE	MIGRATE DATABASE	TERMINATE
CATALOG IPX/SPX NODE	GET MONITOR SWITCHES	PRECOMPILE PROGRAM	UNCATALOG DATABASE
CATALOG LDAP MODE	GET SNAPSHOT	PRUNE HISTORY	UNCATALOG DCS DATABASE
CATALOG LOCAL NODE	HELP	QUERY CLIENT	UNCATALOG LDAP DATABASE
CATALOG NAMED PIPE NODE	IMPORT	QUIESCE TABLESPACES FOR TABLE	UNCATALOG LDAP NODE
CATALOG NETBIOS NODE	INITIALIZE TAPE	QUIT	UNCATALOG NODE

CATALOG ODBC DATA SOURCE	INVOKE STORED PROCEDURE	REBIND	UNCATALOG ODBC DATA SOURCE
CATALOG TCP/IP NODE	LIST ACTIVE DATABASES	REDISTRIBUTE NODEGROUP	UPDATE ADMIN CONFIGURATION
CHANGE DATABASE COMMENT	LIST APPLICATIONS	REFRESH LDAP	UPDATE COMMAND OPTIONS
CHANGE ISOLATION LEVEL	LIST BACKUP/ HISTORY	REGISTER	UPDATE DATABASE CONFIGURATION
CREATE DATABASE	LIST COMMAND OPTIONS	REORGANIZE TABLE	UPDATE DATABASE MANAGER CONFIGURATION
DEACTIVATE DATABASE	LIST DATABASE DIRECTORY	REORGCHK	UPDATE LDAP NODE
DEREGISTER	LIST DATABASE MANAGERS	RESET ADMIN CONFIGURATION	UPDATE MONITOR SWITCHES
DESCRIBE	LIST DCS APPLICATIONS	RESET DATABASE CONFIGURATION	UPDATE RECOVERY HISTORY FILE
DETACH	LIST DCS DIRECTORY	RESET DATABASE MANAGER CONFIGURATION	
DROP DATABASE	LIST DRDA INDOUBT TRANSACTIONS	RESET MONITOR	

IBM DB2 Object Privileges

The following table lists IBM DB2 object privileges.

ALTER	DROPIN
ALTERIN	EXECUTE
BIND	INSERT
CONTROL	REFERENCES
CREATEIN	SELECT
DELETE	UPDATE

SQL Server Permissions

The following table lists SQL Server permissions.

ALTER DATABASE	CREATE INDEX	DUMP TRANSACTION	SELECT
ALTER FUNCTION	CREATE PROCEDURE	EXECUTE	SELECT ALL
ALTER PROCEDURE	CREATE RULE	GRANT	SELECT ANY
ALTER TABLE	CREATE TABLE	GRANT on object	SHUTDOWN
ALTER TRIGGER	CREATE TRIGGER	INSERT	TRUNCATE TABLE
ALTER VIEW	CREATE VIEW	KILL	UPDATE
BACKUP	DATABASE	READTEXT	UPDATE ALL
BACKUP DATABASE	DBCC	RECONFIGURE	UPDATE ANY
BACKUP LOG	DELETE	REFERENCES	UPDATE STATISTICS
BULK INSERT	DENY	REFERENCES ALL	UPDATETEXT
CHECKPOINT	DENY on object	REFERENCES ANY	WRITETEXT
CREATE DATABASE	DRI	RESTORE	
CREATE DEFAULT	DROP	REVOKE	
CREATE FUNCTION	DUMP DATABASE	REVOKE on object	

Sybase Permissions

The following table lists Sybase permissions.

ALTER DATABASE	CREATE VIEW	DROP RULE	RECONFIGURE
ALTER ROLE	DBCC	DROP TABLE	REORG
ALTER TABLE	DELETE	DROP TRIGGER	REVOKE
CREATE DATABASE	DELETE STATISTICS	DROP VIEW	ROLLBACK
CREATE DEFAULT	DISK INIT	DUMP DATABASE	ROLLBACK TRIGGER
CREATE EXISTING TABLE	DISK MIRROR	DUMP TRANSACTION	SELECT
CREATE INDEX	DISK REFIT	EXECUTE	SETUSER
CREATE PLAN	DISK REINIT	GRANT	SHUTDOWN
CREATE PROCEDURE	DISK REMIRROR	INSERT	TRUNCATE TABLE

CREATE PROXY TABLE	DISK UNMIRROR	KILL	UPDATE
CREATE ROLE	DROP DATABASE	LOAD DATABASE	USE
CREATE RULE	DROP DEFAULT	LOAD TRANSACTION	WRITETEXT
CREATE SCHEMA	DROP INDEX	LOCK TABLE	
CREATE TABLE	DROP PROCEDURE	ONLINE DATABASE	
CREATE TRIGGER	DROP ROLE	PRINT QUIESCE DATABASE	

MySQL Privileges

The following table lists MySQL privileges.

ALL	DROP DATABASE	INSERT	SHOW DATABASES
ALTER TABLE	DROP FUNCTION	LOCK TABLE	SHOW VIEW
CREATE DATABASE	DROP INDEX	PROCESS	SHUTDOWN
CREATE FUNCTION	DROP TABLE	REFERENCES	SUPER
CREATE INDEX	FILE	RELOAD	UPDATE
CREATE TABLE	GRANT	REPLICATION CLIENT	USAGE
CREATE TEMPORARY TABLE	GRANT OPTION	REPLICATION SLAVE	
DELETE	INDEX	SELECT	

PostgreSQL Privileges

The following table lists PostgreSQL privileges.

ABORT	CREATE CONSTRAINT TRIGGER	DROP CONVERSION	LOAD
ALTER AGGREGATE	CREATE CONVERSION	DROP DATABASE	LOCK
ALTER CONVERSION	CREATE DATABASE	DROP DOMAIN	MOVE
ALTER DATABASE	CREATE DOMAIN	DROP FUNCTION	NOTIFY
ALTER DOMAIN	CREATE FUNCTION	DROP GROUP	PREPARE
ALTER FUNCTION	CREATE GROUP	DROP INDEX	REINDEX
ALTER GROUP	CREATE INDEX	DROP LANGUAGE	RESET

Table continued on following page

ALTER LANGUAGE	CREATE LANGUAGE	DROP OPERATOR	REVOKE
ALTER OPERATOR CLASS	CREATE OPERATOR	DROP OPERATOR CLASS	ROLLBACK
ALTER SCHEMA	CREATE OPERATOR CLASS	DROP RULE	SELECT
ALTER SEQUENCE	CREATE RULE	DROP SCHEMA	SELECT INTO
ALTER TABLE	CREATE SCHEMA	DROP SEQUENCE	SET
ALTER TRIGGER	CREATE SEQUENCE	DROP TABLE	SET CONSTRAINTS
ALTER USER	CREATE TABLE	DROP TRIGGER	SET SESSION AUTHRIZATION
ANALYZE	CREATE TABLE AS	DROP TYPE	SET TRANSACTION
BEGIN	CREATE TRIGGER	DROP USER	SHOW
CHECKPOINT	CREATE TYPE	DROP VIEW	START TRANSACTION
CLOSE	CREATE USER	END	TRUNCATE
CLUSTER	CREATE VIEW	EXECUTE	UNLISTEN
COMMENT	DEALLOCATE	EXPLAIN	UPDATE
COMMIT	DECLARE	FETCH	VACUUM
COPY	DELETE	GRANT	
CREATE AGGREGATE	DROP AGGREGATE	INSERT	
CREATE CAST	DROP CAST	LISTEN	

PostgreSQL Object Privileges

The following table lists PostgreSQL object privileges.

ALL PRIVILEGES	RULE
CREATE	SELECT
DELETE	TEMPORAR
EXECUTE	TRIGGER
INSERT	UPDATE
REFERENCES	USAGE

ODBC and Stored Procedures and Functions

Stored procedures and functions can be called from languages and frameworks using ODBC. Similar to a stored function, a *stored procedure* is a program stored inside the database that is used to process data. Whereas a function returns a single value to the programmer, a stored procedure can be used to carry out a more complex set of instructions to process data within the database. The Microsoft Oracle Managed Provider is such a framework; it provides efficient communication with Oracle databases. Visual Basic .NET will be used to demonstrate communicating with an Oracle database using the Microsoft Oracle Managed Provider.

In the following example, a stored procedure call retrieves employee information.

1. Import the `OracleClient` object.

```
Imports System.Data.OracleClient
```

2. Declare an `OracleConnection` connection object.

```
Dim Conn As New OracleConnection("Server=acme:database:1521;
Uid=test;Pwd=1234")
```

3. Open the connection.

```
Conn.open()
```

4. Declare an `OracleCommand` object.

```
Dim query As New OracleCommand()
```

5. Customize the `OracleCommand` object. Necessary values are shown.

```
query.Connection = Conn
query.CommandType = CommandType.StoredProcedure
query.CommandText = "ACME_Employee.retrieve_employee_data"
```

6. Register in and out parameters. In this example, the in parameter is a number, n_section. The out parameter is a cursor, o_cursor.

```
query.Parameters.Add(New OracleParameter("n_section", OracleType.Number)).Value = 3
query.Parameters.Add(New OracleParameter("o_cursor", OracleType.Cursor)).Direction
= ParameterDirection.Output
```

7. Declare an OracleDataAdapter object based on the OracleCommand.

```
Dim ODA As New OracleDataAdapter(query)
```

8. Declare a DataSet object.

```
Dim EmpDataSet As New DataSet
```

9. Fill the DataSet using the OracleDataAdapter (error-handling code is omitted).

```
ODA.Fill(EmpDataSet)
```

10. Close the connection.

```
Conn.Close()
```

It is important that the programmer close the Connection object when it is no longer needed. If the Connection object is not closed, it will tie up valuable database resources.

JDBC and Stored Procedures/Functions

Using JDBC it is a simple task to call a stored procedure. The difficulty in making this scenario work may lie on the database side, depending on the database in use. MS SQL Server and Sybase both allow stored procedures to return data from stored procedures via a SELECT statement. Oracle, however, does not provide this convenience. With Oracle, cursors must be used. Regardless, to the Java programmer, all of these databases work the same.

In the following example, a simple user validation is performed by calling an Oracle stored procedure. This example can be extended to any JDBC-compliant database by switching JDBC drivers and changing the connection URL.

Following are the steps used in retrieving data using JDBC (error-handling code is omitted):

1. Register database driver. For pure Java JDBC drivers (Type 4), make sure the driver's JAR file is in the classpath.

```
Import oracle.jdbc.driver.*; // at top of class
Class.forName("oracle.jdbc.driver.OracleDriver"); // in class
```

2. Create a connection to the database.

```
String url = "jdbc:oracle:thin:@192.168.0.1:1521:database";
String user = "test";
String pass = "1234";
Connection conn = DriverManager.getConnection(url,user,pass);
```

3. Create a statement that will call the stored procedure.

```
String query = "{ call ? := getValidUser(?,?) }";
CallableStatement st = conn.prepareCall(query);
```

4. Register all data types in the statement. Every question mark in the statement represents a data type. The statement in Step 3 contains three data types to register.

```
st.registerOutParameter(1,OracleTypes.CURSOR); // data object
st.setString(2,user); // in parameter 1, username
st.setString(3,pass); // in parameter 2, password
```

5. Call the procedure.

```
St.execute();
```

6. Store any results in a ResultSet (if applicable). Note the cast from Object to ResultSet. The Oracle cursor data type maps to a generic Java Object type. The exact Object type must be specified by casting.

```
ResultSet rs = (ResultSet)st.getObject(1);
```

7. Close the Statement and Connection.

```
st.close();
conn.close();
```

8. Process any results (if applicable).

```
while (rs.next()) {
  if (rs.getInt(1) == 1)
  validUser = true;
}
```

9. Close the ResultSet.

```
rs.close();
```

It is important that the Java programmer not forget to close the necessary three objects when working with JDBC. The Statement, ResultSet, and Connection should all be closed when they are no longer needed. If not properly closed, these objects will tie up valuable database resources.

Glossary

Ad hoc query — A specialized query that is outside the scope of the current implementation of standardized reports.

Aggregate function — A function that performs a computation on a set of values rather than on a single value.

American National Standards Institute (ANSI) — A voluntary organization that creates standards for the computer industry (among others).

Analytic function — A function that returns a set of values, rather than a single value.

Analytical processing database architecture — A database model that is optimized for direct queries of the data to analyze the contents.

ANSI SQL:1989 (SQL 89) — The ANSI SQL standard implemented in 1989.

ANSI SQL:1992 (SQL 92) — The ANSI SQL standard implemented in 1992.

ANSI SQL:1999 (SQL 99) — The ANSI SQL standard implemented in 1999.

ANSI SQL — The accepted standard for Structured Query Language (SQL) that software vendors use as a guide when developing database software.

Array — A series of objects, all of which are the same size and type.

Back end (code generator) — The part of the compiler that translates the source code into object code.

BLOB — A large object data type used to store binary data up to 4 GB.

Boolean — Data type introduced in the SQL 99 standard that takes a true or false value.

Business Intelligence (BI) — The tools and systems that help analyze company data to better plan strategic policy.

By reference — When passing parameters to a function, the actual variable containing the passed value is made available to the function.

By value — When passing parameters to a function, a copy of the passed value is provided to the function.

Character function — A function that is applied to character data types.

Classification — Grouping together things that share common attributes and/or characteristics.

Clauses — Statements in SQL commands that specify additional information other than the base command.

CLOB — A large object data type used to store variable-length character data.

Code block — A logically distinct piece of code.

Code generation optimization — A new feature in Oracle 10g that allows the compiler to see the entire procedure execution and find shortcuts to optimize execution.

Column function — A function that acts on a "vertical" set of values.

Conference on Data Systems and Languages (CODASYL) — An organization founded in 1959 that developed programming languages, including COBOL.

Compiled module — One of the stored procedures and functions of an RDBMS. See also *Relational Database Management System (RDBMS)*.

Configuration function — A function that returns information about the current configuration of the RDBMS server, and state of the processes. See also *Relational Database Management System (RDBMS)*.

Control structures — A feature of third-generation programming languages (3GLs). See also *Third-generation language (3GL)*.

Conversion function — A function that assists in conversion between data types.

Cursor function — A function that returns information about the CURSOR state.

Cursors — A feature of third-generation programming languages (3GLs). See also *Third-generation language (3GL)*.

Custom data types — A feature of third generation programming languages (3GLs). See also *Third-generation language (3GL)*.

Data dictionary — The file that contains a list of all files in the database, the number of records in each file, and the names and types of each field.

Data-heavy — An application process that returns large result sets.

Data Manipulation Language (DML) — The set of statements used to store, retrieve, modify, and erase data from a database.

Data migration process — The process of moving data from one database to another.

Data scrubbing — The filtering of individual data columns on their way to the data warehouse. See also *Data warehouse*.

Data warehouse — Data that is presented in an easy-to-understand manner.

Data type conversion function — A function that converts one data type to another data type.

Date and time function — A function that performs operations on date and time values.

DBCLOB — A large object data type used to store variable-length character data.

Debugee session — The session that sets breakpoints, query variables, and so on, to debug code.

Debugger session — The session that runs the PL/SQL code to debug it.

Declarative language — A language that specifies what must done without stating how it should be accomplished.

Declarative programming — A combination of functional and relational programming.

Deterministic function — A function that returns exactly the same result every time it is called with the exactly the same set of arguments.

Direct — Allows direct implementation of SQL in the RDBMS instance. See also *Relational Database Management System (RDBMS)*.

Dynamic SQL — Embedded SQL that allows the program to build the query and pass it directly to the RDBMS. See also *Relational Database Management System (RDBMS)*.

E/R schema — One structure of a data warehouse.

Embedded — Placing SQL statements within a program separate from the RDBMS instance. See also *Relational Database Management System (RDBMS)*.

Embedded functions — Functions written in a 3GL that uses embedded SQL (ESQL). See also *Third-generation language (3GL)*.

Encapsulation — A variable declared within a code block that is accessible only within that block.

Fourth-generation language (4GL) — A high-level programming language that has a human language–like syntax, such as SQL and other modern database languages. See also *Third-generation language (3GL)*.

IBM DB2 UDB — IBM Corporation's RDBMS software. See also *Relational Database Management System (RDBMS)*.

INSERT — One Data Manipulation Language (DML) keyword used to insert data into a table. See also *Data Manipulation Language (DML)*.

Glossary

International Standards Organization (ISO) — The international organization that aids in defining computer standards across member standards bodies.

Java Database Connectivity (JDBC) — Application program interface (API) used with the Java programming language that provides cross-DBMS connectivity to a wide range of SQL databases.

Lazy developer — A DBA who uses advanced administrative features such as task automation to make his or her job easier.

Levels of compliance (entry, intermediate, and full) — Three levels (entry, intermediate, and full) of compliance with an ANSI SQL standard that a database company can claim about its version of database software.

Mathematical function — A function that performs mathematical calculations on input parameters and returns a numeric result.

Metadata function — A function that supplies information about various database objects (such as tables, columns, and so on).

Microsoft SQL Server — Microsoft Corporation's RDBMS software. See also *Relational Database Management System (RDBMS)*.

Miscellaneous function — A function that, not fitting neatly into any of the other categories, has a unique classification.

Module — The component used to make calls from procedures within programs, and return a value to the calling program.

MySQL — One of the most popular versions of an Open Source RDBMS. See also *Relational Database Management System (RDBMS)*.

MySQLGUI — MySQL's graphical SQL client.

Network functions — Functions that perform calculations and transformations of network-related data.

Niladic — A function that takes no arguments.

Non-deterministic function — A function that may return different results any time it is called, even with exactly the same set of arguments.

Numeric — A category of ANSI SQL data types that includes all data types that deal with numbers.

Numeric function — A function that accepts numeric arguments and returns numeric results.

Object reference function — A function that manipulates object data types.

Open Database Connectivity (ODBC) — Protocol that abstracts the database from its physical location and makes it available over a network connection.

Oracle — Oracle Corporation's RDBMS software. See also *Relational Database Management System (RDBMS)*.

Oracle Call Interface (OCI) — Oracle's application program interface.

Outer joins — New in SQL 92, the ability to gather information from a join process even if no matching data is present.

PostgreSQL — A popular Open Source RDBMS. See also *Relational Database Management System (RDBMS)*.

Precompiler — An application that separates SQL statements from the base programming implementation, compiles them, and binds them to the RDBMS. See also *Relational Database Management System (RDBMS)*.

Procedural language — A language that emphasizes how a task is to be done.

Project creep — Describes when a project grows beyond its initial scope because boundaries were never clearly defined.

Pull — Method of reporting where the user actively makes a request for a report that is fulfilled at that time.

Push — Method of reporting involving sending reports to user base without an active request from the user.

Query analyzer — Microsoft's SQL Server's SQL client.

Relational data model — The data model that abstracts the logical implementation of the data from the physical implementation, and provides a declarative interface.

Relational Database Management System (RDBMS) — The general term for any system that allows for remote database management and administration.

Reporting — The process of allowing the user base to gain access to the information contained within the database implementation.

Rowset function — A function that returns an object (a virtual table) that could be used in a SQL query's FROM clause. Similar to a table function.

Scalar function — A function that is applied to each and every row returned by a query.

Scope — The characteristics and limitations of the project that must be accomplished.

Security function — A function that returns information about security arrangement within the system.

SELECT — One Data Manipulation Language (DML) keyword used to query and return data from a table. See also *Data Manipulation Language (DML)*.

Sequence manipulation function — A function that manipulates sequences and returns information about past, present, or future values of the sequence.

SQL implementation — The version of SQL used in the RDBMS. See also *Relational Database Management System (RDBMS)*.

SQL station — An integrated development environment.

Glossary

SQL:2003 — The ANSI SQL standard implemented in 2003.

SQL client — The feature of most SQL implementations that allows for issuing SQL commands.

SQLJ — The dialect used to create Java functions and procedures.

SQL-PLUS — One of Oracle Corporation's SQL client implementations.

SQLPlus Worksheet — One of Oracle Corporation's SQL client implementations.

SQL Server — The general term for the server running the RDBMS. See also *Relational Database Management System (RDBMS)*.

Standardized reports — Reports that try to capture the basic essentials of the business environment in which the particular RDBMS works. See also *Relational Database Management System (RDBMS)*.

State schema — One structure of a data warehouse.

Static SQL — Embedded SQL with a predetermined pattern with which to access the database.

String — A category of ANSI SQL data types that includes all data types that deal with characters.

String functions — Functions that perform operations on string data types.

Strongly typed variables — A feature of third-generation programming languages (3GL). See also *Third-generation language (3GL)*.

Structured Query Language (SQL) — A standardized language used to interact with database systems.

Stub — A SQL wrapper for a Java static method.

Subquery — A query within a query.

Subscription — Method of reporting in which the user decides which reports are needed and subscribes (via an active request) to receive the reports on a scheduled basis.

Sybase Adaptive Server Enterprise (SASE) — Sybase Incorporated's RDBMS software. See also *Relational Database Management System (RDBMS)*.

System function — A function that returns information about values, objects, or system settings within the RDBMS server. See also *Relational Database Management System (RDBMS)*.

System resources — Hardware allocations such as disk space and memory that the database relies on to function optimally.

System statistical function — A function that returns statistical information about the system.

Table function — A function that returns data in the form of a table that can be used by in the FROM clause of a query.

Text and image functions — Functions that perform operations on text or image data type input parameters and return results that contain information about these.

Third-generation language (3GL) — High-level programming language between assembly languages and fourth-generation programming languages. See also *Fourth-generation language (4GL)*.

TOAD — An integrated development environment created by Quest.

TOP N — Analysis used to return the first *n* number of rows from a query.

Transaction heavy — An application process that has many calls to the database.

Transactional database architecture — Database model built to process INSERT, UPDATE, and DELETE statements.

Unary system functions — Argumentless (niladic) functions.

Undocumented functions — Functions that are not currently supported by an RDBMS. See also *Relational Database Management System (RDBMS)*.

Unfenced mode — Running a procedure in the same memory space as the database engine.

User-defined function (UDF) — A function that is created and defined by the user, not already packaged with the product.

User-defined type (UDT) — A subset of a system data type that has been defined by the user.

View — A virtual table created within a database that is defined by a query and contains the data of that query.

Index

P

package, function

Microsoft SQL Server, 25

Oracle, 424, 428, 437–438, 446

overloading package prerequisite, 440

referencing, 438

Sybase, 25

UDF, 424, 428, 437–438, 446

`@@PACKET_ERRORS` **function (Microsoft SQL Server), 481**

`@@PACK_RECEIVED` **function (Microsoft SQL Server), 481**

`@@PACK_SENT` **function (Microsoft SQL Server), 481**

parallelism, intra-partition, 171

parameter, passing to function, 22–24, 714

`PARAMETERS` **view, 504**

parentheses ( ) expression group delimiters, 532

partition connected to, returning, 173

password

encryption, 168, 169, 241–242

login application password processing, 608–610, 611–612

view, replacing with asterisk display in, 646

path

mathematical, 406–408

statement, resolving path of dynamic, 173

`PATINDEX` **function**

Microsoft SQL Server, 191

Sybase, 248, 253–254

`PCLOSE` **function (PostgreSQL), 404, 407–408**

percent sign (%)

modulo operator, 71, 78

wildcard character, 253

`PERCENTILE_CONT` **function, 44**

`PERCENTILE_DISC` **function, 45**

`PERCENT_RANK` **function, 34, 45**

performance

archiving older data, via, 548

average calculation, optimizing, 632

code, improving via removing redundant, 629

database connection pool, improving using, 602, 631

diagnosing performance issue, 207

dynamic SQL overhead, 606

extension, improving using proprietary, 47

function, optimizing, 629–633

index, improving using, 373

I/O performance, optimizing, 631

JDBC API, improving using vendor-specific, 603, 604

procedure, optimizing, 56, 629

query, optimizing, 140, 174, 256, 627, 630–633

security, balancing with, 633

transaction processing, optimizing, 627–628

UDF performance, optimizing, 425, 442, 453, 632

period (.) UDT attribute indicator, 532

`PERIOD_ADD` **function (MySQL), 355, 362–363**

`PERIOD_DIFF` **function (MySQL), 355, 363**

permission

application, acquiring from, 602

bitmap, returning, 231

denying, 478

granting, 423, 450, 477–478

IBM DB2, 450–451, 703–705

Microsoft SQL Server, 218, 231, 477–478, 706

MySQL, 521, 707

Oracle, 422–423, 426, 699–703

PostgreSQL, 532–533, 707–708

Privileges System Catalog, 636

procedure, 423

revoking, 451, 533

SQLJ, 509

Sybase, 509, 706–707

view, 617

`PERMISSIONS` **function (Microsoft SQL Server), 218, 231**

Persistent Stored Module (PSM), 415

`Pg_indexes` **view, 645**

`Pg_locks` **view, 645**

`PG_PROC` **functions (PostgreSQL), 539–540**

`Pg_rules` **view, 645**

`Pg_settings` **view, 645**

`Pg_shadow` **system table, 646**

`Pg_stats` **view, 645**

`Pg_tables` **view, 645, 646**

`Pg_user` **view, 645, 646–647**

`Pg_views` **view, 645, 647**

phone number, formatting, 630

`PI` **function**

ANSI, 71, 79

MySQL, 321, 330

PostgreSQL, 389, 395

Sybase, 277, 282

planning

database migration, 557–558

function development, 605–606

PL/SQL compiler, 421

PL/SQL (Procedural Language/SQL), 20. *See also specific Oracle function*

PL/SQL Virtual Machine (PVM), 421–422

plus sign (+) concatenation operator, 68

polygon

box height, returning, 406

box width, returning, 408

boxes, returning intersection of two, 405

corner points, returning number of, 407

`POPEN` **function (PostgreSQL), 404, 408**

T

X

Y

Z